Public Budgeting Systems
Sixth Edition

Robert D. Lee, Jr.
The Pennsylvania State University
University Park, Pennsylvania

Ronald W. Johnson
Research Triangle Institute
Research Triangle Park, North Carolina

AN ASPEN PUBLICATION®
Aspen Publishers, Inc.
Gaithersburg, Maryland
1998

Library of Congress Cataloging-in-Publication Data

Lee, Robert D.
Public budgeting systems/
Robert D. Lee, Jr., Ronald W. Johnson.—6th ed.
p. cm.
Includes bibliographical references and index.
ISBN 0-8342-1044-4
1. Budget—United States.
2. Budget process—United States.
3. Program budgeting—United States.
I. Johnson, Ronald Wayne. II. Title.
HJ2051.L4 1998
352.4′973—dc21
97-47672
CIP

Orders: (800) 638-8437
Customer Service: (800) 234-1660

About Aspen Publishers • For more than 35 years, Aspen has been a leading professional
publisher in a variety of disciplines. Aspen's vast information resources are available in both
print and electronic formats. We are committed to providing the highest quality information
available in the most appropriate format for our customers. Visit Aspen's Internet site for
more information resources, directories, articles, and a searchable version of Aspen's full
catalog, including the most recent publications: **http://www.aspenpub.com**
Aspen Publishers, Inc. • The hallmark of quality in publishing
Member of the worldwide Wolters Kluwer group.

Editorial Services: Jane Colilla
Library of Congress Catalog Card Number: 97-47672
ISBN: 0-8342-1044-4
Printed in the United States of America

3 4 5

Dedicated to
Barbara, Robert, Craig, Cameron, and Leslie
and to
Sally, Ron, and Jennifer

Table of Contents

Preface ix

Acknowledgments xiii

Chapter 1—Introduction 1

    Distinctions Regarding Public Budgeting .2
    Responsible Government and Budgeting .7
    Budgets and Budgeting Systems 14
    Information and Decision Making 17
    Summary. 20

Chapter 2—The Public Sector in Perspective 25

    Relative Sizes of the Private and Public Sectors 25
    The Magnitude and Growth of Government 31
    Sources of Revenue and Purposes of Government
        Expenditures 38-42
    Summary. 42

Chapter 3—Budget Cycles 47

    The Budget Cycle. 47
    Scrambled Budget Cycles. 53
    Summary. 57

Chapter 4—Budget Preparation: The Revenue Side.................. **59**

Revenue Sources.................................59 *60-63*
Special Concerns 83 *73-75*
                                                 83-86
Summary.......................................86. .88

Chapter 5—Budget Preparation: The Expenditure Side **95**

Early Developments ....95 *-98*
Structuring the Request Process ....98 *-102*
Systems of Budgeting............................107 *102-109*
                                                    109-121
Summary.......................................121

Chapter 6—Budget Preparation: The Decision Process **129**

Decisions on Budget Requests 129
Budget Documents 151
Summary...162

Chapter 7—Policy and Program Analysis **171**

Focus of Analysis 171
Methods and Techniques of Analysis......................177
Organizational Locus and Use of Analysis 190
Summary...195

Chapter 8—Budget Approval: The Role of the Legislature **201**

Parameters..201
Legislative Roles 211
Summary...222

Chapter 9—Budget Approval: The U.S. Congress **227**

Experience Prior to the 1974 Reforms 228
Budget Reforms, 1974–1985 230
The Later Reagan Years and the Bush Years...............236
The Clinton Years....................................242
Proposed Reforms and Their Prospects 247
Summary...257

Chapter 10—Budget Execution **265**

  Budget Office and Agency Relations 265
  Tax Administration and Debt Collection 275
  Cash Management 282
  Procurement 292
  Risk Management 299
  Summary 301

**Chapter 11—Financial Management: Accounting, Auditing, and
   Information Systems.** **309**

  Governmental Accounting 309
  Governmental Auditing 337
  Information Systems 343
  Summary 356

Chapter 12—Financial Management: Capital Budgeting and Debt **363**

  Capital Planning, Budgeting, and Asset Management 363
  State and Local Bond Financing. 378
  Debt Capacity and Management. 392
  Summary 400

Chapter 13—Government Personnel and Pensions. **407**

  Personnel Impacts and Pension Plans. 407
  Personnel Operations 419
  Summary 423

Chapter 14—Intergovernmental Relations **429**

  Structural and Fiscal Features of the Intergovernmental
    System 429
  Patterns of Interaction among Levels of Government 437
  Types of Fiscal Assistance 454
  Restructuring Patterns of Intergovernmental Relations 459
  Summary 468

**Chapter 15—Government, the Economy, and Economic
Development** **473**

The United States and the World Economy 474
Objectives of Economic Policy 476
Anticipating Economic Conditions. 488
Tools Available To Affect the Economy 495
Redistributional Effects of Economic Policy 504
Summary. 506

Concluding Remarks. **511**

Bibliographic Note. **515**

Index **521**

Preface

This is a general book on public budgeting. Our purpose is to survey the current state of the art among all levels of government in the United States. Where illustrative, we also use examples from other countries. We emphasize methods by which financial decisions are reached within a system and ways in which different types of information are used in budgetary decision making. We stress the use of program information, since budget reforms for decades have sought to introduce greater program considerations into financial decisions.

Budgeting is considered within the context of a system containing numerous components and relationships. One problem of such an approach is that, since all things within a system are related, it is difficult to find an appropriate place to begin. We have divided the text into chapters, but the reader should recognize that no single chapter can stand alone. Virtually every chapter mentions some topics and issues that are treated elsewhere in the book.

A discussion of budgeting may be organized in various ways. Historical or chronological sequence is one method of organization, although this approach would require discussing every relevant topic for each time period. Another method is to arrange topics by level of government, with separate sections for local, state, and federal budgeting. Such an approach again would involve extensive rehashing of arguments and information. Still another approach is to focus on phases of the budget cycle, from preparation of the budget through auditing past activities and expenditures. Rigid adherence to this approach would be inappropriate, because the budget cycle is not precisely defined and many issues cut across several phases of the cycle. Another approach would be to organize the discussion around the contrast between the technical and political problems of budgetary decision making.

The organization of this book is a combination of these approaches. Chapter 1, "Introduction," provides a general discussion of the nature of budgetary decision making, including distinctions between private and public budgeting, the concepts of responsibility and accountability in budgeting, the possibility of rationality in decision making, and the nature of budgeting and budget systems. Chapter 2, "The Public Sector in Perspective," reviews the scope of the public sector, the magnitude of government, the sources of revenues, and the purposes of government expenditures. Budget cycles are the topic of Chapter 3, which summarizes the basic steps in budgeting—preparation and submission, approval, execution, and audit. Together these chapters provide a basic framework for the remainder of the book.

The next three chapters focus upon the budget preparation process. The purpose of these chapters is to provide the reader with an understanding of the types of deliberations involved in developing a proposed budget. Chapter 4, "Budget Preparation: The Revenue Side," considers the different sources from which governments obtain their funds, the special concerns associated with limitations on taxing and spending, and estimating revenue for the next budget year. Chapter 5, "Budget Preparation: The Expenditure Side," discusses early budget reform efforts and contemporary approaches to developing proposals for funding government programs. Chapter 6, "Budget Preparation: The Decision Process," examines the process of putting together a budget proposal that includes recommended revenue and expenditure levels and then reviews the types of budget documents that are used in government.

Chapter 7, "Policy and Program Analysis," is a transitional chapter that discusses the role of analysis in both budget preparation and approval. It covers techniques of analysis as well as their use in the executive and legislative branches.

Chapters 8 and 9 deal with the budget approval process. Chapter 8, "Budget Approval: The Role of the Legislature," provides a general account of the processes used by legislative bodies. Chapter 9, "Budget Approval: The U.S. Congress," treats separately the special factors and problems associated with congressional budgeting.

The next three chapters concentrate on the execution phase of budgeting. Chapter 10, "Budget Execution," considers the roles played by the chief executive, the budget office, and the line agencies and treats separately the topics of tax administration, cash management, procurement, and risk management. Chapter 11, "Financial Management: Accounting, Auditing, and Information Systems," presents the basic features of accounting systems and processes, explains the types of audits that are conducted, and discusses the nature of information systems used in budgeting and finance. Chapter 12, "Financial Management: Capital Budgeting and Debt," examines capital budgeting as a decision process and the financing of long-term capital investments through debt instruments.

The final three chapters deal with special topics in government budgeting. Chapter 13, "Government Personnel and Pensions," reviews the effects of personnel expenditures on budgets, with particular attention to public pension systems. Chapter 14, "Intergovernmental Relations," examines the financial interactions among governments, the types of fiscal assistance in use, and possible means of restructuring intergovernmental relationships. Chapter 15, "Government, the Economy, and Economic Development," surveys the federal government's role in managing the economy and the ways economic conditions affect state and local governments.

The book closes with some brief Concluding Remarks on themes that can be expected to receive considerable attention from budgeting practitioners and scholars in the next several years. The Bibliographic Note provides guidance on keeping informed about changes in the field of budgeting.

Overall, this edition retains the structure of the fifth edition but gives increased attention to some topics, such as program information and government's role in the economy. New to this edition is a discussion of the Internet and the information about budgeting and finance it makes available. Chapter endnotes throughout the book cite relevant Web sites, helping to guide the reader to locations that provide bountiful information. Text, tables, and exhibits have been completely updated.

The authors began the first edition as faculty members in the Institute of Public Administration at The Pennsylvania State University. Five editions later, Dr. Lee is Professor of Public Administration and Professor of Hotel, Restaurant, and Recreation Management at Penn State, and Dr. Johnson is Vice President for Social Sciences and International Development at the Research Triangle Institute.

Our hope is that this new edition will be useful to readers from many backgrounds and with diverse purposes.

Acknowledgments

Having gone through six editions, this book is necessarily the product of numerous individuals and not just two authors. We are indebted to colleagues at The Pennsylvania State University and the Research Triangle Institute. Colleagues at other institutions, including various colleges and universities, have provided valuable advice, as have students at a variety of schools. In preparing the book, we received considerable advice from expert practitioners in both the executive and legislative branches of federal, state, and local governments, as well as from other countries and nonprofit organizations. The responsibility for the final product, of course, belongs to us alone.

CHAPTER 1

Introduction

The headline in the July 29, 1997, edition of *USA Today* read "'Dream' budget deal Ok'd." President Clinton had just signed a bill passed by Congress approving tax cuts and expenditure reductions, and a balanced federal budget by the year 2002. What made the budget deal "dream" in the eyes of the editor who wrote that headline? What exactly was behind the budget "deal" approved? After years, decades of debate, a Congress and a president had hammered an agreement out that many thought unreachable—a balanced budget. This book is about budgets, budgeting systems, and budgeting processes—the nature of the decisions that are made and the processes by which those decisions are made while arriving at a "dream deal."

Public budgeting involves the selection of ends and the selection of means to reach those ends. It involves the division of society's economic and financial resources between the public sector and the private sector and the allocation of such resources among competing public sector needs. Public budgeting systems are systems for making choices of ends and means. These choices are guided by theory, by hunch, by partisan politics, by narrow self-interest, by altruism, and by many other sources of value judgment.

Public budgeting systems work by channeling various types of information about societal conditions and about the values that guide resource allocation decision making. Complex channels for information exchange exist. Through these channels, people process information on what is desired, make assessments of what is or is not being achieved, and analyze what might or might not be achieved. Integral to budgeting systems are intricate processes that link both political and economic values. In making decisions that ultimately determine how resources are allocated, the political process uses sometimes bewildering and often conflicting information about values, about actual conditions, and about possible condition changes. This book is an analysis of procedures and methods—past, present, and prospective—used in the resource allocation process.

This chapter examines some basic features of decision-making and budgeting systems. First, some major characteristics of public budgeting are explained through comparison and contrast with private forms of budgeting. Second, the development of budgeting as a means of holding government accountable for its use of society's resources is reviewed. Next, budgets and budgeting systems are defined. Finally, the role of information in budgetary decision making is considered.

DISTINCTIONS REGARDING PUBLIC BUDGETING

Budgeting is a common phenomenon. To some extent everybody does it. People budget time, dollars, food—almost everything. The corner grocer budgets, General Electric budgets, and so do governments. Moreover, important similarities exist in the budgeting done by large public and private bureaucracies.[1]

Budgeting is intended as a mechanism for setting goals and objectives, for measuring progress toward objectives, for identifying weaknesses or inadequacies in organizations, and for controlling and integrating the diverse activities carried out by numerous subunits within large bureaucracies, both public and private. Budgeting is the manifestation of an organization's strategies, whether those strategies are the result of thoughtful strategic planning processes, the inertia of long years of doing approximately the same thing, or of the competing political forces within the organization bargaining for shares of resources. Once resources are allocated through the budgetary process, the organization's strategies become apparent even if they have not been articulated as strategies. Budgeting means examining how the organization's resources have been used in the past, analyzing what has been accomplished and at what cost, and charting a course for the future by allocating new resources for the coming budget period. Whether this process is done haphazardly or after exhaustive analyses prepared by staff, whether it is carried out by order of the chief executive officer or requires the development of a consensus among many individuals, it still is budgeting.

Public and Private Sector Differences in Objectives

Resource Availability. Important differences exist between the private and public spheres. In the first place, the amount of resources available for allocation varies greatly. Both family and corporate budgeting are constrained by a relatively fixed set of available resources. Income is comparatively fixed, at least in the short run, and therefore outgo must be equal to or less than income. Of course, income can be expanded by increasing the level of production and work or temporarily by borrowing, but the opportunities for increasing income are limited.

Government, on the other hand, is bound by much higher limits, and in the United States at least, government does not use nearly all of the possible resources available to it. Only in times of major crises, such as World War II, has government in the United States begun to approach the limits of its resources. Then the federal government borrowed an amount that eventually came close to equaling the total production of the economy in a year. Rationing, price controls, and other measures were imposed in order to limit severely private sector consumption in order to allocate most of society's resources to the government. During other times, much is left to the private sector, with government using only a fraction of society's work force, goods, and services. Government has the power to determine how much of the society's total resources will be taken for public purposes; private parties operate within the limits of their ability to acquire resources through their market activities—selling their labor, selling goods, and so forth.

Profit Motive. Another major distinction between private and public budgeting is the motivation behind budget decisions. The private sector is characterized by the profit motive, whereas government undertakes many things that are financially unprofitable. In the private sector, profit serves as a ready standard for evaluating previous decisions; successful decisions are those that produce profits (as measured in dollars).

The concept of profit, however, can lead to gross oversimplifications about corporate decision making. Not every budget decision in a private firm is determined by the criterion of making an immediate profit. Sometimes corporations forgo profits in the short run. In the case of price wars, they attempt to increase their share of a given market even if it means selling temporarily at a loss. At other times, they incur large debt and take other apparently unprofitable actions to combat a hostile takeover—an attempt by an outsider to purchase enough stock to exercise control over a corporation's assets. Sometimes their major objectives are to produce a good product and to build public confidence. They have enough confidence in their pursuit of customer service that the result will be sustained long-run profits. At other times they undertake actions for mainly social motives, wishing to make a contribution to the society that sustains their corporate existence.

Large firms budget significant resources for research and development (R & D) activities, only a few of which eventually lead to a product that generates large sales and profits. An R & D division can be evaluated over the long term by how many of its developments contribute to profits, but this kind of evaluation is difficult. Often, the results of R & D are subtle improvements in existing products, and measuring the amount of investment relative to the incremental profit gain is impossible. In this regard, private budgeting for R & D is no less difficult than the federal government's support of R & D.

Despite the inability to tie specific expenditures to the results of R & D, firms and governments continue to budget resources for R & D to create future productive capacity. A Congressional Budget Office review of studies estimating the value generated by R & D expenditures noted that although precise achievements are difficult to estimate, R & D spending does yield positive returns.[2]

Regardless of the role profit plays in the private sector, government decision making in general lacks even this standard for measuring activities. Exceptions to this generalization are government activities that yield revenues. State control and sale of alcoholic beverages, whether undertaken for profit or for regulation of public morals, can be evaluated, like any other business, in terms of profit and loss. Similarly, the operation of a water system, a public transit authority, or a public swimming pool can be evaluated in business profit-and-loss terms. This does not mean that each of these should turn a profit. After all, operating a public swimming pool may be the result of a decision to provide subsidized recreation to a low-income neighborhood whose residents cannot afford other private recreational alternatives. The budgeting process, however, can be used to assess the operation as a business in order to clarify the subsidy level and to aid decision makers in comparing costs with those for other public services provided free of direct charge.

Still, the majority of private sector budget decisions pertains to at least long-term profits, and most public sector budget decisions do not. Governments undertake some functions deliberately instead of leaving them to the private sector. Public budgetary decisions, for example, frequently involve allocation of resources among competing programs that are not readily susceptible to measurement in dollar costs and dollar returns. There are no easy means of measuring the costs and benefits of a life saved through cancer research, although the value of future earnings sometimes is used as a surrogate measure of the value of life. Nor is there a ready means of clearly separating private incentives from public incentives. For example, although the National Cancer Institute spends millions of public dollars annually on cancer research, the amount is minuscule compared with the amount spent by private companies on research for cancer prevention and treatment.

Even while most public sector activities are not intended to be profitable, it does not mean that business-like measurement of results in relation to costs are rendered useless. Although not susceptible to bottom-line or profit-and-loss measurement, many government programs are able to measure their results in terms of output (efficiency) and outcome (effectiveness). Legislation passed in 1993 mandated the use of performance measures to improve the federal government's accountability for the results of its expenditures.[3]

Public and Private Sector Differences in Services Provided

Public Goods. Some government services yield public or collective benefits that are of value to society as a whole, whereas corporate products are almost always consumed by individuals and specific organizations. When Ford Motor Company produces automobiles, persons buying the automobiles use them to meet their own personal needs. When the Department of Defense produces a network for detecting a possible launching of intercontinental missiles against the United States, that network benefits the public in general. Economists call these kinds of products and services *public goods;* they have the property of nonexclusion. Once the detection network is in place, no one can be excluded from its benefits.[4] Few public products and services qualify as pure public goods, and many goods and services produced by governments are also produced by the private sector.

Externalities. Another class of government services consists of those from which individuals can be excluded but for which the benefits, or costs, extend beyond those involved in the immediate service provision. When Ford Motor Company sells a car, its stockholders enjoy the benefits of the profits, and those profits do not spill over to society at large. However, when a child is educated through a school system, not only does the child benefit, but also society's productive capacity is enhanced. It certainly is common to have private schools that educate children for a profit, and the owners of the school enjoy the benefits of the profits along with the child and society. However, it seems unlikely that these same for-profit schools would willingly provide equivalent education to all children who cannot make tuition payments. Economists label the benefits that spill over to the rest of society *externalities.*[5] Governments provide at least some services that produce significant externalities because the private sector would provide these only to the extent that profit could be made. Education, if left entirely to the private sector, presumably would be available only to those who could pay, or would be provided in insufficient quantity and quality for the needs of society.

Pricing Public Services. Defining just what is clearly public in nature and determining what the private sector presumably cannot provide is controversial. Because the federal government during the 1980s and 1990s cut back on transfers to state and local governments, which also faced more stringent tax and spending limitations inspired by their voters (see Chapter 4), many services once thought to be exclusively public were converted into private services or to public services provided by private firms on a contract basis. This trend advanced throughout many developing countries with public sectors even larger than in the United States.[6] Although this type of conversion is not a new idea, one of the lessons learned throughout the world seems to have been that government may grow larger than most feel is beneficial and may be difficult to cut back when unconstrained by any kind of pricing mechanism, such as the private sector ultimately always faces.[7] One consequence of that lesson is that much more extensive user charges and various other fees now force those who benefit directly from a government service to pay for its cost (see Chapter 4). For example, the U.S. Coast Guard no longer provides towing services to disabled boats unless a genuine emergency exists but instead notifies private operators, who charge the cost to the disabled boat captain. That practice has cut back significantly on calls for towing in general, with prices providing a rationing mechanism.

Other Public and Private Sector Differences. Whatever objectives other than profit private corporations may have, to stay in business they must seek economic efficiency and obtain the greatest possible dollar return on investments. In contrast, governments may be intentionally inefficient in resource allocations, undertaking services the private sector would be reluctant to provide at all. For example, government-financed medical care for the elderly may be inefficient in the sense that, whereas other government programs might provide greater economic returns to society, it has been agreed that at least some support should be provided to the elderly. Governments are also charged with other unique responsibilities, such as intervention in the economy (see Chapter 15).

Another difference between private and public organizations lies in the clientele and the owners of the means of production. In theory, at least, both corporations and governments are answerable to their stockholders and clients, but in the private sector these individuals can disassociate themselves from firms. Their counterparts in the public sector are denied this choice, except through the extreme act of emigration. Private stockholders expect dollar returns on their investments, but because government costs and returns are not easily evaluated, the electorate has no simple measure for assessing the returns on the taxes they pay. Still, state and local governments increasingly are providing annual reports to citizens that are similar in purpose to stockholder reports. These reports emphasize the investments government is making and the benefits citizens are receiving in lieu of profits.

Corporate budgetary decision making is usually more centralized than government decision making. Corporations can stop production of economically unprofitable goods such as Edsels and DeSotos. Given the nature of the public decision-making process, however, governments encounter more difficulty in making decisions both to inaugurate programs and to eliminate them. For example, it seems evident that welfare programs intended to aid the poor have not provided the kinds of results desired by either the electorate in general or welfare recipients in particular. Nevertheless, to change existing programs requires years of debate, negotiations, and political bargaining; in the 1990s, major welfare reform finally was achieved limiting the benefits individuals may receive in a lifetime (see Chapter 14).

RESPONSIBLE GOVERNMENT AND BUDGETING

The emergence and reform of formal government budgeting can be traced to a concern for holding public officials accountable for their actions.[8] The "reinventing government" movement of the 1990s represents the most recent manifestation of a rather ancient concern that public officials be held accountable for their actions.[9] In a democracy, budgeting is a device for limiting the powers of government. Two issues recur in the evolution of modern public budgeting as an instrument of accountability—responsibility to whom and for what purposes.

Responsible to Whom?

Responsibility to Constituency. Basically, responsibility in a democratic society entails holding elected officials answerable to their constituents. Elected executives and legislative representatives at all levels of government are, at least in theory, held accountable for their decisions on programs and budgets. In actuality, however, budget documents are not the main source of information for decisions by the electorate. Obviously, most voters do not diligently study the U.S. budget before casting their votes in presidential and congressional elections. However, as the government's share of the total economy grows, it is increasingly clear that voters do hold elected representatives responsible for the overall budget, the budget deficit, and the general performance of the economy. That the electorate holds presidents responsible for the economy was evidenced in 1992 by President Bush's defeat in his bid for re-election and President Clinton's successful 1996 re-election bid. In addition, state and local governments have specific creditors, the purchasers of bonds issued to finance long-term capital improvements. The interest rates that state and local governments have to pay on their bonds are affected by their ability to provide creditors with convincing evidence of their creditworthiness (see Chapter 12). Hence, financial institutions that purchase bonds and ratings institutions that rate state and local bonds are important constituents to whom these governments are accountable.

Because the public in a large society cannot be fully informed about the operations of government, the United States has used the concepts of *separation of powers* and *checks and balances* as means of providing for responsible government. Power is divided among the executive, legislative, and judicial branches, and each provides some checks on the others. Thus, although the president is held responsible to Congress for preparation and submission of an executive budget, only Congress can pass the budget. In most states and many localities, the chief executive has a similar responsibility to recommend a plan for taxes and expenditures. The legislative body passes judgment on these recommendations and subsequently holds the executive branch responsible for carrying out the decisions.

Development of the Executive Budget System. The development of an executive budget system for holding government accountable was a long process that can be traced as far back as the Magna Charta (1215). The main issue that resulted in this landmark document was the Crown's taxing powers. The Magna Charta did not produce a complete budget but concentrated only upon holding the Crown accountable to the nobility for its revenue actions.[10] At the time, the magnitude of public expenditures and the use of these funds for public services were of less concern than the power to levy and collect taxes. It was not until the English Consolidated Fund Act of 1787 that the rudiments of a complete system were established, and a complete account of revenues and expenditures was presented to Parliament for the first time in 1822.[11]

The same concern in eighteenth-century England for executive accountability was exhibited in other countries. It was carried over to the American experience even prior to the ratification of the Constitution (1789). Fear of a strong executive was evidenced by the failure to provide for an executive in the Articles of Confederation (1781). Fear of "taxation without representation" probably explains why the Constitution is more explicit about taxing powers than the procedures to be followed in government spending.

The first decade under the Constitution saw important developments that could have resulted in an executive budget system, but the trend was reversed in subsequent years. The Treasury Act of 1789, establishing the Treasury Department, granted to the secretary the power "to digest and prepare plans for the improvement of the revenue . . . [and] to prepare and report estimates of the public revenue and expenditures."[12] Alexander Hamilton, secretary of the treasury, in interpreting his mandate broadly, asserted strong leadership in financial affairs. Although the act did not grant the secretary power to prepare a budget by recommending which programs should and should not be funded, such a development might have subsequently occurred.

Instead, Hamilton's apparent lack of deference to Congress strengthened that body's support for greater legislative control over financial matters. To curtail the discretion of the executive, Congress resorted to the use of increasing numbers of line items, specifying in narrow detail for what purposes money could be spent.[13] The pattern emerged that each executive department would deal directly with Congress, thereby curtailing the responsibilities of the secretary of the treasury. The budgetary function of the Treasury Department became primarily ministerial. The Book of Estimates, prepared by the secretary and delivered to Congress, could have become the instrument for a coordinated set of budgetary recommendations; instead it was simply a compilation of departmental requests for funds. A. E. Buck wrote, "Thus budget making became an exclusively legislative function in the national government, and as such it continued for more than a century."[14]

Modern Executive Budgeting. By the beginning of the twentieth century, changing economic conditions stimulated the demand for more centralized and controlled forms of budgeting. E. E. Naylor has written that before this time there was little "enthusiasm for action . . . since federal taxes were usually indirect and not severely felt by any particular individual or group."[15] By 1900, however, existing revenue sources no longer consistently produced sufficient sums to cover the costs of government. At the federal level, the tariff could not be expected to produce a surplus of funds, as had been the case. Causes of this growing deficit were the expanded scope of government programs and, to a lesser extent, waste and corruption in government finance. The latter is often credited as a major political factor stimulating reform.

Local government led the way in the establishment of formal budget procedures. Municipal budget reform was closely associated with general reform of local government, especially the creation of the city manager form of government. In 1899 a model municipal corporation act, released by the National Municipal League, featured a model charter that provided for a budget system whose preparation phase was under the control of the mayor. In 1907, the New York Bureau of Municipal Research issued a study, "Making a Municipal Budget," that became the basis for establishing a budgetary system for New York City.[16] By the mid-1920s, most major U.S. cities had some form of budget system.

Substantial reform of state budgeting occurred between 1910 and 1920. This reform was closely associated with the overall drive to hold executives accountable by first giving them authority over the executive branch. The movement for the short ballot, aimed at eliminating many independently elected administrative officers, resulted in granting governors greater control over their bureaucracies. Ohio, in 1910, was the first state to enact a law empowering the governor to prepare and submit a budget. A. E. Buck, in assessing the effort at the state level, suggested that 1913 marked "the beginning of practical action in the states."[17] By 1920, some budget reform had occurred in 44 states, and all states had a central budget office by 1929.[18]

Simultaneous action occurred at the federal level, and much of what took place there contributed to the reforms at the local and state levels. Frederick A. Cleveland, who was director of the New York Bureau of Municipal Research and who played a key role in national reform, asserted that "it was the uncontrolled and uncontrollable increase in the cost of government that finally jostled the public into an attitude of hostility."[19] In response to this public concern, President Taft requested and received from Congress in 1909 an appropriation of $100,000 for a special Commission on Economy and Efficiency. Known as the Taft Commission, the group was headed by Cleveland and submitted its final report in 1912, recommending the establishment of a budgetary process under the direction of the president. This report was to spur activity at the state and local levels.

However, the Budget and Accounting Act, which established the new federal system, was not passed until 1921.[20] In the interim, deficits were recorded every year between 1912 and 1919 except 1916. The largest deficit occurred in 1919, when expenditures were three times greater than revenues ($18.5 billion in expenditures as compared with $5.1 billion in revenues). During this period, vigorous debate centered on the issue of whether budget reform would in effect establish a superordinate executive over the legislative branch. President Wilson in 1920 vetoed legislation that would have created a Bureau of the Budget and a General Accounting Office on the grounds that the latter, as an arm of Congress, would violate the president's authority over the executive branch. The following year President Harding signed virtually identical legislation into law.

Thus, an executive budget system was established, despite a historical fear of a powerful chief executive. In 1939, the Bureau of the Budget was removed from the Treasury Department and placed in the newly formed Executive Office of the President. This shift reflected the growing importance of the bureau in assisting the president in managing the government. Ten years later the budgetary task force of the First Hoover Commission on the Organization of the Executive Branch recommended that the Bureau of the Budget be reinstated in the Treasury Department, but the commission as a whole opposed the recommendation.[21] The Budget and Accounting Procedures Act of 1950 reinforced the trend of presidential control by explicitly granting the president control over the "form and detail" of the budget document.[22] The Second Hoover Commission in 1955 endorsed strengthening the president's power in budgeting as a means of restoring the "full control of the national purse to the Congress."[23] A president who had full control of the bureaucracy, then, could be held accountable by Congress for action taken by the bureaucracy.

One of the stated goals of the reform movement was to bring the sound financial practices of business to the presumably disorganized public sector—a goal often expressed by current reformers. Available evidence, however, indicates that business practices were not particularly exemplary at the turn of the century, suggesting that the reforms were largely invented within the public sector rather than being transferred into government from the outside.[24]

Responsible for What?

Revenue Responsibility. The earliest concern for financial responsibility centered on taxes. As indicated above, the Magna Charta imposed limitations not on the nature of the Crown's expenditures but on the procedures for raising revenue. This same concern for the revenue side of budgeting was characteristic of the early history of budgeting in this country. The Constitution is more explicit about the tax power of the government than about the nature or purposes of government expenditures.

Expenditure Control, Management, and Planning. The larger the budget has become, the more the concern has shifted to expenditures. Increasing emphasis has been placed on the accountability of government for what it spends and for how well it manages its overall finances. Expenditure accountability may take several different forms. By the 1960s, expenditure accountability had gone through three stages.[25] The first stage was characterized by legislative concern for tight control over executive expenditures. The most prevalent means of exerting this type of expenditure control is to appropriate by line item and object of expenditure. Financial audits are then used to ensure that money in fact is spent for the items authorized for purchase. This information focuses budgetary decision making on the things government buys, such as personnel, travel, and supplies, rather than on the accomplishments of government activities. In other words, responsibility is achieved by controlling the resources or input side.

The second stage was a management orientation, with emphasis on the efficiency of ongoing activities. Historically, this orientation is associated with the New Deal through the First Hoover Commission (1949). The emphasis was on holding administrators accountable for the efficiency of their activities through methods such as work performance measurement.

The third stage of budget reform is identified with post–Hoover Commission concern regarding the planning function served by budgets. The traditional goal of controlling resource inputs may be accommodated in the short time frame of the coming budget year. Managerial control over efficiency, although aided by a longer time perspective, also may be accommodated in a traditional budget-year presentation. When the emphasis is shifted to accomplishing objectives, however, a longer time frame is necessary. Many objectives of government programs cannot be accomplished in one budget year. A multiyear presentation of the budget is thus necessary to indicate the long-range implications of current budget decisions.

Financial Management, Financial Condition, and Program Planning Revisited. While it may be premature to suggest fourth and fifth stages, a significant increase in the concern for sound financial management has been evident since the late 1970s and renewed interest in program planning has been evident since the late 1980s. Financial management can mean many things. It encompasses the desire for appropriate control over public funds. It certainly includes the desire for efficient public sector management. And financial management entails the cost-effective accomplishment of the objectives of government programs, which has already been labeled a planning focus. But a new emphasis has been placed on mechanisms for ensuring that the government remains in a sound financial position. Such mechanisms entail not only budgetary concerns regarding resource allocation but also the development of sound financing plans for meeting both short- and long-term resource requirements. Most recently, it has meant a renewed emphasis on performance measurement and performance improvement.[26]

One of the motivations behind the concern to hold government accountable for its long-run financial position was the New York City budget crisis of the mid-1970s. Following on the heels of that near bankruptcy, both financial institutions that purchased municipal bonds and citizens who wondered about their own cities sought to improve the reporting of the long-term financial position of governments.[27] The issue is that the general operating budget and related accounting reports often do not reveal the overall financial position of the government entity. All state governments, most local governments, and, of course, the federal government have some level of indebtedness. All three types of government also have various assets against which to compare that level of indebtedness. However, the long-run planning for debt retirement and the general strategies for managing existing assets do not receive much attention in budgeting systems. Concern at the federal level has led to a much greater emphasis on fixed asset management and an increase in attention in the annual budget to capital investment budgeting (see Chapters 11 and 12).

Since the late 1980s, governments have sought techniques for improving how seemingly dwindling resources can be distributed effectively to meet increasingly evident needs for government services and assistance. As a result, a renewed interest in program and performance measurement has emerged, with significant efforts occurring at all levels of government. The reinventing government movement and the National Performance Review of the Clinton administration are just two examples of this trend.[28] Emphasis is placed on setting objectives and then motivating managers to be entrepreneurial in their pursuit of those objectives.[29] Other countries too have given the same emphases to results-oriented or value-driven budgeting as a primary tool in increasing the efficiency and reducing the size of the public sector.[30]

The notion of stages in budgeting can be overemphasized. Budget reform efforts for many decades have attempted to improve the capacity for decision-making systems to concentrate on accomplishing desired ends. Identifying three, four, or even five stages helps focus attention on what government is expected to be accountable for and where the locus of that accountability lies. The first stage would place the responsibility on the legislative branch as the principal authority for determining how resources should be allocated. The administrators' job, then, is perfunctory. The second stage may be seen as the beginning of a shift toward broader executive duties but limited to a concern for efficient management. The third stage is typified by program budgeting and management by objectives; it reflects the development of executive responsibility for formulating programs to achieve desired ends. The fourth stage, emphasizing overall financial planning, provides for executive responsibility in tying budgeting for current operations, capital facilities planning, asset management, and long-range debt financing into an integrated financial and management plan. The fifth stage renews the emphasis on program measurement and evaluation within the context of budgetary allocation of resources and reinforces the notion of holding officials accountable through the budgetary decision-making process.[31]

Investment versus Consumption. Recent discussion about the adequacy of contemporary budgetary systems focuses on whether budgetary forms and the budgeting process give sufficient attention to the investment role of government expenditures.[32] The Clinton administration has given much greater emphasis to capital investments, although an initial focus on long-term investments in the nation's public infrastructure as a means of increasing economic productivity fell to the pressures of a balanced budget. Some government expenditures are really investments in future economic productivity while others primarily consume resources with little future payoff.[33] Investment means creating additional productive capacity, such as improving transportation networks that reduce the cost of private sector economic activity through more efficient means of transportation and upgrading education systems that enhance the long-term ability to develop new products and new processes. All governments budget for these activities, but not all government budgeting systems make explicit the consumption versus investment tradeoffs in budget decisions. The argument can be made that some funds should be diverted away from social welfare programs that fail to produce new capability and toward investment opportunities that stimulate regional and national economic development.

Most of the emphasis in this book is on the budget as an instrument for financial and program decision making at all levels of government—federal, state, and local. The one responsibility that most sharply differentiates federal budget decisions from state and local decisions is the federal responsibility for the overall state of the economy. The federal budget not only allocates resources among competing programs but it is also an instrument for achieving economic stability and growth (see Chapter 15). The responsibility to use it as an instrument of economic policy has been a part of the federal budgetary process since the Employment Act of 1946.[34]

Budgeting, then, is an important process by which accountability or responsibility can be provided in a political system. As has been discussed, responsibility varies both in terms of the people to whom the system is accountable and in terms of its purposes. Given the various forms of accountability and the types of choices that decision makers have available to them, different meanings can be attached to the terms *budget* and *budgeting system*. Depending on the purposes of a budget, decision makers will need different kinds and amounts of information to aid them in making choices. The following sections and subsequent chapters therefore focus on the kinds of information required for different budgetary choices and the kinds of procedures for generating the necessary information.

BUDGETS AND BUDGETING SYSTEMS

What Is a Budget?

Budget Documents. In its simplest form, a budget is a document or a collection of documents that refers to the financial condition of an organization (family, corporation, government), including information on revenues, expenditures, activities, and purposes or goals. In contrast to an accounting operating statement, which is retrospective in nature, referring to past conditions, a budget is prospective, referring to anticipated future revenues, expenditures, and accomplishments. Historically, the word *budget* referred to a leather pouch, wallet, bag, or purse. More particularly, "In Britain the term was used to describe the leather bag in which the Chancellor of the Exchequer carried to Parliament the statement of the Government's needs and resources."[35]

The status of budget documents is not consistent across political jurisdictions. In the federal government, the budget has limited legal status. It is the official recommendation of the president to Congress, but it is not the official document under which the government operates. As will be seen later, the official operating budget of the United States consists of several documents, namely appropriation acts (see Chapters 8, 9, and 11). In contrast, local budgets proposed by mayors may become official working budgets adopted in their entirety by the city councils.[36]

In still other instances, there may be a series of budget documents instead of one budget for any given government. These may include (1) an operating budget, which handles the bulk of ongoing operations; (2) a capital budget, which covers major new construction projects; and (3) a series of special fund budgets that cover programs funded by specific revenue sources.[37] Special fund budgets commonly include those for highway programs, which are financed through gasoline and tire sales taxes. In such cases, revenue from these sources is earmarked for highway construction, improvement, and maintenance. As another example, fishing and hunting license fees may constitute the revenue for a special fund devoted to the stocking of streams and the provision of ample hunting opportunities.

The format of budget documents also varies. On the whole, budget documents tend to provide greater information on expenditures than on revenues, which are usually treated in a brief section. On the expenditure side, budgets are multipurpose, in that no single document and no single definition can exhaust the functions budgets serve or the ways they are used. At the most general level, however, budgets can be conceived of as (1) descriptions, (2) explanations or causal assertions, and (3) statements of preferences or values.

Budgets as Descriptions. Budgets are first descriptions of the status of an organization, whether it is an agency, a ministry, or an entire government. The budget document may describe what the organization purchases, what it does, and what it accomplishes. Descriptions of organizational activity are also common in budget documents; expenditures may be classified according to the activities they support. For example, a university budget may be divided into such major activities as instruction, research, and public service. Another type of description, organizational accomplishments, states the consequences of resource consumption and work activities for those outside the organization. For example, successful job placements for individuals finishing a vocational rehabilitation program constitute one type of outcome or consequence of a public expenditure. These statements require external verification of the impact of the organization on its environment.

As descriptions, budgets provide a discrete picture of an organization at a point or points in time—in terms of resources consumed, work performed, and external impact. The dollar revenues and expenditures, according to these types of descriptions, may be the only quantitative information supplied. Or information may be supplied about the number and types of personnel; the quantity and kinds of equipment purchased; measures of performance, such as the number of buildings inspected or the number of acres treated; and measures of impact, such as the number of accidents prevented, the amount of crop yield increases, and so forth. Generally, the more descriptive material supplied, the more the organization can be held accountable for the funds spent, the activities supported by those expenditures, and the external accomplishments produced by those activities. Much of the history of budget reform reflects attempts to increase the quantity and quality of descriptive material available both to decision makers and to the public.

Budgets as Explanations. When they describe organizations in terms of purchases, activities, and accomplishments, budgets also at least implicitly serve a second major function—explanation of causal relationships. The expenditure of a specific amount for the purchase of labor and materials that will be combined in particular work activities implies the existence of a causal sequence that will produce certain results. Regardless of how explicit or how vague the budget document or the statements of organization officials may be, budgetary decisions always imply a causal process in which work activities consume resources to achieve goals. Some organizations may have little accurate information about accomplishments, especially public organizations whose accomplishments are not measured as profit and loss. Governments may choose not to be explicit about particular results because they are either difficult to measure, politically sensitive, or both. Regardless of the availability of information or the willingness of an organization to collect and use it, the budget is an expression of a set of causal relationships.

Budgets as Preferences. Budgets are statements of preferences. Whether intended or not, the allocation of resources among different agencies, among different activities, or among different accomplishments reveals the preferences of those making the allocations. These may be the actual preferences of a few decision makers, but more often they are best thought of as the collective preferences of many decision makers arrived at through complex bargaining. A preference schedule reflects, if not any one individual's values, an aggregate of choices that become the collective value judgment for the local government, state, or nation.

What Is a Budgeting System?

Systems. Budgeting can best be understood as a kind of system—a "set of units with relationships among them."[38] Budgetary decision making consists of the actions of executive officials (both in a central organization such as the governor's office or the mayor's staff and in executive line agencies), legislative officials, organized interest groups, and perhaps unorganized interests that may be manifested in a generally felt public concern about public needs and taxes. All these actions are related, and understanding budgeting means understanding the relationships. Such understanding is best achieved by thinking in terms of complex systems.

A complex social system is composed of organizations, individuals, the values held by these individuals, the norms they act upon, and the relationships among these elements. A system may be thought of as a network typically consisting of many different parts, with messages flowing among the parts. The elements of systems interact with each other to produce system results, or consequences, and the network of interactions may produce the same set of results through several different paths, or the same path may from time to time produce different outcomes.[39] Budgeting systems involve political actors, economic and social theories, numerous institutional structures, and competing norms and values, all of which produce outputs in patterns not immediately evident from studying only budget documents.

Budget System Outputs. In a budgetary system, the outputs flowing from the network of interactions are budget decisions, and these vary greatly in their overall significance. Not every unit of the system will have equal decisional authority or power. A manager of a field office for a state health department is likely to have less power to make major budgetary decisions than the administrative head of the department, the governor, or the members of the legislative appropriations committees. Yet each participant does contribute some input to the system. The field manager may alert others in the system to the rise of a new health problem and in doing so may contribute greatly to the eventual establishment of a new health program to combat the problem.

Like the outputs of any other system or network, budget decisions are seldom final and more commonly are sequential. Decisions are tentative in that each decision made is forwarded for action to another participant in the process. This does not mean that all decisions are reversible. Major breakthroughs, such as passage of the Elementary and Secondary Education Act of 1965, which provided substantial federal aid to education, are abandoned only in response to powerful political pressure.[40] Subsequent budget decisions, therefore, are in large part bounded by previous decisions. The subsequent decisions tend to center on the question of changing the level of commitment—allocating more resources, fewer resources, or different kinds of resources to achieve desired levels of impact or different types of impact.

System Interconnectedness. Another feature of a system is that a change in any part of it will alter other parts. Because all units are related, any change in the role or functioning of one unit necessarily affects other units. In some instances, changes may be of such a modest nature that their ramifications for other parts of the system are difficult to discern. However, when major budgetary reforms are instituted, they assuredly affect most participants. For example, if one unit in the system is granted greater authority, individuals and organizations having access to that unit have their decisional involvement enhanced whereas those groups associated with other units have diminished roles.[41] Thus, each individual and institution evaluates budget reforms in terms of how political strengths will be realigned under the reforms.

INFORMATION AND DECISION MAKING

Types of Information

To serve the multiple functions described in the preceding section, budgeting systems must produce and process a variety of information. Most of the major reforms, attempted or proposed, in public budget systems have been intended to reorganize existing information and to provide participants with different types and greater quantities of information. Basically, there are two types of information: program information and resource information. The latter type is more traditional. People are accustomed to thinking of budgets in terms of resources like monetary units and personnel. A budget would not be a budget if it did not contain dollar, ruble, or other monetary figures. Similarly, budgets commonly contain data on employees or personnel.

Conventional accounting systems provide much of the information that public organizations use for budgetary decisions. This type of information, however, is limited to the internal aspects of organizations—the location of organizational responsibility for expenditures and the resources purchased by those expenditures. When the decision-making system incorporates information about the results or impacts of programs, however, one must leave the boundaries of the organization to examine consequences for those outside. This step requires more extensive and more explicit clarification of governmental goals and objectives (see Chapter 5) and increases the importance of analysis (see Chapter 7).[42] This feature of budget reforms, such as program budgeting, management by objectives, and zero-base budgeting, with their emphasis on program information and priority setting, has generated the most heat among critics of budget reform.[43]

Decision Making

Much of the criticism of reform has involved the argument that decision-making systems must take into account the limitations on human capabilities to use all the information that might be collected. Although there are sometimes subtle differences among theories of decision making, the various theories can generally be classified into three basic approaches: pure rationality, muddling through or incrementalism, and limited rationality.[44] These are descriptive theories as well as prescriptions for how decisions ought to be made.

Rational Decision Making. Decision making according to the pure rationality approach consists of a series of ordered, logical steps. First, all of an organization's or a society's goals must be ranked according to priority. Second, all possible alternatives are identified. The costs of each alternative are compared with anticipated benefits. Judgments are made as to which alternative comes closest to satisfying the relevant needs or desires. The alternative with the highest payoff and/or least cost is chosen. Pure rationality theories assume that complete and perfect information about all alternatives is both available and manageable. Decision making, therefore, is choosing among alternatives to maximize some objective function.

The applicability of the rationality model is limited, and few argue that it is a description of how ordinary human beings make decisions. It is most consistent with notions of technical or economic rationality, where objectives can be stated with some precision and the range of feasible alternatives is finite.[45] Also, the model can be of use where accurate predictions of behavior are possible, such as in the private market, where assumptions regarding rational behavior can be used to predict future economic trends.[46] As a description of how government budgeting works, the pure rationality model is obviously misleading. Meeting the complete requirements of even one of the above steps is impossible. It has been argued that the costs of information are so high as to make it rational to be ignorant, that is, to make decisions on the basis of a limited search and limited information. Some attempts at budget reform have been criticized as attempts to impose an unworkable model, pure rationality, on government financial decision making. The use of program information has been a particular target for criticism.[47]

Incrementalism. The second approach to decision making, muddling through (incrementalism), has been advocated by critics of pure rationality, such as Charles E. Lindblom, Aaron Wildavsky, and others.[48] According to this view, decision making involves a conflict of interests and a corresponding clash of information, resulting in the accommodation of diverse partisan interests through bargaining. "Real" decision making is presumed to begin as issues are raised by significant interest groups that request or demand changes from the existing state.[49] Decision making is not some conscious form of pure rationality but instead is a process of incrementally adjusting existing practices to establish or re-establish consensus among participants. This process is known as *disjointed incrementalism*.[50] Alternatives to the status quo are normally not considered unless partisan interests bring them to the attention of the participants in the decision-making process. There is only a marginal amount of planned search for alternatives to achieve desired ends. The decisional process is structured so that partisan interests have the opportunity to press their desires at some point in the deliberations. Decisions represent a consensus on policy reached through a political, power-oriented bargaining process.

The most important characteristic of the muddling through or incrementalist approach as applied to budgeting is its emphasis on the proposition that budgetary decisions are necessarily political. Whereas a purely rational approach might suggest that budgetary decisions are attempts to allocate resources according to economic criteria, the incrementalist view stresses the extent to which political considerations outweigh calculations of optimality. The strongest critics of many budget reforms have tended to equate those reforms with seeking to establish the pure rationality or a solely economic model, a description rarely accepted by those proposing budget reforms.[51] As will be seen throughout this book, any "real" budget reform is forced to accommodate the political nature of decision making.

Limited Rationality. The third approach to decision making, a compromise between the other two approaches, is called *limited rationality*. This model recognizes the inapplicability of pure rationality to complex problems.[52] While acknowledging the inherent constraints of human cognitive processes, limited rationality does not suggest that a deliberate search for alternative approaches to goal achievement is of no avail. Searching for alternatives is used to find solutions that are satisfactory although not necessarily optimal.

Lindblom suggests that incrementalism is a deliberately chosen strategy for decision making and that other strategies short of pure rationality are possible.[53] These strategies would involve some form of comparison among broad alternatives at the planning level and a more focused analysis of the narrower set of alternatives selected. At this lower level, analysts may consider the immediate effects of incremental adjustments in present policies, but explicit attention is also directed at what these immediate effects portend for broader and more long-range concerns. It is possible to be simultaneously incremental and comprehensive by using a short- and long-range perspective.

Limited rationality seems to occupy a nebulous middle ground between incrementalism and pure rationality. The reasons for this are that the middle ground is difficult to define with precision and, further, that some of the theorists who support incrementalism and pure rationality may claim some share of this middle territory. The main point, however, is that decision theories do differ in how they view the values that decision making serves and the capacities of decision makers to serve those values. One model assumes virtually no limits on human capacities for processing information, another suggests that decision making should only be sensitive to partisan political interests, and the third attempts to strike a balance between the others. The history of budgeting and budget reform, we argue, reflects the tensions among these approaches to decision making.

SUMMARY

Public budgeting involves choices among ends and means. Public budgeting shares many characteristics with budgeting in the private sector, but it often requires the application of criteria different from those used by private organizations. Chief among the differences is that few public sector decisions can be assessed in terms of profit and loss. Private sector decisions, on the other hand, ultimately must consider the long-run profit or loss condition of the firm.

Budgeting systems involve the organization of information for making choices and the structure of decision-making processes. Public budgeting systems have evolved as one of the means of holding government accountable for its actions. Budgetary procedures are developed to hold the government in general accountable to the public, the executive accountable to the legislature, and subordinates accountable to their managers. Budgetary procedures also are developed to specify what the executive is accountable for. Concern for the financial solvency of some city governments and the size of the federal budget deficit and total debt has led to reform proposals to use budgeting as a device for holding governments accountable for their long-term financial position. Renewed interest is evident in holding governments accountable for achieving programmatic results that citizens want and demand.

Budgetary systems work through information flows. However, each participant in the budgetary process pays attention selectively to information. The various theories of decision making advanced differ on how much information decision makers are willing and able to consider. The decision-making approach that seems best to characterize budgetary systems is the so-called limited rationality approach, and it is this approach that underlies the discussions throughout this book.

NOTES

1. A. Downs, *Inside Bureaucracy* (Boston: Little, Brown, 1967).

2. Congressional Budget Office, *CBO Staff Memorandum: A Review of Edwin Mansfield's Estimate of the Rate of Return from Academic Research and Its Relevance to the Federal Budget Process* (Washington, DC: U.S. Government Printing Office, 1993).

3. U.S. General Accounting Office, *Performance Budgeting: Past Initiatives Offer Insights for GPRA Implementation* (Washington, DC: U.S. Government Printing Office, 1997).

4. D.N. Hyman, *Public Finance: A Contemporary Application of Theory to Policy*, 5th ed. (New York: Dryden Press, 1996).

5. W. Duncombe, Public Expenditure Research: What Have We Learned? *Public Budgeting & Finance* 15 (Summer 1995): 26–58.

6. IDB Approves $45M for Panama Water Service Privatization, *Wall Street Journal Interactive Edition*, July 30, 1997; accessed December 1997.

7. L.R. Geri, Federal User Fees and Entrepreneurial Budgeting, *Public Budgeting and Financial Management* 9 (1997): 127–142.

8. M.J. White credits W.F. Willoughby's *The Problem of a National Budget* with an early (1919) statement of budgeting as a process for holding government accountable. M.J. White, Budget Policy: Where Does It Begin and End? *Governmental Finance* 7 (August 1978): 2–9.

9. D. Osborne and P. Plastrik, *Banishing Bureaucracy: The Five Strategies for Reinventing Government* (Reading, MA: Addison-Wesley, 1997).

10. C. Webber and A. Wildavsky, *A History of Taxation and Expenditure in the Western World* (New York: Simon & Schuster, 1986).

11. J. Burkhead, *Government Budgeting* (New York: Wiley, 1956), 2–4.

12. Treasury Act, Ch. 12, 1 Stat. 65 (1789).

13. A. Smithies, *The Budgetary Process in the United States* (New York: McGraw-Hill, 1955), 50.

14. A.E. Buck, *Public Budgeting* (New York: Harper and Brothers, 1919), 17.

15. E.E. Naylor, *The Federal Budget System in Operation* (Washington, DC: printed privately, 1941), 22–23.

16. Burkhead, *Government Budgeting*, 12–13.

17. Buck, *Public Budgeting*, 14.

18. Burkhead, *Government Budgeting*, 23; Y. Willbern, Personnel and Money, in *The 50 States and Their Local Governments*, ed. J.W. Fesler (New York: Knopf, 1967), 391.

19. F.A. Cleveland, Evolution of the Budget Idea in the United States, *Annals* 62 (November 1915): 22.

20. Budget and Accounting Act, Ch. 18, 42 Stat. 20 (1921).

21. U.S. Commission on Organization of the Executive Branch of the Government, *General Management of the Executive Branch* (Washington, DC: U.S. Government Printing Office, 1949).

22. Budget and Accounting Procedures Act, Ch. 946, Title I, part I, 64 Stat. 832 (1950).

23. U.S. Commission on Organization of the Executive Branch of the Government, *Budget and Accounting* (Washington, DC: U.S. Government Printing Office, 1955), ix.

24. I.S. Rubin, Who Invented Budgeting in the United States? *Public Administration Review* 53 (1993): 438–444.

25. A. Schick, The Road to PPB: The Stages of Budget Reform, *Public Administration Review* 26 (1966): 243–258.

26. U.S. General Accounting Office, *Management Reform: Implementation of the National Performance Review's Recommendations* (Washington, DC: U.S. Government Printing Office, 1994).

27. R.W. Johnson and A.Y. Lewin, Management and Accountability Models of Public Sector Performance, in *Public Sector Performance: A Conceptual Turning Point*, ed. T.C. Miller (Baltimore: Johns Hopkins University Press, 1984), 224–250.

28. National Performance Review, *Mission Driven, Results-Oriented Budgeting* (Washington, DC: U.S. Government Printing Office, 1993).

29. L.L. Martin, Outcome Budgeting: A New Entrepreneurial Approach to Budgeting, *Public Budgeting and Financial Management* 9 (Spring 1997): 108–126.

30. *Budgeting for Results: Perspectives on Public Expenditure Management* (Paris: Organization for Economic Cooperation and Development, 1995).

31. I.S. Rubin, Budgeting for Accountability: Municipal Budgeting in the 1990s, *Public Budgeting & Finance* 16 (Summer 1996): 112–132.

32. J. Brizius, *Deciding for Investment: Getting Returns on Tax Dollars* (Washington, DC: National Academy of Public Administration, 1994).

33. C.A. Bowsher, *Improving Government: Need To Reexamine Organization and Performance* (Washington, DC: U.S. Government Printing Office, 1993).

34. Employment Act, Ch. 33, 60 Stat. 23 (1946).

35. Burkhead, *Government Budgeting*, 2.

36. J.C. Powdar, *The Operating Budget: A Guide for Smaller Governments* (Chicago: Government Finance Officers Association, 1996); R.L. Bland and I.S. Rubin, *Budgeting: A Guide for Local Governments* (Washington, DC: International City/County Management Association, 1997).

37. P.L. Solano and M.R. Brams, Budgeting, in *Management Policies in Local Government Finance*, 4th ed., eds. J.R. Aronson and E. Schwartz (Washington, DC: International City/County Management Association, 1996), 125–168.

38. G. Miller, Living Systems: Basic Concepts, *Behavioral Science* 10 (1965): 200.

39. P. Senge, *The Fifth Discipline: The Art and Practice of the Learning Organization* (New York: Doubleday, 1990).

40. Elementary and Secondary Education Act, P.L. 89-10, 79 Stat. 27 (1965).

41. L.R. Jones and J. McCaffery, Budgeting According to Aaron Wildavsky: A Bibliographic Essay, *Public Budgeting & Finance* 14 (Spring 1994): 16–43.

42. E. Vedung, *Public Policy and Program Evaluation* (New Brunswick, NJ: Transaction Press, 1997).

43. A. Wildavsky and N. Caiden, *The New Politics of the Budgetary Process*, 3rd ed. (New York: Longman Press, 1997); A. Schick, From the Old Politics of Budgeting to the New, *Public Budgeting & Finance* 14 (Spring 1994): 135–144.

44. G.D. Brewer and P. de Leon, *The Foundations of Policy Analysis* (Chicago: Dorsey, 1983). For alternative theories of budgeting and finance, see G.J. Miller, *Government Financial Management and Theory* (New York: Marcel Dekker, 1991).

45. The terms *technical* and *economic rationality* are the names of two of five basic types of rationality identified by P. Diesing, *Reason and Society* (Urbana: University of Illinois Press, 1962).

46. See M. Friedman, *Essays in Positive Economics* (Chicago: University of Chicago Press, 1953).

47. A. Wildavsky, *Speaking Truth to Power: The Art and Craft of Policy Analysis* (Boston: Little, Brown, 1979).

48. C.E. Lindblom, The Science of "Muddling Through," *Public Administration Review* 19 (1959): 79–88.

49. J. White, (Almost) Nothing New under the Sun: Why the Work of Budgeting Remains Incremental, *Public Budgeting & Finance* 14 (Spring 1994): 113–134.

50. D. Braybrooke and C.E. Lindblom, *A Strategy of Decision* (New York: Free Press, 1963).

51. N.E. Long, Public Policy and Administration: The Goals of Rationality and Responsibility, *Public Administration Review* 56 (1996): 149–152.

52. H. Simon, *Administrative Behavior*, 2nd ed. (New York: Macmillan, 1961); R.M. Cyert and J.G. March, *A Behavioral Theory of the Firm* (Englewood Cliffs, NJ: Prentice-Hall, 1963).

53. C.E. Lindblom, Still Muddling, Not Yet Through, *Public Administration Review* 39 (1979): 517–526.

CHAPTER 2

The Public Sector in Perspective

One danger of generalizing about the size of the public sector of society is that any single generalization necessarily ignores important information. Although the statement "government is vast" may be valid, it fails to recognize the difficulties in determining what is and is not government or the fact that government is also small in some respects. This chapter describes the size and extent of the public sector, discusses the relative and absolute growth rates of government, and considers the general level of taxes and other revenue sources and the societal functions these revenues support.

The chapter explores three main topics. The first is the relative sizes of the private and public sectors of society and the reasons for the growth of government. The second is the magnitude of government and the historical growth of local, state, and federal finances. In the last section, we contrast the purposes of government expenditures with the sources of revenue used by the three main levels of government in the United States.

RELATIVE SIZES OF THE PRIVATE AND PUBLIC SECTORS

Basic to all matters of public budgeting is the issue of the appropriate size of the public sector. This issue is inherently political, not only in the partisan sense but also in the sense that it involves fundamental policy questions about what government should and should not do, can and cannot do. At stake are congeries of competing public and private wants and needs and competing philosophies of the role of the public sector in society. A guiding principle for many of the framers of the Constitution was to keep the central government small to protect individual liberty, while other early leaders, such as Alexander Hamilton, sought a more activist role for the new government.[1]

25

Reasons for Growth

Value Questions. The issue of size relates to the values of freedom and social welfare. Keeping government small has been advocated as a means of protecting individuals from tyranny and stimulating individual independence and initiative.[2] On the other hand, faith in the private sector is sometimes criticized as causing the underfinancing of public programs and the failure to confront major social problems.[3] Debates over the rise of the welfare and warfare states have been especially acrimonious.

The U.S. political system, of course, is not structured in such a way that an overriding decision is made as to the size of this sector. The multiplicity of governments makes it virtually impossible to reach any single decision about the appropriate size of this sector. Decisions relevant to size are made in a political context within and between the executive and legislative branches and among the three major levels of government—local, state, and federal. Each set of decisions contributes to an ultimate resolution of the question, but one must await the tally of all decisions before being able to perceive what has been deemed the appropriate size.

Government Responses. Why government expands has been the subject of extended debate.[4] One of the two main reasons is that government is "responsive" to the demands of society. Wagner's law, originally proposed in the 1880s, holds that economic development creates opportunities for new activities that government alone can perform.[5] The second reason is that government has a supposed propensity to be excessive.[6] In this case, government is seen as growing as a result of empire building by government bureaucrats supported by political leaders.[7]

Among the numerous factors suggested as stimulating responses from government are the following[8]:

- *The need for collective goods.* Since defense, flood control, and some other programs benefit all citizens and cannot be handled readily by the private sector, government becomes involved. When wars occur, governments grow in size and after the conflict tend to remain larger than during the prewar period.
- *Demographic changes.* Increases in total population, newborns, and the elderly stimulate the creation and expansion of government programs.
- *Externalities.* Air and water pollution produced by industrial firms, which are concerned mainly with making a profit, is a social cost and a condition that government is expected to control. Education also has important externalities; uneducated people impose costs on others through the need for

welfare and other social services, while educated people tend to be more productive and increase the total wealth of the society.

- *Economic hardships.* Depressions and other economic situations stimulate the growth of government.
- *High-risk situations.* When risks are high, the private sector is unlikely to invest large quantities of resources, so government is called upon to support programs. Examples are the development of nuclear energy as a source of electrical power and the space program. Once the risks of certain aspects of space activity became manageable as a result of government intervention, commercial interests engaged in space research and moved into the launching of private vehicles and satellites.
- *Technological change.* With the advent of new technology, government has been called upon to provide support, as in the case of roads and airports, to accommodate improved transportation modes and information highways such as the Internet, or to regulate new industries, as in the case of railroads, radio, and television.

While these reasons are helpful in explaining why government enters into the private sector, they do not sufficiently reflect the political considerations at stake when proposals are made for expanding or contracting the scope of the public sector. Any proposal for the expansion of services that results in an increase in taxes is likely to have some unfavorable political repercussions. Therefore, the size issue always relates both to government expenditures and revenues (taxes). Decision makers, no matter how crude or approximate their methods of calculating, attempt to weigh the merits of coping with the current situation with available resources against the merits of recommending new programs that may alleviate problems but at the same time raise the ire of taxpayers. Taxpayer revolts, common since the 1970s, may have had a significant impact in curtailing the growth of government at the state and local levels.[9]

Private and Public Sector Boundaries

Major problems are encountered when attempts are made to gauge the sizes of the public and private sectors and to distinguish between one government and another. Government has become so deeply involved in the society that one may frequently have difficulty discerning what is not at least quasi-public. Moreover, governments have extensive relationships with each other, to the point where a discussion of any single government becomes meaningless without a discussion of its relationships with other governments.

Statistical data on government revenues and expenditures fail to reflect adequately the size of government. For instance, the entire political campaign process is clearly governmental in that funds are expended to elect people to political offices, yet most of these monies are not recorded as government expenditures.[10] Also, in cases where government activities require relatively little money and personnel yet have a substantial impact on the private sector or other governments, the size of government tends to be understated. This is especially true with respect to regulatory activities, such as the control of interstate commerce, occupational safety, and environmental health by the federal government. One suggested means of gauging the effects of governments on society is to examine the output of legislatures in terms of the number of days in session and the number of bills introduced and passed into law. The greater the number of days, bills, and laws, the greater the impact and, presumably, the meddling.[11]

Nonexhaustive Expenditures. Complete reliance on revenue and expenditure data for measuring size is unwarranted for another reason. Sometimes the assumption is made that all government expenditures are a drain on the private economy. However, government expenditures can be nonexhaustive as well as exhaustive. Exhaustive expenditures occur when government consumes resources such as facilities and manpower that might otherwise have been used by the private sector. Nonexhaustive expenditures occur when government redistributes or transfers resources to components of the society instead of consuming them. Interest payments on the national debt, unemployment compensation, aid to the indigent, and old-age and retirement benefits are major examples of nonexhaustive government expenditures.

Another form of nonexhaustive expenditures is investment for the future, whether for capital facilities or for services, as in education for children. Government aid to small businesses, support of research and development, and like activities are forms of investment in future economic development. As a result of these kinds of expenditures the cost of government is actually less than the total dollar figures reported in budgets in the sense that what is spent will generate future revenue for both society and its governments.

Effects on the Private Sector. Government expenditures have specific effects on industries, occupations, geographic regions, and subpopulations. These effects are especially evident in the field of defense. During the Cold War, clusters of firms and their employees became highly dependent upon defense outlays, resulting in what President Eisenhower in 1961 decried as the military-industrial complex. The case could be made that a dangerous symbiotic relationship developed between the military, with its penchant for new weaponry, and corporations eager to supply such weaponry. Periodic scandals in defense contracting are seeming confirmation of the fears expressed by President Eisenhower.

The impact of defense is particularly pronounced in regard to employment, despite the downsizing that has occurred since the end of the Cold War.[12] In 1993, defense accounted for 0.8 percent of the private sector labor force and about a third of the federal government's civilian labor force. In addition, the federal government hired 1.5 million people for armed forces duty based in the United States. Total military and civilian employment constituted 2.0 percent of total U.S. employment.

The impact of defense expenditures upon specific occupations also has been significant.[13] Defense expenditures account for more than half of all shipfitting jobs, nearly 40 percent of aero-astronautic engineering jobs, and 20 percent or more of jobs in physics, machine tool operations, and aircraft mechanics.[14] The creation of defense-related jobs has the effect of attracting people into educational programs that develop the requisite skills. The result is that people are attracted into technical career fields that are dependent upon continued defense spending. These people suffer or flourish depending on what policies prevail.

Geographic and Industry Effects. Military research, development, and procurement are of such great magnitude that many specific industries and corporations become quasi-public institutions. By the early 1990s, the Department of Defense purchased virtually the entire output of the shipbuilding industry, almost 70 percent of the aircraft industry, and 50 percent of the radio and television communications industry.[15] Although cutbacks in defense in the mid-1990s most likely reduced these numbers, defense expenditures still greatly influence these industries. Besides providers of military equipment, such as General Dynamics, General Electric, and General Motors, numerous consulting and research and development firms are dependent on military expenditures. Nondefense contracting firms are similarly dependent, with 60 to 80 percent of their revenues coming from government contracts.

Employees of these varied private sector firms, judging from their length of service on government projects, are in effect career civil servants. One difference is that the pay of managerial staff in these firms is often higher than similarly trained government employees. (Professional salaries, such as for engineers and scientists, tend to be relatively equal, since government must meet private sector salaries in order to recruit and retain professionals.) Another difference is that private sector employees do not constitute a permanent expense to the government. These workers are not protected by civil service laws and are ineligible for government pension benefits. Furthermore, when these workers' services are not needed, government has no obligation to them as it would to its own employees.

The geographic impact of defense expenditures is equally important because they are not uniformly distributed throughout the nation.[16] In 1994, defense contract awards totaled $110 billion, and 41 percent of those awards went to corporations in just four states: California was first, followed by Texas, Virginia, and Missouri. Other heavily dependent states include Florida, Massachusetts, and New York.[17] The metropolitan area receiving the largest infusion of military and civilian defense expenditures is St. Louis, Missouri.

The dependence on defense is hardly a handicap for states when defense expenditures are rising, but the declines in spending rates that began in the 1980s and accelerated in the 1990s have had severe repercussions. Cutbacks in defense contracting affect employment of contractors and their subcontractors, and closures of military installations sap local economies dependent upon the jobs created by spending of military personnel. Members of Congress may be eager to reduce defense expenditures as long as cuts in spending in their individual districts are kept to a minimum, an obviously impossible objective if all congressional districts are to be so protected.[18]

Defense, while the most striking example of private dependence upon public outlays, is not the sole example. Highway construction also involves large sums of public money. The employees of construction firms specializing in bridge and highway construction are in effect government employees. The same is true for suppliers of road-building equipment. It also should be noted that companies of this type are major suppliers of equipment to the Defense Department.

In some cases, the impact of government on an industry is greater as a result of what government does not do than what it does. The impact of the federal government's not taxing interest paid on home mortgages has a far greater effect on the housing industry than all federal expenditures for public housing and redevelopment.

The lack of clear-cut distinctions between the public and private sectors and between one government and another is evident in education. Elementary and secondary education is a function of local school districts, but about half the funds used by these districts come from state governments, with additional funds coming from the federal government. Public higher education is funded by the states, with important federal support, especially student aid and research financing. Governments also selectively subsidize private colleges and universities. Private corporations make important contributions to both public and private schools.

Subpopulation Effects. Taxes and expenditures affect different subpopulations in different ways. In the example above of the federal government allowing income tax deductions for interest paid on home mortgages, the middle class and upper class benefit far more than lower-income groups, who typically are renters rather than home owners. This tax expenditure, namely, the government's not taxing something that could be taxed, has a redistributional effect in favor of the middle and upper classes (see Chapter 4).

Government actions have important effects on generations, including those who will be born in years to come. Taxing and spending policies can help or harm children through health and education programs, the working-age population through transportation programs, and the elderly through government-sponsored nursing care and the like. Future generations benefit from government programs that encourage investment in economic development but may be harmed by excessive debts that governments may accumulate, especially the federal government.

THE MAGNITUDE AND GROWTH OF GOVERNMENT

There are many ways to measure the magnitude of government, but dollars and people are generally the easiest measures to apply. By focusing on revenues, expenditures, and numbers of employees, we can use comparable standards in contrasting governments with each other and with private organizations. These measures, then, are the main ones used in this section.

A couple of words of caution are warranted. Statistical data used in this and the following section are drawn from several sources, some of which are not in agreement. Therefore, some of the data reported here must be considered approximate. Another item to note is that the U.S. census bureau, primarily due to budgetary limitations, has scaled back the data it reports, the frequency of reporting, and the timeliness of the data.

Revenues

One approach to measuring organizations is to consider their revenues or receipts, which allows comparisons among private and public organizations.[19] Table 2–1 ranks the 25 largest governments and industrial corporations in the world as measured by revenues. Significantly, 16 of the 25 are governments, with the U.S. federal government ranked first. Until the Soviet Union disintegrated, it was unquestionably the second largest organization in the world, but the new Russian federation is in sixth place. Three U.S. bureaucracies are included in the list of 25—the federal government, California, and New York State. The listing is replete with intriguing contrasts; for example, China's government budget is smaller than the budget of New York State or Toyota Motor Company.

In a list of the top 50 organizations in the United States, 12 state governments are included (see Table 2–2). These states, in order of appearance, are California, New York, Texas, Pennsylvania, Ohio, New Jersey, Illinois, Florida, Michigan, Massachusetts, North Carolina, and Washington. Ranking ahead of all of these states except California and New York is New York City.

These statistics dramatically underscore the need for caution in generalizing about governments or private corporations. It is necessary to recognize the important differences in the functions of government and industry and the methods by which these organizations make decisions. Differences also abound within each of these two types of organizations. The services provided and methods of decision making are not identical in the governments of Russia, Germany, and

Table 2–1 Twenty-Five Largest Governments and Industrial Corporations in the World by Revenues, 1992 (in Billions of Dollars)

Rank	Governments	Revenues	Industrial Corporations
1.	U.S. Federal Government	1,259	
2.	Germany	704	
3.	Italy	581	
4.	Japan	571	
5.	United Kingdom	439	
6.	Russia and Russian Federation	310	
7.	France	249	
8.	Spain	140	
9.	Canada	138	
10.		133	General Motors
11.	Netherlands	122	
12.		104	Exxon
13.	California	102	
14.		101	Ford Motor
15.		99	Royal Dutch/Shell Group
16.	Sweden	83	
17.	Iran	80	
18.		79	Toyota Motor
19.	Australia	78	
20.	New York State	74	
21.		68	IRI
22.	China	66	
23.		63	Daimler Benz
24.		62	General Electric
25.		61	Hitachi

Source: Data from *Compendium of Government Finances,* 1992 Census of Governments, 1997, U.S. Bureau of the Census; Fortune's Global 500, *Fortune,* p. 191, © 1993; and *The World Almanac and Book of Facts,* 1994, Funk and Wagnalls.

the United Kingdom, nor are they the same in such private corporations as General Motors, IBM, and Hitachi.

On the other hand, using the standard of size may provide more insights into the operations of organizations than simply classifying organizations as public or private, national or local, and so forth. Not all industrial firms are like General

Table 2–2 Fifty Largest U.S. Organizations by Revenues, 1992 (in Billions of Dollars)

Rank	Organization	Revenue
1.	**U.S. Federal Government**	**1,259.4**
2.	General Motors	132.4
3.	Exxon	103.2
4.	**California**	**101.7**
5.	Ford Motor	100.1
6.	**New York State**	**74.2**
7.	American Telephone & Telegraph	64.9
8.	International Business Machines	64.5
9.	General Electric	57.1
10.	Mobil	56.9
11.	Wal-Mart Stores	55.5
12.	Sears, Roebuck	52.3
13.	Philip Morris Cos.	50.1
14.	**New York City**	**44.9**
15.	Kmart	38.0
16.	**Texas**	**37.6**
17.	Chevron	37.5
18.	E.I. duPont	37.2
19.	Chrysler	36.9
20.	Texaco	36.8
21.	**Pennsylvania**	**36.7**
22.	**Ohio**	**33.6**
23.	Citicorp	31.9
24.	Procter & Gamble	30.4
25.	Boeing	30.2
26.	**New Jersey**	**29.1**
27.	**Illinois**	**27.9**
28.	**Florida**	**27.2**
29.	American Express	27.0
30.	**Michigan**	**26.6**
31.	Amoco	25.3
32.	Kroeger	22.1
33.	PepsiCo	22.0
34.	ConAgra	21.7

continues

Table 2–2 continued

Rank	Organization	Revenue
35.	International Telephone & Telegraph	21.7
36.	United Technologies	21.6
37.	**Massachusetts**	**21.1**
38.	Eastman Kodak	20.2
39.	GTE	20.0
40.	JC Penney	19.1
41.	American Stores	19.1
42.	Dow Chemical	19.0
43.	Xerox	18.7
44.	Cigna	18.6
45.	American International Group	18.4
46.	**North Carolina**	**18.0**
47.	Dayton Hudson	17.9
48.	**Washington**	**17.7**
49.	Atlantic Richfield	17.5
50.	Aetna Life and Casualty	17.5

Note: Governments appear in boldface.

Source: Data from *Compendium of Government Finances*, 1992 Census of Governments, pp. 88–139, 1997, U.S. Bureau of the Census; and The Forbes 500s: Sales, *Forbes*, pp. 204 and 206, © 1993.

Motors, nor are all state governments like California's, but perhaps all organizations of any given size, regardless of their private or public character, exhibit some common traits.

Although total revenues or expenditures are useful as approximate guides in measuring the size of government, these data need to be assessed in light of the varied capabilities of societies to support government. Unfortunately, reliable international data are often unavailable, and as a consequence, drawing useful comparisons among international organizations is difficult.

Even given these limitations, it is obvious that the U.S. economy is one of the most prosperous in the world. The high per capita gross domestic product (GDP) in the United States, $28,423 in 1996, has allowed for both big government and a large private sector. The nation has been able to afford government expenditures equal to about 32 percent of GDP ($9,145 per capita expenditures for the total of all governments in the United States).[20] This figure, however, is misleading as regards the size of the public sector in that as we noted above only about half of per capita expenditures goes toward the purchase of goods and services—the other half is used for transfer payments and interest payments on debt.

Expenditures

Because early records on state and local finance are spotty, reliance must be placed upon federal expenditure data to obtain some overall perspective of the growth of government since the eighteenth century. Table 2–3 shows federal spending from 1789 through 2002 (estimated). During this period, expenditures rose from only $4.3 million in the first few years to well over $1 trillion annually (bear in mind that an important contributor to this difference is inflation).

The twentieth century has seen important differences in the expenditure patterns of the federal government and those of state and local governments. Federal expenditures have fluctuated most, primarily because of war-related activities. The first year in which federal expenditures exceeded $1 billion was 1865, the peak year of the Civil War. Later, in response to World War I, federal expenditures jumped from $0.7 billion in 1916 to $18.5 billion in 1919, then dropped to $6.4 billion the following year. They also increased from $13.3 billion in 1941, the year the United States entered into World War II, to $92.7 billion in 1945, then declined to $33.1 billion in 1948. During the Korean War, expenditures rose from $42.6 billion in 1950 to $74.3 billion in 1953, then dropped to $68.4 billion in 1955, after the war. In general, federal expenditures have risen during wartime and then declined, but not to prewar levels, resulting in a cumulative increase over time. The Vietnam War era departed from this pattern: Federal expenditures rose during and after the war. State and local expenditures, on the other hand, have fluctuated less. They have increased annually, except for a period of slight decline during World War II.

Important shifts have occurred in the extent to which the nation relies on different levels of government. At the turn of the century, local governments were by far the biggest spenders, followed by the federal government and then the states. During the Depression, federal spending spurted above local expenditures, and the gap has since been widening. As of 1992, federal expenditures stood at $1,527.3 billion compared with $701.6 billion for states and $661.7 billion for local governments. Caution should be exercised in interpreting these numbers in that each includes intergovernmental transfers, namely, grants from one government to another. Total spending for all governments was $2,494.4 billion.[21]

Just as total expenditures have increased, so have per capita expenditures. In 1902, the total of all government expenditures in the United States was only $20 per capita; in 1996, the comparable figure was $9,145 per capita, an increase of more than 45,000 percent. These data, however, overstate the rising cost of government by not deflating for general price increases.

Table 2–3 Federal Government Expenditures, Selected Years, 1789–2002 (in Millions of Dollars)

Year	Expenditures	Year	Expenditures	Year	Expenditures
1789–1791	4	1870	310	1945	92,712
1800	11	1875	275	1950	42,562
1805	11	1880	268	1955	68,444
1810	8	1885	260	1960	92,191
1815	33	1890	318	1965	118,228
1820	18	1895	356	1970	195,649
1825	16	1900	529	1975	332,332
1830	15	1905	567	1980	590,947
1835	18	1910	694	1985	946,499
1840	24	1915	746	1990	1,253,163
1845	23	1920	6,358	1995	1,515,729
1850	40	1925	2,924	2000	1,814,427*
1855	60	1930	3,320	2002	1,879,717*
1860	63	1935	6,412		
1865	1,298	1940	9,468		

*Estimated.

Source: Data from *Historical Statistics of the United States, Colonial Times—1957*, 1960, U.S. Bureau of the Census and Historical Tables, 1997, U.S. Office of Management and Budget.

One means of controlling for price changes over time is to consider government expenditures as a percentage of GDP (Figure 2–1). From 1929 to 1996 the cost of government rose from 10 percent to 32 percent of GDP. Increases occurred in the 1930s due to the Great Depression, and then World War II brought expenditures to an all-time high, at about half of GDP. A sharp cutback followed in the postwar years, and expenditures dropped to a low of 19 percent. Since that time the percentage rose gradually and then plateaued in the 1990s.

Public Employment

The rise of big bureaucracy in the federal government can be measured in terms of numbers of public employees. In 1816, there were less than 5,000 full- and part-time civilian employees in the federal service. Following the Civil War, however, greater growth was recorded. In 1871, there were over 50,000 federal employees, and this number had doubled to 100,000 by 1881. The period of fastest growth was from the Depression through World War II. In 1931, there were

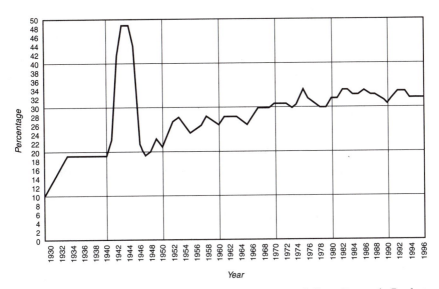

Figure 2–1 All Government Expenditures as a Percentage of Gross Domestic Product, 1929–1996. *Source*: Data from *Historical Statistics on Governmental Finances and Employment*, 1967 Census of Governments, Vol. 6, No. 5, pp. 1, 36–47, 1969, U.S. Bureau of the Census; and *Economic Report of the President*, pp. 300, 394, 1997, Council of Economic Advisers.

still only 610,000 employees, but by 1945, the peak of the wartime economy, the federal civilian work force had climbed to nearly 4 million. Within a year, it was reduced to less than 3 million. Since then, only once, in 1950, has the federal work force dropped below 2 million. Federal civilian personnel have totaled about 3 million or a little less since the 1970s.

Although the size of the federal bureaucracy is extraordinarily large, government personnel are geographically dispersed. In 1994, California had 295,000 federal civilian employees, a figure equal to more than half of Vermont's population. If these employees were all in one area, they alone, not counting their families, would form a metropolitan area somewhat larger than Binghamton, New York, or Reno, Nevada. Federal employees are also numerous in other states, including Illinois, with 106,000; New York, with 145,000; and Texas, with 175,000.[22] In the 1990s, states such as these became painfully aware of their dependence on federal employment as the government began to downsize the military, since about one out of three federal civilian jobs are in defense.

At the state and local levels, the number of employees has also increased. State employment grew from less than 1 million in 1947 to 3.9 million in 1994. In the same period, local employment increased from 2.9 million to 10.0 million.[23] Significantly, the growth at the local level has been accompanied by a decline in the number of local governments. In 1992, there were 84,955 local governments, 30,000 fewer than four decades earlier. This decline is largely attributable to school district consolidation. Since 1972, the number of local governments has been rising gradually, due mainly to increases in the number of special districts, governments that typically provide a single service, such as water provision or recreation services.

SOURCES OF REVENUE AND PURPOSES OF GOVERNMENT EXPENDITURES

Government does not simply get money and spend it in general. Revenue is obtained from specific sources and spent for specific public goods and services. The following discussion considers the relationships between income and outgo, between the ways in which revenue is generated and the purposes of government expenditures.

Revenue Sources

Tax structure always has been and always will be a controversial topic. This section provides an overview of taxes and other revenues. Policy and technical issues pertaining to the tax system are covered in Chapter 4.

Table 2–4 displays the sources of revenue for the federal, state, and local governments in 1991–1992. The first important thing to note is that this table covers the sources of revenue but not expenditures. Because of intergovernmental transfers of funds, governments may obtain revenue from many sources but not directly spend it. This is true for all levels of government, including local governments, which provide the states with some revenue (1 percent). As can be seen in the table, 23 percent of state government revenue and 33 percent of local government revenue come from other jurisdictions. Once again it is apparent that there are no clear-cut distinctions among the three levels of government.

Three tax sources provide almost 80 percent of the federal government's revenue. The largest single share (38 percent) is obtained through the individual income tax; 32 percent through social insurance, including Social Security and unemployment compensation; and 8 percent through the corporate income tax. Another 5 percent comes from sales and gross receipt taxes and customs duties. The latter accounted for 94 percent of all federal monies in 1792. Corporate income tax revenues also have declined in importance; they accounted for 30 percent of revenues in 1930.

Table 2–4 Government Revenue by Source and Level of Government, 1991–1992

Revenue Source	All Government Revenues (in Millions of Dollars)	Distribution (Percentage)			
		All	Federal	State	Local
General Revenue	1,651,352	72.9	67.9	81.9	88.4
Intergovernmental Revenue			0.3	22.9	33.3
From Federal Government				21.4	3.1
From States			0.3		30.2
From Local Governments				1.5	
General Revenue from Own Sources	1,218,900	72.9	67.6	59.0	55.1
Taxes		53.8	52.3	44.5	34.9
Property	180,337	8.0		1.0	26.4
Sales, Gross Receipts, and Customs	262,013	11.6	5.1	22.1	5.1
Individual Income	592,103	26.1	37.8	14.1	1.6
Corporate Net Income	124,150	5.5	8.0	2.9	0.3
Other	60,297	2.7	1.4	4.4	1.4
Charges and Miscellaneous General Revenue	432,452	19.1	15.3	14.5	20.2
Utility and Liquor Store Revenue	63,240	2.8		0.9	8.6
Insurance Trust Revenue	552,172	24.4	32.1	17.2	3.0
Total Revenue	2,266,765	100.0	100.0	100.0	100.0
			1,259,383	743,520	655,216

Note: Totals may not equal 100.0 percent due to rounding.

Source: Reprinted from *Compendium of Government Finances*, 1992 Census of Governments, p. 2, 1997, U.S. Bureau of the Census.

As already indicated, one-fifth of state revenue comes from other governments, mostly from the federal government. Of the remainder, sales and gross receipts taxes are the largest revenue sources, providing 22 percent of all state funds. Another 14 percent is obtained from individual income taxes.

Local governments obtain one-third of their money from other governments and the rest mainly through the property tax and other sources. Of all local revenue, 26 percent comes from the property tax. Approximately 30 percent is obtained from charges, miscellaneous general revenue, and utility fees.

Expenditures by Function

Expenditures are the product of a set of choices or decisions made as to what public goods and services should be produced. Total expenditures are the sum of decisions made at all levels of government. Each level of government, however, has discrete financial decision-making processes that are only partially dependent on the other levels. Just as the different levels depend on somewhat different sources for revenues, local, state, and federal governments also spend their funds for somewhat different functions.

The federal government provides financial assistance to state and local governments, the states to local governments, and, in some cases, local governments to states. Thus governments obviously do not spend directly all the money that flows through them. In 1991–1992, direct federal expenditures were $1,341 billion, or 88 percent of all federal expenditures. State governments spent a smaller percentage of their funds—$499 billion or 71 percent of all state expenditures. Local governments spent directly virtually all their funds—$654 billion or 99 percent.[24]

Government expenditures by function and by level of government are displayed in Table 2–5. Like Tables 2–3 and 2–4, this table reports gross finances, including intergovernmental transfers. As the percentage distributions show, social insurance is the largest single function of government, accounting for 22 percent of all expenditures by the federal, state, and local governments. That number increases to 36 percent if social services and income maintenance (welfare) are added.

Defense was the second largest federal expenditure function in 1991–1992, at 23 percent of the federal budget. Some of the financial costs of defense are not reflected in these figures. Veterans benefits and services, which are obviously byproducts of defense, are not included. A portion of the interest paid on the national debt can be ascribed to defense, given that major budgetary deficits have been incurred during wartime. Some aspects of the space program also could be charged to defense, because technological breakthroughs in space exploration have military applications.

Table 2–5 Expenditures by Function and Level of Government, 1991–1992

Function	All Government Expenditures (in Millions of Dollars)	Distribution (Percentage)			
		All	Federal	State	Local
General Expenditure	1,864,166	74.7	70.2	87.3	86.9
National Defense and International Relations	351,684	14.1	23.0		
Postal Service	44,890	1.8	2.9		
Space Research and Technology	13,550	0.5	0.9		
Education and Libraries	351,979	14.1	3.2	30.1	36.8
Social Services and Income Maintenance	341,164	13.7	13.1	29.6	12.2
Transportation	88,236	3.5	1.7	7.7	5.6
Public Safety	94,388	3.8	0.7	4.2	8.8
Environment and Housing	151,337	6.1	6.1	2.5	9.6
Government Administration	68,001	2.7	1.3	3.7	4.7
Interest on General Debt	255,077	10.2	13.1	3.5	4.6
Other	103,860	4.2	4.2	6.0	4.5
Utility and Liquor Store	85,314	3.4		1.4	11.4
Insurance Trust	544,945	21.8	29.8	11.3	1.6
Total Expenditures	2,494,424	100.0	100.0	100.0	100.0
			1,527,311	701,601	661,744

Note: Totals may not equal 100.0 percent due to rounding.

Source: Reprinted from *Compendium of Government Finances*, 1992 Census of Governments, p. 2, 1997, U.S. Bureau of the Census.

Compared with social insurance and defense, all other federal program areas are comparatively small. The next largest "program" is interest paid on the national debt (13 percent). The remainder of federal expenditures are divided into small segments devoted to education, postal service, transportation, the environment and housing, and other functions.

State and local expenditures follow different patterns. In the first place, neither the states nor local governments are responsible for defense, postal service, or space exploration. Education is the largest expense for both types of government, 30 percent for states and 37 percent for local governments, particularly school districts. Social services and income maintenance expenditures at the state level are basically the same size as education and library expenditures (30 percent). "Traditional" local functions, such as transportation (roads and public transit), public safety (police and fire), and housing, together account for only 24 percent of local spending.

Expenditures reported here cover intergovernmental transfers as well as direct outlays. Therefore, federal grants to states, for example, are reported under both federal and state expenditures. In spite of this weakness, the table is useful in indicating the purposes for which governments spend their resources. On the other hand, one should recognize that in many cases governments do not actually spend these funds but rather provide them to other governments. Also, these data do not reveal the relative contributions of different levels of government to a given program area.

Issues of relative contribution are clarified in Table 2–6, which displays federal, state, and local expenditures as percentage contributions to functional areas. For instance, in Table 2–5 environment and housing expenditures constitute only 6 percent of the federal budget, but in Table 2–6 federal expenditures are shown to account for 47 percent of all environment and housing outlays.

SUMMARY

The preceding discussion has shown that government is indeed large, that the growth pattern of the public sector has been an upward one, and that today drawing a definitive line between the public and private sectors is virtually impossible. If present trends continue, government can be expected to become even larger, although at a slower rate, providing more services directly or ensuring the provision of services by regulating the private sector.

Governments in the United States differ in the types of revenue sources used and the functions for which revenues are expended. The federal government relies primarily on personal and corporate income taxes and social insurance deductions; expenditures are concentrated in defense, international relations, and social insurance. States obtain a fifth of their revenue from the federal govern-

Table 2–6 Direct Expenditures by Function and Level of Government, 1991–1992

Function	Distribution (Percentage)			
	All	Federal	State	Local
General Expenditure	100.0	53.8	20.0	26.2
National Defense and International Relations	100.0	100.0		
Postal Service	100.0	100.0		
Space Research and Technology	100.0	100.0		
Education and Libraries	100.0	6.4	24.6	69.0
Social Services and Income Maintenance	100.0	27.4	50.2	22.3
Transportation	100.0	10.7	47.8	41.6
Public Safety	100.0	9.7	29.0	61.4
Environment and Housing	100.0	47.3	10.9	41.8
Government Administration	100.0	24.8	29.2	46.0
Interest on General Debt	100.0	78.3	9.7	12.1
Other	100.0	51.6	20.5	27.9
Utility and Liquor Store	100.0		11.3	88.7
Insurance Trust	100.0	83.4	14.6	2.0

Note: Totals may not equal 100.0 percent due to rounding.

Source: Reprinted from *Compendium of Government Finances*, 1992 Census of Governments, p. 12, 1997, U.S. Bureau of the Census.

ment and the remainder largely from sales and individual income taxes; state expenditures are concentrated in education, social services, and welfare. Local governments receive a third of their funds from other governments and a quarter from property taxes; the most expensive function of local government is education.

NOTES

1. S.H. Beer, *To Make a Nation: The Rediscovery of American Federalism* (Cambridge, MA: Belknap Press, 1993); L.D. White, *The Federalists: A Study in Administrative History, 1789–1801* (New York: Free Press, 1948).

2. M. Friedman and R. Friedman, *Freedom to Choose* (New York: Harcourt Brace Jovanovich, 1980); F.A. Hayek, *The Road to Serfdom* (Chicago: University of Chicago Press, 1945); P. Drucker and H. Finer, *The Road to Reaction* (Boston: Little, Brown, 1945).

3. J.K. Galbraith, *Economics and the Public Purpose* (Boston: Houghton Mifflin, 1973).

4. R.A. Musgrave and P.B. Musgrave, *Public Finance in Theory and Practice,* 5th ed. (New York: McGraw-Hill, 1989); D.N. Hyman, *Public Finance: A Contemporary Application of Theory to Policy,* 5th ed. (Orlando, FL: Dryden Press, 1996).

5. S. Abizadeli and A. Basilevsky, Measuring the Size of Government, *Public Finance* 45 (1990): 359–377.

6. W.D. Berry and D. Lawery, Explaining the Size of the Public Sector, *Journal of Politics* 49 (1987): 401–440; P.D. Larkey et al., Theorizing about the Growth of Government, *Journal of Public Policy* 1 (1981): 157–220.

7. R. Bird, Wagner's Law of Expanding State Activity, *Public Finance* 26 (1971): 1–26; J.M. Buchanan and G. Tullock, The Expanding Public Sector: Wagner Squared, *Public Choice* 31 (Fall 1977): 147–150.

8. M. Beck, *Government Spending: Trends and Issues* (New York: Praeger, 1981); M.S. Lewis-Beck and T.W. Rice, Government Growth in the United States, *Journal of Politics* 47 (1985): 2–30.

9. H.W. Elder, Exploring the Tax Revolt: An Analysis of the Effects of State Tax and Expenditure Limitation Laws, *Public Finance Quarterly* 20 (1992): 47–63.

10. N.W. Polsby, *Presidential Elections,* 9th ed. (Chatham, NJ: Chatham House, 1996).

11. W.F. Shughart and R.D. Tollison, On the Growth of Government and the Political Economy of Legislation, *Research in Law and Economics* 9 (1986): 111–127.

12. Committee for Economic Development, *The Economy and National Defense: Adjusting to Military Cutbacks in the Post–Cold War Era* (New York: Committee for Economic Development, 1991), 4; U.S. Bureau of the Census, *Statistical Abstract of the United States: 1996* (Washington, DC: U.S. Government Printing Office, 1996), 352.

13. R.S. Boles, *Creating a Strong Post–Cold War Economy* (Washington, DC: National Planning Association, 1990).

14. Committee for Economic Development, *The Economy and National Defense,* 26.

15. Committee for Economic Development, *The Economy and National Defense,* 19.

16. R.E. Bolton, *Defense Purchases and Regional Growth* (Washington, DC: Brookings Institution, 1966).

17. U.S. Bureau of the Census, *Statistical Abstract of the United States*, 353; B.G. Lall and J.T. Marlin, *Building a Peace Economy: Opportunities and Problems of Post–Cold War Defense Cuts* (Boulder, CO: Westview Press, 1992), 54.

18. C. Twight, Department of Defense Attempts to Close Military Bases: The Political Economy of Congressional Resistance, in *Arms, Politics, and the Economy: Historical and Contemporary Perspectives*, ed. R. Higgs (New York: Holmes & Meier, 1990), 236–280.

19. The idea of comparing private and public organizations was suggested by Robert J. Mowitz, then Director, Institute of Public Administration, The Pennsylvania State University.

20. Council of Economic Advisers, *Economic Report of the President* (Washington, DC: U.S. Government Printing Office, 1997), 300, 337, 394.

21. U.S. Bureau of the Census, *Statistical Abstract of the United States*, 7.

22. U.S. Bureau of the Census, *Statistical Abstract of the United States*, 28, 40, 347.

23. U.S. Bureau of the Census at http://www.census.gov/govs/www/index.html; accessed December 1997.

24. U.S. Bureau of the Census, *Compendium of Government Finances*, 1992 Census of Governments (Washington, DC: U.S. Government Printing Office, 1997), 7.

CHAPTER 3

Budget Cycles

Public budgeting systems, which are devices for selecting societal ends and means, consist of numerous participants and various processes that bring the participants into interaction. As was seen in the preceding chapters, the purpose of budgeting is to allocate scarce resources among competing public demands and wants in order to attain societal goals and objectives. Those societal ends are expressed not by philosopher kings but by mortals who must operate within the context of some prescribed allocation process, namely, the budgetary system.

This chapter provides an overview of the participants and processes involved in budgetary decision making. First, the phases of the budget cycle are reviewed. Any system has some structure or form, and budgetary systems are no exception. As will be seen, there are steps in the decision-making process; detailed discussions of these steps are presented in subsequent chapters. The second topic is the extent to which budget cycles are intermingled within government and among governments.

THE BUDGET CYCLE

To provide for responsible government, budgeting is geared to a cycle. The cycle allows the system to absorb and respond to new information and thus allows government to be held accountable for its actions. Although existing budget systems may be less than perfect in guaranteeing adherence to this principle of responsibility, the argument stands that periodicity contributes to achieving and maintaining limited government. The budget cycle consists of four phases: (1) preparation and submission, (2) approval, (3) execution, and (4) audit.

Preparation and Submission

The preparation and submission phase is the most difficult to describe because it has been subjected the most to reform efforts. Experiments in reformulating the preparation process abound. Although institutional units may exist over time, both procedures and substantive content vary from year to year.

Chief Executive Responsibilities. The responsibility for budget preparation varies greatly among jurisdictions. Budget reform efforts in the United States have pressed for executive budgeting, in which the chief executive has exclusive responsibility for preparing a proposed budget and submitting it to the legislative body. At the federal level, the president has such exclusive responsibility, although it should be recognized that many factors curtail the extent to which the president can make major changes in the budget. Preparation authority, however, is not always available to governors and local chief executives. While a majority of governors have responsibility for preparation and submission, some share budget-making authority with other elected administrative officers, civil service appointees, legislative leaders, or some combination of these.[1] In parliamentary systems, the prime minister (chief executive) typically has responsibility for budget preparation and submits what is usually called the "government budget" to the parliament.

At the municipal level, the mayor may or may not have budget preparation powers. In cities where the mayor is strong—has administrative control over the executive branch—the mayor normally does have budget-making power. This is not necessarily the case in weak-mayor systems and in cities operating under the commission plan, where each councilor or commissioner administers a given department. Usually, city managers in council-manager systems have responsibility for budget preparation, although their ability to make budgetary recommendations may be tempered by their lack of independence. Managers are appointed by councils and commonly lack tenure. Even in a city in which the mayor or chief executive does not have budget preparation responsibility, it is still likely to be in the hands of an executive official such as a city finance director. Thus, a majority of cities follow the principle of executive budget preparation.[2]

Location of Budget Office. Budget preparation at the federal level is primarily a function of a budget office that was established by the Budget and Accounting Act of 1921.[3] That legislation established the Bureau of the Budget (BOB), which became a unit of the Treasury Department. With the passage of time, the role of the BOB increased in importance, and in 1939 it became part of the newly formed Executive Office of the President. Given that the BOB was thought to be the "right arm of the president"—a common phrase in early budget literature—the move out of the Treasury, a line department, into the Executive Office of the

President placed the BOB under direct presidential supervision. In 1970, President Nixon reorganized the BOB, giving it a new title, the Office of Management and Budget (OMB). The intent of the reorganization was to bring "real business management into Government at the very highest level."[4]

Steps in the Preparation Stage. In the federal government, budget preparation starts in the spring, or even earlier for large agencies. Agencies begin by assessing their programs and considering which programs require revision and whether new programs should be recommended. At approximately the same time, the president's staff makes estimates of anticipated economic trends to determine available revenue under existing tax legislation. The next step is for the president to issue general budget and fiscal policy guidelines, which agencies use to develop their individual budgets. These budgets are then submitted in late summer to OMB. Throughout the fall and into the later months of the year, OMB staff members review agency requests and hold hearings with agency spokespersons. Not until shortly before the budget is to be released, usually in November and December and into January, does the president become deeply involved in the process, which culminates in February with the submission of a proposed budget to Congress.

At the state and local levels, a similar process is used where executive budgeting systems prevail. The central budget office issues budget request instructions, reviews the submitted requests, and makes recommendations to the chief executive, who decides which items to recommend to the legislative body. In jurisdictions not using executive budgeting, the chief executive and the budget office play minor roles; in this type of system, the line agencies direct their budget requests to the legislative body.

Political Factors. The preparation phase, as well as the other three phases in the budget cycle, is replete with political considerations, both bureaucratic and partisan, in addition to policy considerations. Each organizational unit is concerned with its own survival and advancement. Line agencies and their subunits attempt to protect against budget cuts and may strive for increased resources. Budget offices often play negative roles, attempting to limit agency growth or imposing agency budget cuts. Budget offices always are fully conscious of the fact that whatever they propose can be overruled by the chief executive. All members of the executive branch are concerned with their relationships with the legislative branch and the general citizenry. The chief executive is especially concerned about partisan calculations: Which alternatives will be advantageous to his or her political party? Of course there is concern for developing programs for the common good, but this concern is played out in a complicated game of political maneuvering.[5]

Fragmentation. One complaint about the preparation phase is that it tends to be highly fragmented. Organizational units within line agencies tend to be concerned primarily with their own programs and frequently fail to take a broad perspective. Even the budget office may be myopic, although it will be forced into considering the budget as a whole. Only the chief executive is unquestionably committed to viewing the budget as a whole in the preparation phase.

Approval

Revenue and Appropriation Bills. The budget is approved by a legislative body, whether Congress, a state legislature, a county board of supervisors, a city council, or a school board. The fragmented approach to budgeting in the preparation phase is not characteristic of the approval phase at the local level. A city council may have a separate finance committee, but normally the council as a whole participates actively in the approval process. Local legislative bodies may take several preliminary votes on pieces of the budget but then adopt the budget as a whole by a single vote.

States, however, separate tax and other revenue measures from appropriations or spending bills. Some states place most or all of their spending provisions in a single appropriation bill, but others have hundreds of appropriation bills. Most state legislatures are free to augment or reduce the governor's budget, but some are restricted in their ability to increase the budget. Many parliamentary systems similarly allow the parliament to modify, but not increase, the government's budget proposal.

At the federal level, the revenue and appropriation processes have been markedly fragmented and involve numerous committees and subcommittees. Not only have revenue raising and spending been treated as separate processes, but the expenditure side is handled in 13 major appropriation bills instead of being treated as a whole. Reforms introduced in 1974 attempted to integrate these divergent processes and pieces of legislation, but the system had numerous flaws. Additional problems of extraordinary magnitude developed in the 1980s.[6] Gramm-Rudman-Hollings reforms were put into place to attempt to force reductions in budget deficits, but those efforts also failed.[7] In 1990, Congress passed the Budget Enforcement Act, which set aside, at least temporarily, forced budget cuts.[8] President Clinton, upon taking office in 1993, proposed a budget package involving sizable tax increases and spending cuts, which in revised form were eventually passed by the narrowest of margins by the Congress. In 1997, the President and Congress agreed to a series of measures that were intended to bring the budget into balance by the year 2002 (see Chapter 9).

Executive Veto Powers. The final step of the approval stage is signing the appropriation and tax bills into law. The president, governors, and, in some cases, mayors have the power to veto. A veto sends the measure back to the legislative body for further consideration. Most governors have item-veto power, which allows them to veto specific portions of an appropriation bill but still sign it.[9] In no case can the executive augment parts of the budget beyond that provided by the legislature. Chapter 9 discusses the president's item-veto power.

Execution

Apportionment Process. Execution, the third phase, commences with the fiscal year—October 1 in the federal government. Some form of centralized control during this phase is common at all levels of government, and such control is usually maintained by the budget office. Following congressional passage of an appropriation bill and its signing by the president, agencies must submit to OMB a proposed plan for apportionment. This plan indicates the funds required for operations, typically on a quarterly basis. The apportionment process is used in part to ensure that agencies do not commit all their available funds in a period shorter than the 12-month fiscal year. The intent is to avoid the need for supplementary appropriations from Congress.

The apportionment process is substantively important in that program adjustments must be made to bring planned spending into balance with available revenue. Since it is likely that an agency did not obtain all the funds requested, either from the president in the preparation phase or from Congress in the approval phase, plans for the coming fiscal year must be revised. To varying degrees, state and local governments also use an apportionment process.

Impoundment. The chief executive may assert control in the apportionment process through an informal item veto known as "impoundment," which is basically a refusal to release some funds to agencies. Thomas Jefferson often is considered the first president to have impounded funds. President Nixon impounded so extensively that it stimulated legislative action by Congress. The 1974 legislation in a sense was a treaty between Congress and the White House allowing limited impoundment powers for the president. As will be discussed later, the Supreme Court largely negated the agreed procedures.

Allotments. Once funds are apportioned, agencies and departments make allotments. This process grants budgetary authority to subunits such as bureaus and divisions. Allotments are made on a monthly or quarterly basis, and, like the apportionment process, the allotment process is used to control spending during the fiscal year. Control often may be extensive and detailed, requiring approval by the department budget office for any shift in available funds from one item to another, such as from travel to wages. Some transfers may require clearance by the central budget office.

Preaudits. Before an expenditure is made, a form of preaudit is conducted. Basically, the preaudit is used to ensure that funds are being committed for approved purposes and that an agency has sufficient resources in its budget to meet the proposed expenditure. The responsibility for this function varies widely, with the budget and/or accounting office responsible in some jurisdictions and independently elected comptrollers responsible in others. Later, after approval is granted and a purchase is made, the treasurer writes a check for the expenditure.

Execution Subsystems. During budget execution, several subsystems are in operation. Taxes and other debts to government are collected. Cash is managed in the sense that monies temporarily not needed are invested. Supplies, materials, and equipment are procured, and strategies are developed to protect the government against loss or damage of property and against liability suits. Accounting and information systems are in operation. For state and local governments, bonds are sold and the proceeds are used to finance construction of facilities and the acquisition of major equipment. An office of federal management, independent of the budget office, has been proposed that would assume many duties, including setting procurement policy, conducting regulatory reviews, overseeing financial management systems, and controlling agency-operated grant programs that allocate funds to state and local governments.

Audit

The final phase of the budgetary process is the audit. The objectives of the audit are undergoing considerable change, but initially the main goal was to guarantee executive compliance with the provisions of appropriation bills—particularly to ensure honesty in dispensing public monies and to prevent needless waste. In accord with this goal, accounting procedures are prescribed and auditors check the books maintained by agency personnel. In recent years, the scope of auditing has been broadened to encompass studies of the effectiveness of government programs.

Location of the Audit Function. In the federal government, considerable controversy was generated concerning the appropriate organizational location of the audit function. President Woodrow Wilson in 1920 vetoed legislation that would have established the federal budget system on the grounds that he opposed the creation of an auditing office answerable to Congress rather than the president. Nevertheless, the General Accounting Office (GAO) was established in 1921 by the Budget and Accounting Act and was made an arm of Congress, with the justification that an audit unit outside of the executive branch should be created to provide objective assessments of expenditure practices.

GAO Functions. The GAO is headed by the comptroller general, who is appointed by the president, upon the advice and consent of the Senate, for only one term of 15 years.[10] Despite the GAO's title, the organization does not maintain accounts but rather audits the accounts of operating agencies and evaluates their accounting systems.

The GAO provides a variety of legal services. The office gives Congress opinions on legal issues, such as advising on whether a particular agency acted within the law in some specific instance under consideration. GAO also resolves bid protests over the awarding of government contracts.

In recent years, the GAO has been given responsibility for assessing the results of government programs in addition to its traditional responsibility for performing financial audits.[11] This new responsibility has sometimes led to criticism of GAO. In particular, some members of Congress have claimed that GAO has lost its neutrality and become a policy advocate. On occasion, the President has been more enthusiastic than Congress about the GAO's operations, recommending larger appropriations than the Congress was willing to provide.[12]

State and Local Auditors. At the state and local levels, the issue of organizational responsibility for auditing has been resolved in different ways. The alternatives are to have the audit function performed by a unit answerable to the legislative body, to the chief executive, to the citizenry directly, or some combination of these. The use of an elected auditor is defended on the grounds that objectivity can be achieved if the auditor is independent of the executive and legislative branches. The opposing arguments are that the electorate cannot suitably judge the qualifications of candidates for auditor and that the election process necessarily forces the auditor to become a biased rather than an objective analyst. States use primarily elected and legislative auditors.

SCRAMBLED BUDGET CYCLES

Although it is easy to speak of a budget cycle, there is no single such cycle in operation. Rather, a cycle exists for each budget period, and several cycles are in operation at any given time. The decision-making process is not one that simply moves from preparation and submission to approval, execution, and, finally, audit. Decision making is complicated by the existence of several budget cycles for which information is imperfect and incomplete.

Overlapping Cycles

A pattern of overlapping cycles can be seen in Figure 3–1, which shows the sequencing of five budget cycles typical of a large state. Only cycle 3 in the diagram displays the complete period covering 39 months. The preparation and submission phase requires at least 9 months, approval 6 months, execution 12 months, and audit 12 months. The same general pattern is found at the federal level, except that the execution phase begins on October 1, giving Congress approximately 8 months to consider the budget. As is indicated by the diagram, three or four budget periods are likely to be in progress at any point in time.

Budget preparation is complicated particularly by this scrambling or intermingling of cycles. In the first place, preparation begins perhaps 15 months before the budget is to go into effect. Moreover, much of the preparation phase is completed without knowledge of the legislature's actions in the preceding budget period.

Federal Experience. At the federal level, this problem has been especially difficult. Congress has been slow in passing appropriation bills, and the approval phase was rarely completed by the start of the fiscal year when it began July 1. The usual procedure was to pass a continuation bill permitting agencies to spend at the rate of the previous year's budget while Congress continued to deliberate on the new year. Although the budget calendar adopted in the 1970s gave Congress an additional 3 months, which was expected to permit completion of the approval phase, agencies' preparation problems for the following year's budget request remained. In any given year, an agency begins to prepare its budget request during the spring and summer, yet during this same period Congress deliberates on the agency's upcoming budget. Despite the additional time granted to Congress to act on the budget, work on the budget generally has not been completed on schedule, which compounds the problem of scrambled budget cycles.

Links Between Budget Phases. While a budget is being prepared, another one is being executed; this one may be for the immediately preceding budget year, but it can be for the one before. As can be seen in Figure 3–1, in the early stages of preparation for cycle 4 the execution phase is in operation for cycle 2. Under such conditions, the executive branch may not know the effects of ongoing programs yet is required to begin a new budget, recommending changes upward or downward. On occasion a new program may be created, and an agency must then

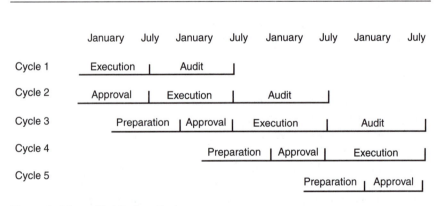

Figure 3–1 Scrambled Budget Cycles

recommend changes in the program for inclusion in the next budget without any time for assessing the merits of the program.

Length of Preparation Phase. The cycle, particularly the preparation phase, may be even longer than indicated above, especially when agencies must rely upon other agencies or subunits for information. For example, in preparing the education component of a state budget, a department of education will require budget information and requests from state universities and colleges early to meet deadlines imposed by the governor's budget office. The reliability and validity of data undoubtedly decrease as the lead time increases. Therefore, the earlier these schools submit their budget requests to the state capital, the less likely it is that such requests will be based on accurate assessments of future requirements.

Other Considerations

Besides the factors already mentioned, others further complicate budget cycles, most notably intergovernmental considerations and the timing of budget years.

Intergovernmental Factors. Another problem arises from intermingled budget cycles because the three main levels of government are interdependent. For the federal government, the main problem is assessing needs and finding resources to meet these needs. A state government must assess its needs and those of local governments and must then search for funds by raising state taxes, providing for new forms of taxation by local governments, or obtaining federal revenues. In preparing budgets, governors take into account whatever information is available on the likelihood of certain actions by the president and Congress. For instance, the president may have recommended a major increase in educational programs that would significantly increase funds flowing to the states, but considerable doubt might exist as to whether Congress will accept the recommendation. In such a case, how should a governor shape the education portion of the state budget? The problem is still worse at the local level, which is dependent for funds on both the state and federal governments.

Budget Years. Budget cycles are further complicated by a lack of uniformity in the budget period. Although most state governments have budget years beginning July 1, four states do not: New York's begins April 1, Texas's begins September 1, and Alabama's and Michigan's begin the same day as the federal fiscal year—October 1. Consistency does not even exist within each state. It is common for a state to begin its fiscal year on July 1 but to have to deal with local governments operating with different start dates, such as January 1, April 1, and September 1.

A case can be made for staggering the budget year for different levels of government; this practice might assist decision makers at one level by providing information about action taken at other levels. For example, the federal government would complete action on its budget by October 1; states could then begin a budget year the following April 1 and local governments July 1. Under such an arrangement, states could base their budgetary decisions on knowledge of available financial support from Washington. Local governments would know the aid available from both Washington and the state capital.

Rearranging the dates for fiscal years is no panacea. Information about financial support from other governments is only one of many items of information used in decision making. Also, any slippage by the legislature in completing its appropriations work by the time a fiscal year begins would void the advantages of staggered budget cycles. In addition, there is no direct translation from appropriations to aid to other governments. Money does not automatically flow to states and communities as soon as an appropriation bill is passed by Congress. Instead, state and local governments must apply for assistance, a process that typically requires many months.

Annual and Biennial Budgets. Not only is there inconsistency in the date budget years begin, but the length of the budget period is also inconsistent. Whereas the federal government and most local governments operate under annual budgets, 20 states have biennial (two-year) budgets.[13] Under these systems, a governor typically submits the budget in January, and legislative action is supposed to be completed by June 30. The execution phase runs for 24 months beginning July 1. Such a system violates the once-standard principle of annuality.[14] The argument is that annual budgets allow for careful and frequent supervision of the executive by the legislature and that this serves to guarantee responsibility in government. The problem with the annual budget, however, is that little breathing time is available; both the executive and legislative branches are continuously in the throes of budgeting. The biennial approach, on the other hand, relieves participants of many routine budget matters and may allow greater time for more thorough analysis of government activities. The 1993 National Performance Review, conducted by Vice President Gore, recommended that the federal government adopt biennial budgeting as a means of eliminating "an enormous amount of busy work."[15] The idea continues to hold interest for some reformers.[16]

One of the greatest dangers of a biennial system is that it may obstruct, if not prohibit, prompt response to new conditions. The costs of not being able to adjust to changing conditions may far outweigh any benefits accruing from time saved. This consideration may explain why most of the more populous states are on annual budget systems and why many states with biennial budgets make provision for "reopening" the two-year budget at midpoint.

Still another consideration is whether under "normal" conditions sufficient amounts of new information become available to warrant annual systems. If program analysis were a well-established part of the budgetary process, then conceivably new insights into the operation of programs would continually occur; in such instances, an annual process might be preferable. In other cases, in which decision makers operate one year with virtually the same information as was available the preceding year, there seems to be little need for annual budgets. Partially for this reason, proposals have been made for selectively abandoning the annual budget cycle. New programs or proposed changes in existing programs would be submitted in any given year for legislative review whereas continuing programs would be reviewed only periodically.

SUMMARY

The four phases of the budget cycle are preparation and submission, approval, execution, and audit. In general, the first and third phases are the responsibility of the executive branch, and the second is controlled by the legislative branch. The fourth phase in the federal system is directed by the GAO, which is answerable to Congress and not the president. Auditing at the state and local levels often is the responsibility of independently elected officials.

A standard criticism of budgeting, especially at the federal level, is that the budget is seldom considered in its entirety during its preparation phase. Within the executive branch, only the president and his or her immediate staff view the budget as a whole, while agencies are primarily concerned only with their own portions of the total. The same disjointed approach has been characteristic of the approval phase at the federal level.

Budget cycles are intermingled. As many as four budget cycles may be in operation at any one time in a single government. This phenomenon complicates decision making; for example, budget preparation often is forced to proceed without knowledge as to what action the legislature will take on the previous year's budget. Moreover, the interdependent nature of the three levels of government contributes to a scrambling of cycles. One possibility would be conversion to biennial budgets, a practice that is common at the state level.

NOTES

1. E.J. Clynch and T.P. Lauth, eds., *Governors, Legislatures, and Budgets: Diversity across the American States* (New York: Greenwood Press, 1991).

2. L.I. Ruchelman, The Finance Function in Local Government, in *Management Policies in Local Government Finance*, 4th ed., eds. J.R. Aronson and E. Schwartz (Washington, DC: International City/County Management Association, 1996), 3–34.

3. Budget and Accounting Act, Ch.18, 42 Stat. 20 (1921).

4. R.M. Nixon, as quoted in the *New York Times*, June 11, 1970; C.G. Dawes, *The First Year of the Budget of the United States* (New York: Harper and Brothers, 1923).

5. A. Wildavsky and N. Caiden, *The New Politics of the Budgetary Process*, 3rd ed. (New York: Longman, 1997).

6. Congressional Budget and Impoundment Control Act, P.L. 93-344, 88 Stat. 297 (1974).

7. Balanced Budget and Emergency Deficit Control Act, P.L. 99-177, Title II, 99 Stat. 1038 (1985); Balanced Budget and Emergency Deficit Control Reaffirmation Act, P.L. 100-199, Title I, 101 Stat. 754 (1987).

8. Budget Enforcement Act, P.L. 101-508, Title XIII, 104 Stat. 1388-573 (1990).

9. Council of State Governments, *Book of the States, 1996–97 Edition* (Lexington, KY: Council of State Governments, 1996), 98–99.

10. The GAO's Web site is http://www.gao.gov; accessed December 1997.

11. H.S. Havens for the U.S. General Accounting Office, *The Evolution of the General Accounting Office: From Voucher Audits to Program Evaluations* (Washington, DC: U.S. Government Printing Office, 1990).

12. E.A. Palmer, House Adopts Final Version of Legislative Spending, *Congressional Quarterly Weekly Report* 54 (1996): 2166.

13. Council of State Governments, *Book of the States*, 227.

14. J.W. Sundelson, Budgetary Principles, *Political Science Quarterly* 50 (1935): 236–263.

15. National Performance Review, *From Red Tape to Results: Creating a Government That Works Better and Costs Less* (Washington, DC: U.S. Government Printing Office, 1993), 17.

16. S.J. Irving, U.S. General Accounting Office, *Budget Process: Comments on S.261—Biennial Budgeting and Appropriations Act* (Washington, DC: U.S. Government Printing Office, 1997).

CHAPTER 4

Budget Preparation: The Revenue Side

This chapter and the next two describe the budget preparation process. We draw attention first to revenues, then to expenditures, and last to the politics of budget preparation. Our discussion begins with the revenue side, for historically taxation has been a fundamental concern of the citizenry. Citizens may be less concerned about how government spends its money than how the money is raised to support programs. In developing a budget package, political leaders are always mindful that program initiatives leading to higher expenditures and therefore higher taxes may have negative effects on the possibility of winning re-election to their offices. Many attribute former President George Bush's failure to win a second term in part to his infamous "no new taxes" promise made, but not kept, during his first term.

This chapter has two sections. The first and longer details various revenue sources; tax equity, tax efficiency, and tax expenditure issues are included in this discussion. Second, we consider special concerns about taxation; the discussion concentrates on taxing limitations and revenue estimating.

REVENUE SOURCES

As mentioned in Chapter 2, governments use myriad revenue sources to support their operations, with taxes usually the most important. In this section, we consider some of the overall concerns about revenue sources and then examine specific sources. Overall concerns focus on the fairness and the efficiency of the tax system. In the discussion of taxes, we are concerned with three types of tax bases: income, wealth, and consumption. Taxes on income apply to the amounts of different types of income earned during the defined tax period. Taxes on wealth apply to accumulated value regardless of the time period; real property is considered wealth, for example. Consumption taxes apply to purchasing transactions, such as retail sales. We then turn to nontax sources of revenue.

Tax Equity, Tax Efficiency, and Tax Expenditures

Besides the obvious concern that a tax source generate whatever is considered an adequate amount of revenue, the chief concern about the tax system is that it treats taxpayers equitably or fairly and that it achieves revenue objectives efficiently.[1] Equity relates to the *ability to pay* principle. A tax should be related to the taxpayer's income or wealth or, more generally, ability to pay the tax. A taxpayer who can afford to pay more should pay more.

An important facet of efficiency relates to the second criterion—the *benefit* principle. Payment for public services or goods should be related to the value of the benefits received from those services. The tax system can be more or less equitable and more or less efficient, not only in terms of what and how taxpayers have to pay, but also in terms of what taxpayers do not have to pay. *Tax expenditures*, tax exemptions, or taxes not collected, can have a major impact on equity and efficiency.

Ability To Pay. This principle implies that a tax imposes the same loss of utility for each taxpayer, or as economists refer to it—the *equal absolute sacrifice*.[2] Equity has both horizontal and vertical dimensions. *Horizontal equity* refers to charging the same amount to different taxpayers whose income levels or ability to pay is the same. *Vertical equity* refers to the principle of charging differently those with different income levels or ability to pay. Confusion immediately develops over whether it is fair for all taxpayers to pay equal absolute amounts, to pay an equal proportion of their incomes, or to pay according to their ability to pay.

A tax or other revenue source can be *regressive, progressive,* or *proportional*. In the last, all taxpayers pay the same percentage, such as a 5-percent state tax on personal income. A progressive tax charges a higher percentage to wealthier taxpayers than to poorer ones, while a regressive tax does the opposite. A tax may seem proportional when it in fact is regressive. A sales tax on purchases seems to treat all taxpayers equally but in fact is often regressive in that poorer families often spend a greater proportion of their incomes on taxed items than wealthier families do. Overall, the entire U.S. system of revenue falls in a range from slightly progressive to proportional.[3]

The revenue system's slightly progressive nature cannot be judged independently of certain government programs. Transfer payments, such as various forms of aid to poor families, are somewhat like "negative" taxes in their effect and increase the progressivity of the tax and transfer system considered together.

Evidence shows that the combination effects of the tax system and the transfer system are "substantially progressive."[4]

Benefit Received. Another concept to keep in mind is that of *benefit received.* Some revenue is derived from payments by recipients for services rendered or benefits received. User charges or fees are noted examples, as in municipal parking garage fees, bus fares, and water and sewer charges. People who park in the garage pay for the service. The principle of payment for services results in an overall efficient allocation of public sector resources, because people will use only the amount of a particular service for which they are willing to pay. The process is similar to the way the private market works. The private market produces no more of those goods than people are willing to purchase.

However, if all government services were paid for by fees, some people would be unable to pay and necessarily would be excluded. Elementary and secondary education, for example, is the most expensive local government service. If government provided this service entirely by charging parents and students the cost of providing education, many parents would be unable to send their children to school. This situation would lead to large segments of the society being uneducated and unable to secure employment that required the ability to read, write, and the like. Because of the *spillover effects* (that lack of education would affect others in the society), many government services cannot be appropriately supported solely through user fees. In addition, the public supports education for equity reasons. Similarly, public goods that benefit all citizens, such as defense, cannot be funded through user fees because citizens who chose not to "purchase" defense would still be basically as secure as their neighbors who did. The benefit received principle simply cannot be applied uniformly to all government services.

According to the related concept of *efficiency*, an efficient tax is one that does not appreciably affect the allocation of resources within the private sector, such as between consumption and saving or among competing items for consumption. Taxes on cigarettes are often cited as efficient in that raising or lowering these taxes does not appreciably influence smokers' spending habits. However, tax provisions that exclude some items from taxation, such as selected tax deferrals on personal income saved for retirement, are designed to influence behavior and may not be neutral or simply efficient. Tax systems that are progressive can be inefficient and have unintentional consequences. If tax rates are particularly high for wealthy persons, then the system may encourage them to spend more time on leisure and less on working and earning more income.

Tax system design generally tries to consider both equity and efficiency objectives. There has been extensive research on how to consider both principles simultaneously focusing on optimal tax structures, designed to achieve an optimal balance between efficiency and equity objectives.[5]

Tax Expenditures. Revenues that could be but are not collected constitute tax expenditures and can aid or hinder achieving an optimal balance. According to federal law, tax expenditures are "revenue losses . . . which allow a special exclusion, exemption, or deduction from gross income or which provide a special credit, a preferential rate of tax, or a deferral of tax liability."[6] Tax expenditures are not new; home mortgage interest payments (on up to two homes) have been deductible from income since 1910.

Numerous exemptions from taxation or deductions from income for corporations have crept into law over the years as well.[7] Tax expenditures grew rapidly through the early 1980s. Measured in constant (1995) dollars, the estimated revenue losses due to these exemptions and deductions grew from just over $250 billion to a high of almost $600 billion in 1987. The Tax Reform Act of 1986 significantly reduced the number and effect of such provisions, and the estimated revenue loss has dropped back to earlier levels.[8]

The federal budget has reported tax expenditures since 1968. In the budget for fiscal year (FY) 1998, analysis indicates that the single largest loss in income tax revenues is due to the exclusion from income of employer contributions for medical insurance premiums and medical care—an estimated $76 billion; exclusion of pension plan contributions is next—$56 billion.[9] Tax expenditures are not automatically bad. The public policy intent of home mortgage interest deduction is to encourage and enable individual family home ownership; exclusion of employer pension and medical insurance contributions are to increase savings for pensions and reduce the cost of health care. The housing exemption may help make housing affordable to moderate-income families, but the exemption also benefits more affluent taxpayers and may be of no benefit to low-income families. Is the housing exemption, then, a factor that furthers or detracts from equity?

Tax exemption of interest earned on municipal bonds cost the U.S. Treasury approximately $20 billion in income taxes in 1996. The interest rate savings to state and local governments may be equal to only about 80 percent of the revenue loss.[10] Not only is there an equity question, but there is also a question of whether the municipal bond interest tax expenditure is achieving its economic goal.

The tax expenditure section of the FY 1998 budget includes analyses of the expenditures that the government otherwise would have had to incur in order to achieve the same effect as the revenue loss from the tax exemptions and exclusions. For example, the FY 1998 budget shows an estimated tax expenditure of $1.2 billion for allowing corporations and others to credit against their tax liability expenses for increasing research and development expenditures. The analysis estimates that the federal government would have had to spend an equal amount in order to achieve the same policy objective, stimulating research and development activities.[11]

Since the 1970s, tax expenditures have become an important issue in debates over tax reform. These measures reduce the revenue flowing into government treasuries and can be "loopholes" for the wealthy. In addition to the federal government, some state governments also routinely report estimates of tax expenditures (see Chapter 6). As the federal government moves toward balancing the budget, tax expenditures increasingly come under scrutiny.[12] Proposals in the FY 1998 budget and in congressional plans rely considerably on reducing and eliminating exclusions and deductions from individual and corporate income taxes to yield the revenue required to move toward a balanced budget.

Personal Income Taxes

As is well known, all levels of government use personal income taxes, but the federal government's income tax is by far the largest in terms of generating revenue; in fact, as noted in Chapter 2, it is the largest revenue source for the federal government.

Tax Base. All taxes begin with identifying what is to be taxed, or the base. In the case of income taxes, not all income is taxable; local governments, for instance, tend to tax earned income as distinguished from other income. For a local government, salary and wages may be subject to an income tax while income from rents and stock investments are not. The federal government includes salaries, wages, commissions and tips, interest, rents, alimony, and unemployment compensation in the income tax base. Excluded are most employee benefits (such as employer-provided health insurance and contributions to pension funds), disability retirement, Workers' Compensation, food stamps, and interest earned on some state and local bonds. (These lists, of course, are only intended to illustrate what items are included and excluded.)

Generally speaking, the more sources of income that are included within the tax base, the more equitable is the income tax. When the base excludes sizable segments of income, vigorous debates immediately arise over whether some interests are receiving undue favoritism as a result of legislative lobbying.[13] Tax changes introduced in 1993 increased the federal income tax base first by taxing employer contributions to pension plans for incomes above $150,000 and second by decreasing the tax-exempt amounts employers contribute to other benefits, such as health insurance. These changes affecting benefits increase the tax base for wealthier taxpayers but leave the tax base unchanged for lower-income individuals.

Adjustments, Exemptions, and Deductions. Tax codes also provide for adjustments to gross income that typically have the effect of removing portions of income from the base. For example, the tax code excludes moving expenses, some job-related educational expenses, and some employer-paid business reimbursements. Individual exemptions further reduce the individual income tax base. For 1996, the federal government allowed an exemption of $2,550 for each filer. The purpose of these provisions is to equalize taxes among families of different sizes.

A final set of adjustments affects the tax base by allowing deductions. Taxpayers usually have a choice between using a standard deduction or itemizing deductions when they exceed the standard deduction. Deductions on the federal income tax include some medical expenses; casualty losses due to theft, fire, and the like; charitable contributions; home mortgage interest; and deductions for some taxes, such as property taxes. Taxes on gasoline and retail sales are not deductible, nor is interest on consumer debt.

The intent of these various exclusions, inclusions, adjustments, and deductions to the income base is to yield income figures for individuals and families that further horizontal and vertical tax equity. These factors together are intended to recognize variations in total income and the circumstances involved in earning that income and meeting living expenses. Individuals earning the same income but having different numbers of family members and expenses will be treated differently, while others with unequal gross incomes ultimately may have the same ability to pay when adjustments and deductions are taken into account.

Rate Structure. The principle of equity is furthered at the federal level by the use of a progressive rate structure. Married taxpayers in 1996 having taxable income below $40,100 paid a 15-percent tax, whereas those with income between $40,100 and $96,900 paid at a 28-percent rate on income in that bracket. Taxpayers in the next bracket paid 31 percent on income up to $147,700. The next two bracket rates were 36-percent and 39.6-percent rate for incomes between $147,700 and incomes up to $263,700, respectively.[14]

Most personal income taxes levied by the states are modeled on the federal tax. The states sometimes use the federal base or a modification of it. Some state income taxes are simply a proportion of the federal tax owed. Other states use flat and graduated tax rates. When the federal government modifies its tax laws, changes inadvertently occur in state taxes. This was the case when Congress adopted the Tax Reform Act of 1986, resulting in would-be revenue windfalls for many states. Many state governments in response modified their laws to avoid collecting more revenue than needed and raising taxpayers' ire.[15] Local income taxes tend to be simple to calculate and involve flat rather than progressive tax rates.

Indexing. The federal government and some states use indexing in various forms to adjust income taxes in accordance with changes in price levels. If tax brackets are not altered and prices rise, then inflation will produce increases in tax revenue because rising incomes place citizens in higher tax brackets without any real increase in buying power. Besides adjusting tax brackets, other indexing techniques include modifying the standard deduction or personal exemption. A controversial issue is the measure of inflation used to adjust tax brackets (and many other revenue and expenditure elements). The consumer price index historically has been used, but many now feel that it overstates inflation, causing taxes to be lower than they should be, and more importantly causing federal benefit programs to extend benefits greater than should be. We discuss this issue in Chapter 15.

Enforcement. A key income tax issue is enforcement. The individual income tax relies heavily on honest self-reporting by taxpayers. Although employers withhold an important proportion of total individual income taxes paid, thus enforcing tax collection for the Internal Revenue Service (IRS), enforcement remains a problem—an especially difficult problem when taxpayers think the tax is unfair. Much income is never identified and thus never becomes part of the tax base. A large underground economy in which transactions occur in trade, payments in kind, and unrecorded payments in cash never become part of the income tax base. Measuring the size of that invisible economy is naturally difficult, but one study of 17 countries estimated that the underground or shadow economy may range from 10 to 20 percent of gross domestic product (GDP) in industrialized countries.[16] For the United States, income equal to an estimated 10 percent of GDP is unrecorded and therefore untaxed.

Corporate Income Taxes

Taxes on corporate earnings have been defended as appropriate given the size of corporate economic power and the fact that some individuals might be able to escape taxation by "hiding" their income in corporations. On the other hand, corporate income taxes may seem to result in double taxation in that first a corporation is taxed and then individuals are taxed on dividends paid on their corporate stock holdings. There have been proposals to replace the corporate income tax with a tax on net business receipts to avoid this double taxation, but these proposals have not attracted much interest.[17]

Tax Base. Corporate taxes use net earnings as a base. Whereas the individual income tax base basically considers income before expenses, except for some deductions and exclusions, corporate income taxes apply only to net profit after operating expenses. In addition, some deductions are allowed for capital losses, operating losses, depreciation of capital investments, charitable contributions, and expenditures for research and development. How these deductions apply is often controversial, such as how rapidly a corporation can depreciate capital investments. The federal tax rates graduate from 15 percent to 36 percent. The two lower brackets of 15 and 20 percent apply to relatively small corporate earnings, up to $50,000 and $75,000, respectively.

Tax Incidence. The primary issue as regards corporate taxation is who actually carries the burden of corporate taxes. Corporations may be able to increase prices and in effect have consumers pay the tax or may limit wage increases to workers and in effect have them pay the tax. The other option is to take taxes out of profits, thereby reducing dividends for investors. Corporations probably use some combination of these shifts.

An issue involving state corporate taxes is whether they affect decisions to locate and expand operations in one state over another. Legislators and executives in a state government fear that any increase in their corporate income taxes will discourage corporations from locating in the state and encourage others to move out of the state. For example, in the mid-1990s Massachusetts adopted a major change in how it taxes corporations manufacturing products in the state. Normally, a corporation would be subject potentially to payroll taxes, property taxes, sales taxes, and possibly others. The Massachusetts reform, which mirrors systems in place for years in Iowa, Nebraska, and Texas, taxes manufacturing companies only on in-state sales. This *single-factor* business tax is getting attention in several other states as well. The expectation is that what the state loses in tax revenue it will gain from companies already there expanding their operations in the state and from companies relocating to the state.[18] In Chapter 15 we discuss interstate (and sometimes interlocal) competition with tax incentives and other benefits to attract business investment, sometimes called *smokestack chasing*.

Property Taxes

Taxes on wealth are based on accumulated value in some asset rather than on current earnings. Personal property, monetary or financial assets, and equipment are important types of wealth that sometimes are subject to taxation. The wealth tax that is most important in the eyes of taxpayers, however, is the real property or real estate tax. It is the tax most reviled by taxpayers, being regarded by many as the most unfair.[19] This tax is the almost exclusive domain of local governments, and despite forecasts of the demise of the tax, it remains the largest single generator of revenue for local governments, although it has declined in recent years relative to other state and local taxes. It funds almost 80 percent of locally raised school district revenues. Some states have considered, and Michigan has even legislated, ending reliance on the property tax altogether, in favor of the state sales tax, as the basis for education financing. It has been challenged in more than half the states as an inequitable or inefficient way to fund education.[20] The argument is that despite state aid to local school districts, almost sole reliance on the property tax to finance education at the local level means unequal education opportunities across the state. The property tax also is the most important source of local revenue for funding urban services in developing countries, although user charges (see later in this chapter) are the fastest growing source of local revenue in the more prosperous emerging market economies.[21]

The justification for using the property tax as the major revenue source for local government is that the services provided by local government supposedly increase the economic value of one's property. It is widely thought that people select their place of residence based on the quality of local schools and other public services. In high-quality service jurisdictions, housing costs are typically higher, reflecting higher costs for delivering services and higher expectations of home buyers for quality services. Property taxes reimburse local government for higher-quality services. The argument is that if more general taxes, such as the sales tax, were used to finance services that benefit property owners, property owners would be less aware of the costs of those services and therefore insist on more and higher-quality services. Evidence has been found to support this argument in developing countries where demand for urban services is much higher in cities that do not use property and other local taxes and charges to finance those services.[22]

One way to tie the benefits of services affecting property values to taxes on property has been through what is called *tax increment financing*. Tax increment financing has been used in redevelopment of inner cities to capitalize on the economic and financial gains that stem from a major rehabilitation project for a contiguous area usually characterized by urban blight and abandoned properties. Prior to city government action, many property owners in such areas derive no benefits from their properties, and the city is able to collect little or no property tax. A redevelopment project changes conditions so that the property in the redeveloped area attains new value, and the property tax gains from that new value are set aside to pay for financing the redevelopment.[23]

The property tax, however, is regressive in its impact. Since higher-income taxpayers tend to have a larger proportion of their wealth in assets not subject to the tax, these taxpayers tend to pay a disproportionately low tax as compared with middle- and lower-income taxpayers, whose only major asset may be their home (in which case basically all of their wealth is being taxed each year). This regressivity fuels controversy over the property tax.

Tax Base. The base of the real property tax is the market value of land and improvements on it, such as homes, factories, and other structures. The value is what the property would sell for if placed on the market. Value for commercial and industrial property sometimes is reflected in the income earned by a corporation from the property or facility.

Property's use and value often do not coincide, with farmland in metropolitan areas being one of the prime examples. As metropolitan areas expand and encroach upon farming areas, the value of the land increases even though the use is unchanged. Situations emerge in which taxes rise beyond what farmers can afford and create a market incentive for the land to be sold and subdivided for homes and other development. All states provide some form of protection for farmland as a means of preserving rural land and discouraging urban sprawl, and reduced tax assessments for farming and other undeveloped land is the most common method. Often these tax breaks are really postponements. If in the future the land is sold for subdivision and housing at a value much higher than the land's worth as farmland, the seller must then pay back property taxes reflecting the residential use tax rate. As with other tax preferences, property tax reductions to preserve farmland can have unintended consequences. One study of Pennsylvania's program concluded that it preserved land in rural areas where population pressure is light, and thus the need for preservation is small.[24] Many states also buy the development rights from property owners as a way of preserving land for open space, or other purposes.

Many properties are completely tax exempt in the United States. Federal and state land is normally exempt from local property taxes, although these jurisdictions may make payments in lieu of taxation. Places of worship, such as churches and synagogues, are tax exempt, as are most parsonages and other related properties. Nonprofit hospitals, YMCAs and YWCAs, nonprofit cemeteries, and the like are usually tax exempt. When tax-exempt properties make up a large proportion of a jurisdiction's potential tax base, the effects of tax exemption can be severe. Some governments are aggressively challenging the tax-exempt status of some nonprofit organizations. The basis for the challenge is that some nonprofit organizations produce for-profit goods and services. Philadelphia is employing a five-part test. To remain exempt from property and other taxes, a nonprofit has to prove that it: "advances a charitable purpose; gives away a substantial portion of its services; benefits people who are legitimate subjects of charity; relieves government of some of its burden; and operates entirely free of profit motives."[25] However, Philadelphia does not have the authority to force those nonprofits that do not meet the tests to pay property taxes. Instead, it is asking, with some success, for voluntary payments in lieu of taxes.

Another challenge is keeping property market value assessments current. When properties are sold, there is an opportunity to measure directly its market value and to revise the assessment, but many properties do not go on sale for decades. Therefore, assessments are revised by using market data regarding similar properties and by periodic assessment surveys in which each property in the jurisdiction receives a direct inspection. Adjustments may be done annually or only once every several years.

Fractional Assessment. Property assessments usually are stated as a percentage or fraction of full market value. A home whose market value is $120,000 would be assessed at only $24,000 if the assessment ratio were 20 percent. In practice, it makes no difference whether full value or a fraction is used; fractional assessment simply requires a higher tax rate than market value assessment to produce the same revenue. Taxpayers may find some psychological solace in fractional assessment, but the opportunity exists for some taxpayers to have their properties over-assessed and therefore taxed more than their share. The trend is to assess all properties at 100 percent of market value in order to be sure that all properties are on an even basis, except where fractional assessment is used to differentiate types of properties. For example, rural property may be assessed at a lower fraction than highly developed property.

Tax Rates. Property tax rates are a percentage of assessed value. The rate is expressed in *mills,* with one mill being one-tenth of a percent. As applied to property taxes, a one-mill rate yields $1 of revenue for every $1,000 of assessed value. A property tax rate of 68.5 mills as applied to a $120,000 property assessed at 20 percent of market value would yield $1,644 ($120 \times 0.2 \times 68.5 = 1,644$).

Local jurisdictions often determine the annual property tax rate by calculating backward from projected expenditures minus other revenues. The property tax then is expected to make up the budget gap. The community's decision makers simply determine how many additional mills will be needed to close the gap. Of course, attempts are made to avoid such tax increases by keeping expenditures as low as considered possible. The process of adjusting the tax rate to match expenditure requirements probably accounts for the great popularity of the property tax among local officials. This tax is one over which officials have considerable control, unlike other taxes that depend on the economy (income and sales taxes) or intergovernmental aid.

Circuit Breakers. As taxes rise, some property owners may encounter considerable difficulty in paying their tax bills and may even be forced to sell their homes and move into rental housing. To alleviate this problem, several states use circuit breaker systems that set a limit on taxes, particularly for low-income elderly persons. A qualified homeowner pays an amount up to the limit, and the state pays any additional amount owed. Often a state bases the limit on some income criteria: When property taxes exceed a specified percentage of the taxpayer's income, the state pays the difference.[26]

Databases for Tax Administration. For a local government instituting the property tax for the first time, the valuation process is almost overwhelming. Traditional valuation procedures involve comprehensive tax mapping to locate every property; and an assessor's visiting each property, measuring the foundation to determine square footage, noting construction details, and recording information about the condition of the structure. This type of comprehensive process is now occurring in many developing countries, where property taxes are being newly applied or where existing records are incomplete and largely useless.

For most jurisdictions in the United States, properties have been constructed under building permits that require supplying information about construction details to the local jurisdiction. Periodic inspections of the property when under construction, conducted by a local code enforcement officer or building inspector, provide additional information. A database, then, can be devised using existing building records and information about sales of properties when deeds are transferred. As new structures are built, they can be added to the database.

Orange County, North Carolina, has what is considered a model property tax valuation system. It is fully computerized and includes diverse information about each property in the county (Exhibit 4–1). Besides information about the location of each lot, the size of the structure, and the number of baths in it, a drawing of the lot and the location of the structure on it is included in the computerized file and can be displayed on screen. Of course, hard-copy maps of properties also are available.

Techniques such as those used in Orange County or paper-and-pencil systems used elsewhere help to foster a perception of fairness among taxpayers. Property owners conclude that they are paying their fair share and are not being overcharged while other taxpayers are being undercharged. If these equity consider-

---

Exhibit 4–1 Property Tax Registration Information Base, Orange County, North Carolina

- Property address
- Plot map and reference to deed register
- Size of lot (square footage)
- Size of dwelling (square footage of living space)
- Number of structures
- Number of stories of each structure
- Basement, slab, or crawl space
- Foundation construction method
- Exterior construction method
- Roof type and roofing materials
- Number of bathrooms
- Number of fireplaces
- Special features (spas, etc.)
- Landscaping
- Paved or unpaved driveway
- Last sale price and date

Courtesy of Office of the Tax Assessor, 1996, Orange County, North Carolina.

ations are met, then the likelihood of a taxpayer revolt is minimized. However, it does not make the property tax popular; it still is the most hated tax in the country.[27]

Personal Property. Besides taxing real property, some jurisdictions tax personal property. For individuals, such property includes furniture, vehicles, clothing, jewelry, and the like. Intangible personal property includes stocks, bonds, and other financial instruments such as mortgages. For corporations, personal property includes equipment, raw materials, and items in inventory. Taxes on personal property are unpopular and subject to considerable evasion.

Retail Sales and Other Consumption Taxes

Sales taxes are one of the most important sources of revenue for state governments. Forty-five of the fifty states levy a sales tax, and it is the largest state-generated source of revenue for many of those. Overall the sales tax accounts for 27 percent of state general tax revenues from own sources; the second largest single general revenue source is the income tax, which accounts for 17 percent of revenues. Both are declining in importance relative to user charges, which are approaching 10 percent of general revenue.[28]

Tax Base. While all three levels of government rely on some form of consumption tax, state governments are the most reliant, particularly on retail sales taxes. The base of any consumption tax is a product or class of goods (sometimes services) whose value is measured in terms of retail gross sales or receipts. The base is a function of what products and services are included and excluded. Almost all states exclude prescription medicines, and 22 states exclude food, except for that sold in restaurants. The number of states excluding food from the sales tax has been growing, but at considerable expense to state revenues. Some states have opted for reducing the sales tax rate on food, compared to other taxed items, rather than eliminating it altogether. The food exemption costs states an estimated 20 to 25 percent of the potential revenue from sales taxes.[29]

Other commonly excluded items are clothing, household fuels, soaps, and some toiletries. Some items may be exempt from the general sales tax since they are subject to another sales tax; cigarettes, gasoline, and alcoholic beverages are examples. However, states generally are not precluded from levying two taxes on one sale, such as a general and specific sales tax placed on cigarettes.

The most notable items not included in most sales tax bases are services, such as the professional services of doctors and lawyers. A Council of State Governments study found that consumption expenditures for tangible goods are less than for services; states that exclude services from the sales tax base forgo considerable revenue. However, in several states that have added services to the list of taxable items, the policy has created so much controversy that many of the services have been quickly removed from the sales tax base.[30]

States currently have only limited authority to tax mail-order sales and have been lobbying for Congress to pass legislation allowing such taxation. The reason is a simple one. Mail-order sales vastly increased starting in the 1980s and constitute a potentially lucrative source of revenue. U.S. Supreme Court interpretations of the due process and interstate commerce clauses have been fairly restrictive on states' ability to tax interstate sales. A 1967 case (*National Bellas Hess, Inc. v. Department of Revenue, State of Illinois*) concluded that the mail-order firm had to have a substantial nexus of business in the state, in the form of a physical presence. A 1992 case (*Quill Corporation v. North Dakota*) relaxed the so-called nexus doctrine, holding that the due process clause of the Constitution does not bar enforcement of North Dakota's use tax on the Quill Corporation, but on other grounds it still refused to overrule *Bellas Hess*.[31]

An additional complication is the growth of sales through cable and satellite television and other electronic commerce. Use of the Internet as a mechanism to place orders shipped interstate has only recently been a significant mode of commerce, and it is likely to burgeon as more users gain access to electronic sources. Although not tested in any court case so far, Internet commerce is being treated the same as interstate mail-order and phone sales. One estimate placed the 1994 losses to sales tax revenues from mail-order sales at $3.5 billion. If estimates of electronic commerce of $7 billion in sales by the year 2000 prove to be accurate, then sales tax losses from such sales could be between $500 million and $1 billion.[32]

Sales taxes are regarded as regressive in that higher-income consumers typically have more discretionary income and may spend it on items not subject to sales taxes. The more the base of the sales tax includes luxury or nonessential goods and services, therefore, the less regressive the tax is likely to be.

Tax Rates. State sales tax rates vary from as low as 3 percent (Colorado) to 7 percent (Mississippi and Rhode Island).[33] To avoid levies of a fraction of a cent, bracket systems are used in which a set amount is collected regardless of the specific sale. For example, a 5-percent tax might yield 5 cents on any purchase starting at 81 cents or 90 cents. With computers and electronic scanners at checkout counters in stores, determinations can be quickly made as to whether an item is taxable and how much tax, if any, should be charged.

Other Consumption Taxes. Some taxes are considered to be *luxury excises*. At one time, federal excise taxes were levied on a wide range of luxury goods such as jewelry, yachts, expensive automobiles, and so forth. The logic of these taxes rests on the assumption that the purchase of such goods is prima facie evidence that the consumer can afford the tax.

Sumptuary excises are regulatory in nature. Taxes on alcohol and tobacco have been justified as deterring people from consuming these commodities. However, the evidence suggests that the demand for these products is relatively inelastic, casting doubt on whether taxes discourage usage. A substantial tax increase on tobacco was proposed as an important source of financing for health care reform. The rationale was that smokers are one of the major sources of health care insurance utilization and that those who create those costs should be the ones to pay taxes to fund them—a sort of *reverse benefit* principle. The proposal, however, did not get serious review in Congress.

Benefit-based excises are linked to the benefit received concept discussed earlier. Motor vehicle fuel taxes are the classic case. Revenues from taxes on gasoline and diesel fuels are used for road and bridge construction and maintenance. Other such excises include taxes on airline tickets; the revenues from these taxes are used to maintain airports and airport security.

User Charges

All governments have user charges, and almost all public sector functions are partially supported by user charges. As noted earlier, user charges and fees for services are the fastest growing state and local revenue source. For example, there are admission charges to national and some state parks and to local tennis courts, other recreational facilities, and exercise and athletic programs. Some elementary and secondary schools charge for textbooks, and higher education institutions charge tuition. Hospitals, transit systems, water and sewer operations, and refuse collection revenues are mainly from fees and charges. Some jurisdictions own electric and telephone facilities, which they finance through user fees. Police departments charge fees for fingerprinting and special assignments, such as patrolling at sports events.

Rationale for Fees. The employment of user charges to raise revenues is based on the principle that citizens ought to pay for the cost of public services as a control on the amount of services produced. The more technical argument for their employment holds that the amount of a service provided is closer to the optimal level of service, as determined by consumer preferences, when the cost of service is borne directly by the consumer.[34] If the cost of a service is part of general taxes, then citizens tend to demand more of that service than they are actually willing to pay.

In addition to any conceptual underpinning for user fees, practical considerations made these fees more popular beginning in the 1970s. One factor was that many state and local jurisdictions adopted measures that effectively limited the ability of their governments to raise revenues through taxes; increased use of fees became a logical alternative to increased taxes. Second, cutbacks in federal aid to state and local governments created revenue gaps that resulted in these governments' placing increased reliance on fees. A good example is the substantial increase in wastewater treatment charges for residential customers and discharge fees for industrial facilities. Between 1986 and 1994, wastewater charges increased over 70 percent, and grew more rapidly than water fees, mainly due to cutbacks in federal aid for wastewater treatment plants and to more stringent discharge regulations that local governments were required to meet.[35] Other user charges that have grown include airport facility charges, which show up in increased ticket prices.[36]

At the federal level, the growth in user charges and fees began with the Reagan administration's opposition to tax increases; with massive annual federal deficits and a president opposed to tax increases, federal agencies in need of additional revenues selectively considered fees as an alternative. The philosophy of federal user charges, that "the service, sale, or use of Government's goods or resources provided by an agency to specific recipients be self-sustaining" is expressed in Office of Management and Budget Circular A-25. In the budget proposal for FY 1998, the administration proposed new increases in user fees and charges that would yield more than $47 billion from FY 1998 through 2002.[37] The budget proposal noted that: "An efficient, effective Government needs . . . where appropriate, fees from those who benefit from Government's business-like activities."[38] Proposed new and additional fees included Federal Aviation Administration fees to fund the air traffic control system, and fees charged by Food and Drug Administration and Food Safety and Inspection Service to finance the costs of drug testing and meat and poultry safety inspections, respectively.

Types of Charges. Fees vary in the extent to which they are voluntary. Charges for entrance to a museum or a municipal swimming pool clearly are voluntary; other leisure options are available if citizens prefer not to pay for these public leisure services. On the other hand, charges for sewers and trash collection usually are mandatory; if a municipal sewer system exists, citizens normally have no choice but to use it and pay the requisite fee. Other services lie between these extremes. Paying a bus or subway fare may be voluntary, but for many people without other transit options the fees are required. Differentiating between a mandatory fee and a tax is difficult.

Some fees are continuous whereas others are for special occasions. Transit fares and sewer and water charges are examples of continuous fees. Other charges occur only on certain occasions, such as a building permit fee that a contractor has to pay preparatory to erecting an office building. Although many jurisdictions use general tax revenues to repave and improve streets, other communities levy special assessments on the property owners whose streets are to be improved. Similarly, when a community installs a sewer system for the first time, property owners are assessed fees. These charges are calculated on a front foot-age basis, namely, the number of linear feet that a lot faces or fronts a street. User charges increasingly are being seen as effective revenue sources for social and human services as well.

Special assessments are used in more general ways to support municipal ser-vices. Firms that construct new office buildings in a city may have an option to provide on-site parking or pay a fee that is used to construct municipal parking facilities. Raleigh, North Carolina, finances much of the cost of extending streets, extending water and sewer lines, and expanding parks in new developments through the imposition of *impact fees* on the developers. In addition, other com-munities use impact fees for low- and moderate-income housing and environ-mental programs. Developers have been unsuccessful in challenging the legality of the formulas used for determining impact fees.[39]

Charges and Tax Subsidies. Although user charges can be substantial, they often fail to cover the costs of the services they support. Entrance fees to a municipal swimming pool usually do not provide adequate funds to operate the pool; therefore, tax revenues are used. An important example of such a subsidy is in the operation of municipal transit systems. If transit fares were set high enough to generate the required operating revenues, the rates would be so high that poor commuters could not afford to use the system and higher-income commuters would shift to alternative modes of travel—private vehicles and taxicabs.

Subsidies, however, have the effect of aiding all that use a service. If transit fares are artificially low because of a tax subsidy, then both the wealthy and poor who use the system benefit. Alternative mechanisms include providing free ser-vice to the poor, such as free bus tokens, or setting fees on a sliding scale. For example, a government-operated mental health clinic might charge poor and moderate-income families little or nothing for services while charging higher-income families at a rate that covered costs.

Some local governments that own profitable utilities, such as public electricity companies and sometimes water enterprises with substantial industrial custom-ers, use utility fee revenue to decrease the taxes otherwise needed to finance other, unrelated services. It appears that for those local governments owning such profitable enterprises, the overall cost of other government services to citizens is lower per capita than for other comparable local governments.[40] Austin, Texas, is an example of a city that uses sales of electricity from its municipally owned util-ity to subsidize the costs of other services. Caution is in order before one assumes that local governments should seek to become utility owners. The sometimes hid-den costs of diverting public management talent to the operation of an essentially private business could adversely affect the municipality's overall management efficiency, although that may be difficult to quantify.[41]

Insurance Trust Revenues

Insurance trust funds, which are separate accounts set up to hold certain earmarked revenues (see Chapter 11), are financed by means of charges on salaries and wages (the charges are paid by employees, employers, or both). These charges are not taxes inasmuchas they do not generate revenue to be used to pay for services; instead, the programs provide insurance to the people who are covered by them. Employers and employees pay into these systems, and people earn benefit credits through contributions made during their working careers. Social insurance receipts rose as a percentage of GDP from 4.5 percent in 1971 (as low as 2.1 percent in the 1950s) to nearly 7 percent in 1995, while corporate income and excise tax revenues fell from 2.5 percent to 2.2 percent and 1.6 percent to 0.8 percent of GDP, respectively.[42]

Social Security. Social Security is a trust program of vast proportions. Its complexities far exceed the scope of this book; all that can be done here is to sketch its overall structure. Three major programs are administered directly by the Social Security Administration. The first program, Old Age and Survivors Insurance, is a benefits program for retired workers and their survivors. Chapter 13 discusses the program as it pertains to retired government employees. The second program, Disability Insurance (DI), provides benefits for covered workers who are disabled and cannot work. In 1995, over 50 million people received benefits under the old-age and survivors program and almost 6 million under the disability program. Benefits paid out from those two programs totaled $363 billion and $61 billion, respectively.[43]

Supplemental Security Income. The third major program under Social Security provides monthly benefits to people who are aged, blind, and disabled; this program is known as Supplemental Security Income (SSI). SSI funds come from general tax revenues and not employer-employee contributions. Unlike disability insurance, SSI does not require work credits for eligibility but does require that recipients are needy. It is possible to qualify for both programs, although qualifying for DI has the effect of reducing SSI benefits. In 1995, 4.7 million people received $21.1 billion in benefits under the SSI program.[44]

Medicare. In addition to these three main Social Security programs, a fourth one, Medicare, is administered by the Health Care Financing Administration in the Department of Health and Human Services. Medicare provides basic health insurance to the elderly, with a separately funded catastrophic coverage component, and is funded by contributions through Social Security, premiums paid by persons covered under the program, and general revenues. By the 1990s, Medicare was one of the major contributors to rapidly rising federal expenditures for health care.

Medicaid. A fifth program often mentioned in conjunction with these other programs is Medicaid; it is funded with federal and state tax revenues as opposed to payroll taxes earmarked for the Social Security Trust Fund. The federal government pays about 60 percent of the costs of Medicaid, the states paying the remainder. From 1970 through 2000 (projected), total Medicaid spending will have increased from $5 to $214 billion with the state share increasing from $2 to $96 billion.[45] Medicaid provides medical care to the poor and the medically indigent (persons who are not classified as poor but cannot afford medical care). Medicaid and SSI are not trust programs as defined above because their funds come from general tax revenues and not revenues earmarked for special trust funds.

Social Security Reform. Legislation in 1983 greatly modified the financing of Old Age and Survivors Insurance to make it solvent for the long term; estimates then were that the trust fund would be insolvent before 1990 unless corrective action were taken. While the increases in both the employer and employee contribution rate and an increase in the amount of annual income subject to the tax met the fund's needs for some decades, the consensus is that the program will need revising again, and the longer reform is postponed, the more dramatic will be the changes required. Different scenarios place the date at which annual disbursements from the Social Security Trust Fund will exceed annual revenues anywhere from 2025 to 2065.

The Advisory Council on Social Security, which in 1997 considered alternative reforms to the system, developed both a low growth and moderate growth scenario for population and labor force growth. The low growth scenario shows the trust fund in deficit sometime after 2050, but the moderate growth scenario shows no deficit through the next 75 years[46]—through the 2070s at least. The Bureau of Labor Statistics and the Census Bureau, however, caution that the Advisory Council used extremely pessimistic assumptions about shrinkage in the population birth rate. If birth rates do not fall as rapidly and as far as the Advisory Council assumed, then the work force paying into the Social Security Trust Fund will be larger in mid-century, and the fund will still show a surplus in 2050.

Several issues have fueled the debate over Social Security reform, and the motivations for reform among many groups are not necessarily consistent. First is the issue we might label "violation of trust." This issue is based on the understanding that the fund is supposed to be a trust fund exclusively for financing Social Security benefits. Many citizens assume that the funds they and their employers contribute to the system are being held in trust, invested much like pension funds to yield the benefits that will be paid out to them in the future. In reality, each year's payments into the Social Security Trust Fund are used to pay out to beneficiaries in that year, and for some time to come the payments into the fund will exceed payments out of the fund. Those excess payments create a surplus in the fund, and that surplus in turn is lent to the U.S. Treasury at the equivalent of the 30-year Treasury bond, to finance part of the annual federal deficit.

Thus, one motivation for reform is the political ethic that the fund should behave as a revolving fund, with proceeds paid into the fund invested as in most pension funds. That view somewhat naively assumes that private pension funds pay out benefits commensurate with the results of investment of funds paid in, but the majority of private pension funds are set up to pay out defined benefits regardless of whether the fund investments are sufficient to meet those benefit payouts (see Chapter 13 for more detailed discussion of defined benefits and the growing category of defined contributions pension programs). Just as an employer with a defined benefits pension fund is obligated to meet the benefit payouts defined in the plan, from business net profits if necessary, the federal government is obligated to meet whatever Congress determines will be the benefit structure, first from the trust fund itself and then from other federal revenues as necessary.

A second motivation for reform is closely linked to the debates on balancing the federal budget. Since the fund shows a surplus, and all revenue to the fund is counted part of the federal government's revenue total, the size of the federal deficit is disguised. The more fiscally conservative feel the practice of using the trust fund surplus to finance part of the deficit, the equivalent of investing the surplus in 30-year Treasury bonds, has been used to postpone addressing the need for a balanced budget (see Chapter 12 for discussion of debt and balanced budgets).

A third issue involved in demands for reform is that the funds being paid into Social Security according to many should be earning more than the implicit 30-year Treasury bond rate. The bull market of the 1990s particularly fueled this aspect of the debate as stocks dramatically earned returns two and three times the rate of the 30-year Treasury bond. Proposals have been advanced to invest the funds flowing into the trust fund in the stock market, to earn higher benefits for future pensioners. In 1996, the Advisory Council on Social Security, unable to reach a consensus, presented three options for reforming the way Social Security funds are invested.

One option, favored by six of the Council's 13 members, is that 40 percent of the trust fund's money should be invested in the stock market. A second option, favored by two members, recommended that workers put 1.6 percent of their pay (just under one-third of their own contributions) into personal retirement accounts with the rest of the employee and all the employer contributions going into the Social Security Trust Fund as it does now. Individuals would have some say in how the personal retirement accounts would be invested, although Social Security would administer the accounts. The third option, favored by the remaining five members of the Council, would replace the current guaranteed benefit system with a system into which workers would be required to put 5 percent of their pay into personal accounts, and individuals would bear all the responsibility for determining investments.[47] The President of Chile in a state visit to the United States in 1997, even got into the act, recommending that the United States fully privatize the entire Social Security system, much as Chile has done. That a non-partisan council after two years of deliberations could not agree to support any single reform showed how difficult it is to make a major change in the way Social Security funds are invested.

A final important proposed reform in the system is tied up with a broader proposal to recalculate the consumer price index, which would affect a variety of federal revenue and expenditure programs as noted previously in this chapter.[48] Currently, Social Security benefits change annually, as does the calculation of income tax brackets, to take into account the effects of inflation, measured by changes in the consumer price index. The Advisory Council noted that a 0.3-percent increase in the payroll tax and changing the formula to produce what many feel is a more accurate estimate of inflation—lower—would ensure Social Security system solvency through the next century, without changing the employer and employee contribution rates or changing the age at which people may begin drawing Social Security benefits. A Senate Finance Committee–appointed commission recommended that the consumer price index be cut 1.1 percent a year. This recommendation met with substantial opposition from groups such as the American Association of Retired Persons.[49]

Medicare reforms also have been an important part of the Social Security system reform debate. In 1997, estimates were that Medicare would be insolvent before the end of the decade. The hospital insurance portion of Medicare in particular would have run at a deficit by 1995 had premium increases not shored it up. Reform proposals especially have aimed at reducing the incentives for physicians and hospitals to order expensive treatments for Medicare patients and to reduce the possibilities for fraudulent charges. Holding down reimbursement rates slowed the slide toward a Medicare deficit, and on the agenda for longer-term reform is moving more people into managed care organizations away from individual physicians. Almost inevitable is eventually raising the age at which one is eligible for Medicare from 65 to perhaps 67.[50] Medicare reform is tied up in the debate over the balanced budget. Medicare's impact on the budget has become so significant that most agree that it will be almost impossible to balance the federal budget early in the 21st century without either increasing Medicare costs or reducing benefits or both.

Employee Retirement. The largest type of insurance trust fund at the state and local levels is for government employee retirement. These retirement programs, as well as the federal government's, are discussed at length in Chapter 13.

Unemployment Insurance. The second largest insurance trust for state governments is unemployment compensation. The program is administered by the states within a framework imposed by the federal government. A floor on benefits is set nationally, although states have the option of exceeding the floor. The program is supported by payroll taxes paid mainly by employers, but in a few states employees are required to make supplementary payments. The program is expected to generate sufficient revenues during prosperous periods to cover payments to unemployed workers during recessionary periods. Sometimes state programs can run into a deficit situation, such as during a sustained recession, or occasionally for temporary, timing differences between payments into the funds and payments out. In such cases, the federal government loans money to the states but expects repayment with interest. As is obvious, a state that has a declining tax base can face severe problems financing its unemployment insurance program.

Workers' Compensation. Another important insurance trust at the state level is Workers' Compensation, which provides cash benefits to persons who, because of job-related injuries and illnesses, are unable to work. Accidents at work may disable people temporarily or permanently; working conditions can cause physical and mental health problems. In addition to cash benefits, the program pays for medical care and rehabilitation services.

Private Sector Provision of Services

Governments that are feeling the pinch from deficits and taxpayer reluctance to support tax increases have increasingly turned to the private sector to finance many services traditionally thought to be the province of the public sector. Harnessing the entrepreneurial spirit of the private sector to provide services and thus to reduce need for public taxes has become virtually nonpartisan.

The number of public services considered for privatization is almost unlimited. Private police and fire services are not exempt. Increasing use of toll roads and turnpikes is common.[51] Privatization of water and wastewater utilities is seen by some as the only way to finance badly needed new investment.[52] There also are numerous local school districts that have turned to the private sector to operate schools, or elements of schools on a contract basis.[53] Because it is not really a revenue-raising measure but more a case of turning over a formerly public service to the private sector, we discuss privatization in a separate chapter (Chapter 10).

Tools for achieving private sector participation that do involve private sector financing are concession contracting and various forms of build-operate-transfer (BOT) and build-operate-own (BOO).[54] Under contracting arrangements, a private organization or consortium contracts with a public agency to rehabilitate, build, operate, and perhaps at a specified future time transfer a facility to the public agency. In the concession contract, the private party operates the facility under a long-term concession, may be required to make significant capital investments in the facility, but never assumes ownership. In BOT/BOO arrangements, at least for a period of time, the private party has legal ownership of the facility. In Sydney, Australia, for example, a BOO contract was awarded in 1996 to a consortium led by the French water company Lyonnaise des Eaux, calling for a $200 million capital investment on the part of the private consortium. The consortium constructs and rehabilitates facilities, is the outright owner of the facilities constructed during the concession period, and is the fully responsible operator for the 25-year period.[55] The issue for Sydney was the cost to the city and taxpayers of financing the needed capital investments, the ability of public officials to manage as efficiently as the private consortium, and the need to expand services much more rapidly than the city could manage.

Concession projects increasingly are being used in many developing and emerging market countries, including Chile, Colombia, Peru, the Philippines, and Poland for water, wastewater, and solid waste treatment services. Buenos Aires turned over the entire city water system on a concession basis, resulting in the removal of thousands of employees from the city payroll.[56]

BOT/BOO and other concession contracting approaches to private sector participation are advantageous to the public sector primarily by eliminating or reducing the need for additional public sector debt to construct expensive infrastructure facilities and by reducing or holding constant the size of the public sector payroll. That latter advantage is particularly important where public sector employees tend to be paid higher wages and better benefits than employees of comparable private operations. Research has shown that U.S. cities that experience fiscal distress are characterized by larger numbers of municipal employees and higher-than-average wages for municipal employees (these cities typically increased hiring and pay rates when large federal grants were plentiful during the 1960s and 1970s).[57] Private concession contracting must bring management expertise, new technology, and operating efficiencies in order to actually reduce the cost of service, given that private parties will require a profitable return on their investment above cost recovery.

Other Revenue

Besides all of these various revenue sources, there are still others that can only be mentioned here. Governments operate revolving loan programs that produce revenue as principal and interest payments are made. Licenses are issued that usually require fees; the purpose of these fees may be to cover costs (for example, building permit fees used to pay the salaries of building inspectors), or to raise revenues beyond costs. Charitable contributions constitute another revenue source, such as gifts to municipal hospitals, county nursing homes, state universities, and the like.

Borrowing also has to be mentioned, not literally as a revenue source, but as a temporary means to obtain revenue while waiting for other revenues to enter the city or state coffers. As will be seen later in discussions of congressional budgeting and budget execution, the federal government's budget is often out of balance, and deficits are routinely financed through the issuance of debt instruments. State and local governments sometimes obtain revenues through borrowing to cover short-term cash flow problems. These governments borrow on a long-term basis to fund capital projects such as highways and government buildings (see Chapter 12).

Lotteries, Casinos, and Other Gambling

Since 1963, when New Hampshire began the first modern state lottery, all but 14 states have launched lottery programs. Lotteries usually produce about 3 to 4 percent of revenues for states, but they range from as low as 0.7 percent in Nebraska to as high as 5.75 percent for Oregon.[58] Revenues generated from the programs can vary considerably from year to year, depending upon lottery activity in adjacent states, the size of jackpots, and the extent to which a lottery has "matured" and lost the public's interest. State lottery revenues rose rapidly in the late 1980s and early 1990s, but leveled off by mid-decade, causing some states to question the long-term value of state lotteries. Iowa in 1996 put before the legislature the question of whether the state lottery was producing sufficient revenue to justify its continuation.[59] Lotteries can be regressive in that lower-income individuals are more likely to participate than middle- and upper-income individuals.[60]

In addition to lotteries, a number of states have legalized casino gambling. Ten states as of 1996 had legalized casinos, and casinos operate on land owned by Indian tribes in 31 states.[61] Although in some states, such as Louisiana, casino gambling has cut into state lottery revenues, some states are generating significant revenues. Illinois, for example, in 1994 earned $167 million for the state treasury, several multiples of the estimated revenues when the legalization proposal was being enacted. Mississippi projected its 1995 casino gambling revenues at $120 million, one of the highest per capita in the country (exceeded by Nevada).[62]

Overall, however, the enthusiasm for tax and economic benefits from lotteries, casinos, and other legalized gambling has waned. Expected economic benefits in the form of job creation and stimulus of related commerce has failed to materialize, and state legislatures are realizing that the state treasury also is absorbing costs associated with the social problems sometimes accompanying gambling. One estimate showed the state of Maryland may have lost as much as $1.5 billion in reduced productivity, unpaid taxes, and other losses. These issues manifested in defeat in over 30 state ballots or legislative proposals to legalize or expand gambling from 1994 through 1996.[63] Even the benefits promised to specific public services have not always materialized; in some states where lottery earnings are earmarked exclusively to support education, state legislatures have cut other state education spending by commensurate amounts.[64]

Value-Added Tax. Increased concern with the robustness of the U.S. tax system, especially the intergovernmental system of taxation and revenue transfers (see Chapter 14), has led some to advocate adoption of a value-added tax (VAT).[65] The United States is one of the few industrialized countries without a VAT. As its name implies, a VAT is a consumption tax on the value added by producers and distributors at every stage in the production, distribution, and sales process. Estimates are that a VAT would raise between $10 and $20 billion a year in new revenue for each 1 percent of tax.[66] Similar to a sales tax, in that the collection burden would be on business, a VAT would be collected not only from retail outlets but also from manufacturers and wholesalers, unlike a sales tax. Proposed during the 1992 election by then candidate Clinton, the VAT tax did not get serious attention in Congress, and during the 1996 campaign was not mentioned at all, superseded by various candidates' proposals for fundamental income tax reform including various flat-tax alternatives.

SPECIAL CONCERNS

Two topics of special interest are considered in this section. The first topic is the limitations that have been imposed on state and local taxes, and the second is the continuous problem of revenue estimating.

Taxing and Spending Limitations

Although citizens seemingly have had little opportunity to affect taxes and spending other than through the process of selecting elected representatives, 1978 changed all that. In that year, California voters approved Proposition 13, an initiative that limited the property tax rate to 1 percent of market value. That provision by itself would have required a rollback in taxes, but an additional provision further cut taxes. Property assessments were to be returned to their values in 1975, when property was considerably less expensive. Although tax limitation measures were not new, Proposition 13 began a new era in which government officials were forced to consider taxpayer reaction and to limit taxes and spending.[67]

Many state and local governments followed California's lead during the late 1970s and early 1980s by passing statutory limits or in some cases adding restrictions to state constitutions. California voters approved Proposition 4 in 1979, which limited state government expenditures as well as local government expenditures. In the following years, restrictive measures were adopted in about half of the states. Massachusetts, which had come to be known as "Taxachusetts," gained notoriety in 1980 as a result of its passage of Proposition 2½. This measure required that local governments reduce taxes by 15 percent each year until they equaled 2.5 percent of market value.[68] "By 1990, 21 states had enacted potentially binding limitations and thirteen had enacted nonbinding limitations on the finances of their local governments."[69] The elections of 1994 and 1996 brought more conservative control to many state legislatures and ushered in a new round of tax limitation proposals.[70] In 1996, California passed Proposition 218, the most severe limitation to date.[71]

Causes and Types of Limitations. The original stimulus behind what came to be known as the taxpayers revolt was the sharp rise in property values and, consequently, tax bills, but a more generally negative attitude emerged—the attitude that government officials have an insatiable appetite for spending. Besides taxing too much, governments allegedly use the revenues to interfere needlessly in the lives of citizens and the operations of corporations. Property taxes remain one of the most criticized. This is probably because of dissatisfaction with the results school systems are producing, which are funded almost entirely by the property tax.[72]

The result has been several types of tax and expenditure limitations. One review classified them into five categories:

1. overall property tax limitation (for example, limit to maximum annual percent increase)
2. specific property tax limitation (for example, limit on use of property tax to finance education)
3. property tax levy limit (for example, ceiling on amount of tax)
4. general revenue or general expenditure increase limit (for example, limit annual expenditure increase to a specific limit)
5. property tax assessment increase limit[73] (limit on the assessed value increase)

In addition, taxpayer concern has caused many state and local governments to increase communication with the public on what is accomplished with taxpayer dollars and how taxes are kept to a minimum. Minnesota, for example, enacted a law requiring the construction of an overall index calculating the cost of everything residents pay to the government as a percent of personal income. Not only are taxes included, but so are all fees, charges, and any other payment to government.[74] The index is kept for different state departments and individual local governments so that citizens throughout the state can compare their own government with others and with limitation guidelines.

Tax Revolt Impact. The effect of these limitations has varied, but in most cases local governments made up for the revenue loss through other sources, usually non–general-revenue sources. Overall, spending may have declined in some jurisdictions but not enough to show up in aggregate figures for individual states. The main effects seem to have been four. First, state legislatures and local governments are much more reluctant to initiate new programs and especially to propose tax increases or new taxes.

Second, combined with major cutbacks in federal aid to states and localities in the 1980s, the limitation movement set these governments on an imaginative hunt for alternative finance measures. The significantly greater use of impact fees, discussed above, and other direct charges to those benefiting from services was an outgrowth of the tax revolt.

Third, states provided increased financial assistance to hard-pressed local governments. For example, when Michigan eliminated the property tax funding for education, the state increased the sales tax, and in turn used state funds for formerly local education funds.[75] Sometimes that state aid has come at a price, namely, various strings attached by states for their aid. One simple example is that local governments could not give their employees salary increases greater than those given state employees.

Fourth, while overall expenditures have been cut somewhat, more services have been reduced, either in quality or quantity, as a means of curbing spending. Essential services such as law enforcement and fire protection have been maintained, but at decreased levels. Budget problems forced cutbacks in maintenance of buildings and purchase of new vehicles and equipment.[76] Overall, however, tax and expenditure limitations did not materially change the relative amounts state and local governments spent on government functions.[77]

Starting in the late 1980s, enthusiasm for the enactment of restrictive measures on government waned, and concern grew among citizens that the reductions imposed over the preceding decade had cut too severely into the level of services. At the same time, there was continued citizen consciousness about tax and expenditure matters. At the federal level, the Budget Enforcement Act of 1990 added the requirement that any additional federal program expenditure proposed in Congress had to be matched with either an equivalent expenditure reduction or a revenue increase (see Chapter 9). The congressional elections of 1994 and the Republicans' Contract with America provided renewed focus on controlling the size of government. Similarly in state governments, more fiscally conservative legislators have continued to focus on reducing the size of government or limiting its growth. By the beginning of the second Clinton term, both parties had made repeated pledges to balance the federal budget with an understanding that this would not be accomplished through massive tax increases. In 1997 those pledges were kept with an agreement expected to achieve a balanced budget by 2002.

Revenue Estimating

Little imagination is required to appreciate the importance of revenue estimating. If a government is required to have a balanced budget, as state and local governments are, then accurate revenue forecasts become critical. Estimates that are too high can create major crises during the execution phase, at which time expenditures must be cut in order not to exceed revenues. Low estimates also cause problems, because programs may be needlessly reduced at the beginning of the fiscal year.

Deterministic Models. Perhaps the easiest method of revenue forecasting involves deterministic models that manipulate the revenue base and tax rate to produce a desired level of revenue. Property tax forecasts are deterministic in that a government can adjust assessments and tax rates to meet desired revenue levels. The main problems to address in such forecasting are the extent that (1) property values overall will rise or possibly decline, (2) new properties will be added to the tax rolls, and (3) old and deteriorating properties will fall into default. Deterministic models are useful for revenue sources over which a jurisdiction has substantial control; the models are not useful for taxes on such items as personal income and retail sales which depend on economic trends.

Simple Trend Extrapolations. Both formal and informal trend extrapolations are used in revenue estimating. In an informal situation, an assumption may be made that a particular revenue source will increase by 5 percent since that is what has occurred for the last several years. In most cases, however, revenues do not increase or decrease by a set percentage or remain constant. Revenue growth may increase on average by 5 percent, but in some years the growth may be 10 percent and in others only 1 or 2 percent. Given this information, what percentage estimate should be used for the upcoming budget year?

One method of dealing with this problem is to use simple linear regression, a statistical technique that fits a straight line to a series of historical data. The formula used is $y = mx + b$. In the equation, y, the forecast revenue, is a function of a coefficient m times a known value x plus a constant b. In the formula, m is the slope of the straight line, x is the actual revenue generated the previous year, and b is a scale factor that adjusts for orders of magnitude differences between values. Computer software is readily available for making the appropriate calculations, but such projections also can be made using simple calculators.

The straight-line calculation of linear regression, however, may not parallel the actual historical series; the fit of the regression can be gauged by calculating the correlation coefficient known as *R*. When the data are random, *R* is 0.00. The closer *R* is to 1.00, the more likely it is that the regression accurately forecasts revenue.

Besides linear regression, other techniques exist for smoothing out fluctuations in a historical series into a straight line. The method called moving averages calculates an average value for each point in the historical series. Starting with a series of, say, eight years, the revenues for years 1, 2, and 3 are averaged. This average becomes the new *smoothed* value for year 2. Then actual values for years 2, 3, and 4 are averaged for a new "smoothed" year 3. Similar averages are calculated for the remaining years. A variant is to weight the most recent years more heavily than early years in calculating the moving average, on the grounds that recent years are better predictors.

Underlying these techniques is the premise that the future will be like the past. The purpose of any projection technique is to reduce historical information to a discernible pattern and then extend that pattern into the future. One way of testing how well the technique works is to "predict" several recent time periods and compare those predictions with what actually occurred. Most local governments, except large cities, still rely on one form or another of trend extrapolation. Evidence suggests that when used in combination with other tools, trend extrapolations produce reliable estimates for local governments.[78] Chesterfield County, Virginia, adds the expert judgment of the county government's program managers, business leaders, state tax experts, and expertise from the Federal Reserve Bank of Richmond convened in a semi-annual forum to discuss underlying trends. This addition of expert judgment allows the county to adjust the results of trend extrapolation methods.[79]

Econometric Models. Several types of econometric models exist.[80] One of the most popular is multiple regression. In multiple regression models, independent variables are sought that can serve as predictors of revenue yield. The assumption is that a linear relationship exists between each predictor and the dependent variable of forecast revenue. Also assumed is that each independent variable is unrelated to the others. A model for sales tax receipts might include the independent variables of population, personal income, and the consumer price index. As each of these variables increases, revenues increase.

Multiple predictor variables are used in simultaneous equation models (multiple regression models rely on a single equation). In simultaneous equation models, individual equations relate each independent or predictor variable to the revenue to be forecast. These individual equations are solved simultaneously. The advantage of simultaneous equation models is that, unlike multiple regression models, they do not assume that each predictor variable is independent of each other predictor variable. Since many of the variables one would use to make a revenue forecast would be expected to be related to each other, the simultaneous equation approach is both more realistic and computationally more valid.

Revenue forecasts can be made using microsimulation models that are dependent on large databases manipulated by computers. Individual taxpayers and corporations are included in the models and exhibit behavior changes in response to projected changes in the economy, tax laws, price levels, personal income, and the like. Data based on the historical performance of actual taxpayers in the jurisdiction are used.[81]

All of these models necessarily use variables that are sensitive to changes in economic conditions. Sales and income tax receipts rise and fall according to economic trends. Many user charges are affected too; when people are unemployed, they curtail their use of public transportation, parking facilities, museums, and zoos. Therefore, these models are most vulnerable with regard to the assumptions made about future economic trends. Also critical are basic demographic shifts. Changing population patterns due to birth rates and migration can undermine the effectiveness of forecasting models that previously had shown themselves to be extremely accurate.[82] Projecting national trends is extremely difficult, and state and local trends are no easier, especially since each subnational jurisdiction has its own economic characteristics and is influenced by national trends.

Politics. Revenue estimating has its political aspects. Presidents, governors, and mayors are loathe to forecast economic hard times and low revenue levels. Political executives tend to campaign for election in part on the promise that they will strive for economic growth. Presidents have the additional problem that the forecast of a recession may be a self-fulfilling prophecy. State and local executives must limit expenditures to available revenue; pessimistic estimates force executives to make difficult choices as to where to cut programs in order to reduce overall expenditures. There seems to be a tendency to underestimate revenues more often than overestimate. Apparently, politicians feel the political risks of underestimating and producing a surplus at the end of the year are less than the consequences of overestimating and having to make program cuts or raise taxes unexpectedly during the year.[83] Since revenue estimates can rarely if ever be certain, establishing *contingency reserves* or *rainy day funds* may be a useful method of protecting against possible shortfalls and the political problems that ensue from such shortfalls.

SUMMARY

Governments use numerous revenue sources to support their operations, with taxes obviously being one of the most important types. In devising a tax system, governments need to consider whether horizontal and vertical equity standards are met. One important consideration is whether to have a person pay based on the benefits received or his or her ability to pay. Taxes on personal and corporate income, property, and retail sales are the largest generators of tax revenue. Each tax has a base, and then a rate or rates are applied to it. Other important revenue sources include user charges, and reliance on charges or fees has increased since the late 1970s. There also is increasing reliance on the private sector to initiate or take over needed services as a means of reducing public payrolls and avoiding an enlargement of public sector debt for capital facilities. Insurance trusts constitute another important source of revenue; included here are Social Security, government employee retirement systems, unemployment insurance, and Workers' Compensation.

Two topics of special concern are limitations imposed on taxing and spending and the procedures used in revenue estimating. Many state and local governments have adopted tax and/or expenditure limitations. Citizens and political leaders alike remain concerned that taxes and spending be kept to a minimum. The 1997 balanced budget agreement between the White House and the Congress and the record low in the federal budget deficit compared with recent decades have not diminished the attention focused on limiting taxes and spending.

Revenue estimating is an ongoing process. Deterministic models, trend extrapolation techniques, and econometric models are among the tools used to forecast future revenues. Increasingly sophisticated merging of mathematical tools with expert judgment improve the accuracy of budget forecasts.

NOTES

1. D.N. Hyman, *Public Finance: A Contemporary Application of Theory to Politics*, 5th ed. (Orlando, FL: Dryden, 1996), 342–346.

2. P. Burgat and C. Jeanrenaud, Do Benefit and Equal Absolute Sacrifice Rules Really Lead to Different Taxation Levels?, *Public Finance Quarterly* 24 (1996): 148–162.

3. J.J. Minarik, *Making America's Budget Policy: From the 1980s to the 1990s* (Armonk, NY: M.E. Sharpe, 1990).

4. J.A. Pechman, *Tax Reform, the Rich and the Poor*, 2nd ed. (New York: Harvester Wheatsheaf, 1989), 23.

5. C.E. McClure, Jr., and G.R. Zodrow, *The Study and Practice of Income Tax Policy*, in *Modern Public Finance*, ed. J.M. Quigley and E. Smolensky (Cambridge, MA: Harvard University Press, 1994), 185.

6. The Congressional Budget and Impoundment Control Act, P.L. 93-344, 88 Stat. 297, 299 (1974).

7. C. Howard, Testing the Tools: Tax Expenditures Versus Direct Expenditures, *Public Administration Review* 55 (1995): 439–447.

8. U.S. General Accounting Office, *Federal Fiscal Trends: Fiscal Years 1991–1995* (Washington, DC: U.S. Government Printing Office, 1996), 21.

9. U.S. Office of Management and Budget, *Analytical Perspectives: Budget of the U.S. Government, Fiscal Year 1998* (Washington, DC: U.S. Government Printing Office, 1997), 79.

10. P. Fortune, The Municipal Bond Market: Part II, Problems and Policies, *New England Economic Review* (May–June 1992): 62.

11. U.S. Office of Management and Budget, *Analytical Perspectives: Budget of the U.S. Government, Fiscal Year 1998,* 82.

12. U.S. General Accounting Office, *Tax Expenditures Deserve More Scrutiny* (Washington, DC: U.S. Government Printing Office, 1994).

13. S. Pollack, *The Failure of U.S. Tax Policy: Revenue and Politics* (University Park, PA: The Pennsylvania State University Press, 1996).

14. Internal Revenue Service, *1040 Forms and Instructions* (Washington, DC: U.S. Government Printing Office, 1996).

15. S.D. Gold, Changes in State Government Finances in the 1980s, *National Tax Journal* 44 (March 1991): 6.

16. Light on the Shadows, *The Economist* 343 (May 3, 1997): 63–64.

17. U.S. General Accounting Office, *Tax Policy: Implications of Replacing the Corporate Income Tax with a Consumption Tax* (Washington, DC: U.S. Government Printing Office, 1993).

18. P. Lemov, Singling Out a Business Tax to Secure Factory Jobs, *Governing* 9 (March 1996): 51.

19. G.W. Fisher, *The Worst Tax? A History of the Property Tax in America* (Lawrence: University of Kansas, 1996).

20. J.E. Petersen, The Schools Are Tumbling Down: The Fiscal Story, *Governing* 7 (March 1994): 90; C. Mahtesian, Ten Legislative Issues to Watch in 1997, *Governing* 10 (February 1997): 23; U.S. General Accounting Office, *School Finance: Three States' Experiences with Equity in School Funding* (Washington, DC: U.S. Government Printing Office, 1995); National Public Radio, *Morning Edition,* September 16, 1997.

21. R.W. Johnson and J.S. McCullough, Case Study on Urban Local Government Finance (Paper presented at the Asian Development Bank seminar on Urban Infrastructure Finance in Asia, Research Triangle Institute, Research Triangle Park, NC, April 17, 1996).

22. R.W. Bahl and J.F. Linn, *Urban Public Finance in Developing Countries* (New York: Oxford University Press); R.M. Bird, *Tax Policy and Economic Development* (Baltimore: Johns Hopkins University Press, 1992).

23. D. Davis, Tax Increment Financing, *Public Budgeting & Finance* 9 (Spring 1989): 63–73.

24. T.W. Kelsey and K.S. Kreahling, Preferential Tax Assessments for Farmland Preservation: Influence of Population Pressures on Fiscal Impacts, *State and Local Government Review* 28 (Winter 1996): 49–57.

25. P. Lemov, Tin-Cup Taxation: Local Governments Are Pressuring Nonprofits to Chip in to Cover the Costs of the Services They Use, *Governing* 8 (October 1995): 25–26.

26. D.H. Monk, *Educational Finance: An Economic Approach* (New York: McGraw-Hill, 1990), 158–160.

27. P. Lemov, The Property Tax Blues: Even the Mayors of Affluent Towns Are Finding That the Tax People Hate the Most Isn't Up to the Job of Paying for Local Government in the '90s, *Governing* 8 (August 1995): 28–32.

28. U.S. Bureau of the Census, 1995 State Finances: http://www.census.gov/govs/www/stsum95; accessed February 1997.

29. P. Lemov, The Tastiest Tax Cut, *Governing* 9 (November 1996): 29–30.

30. D. Olberding, Taxes To Grow With, *State Government News* 36 (February 1993): 11–14.

31. H.A. Coleman, Taxation of Interstate Mail-Order Sales, *Intergovernmental Perspective* 18 (Winter 1992): 9–14; *Quill Corporation v. North Dakota*, 504 U.S. 298 (1992).

32. J. Sharp, Virtual Taxation: Electronic Commerce Poses Problems for State Tax Collections, *Government Finance Review* 12 (August 1996): 36–38.

33. Tax Foundation, *Facts and Figures on Government Finance*, 30th ed. (Baltimore: Johns Hopkins University Press, 1995), 259.

34. Johnson and McCullough, *Case Study on Urban Local Government Finance*.

35. Water Pressure, *Governing* 7 (December 1994): 53.

36. E. Perlman, Taxing Travelers to the Hilt, *Governing* 7 (December 1994): 20–21; C. Kyle, Airport Financing: Let the Passengers Pay, *Governing* 7 (March 1994): 18–19.

37. U.S. Office of Management and Budget, *Analytical Perspectives: Budget of the United States Government: Fiscal Year 1998,* 61.

38. U.S. Office of Management and Budget, *Budget of the United States Government: Fiscal Year 1998* (Washington, DC: U.S. Government Printing Office, 1997), 43.

39. B. Townsend, Development Impact Fees: A Fair Share Formula for Success, *Public Management* 78 (April 1996): 10–15.

40. A. Khan and T.J. Stumm, The Tax and Expenditure Effects of Subsidization by Municipal Utility Enterprises, *Municipal Finance Journal* 15 (1994): 68–81; T.J. Stumm and A. Khan, Effects of Utility Enterprise Fund Subsidization on Municipal Taxes and Expenditures, *State and Local Government Review* 2 (Spring 1996): 103–113.

41. Johnson and McCullough, *Case Study on Urban Local Government Finance*.

42. U.S. General Accounting Office, *Federal Fiscal Trends: Fiscal Years 1991–1995*, 16–18.

43. U.S. General Accounting Office, *Social Security Administration: Effective Leadership Needed to Meet Daunting Challenges* (Washington, DC: U.S. Government Printing Office, 1996), 1; U.S. General Accounting Office, *SSA Disability Redesign: Focus Needed on Initiatives Most Crucial to Reducing Costs and Time* (Washington, DC: U.S. Government Printing Office, 1996), 10.

44. U.S. General Accounting Office, *SSA Disability Redesign: Focus Needed on Initiatives Most Crucial to Reducing Costs and Time*, 10.

45. *U.S. Statistics and Facts*: http://www.instantech.com/users/1260/index.htm#unemp; accessed February 1997.

46. A. Bernstein, Social Security: Is the Sky Really Falling? *Business Week* (February 10, 1997): 92.

47. American Survey: The Pensions Conspiracy, *The Economist* 341 (December 14, 1996): 20, 27–28.

48. J.L. Norwood, The Consumer Price Index, the Deficit, and Politics, *Government Finance Review* 13 (February 1997): 32–33.

49. R. Lewis, AARP Disputes Panel's CPI Call, *AARP Bulletin* 38 (January 1997): 6–7, 13.

50. C. Conte, Capital Hill Moving to Doctor Medicare, *AARP Bulletin* 38 (February 1997): 1, 14–15.

51. A. Daniels, The Turnpike Experiment, *Governing* 9 (May 1996): 31–32.

52. D. Haarmayer, Privatizing Infrastructure: Options for Municipal Systems, *Journal of the AWWA* 96 (March 1994): 43–55.

53. C. Mahtesian, The Precarious Politics of Privatizing Schools, *Governing* 7 (June 1994): 46–51.

54. R.W. Johnson and N.J. Walker, Financing Municipal Infrastructure through Direct Private Investment (Paper presented at Southeastern Conference for Public Administration, Research Triangle Institute, Research Triangle Park, NC, October 7, 1993).

55. *International Water Development: Annual 1997* (World Congress, LLC, 1996), ix.

56. D. Rivera, *Private Sector Participation in the Water Supply and Wastewater Sector: Lessons from Six Developing Countries* (Washington, DC: The World Bank, 1996).

57. A.M. Sullivan, *Urban Economics* (Homewood, IL: Irwin, 1990), 500.

58. The Lottery Loot, *Governing* 8 (October 1995): 45.

59. E. Perlman, The Gambling Glut, *Governing* 9 (May 1996): 49–56.

60. C.T. Clotfelter and P.J. Cook, On the Economics of State Lotteries, *Journal of Economic Perspective* 4 (Fall 1990): 105–119.

61. Perlman, The Gambling Glut, 52.

62. E. Perlman, Gambling, Mississippi Style, *Governing* 8 (April 1995): 40–44.

63. A Busted Flush, *The Economist* 342 (January 25, 1997): 26–28.

64. C.J. Spindler, The Lottery and Education: Robbing Peter to Pay Paul? *Public Budgeting & Finance* 15 (Fall 1995): 54–62.

65. A.M. Rivlin, *Revising the American Dream: The Economy, the States and the Federal Government* (Washington, DC: Brookings Institution, 1992).

66. U.S. General Accounting Office, *Tax Policy, Value-Added Tax: Administration Costs Vary with Complexity and Number of Businesses* (Washington, DC: U.S. Government Printing Office, 1993).

67. I.S. Rubin, *The Politics of Public Budgeting: Getting and Spending, Borrowing and Balancing*, 2nd ed. (Chatham, NJ: Chatham House, 1993), 29–66.

68. H.F. Ladd and J.B. Wilson, Who Supports Tax Limitations: Evidence from Massachusetts' Proposition 2½, *Journal of Policy Analysis and Management* 2 (1983): 256–279; E. Moscovitch, Proposition 2½, *Government Finance Review* 1 (October 1985): 21–25.

69. D.R. Mullins and P.G. Joyce, Tax and Expenditure Limitations and State and Local Fiscal Structure: An Empirical Assessment, *Public Budgeting & Finance* 16 (Spring 1996): 75–101.

70. S.D. Gold, State Tax Cuts of 1995: Is Something New Afoot? *Public Budgeting & Finance* 16 (Spring 1996): 3–22; National Association of State Budget Officers, *1996 State Tax Initiatives*: http://www.nasbo.org/pubs/infobrf/taxib.htm; accessed December 1997.

71. Proposition 218, *Government Finance Review* 13 (February 1997): 3.

72. J.E. Petersen, Why Schools Are Tumbling Down: The Fiscal Story, *Governing* 7 (March 1994): 90.

73. Mullins and Joyce, Tax and Expenditure Limitations and State and Local Fiscal Structure, 77.

74. J. Dunn, A Tax-and-Spend Report Card on Governing in Minnesota, *Governing* 8 (April 1995): 48.

75. S.D. Gold, Steve Gold's Fiscal Notebook, *Governing* 8 (October 1995): 49.

76. T. King-Meadows and D. Lowery, The Impact of the Tax Revolt Era State Fiscal Caps: A Research Update, *Public Budgeting & Finance* 16 (Spring 1996): 102–112.

77. P.G. Joyce and D.R. Mullins, The Changing Fiscal Structure of the State and Local Public Sector: The Impact of Tax and Expenditure Limitations, *Public Administration Review* 51 (May/June 1991): 244–245.

78. G.A. Grizzle and W.E. Klay, Forecasting State Sales Tax Revenues: Comparing the Accuracy of Different Methods, *State and Local Government Review* 26 (1994): 142–152.

79. J.J.L. Stegmaier and M.J. Reiss, The Revenue Forum: An Effective Low-Cost, Low-Tech Approach to Revenue Forecasting, *Government Finance Review* 12 (April 1994): 13–16.

80. J.D. Wong, Options, Challenges, and Incentives for Implementing Systematic Revenue Forecasting in Local Government, *Municipal Finance Journal* 16 (1995): 63–79.

81. S.J. Agostini, Searching for a Better Forecast: San Francisco's Revenue Forecasting Model, *Government Finance Review* 7 (December 1991): 13–15.

82. D.R. Mullins and S. Wallace, Changing Demographics and State Fiscal Outlook: The Case of Sales Taxes, *Public Finance Quarterly* 24 (1996): 237–262.

83. R. Rodgers and P. Joyce, The Effect of Underforecasting on the Accuracy of Revenue Forecasts by State Governments, *Public Administration Review* 56 (1996): 48–56.

CHAPTER 5

Budget Preparation: The Expenditure Side

In the budget preparation phase, important decisions about expenditures are made simultaneously with decisions concerning revenues. The two general types of information relevant for budgeting are program and resource information (see Chapter 1). Program information consists of data on what government does and what those activities accomplish; the resource information consists of the inputs necessary to perform those activities. The input side, which includes dollars, facilities, equipment, supplies, and personnel, has long been an established feature of budgetary systems. The use of program information, on the other hand, has been slow in becoming an integral part of budgeting.

The critical argument relating to these two types of information is that they must be considered in combination if budgeting is to be a sensible process of allocating resources. The budget is expected to relate the accomplishments of government to the costs of resources. The history of budgetary reform can be viewed as a struggle to create such budget systems.

This chapter examines the varied approaches that have been used in assembling the expenditure side of budgets, with the following chapter considering the political concerns of budget preparation. The first section of this chapter discusses early reform efforts, and the next describes the types of program information used to varying degrees in budget systems. The last section discusses the numerous budget systems that have been used, including performance, program, zero-base, and hybrid budgeting systems.

EARLY DEVELOPMENTS

As noted in Chapter 1, budgeting can focus on expenditure control, management control, and planning control.[1] While there is some historical pattern to the development of these three emphases, they are not rigidly fixed to specific time periods, and both the management and planning phases have involved greater utilization of program information. Not only is there a blurring of distinctions between these stages in terms of the dates of their popularity, but use of planning coupled with program information was advocated at least as far back as the early part of the century. (By *planning*, we mean an effort to associate means with ends in order to attain goals and objectives in the future.)

Program Information

1910–1939. Before the establishment of the federal budgetary system, budgeting was often advocated as a means of allocating resources to obtain program results. Two of the most notable proponents were President Taft[2] and the 1912 Taft Commission on Economy and Efficiency. At one point in its report, the commission stated, "In order that he [the administrator] may think intelligently about the subject of his responsibility he must have before him regularly statements which will reflect *results in terms of quality and quantity*; he must be able to measure quality and quantity of results by units of cost and units of efficiency"[3] (emphasis added). Although there was an obvious interest in economizing—in saving dollars—there was also an interest in being able to obtain the best return in program terms for resources spent.

Other important spokespersons for program results in budgeting in the 1910s included Frederick A. Cleveland[4] and William F. Willoughby.[5] The 1920s and 1930s brought Lent D. Upson,[6] A. E. Buck,[7] Wylie Kilpatrick,[8] and the 1937 President's Committee on Administrative Management.[9] A. E. Buck's classic *Public Budgeting* (1929) admittedly lacked a strong program information orientation, but Buck did express interest in reforms that would concentrate upon measuring the products of government activities.

1940–1960. Although the use of program information and planning was advocated throughout the first four decades of the century, this issue received far greater attention beginning in the 1940s. V. O. Key, Jr., challenged previous budgetary literature as largely mechanical and criticized it for failing to focus on the "basic budgeting problem" of comparing the merits of alternative programs: "On what basis shall it be decided to allocate X dollars to activity A instead of activity B?"[10] The 1949 Commission on Organization of the Executive Branch of the Government, known as the First Hoover Commission, recommended that the federal budget be "based upon functions, activities, and projects: this we designate as a performance budget." Budgeting should be in terms of "the work or the service to be accomplished."[11]

More proponents of the same viewpoint emerged in the 1950s. Noted scholars included Verne B. Lewis,[12] Frederick C. Mosher,[13] Catheryn Seckler-Hudson,[14] and Arthur Smithies.[15] The Second Hoover Commission supported the recommendations of its predecessor.[16] Smithies suggested the use of program information in budgeting as a primary means of improving both executive and legislative decision making. Jesse Burkhead's *Government Budgeting*, while basically descriptive rather than normative, devoted considerable discussion to performance and program budgeting.[17]

By the 1950s the use of program information in budgeting had become a mainstream reform issue, while at the same time, another school of thought, led by Charles E. Lindblom, Aaron Wildavsky, and others, challenged the budget reform movement on the grounds that political decision systems were not readily adaptable to program planning. Lindblom advanced the "muddling through" model of decision making (see Chapter 1), which ran counter to budgetary reform efforts. Wildavsky was to become the most outspoken skeptic of the feasibility of using program information in budgeting. In 1969 he concluded, *"No one knows how to do program budgeting."*[18]

Nonbudgetary Developments

An alternative school of thought led by David Novick, Charles J. Hitch, Roland McKean, and others was rooted in a set of theoretical and technological fields that developed after World War II. These fields and technologies were highly compatible with the budget reform movement and served as the theoretical foundation for planning-programming-budgeting (PPB) systems attempted in the 1960s. Of central importance were the following six[19]:

1. operations research, a technique that involves specifying objectives, designing a model representing the situation under investigation, and collecting and applying relevant data[20]
2. economic analysis, a process of determining whether benefits exceed costs of a current or contemplated program[21]
3. general systems theory, an approach which focuses upon how components of a system relate to one another[22]
4. cybernetics, the science of control and communication[23]
5. computer technology, the growth of which made possible a variety of analytic processes that required the manipulation of large amounts of data[24]
6. systems analysis, an eclectic form of analysis that draws upon the previous five items[25]

These fields and technologies were developed outside of the budget reform movement but were highly compatible with it. The six constituted the theoretical and technological foundation for what became the PPB system in the Department of Defense in the 1960s.

The reform efforts from the early 1900s to 1960 that emphasized the use of program information coupled with this series of other nonbudgetary developments constitute the foundation for more recent budget system innovations and for contemporary budget systems.

STRUCTURING THE REQUEST PROCESS

Except in the smallest organizations, the central budget office alone cannot prepare a budget. As noted in Chapter 3, budget preparation begins with the almost simultaneous amassing of supporting information in the operating agencies and the issuance of budget instructions from the central budget office. The information developed at this stage depends in part on how each agency chooses to make its case and in part on the way decisions are expected to be made. If only dollar requests are prepared, there obviously will be no information with which to make judgments on program effectiveness. On the other hand, there is no need to assume that a central budget office necessarily uses program information in its deliberations even if it requires its submission. Still another factor determining what information will be prepared is the known information demands from other budget participants, most notably the legislative body. Much data may be amassed, not because the agency or the chief executive has any intention of using them for decision purposes, but simply because each year the legislative body demands that information.

Preparation Instructions

Budget preparation practices vary considerably within agencies. There will be different degrees of participation by field office staff and other line personnel, but while such variation exists, the overall process is guided by a set of instructions issued by the central budget office of a government.

At the federal level, such instructions are contained in Office of Management and Budget (OMB) Circular A-11, *Preparation and Submission of Budget Estimates*. This document, issued annually, contains considerable detail and, counting text and supporting illustrations, exceeds 300 pages. The circular is available on the Internet, and agencies can submit much of their budget requests through a computer template system.[26] Exhibit 5-1 indicates the vast array of materials that agencies must submit. Much of this information is mandated by various statutes, such as crime control information being required by the Violent Crime Control and Law Enforcement Act of 1994.[27] (Explanations of various items in Exhibit 5-1 are provided in other chapters.)

Instructions such as those contained in Circular A-11 include forms to be completed, reducing uncertainty among agencies as to what the budget office expects

Exhibit 5–1 Selected Materials That Federal Agencies Must Submit as Part of Their Budget Requests

Type of Material	*Description*
General	
Summary and highlight statement	Summarizes major changes that are being proposed
Budget justification	Compares program benefits and program costs; includes information on program evaluations
National Performance Review (NPR) targeted positions	Shows compliance with planned cutbacks in personnel
Financial management	Reports plans for improving financial management (accounting)
Resources for financial management activities and systems	Reports planned expenditures for asset management, accounting and reporting, financial auditing, and financial management systems
Financial management systems	Indicates proposed spending for upgrading financial systems in compliance with the Chief Financial Officers Act
Technology management	Reports how planned improvements in financial management are linked with improvements in information technology (computers)
Rental payments for space and land	Provides information on costs for rent
Receipts estimates	Shows monies that agency expects to collect
Inspector general	Proposes activities and expenditures for inspector general of agency
Credit liquidating accounts	Indicates monies to be carried forward into next fiscal year in order to cover current obligations
Impact of full funding of capital assets	Shows the amount of budget authority needed to fund completely projects that are currently being funded incrementally
Capital asset plan and justification	Indicates spending for projects and their justification, including performance goals
Energy costs	Reports agencies' spending for energy when paid directly to utilities

continues

Exhibit 5–1 continued

Type of Material	Description
Drug control programs	Provides information about drug abuse prevention and treatment and drug law enforcement and prosecution
Annual performance plan	Displays information required by Government Performance and Results Act, indicating linkage between strategic plan and annual performance goals and linkage between annual goals and budget
Violent Crime Control programs	Indicates use of monies provided by the Violent Crime Reduction Trust Fund
Computer and Print Materials	
Budget authority and outlays	Compares proposed authority to commit government to expenditures and expected expenditures
Character classification	Reports investments in physical assets, research and development, and the conduct of education and training
Program, financing, and object class	Shows program activities and finances according to annual performance plans required by Government Performance and Results Act; shows expenditures according to standard accounting structure for object classes (personnel, travel, and the like)
Federal credit	Reports existing credit programs and proposal for extending new credit to potential beneficiaries
Contract authority	Indicates status of contract authority such as amount obligated and amount expiring
Personnel	Indicates full-time equivalents for personnel and proposed compensation
Operations/balance sheet	Provides information on assets, liabilities, and net position for programs with revolving funds
Status of funds	Shows balances, cash income, and cash outgo of main trust funds
Budget plan	Reports for military expenditures multiyear obligations in the year that appropriation is granted

continues

Exhibit 5–1 continued

Type of Material	*Description*
Information on accounts required to submit budget execution reports	Links budget preparation and budget execution data
Status of contingent emergency funding	Indicates funding for emergencies that President requests of Congress separately under the Balanced Budget and Emergency Deficit Control Act of 1995
Appropriations requests (thousands)	Displays net resources included in proposed appropriations language for accounts requesting new spending authority
Unavailable collections	Reports monies received that are unavailable for expenditure due to limitations in law
Print Materials	
Appropriations language	Proposes wording that Congress may eventually use to appropriate funds for each budget unit within an agency
Narrative statements on program and performance	Describes performance goals, outputs, and outcomes
Additional Information	
Grants to state and local governments	Indicates grants going to each state
Motor vehicles	Reports obligations for purchasing, leasing, and operating motor vehicles
Advisory and assistance services	Shows expenses for acquisition of advisory services on management, evaluation, engineering, and other technical services
Baseline estimates of major regulations, management initiatives, administrative actions	Projects resources, outlays, and receipts into future years based on existing laws (current services projections)
Risk categories	Reports risks associated with federal credit programs
Obligations for information technology and conversion of computer systems for the year 2000	Estimates costs of modifying computer software to accommodate date change from 19XX to 20XX

Source: Adapted from *Preparation and Submission of Budget Estimates*, Circular A-11, 1997, U.S. Office of Management and Budget.

of them. Typically, a calendar will be provided explaining when requests are due for submission to the budget office and indicating a period when agencies may be called for hearings with the budget office. The instructions, then, determine the type and amount of information that will be required of the agencies, although the budget office may request additional information from given agencies.

No matter what the jurisdiction, standard items can be found in virtually all budget instruction manuals. Where appropriate, agencies are asked to submit revenue data (e.g., an agency operating a loan program with a revolving fund). Most of the instructions, however, concentrate on expenditures. The expenditures are keyed with the accounting system, using objects of expenditures such as personnel and supplies (see Chapter 11). There also may be detailed breakouts on the number of persons in a given unit, their job titles, and their current salaries. The instructions usually allow for the agencies to provide narrative statements in order to justify the requests.

Separate sets of instructions may be provided for the operating and capital fund budgets. Instructions for the latter, used extensively at the state and local levels, are primarily for requests on major fixed assets such as buildings and equipment. Federal agencies are required to separate out investment in fixed assets (see Chapter 12). The federal government, according to Executive Order 12837 issued by President Clinton in 1993, also attempts to separate administrative expenses from other expenses that provide direct benefits to program participants. According to the executive order, administrative expenses are to be reduced over a multiyear period while other expenses may increase.

Program Information

Budget systems are making increased use of program information, and therefore request instructions specify what types of program data are to be supplied. The measures typically will have been negotiated between the budget office and the agencies before budget preparation time. In other words, when the agencies receive the request instructions, they already know what program information they need to submit. Determining what information to collect and present in budget requests is of concern at all levels of government in the United States and abroad. As of the late 1990s, the umbrella term used to describe the overall field of program information was *performance measurement*.[28] Such measurement is seen as a means for holding agencies accountable for the expenditure of tax dollars and other public resources.[29]

Social Indicators. Of the variety of program information, social indicators are the broadest or most general type. These measures of the physical, social, and economic environments are intended to reflect what sometimes is called *quality of life.* The percentage of the work force unemployed broken out by age, sex, race, and income constitutes a set of important social indicators. OMB lists several social indicators in its annual report, *Analytical Perspectives*. The report includes such measures as the median annual family income of female householders with no husband present and the population living in counties with ozone levels exceeding the standard.[30] Measures of this type are useful in assessing past and current trends and provide decision makers with some insights into the need for programs. In the 1990s, a volunteer network in the Seattle region developed 40 such indicators to determine whether the region was maintaining "sustainability," namely preserving its "cultural, economic, environmental and social" conditions. The group found the region was declining in sustainability in such areas as wetlands, energy use, and children living in poverty.[31]

One limitation of the Seattle measures and other social indicators is their lack of direct linkage with any given government service, meaning that the indicators are of little use for yearly budget decisions. Children living in poverty results from many factors, and no government program alone could be expected to resolve the problem.

Impacts. Measures of more direct relevance to budgeting are impacts (sometimes called outcomes). Measures of this type concentrate on effectiveness—whether desired effects or consequences are being achieved. When a government service has affected "individuals, institutions [or] the environment," an impact has occurred.[32] In the employment case, an impact measure might be the average earnings of nonwhite men who completed a job training program or, even more focused, the average increase in hourly earnings after completion of the program compared with prior earnings. Such a measure needs to be assessed carefully, however, because earnings may have increased in a given time period mainly as a result of inflation or an upturn in the economy. Impacts can be seen as a method of gauging the value of government services or determining whether expenditures for services are *investments*.[33]

Sometimes myths or doctrines lead to problems in the selection of impact measures. In providing funds to police departments, the assumption is often made that crime will be controlled. This assumption leads to the selection of crime rates as impact measures despite the fact that police have only limited control over crime.

Outputs. In contrast with impact measures, output measures reflect the immediate products or services being provided. Returning to the employment example, the number of graduates of the training program would be the output. The percentage of persons enrolled who graduate—the completion rate—can be calculated from year to year. Measures such as this are far easier to calculate than many impact measures because the data sources are within the organization. One needs only to keep accurate records of who enrolled and who graduated. Impacts, on the other hand, are external. In the case of earnings of graduates, a monitoring or follow-up system for the graduates is necessary to obtain the appropriate data.

One drawback of using output measures alone is that an erroneous assumption can be made about causal relationships. Focusing on the graduation rate of the training program makes sense only if it is assumed that training improves employability, but unless data are collected to verify anticipated results, the program is being maintained strictly on faith or doctrine. Outputs, then, may encourage *suboptimization,* which is the improvement of operations for attaining subobjectives while risking the possibility of moving away from rather than toward larger values.

Activities and Workload. Activities are the work that is done to produce outputs. The total hours of instruction could be a measure for a job training program, or the measure might be more focused, such as hours of instruction in lathe operations. Activities are sometimes measured as workload. The number of applications processed and the number of enrollees in a program are workload measures. If the number of applicants increases, though enrollments are kept constant because of space limitations, the workload will still increase, since more applications will need to be screened. Both activities and outputs are far easier to measure than impacts, a factor that contributes to the extensive use of the former and more limited use of the latter in budgeting.

Management by Objectives. Workload is often the focus of management by objectives (MBO) and other participative management techniques.[34] Although many diverse activities have been carried out in government under the rubric of MBO, a common theme tends to be prescribing objectives for organizational units, managers, and workers in terms of the work they are expected to accomplish. Participative management systems such as MBO emphasize involvement of all strata of the bureaucracy in the development of objectives.

Productivity. Another term having many different meanings is productivity.[35] The term is sometimes used to cover virtually all forms of program measurement. A different approach is to limit the concept of productivity to comparisons of resource inputs and work. Ratios are typically used for productivity measurement, such as the total cost of a job training program divided by the number of graduates, yielding an average cost per graduate. If average cost remains constant from one year to another, despite increases in salary rates and various supplies, then the assumption is made that the unit is more productive. Emphasis is placed on making government operations increasingly efficient. OMB Circular A-11 provides that agencies should report gains in productivity, especially when justifying staffing and other resource needs.

Productivity measures often require extensive recordkeeping. If a group of employees together performs several different activities, then a reporting system is needed to account for the hours committed to each activity by each employee.

This accounting is sometimes accomplished by means of daily report forms. State and local police often must submit daily reports on hours spent patrolling, investigating, testifying in court, and report writing itself. Less complicated systems may use weekly, monthly, or quarterly report forms. On the cost side, accounting systems need to capture nonpersonnel expenditures related to activities.

Total Quality Management or Continuous Quality Improvement. Total quality management (TQM)—also called continuous quality improvement—is not a budget system but, as envisioned by its creator, W. Edwards Deming, is a management system that focuses on the end products or results of organizations.[36] Available space does not allow a discussion of TQM, but it should be noted that the system relies heavily on program measurement and that one of Deming's 14 TQM recommendations is to avoid management by objectives. This latter management system is seen as setting quotas for workers rather than empowering them to think creatively and allowing them to achieve results that might well be beyond any expected quotas. The Baldrige Quality System has been devised for the private sector and extended to the public sector. The system, as with TQM in general, emphasizes the use of information, analysis, and planning in order to improve quality and customer satisfaction.[37]

Need. A final type of measure gauges the need for a program. The need measure indicates the gap between the level of service and the need for it. In the case of the job training program, one need measure would be the number of persons who are without adequate job skills and therefore in need of training.

In discussing need, we have come full circle back to social indicators, prompting a few words of caution. We have relied here on several examples to show differences among types of measures, but it should be understood that the differences might not always be so obvious. For example, the dollar value of fire damage in a city might be considered a social indicator, an impact of the fire department, and an indicator of fire service need.

Using Program Measures. A major challenge facing any budget system is deciding how to use these diverse types of information. Which types will be used, in what combination, and to what extent? An initial temptation is to decide to use every imaginable measure of government operations, but such an approach is doomed to failure, since it, if carefully and thoroughly executed, would produce massive amounts of data that could not be comprehended by decision makers. Indeed, such data produce what is called noise rather than information.

Reformers for decades have been concerned that budgeting keep its focus on the missions of government and on the goals and objectives to be achieved. Osborne and Gaebler's popular work *Reinventing Government* stresses the need to keep mission primarily in mind when making decisions in government.[38] *Mission* refers to the fundamental reasons why a government program exists.

Although scholars and practitioners in the field of budgeting have yet to reach any consensus on what constitutes a goal as distinguished from an objective, one approach is to think of goals as broadly stated ideal conditions, such as the absence of crime. *Goals,* given this definition, are unlikely to be achieved but function as desired states that governments can continuously work toward attaining. *Objectives,* on the other hand, are more focused and immediate, and impact data are used to gauge whether a program is moving toward achieving its objectives. A jurisdiction might focus on reducing burglaries and could specify a quantitative target for the future, such as a 10-percent reduction in burglaries. In setting goals and objectives, decision makers must understand that some desired results can be achieved in a comparatively short period, such as a year, while other results will require many years.[39]

Selecting measures for any given program depends on perceptions about the program's mission, and individuals may differ widely on this matter. In a broad sense, the vision one has of a program is related to one's perception of what the public interest is. In a narrow sense, individuals may have specific expectations of what government programs are expected to accomplish. Renters may want a city housing program to focus on affordable rental housing, while homeowners may be largely concerned with city policies that will protect property values and keep taxes low. Owners of rental properties, in contrast, may be chiefly interested in achieving substantial returns on their financial investments. Ultimately, then, the success of many, if not most, government programs will be evaluated in terms of several measures rather than only one or two. The need to use multiple measures makes analysis of a program's achievements more challenging than if a single measure is used (see Chapter 7).

Interpreting measures, especially social indicators and impacts, is an additional problem. Because conditions in society are the result of a wide assortment of variables, isolating government's contribution to any given situation is difficult. One of the most difficult tasks in developing program measures is to select those that reflect what a particular government accomplishes. The federal government faces considerable challenges in this arena, since national programs are carried out through a variety of means, such as through state and local government and nonprofit organizations. If a given program is successful, to what extent is the success due to partial funding by the federal government?[40]

Choosing among Program Results. Inevitably some tradeoffs occur when trying to decide among programs. Consequently, equity becomes a concern—are different segments of the citizenry benefiting according to some standard of fairness? The perceived severity of a problem to be addressed by government enters into such deliberations, such as the perception that a community has a major illegal drug problem or that the nation must address the problem of conquering acquired immune deficiency syndrome (AIDS). In both of these examples, a tempering factor is whether government programs are able to use infusions of resources effectively. Large budget increases for combating drugs or AIDS will not necessarily resolve these problems.

Governments are at a disadvantage in making these difficult choices in comparison with private corporations, which have the profit motive as their primary concern. A private corporation will invest in those product lines that are expected to yield the highest rate of return on investments. Governments utilize some combination of the types of program information discussed here but cannot readily convert these into a single measure of profit. They must choose among disparate commodities such as fire protection, air pollution reduction, and public transit. Making comparisons may help in this situation. Cost-benefit studies, discussed in Chapter 7, can provide insights into the return on public investments.

SYSTEMS OF BUDGETING

If the central budget office simply instructed agencies to request budgets for the coming year, the result most likely would be several different types of responses based on different assumptions about the coming budget year. One agency might respond by requesting what it felt was needed. Another might respond in light of what resources it thought were available, resulting in a much lower request. Others might use combinations of these and other approaches. The consequences would be budget requests based on varied assumptions, and these requests would require different reactions by the budget office. To avoid such disparities in the assumptions made by requesting agencies, budget instructions often provide guidance to agencies.

Preparation Assumptions

Current Services Budgeting. One type of guidance is to assume basically no change in programs. A department's current budget is considered its *base*, and any increases are to be requested only to cover additional operating costs, such as increased costs for personnel, supplies, and so on. An assumption is made that the government is committed or obligated to continue existing programs. This base approach often has been used only implicitly, but since the 1960s and 1970s many governments have had their budgets explicitly indicate levels of commitment for agencies and programs. The federal budget has included current services estimates since the 1970s.

Explicitly determining what are current commitments is difficult because programs often are created without any forthright statement of commitment. The easiest cases are those in which there is an obligation to serve all claimants on the system. School districts, for example, are obligated to serve all eligible children, and therefore budget requests from units within the school district would be based on the expected number of enrolled children. In other cases, the commitment may be in terms of the level of service, specifically outputs and workload. Using job training as an example again, the unit could have a commitment to maintain the same number of graduates or alternatively the same number of students. Budgeting, then, can be seen as adding increments to or subtracting them from the base.

Fixed-Ceiling Budgeting. An alternative to the current commitment approach is fixed-ceiling budgeting. Under this system, a dollar limit is set government-wide, then factored into limits for departments, bureaus, and other subunits. The advantage is that budget requests are created that do not, when totaled, exceed the desired ceiling. The disadvantage is that some organizational units may receive inadequate funding and others may be overfunded in terms of program priorities. This can result from the unavailability of adequate information about program requirements when limits are set. Fixed-ceiling budgeting is most useful during periods of stability.

A weakness of both the base and fixed-ceiling approaches is that by themselves they offer no suggestions for program changes. If the budget office and chief executive have only these types of budget requests, they lack information about alternative resource allocations. In response to this lack of information, several "what-if" approaches to budget requests have been devised. These approaches ask agencies to develop alternatives by asking, for example, What if more dollars were available? Or what if program improvements were to be made in specific areas?

Open-Ended Budgeting. One of the most common what-if approaches is open-ended or "blue-sky" budgeting. The question is asked, What if resources were available to meet all needs? Agencies are expected to ask for what they think they need to deal with problems assigned to them. This approach should not be confused with the absence of guidance, in which some agencies might request "needed" funds and others might ask for lesser amounts. The advantage of the open-ended approach is that it surfaces perceived needs for services. The open-ended budget, in contrast with the current services budget, can serve as the basis for discussions of preferred funding levels. The disadvantage is that open-ended requests may exceed the economic and political capabilities of the jurisdiction, making the requests seem like fanciful wish lists. Such has been the case in the Department of Defense and its use of the Joint Strategic Objectives Plan (JSOP), which is based on the assumption that defense forces should be as strong as necessary to meet all potential threats simultaneously.[41]

Performance Budgeting

A flurry of budget reform activity aimed at bringing greater program data into the budget decision-making process occurred in response to the First Hoover Commission (1949), which proposed the use of performance budgeting. In response to the commission's recommendation, Congress specifically provided in the National Security Act Amendments of 1949 that performance budgeting be used in the military.[42] The following year saw passage of the Budget and Accounting Procedures Act, which in essence required performance budgeting for the entire federal government.[43] State and local governments followed suit.

Among federal, state, and local agencies, performance budgeting was geared mainly toward developing workload and unit cost measures of activities. For the postal service, the number of letters that could be processed by one employee was identified. With this knowledge and an estimate of the number of letters to be processed, postal officials could calculate the personnel required for the coming budget year.[44] In the name of performance budgeting, the Department of Defense in 1950 adopted a single set of budget categories that were applied to all services. These categories, most of which were still in use in the 1990s, included personnel, maintenance and operation, and research and development.

Applying performance budgeting to all aspects of government is difficult. For instance, there is no easy method for determining how much defense is enough. The problem is that defense is mainly a matter of deterrence and preparedness. The military is expected to have sufficient strength to deter an attack by a potential aggressor and to be sufficiently prepared for war or other emergencies if they do occur. The deterrent strategy is working when no attack has been launched. As for preparedness, that can only be tested in real combat and other military situations. When the nation is not fighting a war or deploying troops in emergency situations at home or abroad, it is difficult to prove conclusively that the nation is or is not sufficiently prepared.

Although reconstructing the past is difficult, it seems that the efforts to install performance budgeting in the 1950s failed. There is little evidence that performance budgeting ever became the basis upon which decisions were made in federal, state, or local budget processes. But some lasting effect was evident. Performance budgeting did introduce on a wide scale the use of program information in budget documents, and that type of information gained increasing attention in later years.

Planning-Programming-Budgeting and Program Budgeting

The origin of the term planning-programming-budgeting is uncertain. Mosher used it in his 1954 book on Army program budgeting.[45] During the early 1960s in the Department of Defense, PPB stood for program package budgeting, because a package was presented in terms of the resource inputs (personnel, equipment, etc.) and outputs.[46] By 1965, when President Lyndon B. Johnson extended the system to civilian agencies, PPB had come to mean planning-programming-budgeting. It should be recognized that planning and programming are not distinct from each other but differ only in degree. They have been defined as follows: "*Planning* is the production of the range of meaningful potentials for selection of courses of action through a systematic consideration of alternatives. *Programming* is the more specific determination of the manpower, material, and facilities necessary for accomplishing a program."[47]

Today, PPB is generally used to refer to a series of budgetary reform efforts in the 1960s. The term *program budgeting* is more generic and applies to systems intended to link program costs with results.

Defense. There are several reasons why PPB started in the Department of Defense. Probably the most important one was that, despite having the authority to manage the military, the secretary of defense did not have the necessary management support. Secretary Robert S. McNamara in 1961 had the determination to initiate change. In coming to the Pentagon, he brought with him several people from the RAND Corporation who earlier had done extensive work related to program budgeting. David Novick of RAND published reports in the 1950s recommending such a system for the Department of Defense.[48] The key person for program budgeting under McNamara was Charles J. Hitch, who became assistant secretary of defense (comptroller). McNamara, Hitch, and others made use of the development of operations research, computers, and systems analysis, all of which were complementary to the mainstream of budgetary reform.

The central component of the Department of Defense system is the Five-Year Defense Program (FYDP), which projects costs and personnel according to missions or programs. The programs form what is called the *program structure*, a classification system that begins with broad missions and factors them into subunits and activities. The structure groups like activities together regardless of which branches of the service conduct them, thereby allowing for analyses across organizational lines. The major programs within the FYDP are

- strategic forces
- general purpose forces
- intelligence and communications
- airlift and sealift
- guard and reserve
- research and development
- central supply and maintenance
- training, medical, and other general purpose activities

- administration and associated activities
- support of other nations
- special operations forces

Changes in terminology and process have occurred since the 1960s, but overall the main approach in the Department of Defense has remained constant. Changes in the FYDP are accomplished by the Office of the Secretary of Defense issuing guidance, to which the services respond by preparing program objective memoranda, which contain budget proposals for modifying the FYDP.[49] The program objective memoranda suggest programmatic and resource incremental changes to the base established in the FYDP. While the PPB system is organized around programs, Congress has continued to appropriate funds for defense based on object classifications, the main ones including military personnel, operation and maintenance, procurement; research, development, test, and evaluation; and military construction.

The Department of Defense's PPB system has been in operation for more than three decades, but the system clearly has not been a panacea for defense-related problems. During that period the department was subjected to extensive and severe criticism regarding its conduct of the Vietnam War. Since then, there also have been major cost overruns and failures of various weapons systems, along with scandals involving alleged corruption in weapons contracting. The point is that budget systems may provide useful information for decision makers but do not guarantee that wise decisions will be made.

In 1995, the Commission on Roles and Missions of the Armed Forces, created by the National Defense Authorization Act for Fiscal Year 1994, issued a wide-sweeping set of recommendations, including a major overhaul of the defense budget process. Earlier, the National Performance Review (NPR) had suggested changes in the process, but the 1995 Commission made recommendations that would fundamentally revise the system.[50] The report stated, "The current PPB system reexamines the entire multiyear defense program annually, uses too many people, takes too long, goes into too much detail, and leaves little time for reflection and creativity."[51] The revised system, if adopted, would have two phases, the first concentrating on the broad decisions about defense and the second on how to meet those needs through the budget process. The powers of the secretary of defense would be enhanced and the individual armed services would be brought into closer linkage with one another. Any new system needs to take into consideration that defense is organized simultaneously by type of weapons system (missiles, aircraft, naval ships, and the like), geography (Western Europe, Pacific, etc.), and mission. The latter has changed dramatically since the end of the Cold War so that there is less concern about nuclear attack. Instead, there is an increased emphasis on using the military in attempting to bring stability to various regions of the world and to provide humanitarian relief as the need arises.[52]

Federal Civilian Reforms. Turning to the civilian side of government, use of PPB by federal agencies was announced in 1965 by President Johnson, who had been impressed with the Department of Defense budget system. This action sparked massive reform efforts throughout all levels of government in the United States.

The federal civilian system was intended to be similar to the Department of Defense model. Multiyear plans, known as program and financial plans, were to be devised for each department. Changes were to be made through the submission of program memoranda. However, by 1969, when Richard M. Nixon became president, PPB had not been fully implemented by the civilian agencies, and in 1971 OMB relieved agencies of the duty to prepare program and financial plans and program memoranda. As a major budget system, PPB was allowed a quiet death.[53]

A study conducted by the Bureau of the Budget (now OMB) found there were six factors that characterized the more successful efforts to introduce PPB[54]:

1. The number of analysts was sufficient.
2. Analysts were well qualified.
3. Analysts had formal access to agency heads and managers.
4. Analysts had informal access.
5. Agency heads and managers gave strong support for use of analysis.
6. Analysis was viewed as a valuable tool by agency heads and managers.

This study and others found that lack of understanding of and commitment to program budgeting on the part of leadership tended to deter success, as did an agency's general "underdevelopment" in the use of analytic techniques. Agencies administering "soft" social programs had difficulty devising useful program measures. Bureaucratic infighting also reduced the chances of successful implementation. These findings are instructive for any government that undertakes to restructure the operations of its budget system.

State and Local Reforms. The use of PPB did not revolutionize state and local decision making in the 1960s any more than it revolutionized federal decision making. Most of the states that experimented with PPB emphasized the development of program structure, multiyear plans, and program memoranda, while only a few concentrated on analysis as their main thrust. By the mid-1970s, however, the emphasis had swung away from the structural features of PPB to the use of measures of effectiveness and efficiency and program analysis. In the 1960s, many of the states and municipalities took only cautious first steps and established no timetable for completion of the installation process. Others began the effort on a pilot basis, attempting PPB in one department before expanding its use.

By the close of the 1960s, it was difficult to identify many ongoing PPB systems at the state and local levels. The reasons for failure or lack of major success were similar to those already mentioned for federal agencies. State and local governments usually did not have sufficiently sophisticated management practices to be able to undertake the transformation that was expected. Additionally, people simply expected too much to result from conversion to PPB and did not realize the financial and administrative costs associated with the conversion. Legislative bodies often showed little support for the new budget system, and this fact was interpreted by some as legislative hostility toward change.[55]

Change, however, did occur as a result of efforts to introduce PPB systems. Perhaps the biggest single achievement was that governments began to make greater use of program information in budgetary decision making, albeit information largely of the output variety.[56] The pattern continued through the 1980s but, as is discussed later, may have waned somewhat in the 1990s.

Zero-Base Budgeting

Zero-base budgeting (ZBB) is another form of "what-if" budgeting. "Traditional" ZBB—that is, *not* the type used by the federal government during the Carter administration—asks, What if a program were to be eliminated? Rather than assuming that a base exists, the approach asks what would happen if a program were discontinued. Each program is challenged to justify its very existence in every budget cycle.

Early Use. The U.S. Department of Agriculture engaged in an experiment with ZBB in the early 1960s, and the results were disappointing.[57] ZBB, it was found, wasted valuable administrative time by requiring the rehashing of old issues that had already been resolved. The system was unrealistic; many programs were mandatory within the political arena and could not be dismantled no matter how compelling the available data and analysis. Decision makers within the agency could not adequately review the excessive paperwork that was generated.

The disadvantage of ZBB is analogous to that of open-ended budgeting. Both approaches make basically unrealistic assumptions. Whereas open-ended budgeting assumes unlimited resources, the zero-base approach makes the unrealistic assumption that decision makers have the capacity to eliminate programs. In reality, the political forces in any jurisdiction are such that few programs in any given year can be abandoned. For this reason, ZBB may be better applied to selective programs in any one year rather than government-wide. A cycle of reviews can be established such that some programs are thoroughly reviewed each year using ZBB, and all programs are reviewed in any five-year period.

The 1970s. ZBB gained new popularity in the 1970s.[58] Much attention focused on Georgia and its governor, Jimmy Carter, who subsequently brought a new version of ZBB to the federal government upon becoming president in 1977.[59] The Carter administration's version had three major characteristics[60]:

1. Decision units were identified for which budget requests, called *decision packages*, were to be prepared. Approximately 10,000 of these were prepared each year.
2. Alternative funding levels were used for each package:
   - the *minimum level*, which entailed providing services below present levels
   - the *current level*, which maintained existing services and reflected increased costs for personnel, supplies, and the like
   - an *enhancement level*, which provided for upgraded services
3. Alternative funding levels of decision packages were to be *ranked* by importance.

The ZBB experiment at the federal level was criticized on several counts. The most frequently heard complaint was the amount of time required preparing requests and the corresponding amount of paperwork. The ZBB system, contrary to what President Carter had promised, did not require agencies to justify every tax dollar they received. Administrators puzzled over how there could be a minimum level below current operations when the statute under which an agency operated specified benefits, as in the case of Social Security.

ZBB rarely eliminated unnecessary programs, curtailed their growth, or resulted in reassigning priorities among programs.[61] In some isolated instances savings were achieved by funding programs at the minimum level, but that produced agency resentment. Administrators of these programs saw themselves as being punished because they had identified how their programs could operate with less than the current budget. More often, however, the system was seen as involving excessive paperwork that ultimately had little or no impact on policy making. Shortly after President Reagan took office in January 1981, the new administration announced that ZBB would no longer be practiced.

The experience at the state and local levels was comparable to that of the federal government. ZBB initially seemed to hold great promise but eventually was abandoned, although some governments continued to describe their budget systems as founded on the concept.

Strategic Planning and Guidance

Planning. Some governments, in part following the lead of private sector organizations, have engaged in strategic planning efforts, which focus attention on missions, goals, and objectives.[62] In strategic planning, options are identified and chosen in light of fundamental values and purposes. Annual budgeting is then used to allocate resources according to the established priorities.

Strategic planning can be an extremely time-consuming process in which various plans, often presented in great detail, are drafted, reviewed, and then modified. This process usually involves developing an overall plan and then revising the plan annually to reflect new information and revised priorities. Comparisons can be drawn here with the Department of Defense's JSOP and FYDP mentioned earlier. The process of devising and revising plans is sometimes considered as valuable as the actual written plans in that the process fosters extensive thinking within a government about its core values in serving the citizenry.

Policy and Program Guidance. A less ambitious but nevertheless useful approach is to provide broad policy guidance or more narrowly focused program guidance to departments and agencies before they begin to prepare their budget requests. At the federal level, OMB often instructs specific agencies as to what program funding proposals are likely to receive favorable review and instructs them to prepare issue papers on specific programs for which there is concern about the efficacy of resource utilization. Some state and local budget offices provide program guidelines that indicate to agencies the concerns of their governors or mayors, namely, the issues that have high priority for the coming budget year.

In response to such guidance, agencies prepare detailed program requests. There is likely to be a discussion of the range of available alternatives, possibly with detailed costing of each and the expected results of each. Where guidance is not directed at any one agency, two or more may submit competing requests, each attempting to show how its proposed alternative would deal with a problem. For example, both the city police and recreation departments might submit budget proposals for dealing with juvenile delinquency.

The advantage of such guidance is that agencies prepare requests that are likely to be favorably received by the chief executive and are spared many hours of needless work in preparing requests that are fated for rejection. Policy or program guidance, however, does not ensure executive approval of agency requests. The requests may be rejected simply because of inadequate funds or because the arguments for the proposed changes fail to be persuasive.

Multiyear Requests

All budget requests are multiyear in that they at least cover the current year plus the coming budget year and probably the past year as well. States with biennial budgets obviously have multiyear requests. One issue, however, is whether budget requests should extend beyond the budget year and, if yes, how this is to be accomplished. The argument for multiyear requests is simple: Without looking beyond the budget year, commitments of resources may be made that were never intended. This argument applies particularly to proposed expansions and new programs.

Time Horizons. In theory, the time horizon of a budget request should be geared to the life cycle of each program. This life cycle is clearest in specific projects or programs that have an obvious beginning and conclusion. A weapons system is one of the best examples. The cycle begins with research and concludes when the system is judged to be obsolete.

On the other hand, many government programs have no foreseeable conclusion. The need for education, roads, law enforcement, recreation, and the like will always exist. Each of these may have unique properties that suggest possible time horizons. Given the length of time required to design and construct schools, projections of several years are needed. Multiyear requests can reveal when roads will require major repairs, redesigns, and expansions.

Since an appropriate life cycle for multiyear requests is often not obvious, an arbitrary set of years may be imposed. The most common is the budget year plus the four succeeding years, known as a five-year projection. The federal government makes such projections. Making projections beyond five years is difficult because of the many unknowns. Using the road example, it may be largely unknown what the typical commuting pattern will be ten or more years from now.

Cost and Program Projections. Assuming they can be made, however, projections can be limited to finances or can include program data projections. The state of the art tends to limit projections to finances, showing anticipated future financial requirements. When program impacts and outputs are projected, the requests show what resources will be needed in future years along with the benefits that will be derived.

Multiyear projections using cost and program data can be helpful in coping with severe economic conditions. Where program reductions are necessary, agency requests can illustrate the consequences over a longer time period. Cuts in an agency's budget made this year may seem essential but may produce undesirable future consequences. To live within available revenues, a city may reduce its road maintenance program, with no noticeable reduction in road quality in the first year; however, by the second or third year following these cuts, the city may have a road network of substantially lower quality than before.

Use of Budget Techniques

Hybrid Techniques. Many of the techniques discussed here can be used in combination to form hybrid systems. ZBB, for example, can be used selectively for some agencies undergoing intensive review while others use a fixed-ceiling approach. A government may use fixed-ceiling budgeting to allocate monies among major departments but then allow each department to use what has been called *entrepreneurial* budgeting, namely, allocating funds within the department with only a minimum of control from the central budget office.[63] *Target-base* budgeting is also sometimes used. In this type of budgeting, agencies prepare budget requests based on fixed ceilings but then may propose budget increases above the ceilings.[64] Governments can use a current services budget in conjunction with priority listing of decision packages akin to the Carter administration's version of ZBB. The base approach can be combined with open-ended budgeting, in which agencies request funds for what they perceive to be their needs. Program guidance can be linked with priority listings.

As of the late 1990s, the federal government used a variety of systems. Most agencies used some type of program information in their budgeting, while the Department of Defense continued to use a version of PPB. According to a General Accounting Office (GAO) survey of 103 federal organizations, about three-fourths indicated they collected data to assess program performance. On closer examination, however, GAO found that only 9 of the 103 agencies systematically collected performance data that were used to gauge progress toward goal attainment.[65] The Congressional Budget Office, in a study of six agencies that were purported to use performance measures found that none used these measures in deciding on the allocation of resources among programs.[66]

Federal Initiatives—National Performance Review. Upon taking office in 1993, President Clinton established NPR under the direction of Vice President Gore. NPR's initial report, issued in 1993, contained a host of recommendations intended to streamline all aspects of the government.[67] Prompted by the work of this group, President Clinton issued Executive Order 12862 in 1993 requiring that federal agencies establish *customer service standards*, intended to establish levels of performance by agencies. The executive order instructed agencies to determine what services customers demand, what complaints customers have, and allocate resources—make budget decisions—based on customer satisfaction. Some standards that have been adopted simply indicate that an agency will perform a certain task, such as the National Park Service committing itself to keeping the "Great Smoky Mountains visitor center open every day but Christmas."[68] Other standards are time specific, such as the Highway Traffic Safety Administration committing to mailing a registration form for hazardous material within ten days of receiving a request for the form.[69]

NPR, which continued into President Clinton's second term, had as its focus the *re-engineering* of government. *Benchmarking* was an important component involving finding best practices elsewhere, whether in government or the private sector, and using those practices as a guide for revising how government operates. As NPR reported, benchmarking is "stealing shamelessly" from the best, as in the case of the Social Security Administration learning about "800" telephone service from American Express, AT&T Universal Card, Citibank, and the like.[70]

Other aspects of NPR include an emphasis on regulatory reform and seeking opportunities for privatizing government services. One view is that NPR, while initially focusing upon how to increase the efficiency of government programs, shifted its focus in subsequent years to acting as a mechanism for wresting leadership away from the Republican-controlled Congress that took power following the 1994 elections. Adherents of this view claim that NPR specifically attempted to divert attention away from the Contract with America plan developed by Representative Newt Gingrich (Rep., GA) and other House Republicans. NPR can be seen as a Democratic response to Republican initiatives and as an executive branch response to congressional initiatives.[71]

Federal Initiatives—Government Performance and Results Act. Occurring coincident with the NPR was congressional passage of the Government Performance and Results Act (GPRA, pronounced "gip-ra") of 1993 and the law's ensuing implementation.[72] The law was passed as a result of congressional and presidential concern about "waste and inefficiency" in government and "insufficient articulation of program goals and inadequate information on program performance." The law is based on the premise that (1) agencies need to define their missions and desired outcomes, (2) measure performance, and (3) use the performance information to revise programs.[73] All aspects of GPRA are under the direction of OMB and the Chief Financial Officers (CFO) Council, consisting of the top financial officers of major federal agencies.[74] OMB Circular A-11, which instructs agencies on how to prepare their budgets, provides guidance on the implementation of GPRA.

Federal agencies were required to have strategic planning processes and plans in place by the end of fiscal 1997. Each plan, which must cover at least five years, includes a mission statement, outcome-related goals and objectives, a discussion of factors that are beyond the agency's control and could affect its ability to achieve the goals and objectives, and an explanation of how program evaluations were used in developing the plan. About 70 pilots were initiated to test how these plans and other features of GPRA were to be implemented.[75]

The law, while stipulating that strategic plans are to be developed by agencies in consultation with Congress, provides no specific guidance as to how that consultation is to occur. In 1997, the Republican leadership in the House and Senate along with key committee chairpersons submitted a letter to OMB suggesting broad principles regarding how consultation was to be achieved. OMB, then, was expected to oversee a process by which the consultation process was customized to fit the needs of specific committees and agencies.[76] The GAO has assisted Congress in evaluating the strategic plans.[77]

Beginning with fiscal 1999, annual performance plans are to be prepared as outgrowths of the multiyear strategic plans. OMB did not prescribe a specific format for the annual plans, but Circular A-11 gives agencies overall guidance for what information the plans must contain. The performance plans must include information about outcomes, outputs, and activities. By March 31, 2000, each agency must submit its annual program performance plan to the President and Congress. Given the diversity of agencies within the federal government and the immensity of the task of implementing GPRA, unevenness in the quality of the annual plans is inevitable.[78] The law will have important intergovernmental repercussions in that federal agencies will need to obtain information about federally supported programs that are operated by state and local governments.

OMB Circular A-123, the Paperwork Reduction Act of 1995, and the Information Technology Management Reform Act of 1996 further strengthen the federal government's commitment to program measurement and government reengineering. A-123, which was revised in 1995, requires that agencies establish management controls to "ensure that (1) programs achieve their intended results, (2) resources are used consistent with agency mission, (3) programs and resources are protected from waste, fraud, and mismanagement, (4) laws and regulations are followed, and (5) reliable and timely information is obtained, maintained, reported, and used for decision making."[79] The Paperwork Reduction Act of 1995 requires that OMB ensure that agencies share information through the Government Information Locator Service (GILS).[80] Through the sharing of information, agencies can reduce the demands they make on state and local governments, corporations, and individuals to supply information needed for program measurement. The Information Technology Management Reform Act of 1996 requires that agencies use appropriate information technology when setting goals and establishing program measures.[81]

State Techniques. Various surveys of state budget offices shed light on state budgetary practices.[82] In a longitudinal study of state budgeting, the use of effectiveness measures increased from 29 percent of the states in 1970 to 73 percent in 1995, and the use of productivity measures increased from 45 percent to 80 percent.[83] About three-fourths of the states (72 percent) reported that agencies, when requesting approval of new programs or revisions in existing programs, are required to submit data on estimated program effectiveness. This figure, while substantial, was down considerably from the 95-percent figures of 1985 and 1990, perhaps suggesting some backsliding among the states. A majority of the states (70 percent) reported using written policy guidance (up from 30 percent in 1970 but down from 80 percent in 1990). Only 39 percent reported using written program guidance. More than half of the states (62 percent) used a current services budget, and three-fourths (78 percent) used priority ranking. About half of the states (48 percent) said they use fixed ceilings expressed in dollars.[84] States noted for their involvement in benchmarking include Florida, Minnesota, and Oregon.[85] Texas has gained national attention for its strategic budgeting system, which links strategic planning, performance measurement, budgeting, and program monitoring.[86]

Local Techniques. Use of program information at the local level is more limited than at the state level. A mid-1990s study of members of the Government Finance Officers Association found that 51 percent of local governments still used line-item budgeting.[87] Performance budgeting and zero-base/target-base budgeting were used by 2 to 3 percent, while program budgeting was used by 10 percent of the local governments. Thirty-five percent reported using a hybrid system. In another 1990s study, this one of medium-size cities (population, 25,000 to 1 million), 41 percent of the cities said they used program budgeting and 30 percent said they used ZBB, with the latter being down 15 percentage points from a survey of five years earlier.[88] Surveys of local governments, and specifically cities, have found that from 30 percent to more than 60 percent used performance measurement and monitoring in the budget process.[89]

Although a substantial number of local governments use traditional line-item budgeting, which emphasizes resources consumed rather than results, other local governments have been experimenting with the use of various types of program information in their budget processes. Osborne and Gaebler in *Reinventing Government* discuss local governments that have adopted mission-driven budgeting, which empowers managers by freeing them from many restrictions of line-item budgeting.[90] Charlotte, North Carolina; Dayton, Ohio; Phoenix, Arizona; Portland, Oregon; St. Petersburg, Florida; and Sunnyvale, California, have received national attention for their budget systems.[91] Cities such as these may be in the forefront of budget reform, ahead of states and the federal government.[92]

Techniques in Other Nations. Efforts to include performance measurement in budgeting are common in other countries. New Zealand is said to be furthest along in developing a resource allocation system that relies heavily upon quantified performance.[93] Australia, Canada, and the United Kingdom have received worldwide attention as these governments have embarked on performance measurement projects as means for curtailing budget deficits and for holding government agencies accountable for achieving results.[94]

Multiyear Techniques. Making multiyear projections is difficult, and as a consequence some governments choose not to engage in them. A survey of state budget offices found that a third of the states project measures of program effectiveness and nearly half project measures of productivity.[95] In another study, this one of local governments in Florida, problems cited as deterring the use of expenditure forecasting included the difficulty of anticipating new state mandates, anticipating the impacts of court rulings, and anticipating the cost of employee wage agreements.[96] In a study of cities with populations of 25,000 or more, about two-thirds reported using revenue and expenditure forecasting.[97]

Reasons for Adopting Reforms. Why do some governments adopt budget reforms and others do not—or adopt them at a slower pace?[98] Researchers have identified several factors. Fiscal stress caused by the inability of governments to finance all programs at what seems to be a minimal standard stimulates searches for alternative budget techniques. Governments search for techniques that facilitate dealing with the knottiest of problems and provide them with the sense of being in control of current and future operations. Government structure is sometimes important; cities with professional managers are more likely to adopt program and performance budgeting than strong mayor systems.[99] Having an elected and appointed political leadership that is committed to budget reform is another important ingredient, since reforms that are generated exclusively from lower levels in the bureaucracy are unlikely to be effective. Governments need trained professional staffs and computer capabilities to undertake many budget reforms. Changes that are undertaken should be expected to take time. Expectations of quick results are likely to lead to disappointments.

Reasons for Change in Budget Format

Legal requirements, such as the 1993 federal legislation instructing agencies to prepare strategic and annual performance plans, and other mandates and incentives are important. Another potential influence of major proportions is the professional accounting field, which has shown interest in mandating that accounting systems be linked to program measurement. The Governmental Accounting Standards Board (GASB) intends to adopt a requirement that governments link service efforts and accomplishments to their accounting systems. The Government Finance Officers Association, in opposing the GASB proposal, favors a voluntary system and maintains that GASB, being an accounting organization, would overstep its bounds and area of expertise were it to require service efforts and accomplishments reporting.[100]

Perhaps one of the most difficult barriers to reform is overcoming the past. So-called new management practices arise with great frequency and governments may feel pressure to jump on the most current bandwagon, but then later they jump from that bandwagon to another. Any person involved in policy making and administration can easily become cynical about the prospects for any new management practice actually being implemented. Experienced administrators inevitably question whether the latest technique will have any real effect upon how decisions are made and the outcomes of the decision process.[101] Also, managers often find unpleasant, if not downright repulsive, having their operations compared with operations in other departments or in other governments.[102]

SUMMARY

One of the main themes running through budgetary literature has been the need to use the budgetary process as a vehicle for planning. In particular, this need has facilitated an attempt to incorporate program data into the system along with resource data, such as dollar and personnel costs.

During and after World War II, a set of theoretical fields and technologies emerged that had a great influence on budgetary reform. These include operations research, economic analysis, general systems theory, cybernetics, computer technology, and systems analysis.

Budget requests are prepared by agencies in accordance with instructions provided by the central budget office. In addition to data on finances and personnel, request instructions increasingly require program data, including social indicators, impacts, outputs, workloads and activities, and data on the need or demand for services. Productivity measures are used to relate resource consumption, as measured in dollars and personnel, to the work accomplished and the product of that work.

Budget request manuals take varied approaches to providing guidance on how agencies should request resources. These approaches include current commitment, fixed-ceiling, and open-ended budgeting. Reform efforts since the 1960s have focused on PPB systems, or more generally program budgeting, and also on zero-base budgeting. Strategic planning and policy and program guidance also have been popular. Current emphasis is on what is called performance measurement. Governments tend to use hybrids of these systems.

NOTES

1. A. Schick, The Road to PPB: The Stages of Budget Reform, *Public Administration Review* 26 (1966): 243–258.

2. W.H. Taft, *Economy and Efficiency in the Government Service*, House Doc. No. 458, January 1912, p. 16.

3. Commission on Economy and Efficiency, *The Need for a National Budget*, House Doc. No. 854, 1912: 4–5.

4. F.A. Cleveland, Evolution of the Budget Idea in the United States, *Annals* 62 (1915): 15–35.

5. W.F. Willoughby, *The Problems of a National Budget* (New York: Appleton, 1918).

6. L.D. Upson, Half-time Budget Methods, *Annals* 113 (1924): 69–74.

7. A.E. Buck, *Public Budgeting* (New York: Harper and Brothers, 1929).

8. W. Kilpatrick, Classification and Measurement of Public Expenditures, *Annals* 183 (1936): 19–26.

9. President's Committee on Administrative Management, *Report* (Washington, DC: U.S. Government Printing Office, 1937).

10. V.O. Key, Jr., The Lack of a Budgetary Theory, *American Political Science Review* 34 (1940): 1138–1144.

11. Commission on Organization of the Executive Branch of the Government, *Budgeting and Accounting* (Washington, DC: U.S. Government Printing Office, 1949), 8.

12. V.B. Lewis, Toward a Theory of Budgeting, *Public Administration Review* 12 (1952): 42–54.

13. F.C. Mosher, *Program Budgeting: Theory and Practice with Particular Reference to the U.S. Department of Army* (Chicago: Public Administration Service, 1954).

14. C. Seckler-Hudson, Performance Budgeting in the Government of the United States, *Public Finance* 7 (1952): 327–345.

15. A. Smithies, *The Budgetary Process in the United States* (New York: McGraw-Hill, 1955), 198–225.

16. Commission on Organization of the Executive Branch of the Government, *Final Report to Congress* (Washington, DC: U.S. Government Printing Office, 1955); Commission on Organization of the Executive Branch of the Government, *Budgeting and Accounting* (Washington, DC: U.S. Government Printing Office, 1955).

17. J. Burkhead, *Government Budgeting* (New York: Wiley, 1956), 133–182.

18. A. Wildavsky, Rescuing Policy Analysis from PPBS, *Public Administration Review* 29 (1969): 193.

19. The early thinking on this topic was suggested by Robert J. Mowitz, Director of the Institute of Public Administration, The Pennsylvania State University.

20. C.W. Churchman et al., *Introduction to Operations Research* (New York: Wiley, 1957).

21. For an early survey of the economic analysis field, see A.R. Prest and R. Turvey, Cost-Benefit Analysis: A Survey, *Economic Journal* 75 (1965): 683–735.

22. L. von Bertalanffy, General System Theory: A New Approach to Unity of Science, *Human Biology* 23 (1951): 303–361.

23. N. Wiener, *The Human Use of Human Beings* (Garden City, NY: Doubleday, 1956).

24. W.G. Ouchi, A Short History of the Development of Computer Hardware, in *Information Technology and Organizational Change*, ed. T.L. Whisler (Belmont, CA: Wadsworth, 1970), 129–134.

25. G.H. Fisher, *The Analytical Bases of Systems Analysis* (Santa Monica, CA: The RAND Corporation, 1966).

26. U.S. Office of Management and Budget, *Preparation and Submission of Budget Estimates*, Circular A-11 (1997): http://www.whitehouse.gov/WH/EOP/OMB/html/circulars/a011/toc97.html; accessed December 1997.

27. Violent Crime Control and Law Enforcement Act, P.L. 103-322, 108 Stat. 1796 (1994).

28. J.R. Allen, The Uses of Performance Measurement in Government, *Government Finance Review* 12 (August 1996): 11–15; G.C. Moore and P.M. Heneghan, Defining and Prioritizing Public Performance Requirement, *Public Productivity and Management Review* 20 (1996): 158–173; for a "how-to" CD-ROM, see International City/County Management Association, *Applying Performance Measurement* (Washington, DC: International City/County Management Association, 1996).

29. I. Rubin, Budgeting for Accountability: Municipal Budgeting for the 1990s, *Public Budgeting & Finance* 16 (Summer 1996): 112–132.

30. U.S. Office of Management and Budget, *Analytical Perspectives* (Washington, DC: U.S. Government Printing Office, 1997), 33.

31. Sustainability Seattle, *Indicators of Sustainability Community, 1995* (Seattle: Sustainability Seattle, 1995).

32. R.J. Mowitz, *The Design and Implementation of Pennsylvania's Planning, Programming, Budgeting System* (Harrisburg: Commonwealth of Pennsylvania, 1970), 17.

33. J. Brizius et al., *Deciding for Investment: Getting Returns on Tax Dollars* (Washington, DC: National Academy of Public Administration, 1994).

34. G. Odiorne, *Management by Objectives* (New York: Pitman, 1965); T.H. Poister and G. Streib, MBO in Municipal Government: Variations on a Traditional Management Tool, *Public Administration Review* 55 (1995): 48–56.

35. See current issues of *Public Productivity and Management Review*, a quarterly journal.

36. W.E. Deming, *Quality, Productivity, and Competitive Position* (Cambridge, MA: Massachusetts Institute of Technology Center for Advanced Engineering Study, 1982); T.H. Poister and R.H. Harris, Service Delivery Impacts of TQM: A Preliminary Investigation, *Public Productivity and Management Review* 20 (1996): 84–100.

37. S. George, *The Baldrige Quality System: The Do-It-Yourself Way to Transform Your Business* (New York: John Wiley & Sons, 1992); D.C. Fisher, *Measuring Up to the Baldrige* (New York: AMACOM [American Management Association], 1994).

38. D. Osborne and T. Gaebler, *Reinventing Government: How the Entrepreneurial Spirit Is Transforming the Public Sector* (Reading, MA: Addison-Wesley, 1992); D. Osborne and P. Plastrik, *Banishing Bureaucracy: The Five Strategies for Reinventing Government* (Reading, MA: Addison-Wesley, 1997); see D.F. Kettl and J.J. DiIulio, Jr., eds., *Inside the Reinvention Machine: Appraising Governmental Reform* (Washington, DC: Brookings Institution, 1995).

39. R.S. Kravchuk and R.W. Schack, Designing Effective Performance-Measurement Systems under the Government Performance and Results Act of 1993, *Public Administration Review* 56 (1996): 348–358.

40. U.S. General Accounting Office, *Managing for Results: Analytic Challenges in Measuring Performance* (Washington, DC: U.S. Government Printing Office, 1997).

41. W.A. Lucas and R.H. Dawson, *The Organizational Politics of Defense* (Pittsburgh: International Studies Association, University of Pittsburgh, 1974), 87.

42. National Security Act Amendments, Ch. 412, 63 Stat. 578 (1949).

43. Budget and Accounting Procedures Act, Ch. 946, 64 Stat. 832 (1950); U.S. General Accounting Office, *Performance Budgeting: Past Initiatives Offer Insights for GPRA Implementation* (Washington, DC: U.S. Government Printing Office, 1997).

44. Schick, The Road to PPB, 252–253.

45. Mosher, *Program Budgeting*, 34–47.

46. R.J. Massey, Program Packages and the Program Budget in the Department of Defense, *Public Administration Review* 23 (1963): 30–34.

47. D. Novick, The Department of Defense, in D. Novick, ed., *Program Budgeting: Program Analysis and the Federal Budget* (Cambridge, MA: Harvard University Press, 1965), 91.

48. D. Novick, *Efficiency and Economy in Government through New Budgeting and Accounting Procedures* (Santa Monica, CA: The RAND Corporation, 1956).

49. L.R. Jones, Policy Development, Planning, and Resource Allocation in the Department of Defense, *Public Budgeting & Finance* 11 (Fall 1991): 15–27.

50. National Performance Review, *Creating a Government that Works Better and Costs Less: Department of Defense* (Washington, DC: U.S. Government Printing Office, 1993).

51. Commission on Roles and Missions of the Armed Forces, *Directions for Defense* (Washington, DC: U.S. Government Printing Office, 1995).

52. F. Thompson and L.R. Jones, *Reinventing the Pentagon* (San Francisco: Jossey-Bass, 1994).

53. A. Schick, A Death in the Bureaucracy: The Demise of Federal PPB, *Public Administration Review* 33 (1973): 146–156.

54. E.L. Harper et al., Implementation and Use of PPB in Sixteen Federal Agencies, *Public Administration Review* 29 (1969): 634.

55. R.C. Casselman, Massachusetts Revisited: Chronology of a Failure, *Public Administration Review* 33 (1973): 129–135.

56. D. Sallack and D.N. Allen, From Impact to Output: Pennsylvania's Planning-Programming-Budgeting System in Transition, *Public Budgeting & Finance* 7 (Spring 1987): 38–50.

57. A. Wildavsky and A. Hammann, Comprehensive versus Incremental Budgeting in the Department of Agriculture, *Administrative Science Quarterly* 10 (1965): 321–346.

58. P.A. Phyrr, *Zero-Base Budgeting: A Practical Management Tool for Evaluating Expenses* (New York: Wiley, 1973).

59. T.P. Lauth and S.C. Rieck, Modifications in Georgia Zero-Base Budgeting Procedures: 1973–1981, *Midwest Review of Public Administration* 13 (1979): 225–238.

60. U.S. General Accounting Office, *Streamlining Zero-Base Budgeting Will Benefit Decision Making* (Washington, DC: U.S. Government Printing Office, 1979).

61. A. Schick, The Road from ZBB, *Public Administration Review* 38 (1978): 177–180.

62. P.C. Nutt and R.W. Backoff, Fashioning and Sustaining Strategic Change in Public Organizations, *Public Productivity and Management Review* 19 (1996): 313–337.

63. P. Kobrak, The Social Responsibilities of a Public Entrepreneur, *Administration and Society* 28 (1996): 205–237.

64. I.S. Rubin, Budgeting for Our Times: Target Base Budgeting, *Public Budgeting & Finance* 11 (Fall 1991): 5–14.

65. C.A. Bowsher, Comptroller General of the United States, *Performance Measurement: An Important Tool in Managing for Results* (Washington, DC: U.S. Government Printing Office, 1992); U.S. General Accounting Office, *Program Performance Measures: Federal Agency Collection and Use of Performance Data* (Washington, DC: U.S. Government Printing Office, 1992).

66. Congressional Budget Office, *Using Performance Measures in the Federal Budget Process* (Washington, DC: U.S. Government Printing Office, 1993).

67. National Performance Review, *From Red Tape to Results: Creating a Government that Works Better and Costs Less* (Washington, DC: U.S. Government Printing Office, 1993), 16–17; U.S. General Accounting Office, *Management Reform: Implementation of the National Performance Review's Recommendations* (Washington, DC: U.S. Government Printing Office, 1994).

68. National Performance Review, *The Best Kept Secrets in Government* (Washington, DC: U.S. Government Printing Office, 1996), 31.

69. National Performance Review, *Putting Customers First '95: Standards for Serving the American People* (Washington, DC: U.S. Government Printing Office, 1995), 69.

70. National Performance Review, *Common Sense Government: Works Better and Costs Less* (Washington, DC: U.S. Government Printing Office, 1995), 59–60.

71. J.R. Thompson and P.W. Ingraham, The Reinvention Game, *Public Administration Review* 56 (1996): 291–298; W.D. Eggers and J. O'Leary, *Revolution at the Roots: Making Our Government Smaller, Better, and Closer to Home* (New York: Free Press, 1995).

72. Government Performance and Results Act, P.L. 103-62, 107 Stat. 285 (1993).

73. U.S. General Accounting Office, *Executive Guide: Effectively Implementing the Government Performance and Results Act* (Washington, DC: U.S. Government Printing Office, 1996).

74. U.S. Office of Management and Budget and Chief Financial Officers Council, *Federal Financial Management Status Report and Five-Year Plan* (Washington, DC: U.S. Government Printing Office, 1995); Johnny C. Finch, Assistant Comptroller General, *Managing for Results: Status of the Government Performance and Results Act* (Washington, DC: U.S. Government Printing Office, 1995).

75. U.S. General Accounting Office, *GPRA: Managerial Accountability and Flexibility Pilot Did Not Work as Intended* (Washington, DC: U.S. Government Printing Office, 1997).

76. L. Nye Stevens, U.S. General Accounting Office, *Managing for Results: Enhancing the Usefulness of GPRA Consultations between the Executive Branch and Congress* (Washington, DC: U.S. Government Printing Office, 1997).

77. U.S. General Accounting Office, *Agencies' Strategic Plans under GPRA: Key Questions to Facilitate Congressional Review* (Washington, DC: U.S. Government Printing Office, 1997).

78. U.S. General Accounting Office, *The Government Performance Results Act: 1997 Governmentwide Implementation Will Be Uneven* (Washington, DC: U.S. Government Printing Office, 1997).

79. U.S. Office of Management and Budget, *Management Accountability and Control*, Circular A-123 (1995), Section II.

80. Paperwork Reduction Act, P.L. 104-13, 109 Stat. 163 (1995).

81. Information Technology Management Reform Act, P.L. 104-106, 110 Stat. 186 (1996).

82. For a ranking of states based on budgeting and other practices, see K. Barrett and R. Greene, The State of the States, *Financial World* 162 (May 1993): 43–46.

83. R.D. Lee, Jr., A Quarter Century of State Budgeting Practices, *Public Administration Review* 57 (1997): 133–140.

84. Also see R.D. Lee, Jr., The Use of Executive Guidance in State Budget Preparation, *Public Budgeting & Finance* 12 (Fall 1992): 19–31.

85. Florida Commission on Government Accountability to the People, *The Florida Benchmarks Report* (Tallahassee: Florida Commission on Government Accountability to the People, 1996); C.A. Broom and L.A. McGuire, Performance-Based Government Models, *Public Budgeting & Finance* 15 (Winter 1995): 3–17.

86. A. Merjanian, Striving to Make Performance Measurement Work: Texas Implements Systems Approach to Planning, Budgeting, *PA Times* 20 (June 1997): 1, 19–20.

87. D.E. O'Toole, J. Marshall, and T. Grewe, Current Local Government Budgeting Practices, *Government Finance Review* 12 (December 1996): 25–29.

88. T.H. Poister and G. Streib, Municipal Management Tools from 1976 to 1993: An Overview and Update, *Public Productivity and Management Review* 18 (1994): 115–125.

89. J.R. Fountain, Are State and Local Governments Using Performance Measures? *PA Times Supplement* (January 1997): PM–2, PM–8; Poister and Streib, Municipal Management Tools from 1976 to 1993; P. Tigue, Use of Performance Measures by GFO Members, *Government Finance Review* 10 (December 1994): 42–44; D.N. Ammons, ed., *Accountability for Performance: Measurement and Monitoring in Local Government* (Washington, DC: International City/County Management Association, 1995).

90. Osborne and Gaebler, *Reinventing Government*, 117–124, 161–165.

91. F. Fairbanks, Managing for Results: The Path that Phoenix Has Followed, *Public Management* 78 (January 1996): 12–15; A. Chan and D. Rich, Sunnyvale's Outcome Management: Taking Performance Budgeting One Step Further, *Government Finance Review* 12 (December 1996): 13–17.

92. Brizius et al., *Deciding for Investment*.

93. Organization for Economic Co-operation and Development, *Budgeting for Results: Perspectives on Public Expenditure Management* (Paris: Organization for Economic Co-operation and Development, 1995), 55.

94. U.S. General Accounting Office, *Managing for Results: Experiences Abroad Suggest Insights for Federal Management Reforms* (Washington, DC: U.S. Government Printing Office, 1995); R.C. Mascarenhas, Searching for Efficiency in the Public Sector: Interim Evaluation of Performance Budgeting in New Zealand, *Public Budgeting & Finance* 16 (Fall 1996): 13–27.

95. Lee, A Quarter Century of State Budgeting Practices.

96. S.A. MacManus, Forecasting Frustrations: Factors Limiting Accuracy, *Government Finance Review* 8 (June 1992): 7–11.

97. R.K. Goertz, Target-Based Budgeting and Adaptations to Fiscal Uncertainty, *Public Productivity and Management Review* 16 (1993): 425–429.

98. U.S. General Accounting Office, *Managing for Results: State Experiences Provide Insights for Federal Management Reforms* (Washington, DC: U.S. Government Printing Office, 1994); J.P. Forrester and G.B. Adams, Budgetary Reform Through Organizational Learning, *Administration and Society* 28 (1997): 466–488.

99. G.H. Cope, Juggling Dollars and Making Sense: Budgeting in Local Governments (Paper presented at 1992 Conference on Budgeting and Financial Management, American Society for Public Administration, Arlington, VA, October 1992).

100. Governmental Accounting Standards Board, *Concept Statement No. 2: Service Efforts and Accomplishments Reporting* (Norwalk, CT.: Governmental Accounting Standards Board, 1994); D.K. Clancy and T.K. Patton, Service Efforts and Accomplishments Reporting: A Study of Texas Public Schools, *Public Budgeting and Financial Management* 8 (1996): 272–302.

101. J. Walters, Fad Mad, *Governing* 9 (September 1996): 48–52.

102. J. Walters, Performance and Pain, *Governing* 10 (June 1997): 26–29, 31.

CHAPTER 6

Budget Preparation: The Decision Process

Preparing a budget in an executive budget system involves having agencies prepare requests and then assembling those requests, but the process also involves much more. Indeed, the request process is simple compared with the difficult task that remains—making decisions on the recommended levels for revenues and expenditures. Is a tax increase needed? Which programs should be expanded and which should be reduced? In systems that do not centralize budget preparation in the executive, the same concerns prevail. A legislative committee or a joint group of executives and legislators may be responsible for weighing the citizens' joint demands for increased services and possibly lower taxes and for proposing a budget package that balances these competing demands.

This chapter has two sections. The first considers how a proposed executive budget is assembled; deliberations on the revenue and expenditure sides of the budget are examined. The second section reviews the products of budget preparation, namely, the various types of budget documents and their formats.

DECISIONS ON BUDGET REQUESTS

Budget preparation involves participation by a variety of individuals and organizations along with myriad values associated with taxing and spending. In an executive budget system, the chief executive has the overall responsibility for the preparation process, but numerous other actors have roles, including, of course, the central budget office and other units such as the treasury office. Not all governments have executive systems. A survey of county governments found that fewer than 10 percent placed responsibility for budget preparation in the hands of a chief executive; more typically, the responsibility was shared by others, particularly administrators, auditors, and the members of the legislative branch.[1] In other systems, such as some local governments in Russia, finance departments have reporting responsibilities to both the mayor and the legislative council, and municipal finance officers and/or treasurers sometimes are appointed by the central government, such as in Ukraine.

Legislators or their staffs may be involved in preparation. On occasion, state legislative staff members may be allowed to attend executive budget hearings that review the proposed budgets of line agencies. This practice helps the legislative branch become aware of what budget proposals are being developed and the rationales behind these proposals *prior* to the budget actually reaching the legislature. In small local governments, budget preparation may be a relatively fluid process and may be characterized by close links between executive and legislative officials. Even when legislative officers are not involved, their views on taxing and spending are taken into account.

In some other systems, such as in Egypt, agencies make their recommendations to a ministry of finance, which has the final decision authority without significant legislative review. Egypt's People's Assembly, for example, had little input into the budget until 1996 when it was able to negotiate some budget changes with the government. Subunits of other ministries, without the presence of their superiors, may be called to defend budget requests before the finance ministry, creating a situation in which heads of ministries may have only limited input on their budgets.

Concerns of the Chief Executive

The chief executive—president, governor, mayor, county executive, and the like—may have official responsibility for preparation but usually will have only limited direct involvement until the later stages of preparation. This allows the chief executive extra time to take care of other duties. Having the budget office and other units, such as treasury, involved early in the process provides for the application of professional administrative talent in analyzing problems and options that will later come before the chief executive for review. A professional budget staff endeavors to take preliminary actions on budget requests that are in keeping with the policy objectives of the chief executive, thereby allowing the chief executive to avoid dealing with minor problems and reserving time to deal with major ones.[2]

Strategic Concerns. The chief executive needs to convey to the units involved, and especially to the central budget office, a sense of priorities so that effort is not needlessly wasted on proposals that he or she will reject. There are several concerns with a major one being the overall philosophy of the role of government in contemporary society. What is the overall public interest, and how large should the public sector be in the total economy?[3]

Another concern for many chief executives is the effect the budget may have on the economic environment.[4] Cities, counties, states, and the national government are concerned about budgetary influences on the economy. For local and state chief executives, the concern tends to focus on whether current or proposed taxes will deter businesses from locating or expanding operations in their jurisdictions. The quality of government services is perhaps equally important. While school districts and special districts may have little or no official role in economic development, the quality of education, water systems, sewers, and so on are critical in the location decisions of corporations. The national government has these same concerns and others as well, including international implications and price stability (see Chapter 15).

The chief executive sets ground rules on policies and program priorities.[5] A president conveys an overall sense of priorities to the Office of Management and Budget (OMB) regarding defense and domestic spending and a sense of priorities within each of these categories. Election campaign promises are important in that chief executives usually attempt to pursue the objectives outlined in their bid for voter approval. For many chief executives, the budget is used as a vehicle for strategic planning for the government.[6]

Program priorities also can be viewed from the perspective of achieving some degree of social justice. While space prohibits any extensive discussion of what constitutes social justice, it can be said that budget deliberations include an overall assessment of how different segments of the society will benefit or be burdened by governmental actions. One way of viewing the situation is to think of government redistributing income among the various segments of society. Funding one set of programs at a high level obviously will benefit the programs' clients. If, for example, the elderly benefit from a program, then the young do not. Providing income maintenance checks to the needy redistributes money from the middle and upper classes to the poor. Redistribution also occurs through tax measures, including tax expenditures, such as the policy of not taxing home mortgage interest payments (see Chapter 4).

A major concern of southern border states is social justice as it pertains to illegal immigrants. California voters in 1996 adopted Proposition 209, which attempted to deny many benefits to these immigrants. When taxes are high and yet available revenues cannot seem to keep pace with funding needs, one view is that illegal aliens should be denied access to government services, including health care and various social services. Complaints from citizens arise in such instances as when most mothers giving birth at the Los Angeles County Hospital are illegal aliens.[7] Providing free services to illegal immigrants was seen as an unfair burden to taxpayers.

A suggestion gaining in popularity is that budgeting should be concerned with its generational effects—the extent to which current actions will improve or harm the conditions that older, younger, and future generations must confront.[8] The federal government has reported generational effects in terms of taxes and transfers.

In budget preparation, the projection of a budget deficit becomes an overriding issue that cannot be ignored. For state and local governments, chief executives are often required to submit balanced budgets, and therefore any projections of a deficit must be resolved. For the federal government, deficits have loomed so large since 1981 that most discussions about the budget seem to focus on how to reduce the deficit. Instead of being concerned about which alternatives are more likely to bring positive results in the operation of a program, decision makers worry almost exclusively about the cost of the alternatives and their potential for increasing or decreasing the deficit. Deficits incapacitate decision makers, who presume they are unable to deal with society's problems for lack of funds.[9]

Government indebtedness and borrowing constitute another concern of the chief executive during budget preparation. For a president, indebtedness is a concern in regard to its effect on the economy. For governors and local executives, indebtedness results from the sale of bonds and creates financial burdens for decades.

Tactical Concerns. In addition to a "philosophical" approach to taxation and expenditures, the chief executive conveys a tactical view. An assessment must be made of political reactions to any possible proposed tax increase or cut. Of course, increases are more likely to produce negative reactions than tax cuts.

For governors and the president, intergovernmental relations will be an important component of budget preparation deliberations. Presidents may prefer, where possible, to carry out policies through state and local governments rather than directly through federal agencies. Likewise, governors may prefer to work through local governments. Mandating that state and local governments deliver services, adopt standards, or otherwise implement federal programs is seen by some as a way of achieving a federal policy goal without paying for it. These unfunded mandates, of course, are extremely unpopular with governors, state legislatures, mayors, and city councils (see Chapter 14).

Another set of considerations involves relationships with the legislative body. Stated simply, the chief executive assesses the chances of various recommendations receiving the approval of Congress, the state legislature, or the city council. Executives must decide whether to push for proposals that will meet certain opposition from some legislators in alliance with interest groups.[10] In making such calculations, chief executives do not recommend only policies likely to be approved. A doomed recommendation may be put forth as a means of preparing the legislature to approve the proposal in some future year, or the chief executive may be strongly committed to a proposal despite legislative opposition.

Perceived citizen preferences regarding service and tax levels constitute another consideration. Chief executives have a keen sense for what the general citizenry and interest groups desire. What services do citizens demand and what are they willing to pay in either taxes or fees?[11] Results from national and state polls are watched for important trends. Some cities conduct surveys of citizens and/or hold public hearings at which citizens may testify as a means of identifying prevailing attitudes about existing and desired services. Eugene, Oregon, and Sacramento, California, have received attention for their efforts to go beyond simple polling in an effort to reach out to their communities and engage them in making difficult decisions about government services and corresponding taxes. City leaders use such techniques as contacting neighborhood groups and civic associations as a means of reaching citizens.[12]

Revenue Deliberations

Revenue Estimates. Central to deliberations on the revenue side of budget preparation are revenue estimates. Chapter 4 dealt with some of the technical problems associated with revenue estimating. Here it should be noted that there are important bureaucratic considerations. Sometimes revenue estimating is assigned to the organization responsible for collecting revenues, most often a treasury or revenue department. Such an arrangement may place that unit in competition with the budget office, because the latter may differ on projected revenues. The budget office may be essentially forced into developing a budget package that is perceived to be unnecessarily constrained because of an estimate that anticipates little or no growth in revenue or even a downturn. This is especially a problem in some developing countries where the local treasurer is a central government appointee. At the federal level, the revenue-estimating function is handled jointly by OMB, the Council of Economic Advisers, and the Treasury Department. The Congressional Budget Office makes independent revenue estimates for congressional consideration.

Taxing Limitations. Since the 1970s, taxing limitations have constituted a major consideration at the state and local levels (see Chapter 4). Government officials, in assembling a budget proposal, may be constrained by having to present a balanced budget that allows for no increases in tax revenues. One commonly used alternative to raising taxes is to raise user fees.

Balanced Budgets. For state and local governments, revenue estimating is particularly critical because of the standard requirement that they have balanced operating budgets. Indebtedness is possible but is typically only used for capital investments and other selected expenses. If a budget is built on revenue estimates that are too high, crises will ensue during execution as the government attempts to bring expenditures down in order to balance them against revenues.

While all but a few states have requirements for a balanced budget, the requirements are not uniform among the states. In the first place, "balance" means that expenditures may not exceed revenues, but not all available revenues must be appropriated and spent. Coverage is not all-inclusive, and trust funds and capital expenditures are often excluded; as little as half of all state funds may be covered by the balanced budget requirement. Balancing requirements also vary as to when they apply in the budget process, such as when the budget is presented to the legislature or when it is adopted.[13] Similar variations are found at the local level.[14]

Achieving balance in a state budget is a political process. There are the obvious alternatives of seeking revenue increases or spending decreases, but balance can also be attained through other means. Budget reserves, rainy day funds, or savings from previous years may be drawn upon to increase available revenues. Sometimes payments from one fiscal year may be shifted to the next, even though resources are actually used in the earlier year. Political leaders use this technique and others to make budgets appear to be balanced when the opposite is true.[15]

Elimination of tax expenditures can yield additional revenues without officially raising tax rates; for instance, adding products or services to the list of taxable items on a state sales tax can increase revenues. Decision makers are concerned with whether each tax expenditure serves any major public purpose, and all tax expenditures are particularly subject to challenge when revenues are needed to balance a budget.[16]

Budget gimmickry also is used during economic boom-times. By estimating revenues to be lower than are most likely to occur, decision makers later in the year can "discover" that a budget surplus exists and then use the money for some combination of tax relief and new spending.[17]

Tax earmarking often constrains efforts to balance budgets without necessarily helping the programs officially being benefited. Receipts from state lotteries, for instance, are often earmarked for such good causes as public education or aid to senior citizens. Available evidence indicates that programs with such earmarked revenue do not receive proportionately greater overall funding than other programs, and indeed earmarking is sometimes used as an excuse for not providing more funds to a program, since it is expected to operate within available revenue from the earmarked source.[18] The supposed program that benefits from a lottery, then, may receive no greater funding than it would have without the lottery. Earmarking in effect "Balkanizes" a government's finances and can greatly hamper efforts to resolve budget problems when revenues decline, since monies are compartmentalized and cannot be treated as part of the total resources usable for creating an overall balanced budget.

Revenue gaps are sometimes closed with public employee pension monies. A government may simply not make its full contribution to the employee pension funds or may even have the freedom to withdraw monies in order to balance the budget. More subtle methods involve adjusting actuarial assumptions. By making an assumption that retired employees will die comparatively early in life, fewer dollars will be needed to cover expected retirees when benefit levels are predetermined. Also, by assuming that investments on retirement monies will result in comparatively high returns, increased dollars will be available to cover expected retirement benefits and the government will need to contribute less to the retirement fund.[19]

Whereas the decision makers responsible for state and local budgeting spend substantial time and energy balancing their budgets, the situation is different at the federal level. Whether to require a balanced federal budget has long been a controversial issue, but a law requiring a balanced budget has yet to be adopted (see Chapters 9 and 15).

Spending Deliberations

Entitlements and Other Commitments. Much of the spending side of any budget is determined in advance of budget preparation deliberations. Interest on the debt must be paid, and prior commitments to employees, such as set levels of contributions to retirement plans must be met. Entitlement programs that guarantee benefits to various groups, such as the needy, the elderly, and the ill determine much of the spending side of a budget, and the amount spent is a function of the numbers of people qualifying for various programs. Increased spending for these entitlements is often pegged to increases in the consumer price index, which has been criticized as overstating the rate of inflation. Nevertheless, as long as a law uses the consumer price index, budget makers must use its projected increases as the basis for calculating entitlement costs.[20]

Organizational Competition. Just as there are central administrative organizations that compete in trying to influence revenue decisions, organizations vie with one another on the spending side of the budget. At the top level of a government, personalities become important. The roles of various participants at the federal level depend upon a president's administrative style, his or her confidence in the abilities of key figures, and the roles these figures seek for themselves. A president is not obligated to rely on the advice of any individual and may seek guidance from anyone inside or outside government.

In the international policy arena, there are many participants, such as the State Department, the Department of Defense, and the Central Intelligence Agency (CIA), and each may resist major exercise of control by the central budget office. In addition, the National Security Council (NSC) exists to advise the president on "domestic, foreign, and military policies relating to national security."[21] The NSC is headed by the president and includes as members the vice president and the secretaries of state and defense; the director of the CIA and the chair of the Joint Chiefs of Staff serve as statutory advisers to the council. Also included is the president's national security adviser.

OMB is notably not part of the NSC, although it can be invited to meetings at the president's discretion. OMB can be eclipsed in this arena, performing the largely routine function of assembling budget materials rather than having much influence on how much money is to be allocated to defense and foreign affairs and for what purposes.

In the domestic arena, the competition is also fierce. Cabinet officers seek to gain acceptance and financial support for their agencies' programs. Central advisers to the president are other contenders for attention. In addition to advice provided by the White House Office staff, advice is available from the Office of Policy Development (consisting of the Domestic Policy Council and the National Economic Council) and the Council of Economic Advisers.[22]

One suggestion is that at this level of government, but also at lower levels, misrepresentation and other ethically questionable behavior prevails.[23] The competitive nature of budgeting may emphasize self-interest, both personal and collective, to the detriment of the public interest. As C. W. Lewis notes,"The process depends on and rewards deceit."[24] Agencies may misrepresent their situations to budget offices, such as claiming dire consequences unless budgets are increased for programs that are highly visible and favored by the public. At a higher level, political leaders may deceive the public, such as downplaying the importance of budget deficits and rationalizing the need for greater spending on pet projects even though the budget is out of balance.

Budget Office Roles. The central budget office has numerous roles to perform. Not only does the budget office recommend policies on spending, but it participates in the review of legislative proposals, economic policy, administrative regulations, evaluation of programs, collection of data by agencies, and agency management studies and management improvement efforts (see Chapter 10). OMB during the 1980s was given increased responsibility for functioning as an advocate for legislative policies before Congress. When OMB examines an agency's budget request, all of these other forces come into play. Agency budget proposals will be seen in the context of what legislative changes will be necessary, what regulatory actions will be required by the agency, and whether the agency is perceived as well managed.

Agency Expectations and Deliberations. In approaching the budget process, including the preparation phase, agencies have expectations about what constitutes success. Until the latter half of the 1970s, success often was measured in terms of budget increases approved by the executive and ultimately by the legislative body.[25] This approach of adding increments to a base has been discarded in many locales. Where taxing and spending limits have been imposed at the state and local levels, agencies have been forced instead to concentrate on defending their bases and minimizing the extent of cuts imposed on their budgets. This period has been dubbed the *decremental age*.[26]

By the time a budget request reaches the central budget office, an extensive series of discussions has been completed within the line agency. In large agencies having several layers of organizational units, those at the bottom will have attempted to persuade their superiors to approve requests for additional funding. The force being exerted from the top downward tends to be negative—in the sense that there is pressure to limit the growth of programs and the corresponding rise in expenditures. Yet this does not mean that there is simply a set of petitioners and a set of rejecters who do battle within each agency or department. Middle managers up through department heads are required to take positive and negative positions, rejecting many of the proposals brought to them by subordinates and, in negotiating with their superiors, advocating those proposals that they accept.

Part of the influence within an agency is a function of superior levels attempting to determine what is likely to be salable to the budget office and the chief executive. Agencies are aware that they are likely to get less than they request. Therefore, they will avoid requesting too little but will not ask for exorbitant sums unless an open-ended budget system is in use.

What is eventually requested by the department is necessarily a function of the type of budget system in place. As discussed in the preceding chapter, some systems provide for a base budget and then permit requests for additions to the base. Others use a current services budget and may require that an agency include information about possibly funding activities below and above the current services level. Some budget systems may require reductions. For example, President Clinton issued Executive Order 12837 in 1993, requiring federal agencies to segregate their administrative expenses from other budget items and to reduce these expenses (when adjusted for inflation) each year through fiscal 1997. The executive order was intended to force agencies to improve their productivity, namely, to meet their statutory mandates to provide services but with reduced resources.

Budget Office and Agency Relations. Just as the interplay is extensive and vociferous within an agency during budget preparation, so is the interplay between the central budget office and the agencies. The central office, serving as the agent of the chief executive, must assert a centralizing influence over the diverse interests of administrative units; these, on the other hand, can be expected to favor greater autonomy. Operating departments and agencies will of course favor the advancement of their particular programs (seeking greater funds or defending programs against cuts), while the budget office will be forced usually to say no to program growth and even sometimes to say yes to cutbacks.

When the budget office receives agency budget submissions, examiners are assigned to review these documents. The examiners are the main link between the budget office and line units. With the passage of time, examiners gain considerable knowledge about their agencies, providing substantive expertise within the budget office. Examiners often become advocates for the agencies they review and frequently even shift to an operating agency. Still, the accusation is commonly made by the agency officials that budget examiners often are not program oriented and are insensitive to the needs of operating units.

The structure of budget offices varies from government to government and from time to time. One key concern is whether the central function of examining agency budget requests should be integrated with other functions, notably management functions (discussed in Chapter 10), program analysis, and planning. The argument for their integration is that it gives budget analysts much broader exposure to the operations of government and enhances the analysts' opportunities to make valuable inputs into budget deliberations. The argument against integration is that all too often budget examination activities take top priority, leaving all other activities on the sidelines.

In the 1990s, OMB reorganized itself, under the project name of OMB 2000, using the integrative approach. Five resource management offices were created to cover the full spectrum of the government's operations:

1. natural resources, energy and science
2. national security and international affairs
3. health and personnel
4. human resources
5. general government and finance

Each resource management office is responsible for budgeting, management, and planning/policy issues within its arena.[27]

Budget office discussions with agencies will involve how services are to be delivered to the citizenry as well as the funding for the services. The deliberations will include whether services should be provided directly by agencies, by private corporations operating under contract with government, or some combination of these and other modes.

The nature of the dialogue between the budget office and agencies hinges in large measure on the extent to which the latter consider the former an important ally or an opponent. Only minimal information can be expected from an agency that is suspicious of the central budget office. A common concern is that an agency will not release data that could be used to its detriment. On the other hand, if an agency can win the confidence and support of the examiner, then it in effect has gained a spokesperson for its program on the chief executive's staff.

The budget office holds hearings with agency representatives. Whereas earlier in the process the examiners may have contacted agencies by phone, e-mail, facsimile, or in person to clarify detailed items included in requests, hearings tend to focus on broader concerns. The budget office must decide whether agencies can accomplish what they propose and whether the anticipated accomplishments are worth seeking. The burden of proof rests with the agencies. The operating agency that has a reputation for requesting excessive sums and for over-promising on results will be suspect.

At the same time, winning budget office approval is no guarantee of success for the agency. The resistant or recalcitrant agency, indeed, may be able to increase the caution with which the examiner makes recommendations to reduce the agency's budget. At the federal level, the significance of OMB action is mitigated by the fact that it is Congress that has the power to pass appropriations. It has even been suggested that opposition by the budget office to any agency's request for funds may sometimes be helpful in winning legislative support.

The agencies, not OMB, have had major responsibility for defending their budget requests before Congress, and therefore the office's utility to the agencies has been greater in the preparation phase than in the approval phase of the budget cycle. Some organizational units, such as the Federal Bureau of Investigation in the 1950s and 1960s, were able to secure extensive support within Congress, thereby providing them with some autonomy vis-à-vis their departments and OMB. Beginning in the 1980s, OMB gained greater responsibility for explaining and defending the president's budget before Congress; this role, however, often was negative in the sense that the main task was to explain how and why reductions should be made in agencies' budgets.[28]

Legal requirements and court decisions may force increases in expenditures and preclude some decision making by agencies and the central budget office. State government mandates may require local governments to establish recycling programs for solid waste. Federal officials may require a city to upgrade its sewage treatment facilities. Federal and state court decisions may force a state government to expand prison facilities in order to accommodate increased numbers of prisoners. Court cases may be filed against governments, forcing them to spend considerable sums on legal representation.[29]

Budget Office Recommendations. The response of the budget office to agency requests is in part a function of the office's assessment of its own powers and responsibilities in relation to the operating agencies and other central units. Few would deny to a budget office the ministerial or bookkeeping functions of assembling requests and carrying out the mechanical duties of designing, tabulating, and overseeing the printing of the budget. However, how many additional responsibilities the budget office has depends largely on the competition from other units and the management style of the chief executive.

Because in an executive budgeting system the chief executive has the final say on what to recommend to the legislative body, the budget office attempts to formulate recommendations thought to be in keeping with the executive's priorities.[30] As part of the calculation of what to recommend, the budget office assesses the chances of agencies' making direct appeals to the chief executive, or in the extreme case to the legislature, and thereby overturning the budget office's recommendations. If this strategy—making an end-run around the budget office—is successful, it can severely weaken the budget office's role. If an agency knows it can get what it wants by making direct appeals to the chief executive or legislature, the agency is likely to consider the budget office as only a bookkeeper that can be largely ignored.

As a staff unit of the chief executive, the budget office is expected to develop recommendations that are compatible with executive priorities. On the other hand, budgeters as professionals are said to have a responsibility to report to the chief executive their views on the worthiness of programs. To report that a given program is operating well simply because the chief executive wants to hear that does a disservice. So does recommending severe budget cuts to the chief executive when the budget office knows these cuts could have devastating results on the affected programs. *Neutral competence* has been proposed as the appropriate role for the budget office: The office should retain its professional approach in developing its budget recommendations but simultaneously should develop recommendations in tune with executive priorities.[31]

Downsizing, Rightsizing, and Spending Cutbacks

For many government programs, the 1980s marked the beginning of a new era that continued into the 1990s—an era of downsizing, rightsizing, and spending cutbacks. The long-standing pattern of spending increases was replaced in many governments by a pattern of reductions or cutbacks. So-called uncontrollable segments of the budget were not immune from these reductions.

The financial problems that materialized were due to several factors. For the federal government, deficits in the total budget during the 1980s attained new magnitude, often in the range of $200 billion or more each year. The deficits resulted in part from the massive tax reduction measures initiated in 1981 based on President Reagan's claim that tax cuts would so stimulate the economy that increased tax revenues would be produced. That bonanza of revenues never materialized. Programmatic cutbacks have been necessary as governments have tried to keep pace with rising salaries and wages in the private sector, health care costs for workers, and the employer portion of Social Security payroll taxes. In order to meet these costs, the number of personnel has been reduced and program operations have been curtailed.

Government sometimes has been viewed as bloated by years of excessive budget increases, and the response has been to reduce the size of operations. Whether this process is called downsizing or rightsizing, the result is the same, namely that agencies are faced with trying to provide the same or even more services with fewer personnel and other resources.

Fiscal Stress. Many state and local governments entered into an era of prolonged fiscal stress or distress.[32] Some of their problems were due to extended economic declines in their economies as well as a lack of robustness in the national economy. When the economy slumps, state and local sales and income tax revenues fall. So-called rust belt states and communities faced a different set of economic woes, namely a long-term erosion in their tax bases. Additional fiscal stress was caused by major reductions in aid from the federal government. During the 1980s, the national government permanently reduced funding of many grant programs and totally eliminated general revenue sharing (see Chapter 14). Compounding the problems of economic decline is the fact that many hard-hit governments had management practices that were inadequate for coping with their problems.[33]

The tax revolt movement discussed in Chapter 4 imposed additional constraints on spending. In some instances, a jurisdiction's economy may have been vibrant, but the government was precluded from taxing that economic base to the extent it perceived was needed to fund government programs.

Cutback Management. In response to their financial problems, governments engaged in cutback management, retrenchment, downsizing, or rightsizing.[34] It should be noted that governments in other countries have experienced similar problems. Also, sometimes retrenchment programs are undertaken not because of fiscal stress but because of the preferences of the political leadership, namely a desire on the part of officials to reduce the size of government. When Margaret Thatcher became Prime Minister of Great Britain, she and the Conservative Party led a massive program of privatization that considerably reduced the size of government. Later, when the Labour Party gained control, no attempts were made to re-nationalize the now private companies, so essentially a permanent reduction in the size of government was achieved.

How to deal with a budget shortage depends in part upon its perceived duration. If the shortage is considered to be short term, perhaps only for the current year, then modest adjustments can be made, such as imposing temporary cuts on programs and drawing on *budget reserves* or *rainy day funds*.

When long-term budget retrenchment is seen as necessary, then decision makers must manage the immediate problems of the current and upcoming budget years and anticipate problems in future years. Where budget cuts must be imposed several years in a row, then decision makers must be prepared to make extraordinarily difficult choices. Sometimes across-the-board cuts are ordered, as in the case of President Clinton's 1993 Executive Order 12837, in which agencies were instructed that they were to submit reduced administrative budget requests by specified percentages through fiscal year 1997.

Which budget cuts will be made ultimately hinges on the extent to which various groups in the society will suffer from program reductions or eliminations. Budget cuts are less likely to be imposed on groups that are politically organized and vocal than on other groups. Applying the budget knife to programs for the elderly is often politically dangerous whereas cutting programs for the poor, since they tend to be politically less active, may seem "safer" for decision makers. In relatively homogeneous communities, budget cutback procedures do not pit one segment of the community against another.

Budget Office Roles during Cutbacks. When jurisdictions confront fiscal stress, the decision process initially tends to be centralized, for without central instruction to begin a process of cutting, agencies might well submit budget requests based on unrealistic assumptions. The central budget office, working with the chief executive, attempts to instruct departments as to priorities for funding. Efforts are made to avoid across-the-board cuts in all programs since such an approach can cause severe harm to essential services.

If some programs are set aside as immune from budget cuts, there may be few incentives for these programs to be efficient in their spending. Moreover, achieving the level of budget reductions needed to balance a budget may be impossible if many key programs are immune from cuts. This problem existed at the federal level during the Reagan administration, where Social Security and the Department of Defense were protected from cuts.

In a retrenchment environment, agencies normally can expect budget office approval of no more than their projected current services budgets. In other situations, the central budget office may provide specific budget ceilings to each department. These figures, which most likely are below the current services levels, are used in preparing budget requests. The process has all the strengths and weaknesses of fixed-ceiling budgeting. Where such approaches are taken, the process of cutting often starts earlier in the calendar than in a budget situation where growth, rather than reduction, is predominant.[35] More time may be needed to determine what programs will be cut than to introduce new programs or expand existing ones, although some governments may find themselves in crisis situations in which cuts must be imposed immediately in order to avert a collapse of their financial situation.

Legislative Roles. If legislative preferences can be identified at the beginning of budget preparation, then cuts can be planned that later are likely to meet with legislative approval. Some communities have used confidential questionnaires and other techniques for soliciting legislative input when budget cutting must be part of the preparation phase. Members of local legislative bodies, however, may prefer not to reveal their preferences until later, when more is known about the options for cutting and citizens' attitudes. Of course, legislatures are not always on the "cutting" side of the budget process in that sometimes legislatures are in the position of restoring cuts proposed by the executive.

Items To Cut. When reductions must be made in expenditures, there are standard areas that are considered, one of them being personnel costs.[36] Since much of any government's operating budget is in personnel, it is difficult to make any appreciable reduction in expenditures without reducing personnel. Holding down general pay increases for workers is a common practice, although this technique can make compensation for government jobs noncompetitive with that for private sector jobs. Commonly used techniques for reducing personnel expenditures include delaying filling vacant positions, leaving other positions empty as they become vacant, and, if necessary, laying off workers. Financial incentives may be offered senior workers to encourage them to retire early, nonpaid furloughs of one day per week may be required of all employees, and, depending on legal restrictions, some workers may be required to accept pay cuts. Governments must be cautious in instituting personnel and other cutbacks in that intergovernmental aid can be reduced accordingly, especially if grants include matching provisions.

Equipment and facilities are other areas in which cutting can occur. Decisions may be made to delay purchase of major equipment and to defer maintenance, such as postponing the repair of city-owned sidewalks, roofs on government buildings, and potholes in city and state roads. The savings here can be short lived: The failure to repair a roof, for example, might result in water damage costing many thousands of dollars. There may be a tendency to use the deferred maintenance approach on less visible facilities, especially water and sewer lines, although highways and bridges have suffered notably due to state and local fiscal problems.

In so-called tight budget periods, major emphasis is given to making operations as efficient as possible. The expectation is that organizational units should be able to operate with fewer resources while maintaining existing service levels. On the other hand, no single agency is eager to relinquish resources through increased efficiency if other agencies are not compelled to take the same route. Each agency is fearful of being the first to show how savings can be accomplished in its operations. This same attitude prevails in the approval phase among legislators, who are not eager to agree to budget cuts in their favored programs even though it is well understood that major cuts will be necessary. Some propose that agencies will have greater incentives to be efficient if they are allowed greater discretion in how they spend their funds and if they are allowed to carry over unspent funds into the next year.[37] However, this requires budget offices and legislatures to take a leap of faith in agency executives and to exercise restraint, namely not eliminating carryover funds during budget cutback periods.

Budget cutting creates havoc, low morale, and some inefficiencies in agencies. Personnel rightfully become concerned that their positions will be eliminated in the agency's budget request. Political appointees in an agency may be at odds with career personnel over which activities are essential and which expendable. Some budget cuts necessitate agency reorganization, which causes disruptions in operations. Uncertainty in funding can require stretching the completion of projects. Defense is a major example of this problem, where changes in project schedules can result in billions of dollars of increased costs.

Budget Systems and Cutbacks. A final consideration regarding cutback budgeting is how the various budget systems discussed in the preceding chapter assist in retrenchment efforts. As already noted, central budget offices use variations on fixed-ceiling budgeting to indicate to agencies what funding levels are acceptable in the budget preparation process. It may be that most other budget systems have been developed on the stated or unstated premise that budgets will increase from year to year and therefore that these budget systems are less central to decision making when budget cuts must be imposed. At the same time, program budgeting and various forms of zero-base budgeting in theory should be highly useful in budget-cutting situations. During prosperous times, budgeting may be largely a process of considering possible incremental additions to the budget bases of programs, and during declining times, the process may become one of subtracting increments from the base.

Credit and Insurance Liabilities

In assembling a proposed budget, there are obvious and not-so-obvious expenditures that must be anticipated. Much of any budget will be committed to funding the operations of government, either for direct services provided by the government's departments or through grant programs, as in the case of state aid to local school districts. Monies also must be set aside for making payments on the principal and interest for outstanding debt. As is discussed in subsequent chapters, sustained federal budget deficits have yielded an increasingly large total federal debt that requires massive interest payments every year—so massive that they now constitute one of the most important components of federal expenditures. In addition to debt accumulated through borrowing by the U.S. Treasury Department, federal debt has grown through borrowing by federal agencies such as the U.S. Postal Service and Tennessee Valley Authority.[38]

Beginning in the late 1980s, political leaders, public administrators, leaders in private financial institutions, and the citizenry became painfully aware that the federal government had other liabilities that until then had seemed innocuous or almost nonexistent.[39] Hundreds of savings and loan institutions failed, forcing the federal government to meet its financial commitments to depositors. The Resolution Trust Corporation was established, as a temporary agency, to manage the resources of thrifts going into receivership at a staggering cost to taxpayers. Further liabilities were encountered when the government had surviving banks acquire many of the failed thrifts.[40]

Types of Liabilities. Appreciating the nature of government liabilities is difficult due to the complex nature of the institutions that are involved. There are at least three methods for differentiating these institutions and the programs that they administer: (1) the ownership of the institution, (2) the purpose that it serves, and (3) the type of service that it provides.

Figure 6–1 indicates how ownership can vary from an agency within a regular department of government to a separate government corporation, such as the Rural Telephone Bank, to a government-sponsored enterprise, such as the Federal National Mortgage Association (Fannie Mae), and finally to a privately owned corporation.[41] As the figure illustrates, a government corporation is owned by the public but may be only partially funded by government, may be largely independent of any government department, and is usually created for a business purpose. A government-sponsored enterprise is a "federal chartered, privately owned, for-profit corporation designed to provide a continuing source of credit nationwide to a specific economic sector."[42] As might be expected, institutions in this obscure realm do not always fit nicely into one of the four categories suggested by the figure. Indeed, Congress has recognized in legislation that some government corporations have mixed ownership, including the Federal Deposit Insurance Corporation (FDIC) and Amtrak.[43]

A second way of viewing these institutions is to consider them in terms of the purposes that they serve. They bolster and foster growth of the financial system of the nation, housing, education, agriculture, and the like.

A third approach is to consider the methods they use in serving these purposes. Here, four approaches are used, as illustrated in Exhibit 6–1. As can be seen, the instruments used and the consequent categories of liabilities are direct loans, guaranteed loans, insurance, and government-sponsored enterprises.

Before discussing these, it should be noted that other major liabilities are not included, such as the costs of environmental clean up of nuclear weapons production plants, defense installations that are being abandoned both in the United States and overseas, and other federal agency facilities. Other exclusions are federal research and development centers, such as the RAND Corporation, which are primarily the creations of the Departments of Defense and Energy, and congressionally chartered, nonprofit corporations, such as the American Red Cross.

Direct loans involve operations at home and abroad. Monies are available to help farmers acquire homes, electrify their farms, and engage in overseas com-

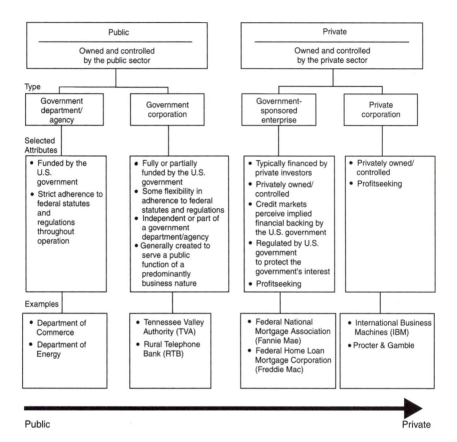

Figure 6–1 Comparison of Public and Private Entities. *Source:* Reprinted from *Government Corporations: Profiles of Existing Government Corporations*, p. 5, 1995, U.S. General Accounting Office, Washington, D.C.: U.S. Government Printing Office.

merce. International operations include loans to support defense and economic development of other nations and to stimulate the growth of the private sectors in these countries. Immense political risks exist, because a change in a government may lead to the renunciation of previous commitments to repay loans. In other situations, developing countries may be too poor to repay loans so that these become *de facto* grants.

Guaranteed loans entail agreement by the government to pay loans when customers default. A major segment of the housing mortgage market in the United States is backed by federal government loan guarantees. The category has included student loans, which have had a history of high rates of default. In the

Exhibit 6–1 Long-Term Federal Government Obligations and Risks

1. Direct Loans
   - Agency for International Development
   - Disaster Assistance
   - Export-Import Bank
   - Farm Service Agency, Rural Development, Rural Housing
   - Federal Direct Student Loan Program
   - Foreign Military Financing
   - Public Law 83-480—Agriculture
   - Rural Electrification Administration and Rural Telephone Bank
   - Small Business
   - Other Direct
2. Guaranteed Loans
   - Commodity Credit Corporation (CCC) Export Credits
   - Export-Import Bank
   - Farm Service Agency and Rural Housing
   - Federal Family Education Loan Program
   - Federal Housing Administration General Insurance and Special Risk Insurance (GI/SRI) Fund
   - Federal Housing Administration Mutual Mortgage Insurance (MMI) Fund
   - Small Business
   - Veterans Affairs Mortgage
   - Other Direct
3. Insurance
   - Deposit Insurance
     - Commercial Banks and Thrifts—Federal Deposit Insurance Corporation
     - National Credit Union Share Insurance Fund
   - Disaster Insurance
     - Federal Crop Insurance Corporation
     - National Flood Insurance Program
     - Pension Benefit Guarantee Corporation
4. Government-Sponsored Enterprises
   - Federal National Mortgage Association (Fannie Mae)
   - Farm Credit System
   - Federal Home Loan Banks
   - Federal Home Loan Mortgage Corporation (Freddie Mac)
   - Student Loan Market Association (Sallie Mae)

Source: Adapted from *Analytical Perspectives, Budget of the United States Government*, 1997, U.S. Office of Management and Budget, Washington, D.C.: U.S. Government Printing Office.

international arena, the federal government has guaranteed billions of dollars of loans made by U.S. financial institutions to developing countries under the Housing Guaranty Loan Program.

Federal insurance programs cover deposits in financial institutions and private pension deposits. Not only have thrift institutions failed, but so have some commercial banks. Pension guarantees present other problems. Corporate failures, as in the case of Eastern Airlines and Pan Am Airlines, leave pensioners and employees with credits into pension plans that lack adequate financial backing. The Pension Benefit Guarantee Corporation deals with these problems, with the support of the federal government. Other programs include crop insurance for farmers.

Government-sponsored enterprises are another source of liability. The institutions listed in Figure 6–1, including Freddie Mac and Fannie Mae, involve largely secondary credit markets, in which these institutions purchase debt instruments, such as mortgages, and in turn release funds to lending institutions for further loan activity.[44]

Federal Liability Reforms. Efforts are under way to bring some clarity to what liabilities the government has, and proposals exist for reforming this immense area of finance. The concerns about such liabilities are not new but rather date back to 1945 when Congress passed the Government Corporation Control Act.[45] At the time, there was concern that government corporations were operating without sufficient guidance and control by the government. The argument can be made that despite the numerous revisions Congress has made in the law over the years, the law is inadequate in controlling these major institutions.[46]

The Financial Institutions Reform, Recovery, and Enforcement Act of 1989 dealt with failed thrift institutions and required the General Accounting Office (GAO) to investigate the financing of government-sponsored enterprises.[47] The GAO has designated some programs as "high risk," such as Farm Loan Programs.[48] The GAO's intent is to train attention on those programs that have the potential for creating large economic losses for the government.

The Federal Credit Reform Act of 1990 required the government to upgrade its accounting for credit programs.[49] OMB has issued Circular A-129 (1993), which provides a uniform set of procedures for agencies engaged in loan programs, both direct and guaranteed. The procedures indicate how agencies are to estimate the costs of loans and loan guarantees, a function that is difficult to accomplish.[50] The purpose of Circular A-129 is to reduce risks and place the federal government's credit operations on a better financial foundation. Agencies that guarantee loans must estimate potential defaults and include those estimates in their current appropriations requests. This reform places potential defaults in direct competition with current spending requests, a practice expected to make decision makers more cautious in extending loans and loan guarantees.

Efforts are under way to improve the collection of debts rather than simply writing off bad debts. The Debt Collection Improvement Act of 1996 strengthened the government's ability to retrieve monies owed.[51] Agencies may refer bad debts to private collection companies and may share information with one another in locating those in arrears.

These significant changes, however, have not addressed the main issue, namely, what should be the federal government's responsibilities in this area and how can liabilities and risks be curtailed? One line of criticism is that the federal government has been too generous. Fostering a credit market is important to national economic growth, but should the federal government assist three-fifths of all nonfederal credit in the nation, as is currently the case? Agencies, under pressure to justify their continued governmental support, have issued reports explaining how their operations contribute to the well-being of the nation.[52]

Credit programs subsidize risk taking on the part of individuals and corporations. When the federal government provides full backing for a venture, then it assumes 100 percent of the risk. Crop insurance, for example, is available at comparatively low cost to farms, but only about one in four farms uses the insurance, because when droughts, floods, and other conditions destroy crops, the government usually passes legislation that fully covers all damage. Prescriptions for reform, therefore, tend to favor increasing the risk of the private sector and decreasing that of the public sector. Such action was taken in 1996 by passage of the Student Loan Marketing Association Reorganization Act, which provides for the privatization of Sallie Mae (student loans) and Connie Lee (college construction loans).[53] The student loan program was one the GAO identified as a high-risk program.[54]

Another reform theme is that structural changes should bring greater coordination among the various institutions involved and greater oversight of their operations. It may be desirable to have a single regulatory body that would oversee many government-sponsored enterprises and related institutions. An oversight board specifically dedicated to this function might be more energized than OMB, which must oversee the operations of these varied institutions as well as all of the regular departments and agencies of the government.[55]

Although one line of concern is that credit and insurance institutions have become burdensome on government, perhaps suggesting that they should be totally privatized, the reality is that they serve important functions. Proposals exist for creating still more of these bodies. Government corporations have been proposed for air traffic services, managing petroleum reserves, and the development of national infrastructure.[56]

State and Local Governments. Similar liability and risk problems exist at the state and local levels. The Governmental Accounting Standards Board has prescribed how these governments are to report risks and insurance (see Chapter 11).

Potential losses can be due to "torts; theft of, damage to, or destruction of assets; business interruptions; errors or omissions; job-related illnesses or injuries to employees; acts of God; and any other risks of loss assumed under a policy or participation contract issued by a public entity risk pool."[57] Torts are civil wrongs that occur independent of contract, as when a city refuse truck accidentally backs into a person's vehicle and causes personal harm and property damage. Among the greatest liabilities of state and local governments are their pensions systems, which are often actuarially unsound (see Chapter 13).

Final Preparation Deliberations

The chief executive becomes most active in the preparation phase during its final weeks, a frustrating period for the budget office. Decisions are seemingly reached but then may be reversed. The chief executive may instruct the budget office to include an agency's proposed change in the budget but later reject the proposal after considering revenue estimates. The chief executive may tentatively decide to recommend tax increases and then reverse that decision. Materials prepared during evenings and weekends by the budget office may find their way to the paper shredder as decisions are changed. The process may seem haphazard—and it probably is in many respects—but it is necessarily complicated because of the numerous factors being evaluated simultaneously.

A common complaint about the preparation phase is that only the chief executive and the director of the central budget office consider the budget as a whole. An organizational unit within a department or agency is concerned primarily with its own piece of the budget, and the same is true of a department vis-à-vis other departments and the rest of the budget. Even within the central budget office, budget examiners focus mainly on one or a few segments of the budget and not on the total package. The chief executive, assisted by the budget director, must pull together pieces of information and intelligence provided by various sources into a set of decisions that can be defended as a whole. The budget that is to be submitted to the legislative body is the chief executive's creation.

The decision process involves tradeoffs. A $1 million increase in a city police department's budget means there is that much less available for other departments in the government. A one-mill increase in property taxes makes more money available to provide services that citizens want but at the same time may anger those same citizens because of the increase in their tax bills. Planning personnel layoffs may seem a reasonable choice for avoiding tax increases, but will layoffs be imposed on all agencies, including highly visible units such as the police and fire departments? Chief executives take seriously the justifications that agencies make for budget increases or for avoiding budget cuts, and perceptions about the effectiveness of agencies' programs and activities influence executive decisions in the preparation phase of budgeting.

BUDGET DOCUMENTS

The final product of the preparation phase of budgeting is a budget document (or documents) that contains the decisions reached in the months of agency requests and executive reviews. The budget at this point is only a proposal, a set of recommended policies and programs set forth by the chief executive. The budget remains a proposal until the legislative body acts on it.

Number and Types of Documents

The budget for any government may consist of one or several documents. Small jurisdictions often have only one-volume budgets whereas larger governments usually package their budgets in several volumes. The size of a jurisdiction's budget, as measured in receipts or outlays, does not always determine the size of its documents, however. Documents are printed on different sizes of paper and vary considerably in their graphics. Some volumes have mainly text and tables while others include charts, graphs, photographs of citizens and government buildings, and magazine-style articles on special topics—for example, nursing home care for the elderly.

The preparers of budget documents are giving increasing attention to making the documents more "user friendly," reflecting the fact that these documents are expected to communicate the proposals contained within not only to technical budget analysts but to executive and legislative political leaders, the news media, and the general citizenry. Budget documents often include glossaries that define technical terms in everyday language. Explanations are provided as to how tables are to be read. Sections are sometimes color-coded and tabbed or have markings on page edges to help readers find the topics of interest to them. Since 1984, the Government Finance Officers Association has given its Award for Distinguished Budget Presentation to hundreds of state and local governments.[58]

A government will produce one main document and then may have one or more additional documents. A *budget-in-brief* may be prepared for general consumption with emphasis on graphics and readability. Documents can be made of greater interest to general readers through attractive formats made possible by the widespread availability of affordable desktop publishing computer software.

Federal Documents. Some years the federal government publishes numerous budget documents and other years much fewer documents. The main budget document is the *Budget of the United States Government*, which is backed up by a second and much larger document—the *Budget Appendix*. In addition to preparing these documents, OMB prepares *Analytical Perspectives*, which provides more detailed information about specific aspects of the budget. Topics in this document include the government's balance sheet, expenditures for research and development, federal credit and insurance, aid to state and local governments, borrowing and debt, current services estimates, and compliance with the Budget Enforcement Act (see Chapter 9). *Historical Tables* provides multiyear financial data on a variety of subjects. *Budget System and Concepts* gives an overview of federal budgeting, and *A Citizen's Guide to the Federal Budget* presents a general overview of the budget. *Principles of Budgeting for Capital Asset Acquisition* reports the basic concepts used in budgeting for capital projects.

OMB produces other important documents, such as budget circulars (for example, A-11, which is about budget preparation) and annual publications covering procurement and the midyear status of the budget. Some documents may be prepared for a few years and then are replaced or superseded. For instance, sometimes separate annual volumes have been prepared that describe the policy initiatives being advocated by the president and the information being collected by federal agencies.

The *Economic Report of the President* is prepared by the Council of Economic Advisers and is released at about the same time as the other main budget documents. The *Economic Report* discusses expected economic trends for the coming fiscal year and is the basis upon which the president's economic policy is formulated. The economic assumptions reflected in this report are used for estimating revenues and expenditures for the budget year.

The Treasury Department has an extensive publishing program and produces several documents specifically related to budgeting. The *United States Government Annual Report*, mandated by the constitutional provision for reporting of the government's finances, provides information about receipts, outlays, deficits, borrowing, and debt. The document *Consolidated Financial Statements* was introduced in 1990 and is intended to report on the financial condition of the government (see Chapter 12). The *Treasury Bulletin*, issued quarterly, reports information about the economy, government receipts and outlays, and federal debt. This document provides details on the various forms of federal securities. In addition to these documents, the department publishes monthly and daily reports on the government's financial transactions and separate reports on trust funds, such as the unemployment, highway, and disability insurance trust funds.

Other Specialized Documents. Governments sometimes publish specialized budget-related documents in addition to those already mentioned. Some states and many local governments publish capital budgets, showing planned construction projects and major pieces of equipment to be purchased (see Chapter 12) and some publish separate volumes on personnel (see Chapter 13).

The federal government and some states publish discussions of tax expenditures, which are losses in government revenue due to tax provisions that exempt some items from taxation or provide favorable tax rates.[59] In its annual publication *Analytical Perspectives*, OMB provides an extensive itemization of tax expenditures and projects each of these into the future for five years. California and Massachusetts have published separate volumes on tax expenditures. Exhibit 6–2

Exhibit 6–2 Pennsylvania Personal Income Tax Expenditures, Exclusions from Income, 1995–2002

RETIREMENT INCOME

Description: Payments commonly recognized as old-age or retirement benefits paid to persons retired from service after reaching a specific age or after a stated period of service are exempt from taxation.

Purpose: The exemption limits the impact of the tax on retired persons. It also prevents taxation of previously taxed employee contributions to retirement plans.

(Dollar Amounts in Millions)

Estimates:	1995–96	1996–97	1997–98	1998–99	1999–00	2000–01	2001–02
	$1,058.7	$1,122.9	$1,191.1	$1,263.4	$1,340.1	$1,421.4	$1,507.7

Beneficiaries: Approximately 1.5 million retired residents benefit from this tax expenditure.

RETIREMENT CONTRIBUTIONS BY EMPLOYERS

Description: Payments made by employers for programs covering employee retirement and employer Social Security contributions are exempt from taxation.

Purpose: This provision lessens the burden of the tax upon Pennsylvania wage earners and maintains fairness, since the employee often does not have the right to possess the funds in the retirement plan except for retirement or separation from the company after a set number of years of service.

(Dollar Amounts in Millions)

Estimates:	1995–96	1996–97	1997–98	1998–99	1999–00	2000–01	2001–02
	$460.6	$477.2	$493.8	$513.3	$537.0	$561.2	$584.7

Beneficiaries: As many as 5.5 million employees benefit from this tax expenditure.

Note: This exhibit does not include all exemptions listed in the budget document.

Source: 1997–98 Governor's Executive Budget, courtesy of Office of the Budget, 1997, Harrisburg, Pennsylvania.

presents two types of tax expenditures that are part of the Pennsylvania tax code. If the state chose to tax some forms of retirement income and employers' contributions to retirement plans, then tax revenues would increase.

Budget Messages. Another feature of budget documents is the budget message, in which the chief executive highlights the major recommendations in the budget. The message sometimes is presented orally to the legislature. The president's budget message is included in the *Budget of the United States Government* itself. State governments vary widely, with some having no message and others having lengthy ones, sometimes as long as 100 pages. State and local jurisdictions on occasion publish their budget messages as separate documents.

Approved Budgets. Some jurisdictions publish their approved budgets (i.e., budgets that reflect action taken by the legislative bodies). North Carolina, for example, publishes a *Post-Legislative Budget Summary.* The federal government does not provide such a volume.

Coverage

Budget documents vary with regard to the extent of their coverage. All report information about government receipts and expenditures. Intergovernmental transactions also are reported. A state budget highlights funds it receives from the federal government and funds it provides local governments within the state. Issues arise over how much detail to provide on these items.

General and Special Funds. Confusion is common in the handling of funds in budget documents. State and local governments are major users of special funds, which basically are financial accounts for special revenue sources, such as the Casino Revenue Fund in New Jersey, and which can be used only for specific purposes. A jurisdiction's general fund consists of revenue that can be used for all functions of the government. These different types of funds are discussed elsewhere in conjunction with accounting problems (Chapter 11), but here it should be noted that many jurisdictions have a general fund budget document and then one or more documents for special funds. One result of having separate budgets is confusion over the size of the total budget and the amount spent by any given agency, because the agency may be receiving support from several funds.

Federal Coverage Prior to 1969. The coverage issue at the federal level is similar.[60] Until the late 1960s, there were really three types of federal budgets: the administrative budget, the consolidated cash statement, and the federal sector of the national income accounts. The differences among these need not bother us here. What is important is that using three types of budgets resulted in much confusion. Because each of the three types had a different coverage, total revenues and expenditures varied from one to another, leading to different statements of budget surpluses and deficits. Different pictures of federal finances—gloomy or bright—could be painted by choosing to discuss one budget statement and ignoring the other two. In response to this problem, President Johnson in 1967 appointed the President's Commission on Budget Concepts, whose eventual recommendation for a unified budget was incorporated into the budget document beginning with fiscal year 1969.[61]

Unified or Consolidated Budget. In the revised format, all federal agencies and programs are included, with some important exceptions noted below. Receipts, budget authority (appropriations), outlays (expenditures), and the resulting deficit or surplus are shown. Information is supplied for the means of financing the deficit and about the size of the federal debt.

Off-Budget. Since adoption of the unified budget, important changes have been made. One trend was toward greater use of what is known as the *off-budget*. Congress determined what was included in this budget, which varied somewhat from year to year. The postal service, for example, was placed in the off-budget, because it was expected to operate like a business, largely independent of the government. Other federal entities were removed from the budget or *on-budget* because they operated largely with revolving funds rather than annual appropriations and made direct loans to the public. For example, the Rural Telephone Bank, the Federal Financing Bank, and the U.S. Synthetic Fuels Corporation were placed in the off-budget. The Gramm-Rudman-Hollings Act of 1985, however, required that all federal entities be placed in the on-budget, with one set of important exceptions. The Old Age and Survivors Insurance, Disability Insurance, and Hospital Insurance trust funds were left outside of the budget. In the 1990s, the Social Security Trust Fund and the postal service constitute the off-budget. Receipts in the off-budget are equal to 25 percent of all receipts, and outlays equal close to 20 percent of all outlays.

Exclusions from the On-Budget and Off-Budget. Government-sponsored enterprises are included in neither the on-budget nor the off-budget. The same is true for the Board of Governors of the Federal Reserve System. Information about these bodies, however, is provided in the Bibliographic Note and in OMB's *Analytical Perspectives*.

Alternative Budget Presentations. The decades of debate about how best to present the overall budget of the federal government have made clear that probably no single format is ideal. As a result, the OMB attempts to satisfy the needs of different participants in the budget process by presenting information in a variety of formats. The exact coverage of the *Budget of the United States Government* varies from year to year. The document may show outlays divided into mandatory and discretionary categories along with revenues and the seemingly inevitable deficit. Mandatory outlays include deposit insurance, federal retirement, Medicaid, Medicare, and the like. An alternative presentation is usually provided using national income and product accounts (see Chapter 15). Presentations may be based on a format suggested by the GAO or one similar to a typical state government format. The budget may be displayed in terms of its effects upon various age groups or generations. Although the federal government does not have a capital budget, a presentation usually is provided to show federal investment expenditures as distinguished from operating costs.

Information Displays

Receipts. Turning to other aspects of the budget document, budgets present both revenue and expenditure data. The coverage of receipts or revenues usually is substantially less extensive than the coverage of expenditures. Budgets show receipts from taxes, such as individual and corporate income taxes; from user charges, such as water service fees; and from other governments, such as state grants to local government. Table 6–1, taken from a Tennessee budget, shows the state, federal, and other revenue that support a mental retardation center. Budget documents usually discuss proposed changes in tax laws, especially proposed tax rate changes. For the federal government, some revenues are treated as expenditures. OMB treats receipts generated by an agency as an "offsetting collection" and deducts that from outlays rather than treating the amount as revenue.

Expenditures. The bulk of the budget document is devoted to the expenditure side of government finance, with the main classification usually based on organi-

Table 6–1 Tennessee Base and Improvement Budget, Clover Bottom Developmental Center, 1995–1998

	Actual 1995–1996	Estimated 1996–1997	Base 1997–1998	Improvement 1997–1998	Recommended 1997–1998
Full Time	1,224	1,149	1,149	0	1,149
Part Time	2	2	2	0	2
Seasonal	0	0	0	0	0
Total	1,226	1,151	1,151	0	1,151
Payroll	25,777,300	33,780,500	32,598,100	83,600	32,681,700
Operational	15,012,100	12,248,000	13,430,400	0	13,430,400
Total	$40,789,400	$46,028,500	$46,028,500	$83,600	$46,112,100
State	1,803,800	1,486,900	1,486,900	0	1,486,900
Federal	0	0	0	0	0
Other	38,985,600	44,541,600	44,541,600	83,600	44,625,200

Source: The Budget, 1997–98, courtesy of Budget Division, 1997, Nashville, Tennessee.

zational unit. Each department presents a budget within which subunits are given separate treatment. A generally uniform format is used for each subunit, including a brief narrative description of the subunit's responsibilities and functions. Narratives contained in the federal appendix section also contain proposed appropriations language that may be quite specific: For the Commodity Futures Trading Commission's budget of $60 million, not more than $1,000 was to be used for "official reception and representation expenses."[62]

In addition to the narrative are various tabular displays. Expenditures are reported by object classes, such as personnel, equipment, and travel (see Chapter 11).[63] These financial tables may be primarily for information purposes or may later be incorporated into the appropriation bill. When this practice is used, the legislative body is said to have adopted a line-item budget, which reduces the president's, governor's, or mayor's flexibility in executing the budget.

Budget presentations sometimes show for the past fiscal year the budgeted amounts and actual amounts, for both receipts and expenditures. This information is helpful in understanding the accuracy with which the government is able to estimate its revenues and keep its expenditures within budgeted amounts.[64]

Current Services. Governments sometimes display current services budget data, which are intended to show decision makers what receipts and expenditures will be without any changes being made in tax laws, other revenue sources, and spending levels. Table 6–2 shows current services projections for the federal government from 1996 through 2002. In addition to receipts, the table reports outlays subdivided into discretionary spending and mandatory or entitlement spending. The table also shows the differences between receipts and outlays for the on-budget and off-budget for each year.

Program Information. Since World War II, program data have become increasingly common in the budget documents of most governments. Federal program data are presented in the *Appendix* volume of the *Budget of the United States Government*, but only for a small number of agencies, and the information tends to be in terms of workload or outputs rather than impacts. Table 6–3 illustrates the workload of the Department of Justice in representing the government before the Supreme Court. The table indicates the number of cases pending at the beginning of the Court's term (October of each year), received, and terminated as well as the number of cases pending at the end of the term, but it provides no clues to the effectiveness of the department's activities. Greater program information can be expected to appear in the budget as federal agencies begin to implement fully the Government Performance and Results Act of 1993 and President Clinton's 1993 Executive Order 12862, which requires agencies to establish customer service standards (Chapter 5). With regard to state governments, 73 percent reported in 1995 that their documents contained effectiveness measures for some or most agencies, and 80 percent reported using productivity measures.[65]

Table 6–2 Current Services Estimates, U.S. Budget, 1996–2002 (in Billions of Dollars)

	1996	1997	1998	1999	2000	2001	2002
Receipts	1,453.1	1,503.8	1,573.8	1,644.7	1,731.0	1,813.8	1,901.6
Outlays							
Discretionary:							
Defense	266.0	268.7	265.4	276.7	282.2	290.5	297.1
Nondefense	268.4	282.0	288.0	298.7	304.4	311.3	320.3
Subtotal, discretionary	534.4	550.7	553.4	575.4	586.6	601.8	617.4
Mandatory:							
Social Security	347.1	364.2	380.9	398.6	417.7	438.0	459.7
Medicare	171.3	191.6	208.6	228.2	248.8	271.1	295.1
Medicaid	92.0	98.5	104.5	111.2	119.6	129.1	139.2
All other	174.6	178.9	196.0	218.9	235.7	233.0	243.8
Subtotal, mandatory	784.9	833.2	890.0	957.0	1,021.8	1,071.2	1,137.7
Net interest	241.1	247.6	249.9	252.4	250.2	249.4	247.2
Total, outlays	1,560.3	1,631.5	1,693.4	1,784.8	1,858.6	1,922.3	2,002.3
Deficit (−)	−107.3	−127.7	−119.5	−140.1	−127.6	−108.5	−100.8
On-budget	−174.3	−201.6	−195.7	−227.0	−223.2	−210.9	−209.4
Off-budget	67.0	73.9	76.2	86.9	95.7	102.4	108.7
Memorandum							
With discretionary spending at BEA caps:							
Discretionary	534.4	550.7	548.2	563.0	578.2	593.8	609.8
Deficit (−)	−107.3	−127.7	−114.2	−127.1	−118.2	−99.1	−91.4

Source: Reprinted from Analytical Perspectives, Budget of the United States Government, p. 249, 1997, U.S. Office of Management and Budget.

Table 6–3 Supreme Court Workload, U.S. Department of Justice, 1996–1998

	1996 Actual	1997 Estimate	1998 Estimate
Cases:			
Pending, beginning of term	304	377	450
Received	2,972	2,987	3,002
Terminated	2,899	2,914	2,929
Pending, end of term	377	450	523
Other Activities:			
Appellate determinations	920	925	929
Certiorari determinations	728	732	735
Miscellaneous recommendations	786	790	794
Oral arguments participation*	67	67	67

*The government participated in 67 cases in 1996, which include consolidated cases.

Source: Reprinted from *Appendix: Budget of the United States Government*, p. 662, 1997, U.S. Office of Management and Budget.

Program Structure. An alternative to arranging the budget document by organizational unit is to arrange it by program structure. The structure consists of a number of broad programs that are subdivided into more narrowly focused subprograms, which are themselves subdivided. Terminology varies, but one approach is to have programs divided into program categories, which are divided into subcategories and then into elements.

The federal government does not have a program budget but does use broad functional classifications to summarize the budget: national defense, natural resources and environment, agriculture, transportation, and the like.[66] The functional classifications are useful for highlighting the changing character of government expenditures over time, such as changes in the proportion of the budget committed to social services, but these classifications are not linked explicitly to program descriptions or specific agency activities.

Using a program structure for the main outline of a budget has both advantages and disadvantages. On the positive side, the budget shows how the various activities of different programs relate to each other, regardless of the agency location of the activities, since they are juxtaposed with one another in the document. As a result of being placed in the same program, agencies are forced to recognize their dependence on each other and the need for cooperation. For example, a city transportation department and police department are forced to recognize that they both influence traffic safety.

On the negative side, the "pure" program structure type of budget disperses parts of agencies throughout the budget, making it difficult to determine what the budget is for any one agency. One solution to this problem is known as *crosswalking*, in which information organized by program is reconfigured into an organizational format. Crosswalking, while a successful technique when computer technology is employed, is cumbersome and may force a government to produce two budgets—a program budget and an agency budget.

The state of Vermont has used a budget format that is a compromise between a program structure format and an organizational unit format. The budget is divided into major programs first, such as protection of persons and property, human services, employment and training services, and general education. These are then subdivided into organizational units. The protection program includes such units as the Office of the Attorney General, the Military Department, and the Department of Labor and Industry. The latter department has its operations divided into such activities as fire prevention and occupational safety and health.

Exhibit 6–3 displays the programmatic format used by Lakewood, Colorado. The exhibit shows the description, city council goal, departmental goals, program objectives, and standards of performance for police services. Data are presented regarding traffic accidents, driving-under-the-influence (DUI) arrests, police commendations, and complaints about police.

Program Revisions. Chief executives often wish to use the budget to highlight the programmatic initiatives they are recommending to their respective legislative bodies. Budget documents frequently contain a section that sets forth themes that summarize the major recommendations being made. The federal government's budget for fiscal year 1998 had ten such themes, including strengthening health care, restoring the American community, and supporting the world's strongest military force.

Exhibit 6–4 illustrates another type of information display provided in budget documents. The exhibit first shows that the Pennsylvania budget has five program revision "themes," with one being "community building." The exhibit then shows that three departments plus executive offices are part of this set of revisions. Then program measures are presented along with recommended spending levels for each activity within each department. The information is displayed on a multiyear basis.

Future Years. Budget reformers have tended to advocate multiyear projections as a method for helping decision makers understand the long-term implications of policy and program issues. However, given the uncertainty of the future, one might expect few governments to attempt to make projections beyond the budget year or biennium. Perhaps somewhat surprisingly, then, there has been a steady increase in the use of multiyear projections. A longitudinal study of state budgeting found that while only 2 percent of the states responding in 1970 said they

Exhibit 6–3 Program Data for Patrol Services, City of Lakewood, Colorado, 1994–1997

Description

The Patrol Services Program provides first response to citizen requests in emergency and nonemergency incidents. It also includes traffic enforcement, prevention and detection of crime, apprehension of offenders, and assistance in the safe and expedient movement of vehicular and pedestrian traffic.

Council Strategic Goal

Safety: Continue Lakewood's commitment to community safety by emphasizing community policing in cooperation with other cities and counties, gang control and alternatives, and increased focus on domestic violence.

Departmental Goals

- Create with citizens a long-term vision for Lakewood and encourage diverse input to the process to create a safe and secure Lakewood community.
- Continue to research creative techniques that will enhance the service provided to the citizens of Lakewood by developing programs with the resources available.

Program Objectives for 1997

- To provide police service to the community in a timely and professional manner, resulting in a sense of safety and security among the residents of our community.
- To continue to promote a community partnership by aggressively implementing community-oriented policing strategies.
- To continue to use the Traffic Team in the solution of community problems.
- To dedicate four agents from the Special Enforcement Team (SET) to gang-related crime suppression.
- To evaluate delivery of services, and make improvements as necessary.
- Respond aggressively to the challenge of ensuring community safety and security.
- The three Area COPS [Community Oriented Problem Solving] Projects will continue to address neighborhood concerns with combined efforts from business people and citizens while developing techniques to solve problems.

Standards of Performance

- Reflect customer satisfaction with police services in the published results of citizen surveys and in the department receiving more commendations than complaints.
- Devote 70 percent of available sworn man-hours to patrol-type (operational) duties versus nonoperational activities such as court appearances, administrative duties, vehicle maintenance, etc.

continues

Exhibit 6–3 continued

Operational Data

	1994 Actual	1995 Actual	1996 Revised	1997 Budget
Traffic Accidents Reported	4,847	5,254	5,232	5,111
Traffic Summonses Issued	11,148	11,310	10,346	10,935
DUI Arrests	1,014	842	735	780
Total Arrests	10,054	10,421	9,939	10,138
Percentage of Time Spent on Patrol-Type Duties	71%	71.8%	71.1%	71%
Commendations versus Allegations of Misconduct	507/52	481/70	408/63	477/74

Source: Lakewood Annual Budget, 1997, pp. 185–186, courtesy of Lakewood Police Department, 1997, Lakewood, Colorado.

projected effectiveness measures in budget documents, 33 percent reported they made such projections in 1995; comparable figures for the use of productivity measures were 8 percent and 44 percent.[67]

Space Limitations. Not all available program and resource information can be presented in budget documents without making the documents unwieldy. The budget formats of some jurisdictions rigidly prescribe allowed space—one page, for example, for each bureau, program, or activity. This type of format may increase the readability of the document. The disadvantage is that not all subunits are of equal importance, either in terms of budget size or political interest. Therefore, many jurisdictions use more flexible formats, providing more information on some agencies and programs and less information on others. With this type of format, larger agencies commonly receive more extensive coverage because they are more complex and have more varied activities. However, agencies that are particularly popular or unpopular may receive more extensive coverage regardless of their size.

SUMMARY

In beginning the preparation phase, the chief executive conveys to agencies some sense of priorities, either formally in writing or by more subtle means. The executive's view of the role of government in society is indicated to agencies as well as more specific priorities.

Exhibit 6–4 Pennsylvania Program Revisions: Community Building, 1995–2002

Program Revision Themes
Creating Economic Opportunity
Community Building
Preparing for the Future
Enhancing Services and Promoting Self-Sufficiency
Information Technology for Pennsylvania

Community Building Theme
Executive Offices:
  Community Crime Prevention
Department of Community and Economic Development:
  Community Development Bank
  Family Savings Accounts
Department of Health:
  Maternal and Child Health
  Maternal and Child Health Service Block Grant—Program Services
Department of Labor and Industry:
  General Government Operations
  Job Training Partnership Act—Administration

Program Measures for Community Building (based on program revision)

	1995–96	1996–97	1997–98	1998–99	1999–00	2000–01	2001–02
Pennsylvania Community Development Bank							
Value of Loans	0	0	5,000	16,800	16,800	16,800	16,800

continues

Exhibit 6–4 continued

	1995–96	1996–97	1997–98	1998–99	1999–00	2000–01	2001–02
Jobs Created or Retained	0	0	411	1,547	1,547	1,547	1,547
Family Savings Accounts							
Families Participating	0	0	2,500	2,500	2,500	2,500	2,500
Self-Employment Assistance Program							
Individuals Assisted	0	0	1,000	1,000	1,000	1,000	1,000
Businesses Started	0	0	580	580	580	580	580
Program Revision Costs by Appropriation (in thousands of dollars)							
Department of Community and Economic Development							
Community Development Bank	0	0	$15,000	$5,000	$5,000	$5,000	$5,000
Family Savings Accounts	0	0	1,250	1,250	1,250	1,250	1,250
Department of Labor and Industry							
General Government Operations	0	0	851	851	851	851	851
Executive Offices							
Community Crime Prevention	0	0	1,000	1,000	1,000	1,000	1,000
Department of Health							
Maternal and Child Health	0	0	1,050	1,400	1,400	1,400	1,400
Total General Fund	$ 0	$ 0	$19,151	$9,501	$9,501	$9,501	$9,501

Source: 1997–98 Governor's Executive Budget, courtesy of Office of the Budget, 1997, Harrisburg, Pennsylvania.

The revenue side of the budget is examined carefully, especially because state and local governments are not permitted to have operating budgets that exceed available revenues. Requiring the federal government to balance its budget is a proposal that has gained considerable acceptance but has not been put into law (see Chapter 9).

Budget preparation begins in agencies and involves extensive debate; similar debate develops between agencies and the central budget office, which in turn must compete with other central staff units. Since little formal authority is granted to a central budget office, it must always be concerned with being overruled by the chief executive.

The 1980s ushered in a new era in budgeting, where the focus is on budget cutbacks rather than program expansion. Fiscal stress, taxing and spending limitations, and an increase in anti–big government attitudes among political leaders have resulted in retrenchment efforts.

Decision makers have come to realize that they can be forced to deal with immense problems associated with credit and insurance liabilities. The collapse of hundreds of federally backed thrift institutions amply demonstrated the risks that are involved.

The product of the preparation phase is a budget or set of budget documents that reflect executive decisions on policies and programs. The federal government has what is called a *unified budget*. Revenue and expenditure data are treated in all budgets, but the latter receive much more extensive treatment. One common budget format has a structure based on organizational units and includes supporting narratives and tabular displays that present costs, personnel, and program data.

NOTES

1. S. Duncombe et al., Factors Influencing the Politics and Process of County Government Budgeting, *State and Local Government Review* 24 (1992): 19–27.

2. K. Thurmaier, Budgetary Decision Making in Central Budget Bureaus: An Experiment, *Journal of Public Administration Research and Theory* 2 (1992): 463–487.

3. M.L. Whicker and L. Sigelman, Decision Sequencing and Budgetary Outcomes: A Simulation Model, *Public Budgeting and Financial Management* 3 (1991): 7–34.

4. J.E. Stapleford, Economic Impact of Budgeting, in *Handbook of Public Budgeting*, ed. J. Rabin (New York: Marcel Dekker, 1992), 401–418.

5. J.J. Gosling, Patterns of Stability and Change in Gubernatorial Policy Agendas, *State and Local Government Review* 23 (1991): 3–12.

6. L.R. Jones, Strategic Planning and Resource Allocation for Defense, *Public Budgeting and Financial Management* 3 (1991): 355–370; D.E. O'Toole and B. Stipak, Strategic Planning and

Budgeting in Local Government, *Public Budgeting and Financial Management* 3 (1991): 317–331.

7. C. Mahtesian, Immigration: The Symbolic Crackdown, *Governing* 7 (May 1994): 52–57.

8. L. J. Kotlikoff, *Generational Accounting: Knowing Who Pays, and When, for What We Spend* (New York: The Free Press, 1992).

9. J.H. Makin et al., eds., *Balancing Act: Debt, Deficits, and Taxes* (Washington, DC: AEI Press, 1990); A. Schick, *The Capacity To Budget* (Washington, DC: Urban Institute Press, 1990); J.L. True, Is the National Budget Controllable?, *Public Budgeting & Finance* 15 (Summer 1995): 18–32.

10. J. Gill, Formal Models of Legislative/Administrative Interaction: A Survey of the Subfield, *Public Administration Review* 55 (1995): 99–106.

11. M.A. Glaser and W.B. Hildreth, A Profile of Discontinuity between Citizen Demand and Willingness to Pay Taxes: Comprehensive Planning for Park and Recreation Investment, *Public Budgeting & Finance* 16 (Winter 1996): 96–113.

12. J. Marengo, Bringing Communities Together: How the City of Sacramento Used Community Input to Solve Its Budget Problem, *PA Times* 20 (June 1997): 1, 10; also see D. Osborne and P. Plastrik, *Banishing Bureaucracy: The Five Strategies for Reinventing Government* (New York: Addison-Wesley, 1997).

13. Council of State Governments, *Book of the States, 1996–97 Edition* (Lexington, KY: Council of State Governments, 1996), 230–231.

14. C.W. Lewis, Budgetary Balance: The Norm, Concept, and Practice in Large U.S. Cities, *Public Administration Review* 54 (1994): 515–524.

15. R. Briffault, *Balancing Acts: The Reality Behind State Balanced Budget Requirements* (New York: Twentieth Century Fund, 1996).

16. J.E. Harris and S.A. Hicks, Tax Expenditure Reporting: The Utilization of an Innovation, *Public Budgeting & Finance* 12 (Fall 1992): 32–49.

17. P. Lemov, Fiscal Tricks for the Fat Years, *Governing* 10 (February 1997): 44–46.

18. R.F. Dye and T.J. McGuire, The Effect of Earmarked Revenues on Level and Composition of Expenditures, *Public Finance Quarterly* 20 (1992): 543–556.

19. A. Deutschman, The Great Pension Robbery, *Fortune* 12 (January 13, 1992): 76–78.

20. U.S. General Accounting Office, *Social Security Administration: Effective Leadership Needed To Meet Daunting Challenges* (Washington, DC: U.S. Government Printing Office, 1996); H.C. Grossman, Stunting the CPI Would Help Slow Spending But Hinder Revenues, *Government Finance Review* 13 (April 1997): 50.

21. National Security Act of 1947 and Amendments of 1949, 50 U.S.C. § 401–402.

22. S.A. Warshaw, White House Control of Domestic Policy Making: The Reagan Years, *Public Administration Review* 55 (1995): 247–253.

23. L.R. Jones and K.J. Euske, Strategic Misrepresentation in Budgeting, *Journal of Public Administration Research and Theory* 1 (1991): 437–460.

24. C.W. Lewis, Public Budgeting: Unethical in Purpose, Product, and Promise, *Public Budgeting and Financial Management* 4 (1992): 667–680.

25. A. Blais and S. Dion, eds., *The Budget-Maximizing Bureaucrat* (Pittsburgh, PA: University of Pittsburgh Press, 1991).

26. A. Schick, Incremental Budgeting in a Decremental Age, *Policy Sciences* 16 (1983): 1–25.

27. U.S. General Accounting Office, *Office of Management and Budget: Changes Resulting from the OMB 2000 Reorganization* (Washington, DC: U.S. Government Printing Office, 1995).

28. D.A. Stockman, *The Triumph of Politics: How the Reagan Revolution Failed* (New York: Harper & Row, 1986); A. Wildavsky and N. Caiden, *The New Politics of the Budgetary Process,* 3rd ed. (New York: Longman, 1997).

29. S.A. MacManus, Litigation: A Real Budget Buster for Many U.S. Municipalities, *Government Finance Review* 10 (February 1994): 27–31; C. Mahtesian, The Endless Court Order, *Governing* 10 (April 1997): 40–43.

30. K. Thurmaier, Decisive Decision Making in the Executive Budget Process: Analyzing the Political and Economic Propensities of Central Budget Bureau Analysts, *Public Administration Review* 55 (1995): 448–460.

31. H. Heclo, OMB and the Presidency: The Problem of "Neutral Competence," *Public Interest* 38 (1975): 80–98.

32. W.J. Pammer, Jr., *Managing Fiscal Strain in Major American Cities: Understanding Retrenchment in the Public Sector* (New York: Greenwood Press, 1990); T.N. Clark, Municipal Fiscal Strain: Indicators and Causes, *Government Finance Review* 10 (June 1994): 27–29.

33. G. Mattson, Fiscal Stress, Retrenchment and Small Cities: The Financial Management Practices of "Free Standing" Iowa Cities, *Public Budgeting and Financial Management* 3 (1991): 119–150.

34. S.B. Dewhurst, Downsizing, A View from the Inside, *Public Budgeting & Finance* 16 (Spring 1996): 49–59.

35. A. Schick, Macro-budgetary Adaptations to Fiscal Stress in Industrialized Democracies, *Public Administration Review* 46 (1986): 124–134.

36. M.J. Druker and B.D. Robinson, States' Responses to Budget Shortfalls: Cutback Management Techniques, in *Handbook of Comparative Public Budgeting and Financial Management*, eds. T.D. Lynch and L.L. Martin (New York: Marcel Dekker, 1993), 189–204.

37. Osborne and Plastrik, *Banishing Bureaucracy.*

38. U.S. General Accounting Office, *Financial Management: Federal Entities with Treasury and Federal Financing Bank Borrowing Authority* (Washington, DC: U.S. Government Printing Office, 1992).

39. Committee on the Budget, U.S. House of Representatives, *Hidden Exposure: The Unfunded Liabilities of the Federal Government: Hearing*, 102nd Cong., 1st sess. (Washington, DC: U.S. Government Printing Office, 1991).

40. R. Feldman, How Weak Recognition and Measurement in the Federal Budget Encouraged Costly Policy: The Case of "Supervisory Goodwill," *Public Budgeting & Finance* 16 (Winter 1996): 31–44.

41. U.S. General Accounting Office, *Government Corporations: Profiles of Existing Government Corporations* (Washington, DC: U.S. Government Printing Office, 1995).

42. U.S. General Accounting Office, *Government-Sponsored Enterprises: A Framework for Limiting the Government's Exposure to Risk* (Washington, DC: U.S. Government Printing Office, 1991), 16.

43. Government Corporations, 31 U.S.C.§ 9101.

44. U.S. Congressional Budget Office, *Assessing the Public Costs and Benefits of Fannie Mae and Freddie Mac* (Washington, DC: U.S. Government Printing Office, 1996).

45. Government Corporation Control Act, Ch. 557, 49 Stat. 597 (1945).

46. A.M. Froomkin, Reinventing the Government Corporation, *University of Illinois Law Review* 3 (1995), 543–634.

47. Financial Institutions Reform, Recovery, and Enforcement Act, P.L. 101-73, 103 Stat. 183 (1989).

48. U.S. General Accounting Office, *High Risk Series: Farm Loan Programs* (Washington, DC: U.S. Government Printing Office, 1995); U.S. General Accounting Office, *Farm Loans: Information on the Status of USDA's Portfolio* (Washington, DC: U.S. Government Printing Office, 1997).

49. Federal Credit Reform Act, P.L. 101-508, 104 Stat. 1388-610 (1990), as part of the Omnibus Budget Reconciliation Act of 1990.

50. U.S. General Accounting Office, *Credit Reform: U.S. Needs Better Methods for Estimating Cost of Foreign Loans and Guarantees* (Washington, DC: U.S. Government Printing Office, 1994).

51. Debt Collection Improvement Act, P.L. 104-34, 110 Stat. 1321-358 (1996); also see Federal Debt Collection Procedures Act, P.L. 101-647, 104 Stat. 4933 (1990).

52. U.S. Department of Treasury, *Government Sponsorship of the Federal National Mortgage Association and the Federal Home Loan Mortgage Corporation* (Washington, DC: U.S. Government Printing Office, 1996).

53. Student Loan Marketing Association Reorganization Act, P.L. 104-208, 110 Stat. 3009-275 (1996), as part of the Omnibus Consolidation Appropriations Act of 1997.

54. U.S. General Accounting Office, *High Risk Series: Student Financial Aid* (Washington, DC: U.S. Government Printing Office, 1995).

55. R.C. Moe, Congressional Reference Service, *Managing the Public Business: Federal Government Corporations* (Washington, DC: U.S. Government Printing Office, 1995).

56. U.S. General Accounting Office, *Government Corporations: Profiles of Recent Proposals* (Washington, DC: U.S. Government Printing Office, 1995).

57. Governmental Accounting Standards Board, *Accounting and Financial Reporting for Risk Financing and Related Insurance Issues*, Statement No. 10 (Norwalk, CT: Financial Accounting Foundation, 1989).

58. E.A. Lehan, Budget Appraisal: The Next Step in the Quest for Better Budgeting? *Public Budgeting & Finance* 16 (Winter 1996): 3–20; P.G. Joyce, Appraising Budget Appraisal: Can You Take Politics Out? *Public Budgeting & Finance* 16 (Winter 1996): 21–25.

59. J.E. Harris, ed., Symposium on Tax Expenditures, *Public Budgeting and Financial Management* 5 (1993): 189–528; U.S. General Accounting Office, *Tax Expenditures: Information on Employer-Provided Educational Assistance* (Washington, DC: U.S. Government Printing Office, 1996).

60. S.E. Harris, ed., Budgetary Concepts: A Symposium, *Review of Economics and Statistics* 45 (1963): 113–147; R.W. Johnson, Evolution of Budget Concepts in the President's Message: 1923–1968, in President's Commission on Budget Concepts, *Staff Papers and Other Materials Reviewed* (Washington, DC: U.S. Government Printing Office, 1967), 93–103.

61. President's Commission on Budget Concepts, *Report* (Washington, DC: U.S. Government Printing Office, 1967).

62. U.S. Office of Management and Budget, *Appendix, Budget of the United States Government* (Washington, DC: U.S. Government Printing Office, 1997), 1018.

63. U.S. General Accounting Office, *Budget Object Classification: Origins and Recent Trends* (Washington, DC: U.S. Government Printing Office, 1994).

64. U.S. General Accounting Office, *Budget Issues: Fiscal Year 1994 Budget Estimates and Actual Results* (Washington, DC: U.S. Government Printing Office, 1995).

65. R.D. Lee, Jr., A Quarter Century of State Budgeting Practices, *Public Administration Review* 57 (1997): 133–140.

66. U.S. General Accounting Office, *Budget Function Classification: Relating Agency Spending and Personnel Levels to Budget Functions* (Washington, DC: U.S. Government Printing Office, 1995); U.S. General Accounting Office, *Budget Issues: Fiscal Year 1996 Agency Spending by Budget Function* (Washington, DC: U.S. Government Printing Office, 1997).

67. Lee, A Quarter Century of State Budgeting Practices.

CHAPTER 7

Policy and Program Analysis

The use of policy and program analysis is part of a long-standing trend toward linking financial and program decision making. As preceding chapters have shown, reformists since the early 1900s have advocated decision systems that focus on the results of public expenditures. Analysis, though in no sense new, has gained recognition as a means of relating what government does and costs to what government accomplishes. Measuring, monitoring, and analyzing governmental performance is as much a part of the landscape of modern public budgeting systems as financial tracking and accounting. Today, there is little issue over whether analysis is useful. The issues are: How should we conduct analysis, and how should we use analysis in the decision-making system?

We discuss three main topics in this chapter. The first section considers the purposes or roles of analysis, the second section reviews analytical techniques, and the third discusses the limitations of analysis within a political framework.

FOCUS OF ANALYSIS

There are as many types of analysis as there are potential subjects for analysis and persons to conduct the analyses. In budgeting and finance, financial analyses can focus on revenue projections, the expected costs of proposed program changes, alternative methods for financing debt, and so on.[1] The concern in this chapter, however, is less with financial matters and more with serving public policy and program goals and objectives. The main emphasis here is on government expenditures, but the revenue side should not be forgotten. Important policy goals, such as redistributing income among groups in society and encouraging increased retirement savings, can be achieved through tax measures, such as progressive income tax rates and expanded individual retirement account incentives, respectively, in addition to expenditure programs that provide benefits to lower-income families or individuals or increased Social Security benefits.

Intellectual Roots

Analysis has many intellectual roots. Chapter 5 noted some of these as they relate to the beginning of program budgeting in the 1950s and 1960s. Several disciplines and cross-disciplinary perspectives have influenced the development of the analysis techniques and perspectives that typically are applied to public sector programs.

Economics. Some argue that analysis of public policies and government programs has its roots in the discipline of economics. Cost-benefit analysis, whose origins are in economics, is an early example of how to improve public policy or program choices by applying an analytical perspective.[2] The tools and concepts of microeconomics, including resource allocation efficiency and the role of government in correcting market failures, have contributed greatly to the increase in use of analysis to decide which programs to fund at what levels. The welfare economics branch of microeconomics particularly concerns identifying and evaluating alternative decisions. Since Keynes, macroeconomic analysis of government's effects on the economy also has played a major role in government policy decisions (see Chapter 15).[3]

Policy Sciences. In the broadest perspective, policy and program analysis is simply using knowledge in public sector decision making. The main question is, how can information or knowledge improve the quality of decision making? We can call this broad perspective *policy sciences*, a term that includes a wide range of types of intellectual inquiry.[4] *Public choice* is another possible unifying term that encompasses numerous forms of analysis. Generally, public choice refers to collective decisions made on behalf of societal interests as distinct from individual choices made in market situations.[5]

Social Sciences. Political science, sociology, and public administration are social science disciplines relevant to policy and program analysis. Political science studies government institutions and processes, including policy formulation and implementation, and individual political behavior. Sociology examines group behavior, including decision making in governments and related bodies.

Public administration or management, of course, is deeply committed to analysis, but whether this field is another social science discipline or is an applied specialty of the traditional social sciences is open to question. Also open is whether distinctions can be made between a public management approach to analysis and a public administration approach. Whatever the case, public administrators engage in a wide range of analyses intended to have impact on policy and program deliberations.

Policy Analysis. Another elusive term is *policy analysis*; it is elusive in the sense of defying simple definition. Policy analysis sometimes refers to the application of rational thought processes to political decisions, but that perspective seems to ignore that analysis and political argument about policy choices cannot be separated so easily.[6] Despite varying formal definitions, the heart of policy analysis is in its product, which is "advice relevant to public decisions."[7] This definition distinguishes policy analysis from academic policy research, social criticism, journalistic investigation, and other activities that may analyze public programs and government successes and failures but do not purport to provide information deliberately to policy makers to aid them in making choices.

A broader term often used in conjunction with policy analysis is *systems analysis* (discussed later in this chapter). One may conduct a systems analysis in the course of policy analysis, but systems analyses also may be carried out in technical, engineering, and other arenas in which *policy* is not relevant. There is no single, widely accepted paradigm that clearly differentiates among policy analysis, systems analysis, and the numerous other terms that are used regularly in discussion of analysis.

Uses of Analysis

Policy Formulation. One way of reducing confusion is to think of how analysis is used. There are several types of uses, the first being policy formulation. Sometimes analysis starts when a problem is identified. One useful form of analysis might focus on the causes of the problem, while other analyses might identify tradeoffs among different options for handling the problem and the probable consequences of selecting among those options.[8] These types of analyses are prospective in that they look at possible events in the future. A good example of the broadest use of analysis in policy formulation is the appointment at the beginning of the Clinton administration in 1993 of a broad-based group to examine the entire array of problems preventing many Americans from gaining access to adequate health care. Initially the advisory group considered a broad array of possible solutions ranging from modest improvements in the private health insurance system to radical changes in methods for reimbursing costs. Ultimately, no recommendation by the group was found acceptable in Congress and no major policy changes came out of the broad-based policy exercise.

Another broad type of policy problem is the illegal use of narcotics; conceivable responses may include a variety of law enforcement and preventive options, such as public education programs aimed at increasing general awareness of the health hazards of drug use. Policy issues associated with this type of social problem might include weighing the merits of law enforcement strategies against the value of strategies to reduce demand for illegal drugs. Other analyses might be more narrowly focused—only on options that relate to law enforcement, for example. Analysis also can be limited by the costs of options, as in the case of only examining drug treatment program options that cost no more than some specified maximum amount.

The uses of policy analysis in broad policy formulation, or policy reform, often are cited as accomplishing major turnarounds in national economic performance.[9] The Chilean economy, one of the most dynamic in Latin America in the 1990s, experienced significant improvement as a result of major policy reforms that decreased the role of government in the economy in general and decentralized many government functions.[10] The adoption of population control policies in Indonesia and Thailand is credited with contributing to substantial economic progress. In Jamaica, in the 1980s, export manufacturing improvements were linked to broad policy reformulation arising from deliberate policy analysis.[11] Contemporary theory guiding development assistance programs for such international agencies as the World Bank and bilateral assistance agencies such as the U.S. Agency for International Development recognizes that the mere transfer of funds, even accompanied by technical assistance, is not sufficient to promote sustainable development in the absence of sustained policy change.[12]

Program Monitoring. A second general type of analysis measures or monitors program results.[13] Lent D. Upson in 1924 wrote, "The budget should be supplemented by an operation audit that will measure the effectiveness of expenditures as thoroughly as the financial audits measure the legality of expenditures."[14] Program monitoring, especially when used in conjunction with a budget system, often focuses on keeping agencies honest in the sense of seeing that promised results are indeed produced with the resources provided. The U.S. General Accounting Office has an important program monitoring function, providing Congress with the data necessary for exercising its legislative oversight responsibilities.[15]

One important consideration, in addition to performance, is the actual implementation process itself. Considerable congressional attention centers on whether or not programs once enacted are being implemented as Congress intended. Another term is *accountability,* which is used to connote that agencies should be held answerable for promised results.

Program Evaluation. The third type of analysis is evaluation of ongoing programs.[16] This type of research can involve a host of research questions. One task of an inquiry may be to look at the intended goals and objectives of a program, since sometimes these are not stated clearly. Former Director of the Budget Charles Schultze suggests, "Systematic analysis does not simply accept objectives as immutably given and then proceed to seek the most effective or efficient means of achieving these objectives. One of its major contributions to the complex decision making process lies precisely in its consideration of both objectives and means, allowing analysis of each to influence the other."[17] Schultze warns that he does not mean that analysts determine objectives for persons in decision-making positions. Analysts may suggest objectives previously not considered, and a good analyst may argue for their importance, but decision makers still have the final choice.

Analysts of course have their own values and cannot be totally neutral in dealing with goals and objectives. At the same time, analysts are "scientific" in their pursuit of knowledge. Social scientists sometimes unrealistically expect greater objectivity of themselves than is possible even in the physical and biological sciences.[18]

When the objectives of a program are unknown or not clearly delineated, the nature of the analysis is more qualitative and less quantitative. This type of research has been called *social evaluation* to distinguish it from *technical evaluation*. An example of technical evaluation might be the examination of an air pollution control program's impact on the environment given the agreed objective of reducing pollutants to a specified maximum level. Social evaluation, in contrast, might include interviewing policy makers and administrators in regard to their objectives in creating and maintaining the pollution program.

Program evaluation as a rigorous analysis of ongoing program costs and results became institutionalized in the federal government in the 1960s. Some legislation, such as that for the Women, Infants and Children Supplemental Feeding Program, contains requirements for a portion of program funds to be spent on research and evaluation. Even congressional critics of many social programs endorse requirements for evaluating program costs and program results. Program evaluation results also can feed into prospective policy analysis.[19]

Service Delivery Alternatives. Analysis also can consider the delivery mechanism for meeting objectives. Obvious choices are the direct delivery of services, delivery in conjunction with another organization (called *coproduction*), contracting with a private for-profit firm or nonprofit agency, leaving it up to private parties without government involvement, and policy setting through regulation.[20] Achieving policy goals by regulation had become such a concern among many advocates of smaller government by the early 1980s that President Reagan ordered agencies to consider the expected costs of regulations before adopting them. Executive Order 12291 required evaluation of costs imposed on the federal government, state and local governments, individuals, and corporations along with the benefits derived for all major regulations. President Clinton strengthened that position on limiting regulation only to that "made necessary by compelling public need . . ." in Executive Order 12866. The Paperwork Reduction Act of 1995 requires federal agencies to analyze the costs and benefits of collecting information from the private sector and from state and local government (see Chapter 10).

Criteria for Judgment in Analysis

Analysis gathers information intended for use in policy and program decision making. The analytical tools of analysis typically organize that information around key concepts that focus attention on the judgments that decision makers have to make. Adoption of a policy change, introduction of a new program, modification of an existing program, and similar decisions may be based on several criteria, including efficiency, effectiveness, productivity, and equity.

Effectiveness and Efficiency. Policy analyses and program evaluations commonly deal with issues of effectiveness and efficiency. The use of resources is considered effective if in fact it has the impact on persons or the environment that was intended. Using effectiveness as a criterion for evaluating a program involves determining that the program does in fact achieve its goals and objectives. In effectiveness analysis, the focus is on program outcomes. For example, health outcomes may be described "in terms of generic health states (including death)."[21] Impact assessments are common types of program evaluations and are designed to help decision makers decide on program continuation or program change. For example, one prenatal health care effort may be favored over another because it achieves a greater reduction in infant mortality.

Judgments of *efficiency* always imply comparison. The focus may be on operational efficiency, such as how best to reduce the cost of a particular activity, or it may be on broader questions, such as how to allocate societal resources to best advantage. Operational efficiency criteria may be used, for example, to choose the most efficient routes for different sizes and types of garbage trucks. Focusing on different ways of allocating resources can aid in determining whether it is really better overall for the economy to undertake a particular public sector expenditure. An expenditure is considered optimally efficient from the total economy's point of view if it results in an excess of benefits over costs that is greater than the excess that would result from spending the same amount in any other way.[22] This is basically the concept of *opportunity cost.* An efficient expenditure is one that does not cause us to forgo an opportunity that would have greater benefits either in the public or the private sector.

Efficiency analysis always involves either direct comparisons among alternatives or indirect comparisons in which the rate of return from a particular public expenditure is compared with the typical rate of return for private investments. A public sector expenditure is said to be efficient if the economic rate of return for the program is equal to or greater than the interest rate that could be earned if the expenditure were simply left to the private sector to invest.[23] We will discuss the concept of *discount rate* in this context in the following section.

Productivity. The terms *productivity analysis* and *performance measurement* also have received much publicity in recent years. Sometimes the terms are used interchangeably and encompass effectiveness and efficiency concerns. On other occasions, the term productivity is restricted to the efficient use of resources in conducting work, with little or no consideration given to results or impacts. The concepts of *reengineering* and *reforming*, at least as they have been applied to government in the 1990s, mainly refer to improving productivity without much focus on the value of results achieved.[24]

Equity. Another concern of evaluation is equity, namely, whether program benefits are distributed according to some concept of fairness.[25] An analysis of special low-interest mortgages subsidized by government might consider how various income groups benefit. Or an analysis might be done of the delivery of city services to poor, middle-income, and upper-income neighborhoods to determine if the distribution of services is fair.

METHODS AND TECHNIQUES OF ANALYSIS

Some policy and program analysis techniques are relatively simple and some are extremely complex. Depending on the precision of policy definition, the susceptibility of the problem to quantification, and the questions asked of the analysis, an analysis might be primarily qualitative in nature or it might be highly quantitative.

Approaches to Analysis

Numerous formulations of analysis describe it as a basic methodology consisting of a number of steps. One basic text divides those steps into two stages: problem analysis and solution analysis.

Problem Analysis
1. understanding the problem
   a. receiving the problem: assessing the symptoms
   b. framing the problem: analyzing market and government failures
   c. modeling the problem: identifying policy variables
2. choosing and explaining relevant goals and constraints
3. choosing a solution method

Solution Analysis

4. choosing evaluation criteria
5. specifying policy alternatives
6. evaluating: predicting impacts of alternatives and valuing them in terms of criteria
7. recommending actions[26]

Throughout these seven steps, analysts find and organize relevant data and theories and use them to estimate future consequences of current and alternative actions. The ultimate step is the communication of recommendations to policy makers. Any reduction of a complex analysis process to a series of steps inevitably oversimplifies. The most important oversimplification perhaps is the implication that analysis is always an ordered process performed by rational analysts, ignoring the reality that analysis takes place in a disorderly, highly political process. Analysis and argumentation over normative issues are entwined. In formulating the problem, in articulating the goals, in choosing evaluation criteria and in recommending actions, the analyst inevitably is a part of the political argument about what should, and should not, be done.[27] Nevertheless, the above outline is useful in calling attention to the several phases of the research process that should not be overlooked.

Analytic Models

Operations Research. Most techniques of analysis predate program budgeting, being derived in large part from such antecedent fields as systems analysis and operations research (OR). Although some consider OR synonymous with the application of the scientific method to problem solving,[28] in the narrower sense in which it was defined in Chapter 5, OR refers to a set of algorithms, generally mathematical, for solving recurrent problems that can be expressed quantitatively. Several types of quantitative problems recur with such frequency in private business applications that prototype models have been developed to solve them. These include problems in allocation, inventory, replacement, queuing, sequencing and coordination, routing, and search. The task of routing overnight express packages efficiently is a good example. Specific techniques for solving these problems include linear programming, queuing theory, Monte Carlo or randomizing methods, and gaming theory.[29]

When government programs involve similar problems, such as problems in transportation scheduling, warehousing, inventory, or other routine tasks, OR techniques readily apply. Problems associated with routing garbage trucks or with mail service, for example, are susceptible to such analytic techniques. The basic requirement for applying them is that a single objective be stated in a quantifiable form. The usual form is to maximize some specific measure of production (output) or to minimize a measure of cost (input). Numerous linear and nonlinear programming techniques also exist for solving *optimization problems* involving multiple inputs and multiple outputs, although interpreting the results is still largely an art rather than science, as these methods yield numerous mathematical solutions as opposed to a single optimal solution.[30]

Systems Analysis. The techniques of OR as well as techniques associated with economics may be used in systems analysis, but a distinguishing feature of systems analysis is that it may deal with issues that go beyond quantitative techniques. For example, OR may aid in designing methods for providing logistical support to combat troops, but systems analysis might go beyond this issue to ask, are there other means of handling a situation that would reduce the need for logistical support? Systems analysis tries to avoid the danger of myopic vision in which techniques are emphasized over purpose and takes a more holistic view of both problem definition and solution.[31]

Cost-Benefit and Cost-Effectiveness Analysis. We can distinguish between cost-benefit and cost-effectiveness analysis.[32] Both attempt to relate costs of programs to performance and both quantify costs in monetary terms, but they differ in the way they measure the outcomes of programs. Cost-effectiveness analysis measures outcomes in quantitative but nonmonetary form. For example, it might focus on the number of lives saved through a highway traffic control program or on the time a new supersonic passenger aircraft saves travelers.

Cost-benefit analysis, on the other hand, measures program outcomes in monetary form, thereby allowing for the development of ratios or other measures of the extent to which returns exceed costs or vice versa. For example, cost-benefit analysis would estimate the dollar value of time to travelers and would use the figure to calculate the dollar value of the time saved by flying on the supersonic aircraft.

The potential merit of cost-benefit analysis over cost-effectiveness analysis is that the former allows for analysis across subject areas. When the expressed ratio of benefits to costs of a program is 1.0, costs are equal to benefits. As the ratio increases, the benefits accruing have increased. In theory, if a supersonic transport program yielded a ratio of 1.7 and a highway traffic control program yielded a ratio of 2.5, then, based on the standard of economic efficiency (and assuming the difference in the magnitude of the programs was not great), government would be advised to favor the traffic control program over the air transportation program. Cost-effectiveness analysis, in contrast, would not allow such direct comparisons because the effects would be expressed in time saved for one program and lives saved for the other.

As noted in Chapter 5, cost-benefit analysis was seen at the time of introducing planning-programming-budgeting (PPB) into government budgetary decision making as a key analytical tool for making rational budget allocation decisions. With the demise of PPB, cost-benefit analyses increasingly were applied only to a limited set of analysis problems. However, in recent years, both cost-benefit and cost-effectiveness analysis have gained some new stature in federal program and policy analyses. Environmental regulations particularly have sparked interest in cost-benefit analysis. Controversy over many Environmental Protection

Agency requirements led Congress to numerous attempts, none of which passed, to require the Environmental Protection Agency to show that environmental regulations not only abate risks but also produce benefits that exceed their costs.[33]

Similarly, cost-effectiveness analysis is being used increasingly in regard to medical devices and pharmaceutical products. In Canada and Australia, drugs are placed on the national health system approved list only after they are shown to be safe and effective and are cost effective. That does not mean the drugs cannot be produced, only that they will not be provided through national health service. While not required in western European countries with national health systems, cost-effectiveness analyses of drugs and medical products are becoming the norm, and in the United States managed care organizations are the stimulus for pharmaceutical companies increasingly using the techniques of cost-benefit and cost-effectiveness analysis to evaluate which drugs and products will be put on their approved lists.[34]

Strategic Analysis. Not all analyses will be as quantitative as the preceding examples suggest. One analytic approach engages decision makers in the process of *scenario writing.* Scenario writing may be an analytic tool itself, or it may be the first stage in a more extensive policy formulation process. It requires policy makers, typically assisted by analysts, to engage in speculative consideration of a plausible sequence of events leading from a current state to alternative end states. A now relatively famous example of scenario planning was undertaken by the Royal Dutch Shell company in the mid-1970s. Although many within the company thought the scenario preposterous, the organization considered what steps should be taken if the major oil producers in the Middle East and Latin America should form a cartel to control the world oil supply. Extensive analysis did not produce a set of firm prescriptions, but prepared Shell decision makers to react quickly and decisively when the seemingly unlikely event actually happened.[35]

Military policy analysts commonly use scenario writing to help identify the circumstances that might lead to committing troops to a hostile situation. The purpose of the scenario writing exercise is to describe a logical sequence of events or circumstances that then would require a response. Thinking out the scenario, the decision-making team may decide to explore ways to prevent the sequence of events from occurring. Or based on the logical outcomes of the scenario exercise, an existing plan for response may be rethought because it may seem, in light of the scenario, to be too drastic a response to a likely sequence of events.

A related perspective looks on analysis, not as a process directed toward finding an optimal allocation of resources, but as an extension of the policy-making institution's strategic planning process. According to this view, the problem definition phase should be more holistic, examining the organization's ability to adapt to its changing environment. A variety of OR and cost-benefit techniques could be used, but the problem would be framed more in systems terms in order to focus on the interaction between the organization and the environment. This approach is useful in directing attention to how the organization might implement a policy change to achieve the desired results. The other analytic approaches tend to stop at the selection of "best choice" and assume that implementation will follow.[36]

Problems in Conducting Analysis

Even though there are different approaches to analysis, several problems are common to most.

Multiple Goals. One common problem in policy and program analysis is that people expect most policies, and even most individual programs, to serve more than one goal. Even when a program's goal is stated in narrow terms, such as reducing the morbidity from childhood diseases through an inoculation program, people may have different reasons for supporting that goal. For example, some may compare the inoculation program with other health measures as a means of decreasing future health costs, but others may evaluate the program as one among several poverty alleviation alternatives. The clearly stated goal, morbidity reduction, in reality reflects more than one goal. In this case, the policy analyst either may have to guess at which goals are more important or may attempt to get explicit weights from the client decision makers in order to carry out the analysis.[37]

The problem of assigning weights among multiple goals reflects the reality that decision makers use different criteria to make policy choices. The political process in most systems deliberately pits various groups against each other, relying on advocacy and checks and balances to protect the public interest. This is the basis for the separation of powers among the executive, legislative, and judicial branches in the U.S. system, and there are similar checks and balances built into most constitutional systems. This political reality requires policy analysis to consider multiple criteria and to consider multiple perspectives on what is the best choice.

Causal Relationships. Closely related to the multiple goals problem is understanding the pattern of causal relationships. In examining alternative programs, the analyst must make some assumptions about causation in order to proceed. But many effects have multiple causes, and sorting out the subset of causes that are under the program's control is not easy. The analyst can rely somewhat on earlier experiences or evaluations of existing programs of similar character for guidance. For example, in analyzing a possible advertising program to persuade smokers to quit, available research on advertising programs aimed at reducing drunk driving may be useful.

Another problem analysts face in understanding the causal relationships involved in a program is that a single evaluation study, unless it is extensive, may be unable to detect relatively small effects. One strategy for addressing this problem is to pool data from many different studies and evaluations of the same program. Called *meta-analysis*, this approach takes advantage of numerous smaller studies to create a larger data set. This helps detect small increments of program impact and helps identify causal relationships.

A good example of a meta-analysis is a study of the DARE program, a drug use prevention program in which police officers work closely with elementary school children. Many specific evaluations of different DARE sites have had difficulty detecting any results. A meta-analysis of many of these evaluations revealed that DARE seems to have little effect on drug use but does seem to increase positive attitudes toward police and to improve youngsters' social skills.[38]

In some cases, there may be little available information from which to assess causal relationships. This is the case particularly when new technologies and materials must be developed as part of the project being analyzed or when the problem is new. Early attempts to understand the means by which human immunodeficiency virus (HIV) infections are transmitted is a good example of a new problem. The analysis of a new fighter aircraft might require an assessment of person-hours, materials, and equipment needed to develop new lightweight metals and design new instrumentation. Estimates must be made of the relationships between resource inputs and technological breakthroughs.

Identifying Costs and Benefits. Then there is the issue of what counts as a cost and a benefit. Determining the financial costs of existing programs is often difficult because accounting systems are designed to produce information by organizational units and not necessarily by program. Only if a program is unique to an organizational unit specified in the accounting system will the financial costs be easy to measure. Even when this matter is resolved, all that is produced are the direct financial expenditures of government rather than costs as would be derived by a cost accounting system (Chapter 11). Indeed, critics often charge that analyses overlook the costs imposed on others. Failure to consider all costs tends to weight the analysis in favor of the proposed project under review.

Related problems are that the financial accounts for a program agency may not distinguish between capital and current costs and may not include services provided to that agency by a central service unit. For example, many evaluations of federal programs involve collecting data on costs and impacts from state and local and even voluntary agencies that are implementing the program. But in one state's accounting system, all the costs of a facility improvement might show up in the budget outlays in the year the improvement is built, whereas in another state the same costs might show up only as a one-year depreciation charge. Similarly, utility costs might be associated with the building that houses the program in one location and might be part of a central account in another location. The analyst must be sure to measure all costs on the same basis across multiple program sites.[39]

Externalities. Indirect costs as well as benefits granted to others are called *externalities*, or *spillover, secondary*, and *tertiary effects*.[40] These are costs and benefits that affect parties other than the ones directly involved. In the private sector, air and water pollution from industrial plants are externalities. The main concern of a private enterprise is making a profit, but part of the cost of production may be imposed on persons living in the area. Residents of the area downstream and downwind of the plant pay the costs of discomfort, poor health, and loss of water recreation opportunities. And they may experience an actual decrease in the value of their assets, such as their homes, if the pollution is bad enough to make it difficult to sell property. If a municipality downstream has to treat water that has been polluted by the plant, the costs imposed are relatively easy to identify.

Most government expenditure decisions involve similar spillover effects. The costs of an urban renewal program are not just the financial outlays required for purchasing and clearing land but also the costs imposed on the families and businesses that must relocate. One government's decision can affect thousands of individuals, businesses, nonprofit organizations, and other governments, including national governments throughout the world.

Some argue that there are no such things as secondary or spillover effects, that all effects of a program should be part of the explicit benefits and costs of that program. The way this is sometimes put is that every affected individual or organization should have *standing* and should thus be taken into account in any analysis of the program.[41] Affected parties are said to be *stakeholders* in that they have interests regarding the outcomes of the program and any decisions that may change it.[42]

Redistributive Effects. Related to spillover costs and benefits are redistributive effects, which analysts once tended to ignore. Now, consideration of major policy changes commonly encompass their potential redistributive effects. For example, the federal budget in recent years has displayed a summary table of the redistributive effects of taxing and spending decisions as part of the budget presentation. Involved here is the matter of whether some groups in the society will benefit more than other groups.[43] In the example of a supersonic transport program mentioned earlier, the program presumably would benefit middle- and upper-income groups who would be the only ones likely to take advantage of this means of transportation. Other criteria for judging redistribution include race, educational level, and occupational class.[44] The effects of programs on different generations in the population have increasingly become a focus of attention.

Common tools for analyzing redistributive effects include *Lorenz curves* and *Gini coefficients of inequality*.[45] A Lorenz curve plots the cumulative percentage of income held by income groups against the cumulative percentage of income groups. For example, in a perfectly equal distribution of income, the lowest population decile in income would have 10 percent of the income, the first and second lowest deciles would have 20 percent of the income, and so forth. That perfectly equal distribution would plot as a straight 45-degree line on an *x,y* graph (Figure 7–1). The difference between the actual plotted Lorenz curve and the perfectly equal distribution is measured as the area between the two curves—the Gini coefficient of inequality.

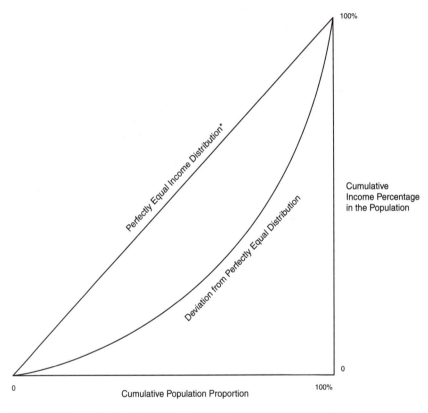

* The first 10% of the population has 10% of the income; the first 50% of the population has 50% of the income; and so forth.

Figure 7–1 Illustration of Lorenz Curve Deviation from Perfect Equality

Subjective Information. Analyses often must rely on subjective, attitudinal data as distinguished from data that gauge behavior. One objective measure of a city road program might be the miles of roads resurfaced while an attitudinal measure might be citizen satisfaction with road conditions. It is indeed possible for citizens (stakeholders) to exhibit no increase in satisfaction even though road conditions may have improved markedly. The same type of situation can develop regarding police protection. Citizens' fear of being burglarized may not decrease despite a decline in the burglary rate. Analytical models such as cost benefit and cost effectiveness are based on rational behavior models in which individuals are presumed to respond to choices based on maximizing their personal utility. Behavioral research calls into question these underlying assumptions with the consequence that a supposedly rational result of policy analysis still may not be the actual preferred result of those affected by the policy.[46]

Internal Validity. When costs, benefits, and expected relationships among them are defined, analysis must consider whether other possible variables may influence outcomes. Such influence is a threat to internal validity. For example, a school program working to increase employment among disadvantaged teenagers may seem to be effective when in fact the program may be having little influence on employment. Any increase in employment might be attributable, not to school district efforts, but to some other program, such as one operated by a nonprofit agency or church. Or a general improvement in the local economy may be increasing the number of jobs for everyone. This type of problem is common in the area of social services, where several agencies may be working with some of the same clients or may be engaged in the joint production of services.

Problems of Quantification

Even if an ideal model is designed displaying all of the relevant types of costs and benefits or effects of a program, the problem of quantifying them remains. What are the monetary costs imposed on families relocated by urban redevelopment activities? Part of the costs will be moving expenses, perhaps higher rents, and greater costs for commuting to work. While these can be measured, it is much more difficult to set a dollar value on the mental anguish of having to move and leave friends behind.

Shadow Pricing. Much of the problem of setting dollar values in the analysis stems from the fact that government programs do not have market prices. Despite various limitations, the private market does provide some standard for measuring the value of goods and services by the prices set for those. Much of analysis in the public sector, however, must impute the prices or values of programs. One such method is known as *shadow pricing.*[47]

Suppose an analyst is given the task of predicting the benefits of a proposed outdoor recreation project. The average hourly value (the shadow price) to a person attending the proposed new public facility can be assumed to be what individuals on the average spend per hour for other similar forms of outdoor recreation. This figure times the number attending will yield an approximate value of the recreational opportunities to be provided by the facility under study.

More detailed approaches can examine each form of outdoor recreation—hiking, swimming, tennis, golfing, picnicking, and so forth. In the case of swimming, the average spent per person for one hour of swimming at a private beach can be imputed to be the value of swimming at a public beach. One danger of such an assumption, however, is that it ignores the possibility that the quality of swimming may be different at the two beaches. If there is a difference, the shadow price should be adjusted accordingly. Another danger is that building the new public swimming facility will change the overall market value of swimming in the area; in that instance, the shadow price must take into account the changes in demand.[48]

Shadow pricing becomes increasingly difficult and the analysis more tenuous when the subject matter for study involves functions that are primarily governmental. There is no apparent method by which a dollar value can be set for the defense capability of killing via intercontinental missiles x million people of an aggressor nation within one hour. Similarly, it is difficult to calculate the dollar value of avoiding one traffic fatality. The calculations employed require assessing what kinds of people are killed in automobile accidents, how old they are, and what income they would have earned in their lifetimes.

Given the questionable assumptions that must be made in estimating the dollar value of saving a life, the argument can be made that cost-effectiveness analysis is preferable to cost-benefit analysis. The former does not attempt to place a dollar value on life but leaves the estimation of that value to decision makers. The disadvantage is that cost-effectiveness analysis, unlike cost-benefit analysis, seldom will yield a single measure of effectiveness. A traffic safety program might be measured by the number of lives saved and by the dollar value of property damage caused by crashes. Like apples and oranges, these benefits cannot be added together.

Contingent Valuation. The amount the public is willing to pay for a particular benefit or to avoid a particular cost also can be measured by means of formal surveys. The methodology, known as *contingent valuation*, describes to survey respondents a particular service or government action and asks through various contingency statements what the respondent would be willing to pay. For example, "Would you be willing to pay a $.75 per day per family fee to avoid the smoke and other pollution emitted by a nearby power plant?" Guidelines for federal government cost-benefit analysis, contained in Office of Management and

Budget (OMB) Circular A-94, recommend willingness to pay as an appropriate concept for measuring costs and benefits. A contingent valuation survey includes a series of questions gradually increasing the price the respondent is asked to consider in order to determine at what price point the survey respondent no longer would be willing to pay. Contingent valuation is used by both government and private industry in the valuation of resource losses due to damages, such as in the *Exxon Valdez* oil spill, and by government to assess the benefits of projected recreational and natural resource preservation programs.[49]

Discount Rates. Another problem for analysis involves the diversion of resources from the private to the public sector and from current consumption to investment in future returns. Investment in a public project or program is warranted only if the returns are greater than they would be if the same funds were left to the private sector and if the future returns are worth the current sacrifice. Thus, the relevant concept of the cost of a public expenditure is the value of the benefits forgone by not leaving the money in the private sector to be consumed or invested.

A dollar diverted from the private to the public sector is not just an equivalent dollar cost or dollar benefit forgone. Presumably, had the dollar not been collected as taxes, it would have been available for the private citizen's use in some enjoyable, immediate consumption. Or it would have been available for the private citizen to invest in some kind of interest-bearing security. If the tax is used to finance a public project that produces a benefit to that citizen, or to citizens in general, then the benefit may offset the sacrifice the taxpayer had to make in private consumption or investment. But what if the public benefit occurs at some future time, whereas the private consumption would have been in the more or less immediate time period? The future public benefit even if it could be said to be exactly equal to the benefit of private consumption will not be as valuable because of the simple fact of its being postponed into the future. Some charge must be made against that dollar removed from consumption to arrive at the current value of future consumption forgone. This charge is known as the *discount* or *interest rate.*

The discount rate serves two purposes. First, it is similar to an interest charge that reflects the cost of removing a dollar from private sector use and diverting it to the public sector. If a dollar could earn 6 percent in the private sector, investment in the public sector would be warranted (in an economic sense) only if the rate of return from the public investment would be at least 6 percent. Second, the discount rate must take into consideration the time pattern of expenditures and returns. In general, people prefer present consumption to future consumption. A dollar that might be spent for current consumption is worth more than a dollar that might be consumed 10 years from now. Normally people do not willingly save unless they receive interest in compensation for the temporary loss of consumption. A discount rate, then, provides a means of showing the present value of dollars to be spent or returned in the future.

The relationships among costs, returns, and time are depicted graphically in Figure 7–2. Most investment projects involve heavy capital costs early on, followed by a tapering off to operating costs. Returns are nonexistent or minimal for the first few years and then increase rapidly. The shape of the return curve after the initial upturn depends on the nature of the particular investment and is drawn arbitrarily for illustrative purposes in the figure. The comparison of costs to benefits over time makes the necessity for discounting obvious. Higher costs occur earlier in most projects. The higher benefits that occur later are valued less because they occur later in time.

Costs and benefits must therefore be compared for each time period (usually each year), and the differences summed over the life span of the project. That is in essence what a discount rate accomplishes. The longer it takes for returns to occur, the more their value is discounted. In effect, it is compound interest in reverse. Costs occurring earlier are subject to less discounting. Thus, for a project

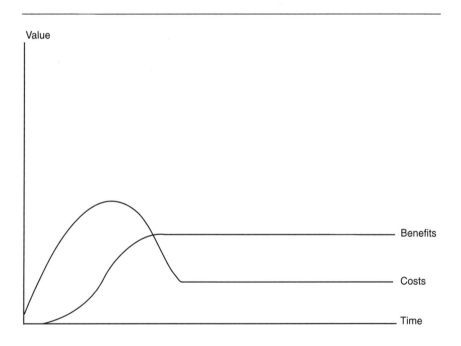

Figure 7–2 Relationship of Costs and Benefits to Time. The value scale is expressed in common units, usually dollars. The time scale goes from one unit, such as one year, through the expected life span of the project.

to be economically feasible, total discounted benefits must exceed total discounted costs. This excess of discounted benefits over discounted costs is known as the *net present value*. Government expenditures are efficient allocations of a society's resources when the net present value is positive.

It is obvious that the choice of a discount rate has an important influence on investment decisions. Too low a rate understates the value of current consumption or of leaving the money to the private sector. Too high a rate uneconomically favors current consumption over future benefits and results in less investment than is worthwhile. The choice of a discount rate may thus determine the outcome of the analysis.

Selecting appropriate discount rates is difficult. Private market rates are inappropriate because they include calculations of the risks of loss involved in making loans. On the other hand, interest rates charged governments often are artificially low because of various guarantees against defaults and sometimes the loans' tax-exempt status. The appropriate discount rate lies between these extremes. OMB annually provides guidance to federal agencies on the discount rates that should be used for federal projects (Appendix C, Circular A-94). In early 1997, the discount rate for costs and benefits over a 10-year period, for example, was 5.6 percent, the equivalent nominal interest rate for a 10-year federal Treasury bond.[50]

Several discount rates may be applied to program alternatives to determine the *sensitivity* of the analysis to discounting. If the cost-benefit ratios of a project are well above 1.0 regardless of the discount rate used, there is little problem, but a different situation arises if some plausible discount rates yield results well below 1.0. In other situations, one discount rate might result in a favorable cost-benefit ratio for alternative A and another ratio for alternative B. The point is that an arbitrary choice of a discount rate without consideration of other ranges can produce misleading results.

Problems of Implementation

Analyses that are conducted with due regard to all the preceding issues will not ensure that the intended effectiveness, efficiency, or equity gains in fact are achieved. Cost-effectiveness analysis, cost-benefit analysis, and other analyses conducted at the policy formulation or program design stage are worthless unless the implementing public agency is capable of carrying out the program. For that reason, analysts now pay increased attention to the various factors that will influence implementation once the program is started. One of the more consistent findings from research on implementation is that involvement of the intended clients or beneficiaries of the program in its design is one of the most important factors affecting the achievement of intended results.[51] Involvement of the client at the design stage helps ensure that factors affecting success are accounted for and helps mold the program to the needs as perceived by the beneficiaries rather than by the bureaucrats. Continued involvement of the program beneficiaries in modifying the design of the program as it is implemented is one aspect of the application of concepts such as total quality management to government programs.[52]

ORGANIZATIONAL LOCUS AND USE OF ANALYSIS

Analytic Units

With the increasing interest in analysis has come a proliferation of analytic units. Central budget offices, other central units such as planning departments, line agencies, and offices of inspectors general have developed analytic capabilities. Legislative analytic units have been established. The 1974 Congressional Budget and Impoundment Control Act specifically empowered standing committees and the comptroller general to "review and evaluate the results of Government programs and activities." The Congressional Budget Office, which initially restricted its work to economic trend analysis, has broadened its scope to include policy and program analysis. State legislative staff units, such as the Virginia Legislative Audit and Review Commission, have gained national prominence in the field of program evaluation. Just as with the U.S. General Accounting Office transition, many state audit agencies have incorporated analyses of economy and efficiency into their traditional auditing roles.[53] While federal line agencies led the way in formal evaluation of their programs in the 1970s, the subsequent years have seen a drastic decline in executive branch evaluation.

Part of the decrease in federal program evaluation we can attribute to a shift in focus. In the 1970s, the major federal anti-poverty programs were the focal points of large-scale, longitudinal studies. Some of the largest social science research projects ever conducted were evaluations of the income maintenance and housing allowance experiments funded in the 1970s by the Departments of Health and Human Services and Housing and Urban Development, respectively. Then, along with significant reorientation of the role of the federal government, the Reagan administration shifted the focus from the impacts of federal programs to more management-oriented studies of administrative efficiency—how to reduce the costs of federal programs.[54] This resulted in the significant decrease in executive agency use of large-scale program evaluation research studies but growth in the role of offices of inspectors general as they performed more management-oriented program reviews.[55]

Analysis had become widespread at the state level by the beginning of the 1990s, but seems to be declining somewhat now, as revealed by surveys of state budget offices. Whereas in 1970 only 18 percent of state budget offices reported that they conducted effectiveness program analysis, by 1990, 66 percent reported engaging in such analysis. In 1995, that figure had dropped to only 46 percent. Similar patterns are observed for conducting productivity analysis—31 percent in 1970, a whopping 94 percent in 1990, and a drop to 72 percent in 1995.[56] To some extent, the decline in state government budget agencies' conduct of analysis has been offset by increased program analysis in other central agencies, but there seems no doubt that state executive agencies have decreased their reliance on analysis in the budgetary process. This shows up, for example, in the decrease in the presentation of program information in budget requests (see Chapter 5). Local governments also engage in analysis, but many are too small to be able to afford large analytic staffs.

Greater dissemination of analyses may be of help in allowing more than one community to benefit from the findings of a given study. While some cities may be reluctant to apply the results achieved in other cities, comparison with comparable communities is irresistible to many local politicians. Popularized in the management literature as *benchmarking*, the idea of seeing what other communities have achieved as an aid in one's own local decision-making process is entrenched. Comparisons with other school districts' capital expenditures for school construction, for example, changed one county commission's near unanimous opposition to a bond issue for school construction to near unanimous support for putting the bond issue on the ballot.[57]

Universities and contract research organizations also perform analyses of various kinds. Faculty and staff in a wide range of research and academic units conduct research that is of direct relevance to policy deliberations in government. Contract research organizations conduct research relevant to policy issues for a wide variety of clients.

A consistent finding from World Bank project preparation activities has been that many developing countries lack a strong analytic unit capable of evaluating the possible consequences of alternative policy decisions. Somewhat greater institutional capacity for conducting project analyses to assess the financial and economic impact of pending projects exists in most developing countries, but even that capacity is plagued by lack of coordination among different agencies.

Regardless of the location of the analytic unit, it necessarily has limited resources and must choose carefully the targets of analysis. If an analytic unit in a government commits all of its resources to one study each year, that means many programs will go unreviewed. At the opposite extreme, numerous "quick-and-dirty" studies can be conducted in a year, but at the risk of excessive superficiality. Central analytic units may use a mixed strategy of conducting brief analyses and more thorough analyses and diversifying them over a wide range of programs and departments. Criteria used in selecting targets for analysis include the dollar magnitude of programs and the political feasibility of changing them.

Analysis in Decision Making

Producing reports and studies is not the same as using them in policy deliberations. In the state budget office survey mentioned above, only 18 percent of the
states reported that executive budget decisions were based substantially on effectiveness analyses, and 30 percent used productivity analyses to a substantial
degree. These 1995 results, as with the decline in conduct of analysis, were down
from a previous trend in increasing use of analysis in decision making. Another
53 and 54 percent of the states, respectively, reported analyses being used somewhat in executive decision making, also down from previous years.[58] The complaint from analysts that their findings and recommendations are often unheeded
is common.

One reason for the limited use of analyses may be the analyses themselves.
Any decision maker needs to examine an analysis before using it. Of course, the
analytic process requires an initial selection of possible causal relationships to
consider and benefits and costs to count, and this obviously occurs before the
decision maker sees the analysis results. The decision maker needs to maintain a
healthy skepticism and be aware of the technical difficulties, discussed in the preceding section, that might influence or determine the outcome of a study. The
database of a study may have been weak, resulting in highly qualified and tentative conclusions; in such a case the decision maker will probably rely on his or
her hunches more than on those of the analysts. Further, the analysts themselves
are acutely aware of the political realities involved in budgetary decisions, and
blend both political issues as well as economic issues in their analyses, leading
decision makers to treat the analyses not as answers to their policy questions but
as additional data to be considered.[59]

Some analyses may be self-serving, produced by analysts eager to secure funding for their departments. A state department of transportation study that concludes that the department needs more funds may be the product of overzealous
analysts eager to serve the needs of their department. Analysts face serious ethical conflicts over loyalty to their agencies and loyalty to some degree of objectivity.

There are many other factors that can make an analysis of limited use. The
topic may be politically too hot or excessively trivial for decision makers to act
upon. If research reports are not relevant to decision makers, the reports will not
be used. Sometimes "windows" open on program areas in which major decisions
can be made—at which time analyses can be influential. At other times, these
same program areas are unlikely to be influenced greatly by analyses because of

political conditions. Overtly including political factors into the analysis, involving decision makers in assigning weights to those factors, and linking evaluation researchers more closely to the program and policy issues they are being asked to address may increase the likelihood that even intensely political decisions will to some extent be affected by more objective analysis.[60]

Beyond the analyses is the nature of the decision system. It may be that a program budget system, for instance, is more likely to use available analyses because the decision structure is specifically geared to that. However, most budget systems may be biased largely in favor of maintaining existing programs and organizations. It is possible that analyses often are directed toward revising and perhaps salvaging existing operations rather than toward exploring alternative opportunities for dealing with society's problems.

Analyses of major projects have far greater appeal than more mundane operational analyses of ongoing activities. It is much more satisfying to analysts to be involved in a major study of a controversial new program than to be conducting detailed analyses of costs and outputs of a necessary but long-standing program. However, much of what government does consists of day-in and day-out continuation of basic operational processes, such as cleaning out and maintaining the city's storm sewers, and analyses of these operational activities can discover important economies of operation.[61]

The organizational location of analytic units can sometimes virtually ensure visibility or obscurity for their products. An analytic unit buried in an agency is unlikely to have much influence on decision making. Having an analytic unit within a budget office can give it visibility but, on the other hand, can result in analysts' being regularly assigned to deal with brush fires so that no time is left for analysis.

The political and administrative cultures of a government and the agencies within it influence the use of analysis. Some units operate in an environment where analysis and the use of information is taken as a given, whereas other organizations find analysis to be a new commodity. The use of analysis is related to the incentives for conducting it. There is an inherent tension between the manager's job and the evaluator's job. The program manager feels that the evaluator demands unreasonable standards of social scientific rigor to "prove the program is working," while the evaluator often feels the manager is too quick to rely on unscientific anecdotal evidence.[62] Furthermore, analytical studies can identify ways to reduce costs, but if such studies result in agency budget cuts, then there is little incentive for agencies to perform them.

Evaluations may be mandated by legislatures, but executive agencies may be reluctant to conduct these with vigor, since most, if not all, analyses are regarded as threats. Negative findings are seen as indicators of administrators' failures and can be used as the rationale for budget cuts. This is related to a more general observation that program managers should have permission to experiment and to fail. Managers will resist analysis as long as any admission that a program is not working as it was originally intended is taken as evidence that the program should be eliminated rather than as an opportunity to redesign or to learn from failures.[63]

Implementation of analysis is further complicated by interagency and intergovernmental relations. The benefits of an improved municipal law enforcement program may not be realized if courts are unable to cope with increased numbers of arrests and prosecutions (assuming that increased arrests yield reductions in crime). Moreover, societal problems do not respect political boundaries, and problems do not coincide with each other. One mix of government units may be appropriate for dealing with air pollution problems and another for dealing with physical health. The increasing partnership between government and community groups such as volunteer associations further complicates analysis, as the number of actors involved in a program and the actions they take may be difficult to determine during the course of a program evaluation.

Institutionalizing the Use of Analysis

In addition to institutionalizing analysis through the creation of analytic units within agencies, within central budget offices, and within groups supporting legislatures, increasing use of analysis can be seen in the trend to make performance measures as integral a part of government reporting as financial statements.[64] Long recommended by the General Accounting Office, the inclusion of program performance measures as part of federal agency financial reporting practices now is mandated by the Government Performance and Results Act of 1993 (see Chapter 5).[65] Similarly, the Governmental Accounting Standards Board has considered performance reporting standards for state and local governments.[66]

The adoption of formal standards and the imposition of regular reporting requirements for government financial accounts (see Chapter 11) contributed to the increase in cost analysis and other financial analysis of government programs. Regular reporting on the service accomplishments of government agencies could similarly lead to an increase in the analysis of the results of government expenditures. To the extent that performance indicators measure program outputs, the types of analysis will be of government productivity or operational performance. To the extent that performance indicators focus on the impacts on the intended beneficiaries, the types of analysis will be of governmental effectiveness.

The more extensive the regular capture of information on the outputs and outcomes of government programs at the time the events occur, the less costly the analysis. Prospective analyses of the potential results of pending programs typically rely on analytical models to extrapolate the results from similar programs to the new programs. Research in this type of prospective analysis tends to be reviews of previous analyses. Evaluation of program outcomes, after programs already are operating, can be expensive and time consuming. Often external contractors are hired by government agencies to send teams to collect extensive field data, frequently after some records are no longer maintained or after the opportunity to structure recordkeeping related to program results has been missed. Designing evaluations into a pilot or demonstration program as part of program implementation puts the evaluation contractor, the implementing agency, and the sponsoring funding source together at the beginning of program implementation and allows them to structure data collection that will be useful for evaluating the program's operations and results on a continuing basis.[67]

These trends undoubtedly will increase the use of analysis in decision making. But they will not cause analysis to supplant political judgment. Government will continue to weave analysis into the fabric of public sector decision making—but as a tool to enhance judgment rather than as a substitute.

SUMMARY

There are related but divergent fields of study that impinge upon analysis. Included are policy science and public choice and the disciplines of political science, sociology, economics, and public administration or management. Operations research and systems analysis are also included.

Much of this chapter has focused on cost-benefit and cost-effectiveness analysis. These are similar, except that cost-benefit analysis quantifies program outcomes in monetary terms whereas cost-effectiveness analysis quantifies outcomes in programmatic terms, such as the number of lives saved. Many of the problems associated with analysis relate to the assumptions that must be made in order to derive cost and benefit data, particularly through the use of shadow prices and discount rates.

Numerous political and institutional factors limit the use of analysis. Because analysis is part of the political process, some analyses will undoubtedly be designed to produce the desired conclusions. Even when studies conclude that existing programs are not yielding the intended impacts, these studies can serve as justification for expanding rather than shrinking these programs. Beyond the politics of the situation are institutional constraints that deter the translation of analytic findings into program decisions for the coming budget year. Analysis is now a maturing field; gone is the era in which analysis was viewed as a novel activity.

NOTES

1. R. Berne, Governmental Accounting and Financial Reporting and the Measurement of Financial Condition, in *The Handbook of Municipal Bonds and Public Finance*, eds. R. Lamb, J. Leigland, and S. Rappaport (New York: New York Institute of Finance, 1993), 257–315.

2. Prest and Turvey, in their survey of cost-benefit analysis, date program analysis in the United States back to the River and Harbor Act of 1902, which required analysis of the costs of river and harbor projects undertaken by the Army Corps of Engineers in comparison with the amount of commerce benefited by these projects. A.R. Prest and R. Turvey, Cost-Benefit Analysis: A Survey, *The Economic Journal* 75 (1965): 683–735.

3. D.N. Hyman, *Public Finance: A Contemporary Application of Theory to Policy*, 5th ed. (New York: Dryden, 1996).

4. Credit for "inventing" the term *policy sciences* often goes to H.D. Lasswell, The Policy Orientation, in *The Policy Sciences*, eds. D. Lerner and H.D. Lasswell (Stanford, CA: Stanford University Press, 1951), 3–15; see P. Deleon, Reinventing the Policy Sciences: Three Steps Back to the Future, *Policy Sciences* 27 (1994): 77–95.

5. I. McLean and A.B. Urken, eds., *Classics of Social Choice* (Ann Arbor: University of Michigan Press, 1993).

6. F. Fischer and J. Forester, eds., Editors' Introduction, in *The Argumentative Turn in Policy Analysis and Planning* (Durham, NC: Duke University Press, 1993), i–ix.

7. D.L. Weimer and A.R. Vining, *Policy Analysis: Concepts and Practice*, 2nd ed. (Englewood Cliffs, NJ: Prentice Hall, 1992), 1.

8. S.J. Irving, *Budget Process: History and Future Directions* (Washington, DC: U.S. Government Printing Office, 1995), 5.

9. J.P. Chudy, Political Management and Economic Policy Reform: An Exploration of Structural Adjustment Experience, *Public Budgeting and Financial Management* 6 (1994): 542–565.

10. D. Hachette and R. Luders, *Privatization in Chile: An Economic Appraisal* (San Francisco: ICS Press, 1993).

11. M.S. Grindle and J.W. Thomas, *Public Choices and Policy Change: The Political Economy of Reform in Developing Countries* (Baltimore: Johns Hopkins University Press, 1991).

12. L.A. Crouch, E. Vegas, and R.W. Johnson, *Educational Policy Dialogue in Latin America* (Research Triangle Park, NC: Research Triangle Institute, 1992).

13. K.E. Newcomer, Opportunities and Incentives for Improving Program Quality: Auditing and Evaluating, *Public Administration Review* 54 (1994): 147–154.

14. L.D. Upson, Half-Time Budget Methods, *Annals* 113 (1924): 74.

15. G.L. Dodaro, *Managing for Results: Strengthening Financial and Budgetary Reporting* (Washington, DC: U.S. Government Printing Office, 1995).

16. E. Vedung, *Public Policy and Program Evaluation* (New Brunswick, NJ: Transaction, 1997).

17. C.L. Schultze, *The Politics of Economics of Public Spending* (Washington, DC: Brookings Institution, 1968), 65.

18. H.K. Colebatch, Organizational Meanings of Program Evaluation, *Policy Sciences* 28 (1995): 149–164.

19. D. Mathiasen, The Separation of Powers and Political Choice: Budgeting, Auditing and Evaluation in the United States, in P. Gray et al., *Budgeting, Auditing and Evaluation: Functions and Integration in Seven Governments* (New Brunswick, NJ: Transaction, 1993).

20. C.C. Barnett and R.W. Johnson, *Urban Services Delivery in Central and Eastern Europe and the Newly Independent States* (Research Triangle Park, NC: Research Triangle Institute, 1996); R.W. Johnson and J.S. McCullough, Case Study on Urban Local Government Finance (Paper presented at the Asian Development Bank seminar on Urban Infrastructure Finance in Asia, Research Triangle Institute, Research Triangle Park, NC, April 17, 1996).

21. M.R. Gold et al., Identifying and Valuing Outcomes, in *Cost-Effectiveness in Health and Medicine*, eds. M.R. Gold et al. (New York: Oxford, 1996), 83.

22. T.F. Nas, *Cost-Benefit Analysis: Theory and Application* (Thousand Oaks, CA: Sage, 1996).

23. A. Wildavsky, The Political Economy of Efficiency: Cost Benefit Analysis, Systems Analysis, and Program Budgeting, *Public Budgeting and Financial Management* 1 (1989): 1–41 (originally published in *Public Administration Review*, December 1966, 292–310).

24. P.F. Drucker, Reinventing Government, in P.F. Drucker, *Managing in a Time of Great Change* (New York: Truman Talley Books, 1995), 285–306.

25. J. Rawls, *Political Liberalism* (New York: Columbia University Press, 1993).

26. Weimer and Vining, *Policy Analysis*, 205.

27. J.S. Dryzek, Policy Analysis and Planning: From Science to Argument, in Fischer and Forester, *The Argumentative Turn in Policy Analysis and Planning*, 213–232.

28. R.L. Ackoff and M.W. Sasieni, *Fundamentals of Operations Research* (New York: Wiley, 1968).

29. F. Hillier and G. Lieberman, *Introduction to Operations Research*, 6th ed. (New York: McGraw-Hill, 1995).

30. H.O. Fried et al., *The Measurement of Production Efficiency* (New York: Oxford, 1993).

31. P.M. Senge, *The Fifth Discipline: The Art and Practice of the Learning Organization* (New York: Doubleday, 1990).

32. Nas, *Cost-Benefit Analysis*, 2–3.

33. Bills HR 690, HR 961, HR 1022 S 100, S 123, S 221, S 229, S 343.

34. J.L. Bootman et al., *Principles of Pharmacoeconomics*, 2nd ed. (Cincinnati, OH: W. Harvey Whitney Books, 1996).

35. P. Schwartz, *The Art of the Long View* (New York: Doubleday, 1991).

36. D.L. Weimer, The Current State of Design Craft: Borrowing, Tinkering and Problem Solving, *Public Administration Review* 53 (1993): 110–120.

37. Vedung, *Public Policy and Program Evaluation*.

38. S.T. Ennett et al., How Effective Is Drug Abuse Resistance Education? A Meta-Analysis of Project DARE Outcome Evaluations, *American Journal of Public Health* 84 (1994): 1394–1401.

39. B.J. Hayward, *A Longitudinal Study of the Vocational Rehabilitation Service Program: Third Interim Report* (Washington, DC: U.S. Department of Education, 1997).

40. Hyman, *Public Finance*, 87–122.

41. D. Whittington and D. MacRae, Jr., The Issue of Standing in Cost-Benefit Analysis, *Journal of Policy Analysis and Management* 5 (1986): 665–682; W.N. Trumbull, Who Has Standing in Cost-Benefit Analysis? *Journal of Policy Analysis and Management* 9 (1990): 201–218.

42. J.A. Altman and E. Petkus, Jr., Toward a Stakeholder-Based Policy Process: An Application of the Social Marketing Perspective to Environmental Policy Development, *Policy Sciences* 27 (1994): 37–51.

43. A. Wildavsky, Political Implications of Budget Reform: A Retrospective, *Public Administration Review* 52 (1992): 597.

44. R.W. Johnson and J.M. Pierce, The Economic Evaluation of Policy Impacts: Cost-Benefit and Cost Effectiveness Analysis, in *Methodologies for Analyzing Public Policies*, eds. F.P. Scioli, Jr., and T.J. Cook (Lexington, MA: Lexington Books, 1975), 131–154.

45. R. Hemming and D.P. Hewitt, The Distributional Impact of Public Expenditures, in *Public Expenditure Handbook: A Guide to Public Policy Issues in Developing Countries*, eds. K. Chu and R. Hemming (Washington, DC: International Monetary Fund, 1991), 119–129.

46. J.L. Knetsch, Assumptions, Behavioral Findings and Policy Analysis, *Journal of Policy Analysis and Management* 14 (1995): 68–78.

47. R.N. McKean, The Use of Shadow Prices, in *Problems in Public Expenditure Analysis*, ed. S.B. Chase, Jr. (Washington, DC: Brookings Institution, 1968), 33–65; T. Boeri, *Beyond the Rule of Thumb: Methods for Evaluating Public Investment Projects* (Boulder, CO: Westview Press, 1990).

48. Nas, *Cost-Benefit Analysis*, 97–99.

49. W.H. Desvousges et al., *Measuring Nonuse Damages Using Contingent Valuation: An Experimental Evaluation of Accuracy*, Monograph 92-1 (Research Triangle Park, NC: Research Triangle Institute, 1992).

50. OMB Circular A-94, *Appendix C, Discount Rates for Cost-effectiveness, Lease Purchase, and Related Analyses*: http://www.whitehouse.gov/WH/EOP/OMB/html/circulars/a094/a094/html; accessed May 1997.

51. J.C. Thomas, Public Involvement and Governmental Effectiveness: A Decision-Making Model for Public Managers, *Administration and Society* 24 (1993): 444–469.

52. D. Osborne and P. Plastrik, *Banishing Bureaucracy: The Five Strategies for Reinventing Government* (New York: Addison-Wesley, 1997).

53. R.T. Wagner, Jr., and R.M. Malan, Economy and Efficiency Auditing: Difficult, Doable and Cost-Effective in the State of Delaware, *Government Finance Review* 11 (February 1995): 11–16.

54. R.C. Rist, The Organization and Function of Evaluation in the United States: A Federal Overview, in *Program Evaluation and the Management of Government*, ed. R.C Rist (New Brunswick, NJ: Transaction, 1990), 1–17.

55. K.E. Newcomer, Opportunities and Incentives for Improving Program Quality, 148.

56. R.D. Lee, Jr., The Use of Program Analysis in State Budgeting: Changes Between 1990 to 1995, *Public Budgeting & Finance* 17 (1997): 18–36.

57. L.S. Stewart and R.W. Johnson, *Can Vance County Afford a New School Bond? An Independent Analysis of Vance County's Comparative Ability to Finance School Improvements* (Research Triangle Park, NC: Research Triangle Institute, 1995).

58. R.D. Lee, Jr. A Quarter Century of State Budgeting Practices, *Public Administration Review* 57 (1997): 133–140.

59. K. Thurmaier, Decisive Decision Making in the Executive Budget Process: Analyzing the Political and Economic Propensities of Central Budget Bureau Analysts, *Public Administration Review* 55 (1995): 448–460.

60. F.P. Williams III et al., Barriers to Effective Performance Review: The Seduction of Raw Data, *Public Administration Review* 54 (1994): 537–542.

61. D.N. Ammons, Overcoming the Inadequacies of Performance Measurement in Local Government: The Case of Libraries and Leisure Services, *Public Administration Review* 55 (1995): 37–47.

62. E. Albaek, Between Knowledge and Power: Utilization of Social Science in Public Policy Making, *Policy Sciences* 28 (1995): 79–100.

63. R.A. Pielke, Jr., Usable Information for Policy: An Appraisal of the U.S. Global Change Research Program, *Policy Sciences* 28 (1995): 39–77.

64. G.T. Henry and K.C. Dickey, Implementing Performance Monitoring: A Research and Development Approach, *Public Administration Review* 53 (1993): 203–212; U.S. Congressional Budget Office, *Using Performance Measures in the Federal Budget Process* (Washington, DC: U.S. Government Printing Office, 1993).

65. J.F. Hinchman, *Managing for Results: Using GPRA to Assist Congressional and Executive Branch Decisionmaking* (Washington, DC: U.S. Government Printing Office, 1997).

66. J. Harris, Service Efforts and Accomplishments Standards: Fundamental Questions of an Emerging Concept, *Public Budgeting & Finance* 15 (Winter, 1995): 18–37.

67. General Accounting Office, *Agencies' Strategic Plans under GPRA: Key Questions to Facilitate Congressional Review* (Washington, DC: U.S. Government Printing Office, 1997).

CHAPTER 8

Budget Approval:
The Role of the Legislature

The struggle over the budget has only begun when the budget document goes to the legislative body. Executive budget preparation at the state and federal levels will have consumed months, but the product of the process is only a proposal. The distinction between preparation and approval is alluded to by the phrase "the executive proposes and the legislature disposes." The process is different from that used in parliamentary governments such as the British one, in which the executive and legislative functions are controlled by the same political party. In such systems, the approval phase is largely pro forma. Parliaments generally can alter the government's budget but often are prohibited from increasing it. Party discipline generally means that the changes made by a parliament are typically minor. In the United States, however, the legislative body may approve a budget that diverges in important respects from the budget proposed by the executive.

In this chapter, major emphasis is given to the similarities in the approval phase across levels of government—local, state, and federal. The next chapter, in contrast, focuses exclusively on Congress, because that body is unique in the American political system and has unique budgetary roles, procedures, and problems.

This chapter has two main sections. The first discusses the parameters that constrain how legislative bodies operate and the processes used in approving government budgets. The second section examines the relationships between the legislative and executive branches and the changing role of the legislature as an overseer of the executive branch.

PARAMETERS

Legislative Characteristics

Legislative bodies—city councils, school boards, state legislatures, and Congress—sometimes have had a reputation for being relatively weak, ineffective bodies, but that perception has been changing, especially since the 1970s. Legislative bodies at all levels of government are reasserting their authority to set policy and are taking measures to increase their ability to wield the powers granted to them.

Economic Environment. As with all human enterprise, legislative bodies must operate within a set of parameters; these greatly constrain how they approve the budgets. One of the most important constraints is the economic environment, both short and long term. How a legislative body approaches the task of passing a budget is influenced greatly by whether a surplus of revenues is projected or whether sizable cuts must be made to bring expenditures down to meet anticipated reductions in revenues.

Previous Decisions. Before a local legislative body commences considering the budget, many decisions already will have been made. As explained in previous chapters, the state will have imposed a variety of mandates. A school district will be told how many days it must operate in a school year, possibly what the minimum salaries should be for teachers at different levels, and what courses must be taught. Over half of a school district's budget typically comes from state aid, which greatly reduces what the school district can decide on its own. The state also will have imposed limits on taxation and borrowing authority for each type of local government and may deny taxing power to some jurisdictions, as is sometimes the case with special districts.

Just as many decisions already will have been made before a local legislative body begins its deliberations, so will many decisions have been made for state legislatures and Congress. Entitlement laws that provide open-ended benefits to individuals, such as guaranteed payments to all persons qualifying for disability benefits under Social Security, greatly curtail what Congress can do in a given year.[1] Similarly, some federal grant programs to state and local governments have been on a permanent appropriation basis, providing for no input from Congress over a period of several years. Federal highway funding is an example. State legislatures face this same situation, most notably in the case of aid to local school districts. Additionally, courts force legislative bodies to take actions, as in such situations as legislatures having to revise state funding formulas for school districts in order to comply with court orders (see Chapter 4).

Representation of Interests. Socioeconomic and political diversity influence legislative behavior. At the national level, Congress must deal with a broad range of issues and associated interest groups. States tend to be less diverse and therefore tend to have fewer interest groups that press their preferences upon legislatures; this situation can allow for a relatively few number of interests to influence legislation.[2] The concentration of influence can be even greater at the local level, as in the case of a town that is dominated by a single employer.

Citizen initiatives, allowable in many states, constitute another set of parameters that can have major impacts on the legislative bodies responsible for approving budgets.[3] Under the initiative process, citizens have the power to legislate changes, often by making amendments to state constitutions; if citizens are dissatisfied with tax rates, as was frequently the case in the 1970s, voters may approve new limits on taxes that force jurisdictions to cut tax rates and spending. In 1994, California voters approved Proposition 187, greatly restricting the expenditure of funds for services to illegal immigrants.[4]

The news media are important influences on legislatures. The media bring issues to the public's attention, help frame those issues and their solutions, and focus attention on legislatures in their efforts to resolve issues. However, newspapers, local radio and television stations, and the news networks vary in their abilities to understand complex budget matters and to convey information to the public.[5] The media can be important sources of misinformation as well as information regarding public budgeting and finance.

A responsibility—if not the chief responsibility—of legislators is to represent their constituents. Decisions on the budget can have major positive and negative effects on a legislator's constituents. Although a legislator may be generally in favor of reduced government spending, one common exception is any budget reduction in the legislator's district. Positive budget decisions—increases in government spending or fending off possible decreases in spending—are seen by every office-holder as essential for gaining re-election, which itself is seen as of paramount importance. One hardly can be an effective legislator if one fails to be re-elected to office.

Representation sometimes can be considered along generational lines. Most legislative bodies include new, younger members who may have a zeal for reforming existing processes, including budgeting. Younger members may see their elections as mandates for representing their generation's needs.[6]

Legislative Apportionment. How the duty of representation is met is influenced by how legislators are elected to their jobs. The Supreme Court ruled in the 1960s that state legislatures must have district lines drawn that are proportional to population. The effect has been to apportion legislative election districts on a population basis and in turn to reduce substantially what was once over-representation of rural interests and to increase representation of urban and suburban areas in states.[7]

Local governments are undergoing similar changes. City councils are changing from using at-large seats, because this procedure tends to result in under-representation of minority interests. The movement is to *single-member districts* based on neighborhood populations or a combination of these and at-large seats.[8] Legislative bodies are increasingly diverse in terms of gender and minority representation, although the distinct influence that women and minority legislators have on the legislative process is uncertain.[9]

Race is of great concern regarding how district boundaries are drawn. In an earlier time when efforts were made to deliberately under-represent the interests of minorities, boundaries were drawn such that minority neighborhoods were carved into small segments and then apportioned to several districts. This helped to ensure that a minority person would never be elected to represent any of the districts. In contemporary times, efforts have been made to help ensure minority representation by drawing boundaries to encircle minority neighborhoods. The Supreme Court has held through a series of rulings that when race becomes the dominant factor in deciding on district boundaries that action is a violation of the Equal Protection clause of the Fourteenth Amendment.[10] The result is considerable confusion when a state legislature redraws district boundaries for its own election districts or for congressional districts. Redistricting plans are frequently challenged in courts as being unfair to minorities or as over-representing them.[11]

Term Limits. A related concern regarding legislators is that they not become so entrenched in their positions that they lose a sense of responsibility to the citizens who elected them. One response has been to impose term limits that curtail the number of years a person may serve.[12] The limits typically involve consecutive years of services, such as no more than two terms of four years in a state senate and no more than six terms of two years in a state house. Limits also can be on a lifetime basis, such as limiting the total number of years a person may serve in the house and/or senate for one's entire life. As of 1996, seven states had lifetime limits for membership in their state legislative bodies.[13]

Term limits have been proposed at all levels of government, and many governments now have such limits. Eight of the largest cities in the country, such as New York City and Los Angeles, along with smaller cities such as Honolulu, Omaha, and Spokane have term limits.[14] About half of the states have adopted some form of term limits for their legislatures.

As for the federal government, the Supreme Court has ruled that term limits to be imposed on the Congress must be carried out through a constitutional amendment.[15] Proponents of term limits, convinced that the two-thirds vote necessary for the Congress to pass such an amendment is unlikely to happen without substantial prodding, have taken to using the initiative to adopt state term-limits accountability laws. These laws require the states' delegations to Congress to support a term-limits constitutional amendment and require members of the state legislatures to ratify the amendment. If a member of Congress or the state legislature fails to vote in favor of the amendment or if a candidate for office fails to pledge support for term limits, the ballot indicates such. The constitutionality of such laws is being fought in the courts.

In the meantime, many state legislatures are in the midst of implementing term-limits requirements. One view is that the reform has led to more women and Latinos being elected. Members of the California Assembly in 1997 chose the state's first ever Latino speaker, a feat that would have been highly unlikely without term limits.[16]

The term-limits reform has its downside. Political bodies are automatically denied the experience that can only be gained from long years of service in a legislature. People do not automatically change their family doctors and dentists every six years, so why should they do that with their elected representatives? Effective representatives presumably should be retained in office, while ineffective ones should not be re-elected. Reducing the length of time that someone may stay in office may deter some of the more qualified people from running for office in the first place. Citizens may support term limits less because of any dissatisfaction with their representatives and more because of a general cynicism about government itself.[17]

Fragmentation. An overriding characteristic of state legislatures and Congress is fragmentation in budgeting. Constitutionally imposed bicameralism divides the legislature into two chambers, a house and a senate, which seek to establish their own identities and powers but which must be coordinated if a budget is to be approved. Local governing bodies, in contrast, usually are unicameral and do not face this fragmentation problem. Fragmentation also is apparent within each chamber of a legislative body and between the executive and legislative branches.

Political parties can serve as a unifying force between branches, between legislative chambers, and within chambers. According to conventional practice, whichever party wins a majority of seats in a chamber will control the leadership positions, have a majority of its members on each committee, and have each committee chaired by a member of the party. In theory, if the Democrats hold a majority of the seats in a state senate, then the Democratic party has control of that chamber in handling all legislative matters. Sometimes a ruling party may have the narrowest possible majority or no majority at all. In 1996, Maine, Nevada, and Virginia each had a legislative chamber whose members were evenly divided between Republicans and Democrats. The 1996 elections yielded an evenly divided Indiana House. Indiana law provides that when this occurs, the ruling party will be the same as the party of the governor, in effect providing some degree of coordination between the legislative and executive branches.[18]

Political Party Leadership. In the United States, political parties are weak, and their leaders are unable to control their own party members. On any given issue there may be no guarantee that all or even most of the party's members will vote as a block. Many members of the legislative body, especially those who have gained seniority through numerous re-elections, are not always amenable to supporting the policies of their party's leadership, whether in the legislature or in the executive branch. Leaders often are in a position of having to persuade members for their votes, unlike earlier times when legislative leaders may have ruled with iron fists.[19]

Parties attempt to exert influence on their legislators through caucuses. Republicans in a state house of representatives, for example, will meet periodically to develop party positions on issues and then attempt to exert influence on party members to vote accordingly. The positions approved in caucus meetings do not always coincide with the views of the party's leadership.

The situation is further complicated by the fact that the two chambers can be controlled by different parties, and even if both are controlled by one party, the chief executive might be of another party. In 1996, for example, 27 states had divided governments in which the governor, the lower legislative chamber, and the upper chamber were not all controlled by the same political party.[20] This condition is sometimes seen as leading to *gridlock*, which is one often cited cause for the inability of government to deal with pressing problems. Divided government, however, as will be seen in this chapter and later ones, should not be considered the sole explanation of why governments sometimes fail to address major problems.[21]

Legislative Committees. The extensive use of legislative committees is essential in that acting as a committee of the whole is impractical, but committee structures add to fragmentation. Committees become little legislatures in their own right.[22] Given that the U.S. House of Representatives has 435 members and the Senate 100, a committee structure is inevitable. Among the states, New Hampshire has the largest legislature, with 424 members, and Nebraska the smallest, with 49 members in one chamber. Most states have more than 100 legislators.[23]

In a bicameral legislative body, legislation is handled by parallel committees in each chamber. These committees report out bills that are acted on by the full membership of the house and senate. When differences exist in the two bills, a *conference committee* is usually appointed, which reports a revised bill that again is acted upon by both houses; the conference committee consists of members from the two committees that prepared the legislation. Once the chambers have passed identical bills, the legislation is ready for signing or vetoing by the governor or president.

At the local level, where unicameralism prevails, a budget committee often has main responsibility for reviewing and amending the executive's proposed budget and for submitting a set of recommendations to the full legislative body, such as a city council or school board.

Committees that continue on a permanent basis are known as *standing committees*, whereas ad hoc committees are usually created to deal with specific problems and are then disbanded. Most standing committees consist of selected members of one house of a legislature, but standing committees can be joint in nature, consisting of selected members from both chambers. State legislatures usually have 15 to 20 standing committees in each chamber.[24]

Legislators seek to serve their district's or state's interests by gaining appointment to appropriate legislative committees. Someone from a farming community may seek appointment to a state senate's agriculture committee, and a member of the U.S. House of Representatives from a district that includes major military installations may seek appointment to the Armed Services Committee to help ensure that military funds continue to flow into the district. Similarly, members of the House and Senate will seek appointment to key subcommittees of their chamber's appropriations committee.[25]

Availability of Time. How a legislative body operates is greatly influenced by whether it continues in session throughout the year. City councils usually hold meetings once, twice, or even more times per month throughout the year. Congress is in session much of each year except for holidays and recesses during election periods.

State legislatures vary widely. While about a dozen states have no limits on the length of legislative sessions, the rest control whether the legislature can meet each year, for how many days, and whether the legislature may call itself back into session after adjournment. The legislatures in California, Illinois, Massachusetts, Michigan, New Jersey, New York, Ohio, Pennsylvania, and Wisconsin hold sessions that run during much of the year.[26] When legislatures have time limitations, procedural limits are used to "budget" the available time. For example, a common practice is to set a cutoff date for the introduction of bills, since late submission would carry deliberations beyond the required adjournment.

Similarly, time limits are set on the budget process. Some states allow their spending and taxation committees only a few weeks to consider their relevant portions of the budget, while other states allow 20 or more weeks. In some states, the entire budget approval process must be completed by the legislature within six weeks or less, while other states allow 20 weeks, 30 weeks, or even more.

A major problem facing Congress is not that it has limits on the time that it may be in session but rather that it has difficulty approving the budget within the available time. Until legislation was adopted in 1974, Congress faced a situation in which the president's budget was delivered to it shortly after the first of the calendar year and work was to be completed by July 1, then the beginning of the fiscal year. Although the beginning of the fiscal year was shifted to October 1, which gave Congress an additional three months to complete its work, Congress's track record in completing its work on time often has been poor.

Part of the problem is that every two years Congress has to reorganize itself and in the process loses valuable time. In January and February of odd-numbered years, Congress must reorganize since all members of the House of Representatives and one-third of the members of the Senate have been elected (or re-elected) the previous November. New memberships result in new committee assignments, new chairs of some committees, some new leadership, and a reassignment of offices. When party control of a chamber changes, the disruptions are compounded. Under these conditions, Congress simply has immense difficulty finding sufficient time to act on the budget.

Compensation and Staff. Closely associated with time limits on legislatures is compensation for their members. Annual compensation is low in many states. For example, in 1995, Georgia, Indiana, Mississippi, Nebraska, South Carolina, and Texas paid their legislators $12,000 or less.[27] In these states and others, however, members might be eligible for per diem payments, travel expenses, and other payments. Nevertheless, pay for state legislators overall is low, resulting in most legislators having to have other income sources, such as from law practices. In contrast, members of Congress earn incomes and receive other benefits, such as travel expenses, that allow the legislative job to be a full-time occupation. One of the most important forms of compensation afforded members of Congress is lucrative pension benefits, which can be an incentive for continuing to stand for re-election. Fees for speeches and other appearances are lucrative for some legislators.

Staffing is another factor that influences legislative behavior. Staff dedicated to assist legislators presumably can help them perform more effectively and reduce their reliance on the executive branch and lobbyists for information. Although local bodies, such as county commissioners or city council members, rarely have sizable staffs at their disposal, Congress does, and so do many state legislatures, although some states have small staffs. A predominantly rural state, such as Wyoming, will have a legislative staff of less than 100, while a large state, such as New York, will have a staff in the thousands. Staffs serve individual members, committees, and persons holding leadership positions, as in the case of the speaker of a state house of representatives. In addition, there are some legislative staff units that serve a variety of individuals and committees in both chambers; the Congressional Budget Office is a noted example. Since the 1960s, staffs in state legislatures and Congress have greatly increased their professional training; staff members often have graduate degrees, including doctorates.

Legislative fiscal committee staffs provide a host of services. For example, most state legislatures' fiscal committee staffs conduct fiscal research studies, prepare reports on revenues and taxes, and prepare reports on expenditures and the budget. Other important staff functions include making revenue projections, analyzing budget trends during the fiscal year, and preparing reports on economic conditions.

The increasing bureaucratization of legislatures through the growth of staff has led some critics to claim legislators are creating servants for themselves at the expense of taxpayers. As part of the term limitation movement, some activists, such as those in California, have succeeded in forcing cutbacks in staff.[28]

Ten state legislatures have been classified as "professional" by the National Conference of State Legislatures. This designation means that the legislators work full time at their jobs, staff is well trained and paid, and other support resources, such as computer services, are available to legislators and staff. Professionalism, however, is no guarantee of a smoothly operating legislature, as has been evident in such states as California and Minnesota. One view is that professionalism attracts better-informed individuals who inevitably clash with one another, yielding conflict that is not necessarily productive.[29]

The Legislative Process

Members of the legislature or their staff often participate in preparation deliberations by the executive branch. When the budget reaches the legislature, therefore, there may be relatively few surprises in terms of proposals being advanced; that is, many of the key legislators already will be familiar with the budget's main proposals. Legislative involvement during preparation can help build support for executive budget recommendations.

Committee Responsibilities. When a budget reaches a state legislature or Congress, the document is divided into numerous pieces and sent to committees. Proposals that require new substantive legislation to implement them will be sent to substantive standing committees; these committees exist for areas such as environmental protection, education, recreation, welfare, and, at the federal level, also for defense and international relations. For programs to be implemented, these committees must report bills that will be approved eventually by the two chambers of the legislature. Legislation of this type authorizes the existence of programs, while appropriations provide the necessary funding.

While deliberations proceed on these substantive matters, other committees deal with the financial aspects of the budget. A regular practice is to assign taxing and other revenue matters to one group of committees and spending or appropriations to another. In Congress, taxation is handled by the Ways and Means Committee in the House of Representatives and by the Finance Committee in the Senate; spending is dealt with by each chamber's appropriations committee. These committees actually conduct much of their work at the subcommittee level (see Chapter 9).

Coordination problems and terrain battles among committees are common. A person achieves the position of chair of a committee by serving on the committee a long time and hence, once made chair, is unlikely to look favorably on threats to the committee's powers. The Appropriations Committee of the U.S. House of Representatives was once considered the College of Cardinals, and while the committee has lost the prestige and power that such a title suggests, the committee remains powerful and its members work to retain its powers.[30] Nevertheless, some coordinating mechanisms are essential if realistic budgets are to be adopted. For example, if separate revenue and expenditure committees are free to act independently, then the situation is analogous to a couple, one of whom earns income and the other spends with only occasional reference to how much is earned.

Fiscal Notes. One important mechanism that has been adopted is the requirement that fiscal notes be developed for most draft legislation. A fiscal note is a report that addresses the current and future costs of implementing a proposed bill. The fiscal note may include analysis of the purpose of the legislation, the proposed sources of funding, and the impact on other governments, as in the case of a state law affecting local government budgets. Fiscal notes are typically prepared by legislative staff. At the state level, appropriations committees often have this responsibility. At the federal level, the Congressional Budget Office prepares fiscal notes regarding impacts on state and local governments. The State and Local Government Cost Estimate Act of 1981 requires that fiscal notes be prepared to estimate the impact of proposed legislation affecting these governments.[31] The Unfunded Mandates Reform Act of 1995 not only requires that Congress consider the possible financial effects of draft legislation on state and local governments but basically requires funding of such mandates (see Chapter 14).[32]

The fiscal note is intended to help decision makers be better informed about the implications of draft legislation. For example, if a proposal provides for revising a state program for teenagers to include 13-year-olds, whereas only those 14 years old and older are currently included, the revision could greatly increase the number of clients served and the demand on resources. Fiscal notes also are prepared for revenue proposals, as in the case of forecasting the extra income that would be generated by increasing a state sales tax by 1 percentage point.

Fiscal notes are particularly important at the state and local levels, where balanced budgets are required. Indeed, the revenue estimates prepared by the chief executive coupled with any fiscal note on proposed revenue increases will greatly influence what spending programs the legislature will be able to approve. While nearly all states require that fiscal notes be prepared,[33] in practice this does not always happen or the notes are prepared in an incomplete fashion, such as omitting the all-important cost estimates of bills. This failure to prepare thorough fiscal notes may be a function of short deadlines that are impossible to meet and the lack of qualified staff in sufficient numbers to prepare the notes.[34]

In addition to fiscal notes, other mechanisms are devised to link together the work of committees and ensure that "reasonable" budgets are developed. Some states have used a system by which lump-sum amounts are assigned to program areas, and these funds then are distributed among programs within each area by standing committees and reported back to the appropriations committee for inclusion in their budget bills. Congress uses a variation of this approach. Local governments generally have less of a coordination problem, since most of the budget work will be handled by a single committee.

LEGISLATIVE ROLES

Legislative-Executive Interactions

In this section, we turn to how the executive branch relates to the legislative branch. Because legislatures are not integrated wholes but rather consist of numerous subunits, this section considers how the executive branch relates to those subunits, especially to the two legislative chambers and their committees.

Authority. The executive and legislative branches of government in the United States are typically said to be coequal.[35] The separation of powers, in this case between the executive and legislative branches, is a fundamental feature of U.S. governments. Therefore the two branches tend to be wary of possible diminution of their powers and may seek strategies for demonstrating their independence. Confrontations between the two are sometimes akin to tests of strength, with each branch showing it is not subservient to the other.

In earlier days, the legislature was considered to be responsible for setting policy, but today both the legislative and executive branches are inextricably engaged in policy making. Conflicts arise, not over whether the executive should be involved in policy making, but rather to what extent and in what ways. The movement toward executive budget systems has placed the executive in the policy-making process, because the preparation of budget proposals by the executive is, in effect, the drafting of proposed policies. Congress, state legislatures, and city councils have often found themselves in the position of having to react to executive recommendations instead of formulating policy. To demonstrate their independence, then, legislators may feel a compulsion to alter a proposed budget no matter how compatible its recommendations may be with their own preferences.

Not all governments have executive budgeting systems. In some governments, budgeting powers overlap between the branches, and in others, legislatures dominate the budgeting process.[36] Regardless of the distribution of powers, tensions will exist between the branches of government.

Constitutional and legal constraints greatly affect the extent of executive and legislative powers in budgeting. The Budget and Accounting Act of 1921 and comparable legislation at the state level have granted substantial budgetary powers to the president and governors. Yet, in some states, the governor must share budget-making authority with other relatively independent executive officers and/or legislative bodies. In most states, the legislature is free to adjust the governor's budget either upward or downward, but in a few states (Maryland, Nebraska, New York, and West Virginia), the legislature has limited or no authority to appropriate above what was recommended by the governor.

Relationships between the branches change over time. Changes in political leadership have short- and long-term effects. When a new executive takes office, inevitable discontinuities occur during the transition period, which can last from a few weeks to months.[37] Personalities and the political clout of leaders influence executive-legislative relations. The election of a widely popular political leader in the legislature can lead to diminished executive powers. A newly elected governor, who is more assertive than his or her predecessor, may be successful in demanding that the legislature yield some of its budgetary powers. In periods of fiscal crisis and other challenging times, the executive may tend to garner greater budgetary powers at the expense of the legislature.[38]

Constituency Differences. The legislative and executive branches have different constituencies and as a result have different perspectives on the budget. One common interpretation has been that the chief executive, being elected by the jurisdiction's entire constituency, has a broader perspective on the budget; a governor will attempt to satisfy the diverse needs of citizens throughout the state. Legislative bodies, on the other hand, have been seen as consisting of parochial individuals who may be less impressed with government-wide problems and therefore more likely to cut budgets. The legislature, then, is seen as a protector of the treasury and as a budget cutter.

A competing view of legislative bodies is that, in their desire to represent constituents, they tend to be eager to spend resources far beyond what is financially sound and that, while the requirement for a balanced budget keeps that desire to spend in check at the state and local levels, few constraints are evident at the national level. *Pork barrel*, a basic term of U.S. politics, refers to legislatively approved government projects that are aimed at helping home districts and states.[39] A standard complaint of pork barrel projects is that they have limited utility beyond winning votes for legislators seeking re-election. The item veto, discussed below, may help to reduce the wastefulness of pork barrel spending.

Recent presidents have attempted to advance their own legislative programs while minimizing the gap between high spending and lower revenues. For example, budgets submitted during the Reagan administration were intended to support a buildup in defense, and in order to minimize deficits, sizable reductions in domestic programs were proposed. In this type of situation, almost regardless of political party positions, legislatures tend to be supportive of efforts to restore budget cuts proposed by the executive. Selective cuts may cost the executive few votes in a bid for re-election, whereas those same cuts can have dire effects on the political futures of many legislators.

Deadlock between the branches is a common phenomenon, and when the two cannot agree on a budget, commuters can be greatly inconvenienced due to shutdowns in public transit, welfare recipients can be forced to eke out an existence without their checks, and public employees may have to endure payless paydays. Requirements at the state and local levels that balanced budgets be adopted, while imposing fiscal discipline on decision makers, can lead to delays in adopting budgets, since neither the executive nor legislative branch wishes to take the first step toward compromise lest that be viewed as a sign of weakness. In 1992, California state government operated for months without a budget, during which time employees were issued script rather than dollars.

Executive Fragmentation. An executive budget system provides the chief executive with control over budget preparation, but there is no guarantee that all units within the executive branch will subscribe fully to the budget's recommendations. The chief executive will not be uniformly in support of all portions of the budget; some recommendations will have been approved because of political considerations. Typically, the chief executive will single out a few major recommendations for which approval is sought, with other recommendations being considered low priority. The budget office will be expected to make general presentations on the overall recommendations contained in the budget, although the budget office may be lukewarm to many of those recommendations.

Detailed defense of specific recommendations is normally the responsibility of the operating agencies. Because the heads of the agencies in a strong executive system are the appointees of the chief executive, they have an obligation to defend the budget recommendations, even though higher funding levels may be preferred.[40] Agency representatives, however, may have little enthusiasm for defending budget proposals that call for deep cuts in programs. As a result, agencies attempt to calculate the extent to which they can reveal their preferences for greater resources to the spending committees in the legislature and still be "faithful" to the chief executive. The agencies also seek to head off any budget cuts being contemplated by the appropriations committee and are willing to engage in conflict if necessary to protect their budgets.[41]

During the approval phase, central budget offices may have responsibility for exercising some control over agencies that might seek to garner financial support beyond what the executive is recommending to the legislature and may serve as a major negotiator for the executive in sensitive discussions with legislative leaders. Since the early 1980s, the Office of Management and Budget (OMB) has played a much more prominent role in legislative relations. This role includes activities not just of the OMB director but also of individual budget examiners.[42]

Budget offices commonly perform a *clearinghouse function* on reviewing all proposed legislation and bills that have been passed by the legislature and forwarded to the chief executive for signing. OMB Circular A-19 prescribes for federal agencies that they submit to OMB an annual set of proposals for legislation. If these proposals are not submitted in time for consideration at budgeting time in the latter part of the year, then they are excluded from the President's budget and therefore not endorsed by the President and his administration. Circular A-19 provides that when Congress passes a bill, OMB distributes copies of the *enrolled bill* to affected agencies for their comments. The agencies must respond promptly, either endorsing or opposing the legislation, in order to be considered within the President's limit of ten days. If the President does not act within the ten days (including holidays but excluding Sundays), the bill automatically becomes law.

Influence of Bicameralism. One set of calculations from both the executive and legislative branch perspectives involves the relative roles of the two chambers. At the federal level, the Constitution requires that revenue or tax bills begin in the House of Representatives, in particular, the Ways and Means Committee (Article I, Section 7). Until the 1974 reform legislation, the normal procedure was for the Senate Finance Committee to wait until the House completed action before taking up the tax bill. Appropriations were handled in a similar manner, although the practice was based on custom and not the Constitution; appropriation bills began in the House and later were referred to the Senate. Under that system, strategists were able to concentrate their attentions on first one committee and then another as the legislation worked its way through Congress. Since 1974, the House and Senate have simultaneously commenced work on the budget.

Where appropriations are handled sequentially, that is, beginning in the lower chamber and then moving to the upper chamber, the two chambers tend to take on different roles. Since a house of representatives tends to have more members than a senate, a house appropriations committee tends to have more members than its counterpart in the senate. As a result, house committee members are able to specialize in segments of the budget whereas senators must attempt to become informed on a larger number of areas and consequently may be viewed as amateurs. Members of the senate committee, on the other hand, might consider themselves to have a broader awareness of total budget needs than house members. Also, given the transfers of appropriations from one chamber to another, the house appropriations committee tends to focus on the proposed budget whereas the senate committee focuses on what the house did to the proposed budget.[43]

Federal Aid to States. One particular area of executive-legislative contention at the state level has been control over federal assistance. Historically, legislative bodies did not appropriate federal funds coming into state treasuries. Governors contended that they acted as custodians over federal dollars and were bound by federal regulations that established how and for what purposes monies were to be spent; the conclusion followed that the legislature had no role in deciding about the use of these funds. However, governors on occasion were able to use federal grants to finance services that state legislatures opposed. The legislative view of this situation was and is that, once received, federal dollars become state dollars and can be spent only when approved by an appropriation bill adopted by the legislature. Although the Supreme Court has not ruled on this issue, in 1979 it let stand a lower court's ruling in favor of the legislature.[44]

The issue of state appropriation of federal funds became more important in 1981, when Congress passed legislation creating large block grants to be administered by the states (see Chapter 14). Under these grant programs, the states were given increased flexibility in how they spend some of the grant monies and how they distribute the remainder to local governments. The response has been for state legislatures to require that appropriations be passed before federal dollars can be spent. The legislatures in Florida, Ohio, and Washington, for example, determine in considerable detail how monies are to be spent on programs and subprograms.

Strategies. Regardless of what level of government is considered, executive-legislative relationships inevitably can be characterized as cat-and-mouse games, although it is not always clear who is the cat and who is the mouse. Strategies are devised in each branch to deal with the other. On the executive side, a general strategy that is almost ubiquitous is to cultivate clientele who will support requests for increased funding. Agencies are sensitive to where they locate buildings and other facilities; a new facility in a key legislator's district may gain the support of that legislator. Agencies pursue such strategies continuously as a matter of course.[45]

Contingent strategies, on the other hand, are limited to particular situations. No comprehensive cataloging of them is possible, because they vary from agency to agency and from circumstance to circumstance. They arise out of perceptions of what is possible in a given budget period. In growth periods, when revenue surplus or slack is evident, agencies may seek to expand existing programs or gain approval for the creation of new ones. Even when revenues are scarce, agencies whose areas are favored by the chief executive may seek expansion, as was the case of defense during the Reagan years. Sometimes obtaining approval for a new program may be easier than obtaining approval for expansion of an existing one; executives and legislators alike prefer being able to take credit for creation of a new program over simply improving an existing one. A ploy that may be used is to start a new project with a small appropriation, getting the legislature accustomed to the program and then seeking much greater appropriations in subsequent years.

When funds are less plentiful, one strategy is to defend programs against cuts and to maintain what is called the *base*. An agency's existing budget is often regarded as the base, with the budget process adding or subtracting increments to the base. Agencies have been known to warn that the slightest of budget cuts would necessarily diminish popular programs and thereby erode electoral support of legislators.

When cuts are perceived as inevitable, often because of a declining tax base and/or tax limitations, one strategy is to minimize cuts in the base and to obtain *fair share* funding. An agency will argue, on the one hand, that its programs are essential and should not be cut at all but, on the other hand, will insist that, if cuts must be made, they be no greater than cuts imposed on programs in other agencies.

While various strategies may be influential, there are limits to their effectiveness. Legislatures are influenced by personal values and committee role expectations as well as agency budget strategies and presentations. Agency strategies may also backfire and create negative feelings on the part of members of the appropriations committees, perhaps because they suspect they are being exploited.

In response to agency pressure, legislators also devise a number of strategies for dealing with their budgetary responsibilities. A major problem is the capacity of agencies to produce vast amounts of information in support of their requests— more information than the legislature can process. Legislative strategies, then, may be seen as methods by which complex choices are simplified.

For example, an appropriations committee or subcommittee finds it difficult, if not impossible, to decide rationally if $83.6 million is the exact amount that should be granted to an agency. Thus, legislators in appropriations committees look for other ways to determine what should be granted an agency. They place much of the burden for calculation on the executive and demand that an agency justify its need for certain funds in response to probing questions. Detailed questions, which to outsiders may seem petty and trivial, are designed to determine how much confidence the subcommittee can place in the executive's testimony. Legislators have "discernible patterns" in their line of questioning, suggesting that legislators have their own strategies for dealing with different agencies and that these strategies depend in part upon changes in fiscal conditions.[46] How the various strategies affect the outcomes of appropriations is uncertain and no doubt varies among jurisdictions and over time.

Item Veto. Once appropriations and revenue bills are adopted by the legislature, the approval phase is not necessarily completed. In more than 40 states, governors have item-veto power, which permits reductions in amounts that have been appropriated. In some cases, governors may eliminate selected language in appropriation bills, which can have substantial effects on policy. State legislatures may seek to override these vetoes; usually a two-thirds vote is required to override. As with the general veto power, the threat of the item veto may be as important as its eventual use in that legislators may avoid including some measures in an appropriation bill on the assumption they would be excised eventually by the governor.

The item veto has three uses[47]:

1. It allows chief executives to keep total expenditures within the limits of anticipated available revenue.
2. The executive can reduce or even eliminate funds for projects or programs considered to be unworthy. The item veto can help curtail the excesses of pork barrel projects mentioned earlier.
3. The veto can be used for partisan purposes. This kind of use often occurs in situations where the governor is of one political party and one or both chambers of the legislature are of another party.

Studies have found that the item-veto power sometimes—but not always—has a negative effect on spending, especially pork barrel highway projects, and can be particularly important when at least one chamber is under the control of a political party that differs from the governor's party.[48] From a practical standpoint, the item veto allows action by the governor without forcing the legislature to react unless it chooses to do so. Indeed, legislators may be privately pleased to have the governor item veto some projects that were included in an appropriation bill to satisfy strong lobbying pressure.

At the federal level, the president has always been able to exercise the standard veto power, meaning that he can veto an entire appropriation bill. When this power is exercised, the House and Senate may override the veto by a two-thirds vote, but should the veto be sustained, the legislation is referred back to committee for further review. The disadvantage of the veto power for both Congress and the president is that much time and energy may be consumed in redrafting the legislation and negotiating an agreement between the two branches.

Every president since Ulysses S. Grant, including President Clinton has requested the item-veto power,[49] and in 1996, Congress granted that wish by passing the Line Item Veto Act.[50] The law is discussed in the following chapter, which deals with congressional budget processes.

Legislative Oversight

Not only are the executive and legislative branches typically separated in U.S. governments, but each branch is provided with powers that can be used to limit the powers of the other. The basic structure of this *checks-and-balances system* is set forth in the U.S. Constitution, state constitutions, and city charters. However, constitutional and statutory provisions must be implemented on a daily basis, and the extent to which one branch limits the other may fluctuate over time. In this section, we consider the increasing interest being given to the legislative body's overseeing of executive operations.[51]

Influences on Oversight. When revenues are limited and the demands for expenditures are seemingly limitless, legislators perceive a need for greater efficiency and effectiveness in government operations. Such perceptions increase the interest in oversight operations, which in turn increases the pressure on administrative agencies to improve their operations while curtailing or even reducing expenditures. Agencies are required to provide masses of information to legislative committees to support their quest for ferreting out mismanagement and saving taxpayers' dollars.[52]

There are, of course, other reasons for the current legislative oversight movement. Financial crises in major cities have contributed to the interest in oversight. The Watergate scandal during the Nixon administration and subsequent scandals and abuses of government funds by federal agencies have stimulated interest in greater legislative oversight. Legislators have not been immune from their own scandals, raising the question of whether they have the appropriate credentials to oversee executive branch operations.

Legislators are sincerely interested in using government to alleviate societal problems. Frustrated by what is perceived as inept administration, legislators are attracted to expanding their oversight roles in the hope of improving government operations.

This legislative interest in oversight occurs at a time when executives feel increasingly frustrated with their own efforts to control public bureaucracies. Elected executives often complain that they lack the authority needed to control and redirect agencies. Merit systems that protect civil service employees are often cited as weakening executives and protecting lazy and incompetent employees from disciplinary actions. Tensions exist between the White House and Congress over control of the chief financial officers in federal agencies, with the White House seeing the officers as a means of exerting executive influence and Congress being concerned with extending its oversight function (see Chapter 11).[53]

Methods. Legislative oversight can be performed using numerous methods. Legislation that provides authorizations, revenues, and appropriations constitutes one set of methods. Other familiar devices are laws that prescribe the structure of executive agencies and personnel policies regarding hiring, promotion, and dismissal. An informal type of oversight occurs when a legislator or a legislative staff member contacts an agency about specific day-to-day operations; although legislators may have no official power to command any action by an agency, their wishes will be treated carefully and with some urgency by agency personnel. Oversight is important in advise-and-consent proceedings in which a senate committee screens a nominee for an executive position; the questions asked a nominee can influence that person's actions once in office.

Legislative investigations or the simple threat of investigation are other instruments of oversight. A legislative committee chair may greatly influence an agency by suggesting that investigative hearings will be scheduled unless certain practices are changed within the agency.

Greater specificity of *legislative intent* is being used to reduce executive discretion. In the past, ambiguous language was used as a deliberate tool for delegating responsibilities to the executive and increasing executive flexibility in carrying out policies. The opposite is common today. State legislatures attempt to establish legislative intent through the use of wording contained in line items, footnotes, and concluding sections to appropriation bills; the use of committee reports; and the use of letters of intent delivered to the governor.

A problem of legislatures is enforcing legislative intent. What if an agency stays within the legal prescriptions of legislative intent but violates its spirit? The punitive action of cutting the agency's budget often is not possible; citizens benefiting from agency programs would be harmed as well as the agency itself. Therefore, the main punitive alternative may be to impose more restrictions on the agency, such as making legislative intent more explicit, specifically prohibiting various practices, and perhaps increasing the number of line items in the agency's budget in order to hamstring flexibility.

As part of legislative intent, there is increasing specificity of information that agencies are expected to collect and provide to the legislature. This practice denies agencies the tactic of confessing ignorance about their own programs; if legislation indicates an agency is to collect specific data, the agency will be expected to deliver it at designated times every year.

Congress often adopts appropriation bills that have detailed language. The foreign assistance program is said to be hamstrung by crosscutting legislative requirements built into appropriations. For example, appropriations specify how much each country will receive. In addition, appropriations specify the amounts that will be spent on programs such as child survival, population, the environment, and natural resources. Executives of the Agency for International Development must plan their expenditures within a matrix that links programs with nations even though more flexible planning might better serve foreign policy objectives.

Sunset Legislation and Zero-Base Budgeting. Another type of oversight mechanism consists of sunset legislation coupled with zero-base budgeting. Programs are authorized to exist for a given period, after which they expire (the sun sets on them). Before a program's expiration date, an agency may be required to present a zero-base budget indicating the achievements of the agency's program and the projected consequences if the program is not renewed. Depending on how these proposals are implemented, they can provide greater leverage for the legislature. Sunset legislation is used widely by state legislatures.[54]

Information and Analysis. Program budgeting and analysis constitute another approach to legislative oversight. Legislatures are increasingly demanding impact and output data from agencies; such demands have reinforcing effects on chief executives' efforts to install program budgeting. The Government Performance and Results Act of 1993 and President Clinton's Executive Order 12862 on setting customer service standards are expected to result in increased programmatic information being presented to the Congress as well as to the president (see Chapter 5).

Tensions exist over which organizational units should conduct analyses. Legislatures have sometimes given little attention to oversight, and the function has fallen to audit agencies, which at the state level are often headed by independently elected auditors. When legislative bodies later develop their own analytic capabilities, turf issues arise.[55] Virginia's Joint Legislative Audit and Review Commission is an example of a state legislative analysis unit.

At the federal level, the General Accounting Office (GAO) has an extensive ongoing research agenda that examines the full gamut of government programs.[56] GAO has been embroiled in controversy under the direction of Comptroller General Charles A. Bowsher, who has had GAO serve not only as an evaluator but also as a policy advocate. Critics have contended that GAO, rather than being a neutral evaluator, has become a proponent of policies advanced by the Democrats in Congress and the White House, a charge that Bowsher vehemently denied.[57]

Information technology also makes possible greater legislative oversight. Congress and state legislatures have developed their own information systems that allow them to tap into a variety of databases, including those maintained by agencies. However, the application of this technology is limited by the quality of data being maintained; computer hardware and software cannot compensate for agency neglect in collecting important information.

Legislative Veto. Legislatures are making increased use of their power to veto proposed executive actions. For instance, an agency may be granted authority to issue regulations, but a stipulation in the legislation can require the agency to obtain legislative approval prior to implementation of the regulations.[58] Depending on the governing legislation, a proposed action can be vetoed by a vote in either house or both houses of a legislature or can be implemented only with a vote of approval from both houses. Sometimes legislative committees have veto powers. More than 40 state legislatures exercise some form of legislative veto over executive agency regulations.[59]

The legislative veto is used as a means of furthering policy. Legislative intent is served presumably by allowing the full legislature or designated committees to oversee executive implementation. The veto process can steer executive agencies away from actions that are contrary to what the legislature wishes to see implemented.

Executives have a less positive view of legislative vetoes. The process often delays implementation of actions because the legislature is assured a given number of weeks to consider whether to support or veto a proposal. These vetoes are seen as giving authority to legislatures to meddle needlessly in the details of administration and, more significantly, to infringe upon the constitutional administrative powers of the executive.

A crisis seemed to develop in 1983 when the Supreme Court handed down one of its most controversial decisions in *Immigration and Naturalization Service v. Chadha*.[60] The case dealt with congressional veto power involving the deportation of aliens, but what was significant was not that the Court struck down that legislative veto but that it struck down most if not all such vetoes at the federal level. The Court's reasoning was simple: The Constitution provides for the House and Senate to set policy subject to veto by the President and does not allow for the opposite procedure.

Following the *Chadha* decision, Congress did not rush to adopt statutory measures or seek constitutional revisions that would reinstate the legislative veto. Instead, Congress dealt with matters as they arose and, in some instances, largely ignored the Court's ruling. For example, subsequent appropriation bills have included legislative vetoes. In 1996, Congress passed the Congressional Review Act, which provides a form of legislative veto of agency draft regulations (see Chapter 10).[61]

Oversight Limitations. While numerous methods of oversight are available, the organizational locus of oversight remains a problem because of the fragmentation discussed earlier. A coherent approach to oversight is not possible when committee powers overlap. Every federal agency must deal with at least one substantive committee, the Appropriations Committee, and the Budget Committee (discussed in Chapter 9) in each chamber of Congress. These committees may differ with each other and not have the backing of the full legislative body. Turf battles among committees are routine. For instance, the Chief Financial Officers Act of 1990 (see Chapter 11), by creating chief financial officers in agencies, enhanced the oversight powers of the House Government Operations Committee and the Senate Governmental Affairs Committee at the expense of the Appropriations Committees.[62]

One approach to overcoming fragmentation might be to center oversight in a staff unit of the legislature. For example, GAO at the federal level could be given greater oversight responsibilities. Another option would be to give committee staffs oversight duties. The problem with these suggestions is that they tend to conflict with legislators' desire to have staffs act in subordinate and inferior capacities. For a staff unit to evaluate a program enacted by the legislative body, to find the program inadequate, and to suggest means of improving it is likely to be viewed by many legislators as an affront to their responsibility for setting policy. For this reason, legislative analytic units tend to be cautious in program analysis and tentative in reaching conclusions and recommendations.

A final limitation on oversight is the priorities legislators set for themselves. Re-election is always paramount, and legislators often regard oversight activities as not contributing appreciably to their prospects for winning voter approval. Voters are seen as more supportive of legislators who initiate new programs than of those who serve as watchdogs over the executive branch.

SUMMARY

A variety of factors constrain the budgetary role of legislatures. The availability of revenue greatly influences how the legislature approaches budget approval. Previously reached decisions, such as established entitlement programs, limit action, as do numerous socioeconomic and political factors, such as the influence of interest groups. Fragmentation that results from bicameralism and the use of committees complicates the approval phase of budgeting, although political parties can help to overcome some of the problems.

The budget is approved through the work of substantive standing committees, appropriations committees, and revenue or finance committees. Fiscal notes have become important tools for tracking the financial implications of proposed legislation.

At least since the 1970s, a movement has existed to revitalize the role of legislatures vis-à-vis executives in the budgetary process. While in years past legislatures sometimes had a reputation for being budget cutters, more recently their role has been to represent constituents who would be harmed if proposed budget cuts were implemented. Many executives have the power to item veto appropriations that seem excessive.

Agencies use numerous strategies in seeking approval of their budgets. An administrator's initial objective may be to obtain increased funding for a program, but if that is not possible, then the administrator will concentrate on protecting the base and preventing budget cuts beyond those that constitute a fair share.

Legislative oversight is increasingly popular. Prior legislative approval of some administrative decisions may be required. Legislative investigative hearings serve the oversight function, along with detailed specification of legislative intent. Sunset legislation and zero-base budgeting are other oversight techniques.

NOTES

1. A. Wildavsky and N. Caiden, *The New Politics of the Budgetary Process*, 3rd ed. (New York: Longman, 1997), 163–218.

2. W.J. Keefe and M.S. Ogul, *The American Legislative Process: Congress and the States*, 9th ed. (Upper Saddle River, NJ: Prentice-Hall, 1997).

3. R. Kurfirst, Direct Democracy in the Sunshine State: Recent Challenges to Florida's Citizen Initiative, *Comparative State Politics* 17 (August 1996): 1–15.

4. C.J. Tolbert and R.E. Hero, Race/Ethnicity and Direct Democracy: An Analysis of California's Illegal Immigration Initiative, *Journal of Politics* 58 (1996): 806–818.

5. D.P. Swoboda, Accuracy and Accountability in Reporting Local Government Budget Activities: Evidence from the Newsroom and from Newsmakers, *Public Budgeting & Finance* 15 (Fall 1995): 74–90.

6. T. Loftus, *The Art of Legislative Politics* (Washington, DC: Congressional Quarterly Press, 1994), 6.

7. *Baker v. Carr*, 369 U.S. 186 (1962); *Reynolds v. Sims*, 377 U.S. 533 (1964).

8. *Reno v. Bossier Parish School Board*, 117 S.Ct. 1491 (1997).

9. A.J. Nelson, *Emerging Influentials in State Legislatures: Women, Blacks, and Hispanics* (New York: Praeger, 1991).

10. *Shaw v. Reno*, 509 U.S. 630 (1993); *Miller v. Johnson*, 115 S.Ct. 2475 (1995); *Shaw v. Hunt*, 116 S.Ct. 1894 (1996); *Bush v. Vera*, 116 S.Ct. 1941 (1996).

11. *Abrams v. Johnson*, 117 S.Ct. 1925 (1997); *Lawyer v. Department of Justice*, 117 S.Ct. 2186 (1997).

12. J.L. Sundquist, *Constitutional Reform and Effective Government*, rev. ed. (Washington, DC: Brookings Institution, 1992), 144–198.

13. G. Peery, Transcending Term Limits, *State Legislatures* 22 (June 1996): 20–25.

14. Local Term Limits, U.S. Term Limits Home Page: http://www.termlimits.org/munilimits.shtml; accessed September 1997.

15. *U.S. Term Limits, Inc. v. Thornton*, 115 S.Ct. 1842 (1995).

16. M. Katches and D.M. Weintraub, The Tremors of Term Limits, *State Legislatures* 23 (March 1997): 21–25.

17. J.A. Karp, Explaining Public Support for Legislative Term Limits, *Public Opinion Quarterly* 59 (1995): 373–391.

18. R.X. Browning, Indiana House Equally Divided Once Again, *Comparative State Politics* 18 (February 1997): 41–43.

19. M.E. Jewell and M.L. Whicker, *Legislative Leadership in the American States* (Ann Arbor: University of Michigan Press, 1994).

20. Included in the 27 is Nebraska, which has a nonpartisan unicameral legislature, and Maine, which in 1996 had an independent governor. Council of State Governments, *Book of the States, 1996–97 Edition* (Lexington, KY: Council of State Governments, 1996), 109–112.

21. C.W. Cox and S. Kernell, eds., *The Politics of Divided Government* (Boulder, CO: Westview Press, 1991).

22. G. Goodwin, Jr., *The Little Legislatures: Committees of Congress* (Amherst: University of Massachusetts Press, 1970).

23. Council of State Governments, *Book of the States,* 68.

24. Ibid.

25. G.S. Gryski, The Influence of Committee Position on Federal Program Spending, *Polity* 23 (1991): 443–459.

26. Council of State Governments, *Book of the States,* 64–65.

27. Council of State Governments, *Book of the States,* 80–81.

28. R. Gurwitt, California, Here We Come: The Professional Legislature and Its Discontents, *Governing* 4 (August 1991): 64–69.

29. C. Mahtesian, The Sick Legislature Syndrome, *Governing* 10 (February 1997): 16–20.

30. J. Shear, Power Loss, *National Journal* 28 (1996): 874–878.

31. State and Local Government Cost Estimate Act, P.L. 97-108, 95 Stat. 1510 (1981).

32. Unfunded Mandates Reform Act, P.L. 104-4, 109 Stat. 48 (1995).

33. Council of State Governments, *Book of the States,* 103–104.

34. J.M. Kelly, Fiscal Noting Reconsidered: The Experience of the States with Mandate Cost Estimation, *Public Budgeting and Financial Management* 6 (1994): 1–27.

35. Loftus, *The Art of Legislative Politics,* 61–75; J. Gill, Formal Models of Legislative/Administrative Interaction: A Survey of the Subfield, *Public Administration Review* 55 (1995): 99–106.

36. E.J. Clynch and T.P. Lauth, eds., *Governors, Legislatures, and Budgets: Diversity across the American States* (New York: Greenwood Press, 1991).

37. K. O'Lessker, The New President Makes a Budget: From Eisenhower to Bush, *Public Budgeting & Finance* 12 (Fall 1992): 3–18.

38. Clynch and Lauth, *Governors, Legislatures, and Budgets.*

39. J.L. Payne, *The Culture of Spending: Why Congress Lives beyond Our Means* (San Francisco: ICS Press, 1991).

40. J.P. Dobel, Managerial Leadership in Divided Times, *Administration and Society* 26 (1995): 488–514.

41. C.M. Johnson, *The Dynamics of Conflict Between Bureaucrats and Legislators* (Armonk, NY: M.E. Sharpe, 1992).

42. B. Johnson, The OMB Budget Examiner and the Congressional Budget Process, *Public Budgeting & Finance* 9 (Spring 1989): 5–14.

43. R.F. Fenno, Jr., *Power of the Purse: Appropriations Politics in Congress* (Boston: Little, Brown, 1966); S. Horn, *Unused Power: The Work of the Senate Committee on Appropriations* (Washington, DC: Brookings Institution, 1970).

44. *Shapp v. Sloan,* 480 Pa. 449, 391 A.2d 595 (1978); *Thornburgh v. Casey,* 440 U.S. 942 (1979).

45. Wildavsky and Caiden, *The New Politics of the Budgetary Process,* 49–53, 57–66.

46. K.A. Stanford, State Budget Deliberations: Do Legislators Have a Strategy? *Public Administration Review* 52 (1992): 16–26.

47. G. Abney and T.P. Lauth, The Line-Item Veto in the States, *Public Administration Review* 45 (1985): 372–377; T.P. Lauth, The Line-Item Veto in Government Budgeting, *Public Budgeting & Finance* 16 (Summer 1996): 97–111.

48. J. Alm and M. Evers, The Item Veto and State Government Expenditures, *Public Choice* 68 (1991): 1–15; N. Berch, The Item Veto in the States: An Analysis of the Effects over Time, *Social Science Quarterly* 29 (1992): 335–346; P. Thompson and S.R. Boyd, Use of the Item Veto in Texas, 1940–1990, *State and Local Government Review* 26 (1994): 38–45.

49. C. Bellamy, Item Veto: Dangerous Constitutional Tinkering, *Public Administration Review* 49 (1989): 46–51; Sundquist, *Constitutional Reform and Effective Government*, 281–294.

50. Line Item Veto Act, P.L. 104-130, 110 Stat 1200 (1996).

51. J.D. Aberbach, *Keeping a Watchful Eye: The Politics of Congressional Oversight* (Washington, DC: Brookings Institution, 1990); D. Evans, Congressional Oversight and the Diversity of Members' Goals, *Political Science Quarterly* 109 (1994): 669–687.

52. B.J. Lewis and P.V. Ellefson, Evaluating Information Flows to Policy Committees in State Legislatures, *Evaluation Review* 20 (1996): 29–48.

53. C.C. Lawrence, New Chief Financial Officers Straddle Branches of Power, *Congressional Quarterly Weekly Report* 49 (1991): 2286–2287.

54. Council of State Governments, *Book of the States*, 122–124; M.R. Daniels, Termination, Innovation and the American States: Testing Sunset Legislation, *American Review of Politics* 15 (1994): 507–518.

55. K.S. Walton and R.E. Brown, State Legislators and State Auditors: Is There an Inherent Role Conflict? *Public Budgeting & Finance* 10 (Spring 1990): 3–12.

56. H.S. Havens, U.S. General Accounting Office, *The Evolution of the General Accounting Office: From Voucher Audits to Program Evaluations* (Washington, DC: U.S. Government Printing Office, 1990); National Academy of Public Administration, *The Roles, Mission and Operation of the U.S. General Accounting Office* (Washington, DC: U.S. Government Printing Office, 1994).

57. P. Kuntz, Embattled GAO Fights Back: Bowsher Denies Any Bias, *Congressional Quarterly Weekly Report* 49 (1991): 2046–2050; E.N. Carney, Losing Support, *National Journal* 27 (1995): 2353–2357.

58. M.L. Gibson, *Weapons of Influence: The Legislative Veto, American Foreign Policy, and the Irony of Reform* (Boulder, CO: Westview Press, 1992).

59. Council of State Governments, *Book of the States*, 118–121.

60. *Immigration and Naturalization Service v. Chadha*, 462 U.S. 919 (1983).

61. Congressional Review Act, P.L. 104-121, 110 Stat. 857 (1996).

62. L.R. Jones, Counterpoint Essay: Nine Reasons Why the CFO Act May Not Achieve Its Objectives, *Public Budgeting & Finance* 13 (Spring 1993): 87–94.

CHAPTER 9

Budget Approval: The U.S. Congress

The preceding chapter examined the budget approval process across levels and types of government. This chapter examines the special case of Congress, which is of unique importance in the U.S. governmental system and has unique procedures. Whereas the preceding chapter emphasized similarities among governments, this chapter considers the special budgetary processes used by Congress and the problems it faces.

As will be seen in the following discussion, the process by which Congress acts on the budget has become increasingly complex. One illustration of the complexity is that the Congressional Research Service issued an 11-page, single-spaced report that simply itemized all of the actions that were taken by Congress to pass the budget for fiscal year 1997, and that report did not include a listing of the various actions taken by the subcommittees of the House and Senate Appropriations Committees.[1] This chapter tries to bring some clarity to understanding this intricate budget system.

The chapter has five sections. The first reviews developments in Congress until passage of the Congressional Budget and Impoundment Control Act of 1974. The next section examines the period following passage of the law and notes differences before and after 1981, when Ronald Reagan became President. The third and fourth sections discuss efforts to reduce deficits in the budget, with attention given to the Gramm-Rudman-Hollings reform, the Budget Enforcement Act of 1990, the Omnibus Budget Reconciliation Act of 1993, and the Balanced Budget Act of 1997. The last section discusses a variety of possible reforms.

227

EXPERIENCE PRIOR TO THE 1974 REFORMS

Authorizations, Revenues, and Appropriations

An axiom to remember is that Congress conducts its work in committees. One group of committees, as explained in the preceding chapter, has responsibility for substantive legislation. The committees' job is to develop authorizing legislation, which establishes departments and agencies and the programs they operate. An *authorization* provides a dollar amount as a ceiling for spending; approval to commit the government to spend, however, is given through the appropriation process.[2]

Another set of committees provides the wherewithal for the government to operate.[3] The Ways and Means Committee in the House and the Finance Committee in the Senate fashion legislation that generates revenue for the government. In addition to being responsible for tax legislation, the committees are responsible for some substantive measures, such as Social Security and Medicare. These committees handle legislation permitting increases in the federal debt; such legislation is necessary since the government accumulates debt by spending more than it collects in revenues. Raising the debt is a sensitive matter because members of Congress fear that their voting for debt increases can be used by political rivals as evidence of fiscal irresponsibility.

The Ways and Means Committee includes about 40 of the 435 members of the House, and the Finance Committee includes 20 of the 100 members of the Senate. The number of seats held by each party on the committees is generally proportional to total party membership in the chambers.

Spending is under the aegis of the Appropriations Committee in each house.[4] There are nearly 60 members on the House committee and 30 on the Senate committee. The spending side of the budget is divided among 13 subcommittees in the House and in the Senate that report out appropriation bills. Appropriations permit agencies to commit the government to expenditures, with some outlays occurring in subsequent budget years as a result of contracts signed in the current year.

In addition to the 13 regular appropriation bills covering the executive, legislative, and judicial branches of the government, Congress each year adopts one or more supplemental appropriation bills that are necessary to correct unexpected situations in which agencies have insufficient funds and to handle emergencies, such as relief for victims of the 1994 earthquake in the Los Angeles area and the 1997 flooding in the upper Midwest.

Starting in the 1940s, two major problems with this process became abundantly apparent. Since Congress dealt with the budget through a variety of bills, the budget was handled piecemeal, making difficult the setting of overall comprehensive policy. Second, the piecemeal approach meant that various subcommittees, committees, and the two chambers had to exercise discipline over themselves to complete their work in time for the beginning of the fiscal year.

When appropriation bills are not passed on time, agencies no longer have the funds to operate and are forced to shut down. In order to avoid this situation, Congress passes a continuing appropriation bill that basically permits the affected agencies to operate for a specified time period and to spend at the same level as they did in the just-completed fiscal year. When the federal government's fiscal year began on July 1, it was common for many or most appropriation bills not to have cleared Congress by the deadline, and agencies often operated for an entire fiscal year with continuing rather than regular appropriations.

Early Reforms and Emergence of Backdoor Spending

Congress first attempted to deal with these problems by passing the Legislative Reorganization Act of 1946.[5] The law allowed Congress to agree on an overall budget package before detailed tax and spending bills were developed and approved. In 1947 the House and Senate could not reach agreement, and in 1948 the chambers reached agreement but ignored it. The law was ignored in subsequent years.[6] Next, Congress experimented with using a single omnibus appropriation bill as a means of controlling total spending. The process seemed to work well for fiscal year 1951, but neither the Appropriations Committees nor the White House supported its continuation.[7]

During the 1960s and 1970s, the situation was complicated by what became known as *backdoor spending*, in which spending authority was provided outside of the appropriation process.[8] Backdoor spending may take several forms, including direct actions by substantive committees, such as contract authorizations that allow agencies to commit the government to spend and later may force the Appropriations Committees to provide the necessary funds. Substantive committees have given agencies borrowing authority, which allows them to borrow from the Treasury and spend debt receipts. Some entitlement programs (Medicare and Medicaid, for example) constitute another form of backdoor spending in that the government obligates itself to provide benefits to all qualifying applicants. Other entitlement programs, however, have expenditure limits that are established through the appropriation process.

The effect of backdoor spending was that virtually all committees in Congress came to play important roles in financial decisions, with no mechanism existing to coordinate their diverse activities. As a means of controlling spending, President Nixon vetoed appropriation bills on the grounds that they included too much spending, but that action pleased neither Congress nor the agencies that were covered by the bills. Later in his administration, Nixon went ahead and signed the bills but refused to spend all of the money, a process known as *impoundment*. This action met with great opposition by Congress and led to passage of the Congressional Budget and Impoundment Control Act of 1974, the topic of the next section.[9]

BUDGET REFORMS, 1974–1985

Many objectives underlie the 1974 reform legislation.[10] One goal was to provide Congress with a means for controlling the budget as a whole, namely, linking appropriation bills with each other and linking these with revenue measures. Controlling the budget as a whole was seen as essential if Congress was to influence economic policy. Resolving conflict between Congress and the President was another important objective that required dealing with the impoundment problem. Members of Congress wished to assert their policy-making role vis-à-vis the presidency. A process was needed by which Congress could complete its work on the budget by the beginning of the fiscal year.

It is important to recall the era in which these budget reforms were attempted. The Congressional Budget and Impoundment Control Act was signed into law in July 1974 by President Nixon. At that time, the country was experiencing an energy crisis, inflation, and economic stagnation. One month after the signing, Nixon was out of office, having been forced to resign as a result of the Watergate scandal involving his bid for re-election in 1972. Gerald R. Ford assumed the presidency.

The Ford–Carter Era

Committees and Staff. To provide for coordination among the various components of Congress, the 1974 law established House and Senate Budget Committees, whose members are representatives from the chambers' leadership and relevant committees—the four major money committees and the substantive committees that provide authorizations. There are about 45 members on the House Budget Committee and about 20 on the Senate Budget Committee.

The law provided Congress with additional staff support by creating the Congressional Budget Office to serve as overall staff to the Budget Committees, the other four money committees, and any other committees or individuals in Congress that need assistance in the area of budgeting. The Congressional Budget Office has a staff of about 230. June O'Neill, a professor of economics who earlier worked for the Congressional Budget Office, became the Congressional Budget Office's fourth director in 1995.

Timetable. The discussion here begins by explaining what was prescribed in the law and later turns to analysis of experience under the law.[11] The new process was to begin in November when the President submits to Congress a current services budget that shows future financial requirements without any change in existing laws. The President would then submit his own set of budget recommendations in January.

Working through the House and Senate Budget Committees, Congress would adopt a concurrent budget resolution that established the overall outline of the budget. The resolution would show outlays, budget authority (the authority to commit the government to spend money), the budget deficit (or surplus, if any), and government debt.

Following passage of the concurrent resolution in the spring, Congress then reverted to its old procedures. Subcommittees of the Appropriations Committees considered specific appropriation bills, and the revenue committees considered their portion of the budget. One important difference, however, was that appropriations subcommittees were expected to stay within functional ceilings contained within the concurrent resolution. Another difference was that the Budget Committees were to serve as watchdogs, making sure that legislation was not substantially at variance with the resolution, although these committees lacked authority to overrule other committees. To allow for accommodating changes in policy, a second resolution was to be adopted by September 15. That resolution could be used for *reconciliation*, a process in which committees were instructed to adjust spending and revenue measures upward or downward to conform with the overall budget plan. The beginning of the fiscal year was shifted from July 1 to October 1, thereby giving Congress three additional months for its annual budgetary work.

Adherence to the Timetable. The effort to improve the timing of congressional actions on appropriation bills was moderately successful in the early years under the law. However, by January 1981, the end of the Carter administration, Congress had slipped badly. As in the pre-1974 period, Congress was regularly late passing appropriation bills and sometimes never did pass them for some agencies. The three extra months Congress had given itself seemed to have helped only a little.

New Relationships. The new budget process altered significantly relationships between the House and the Senate. Since a concurrent budget resolution was expected of them in the early spring of each year, the two chambers were forced into coordinating their activities early in the approval cycle rather than waiting until conference committees were convened for particular tax and spending bills. This change in timing also meant that the Senate began its budget work earlier than before and no longer served as an "appeals court" to which agencies brought their complaints regarding actions taken earlier by the House and its Appropriations Committee.[12]

Impoundments. Prior to the passage of the 1974 legislation, the Nixon administration claimed it was simply following in the footsteps of virtually every President since Thomas Jefferson in deciding not to spend all of the funds that were appropriated.[13] The Anti-Deficiency Act of 1950, allowing the executive to establish agency reserves in the apportionment process (see Chapter 10), was used as further justification for impounding monies.[14]

Not only did the Nixon administration use impoundment to control total spending, but the process also was used to halt spending on grant programs that the President wanted consolidated into block grants (see Chapter 14). Several court suits developed, which generally were decided in favor of releasing funds, but the Supreme Court never addressed the issue of whether the President has the constitutional power to impound monies.

The Congressional Budget and Impoundment Control Act represented a compromise between the legislative and executive branches, albeit a compromise that the Nixon administration was forced to accept. Two forms of impoundments were permitted: *rescissions* and *deferrals*. When in the judgment of the President part of or all funds of a given appropriation were not needed, a rescission proposal was to be made to Congress; the rescission would not take effect unless approved by Congress within 45 working days. The other type of impoundment, deferral, was a proposal to delay obligations or expenditures. Like rescissions, deferral proposals had to be submitted to Congress, but these became effective unless either the House or Senate passed a resolution disapproving the proposal.

The impoundment process was dealt a major blow by the Supreme Court in *Immigration and Naturalization Service v. Chadha* (1983), which prohibited most uses of the legislative veto (see Chapter 8).[15] In effect, the 1975 law had given the President a form of item veto coupled with a legislative veto, in which the Congress had an opportunity to veto actions taken by the President, but those provisions were nullified by the *Chadha* decision. The President, then, has been forced to request congressional action on policy rescissions and deferrals. The *Chadha* decision did not deal with the constitutionality of the item veto, a topic that is addressed later in the chapter.

Congress Reoriented. During this period, Congress dramatically changed its mode of operations.[16] In an earlier time, committee chairs were held by the most senior members of Congress. They had become senior by coming from "safe" districts and states where re-election was routine. The chairs of committees tended to be southern conservatives and commonly saw their job as protecting the Treasury from the excessive spending tendencies of Presidents. During the 1970s and later, less senior members were able to gain seats on important committees, such as the Appropriations Committees, and to become chairs of these committees.

During the Nixon and Ford years, spending proclivities were reversed. Congress, which was controlled by the Democratic Party, tended to favor increased spending in contrast to an earlier time when Congress was often seen as miserly.

The White House, controlled by the Republican Party, took the role of protecting taxpayers from an allegedly spendthrift Congress.

There were other important changes in the congressional political environment.[17] Members of the House and Senate asserted greater independence, often taking positions that were at odds with their parties' leadership. There was a greater tendency to allow amendments to bills in floor debate, amendments that might well be opposed by the sponsoring committees. The membership of the Ways and Means Committee was enlarged, allowing less senior members to be added, and subcommittees were established that diluted the power of the committee's chair. Both the House and the Senate became more democratic institutions in regard to the roles played by their members. However, that meant that the leadership of the two parties exercised less discipline, making any coordinated, comprehensive approach to congressional budgeting more difficult to achieve.

The Controllability Problem. The other change to note is that the budget was becoming increasingly uncontrollable, meaning that, barring any major readjustment in commitments to programs, much of the budget could not be altered in a given year. Contributing to this situation were multiyear government contracts with government suppliers, multiyear grants to state and local governments, entitlement programs, and interest on the national debt. Another cause of uncontrollability emerged in the late 1970s, the so-called *federal credit budget*, which consists of direct and guaranteed loans by the government to individuals, corporations, state and local governments, and foreign governments (see the discussion of "hidden liabilities" in Chapter 6). The Office of Management and Budget (OMB) estimated that 73 percent of the 1981 budget was relatively uncontrollable, compared with only 63 percent for the 1970 budget.[18] (That percentage was to climb further during the Reagan years and beyond.)

The Early Reagan Years, 1981–1985

Ronald W. Reagan came into office in January 1981 following a major victory at the polls the previous November. The 1980 election created a phenomenon not seen since the 83rd Congress of 1953—the Senate dominated by a Republican majority, the House remaining under the control of the Democrats, and a Republican President. The new President submitted a set of budget proposals that provided for severe budget cuts in domestic programs, a shift toward the use of block grants to state and local governments (see Chapter 14), and an increase in defense spending. The administration recommended a massive set of cuts in the personal income tax that became law in the Economic Recovery Tax Act of 1981.[19] Although the House of Representatives was under the control of the Democrats, there was little "loyal opposition" to the President's recommendations. Reagan's popularity was of such immensity that few political leaders dared to speak out against his recommended policies.

During the early Reagan years, OMB began to play an increasingly important role.[20] Previously, OMB had had the job of making overall presentations on the budget before congressional committees, but the defense of specific recommended appropriations was left to the affected departments. After Reagan's election, major realignments in policies were being recommended on both the revenue and expenditure sides of the budget, and the defense of these recommendations became the job of OMB.[21]

The Deficit. A cloud soon developed that ended the euphoria of early 1981: The budget deficit began to grow at an alarming rate.[22] The administration had championed the 1981 massive tax cuts as a means of stimulating the economy and thereby increasing revenues. The economy was stimulated but not enough to avoid large deficits. Forecasts indicated that the budget would be considerably out of balance for the foreseeable future. Subsequently, Congress used various tactics to escape having to vote on budget resolutions that would show the budget badly out of balance and avoided voting directly on increases in the federal debt by embedding the provision in an overall budget package. The debt limit had to be raised to $1.1 trillion in 1981 and $2.1 trillion in 1985.

Timetable Problems. Rather than completing its work by the beginning of the fiscal year, Congress became dependent on using stopgap continuing appropriation bills. For example, in 1981 only one appropriation bill cleared Congress by October 1, the start of fiscal year 1982. A stopgap appropriation bill was passed to keep the government operating, but the bill expired in November. Another temporary bill was passed, with its expiration set for a month later. That bill expired before Congress could act, forcing the President to send workers home. Another continuing appropriation bill was passed that expired in March, followed by still another that carried the affected departments through the remainder of the fiscal year. The same problems occurred every year from 1982 through 1985.

Stalemate. Substantive issues were partially to blame for Congress's inability to adhere to the prescribed timetable. President Reagan during these years took a firm stand on priorities. He wanted the tax cuts that had been approved in the 1981 law, wanted a buildup in defense capability, insisted that programs such as Social Security be protected from budget cuts, and at the same time wanted a balanced budget.[23] Those objectives simply could not be met simultaneously. If the budget were to be brought into balance by reducing the unprotected areas of the budget, which included an array of social programs, including Aid to Families with Dependent Children, decimation of the remaining part of the federal government would be required. As a consequence a stalemate between the President and

Congress developed, with the two occasionally reaching agreement on actions that only marginally improved the situation.

Reconciliation. As noted above, reconciliation was intended to provide in one resolution directed guidance to committees on how they should alter authorizing, taxing, and spending legislation. The process was envisioned as coming at the end of the budget approval phase. However, in the years following the 1974 reforms, the House and Senate Budget Committees were reluctant to use reconciliation because it would have been seen as infringing on the domains of powerful committees and as a personal affront to the committee chairs.

The reconciliation process was used for the first time in 1980, the last year of the Carter administration, and from that time forward it became a prominent feature of congressional budgeting.[24] Significantly, reconciliation was used early in the 1981 approval process, with the bill clearing Congress in July rather than in September, as originally intended. Early action was needed in order to give affected committees sufficient time to adhere to the reconciliation instructions, such as reducing amounts in a given appropriation bill.

At least five major observations are to be made about the use of reconciliation.

1. The size and complexity of these bills defy individual comprehension. When these bills are assembled, even the members of the originating committees may not be familiar with all the details spread across hundreds of pages.
2. Large bills are open invitations to pork barrel politics. Some members will be successful in adding pet projects or programs that, if required to stand by themselves for approval, might not be accepted by Congress.
3. Large bills place Presidents at a distinct disadvantage in that they must either accept or reject the bills in their entirety.
4. Large bills are compatible with congressional desires to avoid blame. Members of the House or Senate cannot be held accountable for their votes supporting any one aspect of a bill, since they can say they felt compelled to vote for the bill even though it admittedly was flawed in numerous respects.
5. The use of large bills and Congress's preoccupation with budgeting in the 1980s contributed to centralization of decision making at a time when Congress had been democratized. Power was redirected to those members of Congress most closely associated with the budget process.

Shifts in Power. Power shifted away from substantive committees toward the four long-established money committees and the two relatively new Budget Committees. The balance of power among these committees varies from year to year and from chamber to chamber.

Sometimes members of the Appropriations Committees have expressed concern that their powers are diminished through the reconciliation process, which is under the direction of the Budget Committees. However, reconciliation admittedly involves other members of Congress besides those who serve on the House and Senate Budget Committees. In working out a conference bill between the two chambers, the numerous subconference committees created include conferees who are not members of either the House or Senate Budget Committees. Nevertheless, the Appropriations Committees see the situation as centralizing power in the hands of the Budget Committees.

Controllability and Policy Making. The deficit situation during the 1980s imposed constraints on Congress in regard to what it could and could not fund. The Reagan administration proposed numerous cuts in programs that were not popular in Congress. While Congress had every right to reject the President's recommendations, in rejecting the proposed savings and not wanting to adopt a budget more out of balance than recommended by the President, Congress was forced to find offsetting measures to raise revenues, cut expenditures, or both.

There was a tendency to impose across-the-board budget cuts on programs. This meant that programs became smaller and smaller; advocates of programs struggled to maintain the existence of programs no matter how small they might become. "Staying alive" became an objective, since it would be extremely difficult to revive a program once cut out of the budget. Whether Congress made substantive policy during this period is difficult to determine.[25] While what Congress approved is different from what the President recommended, that does not necessarily mean Congress had a great influence on policy. It should be understood, of course, that each branch takes the other into account when advocating policy.

Impact on Departments. The uncertainty of a department's programs, given recommended cuts by the President, is unsettling; the uncertainty is compounded when Congress delays taking action and resorts to continuing appropriation bills. Congressional budgeting problems resulted in workers being briefly sent home in November 1981 and October 1986. There were numerous other cliffhangers in which Congress narrowly met a deadline before workers had to be sent home for lack of government funding. Crises such as these are administratively disruptive and increase citizen discontent with government.

THE LATER REAGAN YEARS AND THE BUSH YEARS

The situation came to a head in the latter part of 1985. Democrats agreed with Republicans and representatives agreed with senators that the deficit situation had become intolerable. The White House did not exhibit the same level of concern but concurred that something should be done to remedy the situation.

Gramm-Rudman-Hollings

By October 1, 1985, the beginning of the fiscal year, not a single appropriation bill had cleared Congress; a stopgap continuing appropriation bill was passed to keep the government operating. The budget resolution had been adopted on August 1 despite the official deadline of May 15. By November the stopgap appropriation bill was expiring, and the debt-limit ceiling was expiring, forcing another stopgap appropriation bill to be rushed through Congress, along with an increase in the debt ceiling.

Enactment of the Law. It was in this politically charged atmosphere that Congress adopted the Balanced Budget and Emergency Deficit Control Act of 1985.[26] The chief authors were Senators W. Philip Gramm (Republican of Texas), Warren B. Rudman (Republican of New Hampshire), and Ernest F. Hollings (Democrat of South Carolina). As an indication of how Congress had changed, both Gramm and Rudman were serving their first terms in the Senate; in an earlier time, only more senior senators would have authored legislation of such importance.

The main objective of Gramm-Rudman-Hollings was simple: to reduce the size of the budget deficit annually until expenditures were in balance with revenues. Target figures were set, and if the President and Congress could not reach agreement on a budget package that met the target figure for a given fiscal year, then automatic across-the-board reductions in expenditures were to occur—a process known as sequestration. Senator Rudman described the law as "a bad idea whose time has come."[27]

Legal Challenge and Revision. As soon as the law was enacted, it was challenged in court. The case was brought on appeal to the Supreme Court, which ruled in July 1986 that one key provision violated the Constitution.[28] The comptroller general, who heads the General Accounting Office and as such is an officer of Congress, was found to have been granted executive powers in violation of the Constitution. In anticipation of such a ruling, the 1985 law included a fallback procedure, but it was one that did not have sufficient restrictions to force compliance with the deficit targets that had been established.

After much debate, Congress in September 1987 adopted the Balanced Budget and Emergency Deficit Control Reaffirmation Act, which modified the original Gramm-Rudman-Hollings legislation.[29] In the interim between the Supreme Court's ruling and the 1987 revisions, the Republicans lost control of the Senate in the November 1986 elections. When Congress convened in January 1987, the Democrats controlled both chambers while the White House was still occupied by President Reagan.

Timetable. Gramm-Rudman-Hollings, as amended, provided a new timetable for Congress to act on the budget and set new target figures for annual budget reductions until the budget was supposed to be balanced in fiscal 1993. The Gramm-Rudman-Hollings process began with the President's submitting his budget in early January. Provisions were made for calculating a baseline, which is analogous to current services calculations. The baseline projects budget authority, outlays, revenues, and the resulting deficit or balance for the budget year and subsequent ones. For these calculations, the off-budget was included with the on-budget (see Chapter 6). Government-sponsored enterprises (see Chapter 6), however, were not part of the baseline, nor were tax expenditures. Congress then was to prepare its budget resolution in response to the President's recommendations. Reconciliation was to be completed in June, after which the President was to prepare a midsession budget due in July. Baselines were to become a driving force, since available spending was a function of the projected caps on mandatory and discretionary spending.[30]

Sequestration. The procedure to force reductions in the deficit—sequestration—was slated to begin in August. At this point baseline calculations became critical, since the results indicated how much spending must be eliminated from the budget unless revenues were to be increased through higher taxes and the like. The President was to issue his initial sequester order, indicating cuts to be made in programs, projects, and activities (PPAs), and that order was to become effective on October 1, the beginning of the fiscal year, unless Congress and the President agreed on an alternative plan for reducing the deficit. Waiver of these rigid provisions was allowed only when specific conditions of economic recession existed or when war was declared. Half of the cuts were apportioned to defense and the other half to domestic programs. A percentage was derived for determining how much to cut each PPA so that the President did not have authority to impose more severe cuts on some programs and less severe ones on others.

Special rules applied to some domestic programs, such as Medicare and guaranteed student loans; the rules generally limited the severity of sequestration. Other PPAs were totally protected from sequestration. These included the basic retirement program under Social Security, Aid to Families with Dependent Children, civil service retirement funds, and the like. The budgets of Congress and the courts were subject to sequestration.

Sequestration was intended as a procedure of last resort. The process was to be used only in the event that Congress failed to develop a budget that was within the deficit limit specified in the law and that met with the approval of the President, who of course could veto whatever Congress developed. Sequestration was thought to be so unpalatable to both Congress and the President that it would force the two sides to work together in order to avoid triggering the process.

1987 Budget Accord. Gramm-Rudman-Hollings may have been a bad idea whose time had come, but it was overtaken by events in 1987. Less than a month after Congress passed the Reaffirmation Act of 1987, the stock market crashed.

On Tuesday, October 19, the Dow Jones Industrial Average dropped 23 percent (508 points), a greater drop than the 13-percent decline on October 28, 1929.[31]

The crash, as would be expected, had a startling effect on private and public sector leaders. Although a feared depression did not materialize, the situation served as a catalyst to force an agreement on budget deficit reduction. In November a two-year agreement was reached by the President and Congress on cutting the deficit but by no means eliminating it. After four stopgap measures, Congress on December 22 passed a huge continuing appropriation bill, along with a reconciliation bill, for the remainder of the fiscal year.

Gramm-Rudman-Hollings and the 1987 budget accord contributed to the trend toward centralization mentioned earlier. Both provided for decision making to be handled by central players, with lesser figures being told what the parameters of the budget would be.

The 1980s closed without Gramm-Rudman-Hollings having appreciably affected the overall budget deficit situation of the government.[32] Reagan's vice president, George W. Bush, was elected as President in 1988. One of his pledges was "Read my lips: No new taxes." With both the new President and the Congress fearful of citizen revolts against possible tax increases, cutbacks in aid programs such as Medicare, and further cuts in services, reducing the deficit to zero as planned under Gramm-Rudman-Hollings had low priority.[33]

The 1990 Crisis and Accord

Another Crisis Situation. By late summer 1990, the budget situation reached another crisis stage. If Congress proceeded on its existing course, Gramm-Rudman-Hollings would trigger a huge sequestration that would have severe effects on all programs. Political leaders were not only concerned with immediate consequences in the upcoming November elections but also with the prospect that the situation would only worsen in subsequent years. Neither Republicans nor Democrats wanted to be facing an explosive budget situation during the 1992 presidential election.

The Budget Enforcement Act of 1990 was created in a period of turmoil.[34] Congress was unable to complete its budget work by October 1990, an all-too-familiar problem, and the use of a continuing appropriation bill and a brief shutdown of nonessential government services were required. President Bush had threatened to lay off air traffic controllers along with other federal workers, which would have forced the closing of the nation's airports and created havoc for business and other travelers. The law, which was approved in November, was the result of negotiations between congressional leaders and the President similar to those in 1987.

Main Features of the 1990 Compromise. The Budget Enforcement Act had two main features.[35] It included a package of revenue increases and expenditure cuts aimed at reducing the budget deficit on a multiyear basis and provided for a new budget process that officially only temporarily replaced Gramm-Rudman-Hollings. The package included substantial tax increases, which President Bush would later regret having approved, since he was attacked in the 1992 election campaign for having reneged on his pledge of no new taxes. The law was projected to reduce the deficit by $500 billion over its five-year life.

The 1990 law shifted emphasis away from budget deficits, although the focus on the deficit was to return in subsequent years. In effect, the law was based on the premise that Congress had little control over the total annual deficit and that the emphasis should therefore be on controlling those areas over which control was possible. Entitlement program expenditures were allowed to fluctuate according to shifts in the eligibility pools. Social Security and Medicare top the list of entitlements programs, costing nearly $400 billion in 1990–1991.[36] The law also exempted the budget from emergencies; the Persian Gulf War and the bailout of failed savings and loan institutions were to fall under this heading. While the law allowed setting aside discretionary spending limits during economic recession (1991 and 1992 met the criterion for recession), Congress chose to abide by the limits, since setting them aside might have been politically destabilizing.

Spending limits, then, were set for the remainder of the budget, based on the development of baseline projections. A politically advantageous aspect of baseline budgeting is that it allows political leaders to increase spending but claim they have cut the budget as in the case of funding a program below the projected budget figure but above the current budget.[37] Conversely, political leaders can claim they are not cutting an agency's budget when funding the unit below the baseline figure, but the reality is that the agency is not receiving funds that keep pace with inflation or workload increases. Whatever the case, baseline budgeting leads to much confusion and can be a helpful tool for those who wish to obfuscate what is happening at budget time.[38]

The Budget Enforcement Act established so-called *fire walls* separating the three areas of defense, international aid, and domestic spending. Spending caps were set for each of these for fiscal 1991, 1992, and 1993, and overall budget caps were set for 1994 and 1995. The significance of the fire walls was that each area was protected from possible budget cuts in response to budget increases in one of the other areas. For instance, the rules prevented defense advocates from trying to avoid cuts by proposing extra cuts in domestic programs. As the Soviet Union crumbled and Eastern European nations dismantled their communist governments, critics of defense spending advocated extraordinary defense cuts as a means of creating a "peace dividend" that could be used for augmenting domestic program expenditures. However, the fire walls of the Budget Enforcement Act disallowed such shifts in spending.

Due to the fire walls, the law pitted domestic programs against one another and provided for a *pay-as-you-go* (PAYGO) mechanism to enforce adherence to spending caps. When supporters of a program wished to increase its funding, then corresponding decreases in funding were required in other programs or additional revenues had to be raised. Similarly, any effort to reduce taxes forced reductions in spending in order to avoid exceeding the deficit limits in the law. The caps in effect gave an advantage to those programs already budgeted and made difficult the inclusion of new or expanded initiatives. The Office of Management and Budget was required by the law to sequester funds when limits were exceeded.

Timetable. The law revised once again the timetable for action on the budget. Table 9–1 shows the new timetable as applied to the fiscal 1998 budget. Submission of the President's budget to Congress was shifted to no later than February 1

Table 9–1   Federal Budget Process Timetable, Fiscal 1998

Date	Action To Be Completed
Between the first Monday in January and the first Monday in February	President transmits the budget, including a sequester preview report
Six weeks later	Congressional committees report budget estimates to Budget Committees
April 15	Action to be completed on congressional budget resolution
May 15	House consideration of annual appropriations bills may begin
June 15	Action to be completed on reconciliation
June 30	Action on appropriations to be completed by House
July 15	President transmits Mid-Session Review of the budget
August 20	OMB updates the sequester preview
October 1	Fiscal year begins
15 days after the end of a session of Congress	OMB issues final sequester report, and the president issues a sequester order, if necessary

Source: Reprinted from *The Budget System and Concepts*, p. 6, 1997, U.S. Office of Management and Budget.

so that when a new President takes office, the budget is submitted by the new President and not the lame-duck President. As with Gramm-Rudman-Hollings, Congress was to complete action on a concurrent budget resolution by April 15 and complete reconciliation by June 15. The result is an annual spring ritual in which the House and Senate Budget Committees must each work with its chamber's committees and members to forge an agreement that will withstand later challenges as the details of the budget are prepared. As noted earlier, reconciliation often involves giving unpopular instructions to committees to reduce spending and increase revenues.

The Budget Enforcement Act along with its companion Omnibus Budget Reconciliation Act of 1990, were successful inasmuch as they limited the growth in programs, but they were not intended to eliminate the annual deficit and had no such effect.[39] The laws successfully kept the budget process under control through the 1992 presidential election, a primary objective of many political leaders. Members of Congress came to the realization that whatever proposals they wished to advance, a price was to be placed on them. Neither tax cuts nor spending increases could be advocated without taking into account their effects on the overall deficit.

THE CLINTON YEARS

Coming into office in January 1993, President Clinton attempted to follow through on his campaign promise to bring the budget deficit under control. Bill Clinton was the first Democratic President since Jimmy Carter left office 12 years before.

The 1993 Accord

In its early effort to demonstrate a commitment to reform, the new Clinton administration ran into trouble trying to gain congressional approval of a proposed stimulus package to bolster a weak economy. Critics, who claimed the package was unnecessary in that the economy was on the rebound and that the government could not afford more spending at a time when the deficit was high, were successful in defeating the proposal in the Senate. The attack, which was led by Republicans, left observers wondering whether the new administration would be successful in winning approval for a full budget proposal.

The Omnibus Budget Reconciliation Act, adopted in August 1993, was approved by the narrowest of margins—218 to 216 in the House and 51 to 50 in the Senate (Vice President Gore cast the tie-breaking vote).[40] The measure was passed without any Republican votes and with considerable lobbying on the part of Republican members to have their Democratic colleagues join them in the opposition. Since the Clinton administration knew that the vote would be close, the White House lobbied members with great intensity, and as a result, all members had ample opportunity to be involved in the process of adopting the budget, unlike earlier situations, such as in 1990, when the rank and file complained that the leadership had made all of the decisions.

The 1993 law included four types of actions:

1. tax increases, particularly increases in individual income taxes for the wealthiest Americans, gasoline taxes, and corporate taxes
2. spending cuts, notably cuts in Medicare, Medicaid, and defense but other programs as well
3. spending increases, such as for empowerment zones, which are designated urban and rural areas that are provided with increased social services in order to attract business
4. tax expenditures, such as tax credits for lower-income workers and tax incentives for businesses operating in empowerment zones

Overall, the law was expected to shrink but in no way eliminate the deficit. The spending caps of the Budget Enforcement Act were revised and extended through fiscal 1998.[41] Annual deficits under the law were expected to be around $200 billion, and because nearly $500 billion in deficits was to be eliminated over five years, the debt was expected to increase by "only" $1.1 trillion. The total deficit reductions were expected to be equal to or somewhat less than the reductions that resulted from the Budget Enforcement Act of 1990. If the administration wanted to tackle the budget deficit in earnest, then another round of spending cuts and tax increases would be necessary. Further, the budget would need to be revisited if the President and Congress could reach agreement on a plan for revising health care and its financing, a high priority of the first Clinton administration and one that failed to win congressional approval.

The 1995–1996 Debacle

The November 1994 elections set up a situation for intense executive-legislative conflict that would benefit few, harm many, and add to the skepticism of the citizenry about the worthiness of government and its political leaders. The elections produced victories for the Republicans, giving them the control of both the Senate, which in recent times had been under Republican control for only two years during the Reagan administration, and the House of Representatives, which had not been under Republican rule for 40 years. The House's new Speaker, Newt Gingrich (Republican of Georgia) had championed a Contract with America in the elections, and Gingrich along with a sizeable group of newly elected Republican members felt deeply committed in legislating the various components of the contract.[42] This extensive package of proposals included a balanced budget amendment to the Constitution, the line-item veto, and a requirement that a three-fifths majority vote would be necessary to raise taxes.

The new Republican Congress and the Democratic President found themselves on an unavoidable collision track. October 1, 1995, the start of the new fiscal year, arrived with no budget agreement. The conflict, however, was not simply one between the two branches of government, for Republicans were pitted against Republicans, Democrats against Democrats, and the House and Senate against each other. While the Republicans had numerical control of the Congress, they lacked cohesion in either chamber over the relative importance of balancing the budget in comparison with programmatic priorities. Senate Republicans were especially cautious about supporting severe budget cuts as a means for bringing the budget into balance. Senator Arlen Specter (Republican of Pennsylvania) said that trying to gain agreement on any compromise was akin to "a high-wire act without a net in a typhoon."[43]

The situation disintegrated when Congress sent to the President two unacceptable bills—one a stopgap continuing appropriation and the other, a bill allowing for short-term borrowing by the Treasury.[44] Clinton vetoed the measures, forcing the government to shut down on a partial basis. The debt problem created by the veto on the second bill was temporarily handled by borrowing funds from the civil service employees' retirement fund. In subsequent days, Republicans were able to gather together the necessary votes to pass an omnibus reconciliation bill for the government, but the President vetoed it, opposing program cuts and, most notably, cuts in the rate of growth for programs such as Medicare.[45]

What ensued was a series of partial government shutdowns starting in November 1995 as a result of agencies not having budgets to support their operations. People were inconvenienced in innumerable respects, such as not being able to visit the Grand Canyon and not being able to obtain a passport for overseas travel. While the government continued to distribute Social Security payments, processing was halted on new applications for benefits. Businesses in Washington, relying on patronage from business travelers and tourists, were hurt financially as people stayed away from the city. Stopgap continuing resolutions, which allow agencies to continue operations until an appropriation bill presumably can be passed, were used repeatedly, with the constant uncertainty of whether the Congress and the White House would reach an overall agreement or even the next temporary agreement to keep the government operating. With all of this turmoil, the President never delivered to Congress a complete budget and set of budget documents for the next fiscal year, 1997.

A series of minor compromises eventually was reached, allowing the government to resume operations. All participants were eager to have the battles resolved, if for only a short period, to avoid having this situation continue into the 1996 presidential election. As it was, Republicans probably were held to blame by the electorate for the shutdowns and overall chaos, partially explaining the losses by Republicans in the House of Representatives, although not enough to lose control, and the win by President Clinton in his bid for re-election.

The 1997 Balanced Budget Act

January 1997 ushered in the 105th Congress, with a new collective mindset, and was the beginning of President Clinton's second and final term in office. The congressional leadership realized that a balanced budget could not be achieved without Clinton's support, since it would be virtually impossible to gain enough votes to override any presidential veto. A balanced budget would inevitably involve budget cuts, which are always unpopular with anyone affected by them, and as a consequence, the Republicans were eager for a bipartisan budget agreement as a means for spreading the blame for cuts in programs. President Clinton, who had earlier championed the idea of a balanced budget, may well have seen 1997 as an opportunity to achieve this goal and consequently to enhance his record of achievement. Working behind the scenes were a group of largely conservative Democrats in the House, who billed themselves as the "Blue Dogs," eager to find some middle-road compromise that would avoid elimination of programs as a budget reduction effort and yet bring spending under control in order to balance the budget.[46]

In May 1997, President Clinton and the Republican leadership in Congress agreed on the outline for a package of decisions that was supposed to balance the budget by the year 2002.[47] Just prior to the agreement, congressional Democrats threatened to oppose the measure, because they had not been included in the negotiations. Also, the Republican chairs of standing congressional committees, such as the ones dealing with highways, had not been included. Many Democrats and Republicans wondered about the adequacy of leadership in their respective parties.

Greatly facilitating the negotiations was a robust economy, which allowed budget forecasters to raise revenue estimates, which in turn automatically reduced a good portion of the gap between high expenditures and lower revenues.[48] The unemployment rate was at its lowest level in nearly a quarter century.[49]

The agreement was followed up by passage of two key laws—the Balanced Budget Act and the Taxpayer Relief Act—both of which were signed by President Clinton at a special ceremony on August 5, 1997. At the ceremony, President Clinton said:

> We come here today, Democrats and Republicans, Congress and President, Americans of goodwill from all points of view and all walks of life, to celebrate a true milestone for our nation. . . . I will sign into law

the first balanced budget in a generation—a balanced budget that honors our values, puts our fiscal house in order, expands vistas of opportunity for all our people, and fashions a new government to lead in a new era.[50]

At the same ceremony, Speaker of the House Gingrich said:

We have proven together that the American constitutional system works, that slowly, over time, we listen to the will of the American people, that we reach beyond parties, we reach beyond institutions, and we find ways to get things done.[51]

The Balanced Budget Act is an immense piece of legislation covering such topics as food stamps, housing, communications, welfare, education, civil service retirement, and much, much more; and the Taxpayer Relief Act provides tax benefits for college education, capital gains tax cuts, family tax credits for children, and other relief measures.[52] Cuts in domestic programs were included, and Medicare expenditures were shaved back. Although spending for Medicaid, which serves the needy, was reduced, the cuts were not as severe as some had advocated.

The Balanced Budget Act included important "budget enforcement" provisions. The law made permanent the requirement that budget resolutions cover a five-year period. Discretionary spending limits, to be enforced through sequestration, were extended through fiscal year 2002 as were PAYGO requirements.

The 1997 laws, however, did not adopt several changes that had been advocated. Instead of overhauling Medicare, the Balanced Budget Act provided for the appointment of a National Bipartisan Commission on the Future of Medicare, with members appointed by the President and congressional leaders. The commission's task was to make a set of recommendations on the financing of the health care system for the elderly by March 1, 1999. There was reason to wonder whether the timing presented a problem in that the commission's recommendations would be forthcoming just as the presidential election of 2000 would be getting into gear.

Perhaps the most important matter not covered by the 1997 legislation was any restructuring of the retirement portion of Social Security. That fund was generating a surplus that had been drawn upon to help fund government operations, with the government in effect providing an IOU to the fund for monies borrowed and additional IOUs for supposed interest payments. As political leaders well knew at the time of the budget deal, some reform of Social Security was needed if the budget was to be truly balanced, but the knotty issues involved were set aside for another time. One proposal that had circulated and which was not part of the Balanced Budget Act, was to revise the consumer price index in order to avoid what seemed to be a windfall for Social Security recipients every time prices rose. The consumer price index was seen as exaggerating the rate of inflation and therefore providing unwarranted payment increases for Social Security retirees.

Reaching the agreement and translating the agreement into legislation were difficult tasks but certainly as difficult, if not more difficult, would be maintaining the agreement over time. With important segments of both parties displeased with the package of changes, one could envision the day when forces would be mustered to revise some portions of the package. One such revision that surfaced from the outset was the proposal to increase highway spending. Although proponents of the agreement successfully rebuffed the proposal in 1997, it was unclear whether they would be equally successful in subsequent years.[53] Asked at a press conference why he thought subsequent Congresses would adhere to the package, President Clinton said that fiscal responsibility and a balanced budget lead to good economic times. "If you spend a lot of money you shouldn't be spending and you run big deficits in good economic times, the international financial markets will punish the United States."[54]

An important threat to the agreement was whether economic assumptions would hold up over time. The economic boom of 1997 could not last indefinitely, and when there was a downturn, revenue would fall and could push the budget well out of balance. An inescapable reality is that optimistic budget assumptions often prove false as time progresses.[55]

A final threat was the item-veto power exercised by President Clinton. In using this power for the first time by excising portions of the Balanced Budget Act and the Taxpayer Relief Act, he triggered a constitutional challenge to the item-veto power and left hanging in the balance the legal status of these two laws. The item veto is discussed in the next section of this chapter.

PROPOSED REFORMS AND THEIR PROSPECTS

Problems Facing the Congress, the President, and the Nation

The Congress, the President, and the nation face a complex set of interwoven problems. The 1997 budget agreement may have taken major steps in balancing the budget, but important problems remain. Some problems concern substantive issues and others concern budget process issues.

Substantive Issues. As noted in Chapter 6, deficits are perceived as demons that haunt all aspects of decision making, including budgetary decision making, but deficits are only a simple manifestation of a much more complex array of problems.[56] Starting in the early 1980s, a structural deficit of giant proportions developed that could only be remedied with major refashioning of the federal budget. Cutting the deficit is seen as essential, since the deficit may thwart economic growth at a time when the government needs to foster growth, given the fierce competition in the global market. Federal borrowing is seen as absorbing national savings that otherwise would be used for capital formation.[57]

Another group of substantive problems involves the question of what is the proper role of government in a new era in which international trade is critical. Are the nation's interests best served simply by having tax policies that favor corporate activities or should government forge closer links with certain industries? And if the latter, which industries?

Still another group of problems concerns defense in the post–Cold War era. A perennial question is how much defense is enough? Defense policy must be rethought given the absence of the threat of nuclear attack by Russia and an increase in demands that the United States assist in resolving conflicts in places like the Middle East, Somalia, and what was once Yugoslavia, as well as defend against terrorism.

Domestic problems are not to be ignored. To many observers, the 1980s bolstered defense at the expense of needed domestic programs, including programs to aid the nation's cities, the educational system, and the health care system. Yet, increasing spending in these and other areas in the 1990s seems infeasible given the size of the deficit. Mounting costs for entitlements drive up the size of the budget.[58] Congress in 1995 passed a massive welfare reform law that was aimed at reducing federal expenditures in this field and shifting responsibilities to the states (see Chapter 14).

As was noted, the 1997 budget agreement may have made progress toward achieving a balanced budget, but painful decisions still must be made to bring the budget into balance. The lives of everyone are potentially affected, from the farmer in Idaho, to the elementary school child in inner-city St. Louis, to the shop owner in a military town where the local Air Force base may be closing, to the IBM executive who fears being furloughed, to the retiree in Miami who worries that health and pension programs will be cut back. The issues raise fundamental questions about individual responsibility, corporate independence in a highly competitive environment, and the proper responsibilities of government. An assessment and almost continuous reassessment of program objectives is essential coupled with an evaluation of who should benefit from programs and in what ways.

Process Issues. Can Congress better organize itself in order to deal effectively with this daunting set of problems?[59] If Congress's primary role is to set policy and provide leadership in furthering the nation's interests, then do means exist for improving the processes of that august body to help it meet its responsibilities?

Fundamental questions are at stake. For example, how should power be distributed between the leadership and the individual members? Placing power in the hands of those in leadership positions can help facilitate decision making but at the same time can subjugate the voices of individual members, who have been chosen by their voters to represent them.[60] How should responsibilities be distributed between new members and those with seniority? How should power be shared by the two chambers of Congress? To what extent should policy decisions be made in committees and subcommittees, with the chamber as a whole, whether it be the House or Senate, being restricted from influencing the details of legislation?[61] What are the appropriate powers of committee and subcommittee chairpersons vis-à-vis their members? To what extent should or must members delegate powers to their own staffs, who in turn may seem to obtain unbridled influence in some situations?[62] How can Congress begin to comprehend the vastness of societal problems and the information available on these problems?[63] To what extent should or must Congress delegate powers to the President and to others in the executive branch of government?[64]

These questions of process cut to the core of any congressional member's future. For example, getting appointed to the "right" committee—any committee in a position to divert funds to one's home district—is considered critical, and any plan to reorganize the committee structure is necessarily regarded as threatening.[65] One view is that Congress will never be able to deal with fundamental problems as long as campaign funds must be obtained largely through contributions from constituent organizations, since those organizations are likely to donate substantial funds only on the condition that members provide pork barrel spending and other immediate benefits.

The Item Veto

As discussed in Chapter 8, most governors have item-veto power, allowing them to reduce or eliminate line items in appropriation bills, but the President of the United States has lacked such power. The power could be provided in a statute or, as many would advocate, in an amendment to the Constitution. Ulysses S. Grant may have been the first President to ask for the item-veto power.[66]

Pros and Cons of the Item Veto. One of the main justifications for the item veto is that the President needs authority to reduce or eliminate funding of pork barrel projects that have little merit other than pleasing specific constituent groups of individual members of Congress. However, what constitutes excesses in spending is necessarily a function of one's values and priorities, and the executive branch is not immune from advocating spending for programs and projects of questionable utility. One aspect that is clearly *not* a purpose of the item veto is to reduce the budget deficit. The spending cuts that might be made by a President would be unlikely to have any appreciable effect on total spending.[67]

Most proposals for a presidential item veto stop short of allowing deletions in the language of appropriation bills, which is a popular location for embedding pet projects of representatives and senators. A bill might provide $65 million for a worthy activity, and the supporting language of the appropriation might earmark $150,000 of that amount for a project in a specific state—the home state of a key senator on the appropriations subcommittee handling the bill. Some states allow the governor to modify appropriations language, but that can lead to problems, as in the case of governors deleting letters from words to form new words, a procedure that has been referred to as the Vanna White technique, a reference to a popular television game show.[68]

Critics of the item veto contend that it gives the President an unwarranted increase in power, allowing for presidential policy preferences to supplant congressional preferences. If a President needed to muster senatorial votes for an initiative, he could privately threaten to item veto favored projects of individual senators. When the White House was controlled by one political party and the Congress by the other, White House priorities might prevail. One can speculate that if Presidents Reagan and Bush had had the item-veto power, several agencies and programs would have been eliminated, such as the Economic Development Administration, the Appalachian Regional Commission, and urban mass transportation formula grants.

The Rescission Process. Procedures, as initially established by the Congressional Budget and Impoundment Control Act of 1974, provide that the President submit packages of proposed rescissions in appropriations enacted by Congress. The Congress has 45 days in which it is in session to approve each package or approve its own set of cuts. Before adopting an appropriation bill, the Congress is made aware of what items are likely to be cut by the President; presidential priorities are reported to Congress through budget submissions and statements of administration policy, which indicate White House opposition to provisions in draft appropriation bills. When the President does propose rescissions, a consistent pattern has been that Congress makes greater cuts than recommended by the President, albeit using a different set of priorities to determine what items are cut.[69]

Enhanced Rescission and the Line Item Veto Act. After decades of debate, the Republican-controlled Congress enacted the Line Item Veto Act of 1996, but set an effectiveness date of January 1997, when presumably a Republican would move into the White House, replacing President Clinton.[70] The Congress did not want to hand to President Clinton the item-veto power, which he might use to his advantage in the 1996 presidential election. Of course, the Republicans were sorely disappointed when President Clinton easily won re-election.

A general consensus exists that a "true" item-veto power could only be provided to the President through a constitutional amendment, and therefore, the 1996 law is best viewed as *enhanced rescission power.* The law gave the President power to cancel three types of provisions: (1) new budget authority for discretionary spending, (2) new entitlements or increased entitlements, and (3) tax provisions that would benefit 100 or fewer individuals or corporations. The President was required to veto an entire item and not just reduce an amount, and could not veto existing entitlement programs and other forms of mandatory spending. Any savings achieved through this process could not be reappropriated for other purposes but rather would be used to reduce the budget deficit. This *lockbox* provision was important to those who wanted the veto power to be used for deficit reduction. The law had a sunset provision, withdrawing this power from the President on January 1, 2005.

In an effort to circumvent the Supreme Court's ban on legislative vetoes (see earlier discussion of the *Chadha* decision), the 1996 measure provided a convoluted form of veto. The President was to submit a set of proposed budget cuts. The Congress then had 30 calendar days, during a time when it is in session, to consider passing a *disapproval bill*. If the Congress did not act, the proposed vetoes would take effect. The disapproval bill would be on an expedited schedule but would go through the standard procedure of passage in both houses and most likely go through a conference committee procedure for working out the differences between the houses. The President could sign or veto the disapproval bill. A veto of the disapproval bill would mean he was standing behind his original set of decisions to cut items in the budget. The Congress could override the President's veto only by a two-thirds vote.

The law included a section for judicial review, allowing for members of Congress and others to file suit in the U.S. District Court for the District of Columbia, with its decision being appealable directly to the Supreme Court. Well before President Clinton had an opportunity to use this new set of powers, the law was challenged in court by Senator Robert C. Byrd (Democrat of West Virginia), who had been the law's most outspoken critic, calling it "a malformed monstrosity."[71] The district court agreed with Byrd that the law had unconstitutionally delegated congressional powers to the President.[72] That decision was appealed to the Supreme Court, which ruled on a procedural rather than substantive basis. The Court in *Raines v. Byrd* (1997) decided that Byrd and others lacked *standing*, a condition in which the party bringing suit shows an injury has occurred or is about to occur. The Court found that an injury had not occurred, since the President had not yet exercised the new power granted to him.[73] Standing was said to be especially important in cases involving conflict between two branches of the government, in this case, between the Congress and the President. The ruling avoided any discussion of the merits of Byrd's position and set in motion the use of the item-veto power whenever one or more of the three conditions arose—presidential objections to new spending authority, new or increased entitlements, and tax provisions benefiting a small number of people or corporations.

The item veto was first used by President Clinton to cut three items from the Balanced Budget Act of 1997 and the Taxpayer Relief Act of 1997, just five days after signing these laws. The vetoes covered (1) tax shelters for financial service companies, (2) a Medicaid provision that specifically would benefit New York State, and (3) a tax benefit that would go to a small number of agri-businesses, including large corporations that in the President's view did not need such a tax advantage. The President noted that many items were protected from his veto on the grounds that the White House had an obligation to act in good faith in retaining items that had been explicitly approved as part of the bargaining process with the Republican-controlled Congress.[74] He agreed with suggestions from the press that the vetoed items were relatively minor but noted that he expected more significant vetoes to arise when appropriations bills began to reach his desk for approval. He expressed hope that his experience as Governor of Arkansas would be repeated as President, namely that the Congress would restrain itself from including pork barrel projects and programs in appropriations bills, since a presidential veto would surely be used. President Clinton said, "It would suit me if, after a while, the use of the veto became quite rare because there was a disciplined agreement not to have projects that ought not be funded in the first place."[75] The future of the item-veto process was left in doubt as constitutional challenges were lodged in federal court.

Proposed Balanced Budget Requirement

A persistent proposal has been for the federal government to adopt a balanced budget requirement.[76] Expenditures would not be allowed to exceed revenues. Since Gramm-Rudman-Hollings was a type of balanced budget statutory requirement and it failed miserably, a constitutional amendment is favored over a statutory requirement.

Proponents typically refer to the successful use of this requirement at the state level, where all but Vermont and Wyoming require some form of balanced budget.[77] Governors or budget boards are required in 43 states to submit balanced budgets, legislatures in 36 states are required to enact balanced budgets, and 39 states have a requirement for a balanced budget at year's end. In 35 states, the requirement is embedded in the constitution, with the remaining 13 states having statutory requirements. It should be noted that balanced budget requirements in most states do not preclude borrowing for capital investments, and few state budgets are annually balanced when both current and capital expenditures are taken into account. Many states also have limitations on revenue raising and spending, stemming from the Proposition 13 movement of the 1970s.

A major concern regarding implementation of a balanced budget requirement at the federal level is that the measure might impose unwarranted restrictions in times of economic hardship or national security emergencies.[78] Some form of override mechanism must be included for situations when the federal government needs to spend more to counteract economic recessions and to wage war. For the override to occur, both houses might be required to have votes of 60 percent, two-thirds, or a majority of all members (rather than a majority of those voting).

Having some set of enforcement mechanisms is regarded as essential for successful implementation, although such mechanisms do not exist at the state level, where the balanced budget process is regarded as generally successful. States do not use sequestration and other such procedures to force their budgets to be balanced when lawmakers are unable to agree on a balanced budget. Skeptics of congressional abilities to reach agreement on a set of revenue and spending programs that are balanced fear that Congress would resort to "smoke and mirror" techniques that merely give the illusion of a balanced budget. Common devices would include overestimating revenues to be collected and moving some expenditures off-budget so that they would be excluded from official total spending. Attempting to prohibit such practices by outlawing them in the constitutional amendment would be cumbersome, and creative minds might always be able to find loopholes in the amendment's language. In addition, detailed provisions in the amendment could create an inflexibility that later would be detrimental to the nation's best interests.

Critics of the balanced budget proposal contend that it would unduly enhance the powers of the President. A typical requirement of balanced budget proposals is that the President would have to submit a balanced budget, thereby setting the agenda from which Congress might have little latitude to veer. One line of reasoning is that in order for the proposal to be effective, an item veto for the President would be essential.

The balanced budget amendment was part of the Republicans' Contract with America. The party, despite its control of Congress since 1995, has been unable to move the proposal out of the Congress by mustering the necessary two-thirds vote.[79] Were that to occur, then the amendment would be forwarded to the state legislatures for their approval. Until such an amendment is adopted—if at all— the government will operate under the Balanced Budget Act.

Proposed Congressional Reorganization

A perennial topic of discussion in Congress is how it could better organize itself to fulfill its responsibilities, especially its budget responsibilities. Important changes did occur as a result of passage of the Legislative Reorganization Acts of

1946 and 1970 as well as other reorganizations that affected either the House or Senate.[80]

Committees. One typical proposal is to reduce the number of congressional committees and subcommittees. These various bodies create problems in coordination, since their domains often overlap and subject areas are needlessly segmented among committees and subcommittees. Power becomes diffuse, and setting overall policy is complicated by the split jurisdictions. The greater the number of committees, the greater the number of committee assignments members have, meaning that they can easily be scheduled to attend two or more committee meetings at the same time. This problem is more acute in the Senate where 100 members must handle the same work that the 435 members in the House handle.

The large number of committees and subcommittees poses problems for the executive branch as well as Congress. Agency administrators complain that valuable time is wasted in having to prepare for and testify before these panels. The defense area is particularly subject to comprehensive congressional involvement, with Defense Department officials having to testify before dozens of committees and subcommittees.

The size of committee membership is a related concern. Memberships are often large because members want to be placed on committees of relevance to their home districts and states. However, the greater the committee size, the greater the number of committees members serve on and the greater the number of meetings they are unable to attend. The result is a proxy system in which another member, often the chair, votes for absent members on the committee.

Although considerable agreement may exist that Congress needs to reduce the number of committees and subcommittees, the task is difficult. Since chairing one of these committees provides power, prestige, and perquisites, any chairperson or other senior member on the committee is likely to defend continuance of the committee and repel efforts to diminish the committee's powers.[81] Members in both houses have historically sought seats on committees dealing with the various aspects of the budget, as a means of gaining power over congressional actions.

One controversial suggestion has been that the budget process could be streamlined by eliminating the two Appropriations Committees and assigning their duties to the committees that handle authorizations. Rather than appropriation bills emanating from one committee, they would arise from the standing substantive committees in each chamber. Critics of this proposal contend that such a reform would worsen the budget situation, since the Appropriations Committees are far more likely to restrict government spending than the substantive committees, which are often seen as having been captured by the executive branch agencies that they oversee.

Other committee-related proposals involve reconfiguring the House and Senate Budget Committees, possibly even merging them into a joint committee. Another option would be to eliminate these committees on the grounds that they have only added to the complexity of congressional budgeting.

When the Republicans took control of Congress in 1995, they promised a revamping of the committee system. The result was a modest realignment of committees, some reduction in the number of subcommittees, and reductions in the sizes of committees. When the 105th Congress was convened in January 1997, the Republicans showed no inclination to reopen the issue of committee restructuring.

Leadership. Strengthening the powers of the Speaker of the House is another possible reform of how Congress conducts its business.[82] One recommendation is to increase the Speaker's power in determining who chairs committees and how long they retain these roles. Increased power would enhance the abilities of the Speaker to coordinate the diverse components of the chamber and develop a unified set of policies but might stifle the independence of individual members.

Term Limits. Growing interest in limiting the length of time a member may serve continuously in Congress is evident.[83] Imposing term limits, as noted in the preceding chapter, is seen as a way of creating opportunities for removing encrusted members who have lost touch with the real world and infusing "new blood" into the system. However, term limits by themselves would not resolve the serious financial problems facing the government. Term limits, if imposed, would need to be applied to all members, since if only some states adopt this approach, their members will have less seniority than those in other states and consequently will have less influence on policy making. The Supreme Court ruled in 1995 that states could not impose qualifications for federal offices beyond what was contained in the Constitution.[84] The Court rejected the view that the reserved powers clause of the Tenth Amendment gave states the power to set term limits on congressional elections. The Republicans in Congress have sought to initiate a constitutional amendment that would set term limits but have been unable to gain the necessary two-thirds vote.

Proposed Revisions in the Use of Resolutions and Budget Summits

Continuing Resolutions. The institution of automatic continuing resolutions for appropriations is another possible strategy. If Congress failed to pass an appropriation bill, the agencies affected would operate with a continuing appropriation without Congress's having to act. Since congressional failure to act on the budget in a timely fashion has become the norm, the obvious advantage of an automatic continuing resolution is that it would eliminate the crisis handling of appropriation bills. The disadvantage of the proposal is that incentives for Congress to adopt regular appropriation bills would be reduced.

This topic was the subject of much controversy in 1997. Spring floods had devastated the upper Midwest, and Congress was under pressure to pass an emergency disaster relief bill. The Republicans passed the bill but included a rider that would have provided continuous funding in the event that the budget agreement became stalled. President Clinton vetoed the bill, and the Republicans were blamed for playing politics when a critical situation existed. Within a matter of days following the veto, the bill was passed without the poison pill of a continuing appropriation, and the President signed it into law.

Joint Resolutions. A more far-reaching proposal would eliminate the concurrent nature of budget resolutions, which do not require presidential signature, and substitute a joint resolution or law to be signed by the President.[85] In effect, budget summitry would be employed at the outset of the budget process. The hope is that the President and key congressional leaders would develop an annual budget resolution that all would support, thereby helping to ensure more timely action as the details of the budget were worked out at a later time. Budget summits bind all participants so that a President who endorsed a summit agreement could not later renege when Congress passed appropriation bills in conformance with the agreement.

Omnibus Bill. A related proposal provides for an omnibus budget bill that would include all spending and revenue measures in one package. The virtue of the proposal is that it provides for a comprehensive overview of the total budget and gives Congress a good opportunity to develop a coherent set of policies pertaining to programs and the financing of government. The main disadvantage is that large bills tend to include extraneous materials that go unexamined. Without the item veto, the President would be forced either to accept or reject the entire package.

Omnibus budget reconciliation bills have become common. They were passed in 1981 through 1983, 1986, 1987, 1989, 1990, and 1993. Also in 1996 Congress passed the Omnibus Consolidated Rescissions and Appropriations Act. These laws run many hundreds of pages in length. The immensity of these documents, often combined with little time allowed to read them, defy the efforts of the most dedicated member of Congress from appreciating even most of the legal provisions contained within them. The laws contain much more than merely providing for spending authority to line agencies. For instance, the 1996 law mandated a reduction in regulatory requirements and corresponding paperwork for the banking industry among hundreds of other provisions.[86] The reconciliation process has become a standard means for Congress to act on the budget, even though such was not intended when the procedure was established in 1974 by the Congressional Budget and Impoundment Control Act.[87]

Other Proposed Reforms

Biennial Budgeting. One frequently mentioned proposal is to change over to a biennial budget.[88] Since Congress has such difficulty acting on a budget, why not simplify the problem by requiring action only every other year? The 1993 report of the National Performance Review recommended such a reform.[89] Whether Congress would be willing to relinquish annual control is highly questionable. Biennial budgets might be routinely reopened in their second years and completely revised. The budgeting process would need to be coordinated with the election of Congress and the President. No Congress would want the government operating on a budget adopted by the previous Congress; the same concern would exist for a President.

Capital Budgeting. Adoption of a capital budgeting system is another possibility. It is advocated as a way of helping to put the deficit into perspective, since it would show that much of federal spending is of an investment nature and not simply annual consumption. Capital budgeting presumably would encourage better planning of expenditures. On the negative side, capital budgets could be used to downplay the true magnitude of federal budget deficits and total debt (see Chapter 12). If a balanced budget constitutional amendment was adopted, Congress most likely would move capital expenditures off-budget just as states permit indebtedness for investments but not for operating expenses.

Other Proposals. There is an abundance of other possible reforms. A return to Gramm-Rudman-Hollings would be possible. The earmarking of revenue for specific purposes or portions of appropriations for specific purposes might be prohibited or limited.[90] Some proposals pertain to how debt ceiling limits are approved. Accrual accounting and performance evaluation are often mentioned as worthy of consideration. Other technical recommendations pertain to the credit budget and to the treatment of trust funds (particularly Social Security and the Highway Trust Fund).

SUMMARY

Congress has an elaborate system for approving the budget. An authorization process exists independent of appropriations. Meanwhile, the House Ways and Means Committee and the Senate Finance Committee have power to deal not only with tax measures but also with some spending. The Appropriations Committees in the two houses operate by developing a series of bills through subcommittees.

The Congressional Budget and Impoundment Control Act of 1974 attempted to deal with several problems, including congressional tardiness in adopting the budget, impoundments, and piecemeal handling of the budget. New Budget

Committees, along with the Congressional Budget Office, were established. Congress generally adhered to the timetable in the law for the first several years but then slipped badly.

The budget process, because budget resolutions were not passed in a timely fashion, was drastically altered during the first several years of the Reagan administration. Reconciliation was used in budget approval but early in the process rather than at the end, as originally envisioned. Appropriation bills rarely were passed on time, and Congress resorted instead to massive continuing appropriations.

The mounting federal debt alarmed Republicans and Democrats alike in Congress, and the result was the Balanced Budget and Emergency Deficit Control Act of 1985, known commonly as Gramm-Rudman-Hollings. The procedure in the law was revised by the 1987 Reaffirmation Act after the Supreme Court declared unconstitutional a provision pertaining to the role of the comptroller general. Gramm-Rudman-Hollings set target figures for reducing the budget deficit to zero by 1993, but rather than balance being achieved, record deficits materialized in the 1990s. During the Bush and Clinton administrations, laws were passed that substantially reduced projected annual budget deficits, but they still remained high—at the $100+ billion level. The 1997 budget agreement fashioned by President Clinton and a Republican Congress was seen as taking an important series of steps toward budget balancing, but whether the Congress could resist temptations to alter the plan in subsequent years will be determined.

Numerous proposals exist for further revising how the federal government adopts the budget. Major proposals include giving item-veto power to the President and passing a constitutional amendment requiring that the budget be balanced. Other proposals involve restructuring congressional committees, changing the concurrent budget resolution to a joint resolution or law, shifting the government to a biennial budget cycle, and separating the budget into capital and operating components.

NOTES

1. J.M. Anderson and M.F. Bley for the Congressional Research Service, *Federal Budget Chronology: Fiscal Year 1997* (1996): http://www.cnie.org/nle/leg-24.html; accessed December 1997.

2. L. Fisher, *The Politics of Shared Power: Congress and the Executive*, 2nd ed. (Washington, DC: Congressional Quarterly Press, 1987), 91–217; A. Schick, *The Federal Budget: Politics, Policy, Process* (Washington, DC: Brookings Institution, 1995), 70–164.

3. J.F. Manley, *The Politics of Finance: The House Committee on Ways and Means* (Boston: Little, Brown, 1970).

4. R.F. Fenno, Jr., *The Power of the Purse: Appropriations Politics in Congress* (Boston: Little, Brown, 1966); H.E. Shuman, *Politics and the Budget: The Struggle between the President and*

the Congress, 3rd ed. (Englewood Cliffs, NJ: Prentice-Hall, 1992); A. Wildavsky and N. Caiden, *The New Politics of the Budgetary Process*, 3rd ed. (New York: Longman, 1997).

5. Legislative Reorganization Act, ch. 753, 60 Stat. 812 (1946).

6. L. Fisher, Experience with a Legislative Budget (1947–1949), in Senate Committee on Government Operations, *Improving Congressional Control of the Budget: Hearings*, Part 2, 93rd Cong., 1st sess. (Washington, DC: U.S. Government Printing Office, 1973), 237–239.

7. R.A. Wallace, Congressional Control of the Budget, *Midwest Journal of Political Science* 3 (1959): 151–167.

8. S.K. Kim, The Politics of a Congressional Budgetary Process: "Backdoor Spending," *Western Political Quarterly* 21 (1968): 606–623; A. Schick, Backdoor Spending Authority, in Senate Committee on Government Operations, *Improving Congressional Control over the Budget: A Compendium of Materials*, 93rd Cong., 1st sess. (Washington, DC: U.S. Government Printing Office, 1973), 293–302.

9. Congressional Budget and Impoundment Control Act, P.L. 93-344, 88 Stat. 297 (1974).

10. L. Fisher, Ten Years of the Budget Act: Still Searching for Controls, *Public Budgeting & Finance* 5 (Autumn 1985): 3–28.

11. A. Schick, *Congress and Money* (Washington, DC: Urban Institute, 1980), 17–81.

12. J.W. Elwood, Budget Reforms and Interchamber Relations, in *Congressional Budgeting*, eds. W.T. Wander et al. (Baltimore: Johns Hopkins University Press, 1984), 100–132.

13. L. Fisher, The Politics of Impounded Funds, *Administrative Science Quarterly* 15 (1970): 361–377.

14. Anti-Deficiency Act, Ch. 510, §3, 34 Stat. 49 (1950).

15. *Immigration and Naturalization Service v. Chadha*, 462 U.S. 919 (1983).

16. D.J. Palazzolo, *The Speaker and the Budget: Leadership in the Post-Reform House of Representatives* (Pittsburgh: University of Pittsburgh Press, 1992).

17. R. Strahan, Agenda Change and Committee Politics in the Postreforms House, *Legislative Studies Quarterly* 13 (1988): 177–197.

18. U.S. Office of Management and Budget, *Budget of the United States Government* (Washington, DC: U.S. Government Printing Office, selected years); F.T. Hebert, Congressional Budgeting, 1977–1983, in Wander et al., *Congressional Budgeting*, 31–48.

19. Economic Recovery Tax Act, P.L. 97-34, 95 Stat. 172 (1981).

20. B.E. Johnson, From Analyst to Negotiator: The OMB's New Role, *Journal of Policy Analysis and Management* 3 (1984): 501–515; B. Johnson, The OMB Budget Examiner and the Congressional Budget Process, *Public Budgeting & Finance* 9 (Spring 1989): 5–14.

21. D.S. Stockman, *The Triumph of Politics: How the Reagan Revolution Failed* (New York: Harper & Row, 1986).

22. L.T. LeLoup and J. Hancock, Congress and the Reagan Budgets, *Public Budgeting & Finance* 8 (Autumn 1988): 30–54.

23. D.S. Ippolito, *Uncertain Legacies: Federal Budget Policy from Roosevelt through Reagan* (Charlottesville: University Press of Virginia, 1990).

24. R.A. Keith, Budget Reconciliation in 1981, *Public Budgeting & Finance* 1 (Winter 1981): 37–47.

25. M.L. Mezey, The Legislature, the Executive and Public Policy: The Futile Quest for Congressional Power, *Congress and the Presidency* 13 (1986): 1–20; J. Cooper, Assessing Legislative Performance: A Reply to Critics of Congress, *Congress and the Presidency* 13 (1986): 21–40.

26. Balanced Budget and Emergency Deficit Control Act, P.L. 99-177, Title II, 99 Stat. 1038 (1985); H.S. Havens, Gramm-Rudman-Hollings: Origins and Implementation, *Public Budgeting & Finance* 6 (August 1986): 4–24; L.T. LeLoup et al., Deficit Politics and Constitutional Government: The Impact of Gramm-Rudman-Hollings, *Public Budgeting & Finance* 7 (Spring 1987): 83–103.

27. W.P. Gramm, as quoted in E. Wehr, Congress Enacts Far-Reaching Budget Measure, *Congressional Quarterly Weekly Report* 43 (1985): 2604.

28. *Bowsher v. Synar*, 478 U.S. 714 (1986); Symposium: *Bowsher v. Synar, Cornell Law Review* 72 (1987): 421–597.

29. Balanced Budget and Emergency Deficit Control Reaffirmation Act, P.L. 100-119, Title I, 101 Stat. 854 (1987).

30. U.S. General Accounting Office, *Budget Policy: Issues in Capping Mandatory Spending* (Washington, DC: U.S. Government Printing Office, 1994).

31. T. Metz et al., Stocks Plunge 508 amid Panicky Selling, *Wall Street Journal*, October 20, 1987, 1, 22.

32. S.E. Schier, *A Decade of Deficits: Congressional Thought and Fiscal Action* (Albany: State University of New York Press, 1992); R. Thelwell, Gramm-Rudman-Hollings Four Years Later, *Public Administration Review* 50 (1990): 190–198.

33. J.B. Gilmour, *Reconcilable Differences? Congress, the Budget Process and the Deficit* (Berkeley: University of California Press, 1990).

34. Budget Enforcement Act, P.L. 101-508, Title XIII, 104 Stat. 1388-573 (1990); D.P. Franklin, *Making Ends Meet: Congressional Budgeting in the Age of Deficits* (Washington, DC: Congressional Quarterly Press, 1993).

35. P.G. Joyce and R.D. Reischauer, Deficit Budgeting: The Federal Budget Process and Budget Reform, *Harvard Journal on Legislation* 29 (1992): 429–453.

36. G. Hager, Entitlements: The Untouchable May Become Unavoidable, *Congressional Quarterly Weekly Report* 51 (1993): 26.

37. Wildavsky and Caiden, *The New Politics of the Budgetary Process*, 144–146.

38. J. Shear, Fair or Foul? *National Journal* 28 (1996): 2662.

39. Budget Enforcement Act was a component of Omnibus Budget Reconciliation Act, P.L. 101-508, 104 Stat. 1388 (1990); U.S. General Accounting Office, *Budget Issues: Compliance with the Budget Enforcement Act of 1990* (Washington, DC: U.S. Government Printing Office, 1992).

40. Omnibus Budget Reconciliation Act, P.L. 103-66, 107 Stat. 312 (1993).

41. D.P. Oak, An Overview of Adjustments to the Budget Enforcement Act Discretionary Spending Caps, *Public Budgeting & Finance* 15 (Fall 1995): 35–53.

42. J.B. Bader, *Taking the Initiative: Leadership Agendas in Congress and the "Contract with America"* (Washington, DC: Georgetown University Press, 1996); J.G. Gimpel, *Legislating the Revolution: The Contract with America in Its First 100 Days* (Boston: Allyn and Bacon, 1996).

43. Arlen Specter as quoted in J.L. Katz, Intraparty Funding Battles, *Congressional Quarterly Weekly Report* 54 (1996): 869.

44. G. Hager, Budget Battle Came Sooner than Either Side Expected, *Congressional Quarterly Weekly Report* 53 (1995): 3503, 3505, 3508, 3509.

45. R. Doyle, Congress, the Deficit, and Budget Reconciliation, *Public Budgeting & Finance* 16 (Winter 1996): 59–81.

46. J. Shear, The Tale of the Dogs, *National Journal* 28 (1996): 18–22.

47. G. Hager, Clinton, GOP Congress Strike Historic Budget Agreement, *Congressional Quarterly Weekly Report* 56 (1997): 993, 996, 997.

48. U.S. Congressional Budget Office, *The Economic and Budget Outlook: Fiscal Years 1998–2007* (1997): http://www.cbo.gov; accessed December 1997.

49. W.J. Clinton, Statement by the President on Budget Agreement (1997): http://www.white-house.gov/WH/html/briefroom.html; accessed December 1997.

50. W.J. Clinton, Remarks by the President at Signing of the Balanced Budget Act of 1997 and the Taxpayers [sic] Relief Act of 1997 (August 5, 1997): http//www.whitehouse.gov/WH/html/briefroom.html; accessed December 1997.

51. N. Gingrich, Remarks at Signing Ceremony for Budget Agreement (August 5, 1997): http://speakernews.house.gov/signing.html; accessed December 1997.

52. Balanced Budget Act, P.L. 105-33 (1997) and Taxpayer Relief Act, P.L. 105-34 (1997).

53. D. Hosansky and A.J. Rubin, Shuster's Steamroller Stopped—For Now, *Congressional Quarterly Weekly Report* 55 (1997): 1183.

54. W.J. Clinton, Press Conference by the President (August 6, 1997): http://library.whitehouse.gov; accessed December 1997.

55. U.S. General Accounting Office, *Budget Process: Issues Concerning the 1990 Reconciliation Act* (Washington, DC: U.S. Government Printing Office, 1994).

56. U.S. General Accounting Office, *Addressing the Deficit: Budgetary Implications of Selected GAO Work for Fiscal Year 1998* (Washington, DC: U.S. Government Printing Office, 1997).

57. U.S. General Accounting Office, *Budget Policy: Prompt Action Necessary To Avert Long-Term Damage to the Economy* (Washington, DC: U.S. Government Printing Office, 1992); U.S. General Accounting Office, *Budget Issues: GDP Analysis Broadens Budget Debate* (Washington, DC: U.S. Government Printing Office, 1994).

58. G. Burtless et al., The Future of the Social Safety Net, in *Setting National Priorities: Budget Choices for the Next Century*, ed. R.D. Reischauer (Washington, DC: Brookings Institution, 1997), 75–122.

59. L.N. Rieselbach, *Congressional Reform: The Changing Modern Congress* (Washington, DC: Congressional Quarterly Press, 1993).

60. B. Sinclair, *Legislators, Leaders and Lawmaking: The U.S. House of Representatives in the Post-reform Era* (Baltimore: Johns Hopkins University Press, 1995).

61. R.D. Kiewiet and M.D. McCubbins, *The Logic of Delegation: Congressional Parties and the Appropriations Process* (Chicago: University of Chicago Press, 1991); R.L. Hall, *Participation in Congress* (New Haven, CT: Yale University Press, 1996).

62. E. Felten, Little Princes: The Petty Despotism of Congressional Staff, *Policy Review* 63 (Winter 1993): 51–57.

63. W.H. Robinson and C.H. Wellborn, eds., *Knowledge, Power, and the Congress* (Washington, DC: Congressional Quarterly Press, 1991).

64. J. Marini, *The Politics of Budget Control: Congress, the Presidency and the Growth of the Administrative State* (Washington, DC: Crane Russak, 1992).

65. G.S. Gryski, The Influence of Committee Position on Federal Program Spending, *Polity* 23 (1991): 443–459.

66. W.J. Clinton, Statement on Signing the Line Item Veto Act, *Weekly Compilation of Presidential Documents* 32 (1996): 637–638.

67. U.S. General Accounting Office, *Line Item Veto: Estimating Potential Savings* (Washington, DC: U.S. Government Printing Office, 1992).

68. V. Novak, Defective Remedy, *National Journal* 25 (1993): 749–753.

69. U.S. General Accounting Office, *Impoundments: Historical Information and Statistics on Proposed and Enacted Rescissions, Fiscal Years 1974–1995* (Washington, DC: U.S. Government Printing Office, 1996).

70. Line Item Veto Act, P.L. 104-130, 110 Stat. 1200 (1996); P.G. Joyce and R.D. Reischauer, The Federal Line-Item Veto: What Is It and What Will It Do? *Public Administration Review* 57 (1997): 95–104.

71. R.C. Byrd as quoted in A. Taylor, Congress Hands President a Budgetary Scalpel, *Congressional Quarterly Weekly Report* 54 (1996): 866.

72. *Byrd v. Raines*, 65 LW 2660 (DDC 1997).

73. *Raines v. Byrd*, 117 S.Ct. 2312 (1997).

74. W.J. Clinton, Remarks by the President on the Line Item Veto (August 11, 1997): http://www.whitehouse.gov/WH/html/briefroom.html; accessed December 1997.

75. Ibid.

76. G. Hager, Country Comes Full Circle on Balancing the Budget, *Congressional Quarterly Weekly Report* 55 (1997): 278–285.

77. U.S. General Accounting Office, *Balanced Budget Requirements: State Experiences and Implications for the Federal Government* (Washington, DC: U.S. Government Printing Office, 1993).

78. D.W. Kiefer et al., *A Balanced Budget Constitutional Amendment: Economic Issues* (Washington, DC: Congressional Research Service, 1992).

79. A. Taylor, Democrats Doom Amendment, But GOP Sees Silver Lining, *Congressional Quarterly Weekly Report* 55 (1997): 523–525.

80. Legislative Reorganization Act, Ch. 753, 60 Stat. 812 (1946); Legislative Reorganization Act, P.L. 91-510, 84 Stat. 1140 (1970).

81. J. Shear, Power Loss, *National Journal* 28 (1996): 874–878.

82. T.E. Mann and N.J. Ornstein, *Renewing Congress: A Second Report* (Washington, DC: Brookings Institution, 1993).

83. E. Garrett, Term Limitations and the Myth of the Citizen Legislator, *Cornell Law Review* 81 (1996): 623–697.

84. *U.S. Term Limits, Inc. v. Thornton*, 115 S.Ct. 1842 (1995).

85. R.T. Meyers, The Budget Resolution Should Be a Law, *Public Budgeting & Finance* 10 (Fall 1990): 103–112; R.T. Meyers, *Strategic Budgeting* (Ann Arbor: University of Michigan Press, 1994).

86. Omnibus Consolidated Appropriations Act, P.L. 104-208, 110 Stat. 3009 (1996).

87. P.G. Joyce, Congressional Budget Reform: The Unanticipated Implications for Federal Policy Making, *Public Administration Review* 56 (1996): 317–325.

88. J.L. Blum, *Statement on the [Proposed] Legislative Reorganization Act of 1994* (Washington, DC: Congressional Budget Office, 1994).

89. National Performance Review, *From Red Tape to Results: Creating a Government That Works Better and Costs Less* (Washington, DC: U.S. Government Printing Office, 1993).

90. P. Kuntz, Another Stab at Cutting, *Congressional Quarterly Weekly Report* 51 (1993): 377; U.S. General Accounting Office, *Budget Issue: Earmarking in the Federal Government* (Washington, DC: U.S. Government Printing Office, 1990).

CHAPTER 10

Budget Execution

Once the budget has been approved, the execution phase of the cycle begins. Of course, at the federal level it is common for many agencies to enter the execution phase with only a continuing resolution to spend at the previous year's rate rather than spend under a new appropriation. This same practice sometimes occurs at the state level, while local governments usually are required by state law to complete the budget approval phase by the beginning of the new fiscal year.

This chapter has five sections. The first deals with interactions between the central budget office and the line agencies. Then four subsystems of the execution phase are discussed—tax administration, cash management, procurement, and risk management.

BUDGET OFFICE AND AGENCY RELATIONS

As would be expected, relationships—both direct and indirect—are extensive between the central budget office and the line agencies during the execution phase of the budget. In this section, we examine these relationships as they pertain specifically to the budget and then consider a variety of other activities that bring the budget office into contact with agencies.

Interactions on Budgeting

Execution is the action phase of budgeting, the phase in which the plans contained in the budget are put into operation. Every budget either explicitly or implicitly contains plans for the work to be done and the achievements to be gained. Execution, then, involves converting those plans into operations. During this phase, budget office personnel gain important insights into the operations of agencies and this knowledge later becomes important during the next round of budget preparation.[1]

Legislative Intent. In acting on the budget, the legislature provides some indication of legislative intent. Such intent may be expressed in terms of the dollars to be available for an organizational unit. The greater the specificity of these appropriations, the less flexibility afforded agencies and the budget office in how funds will be spent. Some flexibility is essential, if for no other reason than the legislative body is unable to readily specify all aspects of all operations of all agencies. Most legislative action, therefore, leaves the door open to further decision making.

Apportionment and Allotments. At the state and federal levels, an apportionment process is used in which line agencies submit plans to the central budget office for how appropriated funds will be used; the plans often indicate proposed expenditures for each month or quarter of the fiscal year. A primary purpose of apportionment is to ensure that agencies spend at a rate that will keep them within limits imposed by their annual appropriations. Office of Management and Budget (OMB) Circular A-34 governs this process at the federal level. The budget office may require modification of agency proposals and eventually approves apportionments for each agency. Following the approval of apportionments by the budget office, allotments are made within departments. This process grants expenditure authority to subunits. At the local level, this process may be relatively informal.

In the apportionment process, chief executives and their budget offices have greater power to deny authority than to grant authority to agencies. The executive cannot approve apportionments for projects prohibited in the appropriation but may be able to reduce or eliminate some appropriated items. As we saw in Chapter 9, presidents have impounded appropriated funds. Another executive means of denying spending authority is to exercise the item veto. In 1997, President Clinton became the first president to have a form of item veto, which is common among the states and is used in some local governments.

Initial Planning. Agencies at the outset of the fiscal year must accommodate differences between the actual appropriations and the original requests. In addition, some substantive changes may be specified in the appropriations, or an informal understanding may have developed between an agency and legislators over how a program will be redirected.

For agencies that were fortunate in obtaining increased funds for improving or expanding existing programs or for new programs, the budget office plays a key role. Mindful that the legislature will expect a detailed reporting of how these funds were used, the budget office exercises oversight in implementing the program revisions or new programs.

Control of Agencies. From the perspective of the central administration, agencies must live within their budgets; otherwise the budget process becomes an empty exercise. Therefore, various controls are imposed upon agencies, including the *preaudit*. After approval of an apportionment plan and granting an allotment, an agency is still not free to spend but must submit a request to obligate the government to spend resources. The request is matched against the unit's budget to determine whether the proposed expenditure is authorized and whether sufficient funds are available in the agency's budget.

Several different units may carry out the preaudit function. Not only the budget office but also an accounting department may be involved. Often at the state and local levels, independent comptrollers, controllers, or auditors general have preaudit responsibilities. These officials have the duty of providing another, presumably independent, check on financial transactions.

In the case of an agency proposing to hire new staff, not only will the usual preaudit procedure be used, but also a central personnel office may review the request. Such a review, known as *personnel complement control*, is used in part to avoid increasing personnel commitments and corresponding increases in budget requirements over what has been appropriated.

Midyear Changes. As the year progresses, the budget office conducts reviews of agency operations. One problem that often emerges is that resources in some agencies' budgets are insufficient to meet the demand for services. One alternative is for the budget office to approve requesting supplemental appropriations from the legislative branch. However, in other circumstances, the budget office will work with agencies to stay within funding limits. Each July OMB issues the *Mid-Session Review of the Budget*, which discusses economic trends and how these trends are affecting receipts, spending patterns, the activities of credit programs, and whatever sequester and other procedures are in place to attempt to limit the budget deficit. In any event, what is actually spent will be different from what was originally approved.

Midyear crises may emerge because of an unfavorable revenue situation. Government budgets that depend heavily on a single commodity export (as Venezuela's budget relies on oil) may experience severe fluctuation during the year as the world price of the commodity fluctuates. In the United States, a downturn in a state's economy can have devastating effects on sales tax and income tax receipts, forcing across-the-board cutbacks in spending. Since personnel costs usually are the largest single item in operating budgets, these costs must be curtailed when revenue receipts are below projected levels; personnel hiring freezes are common in government. Another more extreme technique is to furlough employees. Some governments have expected all employees to share in the problem by each working, and being paid for, a four-day week rather than a five-day week, thereby creating a 20-percent saving.

End-of-Year Spending. As the fiscal year approaches its end, agencies will attempt to zero out their budgets; an agency having unexpended funds at the end of the fiscal year may be considered a prime candidate for cuts in the upcoming budget. Also, unexpended or unencumbered funds often lapse at the end of the budget year. From the agency's perspective, it is a now-or-never situation for spending the available money. Another factor is that an agency may have delayed some expenditures, saving a portion of its budget for contingencies. This delay results in a spurt in expenditures at the end of the year, with some spending being highly appropriate and other spending utterly wasteful. Congress has reduced this last-minute spurt by limiting the proportion of an agency's funds that may be spent in the final quarter of the fiscal year.

An alternative is to allow surplus funds to be transferred to the agency's new budget without requiring a reappropriation. Some jurisdictions allow this within limits, such as a small percentage of each unit's total budget. Advocates of an entrepreneurial spirit in government argue that agencies should be rewarded for efficiency by being allowed to carry over funds into the next fiscal year.[2] The National Performance Review recommended that agencies should be able to carry as much as 50 percent of their internal operations budgets into the next fiscal year.[3]

Reorganization, Downsizing, and Privatization

The Taft Commission on Economy and Efficiency is best known for its 1912 report recommending the establishment of a federal budget process under the direction of the President. The title of the commission is significant in that a primary thrust was to better use government resources (see Chapter 1). More than eight decades later, the same concerns of the Taft Commission are prevalent at all levels of government. Incentives for economy and efficiency are created by taxing and spending limitation measures, by fiscal stress or distress resulting from the erosion of tax bases of many jurisdictions, and by the increased popularity of a form of conservatism dedicated to reducing the role of government in society.

Budget offices historically have played central roles in examining the structures of departments and agencies, with an eye to possible reorganizations as a means for increasing the efficiency of operations.[4] In addition to structural arrangements, budget offices often seek improvements in management processes as a means of garnering savings. Outside experts are used, as was the case of the Grace Commission during the Reagan administration. The commission, whose full title was the President's Private Sector Survey on Cost Control, consisted of chief executive officers from private corporations.[5] The National Performance Review (NPR), during the Clinton administration, was an in-house effort to improve all aspects of government and recommended the reorganization of several government offices and the elimination of others. OMB was deeply involved in all of these efforts.

A phenomenon that gained special momentum in the 1980s and continued into the 1990s was that of cutback management, downsizing, or so-called "right-sizing" (see Chapter 6).[6] Much of the focus of such efforts is on reducing government employment, with the budget offices often in charge of implementing such initiatives. At the federal level, the Clinton administration adopted the NPR's recommendation to reduce personnel. OMB included as part of the budget preparation process a requirement that agencies specify target reductions in personnel and show how they planned to meet these targeted figures (described in OMB Circular A-11). Defense Department downsizing has included closure of numerous installations as well as a "drawdown" in personnel.[7]

While definitions vary, the core of any definition of privatization is the reassignment of government activities to the private sector. A common mechanism used for this is contracting or *outsourcing*, in which a private firm provides a product or service at an agreed quantity, quality, and price.[8] Other means of encouraging private sector involvement in the provision of public services include grants, loan guarantees, tax expenditures, social regulation, and government corporations.[9] Privatization and contracting out government services are intended to increase government efficiency and reduce government spending.

Although the procedures used in contracting are reviewed later in this chapter, it should be noted here that OMB Circular A-76, Performance of Commercial Activities, provides for a review process to determine when activities of the government should be contracted out. There are two main criteria: that the activity be a "commercial" one and not "governmental" and that the cost be lower in the private sector than in government. Examples of commercial activities include guarding public buildings and providing cafeterias for employees. Policy-making activities are not to be contracted out.

Contracting out differs from privatization in that the former focuses primarily on efficiency while the latter has a policy orientation.[10] Circular A-76 uses an efficiency standard, namely, that contracting out should be used when the unit cost for a service is lower outside of government than inside. The privatization movement endorses use of an efficiency standard but also adheres to the view that the population is better served if service delivery is left, where possible, to the private sector. Contracting out maintains government responsibility and control over a service; privatization often seemingly implies the government's removing itself from both responsibility and control. The advocates of privatization contend that government should be proactive in seeking opportunities for turning over functions to the private sector.

Although critics contend that sometimes too much faith is placed in private enterprise and that privatization leads to supporting nonunionized firms that pay low wages, private sector contracting has become a familiar form of service delivery in the United States and abroad.[11] Contracting out is routinely used for such services as refuse pick-up and towing illegally parked vehicles. Private sector firms under government contract are now handling services once thought to be exclusively the responsibility of the public sector, such as welfare services and the operation of prisons.[12] Ports, such as the one in Miami, are being largely privatized, so that a port authority leases much of its property to private firms, which in turn operate the facilities.[13]

Several lessons have been learned as governments have ventured into privatization, with one of the most important being the need to conduct a thorough analysis before taking the plunge into privatization. There is a need to consider whether cost efficiencies will be attained, whether the private firm will be held accountable for its performance, whether any cost efficiency is attained at the expense of quality, and whether equity or fairness in treating citizens and employees will be achieved.[14] Another important question is whether the market has companies that can provide the agreed upon services in a timely fashion and can respond to unforeseen problems that may arise. Are there any legal barriers that prohibit privatizing a given service, and what liability risks may be created by having a private firm deliver a government service?

The analysis needs to include projected costs for monitoring a firm in its delivery of a service. A government needs to be able to assure itself that a firm is abiding by its commitments and needs to be able to respond when citizens complain about a service. Part of the monitoring process includes determining whether the cost savings that were predicted in the original analysis did indeed materialize.[15]

A dogmatic stance that services should be contracted out wherever possible is unwarranted in that government may well be able to provide some services at costs lower than private firms. Competitive bidding on contemplated privatization projects can include not only private firms but government agencies as well. Phoenix, Arizona, and Fort Lauderdale, Florida, have been leaders in developing and using this approach.[16] Further, a mix in service delivery may be more cost effective than strict privatization. In other words, any given service may be delivered in a cooperative arrangement that includes a combination of government agencies, for-profit firms, and nonprofit organizations.[17]

Management Controls

Budget offices have been assigned a variety of management-related duties beyond the core activities of assembling proposed budgets and overseeing their execution. For instance, budget offices may be partially responsible for establishing standards to be used in accounting systems (OMB Circular A-127). Of course, other units such as the General Accounting Office (GAO) at the federal level also play major roles in this area. Information systems and procurement are other important areas in which budget offices have key roles. Procurement is discussed later in this chapter.

Some budget offices have responsibility for studying agency procedures and for recommending or prescribing new procedures. These organization-and-management (O & M) studies can recommend changes in the department's management processes.

Budget offices set ground rules for many of the routine activities of line organizations. Limitations are set for paying employee travel costs. Centrally imposed standards also circumscribe the use of consulting services.

A *legislative clearinghouse* function is the responsibility of some budget offices. Before an agency may endorse a proposal for new or revised legislation, the proposal must be cleared through the budget office. This practice helps ensure that what is proposed is consistent with the views of the chief executive, both substantively and financially (see OMB Circular A-19).

Since corruption in government often involves finance, budget offices sometimes have major responsibility for protecting the government against fraud, waste, and abuse of government resources. The Inspector General Act of 1978 created relatively independent inspector general offices in major federal departments and gave these offices responsibility for investigating possible cases of fraud and other wrongdoing. The inspectors general meet as the President's Council on Integrity and Efficiency, which is chaired by the OMB.[18]

The OMB also oversees agency compliance with the Federal Managers' Financial Integrity Act of 1982, which requires safeguarding financial systems, particularly accounting and payroll, from fraud.[19] OMB Circular A-123, which is used to implement the law, was revised in 1995 to emphasize that managers should be held accountable for producing government services that yield desired results as well as for providing these services free of fraud and abuse of resources. The revision is in keeping with OMB's responsibility to oversee implementation of the Government Performance and Results Act of 1993 (see Chapter 5).

While Circular A-123 encourages agencies to impose regulations on themselves, OMB also is responsible for implementing Executive Order 12861, which instructs agencies to take a somewhat different course of action. The order, issued by President Clinton in 1993, mandates that agencies reduce by half their internal regulations. Many of these regulations pertain to personnel administration, such as when and how employees may use their annual leave or vacation days, but others are directly related to the objectives of A-123.

Presidents frequently assign OMB responsibility for improving the efficiency of government operations. Executive Order 12837, issued by President Clinton in 1993, called upon OMB to work toward reducing the government's budget deficit and increasing productivity. A companion executive order, 12839, required federal agencies to reduce their staffing by 100,000 positions by June 30, 1996.

Another function of OMB is to deal with alleged instances of postemployment conflicts of interest in which former government employees may be illegally benefiting from their previous experience in government. Of course, OMB is not the sole central agency responsible for handling problems in this area. Other important offices include the Office of Personnel Management, the Merit Systems Protection Board, the Department of Justice, and GAO.

Another significant executive order was 12857, issued by President Clinton in 1993, in response to complaints that spending on entitlement programs was out of control. The order required federal agencies to develop targets for direct spending, and when these targets were exceeded, the agencies were required to submit recommendations for bringing expenditures down to the targeted levels. For many entitlement programs, Congress would need to amend current legislation in order to reduce spending. The executive order was to be implemented by June 30, 1998.

OMB, along with the Council on Environmental Quality, which is a unit of the Executive Office of the President, is responsible for devising means for cleaning up environmental conditions on federal land. Extensive environmental pollution exists on military installations, facilities of the National Aeronautics and Space Administration, and other federal properties.[20]

Agencies must report to OMB on several other matters. According to law, OMB must be given reports on agency activities and expenditures pertaining to crime control and drug control. Agencies must report on how they are complying with the Federal Advisory Committee Act of 1972, Executive Order 12838 (1993), and Circular A-135 (1994), which require agencies to reduce their use of advisory committees.[21] The premise here is that while the government benefits from external advice, such advice often costs more than it is worth.

Besides these areas mentioned, there are other management controls over agencies for which budget offices may have some responsibility. Budget offices may be involved in implementing government-wide affirmative action plans. Some states have right-to-know laws that require employers, public and private, to inform their employees whether they are working with hazardous materials; measures aimed at reducing dangerous conditions obviously have budgetary implications. Budget offices may have some responsibilities in implementing freedom-of-information laws.

Control of Information Collection and Dissemination

Government collection and dissemination of information has constituted another problem area in which budget offices are involved. One of the chief concerns is that federal agencies heap huge burdens on individuals, corporations, and state and local governments in requiring them to submit information. The Paperwork Reduction Act, originally passed in 1980 and thoroughly rewritten in 1995, provides an elaborate process by which the government handles information.[22] The process is under the supervision of OMB's Office of Information and Regulatory Affairs (OIRA). The law is implemented by OMB Circular A-130 and strengthened by requirements in Executive Order 13011, Federal Information Technology, issued in 1996. The order provides for the establishment of the Chief Information Officers (CIO) Council. The council, consisting of representatives from all major federal agencies, provides a forum for improving the management of information.

The Paperwork Reduction Act provides that agencies are to reduce the information collection burden by 5 to 10 percent each year through the year 2001. Agencies must submit plans to OIRA showing what information they collect, the estimated thousands of hours the collection process demands of those required to submit the information, and how the agencies plan to meet the law's requirement to reduce paperwork. OMB publishes annually the *Information Resources Management Plan of the Federal Government.*

Any new collection of information must be approved by OIRA, but before that can occur, an agency must go through an elaborate analytic process. Factors to consider are the importance to the agency in collecting the information (the practical utility of the information), a realistic assessment of the burden imposed on those who would be required to submit the information, and a determination that the information does not exist already in some other form or in another agency. The agency might be expected to pilot a program as a means of evaluating the collection process and the utility of the information collected. Once all of this is accomplished, the agency must post a notice about the proposed collection process in the *Federal Register* and then go through a period in which it accepts comments from the public. Only after these steps are completed may the proposal be submitted to OIRA. That office can reject the agency's proposal on such grounds as the information is nonessential, the information already exists, the process would impose an undue burden, or simply that the proposed forms are unacceptable.

At any point in time, OIRA has many agency proposals under review, and action may take up to several months on each. Examples of agency proposals include the Department of Agriculture's proposal to collect information about Irish potatoes grown in Washington State and the Department of Commerce's proposal on reporting of whale sightings. A listing of OIRA paperwork reviews is available on the OMB homepage of the World Wide Web (Chapter 11).

In addition to controlling the collection of information, OIRA regulates the information dissemination process, including the concern that information not be disseminated that would invade the privacy of citizens or would reveal trade secrets of corporations. Circular A-130 provides guidance on when agencies may charge for their information and for what amounts. The Paperwork Reduction Act requires that information be made available in a timely fashion.

OMB has other important roles in the information arena. The office influences how much information is collected by controlling agencies' budgets, particularly those agencies whose primary mission is information collection. If budgets are cut for the Census Bureau in the Commerce Department or the Bureau of Labor Statistics in the Labor Department, the immediate results are less information being collected or less being made available to the public. An agency might collect information but lack the staff needed to make the information available in useable form, whether in paper, electronic, or other format.

Control of Regulations

In addition to relief from paperwork, budget offices also may be responsible for regulatory relief of businesses and governments. Critics of regulations view them as imposing needless expenses on corporations, which in turn pass these costs on to consumers, or taxpayers in the case of state and local governments. On the other hand, one should keep in mind that regulations are issued pursuant to statutes and that both the regulations and the statutes presumably have important public purposes, such as ensuring the safety of polio vaccine or the nation's food supply.

Beginning in the Reagan administration, OMB was given increased powers over the regulatory process, and those powers have been greatly expanded in subsequent years. Part of this movement has probably had political motivations in which Presidents have sought to show their concern for keeping a potentially runaway bureaucracy in check. President Bush in 1992, the year he sought re-election, imposed a moratorium on issuing new rules on the premise that regulations harm the economy and that the economy was already suffering needlessly from over-regulation.[23]

One line of reasoning is that thorough analysis is needed to determine whether regulations should be issued and then whether they should be retained. The current executive order governing this field at the federal level is 12866, issued in 1993. This executive order coupled with the Paperwork Reduction Act of 1995 (discussed above) give OIRA a veto power over most agency regulatory activity. The order provides for a regulatory planning and review process under OIRA. Each year agencies must submit to OIRA proposed plans for revising, issuing, and rescinding regulations. Any proposals for new or revised regulations must be evaluated in terms of their costs and benefits. OMB provides guidance on how analyses of regulations are to be conducted.[24] There are major technical problems in deciding what should be counted as a cost and what as a benefit (see Chapter 7).

Another area of controversy is that regulations often are written for large entities, and as a result, small ones experience major burdens in attempting to comply with the regulations. In response to that view, Congress passed the Regulatory Flexibility Act of 1980 and made important changes in the law in 1996 through passage of the Small Business Regulatory Enforcement Fairness Act.[25] The 1980 law encourages the use of flexible regulations that require lesser amounts of information from smaller entities, including small businesses and local governments. The 1996 law instructs agencies to prepare guides to show small businesses how they can comply with regulations. The Small Business Administration was given the role of ombudsman in assisting small businesses when they encounter regulatory problems with agencies. In the name of "regulatory relief," agencies may selectively waive the application of regulations to small businesses and waive penalties when these businesses violate the regulations. When small businesses think an agency has failed to comply with the law, they may file suit, claiming the regulation in question is invalid.

The 1996 law also includes within it the Congressional Review Act.[26] This law provides a form of legislative veto of administrative regulations. Before a proposed rule can take effect, it must be submitted to Congress. The Congress has 60 days, excluding days when Congress is in recess for four days or more, to review the regulations and can pass a joint resolution disapproving or vetoing the regulations. The President may veto the resolution, and the Congress may consider overriding the veto.

Given all of the items discussed here, some observers have suggested that the tasks are too great to be left to budget offices. One suggestion is to create a separate office of management that would have nonbudgetary duties ranging well beyond what OMB currently has. The argument against creating an office of management hinges mainly on the fact that the issues addressed have budgetary implications and to assign them to a different agency would automatically create coordination problems.

In addition to relations between the central budget office and the line agencies, several other subsystems are in operation during budget execution. Taxes and other debts must be collected, the cash needs of the government must be met, items must be purchased, and the vulnerability of the government to loss of property and other problems must be managed. These topics are discussed below.

TAX ADMINISTRATION AND DEBT COLLECTION

Tax administration, which is discussed here, and cash management, which is discussed in the next section, are two functions that usually are under the same administrative officer, namely, a secretary of treasury or revenue. Having the two functions linked together administratively facilitates sharing information. The cash manager uses information generated by the tax administrator. At the federal level, the Treasury Department handles these tasks.

Besides taxes, there are of course numerous other revenue sources that must be administered. User charges are common at the local level. State lotteries have become important sources of revenue. Administrators responsible for lotteries focus on marketing to increase sales; as the dollar value of sales increases, the unit cost of administration declines. Governments loan billions of dollars, and loan payments frequently are delinquent.[27]

Main Steps

Tax administration has four main steps:

1. Determining the objects or services to be taxed. Using the local property tax as an example, parcels of land and structures, along with their owners, must be identified.
2. Applying the tax. In the case of the property tax, this is an annual process, while sales tax calculations are made each time a sale occurs. Governments make property tax calculations, and bills are sent to property owners; in contrast, individuals have the responsibility to calculate their income taxes.
3. Collecting the revenues. Funds are paid either directly to the government, as in the case of a corporation's paying income tax, or through a third party, as in the case of employers' remitting individual income tax withholdings to the government.
4. Enforcing the law. Audits are conducted selectively of taxpayers to verify compliance, and some taxpayers are prosecuted for tax evasion.

Tax administration is not concerned with the policy issues of tax equity. Instead, the objectives of tax administration are to generate the revenue that is expected and to gain compliance from the vast majority of taxpayers. The Internal Revenue Service (IRS) has a tax compliance measurement program that samples tax returns in order to judge overall how well taxpayers are complying with the tax laws.[28]

Enforcement

Numerous tax enforcement measures are used, and well-trained and ethical personnel are essential for effective enforcement practices.[29]

- The IRS verifies mathematical accuracy through the use of optical scanning. Proper design of forms and clearly written instructions contribute to improved taxpayer accuracy in filing returns.[30]
- Tax return information supplied by individuals is compared with information supplied by banks and employers.[31]
- Governments share computer tapes to compare information on income being reported (or not reported).
- Taxpayer services are provided to help in preparing tax returns. Services may be available at designated government offices, at other facilities, and by telephone.[32]
- Governments draw samples of taxpayer returns to audit. Regression models are designed to identify cases that are most likely to involve noncompliance with the tax laws.
- One of the most common groups singled out for tax auditing are individuals and corporations for which "leads" have been given. Undercover operations may be used in these situations.
- Delinquent accounts are investigated, as well as accounts in which taxpayers have stopped complying altogether.[33]
- Some taxpayers are prosecuted in court, depending on the "seriousness" of the cases and the availability of resources to pursue the cases in court.
- Special enforcement is reserved for sources of illegal income, such as gambling, prostitution, narcotics, and, more generally, organized crime.

Any government must decide how many resources to commit to these various activities and how resources should be distributed among them. The IRS has been criticized for not having a firm idea of the relative yield in tax revenue generated from these activities.[34]

One of the most prominent objectives in enforcement of income tax laws is to have taxpayers comply with the law and to identify taxpayers who failed to report some of their income. One estimate is that the federal government would gain $100 billion annually if the gap between reported and actual income were closed.[35] Major categories of unreported income are sole proprietors' income and nonwage/nonsalary income.[36] Determining how to detect unreported income is a difficult task.[37] The IRS has decided that its super-audits that required a sample of taxpayers to substantiate every item on their tax returns was ineffective in detecting unreported income and identifying unauthorized or fraudulent claims for tax deductions and tax credits. The complexity of tax laws greatly hinders the effectiveness of audits both for personal and corporate income taxes.[38]

Another consideration is that tax administration would be far less complicated if most, or even all, taxpayers were relieved of having to file tax returns. At least

36 countries have tax withholding systems that free taxpayers of the onerous task of preparing and filing tax returns.[39]

Beginning in the 1980s, tax amnesty became popular as a means of retrieving unpaid state taxes. Taxpayers who were delinquent in their income taxes could file returns during a specified time period in a state without fear of prosecution; the taxpayers, however, were expected to pay all back taxes and interest. The amnesty programs have been successful in getting many taxpayers back on the tax rolls.[40] One possible drawback is that taxpayer compliance declines somewhat following an amnesty program, suggesting that taxpayers feel that government is likely to be less vigilant in ferreting out evaders after having enticed many people to return to the tax rolls. Also, taxpayer evasion is related to tax rates—as tax rates increase, evasion increases.

Computers in Tax Administration

It should come as no surprise that computers are playing increasingly important roles in tax administration:

- Besides routine recordkeeping, computers are used for drawing samples for tax auditing and for cross-checking information between different sources.
- Federal taxpayers may file their personal income tax returns electronically through an on-line service or a tax preparation firm.[41] State and federal tax returns can be filed electronically on a joint basis.
- Many businesses are required to make federal tax payments through the Electronic Federal Tax Payment System, and state and local governments are being phased in, requiring them to submit electronically federal income tax and Social Security withholdings.[42]
- Answers to frequently asked questions (FAQs) pertaining to tax laws are available on some government homepages on the Internet.[43]
- Some local governments have automated tax systems that can make monthly withdrawals for property taxes from taxpayers' bank accounts, providing that taxpayers preapprove such withdrawals.[44]
- In some locales, taxpayers use the telephone to pay their taxes.[45]
- Some governments accept credit and debit (automatic teller machine) cards for payment of taxes, fees, parking tickets, and the like; the cards, of course, are possible only because of today's computer technology.[46] Some states accept electronic fund transfers for corporations making tax payments.
- Auditors on field assignments use portable computers. Computers can be used to manage tax cases, providing on any one case a variety of information and prompting the case manager with reminders about the status of the case.

The conversion of various aspects of tax administration from paper files to computer systems or from one computer system to a more advanced one can result in problems for both tax administrators and taxpayers. The IRS became well aware of this problem in the late 1980s and 1990s as it engaged in an $8 billion Tax Systems Modernization project. The system was intended to aid IRS agents, citizens (through more timely tax refunds), corporations, and executive and legislative decision makers through the provision of more accurate and timely information.[47] In 1997, the IRS's assistant commissioner for technology admitted "Our past modernization plans went badly off track."[48] The IRS halted much of its modernization work and developed a new plan that would rely more heavily upon a prime contractor for modernizing the agency's operations.

Personnel in Tax Administration

Tax administration involves several personnel-related problems, with one being the sheer number of employees. As long as tax recordkeeping and tax filing is a largely paper process, treasury departments need large numbers of employees, especially at tax filing time (often April 15). Sizable numbers of people are needed in auditing and investigating tax returns. Since these employees typically generate far more revenue than their salaries, the argument can be made that such units should be immune from budget cuts that result in furloughing employees. Nevertheless, treasury departments often are expected to suffer with all other departments when across-the-board layoffs occur.

Treasury departments encounter difficulties in training their workers. One of the best forms of training is for new employees to be instructed by senior ones, but if senior employees are used to train new employees, then important resources are being diverted away from the main duty of collecting revenue.

Opportunities abound for unethical and illegal activities by employees. As the IRS has improved its computer operations, employees have gained wide access to the tax files of most private citizens, and some employees have been found browsing out of curiosity through the income tax returns of prominent citizens. In response, Congress passed the Taxpayer Browsing Protection Act of 1997.[49] In other instances, employees have been able to have tax refund checks illegally sent to themselves. Other employees may have important conflicts of interest, such as reviewing tax returns of corporations in which they have financial holdings, making obvious the need for financial disclosure systems in which employees must report their financial investments.

Intergovernmental Relations in Tax Administration

There are intergovernmental aspects to tax administration. As already noted, some governments share information with each other to help detect noncompliance with tax laws. Local governments sometimes work together in joint billing, such as when a county, city, and school district prepare a single bill for property taxes. Tax provisions of governments are sometimes related to each other, which can unintentionally create policy and administrative problems. Changes in the federal income tax laws can affect provisions in state taxes, necessitating adjustments in those laws. This was the case with passage of the federal Tax Reform Act in 1986 (see Chapter 4).[50] The federal government and the states have cooperated somewhat in tax administration.[51]

Debt Collection and Taxpayer Rights

One of the biggest debts owed government is taxes, but there are several other types of debt that individuals and corporations owe government. Loans, both direct and guaranteed, result in some defaults. Federal loan programs exist for college students, low-income housing, ship construction, development in other nations, and small businesses recovering from disasters, to name only a few. Various business transactions with government result in debts, such as farmers owing on crop insurance payments and foreign countries owing on purchases of agricultural commodities. Fines are another form of debt, as in the case of a corporation's being fined for not meeting environmental standards for its mining operations.

The National Performance Review recommended that agencies be allowed "to use some of the money they collect from delinquent debts to pay for further debt collection efforts, and to keep a portion of the increased collections" as a form of incentive.[52] The review also recommended the use of private collection agencies in cases where this would be cost effective. Private collection agencies may be particularly useful regarding delinquent accounts, but it should be noted that these agencies often charge as much as a 50-percent commission for what they collect.

The federal government, as discussed in Chapter 6, is attempting to deal with the "hidden liabilities" of federal credit programs. General information on credit is contained in the *Budget of the United States Government*, and more detailed information is available through other documents produced by OMB and the Treasury Department.

OMB Circular A-129, Policies for Federal Credit Programs and Non-Tax Receivables, requires that agencies review their credit programs in terms of the costs and benefits to society. The circular establishes requirements for "sound" credit programs. As noted in Chapter 6, federal agencies must calculate expected credit losses on both direct and guaranteed loans. These losses can reduce the amount of funding available for future loans. The Debt Collection Act of 1982 and OMB Circular A-129 further require that agencies take steps to improve their credit programs.[53] Loan applications must be examined with an eye toward uncovering the risks that government would take in approving the loans. Delinquent cases can be turned over to collection agencies and can be reported to consumer credit agencies. Salary offsets can be used in the case of federal employees who owe the government, and individuals may have income tax refunds withheld up to the amount owed. State governments also have used this latter technique.

In their zeal to extract as many tax dollars as possible from the public, tax administrators must keep in mind that the citizens are ultimately responsible for setting tax laws and for paying the salaries of tax administrators, in other words, that administrators are employees of the citizenry. To this end, governments have adopted laws that declare a set of rights for taxpayers. Hawaii, for example, has such a law.[54] Congress has passed the Omnibus Taxpayer Bill of Rights of 1988 and the Taxpayer Bill of Rights 2 of 1996.[55] The laws impose several restrictions on the government. In particular, they require the IRS to

- make available a statement on taxpayer rights
- allow taxpayers to make installment payments on taxes owed
- set rules on what conduct is permissible by IRS agents in taxpayer interviews
- refrain from using production quotas for employees[56]

The 1996 law allows a taxpayer to sue the IRS for up to $1 million for reckless collections and makes it easier for a taxpayer to win legal fees in a case. The IRS has a taxpayer advocate office, which assists taxpayers in dealing with the agency.[57]

Tax administration is moving toward setting standards not only for treating taxpayers courteously but in a timely fashion. The IRS has been roundly criticized in this respect. As recently as 1996, four out of five people got busy signals when they tried reaching IRS through its telephone hotline for answering tax questions. The IRS has a standard of issuing refunds within 14 days for taxpayers filing electronically and requesting direct deposit of their refunds and a standard of 40 days for issuing refunds for paper returns. However, the IRS has had great difficulty in meeting its own standards. In 1996, it delayed issuing refunds to 2 million taxpayers due to missing or invalid Social Security numbers, but then after several weeks of delay, issued the refunds without having resolved the problems.[58]

Taxpayers' privacy needs to be protected, and taxpayers need to be treated equally. As noted earlier, some government workers have been found browsing the tax returns of celebrities and other prominent figures. Also, access to files needs to be restricted in order to ensure security and avoid record tampering.[59]

The audit process should not be politically motivated, as has sometimes been alleged.

Matters such as these, along with massive problems in introducing new computer systems have led to proposals for a total revamping of the IRS. In 1997, the IRS, itself, admitted to the National Commission on Restructuring the Internal Revenue Service, that the service's efforts to upgrade computer operations had failed and suggested that outsourcing might be desirable. The commission suggested that a major overhaul of the IRS was needed urgently.[60] One option would be to remove IRS from the Treasury Department and have it controlled by an independent commission.

CASH MANAGEMENT

Cash management is the process of administering monies to ensure that they are available over time to meet expenditure needs and that, when temporarily not needed, they are invested at a minimum risk and a maximum yield. Cash management involves both short- and long-term investments; the latter are used mainly in the case of pension funds, which try to build up reserves for future years when employees retire. The state of the art of cash management is necessarily dependent on the state of the larger financial system. In Eastern European countries and the countries that once constituted the Soviet Union, governments are developing cash management strategies to accommodate emerging market economies.[61]

Cash Flow

An essential aspect of cash management is forecasting when revenues will be received, in what amounts (see Chapter 4), and when expenditures will occur and in what amounts over the course of the fiscal year and beyond. A cash management plan will strive to accelerate the receipt of revenues and delay or minimize expenditures. Chapter 11 discusses cash flows statements as one form of financial reporting.

Inflow of Revenues. Enforcement of tax laws is viewed as one means of maximizing inflow. Other techniques involve depositing government receipts as soon as possible into interest-bearing accounts. For example, when tax payments accompany tax returns, these checks can be deposited immediately in banks and processing of the returns can occur later. Governments attempt to minimize the *float time* between when checks and currency are received and when they are deposited. Accounts receivable, involving payments due from citizens, corporations, and other governments, are kept to a minimum. Inflow can be accelerated by prompt invoicing, such as where airlines are invoiced on a monthly basis for their gate space at an airport terminal.

Lockboxes. Another technique used selectively by the federal government and some state governments is the lockbox system, which uses post office boxes that are under the control of banks. Taxpayers send their payments to designated post office boxes that are opened by banking officials, and the receipts are deposited promptly. The process reduces the amount of float time between when a check is written and when government deposits it and begins earning interest.

Expenditure Planning and Prompt Payment. Some techniques deal, not with inflow, but with outflow; here the concern is to keep money in interest-bearing accounts until it is needed to cover expenses and to avoid having to borrow funds to cover expenses when revenues, such as tax receipts, are unavailable in the projected amounts. Cash flow planning is one of the reasons agencies are required to submit apportionment plans to the central budget office. Agencies may be instructed to shift expenditures in apportionment plans from one month or quarter to another. One rule is to pay promptly, that is, when bills are due and not before or after. This procedure is mandated at the federal level by the Prompt Payment Act of 1982, as amended, and OMB Circular A-125.[62] Paying bills promptly saves money for the government, such as avoiding payment of late fees, and reduces a common problem encountered by government's suppliers, namely, not knowing when they will be paid. Although 95 percent of the federal government's payments to vendors are on time, that still leaves many millions of other payments that are late.[63]

Of course, another concern is that not only should bills be paid on time but that they should be paid to the right party and in the right amount. Lax disbursement systems increase the chances that errors are made in paying vendors and that fraud occurs.[64] Fraud can happen without a government officer being aware of the situation or in conjunction with the officer's assistance.

Borrowing. If forecasted expenditures cannot be adjusted downward to be no greater than expected revenues, then short-term borrowing becomes an important option. State and local governments borrow from banks for up to one year in cases where expenditures are considered essential and funds are unavailable to cover the expenses. The backing of these bank notes consists of future receipt of revenues, and the instruments are known as RANs and TANs—*revenue and tax anticipation notes.*

Governments also may spend from their own reserves and borrow from themselves. *Unrestricted fund balances,* which are in effect contingency funds, may be drawn upon to meet unanticipated expenditure needs.[65] Short-term borrowing from one fund to meet the cash needs of another also occurs, as in the case of a local government's borrowing from its pension funds. State laws, however, may greatly restrict such borrowing as a protection against depleting the funds.

Some governments have established *rainy day funds* or *budget stabilization funds* that can be used during years when revenues decline. Statutes or state constitutional provisions require that monies be placed in these funds when the economy improves and revenues rise and that monies may be withdrawn only when revenues decline by some set percentage. It is common for governments to have in these funds something in excess of 5 percent of their general funds.[66] These funds have been found to reduce fiscal stress during recessions.[67]

Investment Planning

When forecasts show periods during the year when revenues will exceed expenditures, plans are made for investment. Virtually all governments encounter this situation. Often there are spurts in revenue receipts, such as when property taxes are due or when state sales tax receipts are due following the Christmas shopping period.

At least seven factors must be taken into account when devising an investment strategy:

1. *Security.* Financial institutions insure some deposits up to only $100,000.
2. *Maturity date.* Some instruments mature in a few months while others mature in 30 years.
3. *Marketability or liquidity.* If cash is needed before the maturity date, may an instrument be sold to a third party or will the issuer convert the instrument to cash?
4. *Call provisions.* May the issuer repay the investor before the date of maturity?
5. *Denominations.* Minimum amounts for investing range from $1,000 to $100,000 and more.
6. *Yield or return on investment.* Yield is measured in terms of a percentage of the investment and often expressed as an interest rate.
7. *Legal authority.* State laws may prohibit the state government and local governments from some types of investment.

With the collapse of many savings and loan associations and rumors of the possible collapse of major banks, the security of investments became a prominent concern in the 1980s and 1990s. When a government deposits funds with a bank, a typical requirement is that the bank set aside funds as collateral on the deposits as a means of protecting the investment in the event that the bank fails. An alternative that was developed in the 1990s is for the bank to purchase private deposit insurance. This insurance, known as ASSURETY, is available through the

Municipal Bond Investors Assurance Corporation, which is the largest insurer of municipal bonds.

Investment Instruments

The instruments available for state and local investments consist of three general types: federal government securities, corporate securities, and money market instruments. Any government must decide to what extent it wishes to invest in each of these.

Federal Securities. Fully guaranteed federal securities include treasury bills (T-bills), notes, and bonds. T-bills mature in 13, 26, and 52 weeks. They are sold at a discount by auction and consequently have no set percentage return. Treasury notes and bonds, which range in maturity from 1 to 30 years, have coupons that mature every six months. Other securities issued by the federal government may or may not be guaranteed. Bonds issued by the Small Business Administration and participation certificates issued by the General Services Administration are guaranteed, unlike bonds issued by the Tennessee Valley Authority and the postal service.

The Treasury Department in 1997 launched a new instrument, an *inflation-sensitive* 10-year note, with the expectation that similar instruments having other maturity structures will be introduced later. Each note has a fixed interest rate, but its principal rises or falls based upon the U.S. city average of the consumer price index. If the consumer price index rises in a time period, the value of the note rises and then the interest is calculated based on the new principal. If deflation occurs, which is considered only a remote possibility, investors at the time of maturity are guaranteed the original purchase price. These instruments pay about a half-percent less than notes that lack the inflation protection.

Other Federal-Related Securities. Other securities are issued by credit institutions created by the federal government and may have full, limited, or no backing or ambiguous backing of the government. Instruments backed by the federal government include Farmers Home Administration insured notes and Ginnie Maes of the Federal Home Loan Mortgage Corporation. Instruments that do not have the expressed guarantee of the federal government but could be backed in emergency situations include Federal Home Loan Bank bonds, Federal Land Bank bonds, and Federal Intermediate Credit Bank bonds.[68]

Many of these federal-related securities involve mortgages, including mortgages on homes, farms, cooperatives, and overseas investments (Asian Development Bank notes and bonds and Export Import Bank debentures). Collateralized mortgage obligations, which are pools of mortgages held by financial institutions, constitute a relatively recent development in the mortgage market and provide high security and yields above U.S. Treasury instruments.[69]

Corporate Securities. Corporations are a possibility for the investment of state and local monies. Corporate bonds are essentially loans made to the issuers. Stocks, in comparison, represent ownership of the corporation. In the event that a corporation goes into bankruptcy, creditors such as bondholders are paid first, and whatever assets remain, if any, are then distributed among stockholders.

Money Market Instruments. Banks and savings and loan institutions provide numerous investment opportunities. Interest is paid on *negotiable order of withdrawal* (NOW) checking accounts and on savings accounts. Not only can government earn interest on these deposits, but also other benefits may be negotiated through what are called *linked deposit agreements.* In these situations, banks, as a condition of receiving government deposits, may agree to make available more loans for housing in a community or for industrial development in a targeted area.[70]

Monies also can be invested in money market instruments, with *certificates of deposit* (CDs) being one of the most popular. Issuers include banks, savings and loans associations, offshore subsidiaries of U.S. banks, and U.S. branches of foreign banks. The latter two issue what are known as Eurodollars and Yankee CDs, respectively, which are not guaranteed by the federal government. Some, but not all, CDs are negotiable. Issuers may charge interest penalties for early withdrawal of monies.

Other instruments include *bankers' acceptances, commercial paper,* and *repurchase agreements.* Bankers' acceptances are agreements to purchase a bank's agreement to loan money on a short-term basis to a corporation (one usually involved in international trade); the largest banks in the nation issue these instruments. Commercial paper, also available through banks, is a corporate promissory note. A repurchase agreement (repo) is a pool of U.S. government securities held by a financial institution and sold temporarily to state and local governments and other purchasers; the institution agrees to repurchase the securities at a later date.

Repurchase agreements are controversial because a few major firms specializing in repos went bankrupt in the mid-1980s. Some governments, including the local governments of Beaumont, Texas, and Toledo, Ohio, lost many millions of dollars.[71] Congress passed the Government Securities Act of 1986, which brought these securities dealers under the regulation of the Treasury Department and the Securities and Exchange Commission.[72]

State and local governments may purchase combinations of various money market instruments. One technique is to invest in a money market fund, which is a pool of securities; the Securities and Exchange Commission regulates these funds in an attempt to reduce the risks undertaken by investors. Despite these regulations, however, law precludes many governments from investing in money market funds because they often include higher-risk investments such as Euro-dollars.

Derivatives. One of the most controversial financial instruments in the 1990s is known as derivatives.[73] These are highly complex devices, which often are poorly understood by both those who sell them and the state and local governments that buy them. A derivative's value depends upon some underlying security or a market index or in other words, the derivative is a bet on what future interest rates will be. Governments purchase swaps that trade in variable rates for fixed rates, with the underlying gamble by the government being that the return on investment will be better with the fixed rate. Some derivatives take the form of collateralized mortgage obligations, which entail investing in a pool of mortgages with the return being based on changes in interest rates and changes in mortgage prepayment rates. As is discussed below, governments have lost large sums of money in these investments.

Investment Pools. Another technique that has become popular is for jurisdictions to combine their investments into a state-authorized investment pool. By pooling resources, smaller jurisdictions can take advantage of higher-yield investments that require larger investments than passbook savings or CDs. Liquidity is improved in that jurisdictions often can withdraw some of their monies from these pools without the financial loss that would be involved if they held securities themselves and had to liquidate them.

Yield Rates. Table 10–1 is a snapshot of yield rates for some of the instruments that have been discussed. As can be seen from the table, the rates varied considerably between the two years reported. Rates increase with risk and time. Bankers' acceptances, which involve risks, pay a higher return than generally risk-free T-bills. Bonds usually pay a higher rate than notes, and notes a higher rate than bills, because of the time factor involved.

Use of Investment Instruments. Most of the money (over 90 percent) in state and local government trust funds, such as employee retirement systems and workers' compensation, are invested and little is kept on hand, whereas the money for the rest of state and local governments is kept much more fluid (one-third in cash and deposits and two-thirds invested). Retirement systems invest mainly in federal securities (19 percent) and corporate stocks and bonds (53 percent).[74] As noted above, legal constraints affect investment programs. One survey of state and local governments found that 57 percent invested in CDs, 56 percent in state investment pools, 49 percent in T-bills, and 45 percent in T-notes.[75] Generally, governments are conservative investors.

Governments vary widely in their use of instruments. For example, in 1996 Washington State invested 74 percent of its monies in U.S. Treasury securities and securities from other federal agencies compared with only 54 percent by Col-

Table 10–1 Yield Rates of Selected Investment Instruments, September 1992 and 1997

Instrument	1992	1997
Federal securities		
13-week Treasury bills	2.97	5.03
26-week Treasury bills	3.01	5.24
52-week Treasury bills	3.13	5.60
10-year Treasury notes	6.45	6.27
30-year Treasury bonds	7.35	6.36
Other deposits and securities		
Interest checking	2.15	1.33
3-month certificates of deposit	2.77	5.26
3-month bankers' acceptances	3.03	5.46
3-month commercial paper	3.27	5.53
3-month Eurodollars	3.31	5.72

Source: Data from *Barron's: National Business and Financial Weekly,* pp. 101 and 104, © September 28, 1992; and *Barron's: The Dow Jones Business and Financial Weekly,* pp. MW 57 and MW 101, © September 29, 1997.

orado's treasury pool. Washington had 11 percent of its funds invested in repos while Colorado had none.[76]

Investment Risks

Investments are not risk-free. One type of risk involves the credit worthiness of the issuer of a security. Bonds issued by the federal government are nearly risk-free in this sense, and bonds issued by major corporations, such as General Electric, are low risk. Another aspect of risk, however, is whether a particular instrument is volatile in the yield it may produce. In this context, then, fixed-rate, long-term government bonds are risky investments. If a government's portfolio contains high-yield securities at a time when yield rates are declining, then the situation is generally positive, but if trends reverse and yield rates climb above those in the portfolio, the government may have difficulty selling low-bearing securities. In that situation, a government's investments might fail to keep pace with inflation. Derivatives often are singled out as one of the most high-risk investments due to their volatility, even though the issuers of the derivatives may be credit worthy.

Orange County, California, the home of Disneyland and the fifth largest county in the United States, experienced a painful lesson in the risks of investing when it was forced in 1994 to file for bankruptcy protection.[77] The county had been hailed as a shrewd investor, earning close to double the rate of return on investments compared with other governments and investment pools. The county had been so successful that 180 other local governments had deposited money with Orange County with the expectation of reaping the benefits of an investment policy that was more aggressive than the typical one. The reality of 1994 was that this approach resulted in a loss of nearly $2 billion.

What went wrong in Orange County? First, heavy investments were placed in derivatives, which as noted earlier are gambles on what will happen to interest rates. When rates went in the opposite direction than what was expected, the county was in trouble. Second, the situation was exacerbated by the use of *reverse repos*. As noted above, a repurchase agreement or repo is a common instrument for investing money. A reverse repo, on the other hand, is a means for a government to borrow against securities it holds; the instrument is a form of temporary debt for the issuer. Orange County used reverse repos to obtain additional money that was used in turn to purchase additional risky instruments. Subsequently, the Governmental Accounting Standards Board (GASB) issued Interpretation No. 3, Financial Reporting for Reverse Repurchase Agreements, which is intended to force governments to disclose their dealings in reverse repos and presumably rein in their use.

The Orange County debacle underscores the need for careful management of risk in developing a portfolio of investments. Derivatives may be a hedge against other investments that have low yields, but the derivatives, themselves, clearly entail substantial risks. Numerous proposals have been made for limiting the use of derivatives.[78] GASB Technical Bulletin 9401, Disclosures about Derivatives and Similar Debt and Investment Transactions, requires state and local governments to make public their dealings in derivatives.

GASB Statement No. 3, Deposits with Financial Institutions, Investments (including Repurchase Agreements), and Reverse Repurchase Agreements, provides that governments are to report high-risk investments in their comprehensive annual financial reports (CAFRs).[79] While an annual report showing such investments is helpful, more short-term reporting is needed. One option is to mark or report the value of each item in a portfolio on a daily basis.[80] GASB Statement No. 31, Accounting and Financial Reporting for Certain Investments and for External Investment Pools, specifies that governments are to account for and report "fair value" for their investments in (1) interest-earning investment contracts, (2) external investment pools, (3) open-end mutual funds, (4) debt securities, and (5) equity securities, option contracts, stock warrants, and stock rights.

Federal Cash Management

The federal government's cash management system is considerably different from those of state and local governments. Federal monies are kept with the Federal Reserve System (see Chapter 15), which pays a form of interest for deposits, and banks, which also pay interest. The Financial Management Service of the Treasury Department handles transactions. Other departments and agencies, however, handle many transactions in accordance with instructions issued by Treasury.

The inflow of federal receipts comes from taxes and other payments and from the sale of T-bills and other instruments discussed earlier. These sales are handled through the Federal Reserve and are limited according to the total debt ceiling set by Congress (Chapter 9). T-bills are auctioned off weekly and other instruments less frequently; there is, of course, a secondary market for these securities.

Currency and Coins. The federal government in the 1990s began a program of redesigning its currency, introducing change for the first time in more than six decades. The $100 note was redesigned first, followed by the $50 note. The bills use color-shifting ink and microprinting that greatly deter counterfeiting through the use of advanced technology photocopying equipment. A $1 coin is to be introduced with the prospect that it might eventually replace the paper bill.[81] People who are blind or only partially sighted have advocated that currency be printed on different-sized paper and that greater contrasts be used in the design of notes, such as the large "50" in a clear space that appears on the new $50 bill.

Checks. In addition to redesigning currency and introducing a redesigned $1 coin, the government redesigned its checks. The punch-card checks that had been used for decades were replaced by checks that have counterfeiting protections and can be read by high-speed processing equipment. However, despite advances made in checks and their processing, Congress decided in 1996 to phase out most check writing by January 1, 1999 (Debt Collection Improvement Act of 1996).[82]

Electronic Fund Transfers. Advances in computer technology have made possible extensive use of electronic fund transfers. Through the use of electronic fund transfers, monies are moved via computer communication from bank to bank and from account to account. Monies received at one bank through a lock-box system, for instance, can be moved to other accounts in distant banks. Another advantage of electronic fund transfers is that they can be used for recurring payments, such as making direct deposits of Social Security payments into retirees' bank accounts. A form of electronic fund transfer is the *electronic benefit transfer*, which can be used to transfer funds through automatic teller machines; some governments use electronic benefit transfers to make payments to welfare recipients.[83] Electronic fund transfers, which are processed nationally by a few large banking systems, cost much less per transaction than conventional checks. Because of this technology, Congress mandated the virtual elimination of checks, including payments to vendors who provide materials and services to the government.

Letters of Credit. An important cash management technique, especially for the federal government, is the use of letters of credit. These are provided to governments and nonprofit corporations that are awarded grants and contracts. The letters allow recipient organizations to establish credit at banks without the federal government having to provide money until it is needed. Funds then are transferred electronically into these accounts by the federal government. The procedure allows the government to delay until the last moment the transfer of funds, thereby saving the government money. The procedure benefits recipients by allowing them to draw-down on their letters of credit as soon as payments are due.

Other Cash Management Considerations

Computer Usage. New computer technology has greatly altered how financial institutions operate and how governments handle cash. As already noted, electronic fund transfers have greatly modified how government does business. After just a few years in existence, the World Wide Web has become an important source of information about investment opportunities.[84] Another example of computer applications is in municipal water systems. Experiments are being conducted in which new electronic water meters are connected to customers' telephone lines, with the meters being programmed to call in billing information at specified intervals.[85]

Intergovernmental Relations. Cash management has important intergovernmental aspects. States, as noted, have passed laws setting standards for their local governments, which often view these laws as unnecessarily restrictive. Several states have established investment pools for their local governments. Some states provide assistance to local governments in the development of cash management plans. One important issue is the timing of grant payments the federal government makes to state and local governments; the former, for cash management reasons, attempts to provide grant installments at the last possible moment. The Cash Management Improvement Act of 1990 provides that states are to pay interest on federal grant monies if the monies are received earlier than required and that the federal government must pay interest if it is tardy in providing promised grant monies.[86]

Cash and Investment Managers. As is obvious, cash management involves a complex set of interdependent activities that require extensive expertise, and for that reason governments do not attempt to operate solely with their own capabilities. A state or local government will select one or more financial institutions to provide a range of services. Banks will receive checks, clear them, and deposit them in government accounts. A government may have a *bank concentration account* into which monies are first entered and then disbursed to others; each day the bank will move money into accounts requiring deposits to cover checks, and remaining funds will be placed in overnight interest-bearing instruments. Banks provide electronic fund transfer services, lockbox services, armored cars, safety deposit boxes, lines of credit, and more. These institutions can provide a wide range of investment services and can handle the registration of government bonds and payments to bondholders. A preferred method for selecting a bank for everyday transactions or a securities dealer for managing an investment portfolio is to request bids from competing institutions.

PROCUREMENT

Procurement entails the acquisition of resources required in providing government services. While this function is not at the core of budgeting, it has major budgetary implications.

Organizational Configurations

Most jurisdictions have procurement systems that blend centralized and decentralized services. There may be a central purchasing agency that is responsible for acquiring commonly used materials, such as office furniture and supplies, while line agencies have authority to purchase items used primarily by themselves. Centralization, at least in theory, has the advantage of providing overall controls to ensure that appropriate procedures are followed, resulting in fair competition among government suppliers and the purchase of quality goods and services at the lowest possible prices. Decentralization, on the other hand, presumably reduces red tape, allowing individual agencies to make purchases as needed and to custom tailor purchases to their specific needs. The National Performance Review, in recommending greater decentralization in federal procurement, cited instances where buying in bulk through central purchasing cost the government more than it would have spent purchasing smaller quantities on a decentralized basis.[87]

At the federal level, there are several major organizational units responsible for procurement. The General Services Administration provides overall support to departments by procuring buildings, equipment, motor vehicles, computer systems, telephone systems, supplies, day care centers for employees' dependents, and the like. General Services Administration's operations are immense. The agency has a fleet of 145,000 vehicles, spends several billions of dollars every year on construction, manages about 300 million square feet of building space (excluding parking), and keeps many thousands of items on hand in its warehouses.[88]

All federal line departments and agencies carry out procurement, with the Department of Defense having one of the largest procurement operations. The Defense Logistics Agency purchases many items centrally for the department, while the individual services also have purchasing authority.

Having many procurement offices can result in a hodgepodge of operations, each with its own peculiar set of regulations. Congress in 1974 attempted to deal with this problem by creating the Office of Federal Procurement Policy (OFPP) within OMB.[89] President Clinton strengthened the OFPP's role in 1994 by issuing Executive Order 12931, which charged the unit with providing "broad policy guidance and overall leadership" in procurement. The OFPP, while not conducting purchasing activities, is responsible for coordinating the activities of purchasing offices.

Procurement Objectives

A procurement program has several objectives. One chief concern is having the materials and supplies available when needed and avoiding stock outages. Keeping unit costs as low as possible is another objective; often the lowest costs for acquiring items are obtained by ordering large quantities, whether large amounts of office stationery or entire fleets of automobiles. Ordering large quantities, however, conflicts with another concern, namely keeping stocked items to a minimum. Procurement specialists strive to determine *economic ordering quantities*, that is, when to purchase particular types of items and in what quantities. Some purchasing offices have shifted to *just-in-time ordering* in which items are received from vendors when needed, thereby eliminating the cost of warehousing these items.[90] The widespread use of computer systems has greatly increased the ability of organizations—both public and private—to implement just-in-time ordering.

Choices also must be made between *purchasing*, *leasing*, and *privatizing*. In some instances, there may be financial and other advantages to leasing a building rather than purchasing it. The federal government, however, has been criticized for its heavy reliance on leasing office space, since ownership presumably is less expensive in the long run, and for its excessive red tape used in leasing.[91] A wide range of equipment can be leased, including photocopying machines, computers, and dump trucks. *True* or *operating leases* are those in which the government pays for the specified period and gains no ownership of whatever is being leased, whereas *lease-purchase agreements* provide for ownership after a specified period.[92]

Privatizing, as discussed earlier, is another option and may involve contracting with a private firm to use its facilities, personnel, and other resources to deliver a service.[93] In many cases, private contractor employees and government employees work side-by-side producing services in government facilities. Federal agencies must follow the guidance in Circular A-76, which covers contracts for commercial (nongovernmental) activities. While many services can be contracted out, policy making is regarded as a core activity that cannot be privatized. This area is of concern in situations where government relies heavily on consulting firms to the extent that they seem to be responsible for setting policy or conducting other inherently governmental functions.[94] In making a choice among these options, a paramount concern must be to use tax dollars efficiently.

The Contracting Process

Steps. Standard procedures are normally followed when contracting for products or services. Specifications for what is to be purchased are determined. For example, a truck might be required to have a specified ground clearance, load capacity, passenger capacity, and the like. Then, bidding procedures begin through the issuance of *invitations for bid* (IFBs), *requests for proposal* (RFPs), and *requests for quotation* (RFQs). An IFB is used when a government has a reasonably detailed conception of what is to be purchased, such as the painting of the exterior of a building, whereas an RFP or RFQ is used in a situation where some latitude exists on the part of the bidder in terms of what is to be offered. Once bids are received, they are analyzed, and, in the case of IFBs, awards are made to the lowest responsible bidder. In a competition involving an RFP, an award might be made to a higher bidder, one that was thought to have the best approach to dealing with a problem. When the government selects a firm using an RFQ, bilateral negotiations are required before a final selection may be made, whereas with an RFP the government may select a firm without further negotiations. The receipt of a product or service follows the signing of a contract or the award of a grant. Additional steps include inspecting the product or service received and paying the contractor.

In some situations, contracts are awarded not to one company but to several. The federal government, since it serves the entire nation, finds it advantageous to contract with several suppliers in the same industry. This multiple award schedule system makes goods and services available on a standby basis, allowing agencies to order them when needed.[95] All forms of construction, ranging from simple repair and maintenance to the construction of an entire building, can be handled through a job order contracting mechanism in which suppliers agree to provide services at specified costs when needed. For example, a painting firm might sign a contract agreeing to charge a set amount per square foot, and then any agency could hire the firm for painting services.

Another feature of some procurement programs is specification of performance in terms of timeliness and quality. For example, a contract for a highway construction project may stipulate that the project must be completed by a specified date with financial penalties imposed for each day beyond the deadline.

The 1994 Federal Acquisition Streamlining Act instructs federal agencies to develop *results-oriented* or *performance* contracts for acquisitions other than standardized commercial items.[96] In other words, when an agency buys a service, such as using a firm to process grant applications from local governments, standards should be set for evaluating the firm's performance.[97] Measurable performance is increasingly a part of federal contracts for research and development. These contracts contain award fee incentives in which contractors can achieve higher or lower fees or profits based on their performance.

Competition. Competition in procurement is considered one of the best means of ensuring quality products or services at minimum cost. Lack of competition may result from blatant favoritism in awarding contracts or from somewhat more subtle ploys, such as specifying a named product brand and model in the IFB. At the state and local levels, corporations have become more aggressive in challenging contract awards when they seem to violate state legal requirements for competition.

The Competition in Contracting Act of 1984 was passed to encourage greater competition in federal contracting and specifically enhanced the powers of losing bidders in making legal challenges of the awards.[98] In addition to filing a protest with the contracting agency itself or with the GAO, a losing bidder may be able to appeal to the General Services Board of Contract Appeals, the Court of Federal Claims, or a federal district court.[99]

The 1994 Federal Acquisition Streamlining Act contains important provisions that limit bid protests, which often are perceived as needlessly delaying the awarding of contracts. President Clinton's Executive Order 12979 of 1995 instructs agencies to devise alternative dispute resolution procedures such as the use of neutral third parties.[100]

Several factors discourage competition among would-be contractors. Lack of knowledge about how contracts are awarded and how to prepare a bid excludes some companies from bidding, although government reports, books, and World Wide Web homepages exist to facilitate bidding.[101] Many procurements are so large and complex that companies would already have had to make major investments in personnel and technology to become competitive in the bidding process. *Design-and-build contracts* in which several contract awards may be made for the design phase, with the best design being selected for the build or implementation phase, enable more firms to compete for the larger, more complex contracts.

Federal purchasing regulations are available on a computer compact disk (CD-ROM) and the World Wide Web to facilitate easy access by vendors.[102] President Clinton in 1993 issued a directive calling for increased use of *electronic commerce*, which allows businesses greater access to information through computers.[103] The General Services Administration has developed an Access America plan for using electronic commerce.[104] The Federal Acquisition Streamlining Act authorized creation of a computer system known as Federal Acquisition Computer Network (FACNET), which is intended to provide vendors with information about solicitations for bids and to allow the submission of bids through the computer network. Implementation, however, has been rocky. A GAO report said that its benefits have been outweighed by its difficulties.[105] One possible problem is that the technology on which FACNET is based is being passed by with more advanced technology, including the World Wide Web.

Competition is restricted in other ways. A close and long-term relationship between a government agency and a contractor can develop, and when a contract is to be rebid for a new time period, the company already holding the contract usually has a decided advantage.[106] Slow payment by government is one of the biggest deterrents of small bidders, who may be unable to wait extended periods for payment on the services or goods delivered to government.[107] Delays in payments can bankrupt a small firm. Even when payments are prompt, small firms may face other problems. If payments are made but then later the funding agency demands greater documentation on transactions, the small firm may be unable to comply. Factors such as these deter some firms from bidding on government contracts.

Reforms

Numerous efforts have been made to improve procurement practices. The National Performance Review called for sweeping reforms aimed at reducing the red tape involved in purchasing and reducing the quantities purchased and held in inventory. The Advisory Commission on Intergovernmental Relations, the Council of State Governments, the Government Finance Officers Association, and the International City/County Management Association have all encouraged improvement in procurement procedures used by state and local governments. The American Bar Association has developed a model procurement code that is recommended for adoption by governments.

Procurement procedures become increasingly complex as additional, well-intended requirements are imposed. Three Presidential executive orders are instructive. Executive Order 12843 provides restrictions on purchasing that in any way involves ozone-depleting substances. Executive Order 12845 requires that computer equipment be energy efficient. Executive Order 12873 mandates recycling and waste prevention in the acquisition process. While each of these orders has laudable purposes, each requires administrators to establish procedures to ensure compliance with the orders, and the steps that are imposed translate into time and cost.

One prescription is that the government procurement process should be simplified. The 1993 National Performance Review recommended that greater use be made of off-the-shelf purchasing of commercial items rather than specifying items that then might require special designs and types of construction. As an example of the rigidity in government purchasing, the General Services Administration had elaborate specifications for the design and durability of "ash receiver[s], tobacco (desk type)" when a wide variety of commercially available ashtrays probably would have been suitable, especially since smoking is banned in most government buildings. Simplification was one of the chief objectives of the 1994 Federal Acquisition Streamlining Act and President Clinton's Executive Order 12931 of 1994. The law eliminated many contracting procedures for purchases under $100,000 and, in purchases of commercial items, waived more than thirty laws that required bidders to collect and submit detailed information of limited utility as part of their bids. The Federal Acquisition Reform Act (FARA) or Clinger-Cohen Act of 1996 broadened the definition of commercial services, bringing more purchasing activities under the simplified procedures.[108]

Another reform frequently mentioned is to upgrade the quality of the procurement work force. High-quality workers need to be recruited into government and rewarded for creativity in improving contracting practices.[109] The 1994 legislation calls for the establishment of incentives for purchasing personnel.[110] Training in ethics and technical knowledge also has been prescribed. The National Institute of Government Purchasing makes courses available to purchasing officials, as do private firms.

Despite sustained efforts to improve procurement practices, the field has been plagued with scandals involving waste (as in the case of toilet seats that cost the military hundreds of dollars) and charges of bribery and other forms of collusion between government contractors and purchasing offices. Scandals that occur periodically in the Defense Department are especially notable in that military contracts often involve billions of dollars, but defense, of course, has not been the only area subject to such scandals. Unethical and illegal practices in purchasing arise with some degree of frequency in federal domestic agencies and throughout state and local governments. Contract auditing is an important mechanism for revealing and presumably deterring illegal practices.

A long-standing problem is how to allow for indirect costs or overhead in government procurement. When government purchases a service, for example, costs include direct expenses, such as the materials and personnel needed to provide the service, and indirect or overhead expenses, such as costs associated with central administrative offices, including the budgeting and accounting office, personnel office, computer operations, and the like. Other indirect costs include the heating, electricity, and janitorial services used in the building that houses the employees working on the project. These costs, while legitimate, can become large and can greatly inflate the cost of a project. Consequently, government procurement offices have repeatedly attempted to place limits on indirect costs. Part of the problem involves determining what is and is not appropriately assigned to the indirect category. Universities as well as most other types of organizations have been challenged by federal authorities for inflating indirect expenses as a means of increasing their federal grant and contract monies. Several of the larger federal departments have what are called *cognizant audit agencies*, such as the Defense Contract Audit Agency, which focus entirely on auditing, negotiating, and approving contractors' indirect rates. The Department of Health and Human Services is the cognizant agency for approving overhead rates for many universities and nonprofit grantees and contractors.

Problem Areas and Innovations

Procurement is undergoing extensive changes too numerous to discuss here, but a few can be noted. One area is the use of credit. Some governments now provide employees with credit cards so that they may charge their travel expenses and be reimbursed later rather than use travel advances or their personal funds to cover costs until being reimbursed. Credit cards also are being used for small purchases, $2,500 or less in the case of the federal government. The cards are helpful in remote areas that lack ready access to General Services Administration supply centers. Today's technology allows credit cards to work or not work at specific stores, liquor stores being one example where the cards would not work.[111]

A continuing problem is the extent to which procurement should support affirmative action. In 1995 the Federal Acquisition Streamlining Act set nonbinding goals of contracting with minority-owned businesses, and President Clinton issued Executive Order 12928 calling upon agencies to develop methods for encouraging minority businesses and historically black colleges and universities to bid on contracts with the government. In order to avoid charges of reverse discrimination, agencies avoid the use of quotas and instead use outreach and other programs to help make minority businesses aware of contracting opportunities and provide advice on how to prepare procurement proposals.[112] Congressional support for these programs has eroded, however. In the 1996 Foreign Affairs reauthorization, Congress dropped a long-standing requirement, known as the Grey Amendment, that some portion of U.S. Agency for International Development (USAID) contracts be subcontracted to women-owned or minority-owned firms. Although USAID continues to encourage such participation in contracts, it no longer can require it.

Other problems involve the environment and immigrants. Executive Order 12969 of 1995 states that federal agencies should only contract with firms that comply with federal requirements for reporting the use of toxic chemicals. Executive Order 12989 of 1996 prohibits agencies from contracting with companies that the Attorney General has determined to have violated immigration laws by hiring illegal alien workers.

There are important aspects of procurement that involve intergovernmental relations. States, through laws and regulations, set standards for purchasing conducted by their local governments. Cooperative purchasing is used to increase the "buying power" of governments. These agreements are among local governments or sometimes between local governments and their state government. The Federal Acquisition Streamlining Act permits state and local governments to make purchases through the General Services Administration, but the Federal Acquisition Reform Act of 1996 temporarily suspended that provision. A study by GAO suggests that the savings achieved by state and local governments in purchasing through the federal government might be quite limited.[113]

Contracting of services is an important form of intergovernmental relations, with the Lakewood Plan in Los Angeles County, California, probably being the oldest and most extensive in the United States. Cities within the county may contract with the county for virtually all of their services, which are provided at cost and at the same level of quality as the county provides to unincorporated areas. Nearly 40 of the county's 88 cities contract for almost all of their services.[114] Some states contract with each other, such as one state contracting to have another state house some of its prisoners.

RISK MANAGEMENT

To provide services, governments must have property and personnel. Arising from this simple fact are a series of *exposures* or *risks*, such as the risk of property being damaged or lost owing to natural disasters, employee error, and fraud by employees and others. Property damage can lead to major repair or replacement costs and to loss of income (e.g., structural problems in a municipal stadium may force its closing). The destruction of the space shuttle Challenger in 1986 is a dramatic example of how one accident can disable a program for months or even years. The Chicago flood of 1992, in which water from the Chicago River entered buildings throughout the downtown area, is an example of how inattention to a problem, in this case leakage into a tunnel system caused by faulty construction under government contract, can have disastrous effects.

Other risks pertain to financial guarantees. As was discussed in Chapter 6, the federal government is striving to identify the extent of its exposure in loan programs and other activities, such as mortgage guarantees. The government also has been attempting to assess risks to public health when the government regulates activities associated with hazardous substances.[115]

Liability

Governments are vulnerable to suits brought by employees or by corporations and private citizens. Negligence is often the basis of suits in which government is alleged not to have acted the way a "reasonable" person would and inflicted harm as a result. Local governments have been sued for allowing the leakage of harmful chemicals from landfills into privately owned water wells. Governments also may be sued for violating antitrust legislation, as in the instance where a city favors one cable television operator over another. Court-awarded financial settlements can be extraordinarily large; in some suits against local governments, the awards have been greater than the governments' total annual budgets.[116]

Laws, of course, govern liability cases.[117] The federal government may be sued only in federal court. One of the most important federal laws is the Federal Tort Claims Act of 1946, which selectively permits suits against the government in cases not arising out of contract.[118] State and local governments sometimes may be sued in federal courts as well as in state courts. Antitrust cases against local governments, for example, are the domain of federal courts. Discrimination cases can be filed in federal and state courts.

Managing Risks

Governments need a management strategy for dealing with liability exposure. Risk management planning begins by identifying risks and, where possible, eliminating them. A faulty woodworking machine in a school shop should be repaired; the repair will improve the safety of the machine, thereby eliminating some risk when students use it. A road intersection widely known to be dangerous can be redesigned. A community that is subject to hurricanes obviously cannot avoid these fierce storms, but it can take steps to be prepared for such emergencies.

Having eliminated or reduced risks, governments must be prepared to deal with remaining areas of exposure. Commercial insurance is used by governments and awarded through a bidding process similar to any other purchasing arrangement. Another option is self-insurance, where a government sets aside funds on a regular basis to cover awards or simply expends funds from the current budget to cover abnormal expenses (for example, the costs of repairing police cars damaged in the line of duty). In some instances, governments help cover each other's risks through self-insurance pooling. Perhaps nearly half of all state and local governments engage in some form of pooling.[119]

Insurance premiums for liability coverage have become extremely expensive, sometimes so expensive that insurance is beyond the reach of governments—if available at all. Costs are a function of the nature of a policy. Factors include the number of employees and officials of a government, the services covered, the deductibles included, and the loss experience. The latter is not just the experience of a particular government. A given city might have had no major suits filed against it, but because some cities have had major legal problems, as in cases involving landfills, all cities pay heavily for coverage.

The costs of risk management are typically handled centrally. That is, the costs of insurance premiums, court-mandated awards to injured parties, out-of-court settlements, and the like are handled by the central budget and not charged to department budgets. Were line agencies charged for these costs, managers would be more aware of the costs of their operations and would have greater incentives to reduce risks.

According to GASB, governments should report risks in their financial statements. GASB Statement No. 10 covers risks associated with torts, thefts, business interruptions, errors or omissions, job-related illnesses or injuries of employees, and acts of God. Governments, when reporting pension plan risks, are expected to use GASB Statement No. 27 starting in 1998. As noted above, GASB Statement No. 31 covers the reporting of investment risks.

SUMMARY

Execution is the conversion of plans embodied in the budget into day-to-day operations. At stake are factors such as interpreting and complying with legislative intent as prescribed in appropriations and providing the services that have been authorized. Control over line agencies is exercised through apportionment planning and preauditing of expenditures.

Since the 1980s there has been a resurgence of interest in economy and efficiency. This trend was embodied in the Grace Commission and the National Performance Review at the national level. Privatization of services has been used as a means of increasing efficiency of operations.

Budget offices are involved in a host of other activities. OMB exercises major powers related to information collection and dissemination and to agencies issuing regulations.

Tax administration and cash management, which usually are under the direction of a secretary of treasury, are processes aimed at maximizing revenues and minimizing costs. Numerous mechanisms are used to enforce tax laws, ranging from offering assistance in preparing tax returns to prosecuting delinquent tax-payers.

Cash management is the process of administering monies to ensure that they are available to meet expenditure needs and that monies, when temporarily not needed, are invested at a minimum risk and a maximum yield. Many instruments exist for investing state and local funds. The Treasury Department handles federal cash management through the Federal Reserve System.

Procurement entails the acquisition of resources required in providing government services, and risk management is concerned with protecting those resources. Governments often have a central purchasing office but allow individual departments some independence in purchasing products and services. A procurement program attempts to purchase only what is needed, avoid stock outages, and keep unit costs low. Risk management attempts to eliminate or reduce risk exposure and to prepare for such events as damage to government property and liability suits arising out of government operations.

NOTES

1. K. Thurmaier, Execution Phase Budgeting in Local Governments, *State and Local Government Review* 27 (1995): 102–117.

2. D. Osborne and T. Gaebler, *Reinventing Government: How the Entrepreneurial Spirit Is Transforming the Public Sector* (Reading, MA: Addison-Wesley, 1992); D. Osborne and P. Plastrik, *Banishing Bureaucracy: The Five Strategies for Reinventing Government* (Reading, MA: Addison-Wesley, 1997).

3. National Performance Review, *From Red Tape to Results: Creating a Government That Works Better and Costs Less* (Washington, DC: U.S. Government Printing Office, 1993), 19.

4. D. Durning, Governors and Administrative Reform in the 1990s, *State and Local Government Review* 27 (1995): 36–54.

5. President's Private Sector Survey on Cost Control, *War on Waste* (New York: Macmillan, 1984); U.S. General Accounting Office, *Compendium of GAO's Views on the Cost Saving Proposals of the Grace Commission* (Washington, DC: U.S. Government Printing Office, 1985).

6. S.B. Dewhurst, Downsizing: A View from the Inside, *Public Budgeting & Finance* 16 (Spring 1996): 49–59.

7. R.A. Bernardi, The Base Closure and Realignment Commission: A Rational or Political Decision Process, *Public Budgeting & Finance* 16 (Spring 1996): 49–59.

8. See series of privatization articles in *Public Administration Review* 57 (1997): 4–82.

9. L.M. Salamon, ed., *Beyond Privatization: The Tools of Government Action* (Washington, DC: Urban Institute Press, 1989); David R. Warren, U.S. General Accounting Office, *Defense Outsourcing: Challenges Facing DOD as It Attempts To Save Billions in Infrastructure Costs* (Washington, DC: U.S. Government Printing Office, 1997).

10. E.S. Savas, *Privatizing the Public Sector* (Chatham, NJ: Chatham House, 1982).

11. D.J. Gayle and J.N. Goodrich, eds., *Privatization and Deregulation in Global Perspective* (New York: Quorum Books, 1990).

12. R.B. Dixon, Reducing Service Delivery Costs through Public/Private Partnerships, *Government Finance Review* 8 (June 1992): 31–33; U.S. Government Printing Office, *Base Operations: Challenges Confronting DOD as It Renews Emphasis on Outsourcing* (Washington, DC: U.S. Government Printing Office, 1997).

13. A. Henderson, The Ports Go Private, *Governing* 8 (April 1995): 37–38.

14. W.Z. Hirsch, Contracting Out by Urban Governments: A Review, *Urban Affairs Review* 30 (1995): 458–572; U.S. General Accounting Office, *Privatization: Lessons Learned by State and Local Governments* (Washington, DC: U.S. Government Printing Office, 1997).

15. J. Prager, Contracting Out Government Services: Lessons from the Private Sector, *Public Administration Review* 54 (1994): 176–184; K. Verma, Covert Costs of Privatization, *Public Budgeting & Finance* 16 (Fall 1996): 49–62; K.S. Eagle, Contract Monitoring for Financial and Operational Performance, *Government Finance Review* 13 (June 1997): 11–14.

16. J. Flanagan and S. Perkins, Public/Private Competition in the City of Phoenix, Arizona, *Government Finance Review* 11 (June 1995): 7–12; T. Sharp, Privatization or Managed Competition? The Fort Lauderdale Experience, *Government Finance Review* 13 (June 1997): 15–18.

17. R. Miranda and A. Lerner, Bureaucracy, Organizational Redundancy, and the Privatization of Public Services, *Public Administration Review* 55 (1995): 193–200.

18. Inspector General Act, P.L. 95-452, 92 Stat. 1101 (1978); P.C. Light, *Monitoring Government: Inspectors General and the Search for Accountability* (Washington, DC: Brookings Institution, 1992).

19. Federal Managers' Financial Integrity Act, P.L. 97-255, 96 Stat. 814 (1982); President's Council on Management Improvement, *Streamlining Internal Control Processes and Strengthening Management Control with Less Effort* (Washington, DC: U.S. Government Printing Office, 1985).

20. U.S. Council on Environmental Quality and U.S. Office of Management and Budget, *Improving Federal Facilities Cleanup* (Washington, DC: U.S. Office of Management and Budget, 1995).

21. Federal Advisory Committee Act, P.L. 92-463, 86 Stat. 770 (1972).

22. Paperwork Reduction Act, P.L. 96-511, 94 Stat. 2812 (1980); P.L. 104-13, 109 Stat. 163 (1995).

23. S.R. Furlong, The 1992 Regulatory Moratorium: Did It Make a Difference?, *Public Administration Review* 55 (1995): 254–262.

24. Regulatory Working Group, *Economic Analysis of Federal Regulations under Executive Order 12866* (Washington, DC: U.S. Office of Management and Budget, 1996); F. Thompson, Toward a Regulatory Budget, *Public Budgeting & Finance* 17 (Spring 1997): 89–98.

25. Regulatory Flexibility Act, P.L. 96-354, 94 Stat. 1164 (1980); Small Business Regulatory Enforcement Fairness Act, P.L. 104-121, sec. 201, 110 Stat. 857 (1996); J. Kosterlitz, Mom and Pop Get Even, *National Journal* 29 (1997): 457–459.

26. Congressional Review Act, P.L. 104–121, sec. 251, 110 Stat. 857 (1996); R.P. Murphy, General Counsel, U.S. General Accounting Office, *Congressional Review Act* (Washington, DC: U.S. Government Printing Office, 1997).

27. U.S. General Accounting Office, *Debt Collection: Improved Reporting Needed on Billions of Dollars in Delinquent Debt and Agency Collection Performance* (Washington, DC: U.S. Government Printing Office, 1997).

28. U.S. General Accounting Office, *Tax Administration: IRS' Plans to Measure Tax Compliance Can Be Improved* (Washington, DC: U.S. Government Printing Office, 1993).

29. D. Burnham, *The Law unto Itself: Power, Politics, and the IRS* (New York: Random House, 1989).

30. U.S. General Accounting Office, *Tax Administration: IRS Efforts to Improve Forms and Publications* (Washington, DC: U.S. Government Printing Office, 1994).

31. U.S. General Accounting Office, *Tax Administration: Information Returns* (Washington, DC: U.S. Government Printing Office, 1993).

32. U.S. General Accounting Office, *Tax Administration: Making IRS' Telephone Systems Easier to Use Should Help Taxpayers* (Washington, DC: U.S. Government Printing Office, 1996).

33. U.S. General Accounting Office, *Tax Administration: New Delinquent Tax Collection Methods for IRS* (Washington, DC: U.S. Government Printing Office, 1993).

34. U.S. General Accounting Office, *Tax Gap: Many Actions Taken, But a Cohesive Compliance Strategy Needed* (Washington, DC: U.S. Government Printing Office, 1994).

35. U.S. General Accounting Office, *Reducing the Tax Gap: Results of a GAO-Sponsored Symposium* (Washington, DC: U.S. Government Printing Office, 1995).

36. U.S. General Accounting Office, *Tax Administration: Tax Compliance of Nonwage Earners* (Washington, DC: U.S. Government Printing Office, 1996).

37. S. Coleman, Income Tax Compliance: A Unique Experiment in Minnesota, *Government Finance Review* 13 (April 1997): 11–15.

38. U.S. General Accounting Office, *Tax Administration: Factors Affecting Results from Audits of Large Corporations* (Washington, DC: U.S. Government Printing Office, 1997).

39. U.S. General Accounting Office, *Tax Administration: Alternative Filing Systems* (Washington, DC: U.S. Government Printing Office, 1996).

40. New York State had a tax amnesty program in late 1996 and early 1997 covering the tax period prior to January 1, 1995.

41. U.S. General Accounting Office, *Tax Systems Modernization: Cyberfile Project Was Poorly Planned and Managed* (Washington, DC: U.S. Government Printing Office, 1996).

42. P.R. Ferm, The Electronic Federal Tax Payment System, *Government Finance Review* 13 (June 1997): 33–34.

43. See Virginia's homepage: http://www.state.va.us/tax/faq.htm; accessed December 1997.

44. Electronic Tax Return Format Approved as National Standards, *Tax Administrators News* 56 (1992): 85.

45. M. Adams, Innovation through Technology: The Success of Massachusetts' Telefile Program, *Government Finance Review* 11 (December 1995): 13–16.

46. R.G. Michel, Analyzing the Costs of Credit Cards, *Government Finance Review* 12 (June 1996): 61–63; M.L. Kezar, Logging on to Electronic Means of Payment, *Government Finance Review* 13 (April 1997): 57–59.

47. U.S. General Accounting Office, *Tax Systems Modernization: IRS Needs to Resolve Certain Issues with Its Integrated Case Processing System* (Washington, DC: U.S. Government Printing Office, 1997).

48. Arthur Gross as quoted in IRS Unveils Modernization Plan, *Government Technology* 10 (July 1997): 12.

49. Taxpayer Browsing Protection Act, P.L. 105-35, 111 Stat. 1104 (1997).

50. Tax Reform Act, P.L. 99-514, 100 Stat. 2085 (1986).

51. U.S. General Accounting Office, *Tax Administration: Federal-State Efforts Offer Opportunities But Programs Need Improvement* (Washington, DC: U.S. Government Printing Office, 1996).

52. National Performance Review, *From Red Tape to Results*, 107.

53. Debt Collection Act, P.L. 97-365, 96 Stat. 1749 (1982).

54. Hawaii Taxpayers Bill of Rights: http://www.hawaii.gov/tax/pubs/rights.htm; accessed December 1997.

55. Omnibus Taxpayer Bill of Rights, P.L. 100-647, 102 Stat. 3730 (1988); Taxpayer Bill of Rights 2, P.L. 104-168, 110 Stat. 1452 (1996); *Ward v. U.S.*, 1997 U.S. Dist. LEXIS 8827 (D. Colo. 1997).

56. U.S. General Accounting Office, *Tax Administration: IRS Is Improving Its Controls for Ensuring That Taxpayers Are Treated Properly* (Washington, DC: U.S. Government Printing Office, 1996).

57. U.S. General Accounting Office, *Internal Revenue Service: IRS Initiatives To Resolve Disputes over Tax Liabilities* (Washington, DC: U.S. Government Printing Office, 1997).

58. U.S. General Accounting Office, *IRS' 1996 Tax Filing Season: Performance Goals Generally Met: Efforts to Modernize Had Mixed Results* (Washington, DC: U.S. Government Printing Office, 1996).

59. U.S. General Accounting Office, *IRS Systems Security: Tax Processing Operations and Data Still at Risk Due to Serious Weaknesses* (Washington, DC: U.S. Government Printing Office, 1997).

60. Treasury, Postal Service, and General Appropriations Act, P.L. 104-52, 109 Stat. 468, sec. 637 (1996); National Commission on Restructuring the Internal Revenue Service, *A Vision for a New IRS* (Washington, DC: U.S. Government Printing Office, 1997).

61. R.W. Burris, Helping Poles Breathe Fresh Air of Democracy, *Government Finance Review* 6 (June 1990): 11–14.

62. Prompt Payment Act, P.L. 97-177, 96 Stat. 85 (1982); Prompt Payment Act Amendments, P.L. 100-496, 102 Stat. 2455 (1988); U.S. General Accounting Office, *Financial Management: The Prompt Payment Act and DOD Problem Disbursements* (Washington, DC: U.S. Government Printing Office, 1997).

63. U.S. Office of Management and Budget and Chief Financial Officers Council, *Federal Financial Management Status Report and Five-Year Plan* (Washington, DC: U.S. Office of Management and Budget, 1996).

64. U.S. General Accounting Office, *Financial Management: Improved Management Needed for DOD Disbursement Process Reforms* (Washington, DC: U.S. Government Printing Office, 1997); U.S. General Accounting Office, *Contract Management: Fixing DOD's Payment Problems Is Imperative* (Washington, DC: U.S. Government Printing Office, 1997).

65. C.B. Tyer, Local Government Reserve Funds: Policy Alternatives and Political Strategies, *Public Budgeting & Finance* 13 (Summer 1993): 75–84.

66. P. Lemov, Patching the Fiscal Umbrella, *Governing* 9 (December 1995): 39–40.

67. R.S. Sobel and R.G. Holcombe, The Impact of State Rainy Day Funds in Easing State Fiscal Crises During the 1990–1991 Recession, *Public Budgeting & Finance* 16 (Fall 1996): 28–48.

68. M.M. Hackbart and J.R. Ramsey, Public Cash Management: Issues and Practices, in *Handbook of Comparative Public Budgeting and Financial Management*, eds. T.D. Lynch and L.L. Martin (New York: Marcel Dekker, 1993), 289–314.

69. J.D. Nadler and B.D. Klapper, Collateralized Mortgage Obligations as Investment Instruments: What Is the Risk? *Government Finance Review* 8 (October 1992): 25–27, 56.

70. G. Valais, The Power of Linked Deposits, *Government Finance Review* 5 (April 1989): 11–15.

71. G. Miller and M.R. Saddler, Collateralization: Protecting Public Deposits, *Government Finance Review* 3 (October 1987): 23–26.

72. Government Securities Act, P.L. 99-571, 100 Stat. 3208 (1986).

73. I.G. Kawaller and T.W. Koch, What Government Finance Officers Should Know about Derivatives, *Municipal Finance Journal* 17 (Fall 1996): 48–62.

74. U.S. Bureau of the Census, Cash and Security Holdings of Major Public Employee–Retirement Systems (quarter ending December 31, 1996): http://www.census.gov/govs/www/gpr.html; accessed December 1997.

75. Governments Invest Conservatively, *P.A. Times* 18 (August 1, 1995): 2.

76. See Washington's homepage at http://www.wa.gov/tre and Colorado's homepage at http://www.treasurer.state.co.us; accessed December 1997.

77. K.P. Kearns, Accountability and Entrepreneurial Public Management: The Case of the Orange County Investment Fund, *Public Budgeting & Finance* 15 (Fall 1995): 3–21; J.E. Petersen, Managing Cash: Local Officials and the Slippery Slopes, *Governing* 51 (June 1996): 51–52, 54–56.

78. U.S. General Accounting Office, *Financial Derivatives: Actions Taken or Proposed Since May 1994* (Washington, DC: U.S. Government Printing Office, 1996).

79. S.A. Langsam and J.G. Kreuze, An Investigation of the Characteristics of Local Governmental Units Disclosing High Deposit and Investment Credit Risk as Defined by Governmental Accounting Standards Board Statement No. 3, *Public Budgeting & Finance* 11 (Winter 1991): 49–62.

80. P. Lemov, Managing Cash in a Post–Orange County World, *Governing* 8 (May 1995): 60–61.

81. U.S. General Accounting Office, *1-Dollar Coin: Reintroduction Could Save Millions If It Replaced the 1-Dollar Note* (Washington, DC: U.S. Government Printing Office, 1995).

82. Debt Collection Improvement Act, P.L. 104-134, 110 Stat. 1321 (1996).

83. C. Swope, Brains in the Billfold, *Governing* 9 (February 1996): 47–48.

84. See *Investors Business Daily* at http://www.investors.com and *The Wall Street Journal* at http://www.wsj.com; accessed December 1997.

85. R.D. Harrell, The Soul of a Cash Management Machine, *Governing* 8 (June 1995): 69.

86. Cash Management Improvement Act, P.L. 101-453, 104 Stat. 1058 (1990).

87. National Performance Review, *From Red Tape to Results*, 26–31.

88. U.S. General Services Administration, *Annual Report* (Washington, DC: U.S. Government Printing Office, published annually): http:/www.gsa.gov; accessed December 1997.

89. Office of Federal Procurement Policy Act, P.L. 93-400, 88 Stat. 796 (1974).

90. U.S. General Accounting Office, *High-Risk Series: Defense Inventory Management* (Washington, DC: U.S. Government Printing Office, 1997).

91. U.S. General Accounting Office, *Federal Office Space: Increased Ownership Would Result in Significant Savings* (Washington, DC: U.S. Government Printing Office, 1989); U.S. General Accounting Office, *Federal Office Space* (Washington, DC: U.S. Government Printing Office, 1995).

92. F.K. Wallison, A Guide to Leasing in the Public Sector, *Governing* 9 (September 1996): 67–73; B.S. Bunch, The Evolution of Lease-Purchase Guidelines in the State of Texas, *Public Budgeting & Finance* 16 (Winter 1996): 114–124.

93. J. Pragea and S. Desai, Privatizing Local Government Operations, *Public Productivity and Management Review* 20 (1996): 185–203.

94. U.S. General Accounting Office, *Government Contractors: Are Service Contractors Performing Inherently Governmental Functions?* (Washington, DC: U.S. Government Printing Office, 1991).

95. U.S. General Accounting Office, *Multiple Award Schedule Purchases: Changes Are Needed To Improve Agencies' Ordering Practices* (Washington, DC: U.S. Government Printing Office, 1992).

96. Federal Acquisition Streamlining Act, P.L. 103-355, 108 Stat. 3243 (1994).

97. M. Kestenbaum and R.L. Straight, Procurement Performance: Measuring Quality, Effectiveness, and Efficiency, *Public Productivity and Management Review* 19 (1995): 200–215.

98. Competition in Contracting Act, P.L. 98-369, Title VII, 98 Stat. 1175 (1984).

99. R.P. Murphy, General Counsel, U.S. General Accounting Office, *Procurement Reform Opportunities for Change* (Washington, DC: U.S. Government Printing Office, 1995).

100. U.S. General Accounting Office, *Bid Protests at GAO: A Descriptive Guide,* 6th ed. (Washington, DC: U.S. Government Printing Office, 1996).

101. U.S. Department of Defense, *Selling to the Military* (Washington, DC: U.S. Government Printing Office, 1996); National Association of State Purchasing Officials, *How To Do Business with the States: A Guide to Vendors*, 3rd ed. (Lexington, KY: Council of State Governments, 1993); see Texas' Web site on procurement at http://www.gsc.state.tx.us/procinfo.html; accessed December 1997.

102. U.S. General Services Administration, *Federal Acquisition Regulation (FAR)*: http://www.arnet.gov/far; accessed December 1997.

103. W.J. Clinton, Streamlining Procurement through Electronic Commerce, 58 F.R. 58095-58096 (1993).

104. U.S. General Services Administration, Access America: http://www.gits.fed.gov; accessed December 1997.

105. U.S. General Accounting Office, *Acquisition Reform: Obstacles to Implementing the Federal Acquisition Computer Network* (Washington, DC: U.S. Government Printing Office, 1997).

106. S. Kelman, *Procurement and Public Management: The Fear of Discretion and the Quality of Government Performance* (Washington, DC: AEI Press, 1990).

107. S.A. MacManus, with S.A. Watson and D.C. Blair, *Doing Business with Government: Federal, State, Local and Foreign Purchasing Practices for Every Business and Public Institution* (New York: Paragon House, 1992); S.A. MacManus, Why Businesses Are Reluctant To Sell to Governments, *Public Administration Review* 51 (1991): 328–344.

108. Federal Acquisition Reform Act, P.L. 104-106, sec. 4001, 110 Stat. 186 (1996).

109. U.S. Merit Systems Protection Board, *Workforce Quality and Federal Procurement: An Assessment* (Washington, DC: U.S. Government Printing Office, 1992).

110. U.S. General Accounting Office, *Acquisition Reform: Implementation of Title V of the Federal Acquisition Streamlining Act of 1994* (Washington, DC: U.S. Government Printing Office, 1996).

111. C. Swope, Purchasing with Plastic, *Governing* 10 (January 1997): 46, 48.

112. G.R. LaNoue and J.C. Sullivan, Race Neutral Programs in Public Contracting, *Public Administration Review* 55 (1995): 348–356.

113. U.S. General Accounting Office, *Cooperative Purchasing: Effects Are Likely To Vary among Governments and Businesses* (Washington, DC: U.S. Government Printing Office, 1997).

114. Chief Administrative Office, County of Los Angeles, Los Angeles County's Contract Services Program, July 1996.

115. Commission on Risk Assessment and Risk Management as established by the 1990 amendments to the Clean Air Act, P.L. 101-549, 104 Stat. 2399 (1990). See http://www.riskworld.com; accessed December 1997.

116. *Bradshaw v. Rawlings*, 464 F. Supp. 175 (1979); 612 F. 2d 135 (1979); cert. denied 446 U.S. 909 (1980).

117. J.C. Pine, *Tort Liability Today: A Guide for State and Local Governments*, 2nd ed. (Arlington, VA: Public Risk Management Association, 1992).

118. Federal Tort Claims Act, Ch. 753, 60 Stat. 842 (1946).

119. P.C. Young and B.J. Reed, Government Risk-Financing Pools, *Public Budgeting & Finance* 15 (Spring 1995): 96–112.

CHAPTER 11

Financial Management: Accounting, Auditing, and Information Systems

Budget execution requires accounting systems that track projected and actual revenues and expenditures during the budget year. Accounting, as will be seen in the following sections, serves a variety of purposes, but one of the most important has always been maintaining honesty and integrity. Accounting also is important to the functions discussed in the preceding chapter, namely, tax administration, cash management, procurement, and risk management. Accounting systems provide the financial information components of more comprehensive management information systems.

This chapter has three sections. The first and largest is devoted to accounting systems; the second discusses the role of auditing; and the third considers information systems used in accounting and, more broadly, in budgeting and finance.

GOVERNMENTAL ACCOUNTING

"A standard definition of accounting is the art of analyzing, recording, summarizing, evaluating and interpreting an organization's financial activities and status, and communicating the results."[1] Accounting, then, is one type of information system and usually contains mostly financial information on the receipt of funds and their expenditure.

In this section, we explore several aspects of accounting systems, beginning with the purposes and standards of accounting and the organizations that shape accounting systems. Fund accounting, the structure of accounting systems, the classification of expenditures, and the bases for accounting are considered. The section concludes with a discussion of the types of reports that are generated by accounting systems.

Organizational Responsibilities and Standards

Purposes. Accounting systems have been devised for a variety of purposes, with the maintenance of honesty being one of the most prominent ones. Through accounting, people who have wrongly intercepted monies being paid to government or channeled expenditures to their own advantage can be detected. Accounting, then, serves as a deterrent to fraud and corruption as well as prevention of inadvertent loss.

A related purpose is to prevent expenditures from straying beyond legal parameters. Illegal expenditures can occur that do not involve graft, as in the case of agency expenditures that exceed an appropriation or are used for purposes other than those permitted in authorizing legislation. Accounting serves to control agencies so that they act in accordance with policy and administrative directives as well as appropriation legislation.

Accounting systems are intended to provide complete, timely, and accurate information concerning receipts and expenditures. The information is used in billing taxpayers and receiving tax payments, paying employees, ordering goods, receiving goods, and paying vendors or contractors. Accounting systems help control inventory by providing accurate records of what items have been purchased.

Another important purpose is to report on the management of funds that are held in custody or trust. For example, accounting systems are used to handle contributions to employee retirement funds and outlays to beneficiaries.

Decision making is facilitated by accounting systems, which report historical data on revenues and expenditures that are essential for forecasting financial transactions. Without accurate information from an accounting system, decision makers are unable to determine whether a gap exists between proposed spending for the budget year and available revenue. Accounting information is important in determining whether a budget deficit exists and in what amount; in determining the size of the government's total debt, including those debts that are part of credit programs; and for estimating funds required for proposed changes in service levels and service quality.

Accounting is used internally to help managers increase efficiency and effectiveness in delivering services. The utilization of resources is monitored in order to avoid waste and to help ensure that desired programmatic outcomes are achieved. Managerial accounting focuses on calculating the costs associated with providing services to citizens. These derived costs also can be used for setting schedules for service charges. Office of Management and Budget (OMB) Circular A-123, Management Accountability and Control, as revised in 1995, emphasizes that management should be held accountable for achieving results and not just for using resources efficiently and honestly.

Information from accounting systems is used in communication between a government and citizens, investors, and other governments. Financial reports derived from detailed accounting information can help citizens gain confidence that the government's resources are well supervised. Investors in such commodities as state and local bonds and federal Treasury bills use accounting-based information to understand the financial conditions of governments. The federal government, in making grants to state and local governments, wants to be assured that the recipient governments have accounting systems that will protect the assets being invested.

As will be seen, accounting systems are based upon details, but those who operate accounting systems should never lose sight of the main purposes. This is the old familiar problem of losing sight of the forest because of all of the trees. It has been said that the Department of Defense "uses a magnifying glass to check a Tootsie Roll purchase and misses the million-dollar problems."[2]

Accounting Organizations. For accounting systems to serve these purposes, certain conventions or standards must be established, else chaos would reign as each government or department within a government established its own standards and practices. Numerous organizations establish the ground rules for accounting. Both the General Accounting Office (GAO), which is a branch of Congress, and OMB, which is an arm of the Executive Office of the President, set guidelines for federal agencies and to some extent compete with one another over control of accounting.[3] The Federal Managers' Financial Integrity Act of 1982, amending the Accounting and Auditing Act of 1950, requires that each executive agency establish internal accounting and administrative controls in accordance with standards prescribed by GAO and that the agency conduct annual reviews to determine the extent of compliance with those standards.[4] However, since the Supreme Court has ruled that GAO cannot be in a position of instructing agencies in what they must do (see Chapter 9), OMB has the upper hand in establishing financial management practices.[5]

One of the positions at OMB is the statutorily created post of deputy director for management. Under the deputy director is the Office of Federal Financial Management, which is headed by the controller. The Chief Financial Officers Act of 1990 created similar offices and chief financial officer (CFO) positions within the major agencies of the government.[6] For example, the Treasury Department has more than 10 CFOs heading the financial operations of units within the department.[7] OMB's controller, in accordance with the law's instructions that a five-year, government-wide financial plan be developed, has launched an ambitious program to improve organizational arrangements for finance, accounting standards, systems of accounting, internal controls, financial management employee training and development, and the like.[8] Agency CFOs have responsibility for all financial operations, including budgeting, and the CFOs along with

OMB's deputy director for management, the controller, and the fiscal assistant secretary of Treasury meet periodically as the Chief Financial Officers Council for the purpose of coordinating their activities.

In addition to the Chief Financial Officers Act of 1990, that year brought the formation of the Federal Accounting Standards Advisory Board (FASAB), which, as its title suggests, is strictly advisory. The board consists of representatives of GAO, OMB, and Treasury Department plus a representative from the Congressional Budget Office, representatives from civilian agencies and the Department of Defense, and nonfederal members. The board's mission is to develop consensus on accounting standards that can then be adopted by GAO, OMB, and Treasury. Prior to FASAB, the Joint Financial Management Improvement Program played an important role in developing coordinated financial and other management practices among these three organizations and the Office of Personnel Management.[9]

A concern exists that FASAB's work on accounting be fully meshed with budgeting standards set by OMB. Without complete integration, the budgeting standards become preeminent in that agencies are compelled to answer to OMB.[10] Circular A-134, issued in 1993, provides for the adoption of Financial Accounting Principles and Standards.

State and local accounting systems are influenced by several sources. State auditors and comptrollers general set standards for their state and local systems. These systems also are influenced by GAO and OMB, which determine how federal grant monies are handled.

Professional organizations have periodically attempted to establish standards of accounting in the public sector. The former National Council on Governmental Accounting consisted of representatives of such bodies as the Government Finance Officers Association, the American Institute of Certified Public Accountants, and the American Accounting Association and produced what was known as the "blue book" or GAAFR (*Governmental Accounting, Auditing, and Financial Reporting*). GAAFR currently is published by the Government Finance Officers Association and is designed to assist governments at all levels achieve what are considered the standards in the field.[11] The Government Finance Officers Association issues a variety of policy statements not only on accounting, reporting, and auditing but also on cash management, debt management, public employee pensions, and intergovernmental finance.[12]

The private sector has long had a well-established standard-setting organization: The Financial Accounting Standards Board issues authoritative pronouncements on accounting for profit and nonprofit organizations. Also, private accounting firms have major input into determining what constitutes good accounting. The Big 6 accounting firms are Arthur Andersen, Coopers and Lybrand, Deloitte and Touche, Ernst and Young, KPMG Peat Marwick, and Price

Waterhouse. In 1997, Coopers and Lybrand and Price Waterhouse announced plans to merge, as did Ernst and Young and KPMG Peat Marwick. If these mergers occur, the Big 6 will be reduced to the Big 4.[13]

In 1984, a government counterpart to the Financial Accounting Standards Board was established. The Governmental Accounting Standards Board (GASB, usually pronounced "gas-bee") is a comparatively new organization that attempts to speak for government entities. Both the Financial Accounting Standards Board and GASB are under the umbrella of the Financial Accounting Foundation. GASB issues accounting standards, known as statements, first as exposure drafts available for public comment and then in final form. The organization also issues technical bulletins that provide guidance on the implementation of the standards.

While the various organizations discussed here may set standards for accounting, the actual practice of operating accounting systems is typically conducted by individual agencies throughout large governments. The federal government has about 800 systems, a fact that greatly complicates reform efforts.[14] Efforts to streamline accounting include the merger of systems and the use of cross-servicing, in which one agency provides financial services to another agency. In contrast with large governments, small ones, such as a local school district, typically have a single centralized accounting system.

Standards and Principles of Accounting. While GAAFR is useful to state and local governments in evaluating their accounting systems, it is not regarded as an authoritative document. In contrast, GASB has issued a document that is authoritative regarding the standards to be used in public accounting: *Codification of Governmental Accounting and Financial Reporting Standards.*[15] The Government Finance Officers Association has produced a guide showing how GAAFR relates to GASB pronouncements.[16]

GASB and its predecessors have recognized what are considered generally accepted accounting principles (GAAP). While space limitations do not allow a discussion of each of the 12 principles, it should be noted that they are intended as guides to establishing and modifying accounting systems. The first principle provides the foundation for the other 11 by requiring that accounting principles should be followed and that the legal requirements of a government should be met. Adhering to this first principle can be difficult in that laws can require accounting practices that are contrary to the generally accepted principles.

At the federal level, the generally accepted accounting principles contained in Title 2 of GAO's *Policy and Procedures Manual for Guidance of Federal Agencies* are being replaced by new standards developed by FASAB. Since FASAB's products are only advisory, OMB takes authoritative action by issuing statements of federal financial accounting standards (SFFAS, Circulars A-127, Financial Management Systems, and A-134, Financial Accounting Principles and Standards).

Organizational Arrangements and Fraud. Creating organizational arrangements that deter fraud is of paramount interest in accounting.[17] Fraud can be committed by workers handling receipts; an employee might hold taxpayer A's money for personal use and use taxpayer B's money to cover A's taxes and subsequently C's money to cover B's taxes. Employees may steal from petty cash or may steal from inventory. Employees may pay vendors who are due nothing or provide travel reimbursement checks to employees who are due nothing.

In order to prevent these types of fraud from occurring and to reduce other losses due to errors in data entry and the like, internal controls that specify organizational arrangements and procedures are established (Circular A-123). Responsibility needs to be assigned to individuals, and any delegations of responsibility need to be detailed in writing. One standard practice is to segregate duties, so that one individual may have only limited authority over monies and two or more people may be required to approve some financial transactions. The presumption is that if two or more individuals are part of a particular process, they will monitor each other's behavior and limit various abuses. For example, two or more signatures may be required in approving the issuance of checks or in transferring money through electronic fund transfers.

Employees are trained in how to enter transactions properly in accounting systems and what their ethical and legal responsibilities are in handling public resources. Employees who handle funds may be subject to more extensive background checks before hiring and may be bonded. Downsizing can force the elimination of personnel and increase the risk that funds are vulnerable to theft or accidental loss due to the reduced oversight of financial operations.

Auditing bodies are important in preventing and detecting fraud. GAO conducts financial as well as program audits and on occasion finds losses in the billions of dollars. When discrepancies are identified through audits, follow-up is necessary to determine their causes and the corrective measures that need to be initiated.[18]

Fund Accounting

One of the main differences between public and private sector accounting is what is called the *accounting entity*. For the typical private sector organization, the entity is the organization itself, since accounts are designed to reflect its entire resources. Governments, in contrast, separate financial resources into distinct accounting entities called funds. Each fund is set up to record and account for the uses of a specific group of assets or sources of revenue. As provided for in generally accepted accounting principles 2, 3, and 4, there are three general classes of public sector funds and 10 different particular types of funds.[19]

Governmental Funds. The first class, known as governmental funds, consists of four types. The most important one is the general fund. Several revenue sources may flow into a government's general fund, such as property tax and income tax receipts at the local level. The resources in the fund are available for expenditure for virtually any purpose that the jurisdiction is legally empowered to pursue. Most municipalities, for instance, may use general fund receipts for police and road services but not schools, since the latter are the domain of independent school districts.

The other fund types within the governmental class are available for what are thought of as normal government operations, but these types have receipt and/or expenditure restrictions. *Special revenue funds* receive monies from special sources and are earmarked for special purposes. Gasoline taxes are typically accounted for in a special revenue fund, with expenditures limited to transportation, especially roads and highways.

Capital project funds account for receipts and expenditures related to projects, such as construction of a new park or city hall, or for major pieces of equipment, such as vehicles for a city fire department. Monies may come into these funds from bond sales that will be paid for with general fund tax receipts.

Debt service funds are used to account for interest and principal on general purpose long-term debt. The revenue received by this type of fund usually is from the general fund.

Proprietary Funds. The second class of funds consists of those that are proprietary or business-like in nature. *Enterprise funds* operate as businesses whose customers are external to government. Such funds are established for toll roads, bridges, and local water systems. Numerous proposals have circulated recommending that various federal operations be converted to government corporations, which would be run as enterprises.[20] *Internal service funds* operate as businesses whose customers are internal to government. A central purchasing office or a vehicle maintenance garage may operate as an internal service fund, with revenues coming from other departments as services are rendered. When bonds are sold to support the activities of a proprietary fund (for example, bond proceeds might be used to renovate a city sewage system), capital expenditures and payment of debt are handled through the proprietary fund, not through a capital project or debt service fund.

Fiduciary Funds. The third class, known as fiduciary funds, has four types. This class, often called *trust and agency funds*, consists of accounts that are dedicated to a third party. *Expendable trust funds* are used for bequests to government in which both the principal and interest can be spent. *Nonexpendable trust funds* allow for the expenditure of interest but not the principal, as in the case of a continuing university scholarship named in memory of someone. Often the largest set of fiduciary funds are *pension trusts* for government employees. The fourth type in this class consists of *agency funds*. These pertain to government acting as a conduit for another party, such as a city government collecting taxes for the local school district.

Account Groups. According to generally accepted accounting principles 5 through 7, governmental funds use account groups to report fixed assets and long-term liabilities, whereas proprietary and fiduciary funds report these resources and debts within the funds themselves. Governmental funds include only financial assets, namely, assets that will be converted to cash, and therefore the general fixed asset account group (GFAAG) is used to report assets that will not be converted to cash, such as buildings, swimming pools, and aircraft hangars and airport terminals. The GFAAG is simply a reporting of assets and does not involve transactions.

The second account group is the general long-term debt account group. This group reports government debt that is not part of proprietary or fiduciary funds. In other words, the account group reports liabilities of the entity as a whole, as distinguished from specific funds. This account group and the fixed assets group in effect are memoranda that report assets and liabilities that otherwise would not be reported.

Structure and Rules of Accounting Systems

Ledgers. Accounting systems use ledgers as a means of organization or structure. Each fund has a general ledger and subsidiary ledgers. The general ledger records the overall status of revenues and expenditures, while subsidiary ledgers are established for each revenue source and type of expenditure. In a general fund having several tax sources of revenue, a subsidiary revenue ledger is used for each source. OMB and the Treasury Department have established a U.S. Government Standard General Ledger, which indicates how agencies are to organize their ledgers (Circular A-127).[21]

Expenditure subsidiary ledgers control expenditures by appropriation, organizational unit, object of expenditure, and sometimes purpose or activity. Accounting systems are used to track expenditures according to provisions in appropriations; often these appropriations are specific to organizations, as in the case of $2 million appropriated to a city housing department. The appropriation also may contain limitations on how funds will be spent, such as expenditures for personnel or equipment; this aspect of accounting is explained later. Some jurisdictions track expenditures by program or activity (this is done if a government's program budget structure does not match its organizational structure).

Accounting Formula. Accounting systems use equations that allow systematic recording of transactions and double-checking that the transactions have been properly recorded. The basic equation that is used is

assets = *liabilities* + *fund balance*

In the formula, assets can be the revenue in a fund; liabilities are the monies owed others, such as suppliers of office equipment and tires for police cars; and the fund balance comprises the residual, uncommitted monies. Specific accounts are established for each of these three components of the formula. Asset accounts, for example, can include those showing cash on hand as well as monies owed by taxpayers (taxes receivable). FASAB has recommended standards for assets and liabilities.[22]

Double-entry accounting, in which any single transaction is recorded twice (at a minimum), is used as a cross-check. If taxes are received and no additional obligations are incurred, then assets are increased and so is the fund balance. Double entry can be used within one portion of the overall formula. If taxes are received but were already noted in an asset account called taxes receivable, then that account would be reduced while another asset account for cash would be increased; that particular set of transactions would not affect liabilities or the fund balance.

Transactions are recorded in a **T** in which the left side of the **T** constitutes *debits* and the right constitutes *credits*. The terms debits and credits refer only to the left and right sides of the **T** and have no connotation of negative and positive. Rules exist as to when an account should be debited and when credited. In any transaction, the amount debited to one or more accounts must equal the amount credited to other accounts.

Specified Procedures. Flowing out of accounting standards and principles are procedures that determine how transactions will be recorded and in what accounts. These procedures are typically specified in manuals or handbooks so that employees involved in whatever aspects of accounting know how to meet their responsibilities. Manuals may begin with such basics as how to log onto the computer system and proceed to cover receipts and purchases, including, for example, overall purchasing policy, purchase orders, contract payments, and emergency purchases. Payroll procedures will be specified in some detail in a manual and are likely to require the approval of specific individuals, possibly including written signatures confirming which employees are to be paid what amounts.

The typical accounting cycle is as follows.[23] An event occurs and a source document is prepared. The event might be a decision to tax property and the document might be a tax bill sent to a citizen; when the citizen pays the bill, another transaction will occur. On the expenditure side of the budget, one event might be the placing of an order for office supplies and a later event might be the receipt of the supplies and the invoice. These types of transactions will first be posted in a *journal,* which is a chronological listing of events or transactions. The journal entry indicates both the credits and debits involved in the transaction. For example, tax monies received would increase a cash account and decrease a taxes payable account. Entries once recorded in the journal are posted to ledgers, and from time to time the debits and credits of these accounts are totaled to obtain trial and final balances. The balances are used in preparing financial reports (which are discussed later).

Classification of Receipts and Expenditures

Receipts and expenditures are classified in a variety of ways and elaborate coding systems are used to be able to monitor and control financial transactions.[24] Such coding devices help hold government officials responsible for honestly managing the government's business.

Receipts. The monies that government receives need to be recorded according to the source. The money derived from each tax source, such as property and income taxes, needs to be recorded separately and in distinction from user fees, such as charges for using a municipal golf course. The federal government treats user fees as *offsetting collections,* namely that money derived from fees, as in the case of the Tennessee Valley Authority, are used to offset expenditures for Tennessee Valley Authority operations. The net differences in such transactions are reported in the budget.[25]

Fund and Appropriation. Expenditures are accounted for in a variety of ways. One set of characteristics is the fund and appropriation. An appropriation is a legislative approval to spend from a specific fund. Since several bills may be passed that appropriate out of the general fund, the dollar stipulations in each of these bills must be observed vis-à-vis the total assets available in the general fund. Even if a jurisdiction uses only one appropriation bill, each of the expenditure limits in the bill must be observed and consequently must be monitored by the accounting system. When an expenditure is made, it is charged against the appropriated amount and the remaining available balance is shown. In this way, an accounting system can be used to keep agency expenditures within budgeted figures.

If the legislative body earmarks expenditures in detail, then the accounting system becomes increasingly complex. For example, Congress in its annual foreign assistance appropriation bill typically imposes detailed figures on the level of funding for programs within the Agency for International Development and amounts to be available in each country receiving aid. The accounting system, therefore, must monitor expenditures by program (e.g., child survival) and by country to adhere to the stipulations in the appropriation bill.

Organizational Unit. Expenditures are made by organizational units, and accounting systems must track expenditures accordingly. Appropriation bills usually are specific to agencies so that, instead of the government simply being authorized to spend an amount on forest preservation, a specific unit within a department is granted the money. Large governments, then, account for expenditures not only at the department level but also at the bureau, office, division, or regional unit level.

Objects of Expenditure. Accounting systems invariably account in terms of the objects acquired or the objects of expenditure.[26] Broad groupings of objects are called major objects, and their subdivisions are called minor objects. Exhibit 11–1 illustrates the object classes used by the federal government. The object series beginning with the number 11 covers all personnel-related expenditures. Within that series are the three subclasses of direct compensation, benefits for employees, and benefits for former employees.

Exhibit 11–1 Federal Objects of Expenditure Classification

Code	Title
	Personal Services and Benefits
11	Personnel Compensation
11.1	Full-Time Permanent
11.3	Other than Full-Time Permanent
11.5	Other Personnel Compensation
11.7	Military Personnel
11.8	Special Personal Services Payments
11.9	Total Personnel Compensation
12	Personnel Benefits
12.1	Civilian Personnel Benefits
12.2	Military Personnel Benefits
13	Benefits for Former Personnel
	Contractual Services and Supplies
21	Travel and Transportation of Persons
22	Transportation of Things

continues

Exhibit 11–1 continued

Code	Title
23	Rent, Communications, and Utilities
	23.1 Rental Payments to General Services Administration
	23.2 Rental Payments to Others
	23.3 Communications, Utilities, and Miscellaneous Charges
24	Printing and Reproduction
25	Other Contractual Services
	25.1 Advisory and Assistance Services
	25.2 Other Services
	25.3 Purchases of Goods and Services from Government Accounts
	25.4 Operation and Maintenance of Facilities
	25.5 Research and Development Contracts
	25.6 Medical Care
	25.7 Operation and Maintenance of Equipment
	25.8 Subsistence and Support of Persons
26	Supplies and Materials

Acquisition of Assets

Code	Title
31	Equipment
32	Land and Structure
33	Investments and Loans

Grants and Fixed Charges

Code	Title
41	Grants, Subsidies, and Contributions
42	Insurance Claims and Indemnities
43	Interest and Dividends
44	Refunds

Other

Code	Title
91	Unvouchered
92	Undistributed
93	Limitation on Expenses

Source: Reprinted from *Preparation and Submission of Budget Estimates*, Circular No. A–11, 1996, U.S. Office of Management and Budget.

Accounting systems can become unwieldy in their use of minor objects. Travel as a major object can be subdivided in numerous ways.

- mode (personal automobile, government automobile, commercial airline, etc.)
- type of person traveling (elected official, political or career executive, employee, client)
- purpose (meeting, conference, training, inspection)
- location (in state, out of state, out of nation)
- type of expense (lodging, meals, transportation)

The number of possible permutations is great. When an accounting system uses such detail, the entry of many transactions may be delayed due to classification ambiguities.

Despite the administrative problems of detailed minor objects, legislative bodies often incorporate such details in appropriation bills. These line items in an appropriation allow control when there is concern that funds may be abused. Restrictions may be inserted regarding the purchase of newspaper subscriptions, the number of automobiles, and government employee travel. When minor object restrictions are embedded in appropriations, the limits are legally mandated, and the accounting system must ensure compliance.

Executives also use object classifications in an attempt to control agencies and increase their efficiency. President Clinton's Executive Order 12837 of 1993 required agencies to reduce their administrative costs, namely travel and other selected objects that often are viewed as luxuries. Of course, administrative expenses often are central to the missions of agencies. Travel is essential for inspectors of meat and poultry processing plants, mines, and workplaces.

Purpose and Activity. Program-oriented budgets that focus decision-making attention on specific program goals and objectives also require accounting-based information on how much each program costs. The federal government uses broad functional categories, such as national defense, energy, and income security, which are divided into subfunctions. For example, energy is subdivided into supply, conservation, emergency preparedness, and energy information.[27] If a budget based on program classifications cuts across agency lines, then the accounting system needs to cut across agency lines to accumulate the costs according to program. Similarly, preparing a budget that allocates funds according to detailed work activities requires an accounting system that tracks expenditures by those activities. In a 1995 survey of state budget offices, 65 percent reported that their states' accounting systems recorded expenditures at the specific program level.[28] The problem of accounting for finances by program or activity is discussed more fully in the next section in regard to cost accounting.

Performance Measurement. While practitioners and academics in the field of budgeting have long been concerned about how to measure the results of government programs, accountants only became particularly concerned starting in the 1980s. Accountants came to recognize a need for measuring outputs, impacts, efficiency, effectiveness, and the like (Chapter 5).[29] What is significant here is that accountants now back the notion that financial accounting should be tied to *performance measurement.* If one wishes to determine the efficiency of an organization in delivering a service over time, then there needs to be a measurement of the service provided (outputs) and the costs (obtained through accounting). GASB is moving toward adopting an accounting statement that would require *service efforts and accomplishments* (SEA) reporting as part of *general purpose external financial reporting* (GPEFR).[30]

Accounting for performance and then auditing for it require going beyond the boundaries of the organization to where results are produced. In contrast, traditional accounting systems have been structured to capture financial transactions within organizations. Once the accounting system has to take measurements outside the organization, as it must with performance accounting, major problems arise over how to collect information and how to audit it. Measurement errors inevitably occur in such systems, raising issues about the accuracy and utility of them.

The federal government has taken major steps in the direction of greater utilization of performance measurement. The Chief Financial Officers Act of 1990 instructs agency CFOs to develop reporting systems that provide for "the integration of accounting and budgeting information and the systematic measurement of performance."[31] The Government Performance and Results Act of 1993, as explained in Chapter 5, requires federal agencies to develop strategic plans and annual performance plans that are integral to the budget.[32] Of course, one should keep in mind that achieving change is different from simply mandating change. Efforts to include performance measurement within accounting systems surely face major challenges.[33]

Basis of Accounting

The *basis of accounting* refers to the timing of transactions, or when a revenue item is recorded as received by the government and when an expenditure is recorded as having occurred. There are several methods for determining when a revenue or expenditure item is recorded, and each has a different purpose.

Cash Accounting. The oldest system is cash accounting, which is still used today, particularly in small governments, but in general all governments have a cash aspect to their accounting systems. In a cash accounting system, tax receipts are recorded when actually received by the government and expenditures are recorded when payments are made. Minor variations exist; some systems record expenditures when checks are written, but others record expenditures when checks clear the banking system. The major advantages of the cash system are that it is simple in comparison with alternatives and that it presents an accurate picture of cash on hand at any point in time.

The major disadvantage of the cash system is that it does not provide information about the future, namely, anticipated receipts and expenditures. The cash on hand may seem to suggest that one's financial situation is reasonably secure, but a different picture may emerge when considering obligations that must be met, such as payrolls.

Encumbrance Accounting. A step in the direction of anticipating future transactions is encumbrance accounting. Expenditures are recorded when purchase orders are written or contracts are signed; some of the cash on hand, then, is said to be encumbered and not available for covering other expenditures. In the case of a multiyear contract, all of the expenditures for a year may be encumbered at the outset of the fiscal year, or amounts may be encumbered each month as work is completed by the contractor. An encumbrance system helps ensure that a government unit will not overspend its appropriation.

Accrual Accounting. In accrual systems, financial transactions are recognized when the activities that generate them occur. Revenues are recorded when the government earns the income, as when a local government sends tax bills to property owners. Expenditures are recognized when the liabilities are incurred regardless of when payment for those goods or services might actually be made during the year.

The accrual basis has been required of federal agencies for over 30 years, but few federal accounting systems actually use accrual accounting. The obstacle has been the diversity of accounting systems; large departments such as the Department of Defense, for example, have many different accounting systems.[34] Where accrual accounting is used in government, it is normally on a modified basis; not all transactions are accrued and some remain on a cash basis. Full accrual, however, is recommended for proprietary funds (enterprise and internal service funds) and pension trusts.

Despite the obstacles to implementation, the accounting profession continues to endorse strongly the accrual basis of accounting. In 1990, GASB adopted Statement No. 11, Measurement Focus and Basis of Accounting: Governmental Fund Operating Statements (MFBA, pronounced "muff-bah"). The statement provides for extending the accrual process to cover items previously not covered. For instance, the costs of employees' vacations are to be recognized when employees earn their vacation time. When employees are allowed to accumulate vacation leave, the accounting system needs to recognize that government's liabilities have increased. Particularly controversial is the provision that employee pension funds should recognize future payments owed future retirees by recording them in the governmental funds rather than as normally reported in the general long-term debt account group. These provisions are controversial in that they negatively affect fund balances, pushing some governments into negative balances.[35] Chapter 13 discusses defined contribution retirement plans, which reduce the liability of governments for pension benefits.

Cost Accounting. While the cash, encumbrance, and accrual bases of accounting focus attention on resources coming into government and being expended, cost accounting is concerned with when resources are used in the production of goods and services.[36] For example, gasoline purchased for a state highway department could be accounted for when the order is made (encumbrance), when the goods are received (modified accrual method), or when the vendor is paid (cash method). The cost approach, in contrast, records the transaction when the gasoline is consumed.

Managerial cost accounting can be viewed as providing key information needed by managers in conducting their operations and in addition to this internal function, providing information to external parties such as the legislative body, taxpayers, and investors in governmental securities.[37] In a cost accounting system, costs of providing services are matched with measures of those services. For example, a school district might want to know the average cost of graduating someone from the general population compared with the average cost of a student with special needs, for instance, a student with physical disabilities. *Activity-based costing* and *activity-based management* concentrate on collecting costs of delivering services to citizens.[38] The costs of delivering services can be monitored over time, thereby giving an impetus for increased efficiency of operations. Such accounting can determine the costs of producing activities, outputs, and impacts.

The incentives for using cost accounting are markedly different in the private and public sectors. In order to determine their profitability, corporations need to know the cost of providing each product or service. The costs of production, then, can be subtracted from sales receipts to determine profit or loss. Governmental programs, such as police and fire departments, obviously do not seek a profit and consequently may see less need for cost accounting. Other programs, particularly enterprise and internal service funds, while not seeking a profit, do endeavor to break even and consequently have an incentive to know the costs of their services. For example, a centralized photoduplication and printing office has an incentive to calculate its costs in order to set appropriate fee schedules for charging departments for services.[39] A central maintenance garage for city vehicles needs an accurate understanding of its costs for maintaining garbage trucks, police cars, and buses. Keeping costs down in each of these areas is important in linking the production of services with costs and is especially important in an era of privatization. As a means of cutting costs, a police department might be eager to contract out for patrol car repairs rather than using a city maintenance facility. Bureaucratic politics are rampant in such situations.

Besides the reduced incentives to use cost accounting in government, several other impediments exist. One such impediment is that purposes and objectives are not neatly compartmentalized into organizational units, resulting in situations in which one organization may be serving multiple purposes and another organization serving some of those same purposes. In order to resolve this problem, *cost centers* must be used in which the accounting system records financial information for each activity performed within an organizational unit. In a bureau that engages in three activities and which has its personnel working at various times on the three activities, records must be maintained regarding the amount of time each worker spends on each activity. Other bureau costs, such as those for supplies, telephones, and furniture, must be distributed among the cost centers.

Other impediments to cost accounting being used in government pertain to how various financial transactions are currently conducted.[40] Government agencies sometimes provide services to one another at no charge, resulting in a form of subsidy to the recipient agencies, and a consequent understatement of the costs of the services those agencies provide. Salaries, wages, and other personnel expenses, such as pension contributions and health benefits for employees and retirees, may be in central budgets and not in the budgets of units that deliver services. Other support services involving budgeting, legal assistance, janitorial services, and computer support may not be charged to line agencies. The result is that organizational budgets typically fall short of reflecting the costs of activities.

Cost accounting requires that special attention be given to the acquisition and utilization of *fixed assets*—land, structures, and major pieces of equipment. Fixed assets sometimes are financed centrally and, as a consequence, do not appear in the budgets of organizational units that use these assets. Additionally, the purchase of fixed assets or capital goods should not be considered costs in the year of purchase but should be depreciated over the life span of the goods. From a cost standpoint, the cost of police patrol cars might be spread over three years, but from a cash standpoint, the purchase will be recorded in the first year when the purchase is made. Buildings and vehicles then are depreciated over time, showing a truer picture of the cost of services than the cash method does. The life cycle of an asset needs to be considered, that is, how long an asset has utility. Federal law and OMB Circular A-131 instruct agencies to use *value engineering* as a management technique in determining how long assets will be of use.[41] The circular defines value engineering as "an organized effort directed at analyzing the functions of systems, equipment, facilities, services, and supplies for the purpose of achieving the essential functions at the lowest life-cycle cost consistent with required performance, reliability, quality, and safety."[42]

Depreciation rules need to be applied differently according to the assets involved. FASAB has identified four types of property, plant, and equipment (PP&E).[43] The *general PP&E* category includes buildings for which a market value can be derived, such as the value of an office building. The category of *federal mission PP&E* is for the uniquely federal functions of defense and space exploration. Depreciating these assets is extremely difficult since that requires estimating the assets' useful lives. How long will a weapon system be of use or how long will a space satellite continue to operate? The *heritage PP&E* category includes education, culture, and artistic endeavors. The Washington Monument and the White House are in this grouping, since they have special significance and are not just ordinary government buildings. The last category, *stewardship PP&E,* covers government holdings that are entrusted to the government for safekeeping. The category covers federal land held by the National Park Service and the U.S. Forest Service.

In addition to fixed assets, other investments pose major challenges for the use of cost accounting in government. When a government bureau pays for several of its workers to attend a training program, is that an investment and what is the life of that investment? When a state government provides a grant to a local government for construction of a sewage treatment plan, how is the state to record the investment since the new plant will belong to the local government and not the state?

Given the complexities of cost accounting, one can readily see why it is used in only limited cases in government. It is an open question whether FASAB and its participating agencies will be successful in moving the federal government toward the use of cost accounting. A 1995 survey of state budget offices found that virtually all states were unable to track costs in relation to work or tasks performed.[44]

Project-Based Accounting. Another option that is not as elaborate as cost accounting is project-based accounting. Accounts can be established on a temporary basis to track costs for selected activities. Private firms, both for-profit and nonprofit, keep detailed accounting records for contracts, including costs at task or subtask levels. If a consulting firm has been awarded a government contract, a separate set of accounts is established showing what personnel worked on what tasks for what length of time within a given reporting period (weekly, biweekly, or monthly). Accounts of this type are important for reimbursement purposes.

Project-based accounting also is used for monitoring internal operations. If a corporation is developing a new product or group of products, separate accounts can be established to gauge the developmental costs of the project. In the quasi-governmental arena, the World Bank uses account codes and employee time report systems to account for project costs, enabling management to evaluate the cost of preparing, negotiating, and supervising a specific loan to a country.

Cost Finding. In some instances, governments may be satisfied with something less than a complete cost accounting system or even project-based accounting. Rather than having an ongoing cost information system, governments sometimes selectively study costs of specific activities that may be contained within a single organization or spread across several units. The cost of delivering family planning services to teenagers might be derived through analysis of expenditure records and a sampling of employee time commitments. A far more elaborate cost-finding endeavor would be to try to derive the costs of AIDS to a state government; the analysis would attempt to determine the costs of prevention and treatment activities that most likely are not encoded in the accounting system. For example, AIDS may well increase health care costs for prisoners, but such costs would not routinely be segregated in the accounting system.

The analysis of cost data can be useful in identifying fixed costs and variable costs. There may be a minimum or fixed cost for providing a given service up to some particular level, above which costs increase as units of service increase. For example, a preschool program for disadvantaged children begins with a fixed set of costs for essentials such as a school room, a teacher, and some supportive services—costs that are incurred whether one or 10 children are taught. As the number of children in the class increases, variable costs increase, such as those for teaching materials and supplies, teacher aides, another teacher, and possibly another classroom.

Allowable Costs. In the awarding of grants and contracts, governments need to determine what costs are allowable. The federal government's Cost Accounting Standards Board has attempted to set parameters for costs in defense and related contracts.[45] OMB Circular A-87 specifies in great detail what costs are allowable in grants to state and local government. Unallowable costs include entertainment, alcoholic beverages, interest on debt (such as working capital borrowings), and donations as in the case of volunteer services.

Risk and Credit Accounting. Public sector officials have come to recognize that risks arise in carrying out public duties. Not only are revenues raised and expenditures made, but other factors create conditions that can result in major financial loss and/or expenditures. Risk management involves assessing the risk exposure of a government (Chapter 10). In making and guaranteeing loans, the federal government assumes risks that can have major financial consequences, as evidenced by the forced bailout of failed savings and loan associations (Chapter 6). On the other hand, credit programs can yield savings or negative subsidies, particularly at some point in the future. Estimating such savings pose considerable technical problems, plus agencies that administer such programs may be biased in favor of forecasting such savings.[46]

State and local governments are expected to follow the instructions for reporting risks contained in GASB Statement No. 10. That statement covers property and liability, workers' compensation, and employee health care, while State-ments No. 26 and No. 27 cover health care plans of retirees and pension plans. GASB Statement No. 3 provides for reporting risks associated with government investments in corporate stocks and bonds and other instruments. GASB has taken steps toward adopting a set of standards for risks involved in cash management.[47] The reporting of investments in derivatives (Chapter 10) is an important aspect of risk accounting.[48]

Another form of risk involves the imposition of unfunded mandates on state and local governments (Chapter 14), creating huge financial costs for these governments. GASB Statement No. 18 covers the reporting of costs associated with closing landfills and maintaining them after their closure. These costs have been imposed by the standards of the Environmental Protection Agency.[49]

OMB, as prescribed by the Federal Credit Reform Act of 1990, is overseeing a thorough revamping of how the government accounts for credit programs and how decisions are made about these programs. The law is intended to "place the cost of credit programs on a budgetary basis" so that they will compete with all other programs for scarce resources.[50] OMB requires agencies to supply data on direct loans, loan subsidies, guaranteed loans, and guaranteed loan subsidies as part of the agencies' budget submissions (Circular A-129). Prior to passage of the Federal Credit Reform Act, many federal agencies could borrow from the Federal Financing Bank, but they now must borrow from the Treasury Department in order to finance their direct and guaranteed loan programs.[51] Also, different types of accounts are now used for credit transactions.[52] Federal agencies have encountered considerable difficulty in complying with the law, because their existing accounting systems and supporting staff often are inadequate.[53]

Generational Accounting. Of growing interest are the potential effects of government finances on different generations.[54] Expenditures for elementary and secondary education obviously help children whereas alcohol programs help adults and programs such as Medicare help the elderly. Generational accounting is important in considering future benefits or costs imposed on different age groups. Although accounting systems have not been devised for identifying the costs or the benefits of government activities for different age groups, some reporting of such effects occurs.

Need for Different Bases. These different approaches to the basis of accounting are not substitutes for each other. Rather, each satisfies a different type of need. From the standpoint of a treasury department, a cash basis for recording receipts and expenditures is necessary because the department has the legal responsibility to receive revenue and issue checks to cover expenses. This responsibility extends to determining that there are sufficient funds to cover checks to be issued. The encumbrance basis is important in showing the current status of assets and liabilities, including liabilities that will place a demand on cash in the future. Cost accounting is valuable in identifying resources consumed, as distinguished from resources acquired and placed in inventory. Risk accounting provides a more comprehensive overview of obligations than is available through accounting systems that cover only revenues and expenditures. Generational accounting provides insights into the implications of government finances for different generations, from the elderly to the young and to those not yet born.

Reporting

Accounting systems generate reports that are used by managers, policy makers, and people outside of government. Generally accepted accounting principle 12 calls on jurisdictions to prepare interim and annual reports. Interim reports, such as daily and weekly reports, are used for internal purposes, as in the case of checking on appropriated funds that are neither spent nor encumbered. These interim reports are useful in monitoring budget execution and anticipating situations in which agencies might have insufficient funds to operate their programs throughout the fiscal year. A fundamental expectation of all financial reports is that they can be audited, meaning there are accounting records that back up the data in the reports.

Annual reports are particularly useful to people and organizations outside of government. Such reports can show taxpayers how revenues have been used to support services. Annual reports of local governments are helpful for businesses that are considering locating, relocating, or expanding existing facilities. The reports are used to help discover the financial condition of governments and decide whether to purchase their bonds. The Government Finance Officers Association issues certificates of achievement for excellence in financial reporting. The association also issues awards for outstanding *popular annual financial reports* (PAFRs), namely, reports that are prepared for use by the general public and not accountants and budgeters.[55]

Financial Reports. GASB recommends a comprehensive annual financial report (CAFR) that has three sections: introduction, finances, and statistics.[56] The first section includes a letter of transmittal and general information about the government. The section lists the principal officials and provides an organization chart indicating lines of authority and responsibility.

The second section contains a variety of financial statements. Since governments make extensive use of funds, several different types of statements may be provided on each fund. These statements by themselves can be confusing in that they do not provide an overall perspective on the finances of the government. For this reason, GASB and other professional accounting organizations prescribe the use of condensed statements that provide a comprehensive picture of a jurisdiction without some of the confusing detail.

One particularly troubling aspect of these statements is the use of *transfers* among funds. Monies can be moved from one fund to another without affecting the overall assets of a jurisdiction, but if transfers are not carefully noted, they appear as expenditures in one fund and as new assets or receipts in another fund. These transfers need to be clearly identified not only to avoid confusion but to provide important information about a government's operations. Transfers may indicate that enterprises are subsidizing general government operations, such as proceeds from a city airport being used in part to support a city's general fund. This type of transfer may be welcome relief to local taxpayers but may be of concern to holders of airport bonds.[57] Good financial reports clearly label transfers—showing the source of receipts and the recipient of transfers—so that false impressions of asset creation or usage are avoided.

The third section of a financial report contains statistical data. Some tables present trend data assembled from earlier financial reports, such as general revenues by source over the most recent ten-year period. Other tables provide demographic data and indicate the principal taxpayers in the jurisdiction.

Balance Sheets. Of the numerous types of financial statements, balance sheets are one of the most common. A balance sheet can be thought of as a snapshot of a government's finances at a point in time, such as at the end of a quarter or fiscal year.

A balance sheet is organized according to the accounting formula discussed earlier. Assets are first listed, showing cash on hand (bank deposits) and taxes receivable. For proprietary funds and fiduciary funds, fixed assets (buildings, land, etc.) are also reported as assets. The balance sheet then indicates liabilities, namely, accounts that are payable and bonds outstanding, followed by the fund balance, showing items such as monies that are encumbered (see Table 11–1 for an example of a balance sheet from the State of Connecticut).

GASB's Statement No. 11 on measurement focus and the basis of accounting is of critical importance to how balance sheets are calculated for state and local governments. Statement No. 11 requires governments to recognize items as liabilities that were previously excluded, and as a result balance sheet bottom lines went from positive to negative for many governments. When numerous governments complained about the potential political and economic harm of such balance sheets, GASB allowed governments to use the term *fund equity* for the difference between revised assets and liabilities. The term *fund balance* can be used for calculating balance sheets in the format used prior to Statement No. 11. The Government Finance Officers Association took the position that Statement No. 11 should not be implemented until GASB had completed all of its work pertaining to the composition of financial reports.[58]

While a compelling case is often made that governments should operate like private businesses, a balance sheet for the federal government modeled strictly

Table 11–1 Governmental Funds Balance Sheet, State of Connecticut, Fiscal Year Ended June 30, 1995 (in Thousands of Dollars)

	General	Special Revenue	Debt Service	Capital Projects	Total
Assets and Other Debits					
Cash and Cash Equivalents		251,902	47,525		299,427
Investments		25,643	372,639		398,282
Receivables					
Taxes	452,623	49,162			501,785
Accounts, Net of Allowances	232,731	9,438		6,124	248,293
Loans, Net of Allowances		360,026			360,026
Interest	1,248	6,940	6,282	373	14,843
Federal Grants Receivable	51,454	7,183			58,637
Non-Federal Grants Receivable	1,676	538			2,214
Due from Other Funds	22,207	147,820		288,042	458,069
Due from Component Unit		181			181
Receivable from Other Governments	349,903	5,580		68,289	423,772
Inventories and Prepaid Items	47,528	13,210			60,738
Other Assets		120			120
Total Assets and Other Debits	1,159,370	877,743	426,446	362,828	2,826,387
Liabilities, Equity, and Other Credits					
Accounts Payable and Accrued Liabilities	715,837	64,163		144,980	924,980
Due to Other Funds	472,884	3,162	6,283	2,259	484,588
Payable to Other Governments	36,757				36,757

continues

Table 11–1 continued

	General	Special Revenue	Debt Service	Capital Projects	Total
Deferred Revenue	295,638	30,367		21,823	347,828
Liability for Escheat Property	18,950				18,950
Total Liabilities	1,540,066	97,692	6,283	169,062	1,813,103
Equity and Other Credits					
Fund Balances					
Reserved	196,183	395,280	420,163		1,011,626
Unreserved, undesignated	(576,879)	384,771		193,766	1,658
Total Equity and Other Credits	(380,696)	780,051	420,163	193,766	1,013,284
Total Liability, Equity, and Other Credits	1,159,370	877,743	426,446	362,828	2,826,387

Note: Table is based on a combined balance sheet for all funds.

Courtesy of Connecticut Comptroller, *Comprehensive Annual Financial Report for the Fiscal Year Ended June 30, 1995,* 1996, Hartford, Connecticut.

on the basis of that used for private corporations would be incomplete in that important resources and needs of the nation as a whole would be excluded. As can be seen in Exhibit 11–2, the government's balance sheet consists of three components, beginning with the familiar listing of assets and liabilities. The second component consists of resources/receipts and responsibilities/outlays. This section of the balance sheet projects long-run receipts (based on the expected growth of gross domestic product) and outlays (notably those for entitlement programs). The third component reports the assets that have been developed and national needs that require the expenditure of monies.

Operating Statements. A second major type of financial statement is the operating statement, which shows the monies received and expended during a specified period of time. State and local governments refer to these as "statements of revenues, expenditures, and changes in fund balance." Revenues can be reported by source—sales tax and income tax. Expenditures can be reported by major objects, organizational units, or other means. Table 11–2 is an operating statement for the State of Missouri. Tables such as this one and others shown in the

Exhibit 11–2 A Balance Sheet Presentation for the Federal Government

ASSETS/RESOURCES		LIABILITIES/RESPONSIBILITIES
Federal Assets		**Federal Liabilities**
Financial Assets		Financial Liabilities
Gold and Foreign Exchange		Currency and Bank Reserves
Other Monetary Assets		Debt Held by the Public
Mortgages and Other Loans		Miscellaneous
Less Expected Loan Losses	**Federal**	Guarantees and Insurance
Other Financial Assets	**Governmental**	Deposit Insurance
	Assets	Pension Benefit Guarantees
Physical Assets	**and Liabilities**	Loan Guarantees
Fixed Reproducible Capital		Other Insurance
Defense		Federal Pension Liabilities
Nondefense		
Inventories		Net Balance
Nonreproducible Capital		
Land		
Mineral Rights		
Resources/Receipts		**Responsibilities/Outlays**
Projected Receipts		Discretionary Outlays
	Long-Run	Mandatory Outlays
Addendum: Real GDP Projections	**Federal**	Social Security
	Budget	Health Programs
	Projections	Other Programs
		Net Interest
	Change in Trust	
	Fund Balances	Deficit
National Assets/Resources		**National Needs/Conditions**
Federally Owned Physical Assets	**National**	Indicators of economic, social,
State & Local Physical Assets	**Wealth**	educational, and environmental
Federal Contribution		conditions to be used as a guide
Privately Owned Physical Assets		to government investment and
Education Capital		management
Federal Contribution	**Social**	
R&D Capital	**Indicators**	
Federal Contribution		

Source: Reprinted from *Analytical Perspectives*, p. 20, 1997, U.S. Office of Management and Budget.

Table 11–2 State of Missouri Revenues, Expenditures, and Transfers, January 31, 1997

	January 1997	January 1996
Revenues and Transfers In		
Revenues:		
Taxes	$ 655,278,493	$ 620,709,864
Licenses, Fees, and Permits	47,047,985	46,596,332
Sales, Services, Leases, and Rentals	41,192,366	40,799,287
Bond Sale Proceeds	—	—
Contributions and Intergovernmental	284,111,620	289,062,652
Interest, Penalties, and Unclaimed Properties	16,973,173	15,881,762
Refunds	6,531,912	7,444,987
Miscellaneous Revenues	10,383,773	9,274,103
Total Revenues	1,061,519,322	1,029,768,987
Total Transfers In	358,845,732	304,856,220
Total Revenues and Transfers In	1,420,365,054	1,334,625,207
Expenditures and Transfers Out		
Expenditures:		
Personal Service	206,611,594	196,356,600
Expense and Equipment	148,574,090	131,095,533
Capital Improvements	28,854,436	17,753,205
Program Specific	606,400,954	546,256,635
Court-Ordered Desegregation Payments	16,433,092	20,666,048
Total Expenditures	1,006,874,166	912,128,021
Transfers Out:		
Appropriated	260,831,073	218,752,117
Other	98,014,659	86,104,103
Total Transfers Out	358,845,732	304,856,220
Total Expenditures and Transfers Out	1,365,719,898	1,216,984,241
Excess Revenues and Transfers In (Expenditures and Transfers Out)	$ 54,645,156	$ 117,640,966

Courtesy of Office of Administration, *State of Missouri Revenues, Expenditures and Transfers—All Funds, January 31, 1997*, 1997, Jefferson City, Missouri.

chapter typically have notes that explain what is included and excluded in specific entries in the statements and are essential components of the statements.

Cash Flows Statements. A third form of financial statement is for cash flows. The purpose is to show how cash entering and leaving a fund affects an entity's operations. These statements cover cash and cash equivalents, such as short-term investments (U.S. Treasury bills, see Chapter 10). Controversy exists over how these statements should be organized and whether they should be extended from just covering enterprise funds and to include basically all funds.[59] Table 11–3 is a cash flows statement from the Commonwealth of Pennsylvania.

In addition to balance sheets, operating statements, and cash flows statements, governments issue other important financial reports (e.g., disclosures on securities). The Government Finance Officers Association's *Disclosure Guidelines for State and Local Securities* identifies the information to be provided when governments issue bonds and other securities.[60] The statements that are provided are intended to help would-be purchasers understand what is being offered for sale in terms of the backing of the securities and what risks are involved.

By the late 1990s, the status of financial reporting for state and local governments was in turmoil. Many governments faced major problems in complying with accepted standards and were concerned about their ability to comply with possibly new reporting standards. One continuing problem is that existing financial reports are products of years of debate within any government and consequently are difficult to change. Compounding the problem is that sometimes state laws mandate reporting formats that are contrary to accepted standards.

Adding to the woes of state and local governments was GASB's effort in the mid-1990s to revise reporting standards.[61] Perhaps the most significant change under review would be a departure from what has been the standard pyramid approach. That method provides for a summary set of reports at the top of the pyramid with lower layers of reports having increasing detail. The proposed approach would provide different types of information at different levels of detail. The approach is premised on the concept that each financial statement should be designed for the specific needs of its users.[62]

The 1990s also have been stressful times for federal agencies in terms of financial reporting. The Chief Financial Officers Act of 1990 and the Government Management Reform Act of 1994 required agencies to prepare a series of *auditable* financial statements by March 1, 1997, and every year thereafter.[63] Federal agencies have experienced numerous problems in meeting these congressionally imposed deadlines.[64]

Government financial reporting has become much more extensive in the 1990s, but this has come at a cost. Questions arise whether accounting systems have become overloaded and whether some of the resources spent on financial reporting might be better spent on the delivery of services to citizens. Demands

Table 11–3 Commonwealth of Pennsylvania Combined Statement of Cash Flows, Proprietary Funds, June 30, 1996 (in Thousands of Dollars)

	Enterprise	Internal Service
CASH USED FOR OPERATIONS:		
Operating income (loss)	$ (113,716)	$ 6,109
Adjustments to reconcile operating income (loss) to net cash provided by (used for) operating activities:		
Depreciation	6,592	7,728
Net amortization	(10,603)	—
Provision for uncollectible accounts	37,280	11
Nonoperating revenues	212	137
Reclassification of investment income	(105,905)	—
Increase in receivables	(46,156)	(110)
(Increase) decrease in due from other funds	(1,438)	5,778
Increase in due from primary government	—	—
Decrease in due from component units	—	187
(Increase) decrease in due from other governments	(8)	117
(Increase) decrease in inventory	(6,560)	(400)
Decrease in other current assets	331	1,320
Increase (decrease) in accounts payable and accrued liabilities	3,095	(835)
Increase (decrease) in due to other funds	(577)	(2,587)
Decrease in due to primary government	—	—
Increase in due to other governments	296	5
Increase (decrease) in deferred revenue	(9,623)	(1)
Increase in insurance loss liability	213,171	—
Increase in other current liabilities	21,274	—
TOTAL ADJUSTMENTS	101,381	11,350
NET CASH PROVIDED BY (USED FOR) OPERATING ACTIVITIES	(12,335)	17,459
CASH FLOWS FROM NONCAPITAL FINANCING ACTIVITIES:		
Proceeds from issuance of debt obligations	—	—
Principal paid on debt obligations	(357)	(1,322)
Interest paid on debt obligations	(27)	(159)
Operating transfers from primary government	—	—
Operating transfers out	(43,117)	—
Increase in contributed capital	3,516	—
Decrease in contributed capital	—	—
NET CASH PROVIDED BY (USED FOR) NONCAPITAL FINANCING ACTIVITIES	(39,985)	(1,481)

continues

Table 11–3 continued

	Enterprise	Internal Service
CASH FLOWS FROM CAPITAL AND RELATED FINANCING ACTIVITIES:		
Proceeds from issuance of debt obligations	—	—
Principal paid on debt obligations	—	—
Interest paid on debt obligations	—	(205)
Increases in contributed capital	23,425	—
Decreases in contributed capital	—	—
Acquisition and construction of capital assets	(4,972)	(14,975)
Proceeds from sale of capital assets	—	1,517
Oil company franchise tax	—	—
NET CASH PROVIDED BY (USED FOR) CAPITAL AND RELATED FINANCING ACTIVITIES	18,453	(13,663)
CASH FLOWS FROM INVESTING ACTIVITIES:		
Purchase of investments	(2,002,384)	(64,291)
Proceeds from sale of maturities of investments	1,922,847	61,223
Investment income	111,387	761
NET CASH PROVIDED BY (USED FOR) INVESTING ACTIVITIES	31,850	(2,307)
NET INCREASE (DECREASE) IN CASH	(2,017)	8
CASH, JULY 1, 1995	9,954	277
CASH, JUNE 30, 1996	7,937	285

Courtesy of Office of the Budget, *Comprehensive Annual Financial Report for Fiscal Year Ended June 30, 1996*, 1997, Harrisburg, Pennsylvania.

for the streamlining of financial reports are increasing. Congress has authorized OMB to waive some reporting requirements imposed on federal agencies.[65] The accounting profession, itself, has shown some awareness that reporting requirements can create overwhelming burdens.[66]

GOVERNMENTAL AUDITING

Auditing serves a variety of functions and consequently exists in many different forms. One distinction made is between pre- and postaudits, namely, between reviewing transactions before and after they occur. The preaudit occurs before the government commits itself to a purchase and is used to verify, for example, that the police department has sufficient funds to purchase a piece of equipment and that the department is authorized to have that equipment. Not only the budget office but also an accounting department may be involved in preaudits; if personnel are to be hired, a personnel office may have some preaudit responsibility. Often at the state and local levels, independent comptrollers, controllers, or auditors general have preaudit responsibilities.

Postaudits generally involve more extensive procedures and often more participants. The following discussion concerns the function of postaudits in government budgeting and finance. This form of auditing has been defined as "a systematic collection of the sufficient, competent evidential matter needed to attest to the fairness of management's assertions in the financial statements, or to evaluate whether management has efficiently and effectively carried out its responsibilities."[67]

Audit Objectives and Organizational Responsibilities

Purposes. Auditing in the private sector is used largely to ensure that the financial statements issued by a firm fairly reflect its financial status, and this same concern exists in the public sector. Auditing is used to provide some assurance to investors in both the private and public sectors that their investments are secure and are being well managed.

Another purpose of auditing is ensuring that funds are not subject to fraud, waste, and abuse or subject to error in reporting. When financial reports cannot be verified by checking accounting records, the opportunities for dishonesty, waste, or just poor management of funds may exist. GAO has criticized the Internal Revenue Service for being unable to reconcile its account records in terms of receiving $1.3 trillion dollars annually.[68]

Auditing in government also is used for compliance purposes. As has been noted, accounting systems track receipts and expenditures to ensure that they are handled in conformance with restrictions contained in revenue and appropriation bills. Auditing helps ensure that an agency does not spend funds on an activity that, while beneficial to society, simply has not been authorized. Compliance auditing can include ensuring that an agency has accomplished programmatically what it was instructed to do. Another form of compliance auditing involves grants. The federal government, for example, needs to check that only appropriate charges have been made by a state government in the case of a federally funded project or program, such as Medicaid, or by a university in the case of funded research.[69]

Auditing Organizations. Nationally, several organizations influence the practice of governmental auditing. The American Institute of Certified Public Accountants issues *generally accepted auditing standards* (GAAS).[70] GASB, in the process of identifying standards for accounting, inevitably becomes involved in auditing. GAO issues *generally accepted government auditing standards* (GAGAS, known as the "yellow book"), which are applied to federal agencies and may be applied to state and local governments that receive federal financial assistance.[71]

Auditing within a government often is performed by several organizations. Audits are conducted periodically by officers within an agency to provide information to management; these internal audits help maintain managerial control over operations. Other audits are conducted by external officers, who can be from a unit answerable to the legislative body (such as GAO being answerable to Congress), a unit headed by an independently elected officer, or an independent private corporation that has a contract to conduct an audit. Internal financial officers frequently view existing control systems as protecting against waste and fraud, while external auditors remain unconvinced.[72]

The federal government augmented the auditing function during the 1970s and 1980s by creating inspectors general in major federal agencies. Appointed by the President with the advice and consent of the Senate, inspectors general are located within agencies but can only be removed by the President. According to the Inspector General Act of 1978 and the Chief Financial Officers Act of 1990, inspectors general are responsible for conducting audits and for investigating possible cases of fraud, waste, and abuse of government resources.[73] The Chief Financial Officers Act, by creating CFOs in major agencies, greatly increased the attention agencies devote to sound accounting practices and to the auditing of accounts. Agencies have redesigned their central staff units, consolidating considerable powers under the CFOs.

President Clinton's Executive Order 12993, issued in 1996, provides a process for dealing with instances of possible wrongdoing by inspectors general and their deputies. The Federal Bureau of Investigation is authorized to investigate such matters, and the President's Council on Integrity and Efficiency (PCIE) reviews the Federal Bureau of Investigation's findings. The PCIE consists of department inspectors general and selected central administrators, such as representatives from OMB and the Office of Personnel Management.[74]

All levels of government use Big 6 and other accounting firms to conduct or assist in auditing. Depending on the state, a local government may have a choice of paying either the state auditor or a private firm for audit services; state services may be less expensive, while private services may perform audits in a more timely fashion.[75] When a private firm is to be used, a government will use a bidding process to give competing firms an opportunity to indicate what services they can provide, in what time frame, and at what cost.

A common practice in the private sector and one often recommended for the public sector is the use of audit committees. These bodies when they exist in government typically consist of administrators, legislators, and financial experts from outside of the government. The committees can serve as useful interfaces between finance offices and auditors. Such committees, however, are seldom used. One survey of cities with populations over 100,000 found that less than 20 percent used audit committees.[76]

Sometimes the number of organizations involved in auditing in a given situation can seem overwhelming. Within an agency there may be two or more auditors. In the Department of Defense, for instance, audit functions are performed by the Defense Contract Audit Agency (which audits contractors), the inspector general, the comptroller, and the CFO.[77] Large state and local agencies may have similar internal auditors, and all levels of government have their central auditors, such as GAO for the federal government and auditors general for the states. As noted, private accounting firms may have responsibilities as well. Additional auditing occurs because of intergovernmental financial transactions. State government agencies, for example, may be audited by federal funding agencies and GAO, although this level of auditing has changed since passage of the Single Audit Act of 1984 (see below).

Types of Audits and Standards

Audit Types. As already noted, there are pre- and postaudits and internal and external audits. Another means of categorizing audits is to consider the purposes to be served. The definition of auditing provided above suggests that audits can be directed toward finance and performance. According to GAGAS, issued by GAO, financial audits focus on whether financial statements prepared by a government accurately reflect financial transactions and the government's or agency's status. The standards of auditing provide a framework for conducting an audit.

Financial audits also review how financial matters are handled or whether suitable internal controls exist to protect resources. Auditors are concerned with the vulnerability of a financial management system to potential fraud. Are organizational lines of responsibility clearly established to ensure that whoever is in charge has the authority to protect the government's or agency's finances? Are policies and procedures established for maintaining records, and are those policies and procedures adhered to in practice? Are computer systems that handle financial transactions protected against potential fraud?

Guidelines in this area are established at the federal level by the Federal Managers' Financial Integrity Act of 1982; the Chief Financial Officers Act of 1990; OMB Circular A-123, Management Accountability and Control; Circular A-127, Financial Management Systems; and Circular A-134, Financial Accounting Principles and Standards.[78] OMB, working with federal agencies, has established a list of high-risk situations in which fraud, waste, and abuse are more likely to occur. The Federal Financial Management Improvement Act of 1996 requires that each federal agency be audited and a report be prepared stating whether the agency complies with the financial management systems requirements (Circular A-127) and the Standard General Ledger (see above).[79]

Identification of the risks is the first step in eliminating the problems. Auditors make risk assessments to determine what accounting activities or operations to audit, since only a sample of financial activities can be audited, given the auditors' limited resources. The risk assessment determines what activities are most vulnerable to fraud, waste, and abuse and therefore should be audited.

The other major function served is performance auditing, which deals with whether resources are being used efficiently and whether results or objectives are being achieved.[80] This subject is discussed in Chapter 7. All that is necessary here is to note that some audit agencies, most notably GAO, have had their traditional duties expanded to include performance audits. Any audit agency faces the difficult choice of deciding how much effort and resources should be devoted to the competing functions of financial and performance auditing. If major emphasis is given to performance auditing, fraud and other abuses may become more prevalent; conversely, emphasis on financial auditing may keep government honest but do little to encourage agencies to fulfill their missions.

Auditing Standards. GAAS provides overall guidelines as well as standards for conducting fieldwork and preparing audit reports.[81] Overall standards call for auditors to be independent of the agencies under review and to be fully trained in the auditing function. Fieldwork is to be planned adequately in advance and sufficiently staffed to meet the requirements of the work plan. Auditors must keep accurate records of their fieldwork to answer questions that may arise at a later time.

Field auditing involves verifying sample transactions to ensure that transactions did occur as recorded. For example, an expense report of a trip taken by a city employee to a national conference, among numerous expense reports, might be selected for review. The auditor may (1) call the travel agent or airline to verify the ticket price, (2) check that the trip was an authorized budget expenditure, (3) interview the employee to verify unreceipted miscellaneous expenses, and (4) review other receipts and documents to determine the accuracy of the report. The purpose of this fieldwork is not particularly to find cases of fraud, waste, and abuse but to verify that the jurisdiction has procedures to protect against them.

The Single Audit Act. A concern of the federal government for many years has been the large volume of federal financial transfers to state and local governments and to nongovernment organizations, and whether these transfers are being suitably audited. OMB has three circulars that detail how these organizations are to organize their accounts: (1) Circular A-21, Cost Principles for Educational

Institutions (1996), (2) Circular A-87, Cost Principles for State, Local and Indian Tribal Governments (1995), and (3) Circular A-122, Cost Principles for Non-Profit Organizations (1997).

The Single Audit Act of 1984, as amended in 1996, deals with this audit problem by requiring that recipients of federal assistance of $300,000 or more in a fiscal year must undergo a single audit of their accounting systems and the way federal funds are handled.[82] Audits must be submitted within nine months of the audit period's close. The law applies to state and local governments and nonprofit organizations. The law has had the effect of requiring tens of thousands of audits annually. These audits, normally conducted by private firms, are intended to help ensure that recipients use federal resources in accordance with federal laws and regulations. The act is implemented through OMB Circular A-133, Audits of States, Local Governments, and Non-Profit Organizations (revised 1997). A survey of accounting/finance offices in state, county, municipal, and township governments found widespread agreement that the Single Audit Act had improved the handling of federal financial assistance, but there was less of an impact on overall financial management in these governments. While the law was intended to reduce duplication efforts, that was not always accomplished.[83]

GAAS, GAGAS, and the Single Audit Act set standards for audit reporting. Of course, one of the chief concerns with regard to any report is that financial statements are in accordance with generally accepted accounting principles. Audit reports are expected to indicate deficiencies, such as inconsistent use of accounting procedures. Reports indicate whether internal controls exist to protect against fraud, waste, and abuse.

Four types of conclusions can be drawn by the auditing body. (1) The audit might be unqualified, providing a "clean bill" that the accounting system meets standards. (2) The report may be qualified, indicating there are problems but that the system generally meets standards. A qualified audit of a local government might be interpreted unfavorably by would-be investors in the government's bonds. (3) A disclaimer audit indicates that the accounting system is inadequate and that conducting an audit is impossible. (4) An audit can be adverse or negative, indicating that the financial statements fail to provide an accurate report of the entity's finances.

Follow-up after an audit is essential in order to ensure that weaknesses are corrected. Without such follow-up, auditing is an empty exercise. OMB Circular A-50, Audit Followup, sets guidelines for checks to be made after audits have been completed at the federal level. A survey of states found that 41 had a follow-up system, of which 31 prepared periodic status reports to indicate whether corrective action had been taken in response to audit findings.[84]

INFORMATION SYSTEMS

Contemporary approaches to budgeting and accounting obviously require considerable amounts of information for decision making and evaluation. Information systems, then, constitute an effort to bring about greater coordination of organizational units in the collection, storage, manipulation, retrieval, and analysis of information. The following discussion addresses the design of information systems, the use of computers, the information available through the Internet, and problems and issues that are endemic to information systems.

Management Information Systems

The term *management information system* (MIS) is most commonly used to refer to systems of information processing intended to provide assistance to planning, administration, and control functions, and *system* suggests a categorizing or ordering of information processing. A distinction is made between data and information; data refer to facts and information to the usefulness of data. Data that are not information are considered noise, in that they detract from rather than aid the decision-making process. Thousands of pieces of data about individual welfare recipients, for example, may be of little help in deliberations about changing the funding formula for federal welfare aid to state and local governments. The management of information is commonly referred to as *information resources management* (IRM).

A term related to MIS is *decision support system* (DSS), which usually refers to a computer information system that facilitates nonroutine, semistructured decision making. In other words, routine activities are excluded, such as simple recordkeeping for patient appointments at a mental health clinic, but so are unstructured decision-making processes, such as setting relative funding priorities among mental health services, narcotic law enforcement, and national security interests in Central Europe.

Categorization of Information. We have consistently noted that basically two types of information are used in budgetary and financial decision making: program information and resource information. That typology is manifest in Figure 11–1, which is a schematic representation of the types of information used in the federal government. The figure shows how public concerns and those of the legislative and executive branches determine the information requirements of government. Four columns of boxes are depicted. The first column, which represents program information, includes social indicators, impacts, outputs, and other program-related information (see Chapter 5). The other three columns involve resource information—personnel, finances, and property (land, buildings, and equipment).

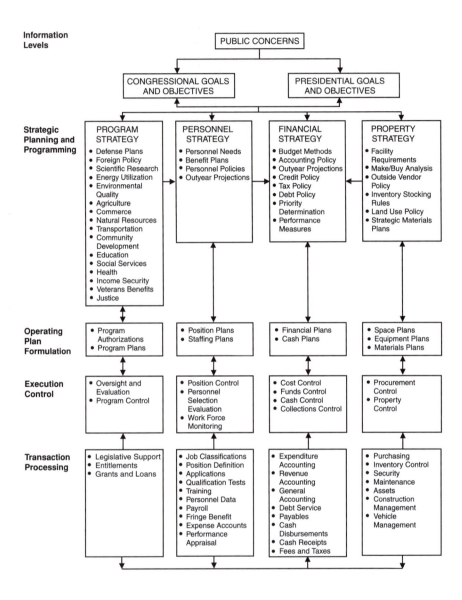

Figure 11–1 Federal Information Requirements Planning Chart. *Source:* Reprinted from *Managing the Cost of Government*, Vol. 2, p. 21, 1985, U.S. General Accounting Office.

The illustration also has several rows depicting the nature of the decisions or the types of transactions involved. The highest level includes strategic planning information and programming information. The second level includes operational planning, and the third includes execution and control. The fourth level includes relatively routine transactions, such as employee payroll, debt service, and construction management.

Structure. The design or structure of an MIS is dependent on the intended users and their information needs. Figure 11–1 is oriented toward the executive branch and its roles in budget preparation and execution. Other major users are the legislative branch in its budget approval and oversight roles and a comptroller office in its auditing role. In addition to needing information pertaining to appropriations and expenditures, legislatures want information on fiscal notes, the status of bills in each chamber, the receipt of grants, and the like.

The public has come to be recognized as a potentially major set of information users in a variety of ways and at a level of intensity not previously experienced. President Clinton and Vice President Gore have championed the formation of a *national information infrastructure* (NII), commonly referred to as linking the general public to the information superhighway.[85]

As part of this effort to make information available to the public, the Government Information Locator Service (GILS) is being developed by the federal government as prescribed by the Paperwork Reduction Act of 1995 and OMB Bulletin 95-01. The objective is to have all federal agencies make known the information in their possession. Some information will become available through the Internet (discussed below) while other information may be available by an 800 telephone number, fax telephone transmission, hard copy, or CD-ROM.

GILS should have many types of users. People of all ages may have access through terminals in schools, public libraries, and their homes. One view is that the chief group of users will be at a secondary level, meaning that a first level already has access. Private citizens who are scientists, for example, already have access to scientific information, but through GILS, much of that information will become available to a much wider group of people. The system also holds potential for federal agencies to share information with each other and for governments to share information. Given efforts to reduce paperwork burdens (Chapter 10), GILS has the potential for reducing redundancy in having two or more agencies collect the same information.

While GILS is an immense project at the federal level, other efforts to serve citizens are under way at the state and local levels. Some states, as in the case of Florida, have their own GILS projects. Numerous communities have created electronic information kiosks located in convenient places, such as shopping malls. Selected Web sites are discussed later.

Organizations vary in how much information they need and how they will use it. A line agency needs much more data about itself than the budget office needs about the agency. Similarly, a personnel department needs much information on agency personnel, while the budget office needs some but not nearly as much. Some users want data simply to have them without necessarily planning to use them. Congress, state legislatures, and city councils often demand detailed financial data that will not be analyzed. Legislative bodies sometimes suspect the executive of hiding something important unless they force the executive to produce detailed expenditure data. The fact that legislators could look at any particular detail helps keep the executive honest.

A budget office needs information for budget preparation, for monitoring budget execution, and possibly for performance auditing and program evaluation. The information needed, as discussed throughout the book, covers such matters as expenditure data based on organizational unit, program, appropriation, and the like. In addition, however, the budget office may want information based geographically, such as by region or by county. Regional data are important for policy and political reasons in order to determine, for example, how programs are influencing different regions or how budget reductions might harm some regions more than others. Local governments may need to have tax data generated by region for special neighborhood assessment purposes, as in the case of a special assessment on downtown businesses. *Geographic information systems* (GISs), as their name suggests, provide data organized by area, such as neighborhoods in a city or counties of a state.[86] A GIS can be helpful in planning for infrastructure improvements, such as water and sewer systems and roads. These systems are especially helpful in considering the impact on utilities of planned construction of new housing or industrial complexes.[87]

Revenue offices, such as the Internal Revenue Service, need extensive information about taxpayers. Property tax systems require information about parcels of land and the structures on them, and sales tax systems need information about corporations and businesses responsible for collecting taxes. The personal income tax, of course, is the major generator of income for the federal government, and the Internal Revenue Service must keep track of millions of taxpayers. Its Tax Systems Modernization project is intended to upgrade its ability to store and retrieve data in a variety of formats. Internal Revenue Service efforts have been plagued with numerous problems, in part perhaps because of the agency's mismanagement, but also because the complexity of tax laws challenge the most sophisticated computer systems.[88]

In addition to central offices such as a budget office and a treasury department, line departments and agencies have a host of information needs and corresponding systems. Agencies that are covered by the Chief Financial Officers Act have about 800 financial systems, plus hundreds of other systems pertaining to the operations of their programs.[89] Some states have publicly accessible information systems for persons seeking government employment. States on occasion have linked their systems with local governments as another means for making information more readily available. The opportunities for networking information on an intergovernmental basis are seemingly limitless.[90]

Timeliness is another criterion. Some data need to be maintained on a daily basis. An accounting department needs daily reports on the status of funds, cash balances, and the like, whereas some organizational units may need only weekly or monthly reports about their budgets. A central budget office does not need daily reports from agencies on program performance, such as outputs and impacts. Some information may need to be available only upon request, with an acceptable lag time of perhaps a week or more before the requested information is provided.

While numerous approaches to designing an MIS exist, seemingly the most viable approach is to develop modules or subsystems that can be linked with each other. Each subsystem need not be computer based, but as computer technology advances, more and more subsystems will be converted from paper and microfiche files to computer files. One essential subsystem of any financially oriented MIS is an accounting system. As has been noted, large governments may have many accounting systems, and in some such cases there is only limited standardization. Over time, standardization will be more prevalent, given the need to compare and analyze data from different accounting systems.

Other subsystems may exist that are largely independent of the accounting system (or systems). There is no compelling need to have a computer-based system containing program impact and output data as part of a financial accounting system. Having both types of information in the same set of files may unnecessarily complicate data input, storage, and manipulation. On the other hand, computer-supported information systems containing program data can be linked to accounting systems as needed. One approach is to download selected information from various subsystems into a temporary file. A state budget office that wants to examine the economic impact of tourism might assemble information from a variety of sources from within the state government but also from external databases.

The modular approach is attractive in concept but difficult to implement. The problem is linking the modules to each other, and in the real world it is not just a matter of literally plugging one module into another. Although a financial module may be suitable for capturing financial transactions, the problem remains of linking those data to program information. In other words, there might be no easy linkage between information about a city department's expenditures and information about its accomplishments. Similar problems exist in linking tax systems with more general information needed for the revenue side of budget preparation or linking appropriations provided to an organizational unit with procurement data about specific purchases. Interfaces among these systems can be difficult to achieve, and when information must be re-entered from one system to another, personnel and time are consumed, errors occur, and information-processing costs rise.

Computers

The rapid advances in computers and related technology are making possible information systems that were only concepts a few years ago, and they are also making these systems affordable for most governments. Powerful mainframe computers, of course, have been a staple for federal agencies, states, and large cities for decades. With the advent of microcomputers, small governments suddenly had easy access to computer technology. By the early 1990s, probably almost every government in the United States had at least one computer. One study found that central cities that relied heavily upon mainframe computing used computing more extensively and used leading-edge technologies more than other cities that relied largely on personal computers.[91] In a 1995 study, all 50 states and the District of Columbia reported using computers for agency budget request preparation, budget request analysis by the central budget office, and preparation of the executive budget.[92]

What exists may well be a hodgepodge of hardware and software. Large jurisdictions may continue to use mainframe equipment but also find a need for mini- and microcomputers that run independently of the mainframes. In some instances, agencies create microcomputer systems that contain duplicates of mainframe files because the central data processing office takes too long to respond to user requests or the mainframe files are not as user friendly with regard to the manipulation of data.

Acquisition Planning. While probably most governments in the United States have at least one computer and while most have applied computer technology to some or a wide range of their financial processes, governments in other countries are just beginning to undertake the process of applying computers to budgeting and finance. Painful lessons are learned in this process, such as the cost of conversion, the time required, the need for skilled personnel, and the like. The introduction of computers in Kenya's accounting systems was found to have strengthened the manual systems and was found to promote effectiveness reforms and rudimentary analysis.[93]

As governments gain experience in computing, they are expending greater effort in planning computer installations and information systems. Once having entered the realm of computing through the purchase of one or more computers, a government must decide what steps to take next; planning for the introduction of new computer-based financial information systems is essential.[94] Steps include designating a group of individuals to be responsible for overseeing the design and installation of the system, making an assessment of what tasks need to be handled by the system, assessing the volume of work to be processed, determining hardware and software needs, identifying employee training requirements, and selecting appropriate vendors.[95] Traditional purchasing procedures that awards contracts to low bidders may be unsuitable in the acquisition of information technology.[96]

The federal government is attempting to take a systematic approach to future acquisition of computer hardware and software. The Information Technology Management Reform Act of 1996 requires each federal agency to establish a position of *chief information officer* (CIO) and requires the head of the agency to work with the CIO and the CFO in integrating financial and information systems.[97] OMB is responsible for overall implementation of the law, including overseeing the acquisition of information technology. Circular A-130, Management of Federal Information Resources, provides guidance on how agencies are to collect, store, and distribute information.

Software Packages. In addition to the acquisition of computer hardware, software or programming is needed. One software problem plaguing governments in the latter part of the 1990s is that many information systems are unable to recognize the year 2000. Since only the last two digits of a year are usually recorded, computers read "00" as "1900," "01" as "1901," and the like. A computer at the turn of the century, then, might think the current year is 1900 and would be unable to recognize the fact that people were born after that date, resulting in denying anyone any benefits that are based on age. Governments and businesses have been scrambling to find solutions to this serious problem.[98]

One of the most common forms of software in budgeting is the *spreadsheet.* A spreadsheet is a chart in which the rows can be organizational units within a department or, at a more detailed level, major and minor objects within a bureau or office and the columns can be time units, such as last year's actual figures, current year projected figures, and proposed figures for the budget year and out-years. Other columns can be included, such as expenditures by quarter. Side-by-side columns can be used to show appropriated amounts and actual expenditures. Spreadsheets can be used for budget proposals and for multiyear budget plans.

The advantage of a spreadsheet program is that it can calculate thousands of adjustments in a few seconds. It can quickly adjust personnel costs, for example, to reflect possible pay increases, such as an across-the-board 3-percent pay adjustment, and can recalculate employee benefits based on projected new pay rates. Spreadsheet programs can accommodate numerous assumptions, such as a pay increase at one level and price increases for supplies and equipment at another level. Among the more popular microcomputer spreadsheet programs are Excel, Lotus, and Quattro Pro.

Agency budget requests can be submitted to a central budget office either electronically or by sending the requests on floppy disks. If the central budget office decides to reduce a request, the computer can readjust figures, such as recalculating all subtotals and totals, without having to consume many hours of staff time.

At the federal level, OMB uses the MAX Decision Support System (MAX DSS). This system is used for preparing the budget and various reports and for ad hoc analysis that commonly arises in any budget office. The system is immense, having more than 100 data tables with the largest having more than two million rows of data.[99] Instructions for the use of MAX DSS in agency submissions of budget requests are contained in OMB Circular A-11, Preparation and Submission of Budget Estimates (Chapters 5 and 6).

A newly emerging form of technology that holds great promise for government is *computer imaging*. Paper records can be scanned into a computer, with the data compressed on optical disks, allowing for the elimination of vast amounts of paper records and the warehouses needed to store them. *Optical character recognition* (OCR) and *intelligent character recognition* (ICR) permit the searching of these scanned records as needed.[100]

Word processing also is an integral part of budget preparation, since substantial textual materials must be drafted each year. Perhaps the biggest advantage of any word-processing software package is that it frees staff from having to retype portions of the budget countless times as decisions, such as whether to fund a particular activity and at what level, are made and adjusted. Changes can be made, the computer can be instructed to check for spelling errors, and the new material then is ready to be presented in a variety of formats.

Database managers constitute another type of software widely used in budget and financial operations. These software packages are intended to handle data pertaining to cases, such as characteristics of welfare clients, paychecks issued to employees, and the status of corporations inspected for compliance with air and water pollution regulations.

Integrated software or suites are desirable because they allow use of word processing, spreadsheets, database managers, and graphics. With an integrated software package, a budget office can prepare the text for the budget document along with tables, charts, and graphs.

The Internet

The Internet has become an essential tool for budgeting and finance. The "Net," as it is called, is a vast system of interconnected computers, originally designed to connect researchers in national defense with one another. The Net, which provides communication links and access to information, has several components:

- *Electronic mail* (e-mail) is one of the Net's most popular features in which people may send messages to one another and may attach lengthy documents to those messages.
- *Usenet News* (Netnews) is what is called a bulletin board system in which people may post inquiries and announcements and then receive comments from others.
- *Mailing Lists* (listservs) are similar to bulletin boards, except that one must join a group, usually at no cost. In a listserv, members automatically receive communications from other members whereas in netnews a person needs to enter the bulletin board to see what messages have been posted.
- *File transfer protocols* (FTPs) allow files of text and data to be sent at high speed to someone requesting the information.
- *Wide Area Information Service* (WAIS) and *Gopher* are tools that facilitate searches for information that has been posted by organizations and individuals.
- *Internet Relay Chat* (chat rooms) allows people to communicate with those having similar interests. A person can enter a chat room and talk with whoever is in the room at the time. Communication is accomplished through the typing of messages but voice communication is becoming available.
- *The World Wide Web* (WWW) is a Windows-based system developed at CERN Research Center in Switzerland. The Web makes a vast array of information available in text and picture forms, sometimes including moving pictures and sound.

The World Wide Web is one of the most popular features of the Internet.[101] Begun only in 1991, the Web has millions of *Web sites* or *homepages* for individuals, nonprofit groups, for-profit companies, and governments. Given the immensity of the Web, devices known as *search engines* have been developed to aid in "surfing" the Web to find information of interest. Popular search engines include Alta-Vista, InfoSeek Guide, and Yahoo.

Exhibit 11–3 lists selected Web sites in the field of budgeting and finance. The first group in the exhibit lists sites of general interest. Government Servers lists sites throughout the world. Thomas is the Web site for the U.S. Library of Congress. Financenet, which is sponsored by the Chief Financial Officers Council, contains a wealth of financial information. Financenet, as with many other Web sites, contains *links* to other sites that can be reached through the click of a computer mouse. Statistical Resources on the Web is a site that provides numerous links to sites that contain data of relevance to the budgeting and finance arena.

Exhibit 11–3 Selected World Wide Web Sites Related to Budgeting and Finance

	Address (http://)
General Sites	
Government Servers	www.eff.org/govt.html
Thomas (U.S. Library of Congress)	thomas.loc.gov
Financenet (sponsored by U.S. Chief Financial Officers Council)	www.financenet.gov
Statistical Resources on the Web	www.lib.umich.edu/libhome/ Documents.center/stats.html
Federal Government	
FedWeb Locator	www.law.vil.edu/Fed-Agency/ fedwebloc.html
FedWorld Information Network	www.fedworld.gov
Federal Statistics Briefing Room	www.whitehouse.gov/WH/html/ briefroom.html#fsbr
Presidential Executive Orders	library.whitehouse.gov/?request= ExecutiveOrder
Office of Management and Budget	www.whitehouse.gov/WH/EOP/OMB/ html/ombhome.html
National Performance Review	www.npr.gov
Council of Economic Advisors	www2.whitehouse.gov/WH/EOP/CEA/ html/CEA.html
Department of Treasury, including Internal Revenue Service	www.ustreas.gov
U.S. House of Representatives	www.house.gov
U.S. Senate	www.senate.gov
Congressional Budget Office	www.cbo.gov
General Accounting Office	www.gao.gov
State and Local Governments	
U.S. State and Local Gateway	www.statelocal.gov
State Government Web Servers	www.state.me.us/states.htm
Council of State Governments	www.csg.org
State of North Carolina	www.state.nc.us
State of Texas	www.state.tx.us
USA Citylink	usacitylink.com
National League of Cities	www.cais.com/nlc

continues

Exhibit 11–3 continued

	Address (http://)
International City/County Management Association	www.icma.org
National Association of Counties	www.naco.org
Blacksburg (Virginia) Electronic Village	www.bev.net
Chicago	www.ci.chi.il.us
San Carlos, California	www.san-carlos.ca.us
Professional Associations	
American Accounting Association	www.rutgers.edu/Accounting/raw/aaa/aaa.htm
American Institute of Certified Public Accountants	www.aicpa.org
Association for Budgeting and Financial Management	www.pubadm.fsu.edu/abfm/index.html
Association of Government Accountants	raw.rutgers.edu/raw/aga
Financial Accounting Standards Board	www.rutgers.edu/Accounting/raw/fasb
Governmental Accounting Standards Board	www.rutgers.edu/Accounting/raw/gasb
Government Finance Officers Association	www.gfoa.org
National Association of State Budget Officers	www.nasbo.org
Private Profit and Nonprofit Organizations	
Arthur Andersen	www.arthurandersen.com
Barron's	www.barrons.com
Bond Buyer	www.bondbuyer.com
Brookings Institution	www.brook.edu
Center on Budget and Policy Priorities	www.cbpp.org
Electronic Policy Network	epn.org
Federal Reserve Board	www.bog.frb.fed.us
FinanceHub	www.financehub.com
FinWeb (Financial Economics)	www.finweb.com

continues

Exhibit 11-3 continued

	Address (http://)
Government Contracts	www.govcon.com
Government On-Line	www.gol.org
Moody's Investors Service	www.moodys.com
OMB Watch	ombwatch.org/ombwatch.html
Regional Economic Models, Inc.	www.remi.com
Wall Street Journal	www.wsj.com
Watchdog Groups	www.voxpop.org/jefferson/watchdog

Federal, state, and local governments each maintain numerous sites as shown in Exhibit 11-3. Federal Web Locator is useful when searching for a particular federal agency's homepage. States sites can be reached by using the site known as State Government Web Servers; a map of the United States is presented, which allows a user to click on the state that is of interest. Many state Web sites have or are developing links to their local governments. State and local sites, as well as policy information of importance to these governments, can be located through the U.S. State and Local Gateway site, a federal interagency project. Finding a site and the information one seeks within the site can require much patience. Many sites have alphabetical indexes and/or keyword search features as aids in locating information. Exhibit 11-3 includes some sample state and city sites.

As is indicated in Exhibit 11-3, numerous other sites are available. Information can be obtained from professional associations, such as the Association for Budgeting and Financial Management and the National Association of State Budget Officers. Private firms maintain many useful sites, as in the case of the *Wall Street Journal* and the Big 6 accounting firms (Arthur Andersen listed in the exhibit). Many sites are accessed without a fee, while other sites may be on a fee or subscription basis. Other sites are maintained by public interest groups. OMB Watch operates a Web homepage and listservs that provide members specific kinds of information as it becomes available, as in the case of action taken by an appropriations subcommittee.

The technology in this area is advancing so rapidly that it is difficult to predict what will occur in the next year or two let alone three or four years into the future. For example, floppy disks have been largely replaced by CD-ROMs for importing software to computers, but CD-ROMs also could be replaced in the future. Not long ago, the *Code of Federal Regulations* (CFR), which is the storehouse of all regulations that citizens, corporations, and governments must obey, was only in paper format and was updated annually. However, the CFR became available on CD-ROM, making quarterly updates feasible. Now with the advent of the Web, the CFR can be continuously updated as federal agencies modify regulations, rescind others, and adopt new ones. One possibility is that these advances in technology will obviate the need for most CD-ROMs.

Issues and Problems

Access to information and information systems is one of the most critical problems in the field of information management. The federal government has hundreds of databanks that contain more than a billion records on individuals. Who should have access to these files? The Privacy Act is intended to protect individuals on whom federal agencies maintain files; on the other hand, the Freedom of Information Act opens many federal records to public inspection.[102] Balancing the two objectives of protecting privacy and maintaining freedom of access obviously is difficult. Agencies that collect information about individuals may be reluctant to share that information with other government units and indeed may be legally prohibited from such sharing.

Another aspect of access is the security of information systems and the computers that support them. Lack of security can result in unwarranted invasions of personal privacy, fraud (as in situations involving tampering with financial records), or breaches of national security. The Federal Managers' Financial Integrity Act requires federal agencies to test their information systems for "integrity," meaning the degree to which unauthorized users are prevented from accessing or altering records. Additionally, the Computer Security Act of 1987 requires federal agencies to develop security plans for computer systems containing sensitive information.[103] When security measures can be circumvented, the information systems can be subjected to so-called viruses, which, when introduced into a program, can shut down systems, alter data, or totally destroy databanks. Each information system should have a plan for dealing with computer failures due to fires, floods, sabotage, and the like.

The introduction of computers in any administrative process should be used as an opportunity to redesign or reengineer the process rather than simply changing it from one based on paper to one based on a computer. Reengineering can result in reduced costs through the elimination or alteration of steps in the process, such as the steps used in encumbering monies in an accounting system.[104]

Computers have greatly expanded the ability of governments to collect, store, and manipulate data; a problem that arises from this is the burden imposed on others in supplying the information. As was discussed in Chapter 10, the federal government has taken important steps to limit the amount of information it collects from citizens, corporations, and state and local governments.

Problems inevitably arise regarding the relative responsibilities of the offices that maintain information systems and the end users of the systems. The demarcation between these two is pronounced when centralized data-processing systems exist, but with the advent of personal computers and *local area networks* (LANs), users increasingly are involved in all aspects of the systems they use. When users are not well trained in computer technology and when the technology is centralized in data-processing offices, special attention must be paid to the interface between users and computer operators.[105]

People need to be taken into account when new technology is introduced. Executives and managers who are unfamiliar with computers may fear having to use them and may resist their use.[106] Computers can be dehumanizing; working all day at a video display terminal can be as tedious and unrewarding as many assembly line jobs. At the same time, technological changes can greatly increase worker productivity, although the advent of extensive computer usage has not led to dramatic increases in the productivity of the American work force. Why such progress has not been achieved is debatable, with one plausible explanation being that traditional measures of productivity simply do not gauge the changes that computers have fostered.[107]

Technological changes and particularly computers can affect relationships among the branches of government and levels of government. Computers hold the potential for increasing the power of legislative branches, which previously may have become dependent on the executive branches for information. New technology may increase the power of the federal government over state and local governments and the power of states over their local governments.

SUMMARY

Governmental accounting is characterized by procedures intended to prevent fraud and to guarantee agency conformance with legal requirements. Information from accounting systems is used in decision making and can help improve the efficiency and effectiveness of services. The GASB was established to help improve state and local government accounting systems, and the Federal Accounting Standards Advisory Board has had similar responsibilities at the federal level. Generally accepted accounting principles allow the use of several different types of funds, with the general fund usually the most important for any government.

Accounting systems are structured by having a general ledger and subsidiary ledgers and follow a relatively simple formula of assets equaling the total of liabilities and fund balance. Within these ledgers, expenditures are accounted for in a variety of ways, including major and minor objects of expenditures.

Bases of accounting include cash, encumbrance, accrual, and cost. Some jurisdictions use project-based accounting and cost finding instead of the more comprehensive cost accounting methods. Regardless of the basis for accounting, reports summarizing transactions are prepared at intervals. Three of the most common types of reports are balance sheets, operating statements, and cash flow statements.

Auditing focuses on whether financial statements are accurate reflections of the status of accounts and/or whether an organization is operating efficiently and effectively. Auditing is used for compliance purposes, namely, to ensure that financial transactions are in accordance with revenue and appropriation legislation. Generally accepted auditing standards constitute the guidelines for auditing in the public sector; in addition, generally accepted government auditing standards are used by GAO.

Management information systems, as applied in budgeting and finance, encompass program and resource information. These systems are used by chief executives, legislatures, and auditors for all four phases of the budget cycle: preparation, approval, execution, and audit. Computers, ranging from mainframes to powerful microcomputers, are greatly increasing the ability to provide the information needed for budgetary decision making. The rapid development of the Internet and especially its World Wide Web have increased the information available to everyone. New problems have arisen as a result of the introduction and expanded use of computer technology, including negative impacts on workers and changes in the relationships among branches and levels of government.

NOTES

1. J.W. Norvelle, *Introduction to Fund Accounting*, 5th ed. (Tucson, AZ: Thoth Books, 1994), 1.

2. T. Harkin, U.S. Senator (Dem., Iowa), as quoted in Report Faults Accounting at Defense Department, *Washington Post,* No. 159 (May 13, 1997): A4; see U.S. General Accounting Office, *Financial Management: Improved Management Needed for DOD Disbursement Process Reforms* (Washington, DC: U.S. Government Printing Office, 1997); U.S. General Accounting Office, *Financial Management: An Overview of Finance and Accounting Activities in DOD* (Washington, DC: U.S. General Accounting Office, 1997).

3. F.C. Mosher, *A Tale of Two Agencies* (Baton Rouge: Louisiana State University Press, 1984).

4. Federal Managers' Financial Integrity Act, P.L. 97-255, 96 Stat. 814 (1982); Accounting and Auditing Act, ch. 946, Title I, 64 Stat. 834 (1950).

5. T.J. Cuny, The Pending Revolution in Federal Accounting Standards, *Public Budgeting & Finance* 15 (Fall 1995): 22–24.

6. Chief Financial Officers Act, P.L. 101-576, 104 Stat. 2838 (1990).

7. U.S. General Accounting Office, *Financial Management: Status of the CFO Act Implementation at the Department of Treasury* (Washington, DC: U.S. Government Printing Office, 1994).

8. U.S. Office of Management and Budget and Chief Financial Officers Council, *Federal Financial Management Status Report and Five-Year Plan* (Washington, DC: U.S. Government Printing Office, 1996).

9. L.R. Jones and J.L. McCaffery, Federal Financial Management Reform and the Chief Financial Officers Act, *Public Budgeting & Finance* 12 (Winter 1992): 75–86.

10. R.N. Anthony, The FASAB's Dilemma, *Government Accountants Journal* 44 (Spring 1996): 31–39.

11. Government Finance Officers Association, *Governmental Accounting, Auditing, and Financial Reporting* (Chicago: Government Finance Officers Association, 1994).

12. Government Finance Officers Association: http://www.gfoa.org; accessed December 1997.

13. Price Waterhouse, Press Release: Coopers & Lybrand, Price Waterhouse to Merge, September 18, 1997: http://www.pw.com/newsflash.htm; accessed December 1997; Ernst & Young and KPMG to combine, October 20, 1997: http://www.eyi.com; accessed December 1997.

14. OMB and CFO Council, *Federal Financial Management Status Report and Five-Year Plan*, 5; U.S. General Accounting Office, *Financial Management: DOC Inventory of Financial Management Systems Incomplete* (Washington, DC: U.S. Government Printing Office, 1997).

15. Governmental Accounting Standards Board, *Codification of Governmental Accounting and Financial Reporting Standards* (Norwalk, CT: Governmental Accounting Standards Board, published biennially).

16. Government Finance Officers Association, *The GAAFR Review Guide to GASB Pronouncements* (Chicago: Government Finance Officers Association, 1996).

17. A.A. Hayes, Jr., Fraud Happens: A Primer on Lying, Cheating, and Stealing, *Government Finance Review* 11 (December 1995): 7–11.

18. U.S. General Accounting Office, *The Accounting Profession: Major Issues, Progress and Concerns* (Washington, DC: U.S. Government Printing Office, 1996), 60–80.

19. Norvelle, *Introduction to Fund Accounting*, 16–18.

20. U.S. General Accounting Office, *Government Corporations: Profiles of Recent Proposals* (Washington, DC: U.S. Government Printing Office, 1995).

21. Standard Government Ledger: http://www.fms.treas.gov/sglhome.html; accessed December 1997.

22. H.I. Steinberg, Financial Management in the Federal Government: A Five-Year Progress Report, *Government Accountants Journal* 44 (Fall 1995): 39–45.

23. Norvelle, *Introduction to Fund Accounting*, 43.

24. U.S. General Accounting Office, *Compendium of Budget Accounts: Fiscal Year 1998* (Washington, DC: U.S. Government Printing Office, 1997).

25. Cuny, The Pending Revolution in Federal Accounting Standards.

26. U.S. General Accounting Office, *Budget Object Classifications: Origins and Recent Trends* (Washington, DC: U.S. Government Printing Office, 1994).

27. U.S. General Accounting Office, *Budget Function Classification: Relating Agency Spending and Personnel Levels to Budget Function* (Washington, DC: U.S. Government Printing Office, 1995).

28. R.D. Lee, Jr., A Quarter Century of State Budgeting Practices, *Public Administration Review* 57 (1997): 133–140.

29. J. Harris, Service Efforts and Accomplishments Standards: Fundamental Questions of an Emerging Concept, *Public Budgeting & Finance* 15 (Winter 1995): 18–37.

30. Governmental Accounting Standards Board, *Concept Statement No. 2: Service Efforts and Accomplishments Reporting* (Norwalk, CT: Governmental Accounting Standards Board, 1994).

31. Chief Financial Officers Act, P.L. 101-576, 104 Stat. 2838 (1990).

32. Government Performance and Results Act, P.L. 103-62, 107 Stat. 285 (1993).

33. L.R. Jones, Counterpoint Essay: Nine Reasons Why the CFO Act May Not Achieve Its Objectives, *Public Budgeting & Finance* 13 (Spring 1993): 87–94.

34. F.S. Redburn, How Should the Government Measure Spending: The Uses of Accrual Accounting, *Public Administration Review* 53 (1993): 228–236.

35. S.J. Gauthier, Implementation of the New Measurement Focus and Basis of Accounting (MFBA) for Governmental Funds, *Government Finance Review* 8 (June 1992): 37–38.

36. C.T. Horngren and G. Foster, *Cost Accounting: A Managerial Emphasis*, 9th ed. (Englewood Cliffs, NJ: Prentice-Hall, 1996).

37. D.R. Geiger, The Emerging Need for Managerial Cost Accounting, *Government Accountants Journal* 44 (Fall 1995): 46–52.

38. W.K. Simpson and M.J. Williams, Activity-Based Costing, Management, and Budgeting, *Government Accountants Journal* 44 (Spring 1996): 26–28.

39. C.K. Coe and E. O'Sullivan, Accounting for the Hidden Costs: A National Study of Internal Service Funds and Other Indirect Costing Methods in Municipal Governments, *Public Administration Review* 53 (1993): 59–63.

40. J.F. Rodriguez, The Usefulness of Cost Accounting in the Federal Government, *Government Accountants Journal* 44 (Spring 1995): 31–35.

41. National Defense Authorization Act for Fiscal Year 1996, Title XLIII, P.L. 104-106, 110 Stat. 186 (1996).

42. U.S. Office of Management and Budget, *Circular A-131: Value Engineering* (1993): http://www.whitehouse.gov/WH/EOP/OMB/html/circulars/a131/a131.html; accessed December 1997.

43. M. Ives, A Fresh Look at Capital Asset Accounting: The New FASAB Proposals, *Government Accountants Journal* 44 (Summer 1995): 24–29; U.S. General Accounting Office, *Budget Issues: The Role of Depreciation in Budgeting for Certain Federal Investments* (Washington, DC: U.S. Government Printing Office, 1995).

44. Lee, A Quarter Century of State Budgeting Practices.

45. U.S. General Accounting Office, *Cost Accounting Standards Board: Little Progress Made in Resolving Important Issues* (Washington, DC: U.S. Government Printing Office, 1994).

46. U.S. General Accounting Office, *Credit Reform: Speculative Savings Used to Offset Current Spending Increase Budget Uncertainty* (Washington, DC: U.S. Government Printing Office, 1994).

47. E.B. Atwood, Sr., Proposed New GASB Standard for Accounting and Reporting for Investments, *Government Finance Review* 12 (June 1996): 55.

48. Governmental Accounting Standards Board, *Technical Bulletin No. 94-1, Disclosures about Derivatives and Similar Debt and Investment Transactions* (Norwalk, CT: Governmental Accounting Standards Board, 1994); G.J. Miller and B.B. Stanko, Disclosure of Financial Instrument Risk by Government Entities, *Government Accountants Journal* 44 (Fall 1995): 29–38.

49. J.D. Beeler and W.A. Morehead, Unfunded Mandates: Federal Regulations, GASB Statement 18 and One State's Response, *Government Accountants Journal* 44 (Spring 1995): 11–16.

50. Federal Credit Reform Act, P.L. 101-508, Title XIII, 104 Stat. 1388-610 (1990).

51. U.S. General Accounting Office, *Financial Management: Federal Entities with Treasury and Federal Financing Bank Borrowing Authority* (Washington, DC: U.S. Government Printing Office, 1992).

52. M. Phaup, Credit Reform, Negative Subsidies, and FHA, *Public Budgeting & Finance* 16 (Spring 1996): 23–36.

53. U.S. General Accounting Office, *Federal Credit Programs: Agencies Had Serious Problems Meeting Credit Reform Accounting Requirements* (Washington, DC: U.S. Government Printing Office, 1993).

54. U.S. Congressional Budget Office, *Who Pays and When? An Assessment of Generational Accounting* (Washington, DC: U.S. Government Printing Office, 1995).

55. B.R. Hennessy and F.P. Daroca, Popular Annual Financial Reports: Current Trends and Future Prospects, *Government Finance Review* 9 (February 1993): 7–13; G. Sanders, E.M. Berman, and J.P. West, Municipal Government Financial Reporting: Administrative and Ethical Climate, *Public Budgeting & Finance* 14 (Summer 1994): 65–78.

56. Governmental Accounting Standards Board, *Codification of Governmental Accounting and Financial Reporting Systems.*

57. W.J. Cox, Jr., Interfund Transfers: A Credit Perspective, *Government Finance Review* 10 (June 1994): 24–25; T.J. Stumm and A. Khan, Effects of Utility Enterprise Fund Subsidization on Municipal Taxes and Expenditures, *State and Local Government Review* 28 (1996): 103–115.

58. J.L. Esser, GASB's Implementation of the New Measurement Focus and Basis of Accounting, *Government Finance Review* 8 (June 1992): 3.

59. G.R. Smith, Jr., and R.J. Freeman, Statement of Cash Flows: The Direct vs. Indirect Method, *Government Finance Review* 12 (February 1996): 17–21.

60. Government Finance Officers Association, *A Preparer's Guide to Note Disclosures* (Chicago: Government Finance Officers Association, 1996).

61. Governmental Accounting Standards Board, *The Governmental Financial Reporting Model: Core Financial Statements*, preliminary views (Norwalk, CT: Governmental Accounting Standards Board, 1995).

62. S. Gauthier, Reporting Model Proposal, *Government Finance Review* 11 (October 1995): 42–43; M. Ives, GASB's Reporting Proposal: Are Two Measurements Better Than One? *Government Accountants Journal* 44 (Fall 1995): 9–16.

63. Government Management Reform Act, P.L. 103-356, 108 Stat. 3410 (1994).

64. A.C. West and D. Clarke, Government as a Business: Five Years Out, Is the CFO Act Working?, *Government Accountants Journal* 44 (Spring 1996): 20–25.

65. Government Management Reform Act of 1995; see OMB and CFO Council, *Federal Financial Management Status Report and Five-Year Plan.*

66. U.S. General Accounting Office, *The Accounting Profession.*

67. Government Finance Officers Association, *Governmental Accounting, Auditing, and Financial Reporting*, 314.

68. Charles A. Bowsher, Comptroller General, *Financial Management: Momentum Must Be Sustained To Achieve the Reform Goals of the Chief Financial Officers Act* (Washington, DC: U.S. Government Printing Office, 1995), 6.

69. U.S. General Accounting Office, *Federal Research: System for Reimbursing Universities' Indirect Costs Should Be Reevaluated* (Washington, DC: U.S. Government Printing Office, 1992);

L. Culter, Can the Single Audit Be Applied to Medicaid?, *Government Accountants Journal* 44 (Spring 1995): 48–54.

70. L.P. Bailey, *Miller GAAS Guide: College Edition, 1994* (Orlando, FL: Dryden Press, 1993).

71. U.S. General Accounting Office, *Government Auditing Standards* (Washington, DC: U.S. Government Printing Office, issued periodically).

72. R.J. Elder, S.C. Kattelus, and D.D. Ward, A Comparison of Finance Officer and Auditor Assessments of Municipal Internal Control, *Public Budgeting and Financial Management* 7 (1995): 336–350.

73. Inspector General Act, P.L. 95-452, 92 Stat. 110 (1978).

74. U.S. General Accounting Office, *Inspectors General: Handling of Allegations Against Senior OIG Officials* (Washington, DC: U.S. Government Printing Office, 1996).

75. M.A. Rubin, Municipal Selection of a State or External Auditor for Financial Statement Audits, *Journal of Accounting and Public Policy* 11 (1992): 155–178.

76. H.M. Nix and D. Nix, The Audit Oversight Function in Municipalities of Greater Than 100,000 Population, *Government Accountants Journal* 45 (Fall 1996): 32–38.

77. U.S. General Accounting Office, *Defense Contract Audits: Current Organizational Relationships and Responsibilities* (Washington, DC: U.S. Government Printing Office, 1991).

78. Federal Managers' Financial Integrity Act, P.L. 97-225, 96 Stat. 814 (1982).

79. Federal Financial Management Improvement Act, P.L. 104-208, 110 Stat. 3009-389 (1996).

80. P. Babachicos et al., Why Performance Audits Preceding Scandals Were Ignored, *Government Accountants Journal* 44 (Spring 1996): 13–18.

81. American Institute of Certified Public Accountants, *Audits of State and Local Governmental Units* (New York: American Institute of Certified Public Accountants, issued periodically).

82. Single Audit Act, P.L. 98-502, 98 Stat. 2327 (1984); Single Audit Act Amendments, P.L. 104-156, 110 Stat. 1396 (1996).

83. G.J. Miller and R.P. VanDaniker, Impact of the Single Audit Act on the Financial Management of State and Local Governments, *Government Accountants Journal* 44 (Spring 1995): 55–63.

84. R.C. Brooks and D.P. Pariser, Audit Recommendation Follow-Up Systems: A Survey of the States, *Public Budgeting & Finance* 15 (Spring 1995): 72–83.

85. National Information Infrastructure Advisory Council, *Common Ground: Fundamental Principles for the National Information Infrastructure* (Washington, DC: National Information Infrastructure Advisory Council, 1995).

86. S.J. Ventura, The Use of Geographic Information Systems in Local Government, *Public Administration Review* 55 (1995): 461–467.

87. J.B. Hokanson, Planning and Financing Infrastructure Using GIS Technology, *Government Finance Review* 10 (August 1994): 19–21.

88. U.S. General Accounting Office, *Tax Systems Modernization: Cyberfile Project Was Poorly Planned and Managed* (Washington, DC: U.S. Government Printing Office, 1996).

89. OMB and CFO Council, *Federal Financial Management Status Report and Five-Year Plan.*

90. M.J. Richter, A Guide to Networking, *Governing* 8 (July 1995): 75, 79–81, 84, 87–89.

91. D.F. Norris, Mainframe and PC Computing in American Cities: Myths and Realities, *Public Administration Review* 56 (1996): 568–576.

92. Lee, A Quarter Century of State Budgeting Practices.

93. S. Peterson et al., Computerizing Accounting Systems in Developing Bureaucracies: Lessons from Kenya, *Public Budgeting & Finance* 16 (Winter 1996): 45–58.

94. K.J. Merz and J. Rosen, eds., *The Handbook of Investment Technology: A State-of-the-Art Guide to Selection, Implementation, and Utilization* (Burr Ridge, IL: Irwin Professional Publishing, 1997); R. Sandlin, *Manager's Guide to Purchasing an Information System* (Washington, DC: International City/County Management Association, 1996); U.S. General Accounting Office, *Assessing Risks and Returns: A Guide for Evaluating Federal Agencies' IT Investment Decision-Making* (Washington, DC: U.S. Government Printing Office, 1997).

95. W. Cats-Baril and R. Thompson, Managing Information Technology Projects in the Public Sector, *Public Administration Review* 55 (1995): 559–566.

96. C. Mahtesian, Low-Bid Hazards in a High-Tech World, *Governing* 8 (March 1994): 64–67, 70.

97. Information Technology Management Reform Act, P.L. 104-106, 110 Stat. 679 (1996); U.S. General Accounting Office, *Information Technology Investment: A Governmentwide Overview* (Washington, DC: U.S. Government Printing Office, 1995).

98. G. Munoz, The Year 2000: Defining the Government Solution, *Government Finance Review* 12 (August 1996): 34–35; E. Perlman, Techno-Terror 2000, *Governing* 9 (September 1996): 22–24, 26; U.S. General Accounting Office, *Year 2000 Computing Crisis: An Assessment Guide* (Washington, DC: U.S. Government Printing Office, 1997).

99. A.M. Schoenbach, MAX Decision System (Presentation at the annual conference of Association for Budgeting and Financial Management, Washington, DC, October 1995).

100. M.J. Richter, Managing Government's Documents, *Governing* 8 (April 1995): 59, 62–64, 66; U.S. General Accounting Office, *Tax Systems Modernization: Imaging System's Performance Improving But Still Falls Short of Expectations* (Washington, DC: U.S. Government Printing Office, 1997).

101. P. Zorn, Use of On-Line Technology: A GFOA/MBIA Survey, *Government Finance Review* 12 (August 1996): 28–30; R.W. Wiggns, Webolution: The Evolution of the Revolutionary World-Wide Web, *Internet World* 6 (April 1995): 33, 36–38.

102. Freedom of Information Act, P.L. 89-487, 80 Stat. 250 (1966); Privacy Act, P.L. 93-579, 88 Stat. 1896 (1974).

103. Computer Security Act, P.L. 100-235, 101 Stat. 1724 (1987).

104. R. Miranda and N. Hillman, Reengineering Financial Management: Pittsburgh's Unisource 2000 Project, *Government Finance Review* (August 1995): 7–10.

105. J.N. Danzinger et al., Enhancing the Quality of Computing Service: Technology, Structure, and People, *Public Administration Review* 53 (1993): 161–169.

106. Z. Nedovic-Budic and D.R. Godschalk, Human Factors in Adoption of Geographic Information Systems, *Public Administration Review* 56 (1996): 554–567.

107. G. Melloan, Global View: Where Is the Information Technology Payoff?, *Wall Street Journal Interactive Edition,* August 11, 1997.

CHAPTER **12**

Financial Management: Capital Budgeting and Debt

Every year, governments spend resources on the construction of facilities or the purchase of equipment that will continue in use for many years beyond the year of purchase. The construction of a new water treatment plant will serve a community for decades, although the actual construction itself may take less than two years. In addition, during the construction phase, the construction costs could equal a large portion of a small community's total budget. Because of the large outlay required in one time period, many communities elect to finance the construction costs over a long period by borrowing or, in fewer instances, by putting aside resources for several years in a capital reserve fund until there is a sufficient amount to pay for the facility.

By constructing the water treatment plant, the community has acquired a capital facility that will operate for perhaps 30 years or more. It has purchased an asset. This chapter focuses on the decision to purchase that asset and related decisions on whether and how to finance that asset through borrowing. We examine in this chapter both the rationale for public sector capital budgeting and the general form of capital budgeting processes. Second, since state and local governments finance much of their capital spending through borrowing, we examine the various types of bonds and other debt instruments. The chapter concludes with a discussion of debt capacity and debt management. We defer discussion of federal borrowing, which is largely unrelated to capital investments, to Chapter 15.

CAPITAL PLANNING, BUDGETING, AND ASSET MANAGEMENT

In this section we define capital and capital investments, discuss the reasons for considering capital spending separately from operating budgets, describe the general form for a capital investment planning and budgeting process, and discuss the issues involved in separating capital from operating budgets. We focus mainly on state and local governments. Although there is much discussion in annual federal budgets of investments and capital expenditures, the federal government, as discussed below, has resisted developing and using a capital budget, or a formal capital budgeting process.

Capital Investments Versus Current Expenditures

Capital Investments. The purchase or construction of a long-lasting physical asset is a capital investment. For a business, the investment typically means acquiring new productive capacity that will increase the business's output in the future. Many public sector physical assets also represent investment in the ability to provide more or higher-quality services in the future. However, public sector assets differ in important respects from private sector assets. In conventional private sector accounting, assets have the capacity to generate future revenues for the enterprise, whereas public sector assets typically do not have as a primary purpose the generation of future revenues.

A limited, accounting-based definition of assets is too restrictive for purposes of public sector budgeting. While a government facility that provides a service to citizens, such as a wastewater treatment plant, may not have as an objective generating future revenues, the facility once built does provide a continuing service through many future years. In that sense, an expenditure on a facility that will provide benefits for many years after its construction is an investment. The fiscal year (FY) 1998 budget for the federal government defined investments as ". . . spending that yields long-term benefits. . . . It can be for physical capital, which yields a stream of services over a period of years. . . ."[1] This investment aspect helps explain why many governments, like businesses, distinguish capital expenditures from current expenditures and have capital budgeting processes, in addition to budgeting processes for current (operating) expenditures.

For governments, it is useful to distinguish among three types of investments. First, a government may purchase physical assets for its own use over many years in the future—assets such as office buildings and machinery. Second, governments may make investments in physical facilities that enhance private economic development, for example, roads and water systems. Third, governments may invest in intangibles, such as education and research. Capital budgeting processes may assist in deciding how much of each type of investment is necessary, although only physical facility investments typically are included in formal capital budgets.

With or without a formal capital budget, focusing some attention on the investment component of a government budget is politically useful because it draws attention to the fact that many public spending programs build for the future. It also reminds citizens that public assets, like highways, may deteriorate to the point of uselessness if not regularly rehabilitated. For example, the federal budget for FY 1998 showed annual investment needs of $42.8 billion (in 1993 dollars) just to maintain federally supported highways at 1993 conditions and performance levels; $127.1 billion (1992 dollars) in sewage treatment facilities; and $29.7 billion for airport development investments.[2]

State and local governments also stress the importance of public capital investment in stimulating economic growth. Massachusetts used public debt issues in 1995 to finance over $400 million in repairs in transportation in order to compete economically with other states that tout their infrastructure facilities.[3] Palm Bay, Florida, found itself in trouble finishing a wastewater treatment facility when the private firm who was to own and operate the facility declared bankruptcy.[4] The city was counting on the facility to convince businesses that the city was committed to supporting development.

Sometimes it becomes difficult to draw the line between investment and noninvestment. The federal budget's definition of investment is very broad, including education, research, and development expenditures, but still it does not include many other elements that it logically could. For example, mental health programs, programs for juveniles, and family counseling programs may be considered investments that help prevent future social and economic problems. A major rationale for the Supplemental Feeding Program for Women, Infants and Children is that the investment in health helps prevent some future federal expenditures for Medicaid.

While it is useful to think of government expenditures in terms of investment or consumption, for budgeting purposes the distinction is more often in terms of capital versus current or operating expenditures. Capital expenditures differ from current expenditures, and some governments therefore distinguish between capital and current budgets.

Physical Nature and Time Duration. Businesses think of capital expenditures as the purchase of physical assets that will be used over a period of several years. Public sector capital expenditures likewise involve the purchase of physical assets whose use extends over a number of years.

Examples of capital expenditures are easy to find. A school building is physically present and will last for many years. On the other hand, paper, pens, pencils, and staples, although physical, are used up and have to be purchased anew each year. The purchase of the building is easy to classify as a capital expenditure and the purchase of the supplies as a current expenditure. Similarly, water mains extending from a treatment plant to neighborhood lines have a physical presence and will serve for many years. Their construction is a capital expenditure. But chemicals used in the water treatment process will be used up and will need to be purchased again and again. Purchase of these chemicals is an operating or current expenditure.

Classification Problems. These examples illustrate that capital expenditures normally are purchases of physical assets that have a long life. Other examples, however, show that the distinction between capital and current is sometimes ambiguous. A big-city police department may purchase more than 50 vehicles a year, and most of these may replace vehicles purchased the previous year. That city may classify the purchase of those police cars as a current expenditure. A small town may purchase two police cars of the same type as the big city's but expect those two cars to last for three to five years. The small town probably would consider purchase of the police cars a capital expenditure.

Even within the same city, some classification problems occur. Books and periodicals bought for a library are expected to be used for many years, and their purchase can be treated as a capital investment. On the other hand, purchase of a periodical by a department of public works, if the periodical has a short useful life, would be an operating expense.

Every government and every business establishes some kind of arbitrary cutoff point that distinguishes current from capital expenditures. In most cases, the cutoff is a combination of the size of the expenditure and the useful life of the asset. Purchase of anything expected to be consumed (or destroyed) during one year normally will be a current expenditure, no matter how large it is. In addition, small expenditures, even for goods that will last several years, also are classified as current. But the size of the government's budget usually determines how small is small. A small town may classify expenditures under $1,000 as current regardless of the useful life. A larger city may use $25,000 as a cutoff—below that, anything is a current expenditure regardless of useful life. One survey found that the threshold for an investment being capital was $1,000 in Utah, but $150,000 in Mississippi.[5] Although some purchases may be classified arbitrarily one way or the other, what constitutes a capital purchase and what constitutes a current one usually is not controversial.

Capital Versus Current Decisions

Separate Capital Budgets. The size of the expenditure and its investment quality distinguish a capital expenditure from a current one. A third distinction, the method of financing the expenditure, leads most state governments and a majority of local governments to pay at least some separate attention to capital expenditures in the annual budget decision-making process. Forty states and over 60 percent of city and county governments have some form of capital improvement plans and/or budgets.[6]

Table 12–1 shows state and local capital expenditures for 1993 as a proportion of total expenditures. Considering only direct capital outlays, about 11 percent of state and local expenditures are for capital purposes. The actual expenditures do not tell the whole story, however, since most of the capital outlays are financed by borrowing and hence have interest costs. With interest included, the figure is closer to 17 percent. Local government capital outlays are a slightly higher proportion of total outlays than state government outlays, 19 percent and 13 percent, respectively. However, these gross percentages obscure the real nature of the decisions to undertake the capital projects. Capital expenditures cluster in only a few government functions. For local governments, of the $86 billion in direct capital outlays in 1993, about $22 billion was for school construction and about $14 billion was for utility capital outlays. The remainder was clustered in roads, sewage, water, and housing construction.

State government capital outlays also cluster in only a few functional categories, and decisions made in one year affect future-year budgets. Of the $50 billion in direct state government capital outlays in 1993, a majority went to highway construction. That level of capital construction implies significant future-year expenditures for highway maintenance. In addition to the $28 billion in new cap-

Table 12–1 Direct Capital Outlays as a Proportion of Total Outlays, by Level of Government, 1993 (in Billions of Dollars)

Government	Total Direct Outlays[a]	Capital Outlays	Capital as Percentage of Total	Interest on Debt[b]	Combined Capital Outlays[c]	Combined Capital as Percentage of Total
All	2,572	221	9	264	485	19
Federal	1,365	85	6	199	85	6
State and Local	1,207	136	11	66	202	17
State	529	50	9	25	75	14
Local	678	86	13	40	126	19

[a]Outlays shown exclude duplicative intergovernmental transfers so that the figures shown are for the level of government making the expenditure even if the source of finance is a transfer from another level of government.

[b]Only interest on general debt and interest on utilities' borrowing is included here.

[c]For state and local governments, interest on general debt plus interest on utility borrowing is attributed in this table to borrowing for capital investment. Federal debt is not considered borrowing for capital investments.

Source: Reprinted from *Statistical Abstract of the United States: 1996*, p. 298, 1997, U.S. Bureau of the Census.

ital spending, state government 1993 current operating expenditures for highways were just over $14 billion, a direct consequence of prior years' capital spending decisions.[7]

Separate Capital Budgeting Processes. These examples demonstrate that decisions about capital spending at the state and local levels are consequential in the year they are made and can have major consequences for future budgets. As discussed in previous chapters, particularly Chapters 5 and 6, it is difficult to incorporate a long-run perspective into budget decisions, especially when the decisions tend to focus on personnel expenditures and only on the current-year implications of starting new programs. The fact that current-year capital budget decisions have significant implications for future operations and maintenance suggests that the effects of capital decisions on future operating budgets must be taken into account in any capital budgeting process. For state and local governments, the logic of having some kind of process for examining capital spending decisions in more detail seems compelling. That does not necessarily entail separate capital budgets, however. In the next section, we illustrate a general approach to capital investment planning and budgeting that satisfies both the requirement to examine capital decisions in more detail and the requirement to consider implications for future-year operating budgets.

Capital Investment Planning

Multiyear Capital Investment Plans. Many governments that distinguish between capital and current budget decisions have an established process for developing a multiyear capital investment plan (CIP) and incorporating elements of that plan into a capital budget.[8] Five years is a common period for projecting capital expenditures, although a longer period is often included in the statements of long-range programs. For example, the Orange County (North Carolina) Water and Sewer Authority distinguishes between its 15-year capital improvements plan and its five-year capital improvements budget.[9] The long-range plan focuses on the expected needs for water supply and sewage treatment for the next decade and a half, while the capital improvements budget includes detailed cost estimates only for the next five years.

Asset Management. Long-term CIPs may be a part of a larger program of asset management. Concern for the condition of America's deteriorating infrastructure base emerged in the early 1980s. Throughout that decade, spectacular incidents, such as the collapse of the Mianus Bridge in Connecticut, and detailed studies of investment deficits heightened attention to the need to rebuild and maintain the nation's physical infrastructure assets.[10] By the middle of the next decade, the value of the nation's infrastructure base that was being depreciated or retired annually was over $110 billion; in one sense, that would be the amount of infrastructure spending needed just to maintain the existing level of infrastructure assets.[11]

The nation's physical infrastructure asset base is primarily because of state and local government investments. As far back as the mid-1950s, state and local capital spending greatly exceeded federal capital spending. In 1956, state and local capital spending on infrastructure amounted to almost $28 billion, whereas federal capital spending was less than $10 billion. A gradual climb in federal spending led to its overtaking state and local capital spending in 1976, and it remained higher until significant federal budget cutbacks affected capital spending in 1986.[12] Figure 12–1 illustrates the pattern for public works facilities specifically, including highways, airports, water transport and terminals, sewage, solid waste, water supply, and mass transit.

Figure 12–1 gives some indication of the relative roles of federal, state, and local governments in public works funding. The figures for federal, state and local are for all direct spending, both capital investments and maintenance and rehabilitation. By far, local governments exceed both federal and state combined. The federal grants figure shows the contribution the federal government makes, for non-defense capital investments only, through intergovernmental grant transfers. Federal grants for physical capital investment peaked in 1980 at $40 billion. Budget estimates show these investments declining out to 2007 as part of the balanced budget program.[13]

Some state and local governments have adopted elaborate systems for assessing the condition of capital assets and linking these "inventories" with the capital planning and budgeting process. Dallas, Texas; King County, Washington; and

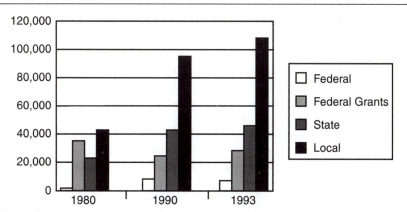

Figure 12–1 Federal, State, and Local Roles in Public Works Funding, 1980–1993, Selected Years. *Source:* Data from *Statistical Abstract of the United States: 1996*, p. 299, 1997, U.S. Bureau of the Census; *Budget of the United States Government: Fiscal Year 1998, Analytical Perspectives*, p. 127, U.S. Office of Management and Budget.

Milwaukee, Wisconsin, for example, have systems of varying sophistication for measuring street conditions and maintaining an updated inventory.[14] Cities throughout developing countries that have underinvested in both maintenance and reconstruction of such critical urban infrastructure assets as paved roadways, water systems, and drainage also have begun to develop more complete systems for taking inventory of existing assets and developing CIPs based on a schedule of needed improvements.[15] These innovations in public sector asset management have begun to alter the way some cities plan, budget, and manage their finances—capital planning and budgeting are now playing a more important role.

Practices vary considerably from city to city, but it is possible to outline a general format for a capital investment planning process. One such model for capital investment planning and budgeting, linked to an inventory of existing facilities, consists of eight steps, which are discussed below (see Exhibit 12–1).

Identifying Present Service Characteristics. The first step is to make an inventory of existing physical or infrastructure facilities and to assess the services provided. For a state or local government that has not previously conducted an inventory, this first step is neither simple nor inexpensive, although maintaining the inventory once established need not be burdensome. Such an inventory involves listing all physical facilities and elements of the physical infrastructure and such related information as date of construction, date of last major rehabilitation, type of construction material (such as type of road surface), and, where relevant, characteristics such as size and capacity. For a building, information may be collected on electrical wiring, fiber optics for computer hookups, plumbing, and elevators.

Quantity of service includes such characteristics as the number of people served, the proportion of total population served, the geographic area covered (area, density, and spatial distribution), and various socioeconomic groupings related to coverage, such as number of clients served by a facility. Different quantity measures are appropriate for different services.

Quality of service in part is a function of the level or the type of service provided. For example, water treatment systems that remove only bacteriological contaminants are qualitatively less effective than those that remove toxins and heavy metals as well as bacteria. Quality also may be indicated by such things as the age of the facility and its condition. The latter may be measured by the frequency-of-repair record. Qualitative measures of service, including records of citizens' complaints and structured citizen satisfaction surveys, are as appropriate as quantitative measures.

Identifying Environmental Trends. The second step looks toward the future. Most city and state governments develop long-range planning forecasts to estimate future service requirements. These forecasts, which project population growth, commercial and industrial growth, demographic and economic changes,

Exhibit 12–1 Capital Facilities Planning and Budgeting

1. Identify present service characteristics (inventory facilities and service levels)
   a. Coverage (quantity)
   b. Quality
   c. Cost per unit of service (efficiency)
2. Identify environmental trends
   a. Population growth projections
   b. Changing regulatory environment
   c. Employment and economic development trends
3. Develop service objectives
   a. Extension of service to new population or area (coverage)
   b. Improvement in quality of service
   c. Opportunities to stimulate economic growth
4. Develop preliminary list of capital projects and cost estimates
   a. Rehabilitation of existing facilities
   b. Replacement of existing facilities
   c. Addition of new facilities
5. Identify financial resources
   a. External assistance
   b. Projected growth in present revenue base
   c. Potential for direct cost recovery for individual projects
   d. Use of credit
6. Select subset of projects for inclusion in five-year capital investment plan (CIP)
7. Identify future recurrent cost impact of CIP on operating budget
8. Include first year of CIP in annual budget estimate

and so forth, are linked to the capital facilities planning process in order to develop plans for required service expansion or contraction. In addition, more detailed analyses of trends in business locations may predict possible shortages or other problems in critical areas, such as the water supply. The capital facilities planning process can provide a means for the jurisdiction to plan expansion of services in an orderly way and can help convince potential investors that the jurisdiction is anticipating future business and residential requirements.[16]

Developing Service Objectives. The process of defining the need for capital investments can take numerous forms. Representation on long-range planning groups, open forums to discuss the need for community facilities, and referendums to approve a specific bond issue to finance a capital investment (see next section) are typical means for generating citizen input.[17] Even in jurisdictions with established channels for citizen input, a special group often convenes every two to three years just to review the current CIP and establish new priorities.[18] Thus a key step is to determine the service objectives that capital investments will need to satisfy.

Preliminary Listing of Capital Projects and Cost Estimates. Based on the service objectives established in the previous step, a preliminary list of capital projects can be developed, along with a timetable for completing the projects. Typically, the preliminary list includes the rehabilitation of existing facilities to improve the quality and/or efficiency of service; the replacement of existing facilities, also for the purpose of improving quality and efficiency; and the addition of new facilities or expansion of existing facilities to meet expansion objectives. The preliminary list typically will not be screened for financial feasibility at this stage.

Identifying Financial Resources. The fifth step, identifying the financial resources potentially available to carry out the preliminary list of capital projects, involves analyzing the jurisdiction's overall financial condition and some of the individual capital projects for possible sources of financing specific to them. Since the 1980s, an important aspect of overall financial management has been the evaluation of the financial condition of local governments.[19] In the wake of public pressure to hold steady or to cut back state and local taxes, major new revenue initiatives in the form of tax increases often are not possible, even when the need to build up infrastructure and rehabilitate existing facilities is obvious. However, because of the expansion of tax bases, making long-range projections of tax yield increases and assessing the performance of other ordinary revenue sources sometimes reveal potential revenues that will be available at some point in the future for capital investment financing.

More commonly, however, state and local governments, particularly the latter, rely increasingly on revenue sources specific to individual capital projects. User fees and property assessments traditionally have been used to finance the major portion of water and other utility capital investments as well as operating expenses. More recently, cities have exacted special impact fees and other charges from residential and commercial developers to pay for roads, water, and sewer lines and drainage intended to serve new developments[20] (see Chapter 4).

Other sources of revenues tied to particular projects include grants from other levels of government and borrowing (typically involving the issuance of bonds). Although federal funding cutbacks were significant starting in the early 1980s, state aid to local governments has in some cases made up for some of the federal cutbacks, and federal funds are still available on a more limited programmatic basis (see Chapter 14).

Selecting Projects for Inclusion in Five-Year Capital Investment Plan. Step 6 involves matching available financial resources with the set of projects included in the preliminary investment plan. Steps 3 through 6 may be iterated to eventually narrow down the list of projects and select a feasible set. Re-evaluation of desired service objectives sometimes is necessary during this iterative process, because financial realities can make it clear that some objectives are impossible without major new financial initiatives. For most state and municipal governments, the application of complex analytical tools such as cost-benefit analysis or rate-of-return analysis plays only a small role in the selection of projects. Further, there is substantial disagreement over the validity of estimates of economic benefits from investments in infrastructure.[21] Instead, the ranking of priorities is often based on the principle that replacing deteriorated facilities should be the first concern, meeting population growth requirements should be the second, and improving quality of services should be the last.

Identifying Implications for Future Recurrent Costs. Decision makers frequently neglect considering the recurrent cost implications of capital investments. It is sometimes difficult to anticipate the costs of keeping a facility operating, and the usually valuable public relations aspects of a new project tend to overshadow the longer-run impact on the general fund's budget. The problem is exaggerated by the fact that the operating and maintenance costs of any new project or facility are lower in the early years of operation, and the heavier costs fall outside the range of normal five-year capital planning cycles. Without an analysis that takes into account this fact, a state or local jurisdiction may find itself 10 or 20 years down the road facing the dilemma of either forgoing new capital investments because of the need to budget greater funds for maintenance or neglecting maintenance in favor of politically more popular capital projects.[22]

The analysis of future operation and maintenance costs is not all negative. If the analysis of the current capital facilities base in step 1 has been carried out well, the jurisdiction will have an idea of the present operation and maintenance costs of existing facilities. Replacing some facilities that require expensive maintenance expenditures may produce significant reductions in operation and maintenance costs in the operating budget.

Including First Year of the Capital Investment Plan in the Annual Budget. Once a feasible set of investments has been selected and the short- and long-term costs have been determined, the next (and last) step is to incorporate the first year of the CIP in the annual budget. To this point, the process, which has been one of planning and programming, may have involved input from the legislative body, but no legal appropriation of funds will have taken place. Some jurisdictions submit the CIP to the legislative body (state legislature, city council, etc.) for formal approval, but the CIP does not necessarily include actual appropriation of funds. Some states appropriate the full costs of capital projects, at least smaller projects, whereas other states appropriate only the annual costs of each project. In the latter case, only a single year's cost actually shows up in the appropriation act.

Evaluation of Capital Budgeting

Much of the argument over the value of capital budgeting at state and local government levels hinges on whether there should be a separate capital budgeting process. There is little argument over the need to examine the full long-term implications of capital spending and not just focus on a single budget year. But it is possible to have a comprehensive capital planning process that concludes with a capital budget plan or statement without a separate capital budgeting process. The amount the city council or state legislature is then asked to appropriate may be for only one year, but the budget request is made in the context of future-year requirements.

Pros and Cons of Separate Capital Budgeting. Capital budgets and statements indicate the extent to which investments are being made with current expenditures. From a political perspective, this gives capital budgets a certain value, since government officials can show citizens that government funds are being used for the acquisition of useful assets and not solely for the payment of bureaucrats' salaries.

On the negative side, capital budgeting can encourage political logrolling, in which various political interests agree to help each other. A capital budget can be a political grab bag, a fund in which every interest can find a project. A state capital budget may provide highway projects in every county, even though real need is concentrated in a small number of counties. In providing everyone with something, some important needs will not be met while less pressing needs will be. Furthermore, if capital costs are presented in a completely separate budget, particularly when financed by borrowing, it may appear as if capital decisions are "costless" in the current year.

On balance, however, the arguments in favor of special attention to capital spending, at least at the state and local level, seem overwhelming. While capital budget decisions are no less political than other budget decisions, the logic of focusing attention on long-run financial and economic consequences of spending or failing to spend for capital facilities is compelling. More than current operating budget decisions, decisions to invest in infrastructure help shape the future direction, location, and extent of private economic investments in the community. Local governments' capital investments may in some cases play a leading role in encouraging future local economic development (see Chapter 15). State and local governments compete for location of major facilities, and they some-times offer large incentive packages comprising infrastructure projects and finan-cial assistance to induce private companies or federal agencies to locate facilities in their jurisdictions.

Once built, major facilities largely will be limited to the uses for which they were designed; inadequate planning of facilities can result in inadequate services, major financial burdens, or the need for expensive alterations. Excess capacity built into a community sewer system cannot be converted into other uses. Too lit-tle acquisition of land for parks in a rapidly growing suburban area may later result in a shortage of recreational opportunities or may force the local govern-ment to pay far more for space than it might have earlier. These arguments do not entail that capital budgets need to be separate from operating budgets. In fact, they suggest the opposite. While capital spending requires attention to some issues that are not germane to operating budgets, capital and operating expendi-tures are inevitably related.

Federal Capital Budgeting. For the federal government, the logic of capital budgeting is less compelling. First, much of the "capital" side of the federal bud-get goes toward defense acquisitions—72 percent in the 1998 budget proposal. These are not investments in the same sense as state and local expenditures for water systems or highways. This does not mean that the purchase of nuclear-powered aircraft carriers, for example, has no implications for future operations and maintenance. But the need to replace a weapons system often is generated, not by its wearing out, but by its inability to cope with new offensive or defensive systems of a potential enemy.

Furthermore, the federal government may undertake many non-defense capital expenditures more for macroeconomic policy reasons than for investment pur-poses. Because of the federal government's role in stimulating the economy, cap-ital spending sometimes has the primary objective of assisting a state or local economy rather than providing a needed facility. Federal grants to state and local governments for non-defense physical capital exceeded $40 billion in 1996.[23] Unfortunately, this use of capital spending often leads to pork barrel decisions that place expensive projects in every congressional district.

There have been periodic calls for federal capital budgeting. At the time the unified budget was adopted at the recommendation of the 1967 President's Com-mission on Budget Concepts, a capital budget for the federal government was again rejected.[24] There was a resurgence of calls for capital budgeting at the fed-eral level in the 1980s. In response to General Accounting Office (GAO) recom-mendations, the federal budget for FY 1996 for the first time used as part of the *Analytical Perspectives* chapter on investment spending a capital budget presen-tation.[25] Table 12–2 is the capital budget table from the FY 1998 budget.

Table 12–2 Capital, Operating, and Unified Budget Concepts, United States Government, Fiscal Year 1998 (in Billions of Dollars)

Operating Budget	
Receipts	1536
Expenses	
Depreciation	77
Other	1567
Subtotal, expenses	1644
Surplus or deficit (–)	–108
Capital Budget	
Income	
Depreciation	77
Earmarked tax receipts	31
Subtotal, income	108
Capital Expenditures	121
Surplus or deficit (–)	–12
Unified Budget	
Receipts	1567
Outlays	1687
Surplus or deficit (–)	–121

Source: Reprinted from *Budget of the United States Government: Fiscal Year 1998, Analytical Perspectives*, p. 135, U.S. Office of Management and Budget.

GAO and others argue that the federal government must adopt more contemporary financial management practices to improve the efficiency of government operations. Federal management practices are inadequate to the task of achieving efficiency or effectiveness in government operations. This does not mean that GAO is in favor of a separate federal capital budget, but that much more systematic attention must be given to physical capital investments, to the value of those assets, and to their management.[26]

The second cause for renewed interest in federal capital budgeting is the concern that the nation is not investing sufficiently in basic infrastructure, to the long-run detriment of the economy. Legislation in 1984 established the National Council on Public Works Improvement and gave it the mandate to assess the state of the nation's capital infrastructure and make recommendations for improvement. The council's 1988 report concluded that infrastructure outlays should increase by 100 percent.[27] Further reports by associations of state and local governments, the Office of Technology Assessment, and researchers have continued to state the case that the nation's infrastructure base is eroding and the level of investment is woefully inadequate.[28]

Many of those concerned that the level of investment in infrastructure is too low argue that the federal budget is biased against such capital investments because it must show the full cost of the outlays in the construction years instead of showing only the annual depreciation of the investments over their long life.[29] A capital budgeting statement might show only one year's depreciation value in the current year budget, spreading the budget implications of such an investment over the expected years of benefits. This approach would more clearly isolate how much of the federal deficit is due to investments that will pay for themselves through future economic growth and might reduce some concern for the size of the deficit.

Developing a federal capital budget would not be simple. The sample capital and operating budget shown in Table 12–2 was developed by the Office of Management and Budget (OMB) with considerable estimation required to determine depreciation values. In addition, what should count as investments in a capital statement is controversial, because as discussed previously, one can make a case for including many government expenditures for programs, such as education and health programs, that do not produce any physical asset, but do produce future benefits. But all program advocates would want their programs included in the capital or investment budget, because only the annual amortized value of those programs would appear as an outlay. Carried to an extreme, the budget might shrink to a small proportion of its present size, covering only obviously current consumption expenditures. Yet the actual cash requirements of the federal government would not have changed.

The debate over federal capital budgeting, meaning a separate capital budget, has subsided. Congress, the Congressional Budget Office, OMB, and the White House in the Clinton administration have all agreed that federal budget analysis must include more focus on investment and the implications of federal investment decisions. Much more extensive attention is being given in the annual budget documents to both investment decisions and to the role of the federal government in developing and maintaining part of the national asset base.

A second defeat of the balanced budget amendment in 1997 also reduced the pressure for distinguishing in a formal budget between capital and current expenditures. A constitutional requirement to balance the budget would make a separate capital budget much more appealing. By including only the single year's depreciation of physical capital assets, plus operating costs, instead of the full cost of construction in the first year, the budget deficit that needs to be covered by spending reductions or revenue increases would be reduced. However, the government's cash flow requirements would not have changed, and for this reason none of the major federal budget participants recommend a formal, separate capital budget.

STATE AND LOCAL BOND FINANCING

State and local governments issue bonds to finance many types of public facilities and infrastructure. Commonly referred to as municipal bonds, bonds are issued by state and local general purpose jurisdictions as well as many nonprofit public institutions, such as hospitals, and single-service authorities, such as school and water districts. The exemption from federal taxes of the interest earned from many of these bonds is a critical feature of their success and a controversial one.

The two main categories of long-term bonds are *full faith and credit* bonds (or *general obligation* bonds) and *nonguaranteed* bonds. Full faith and credit debt is guaranteed by the general revenues of the issuing jurisdiction without regard to the purpose of the expenditures or the potential for direct cost recovery through user charges. Full faith and credit debt thus is considered guaranteed in that the full resources of the jurisdiction are pledged as security to potential investors. Nonguaranteed bonds do not have the full backing of the issuing jurisdiction's resources.

Traditionally, municipalities and local utilities issued bonds in a fairly local market with the main purchasers being banks. Bonds issued were mostly plain vanilla. A general purpose municipal government or school district almost always issued a general obligation bond, backed by the jurisdiction, mainly by property tax proceeds. The water and other utilities issued *nonguaranteed revenue* bonds backed by the future revenue streams from user charges. Local or nearby banks bought most of the issue. These conditions have changed radically. The number of different instruments for debt, while still falling within the two general categories, has increased dramatically, and banks are no longer the largest holders of municipal debt.

For example, in 1996 the City of New York issued a $215 million bond backed solely by expected revenues from collection of delinquent taxes on commercial property. The city sold the property liens to a trustee who in turn issued the bonds, contracted with private parties to collect the delinquent taxes, and returned to New York the difference between amounts required to pay off bondholders and the total collected. This earned the bond issue *Governing* magazine's rating as one of the best municipal bond deals of the year.[30] Although the first major tax lien–backed bond, this issue is only an example of the innovations in municipal bond finance.

Table 12–3 demonstrates the other major change in the municipal bond market—the shift from commercial banks to households as the predominant holders

Table 12–3 Holders of Municipal Debt: 1940–1996 (in Billions of Dollars)

	1940	1950	1960	1970	1980	1985	1990	1996
Commercial Banks	3.6	7.4	16.8	61.2	152.4	231.7	117.4	92.7
Households	NA	NA	NA	NA	129.1	348.2	572.1	441.5

Note: NA, not available.

Source: Data from P.C. Wong, *Role of Private Financial Institutions in the Development of Local Infrastructure in Thailand,* p. 23, 1995, U.S. Agency for International Development; E. Roy, Outstanding Municipal Debt Falls to Lowest Level Since 1991, Fed Says, *The Bond Buyer,* Vol. 318, p. 27, © 1996.

of municipal bonds. Although data on households' municipal debt holdings are incomplete for the earlier years, the reversal between commercial banks and households as the primary investors in municipal debt is striking.

Municipal bonds are debt instruments in that the issuer incurs an obligation to repay and the buyer becomes a lender with a claim on future repayments. The buyer, however, has no claim on the assets of the issuer. Equity ownership, such as is purchased with corporate stocks, is not a feature of municipal bonds. Private equity ownership is a feature of *build-operate-transfer* and *build-operate-own* forms of private financing of public infrastructure facilities (see Chapter 4), but the main form of state and local capital financing is likely to continue to be issuance of municipal bonds.

Importance of Bond Financing for Infrastructure

Debt Financing Versus Pay-as-You-Go. State and local governments finance a major portion of their capital investment spending through long-term debt instruments. In 1995, state and local governments together issued $156 billion in new long-term debt. $60 billion was in the form of general obligation bonds and $96 billion in the form of revenue bonds.[31] Most state constitutions or statutes limit the issuance of long-term debt for both state and local governments to capital investment–type expenditures. Bond financing for infrastructure allows governments to build roads and bridges, schools, hospitals, water and wastewater systems, and numerous other major capital facilities before sufficient capital has been accumulated to pay for these facilities, in much the same way an ordinary consumer often borrows to finance the purchase of a home. The difference between bond financing and a consumer loan is that state and local governments issue debt instruments called bonds that are sold to various investors, giving the government issuing the bonds the cash to build the infrastructure facility and giving the bond purchaser a claim on that government for future repayment of both the borrowed amount and interest.

Some local governments try to avoid indebtedness as much as possible and work on a pay-as-you-go system, which means saving funds in advance until there is cash sufficient to build the infrastructure facility. These governments are like the car buyer who saves money until there are enough funds in the bank to purchase the car for cash. The motivations are similar: Both the government and the consumer avoid the interest costs for borrowing. If the jurisdiction can afford to wait for the facility or can plan far enough in advance to have the funds available when needed, then the prospect of financing without interest costs is attractive. Indeed, as the government is saving funds, it can invest them in interest-earning opportunities, which are becoming increasingly sophisticated for government investors.

Pay-as-you-go local governments tend to be smaller jurisdictions with relatively stable annual capital investment requirements. For example, if a small local government generally needs to spend about $500,000 per year on capital facilities and goods and that is a stable expenditure requirement, over time it will need to spend that same amount, plus interest, each year in debt repayment if it borrows for the capital facilities. So if the jurisdiction can plan far enough ahead or can afford to wait for the facility, by establishing a *capital investment sinking fund* the jurisdiction can accumulate the funds necessary to meet the annual $500,000 per year capital spending requirement. This does not work as well for larger jurisdictions, which tend to have less predictable requirements, and it does not work well for lumpy investment patterns, that is, where large amounts are needed in some years for big construction projects and smaller amounts in other years. Some form of credit financing for most state and local jurisdictions is a necessity.

Role of the Tax System and State and Local Bond Financing. A key reason for the attractiveness of bond financing for state and local government capital borrowing is that federal tax law exempts from the federal income tax interest earned by purchasers of many government bonds. In addition, most states with income taxes also exempt interest earnings from state or local bonds for government entities within that state. This means that an individual who purchases state or municipal bonds retains the interest earnings tax-free in most cases. For individuals in the highest tax bracket, earning 6 percent interest on a municipal bond is equal to earning over 9 percent taxable interest. Because the tax exemption for interest earnings attracts investors to the state and municipal bond market, a ready source of capital for infrastructure financing exists for government. And the tax-exempt status of the earnings enables jurisdictions to offer bonds at lower interest rates than they could get borrowing from commercial lenders or issuing taxable debt securities. Tax exemption for the interest earnings on bonds, then, is the cornerstone of the U.S. system for financing public infrastructure for state and local governments.

Tax-exempt status is somewhat controversial, however. A wave of expansion in use of tax-exempt bonds to finance industrial development parks, incubator facilities to woo private developers to invest in local areas, and a wide variety of other essentially private endeavors led to significant curbs on state and local governments' authority to issue tax-exempt bonds in the Tax Reform Act of 1986 (TRA86) (private purpose bonds are discussed in more detail in a following section). Other features of that tax reform also made municipal bonds a much less attractive investment for commercial banks, accounting in part for the trend noted in Table 12–3.[32]

Concern for equity in taxation leads some to question whether interest on government and certain nonprofit bonds should be exempt. It is generally thought that mostly higher-income taxpayers benefit from this exemption, as they are the most likely purchasers of tax-exempt bonds, and therefore this exemption unfairly benefits those who can most afford to pay higher taxes. The growth of mutual funds in which middle-class individuals are making more and more investments is mitigating this equity argument.

Challenges to the general philosophy of granting tax-exempt status are unlikely to eliminate this fundamental feature of state and local finance in the United States. On the other hand, it is likely that the federal government will increase regulations regarding the issuance of tax-exempt bonds. The state of South Carolina challenged the constitutionality of any federal regulation of state governments' tax-exempt debt issuance in the 1988 *South Carolina v. Baker* case, questioning a law that denied tax-exempt status to bearer bonds (as opposed to registered bonds; see discussion of bond features later in this chapter).[33] The Supreme Court ruled that the Tenth Amendment did not prohibit federal regulation of state and local governments and that there is no constitutional right to state and local immunity from federal tax provisions.[34]

Types of Bonds

General Obligation Bonds and Nonguaranteed Bonds. Since general obligation (full faith and credit) bonds typically are considered safer investments than nonguaranteed bonds because of the full backing of the jurisdiction's resources, these bonds typically carry lower interest rates than nonguaranteed bonds. The interest rate is critical in large bond issues, for a difference of 0.1 percent can affect total interest payments by millions of dollars. However, revenue bonds from a well-managed special purpose authority, such as a water district, with an excellent record of previous borrowing is likely to have a lower interest rate than a general obligation bond from a municipality with a declining property tax base and low personal income. For this reason, bonds not backed by the general revenue resources of a state or local government have become much more common.

In addition, state limitations on general tax revenues, such as Proposition 13 in California, have forced state and local governments to favor revenue bonds over general obligation bonds.

Nonguaranteed debt generally is restricted to the revenue earnings of the specific facility created by the investment. Many sources are used to repay these so-called nonguaranteed bonds. In the case of revenue bonds, the most common type, charges to users generate the funds necessary to repay the loans. Other sources include special assessments, in which the properties affected by an investment are assessed charges, for example, property owners might be assessed charges for sewer installations.

Revenue Bonds. Revenue bonds pledging the revenue from a specific tax or fee have the advantage of placing the burden for financing a facility on those who will use it. For example, using the parking fees from a parking garage to finance its construction places the burden on those who park in the garage. From an intergovernmental perspective, the revenue bond device forces nonresidents who use the parking garage or the highways to pay their fair share regardless of where they reside.

A recent financial invention to finance airport facilities—the pledge of specific charges for use of the airport facility collected from the airlines through increments to the ticket price—is an example of increasingly innovative ways to use revenue bonds to finance facilities. Airport operators (special authorities, municipalities who own the airport) apply to the Federal Aviation Administration to add a few dollars to the price of the ticket of passengers departing from or terminating their flight at the airport. Lansing, Michigan, and Little Rock, Arkansas, both have financed major expansions and renovations through this device.[35]

Tax Increment Financing Bonds. Tax increment bonds combine features of revenue bonds and general obligation bonds. They are used to finance local economic development by pledging future increases in property taxes of areas targeted for development or redevelopment.[36] A city may decide to redevelop an area of the inner city through construction of housing or commercial facilities and may issue a bond to finance the redevelopment. Since the redevelopment will not directly generate revenues, it is not suitable for revenue bond financing. On the other hand, the city may not wish to obligate its full resources to repay the bonds, may be at state debt-limit ceilings for full faith and credit bonds, or may wish to confine the repayment obligations to the direct beneficiaries of the redevelopment. A tax increment financing bond will back up the debt issue with the pledge of increased property tax revenue from the area being developed (the property taxes will rise because the property in the redevelopment area will become more valuable).

Private Purpose Bonds. Starting in the early 1980s, considerable use was made of state and local bonds to finance private construction and ownership of facilities that were then leased back to government entities. Similar use has been made of government bonds for lease and subsequent purchase of privately constructed facilities. In some cases, government bonds have been issued to finance a facility that then is leased to or purchased by the private sector. This last device often has been used to finance industrial development facilities, such as industrial parks and incubator facilities to help small businesses get started. State or local bonds issued for these largely private purposes were quite popular because the interest on the bonds was tax exempt. In 1985, more than half of a record volume in municipal debt issues was for these private purpose activities.[37] This large volume was prompted by legislation under consideration to remove tax-exempt status from this type of bond.

TRA86 contained several provisions to limit tax exemptions. Interest earned on general purpose bonds for construction of facilities or infrastructure to provide essential services remain tax exempt. Private activity bonds for construction of facilities such as airports, docks and wharves, hazardous waste treatment plants, and water supply facilities also retain their tax-exempt status, although the interest is included in the alternative minimum tax base. The law removed the tax-exempt status of bonds for construction of industrial parks, parking garages, sports facilities, and convention or trade show facilities. In addition, each state and its local governments are limited in the amount of private purpose bonds that can be issued in a year, and interest on any otherwise qualified bond issue is subject to tax if the bond issue exceeds the state cap. Since 1986 there has been a fall-off in the issuance of private purpose bonds. Some states, however, issue private purpose bonds to finance facilities tied to economic development promotion, such as industrial parks, considering the economic development benefit is worth the higher-cost, taxable bond.

Municipal Minibonds. Most purchasers of municipal bonds are large purchase investors, including financial institutions that develop tax-exempt investment funds that then may be purchased by both large and small investors. But generally it is harder for all but higher-income individuals to get directly involved in purchasing bonds from their own jurisdiction because purchases often involve minimum amounts of $10,000 or more. Some cities, however, have begun issuing bonds in smaller denominations. For example, in 1990 Denver, Colorado, issued $5.9 million in $1,000 denomination bonds.[38] The minibonds were issued directly by the city without an underwriter (see discussion below on bond issuance), and purchase was possible only by Colorado residents. Almost 2,000 citizens purchased more than twice the amount initially expected. While not appropriate for large-scale bond issues, because it becomes uneconomical to sell and track bonds in small denominations, minibonds have proved popular for financing smaller projects that especially interest local residents.

Certificates of Participation. One form of municipal debt issuance that is not legally classified as debt is the use of certificates of participation. Especially popular in California with its severe restrictions on the ability of local governments to borrow, certificates of participation are municipal debt issues to construct facilities that will be operated by private contractors. The government leases the facility from the private operator and the lease payments are used to retire the debt (principal plus interest) from the debt issue. Increasingly popular, certificates of participation can be risky investments. A school district in California (Richmond County Unified) and Brevard County, Florida, provide two examples where the governmental entity was in the first case financially unable to make the lease payments and in the second case unwilling to make payments, for a time, because of dissatisfaction with the facility.[39] Richmond County Unified School District subsequently defaulted on the lease payments due on the facility built via the certificates of participation debt issue.

State Revolving Funds. In use for decades now, state governments are making increasing use of institutions created to assist local governments obtain better terms for debt financing. The most common form is the *revolving fund*, but other forms include the state bond bank. A revolving fund is created with some initial capitalization, often grants from the federal government plus state government bond issues, to lend to municipal borrowers.[40] The premise is that the state government can get better credit ratings both because of better financial condition and because it can issue debt in larger amounts than individual small local governments. Repayments from the local governments who borrow from the fund keep the capitalization intact, allowing lending and borrowing to continue on a revolving basis.

A bond bank is a variant on the same idea. The state bond bank may pool the borrowing needs of numerous, smaller municipal borrowers into a single state bond issue, and then finance the individual borrowers' requirements from the proceeds of the single state issue. Some state bond banks issue bonds to capitalize a fund for lending; then it is a form of revolving fund. Others accumulate individual municipalities' borrowing needs until a sufficiently large amount is reached and then issue a single bond to meet those specific needs. This is usually called a *bond bank*.

Many of the state revolving funds and bond banks are used to finance federally mandated water and sewer system improvements. One survey found that about 24 percent of municipal sewer authorities/agencies are financed through state revolving funds; this accounted in 1993 for about 8 percent of the funds raised by sewer agencies.[41] 1995 federal legislation—the National Highway System Designation Act—created a pilot program to provide federal grant funding to capitalize state infrastructure banks to finance transportation projects. States were allowed to deposit up to 10 percent of their federal highway transfers into the funds, and in FY 1997, the Department of Transportation's appropriation provided $150 million for capital grants to the pilot states.[42]

Overall, the use of bonds to finance state and local investments continues to increase as state and local financial conditions improve and federal transfers to assist state and local governments decrease. The distinction between general obligation bonds and limited revenue bonds is less important in practice than the financial condition of the borrowing entity. In fact, many water utilities and other users of more limited revenue bonds are in better financial shape than states and general purpose local governments.

Bond Issuance Process

The process of issuing municipal bonds involves numerous steps, and the number of participants in these steps is quite large. Exhibit 12–2 lists the major

Exhibit 12–2 Participants in the Municipal Bond Market

Issuers:	General purpose municipalities, counties, and states; special purpose governmental entities such as school districts and water authorities; and unique public service entities such as airports and transportation terminals.
Financial Advisers:	Finance specialists increasingly used by bond issuers to structure features of the issue to increase attractiveness to borrowers and/or to address a special need of the issuer—features such as issuer options to call the bond before maturity and structuring debt retirement to match cash flow circumstances of the issuer.
Bond Counsel:	Legal advisors to offer legal opinion on the legal authority of the issuer to borrow, on the tax-exempt status of the issue, and the legal obligation of the issuer to repay.
Dealers (Underwriters):	Investment firms, banks, and other financial institutions licensed to trade in municipal securities who sell the issuers' bonds.
Trustee:	Institution that serves mainly bondholders by securing from the issuers bond repayment cash flows and paying out to bondholders when due.
Investors:	Individuals, investment banks, commercial banks, and other financial institutions.

participants, ignoring some of the minor players, for example, the role of bond printers. More detail on the main actors in the bond issuance process is included in the subsections on the major steps.

With as many steps and participants in the process, the costs to the issuing jurisdiction can be high. Numerous legal steps must be followed, numerous documents must be prepared, and numerous transactions with various financial and legal institutions must occur—transactions that require considerable personnel time or the purchase of consulting services. A comprehensive study of the costs associated with the steps discussed in this section found that total costs ranged from a little less than 0.5 percent to just over 1.5 percent of the total value of the bond issue for larger issues.[43] The specific costs of financial advisory services alone range from 0.4 to 0.5 percent added to the borrowing cost (usually referred to as 40 to 50 basis points; 100 basis points equal 1 percent).[44] The percentages are higher for smaller issues generally, because some of the costs are relatively fixed.

Voter Approval. In many states, a general obligation or full faith and credit bond requires a referendum to secure voter approval. Revenue bonds and other forms of limited obligation financing generally do not require voter approval. In some cases, to avoid state limitations on general municipal borrowing, cities have established nonprofit building authorities to issue bonds and construct facilities, as discussed above. Such facilities are then rented to the municipality, and the rental payments secure the bond principal and interest. These special authorities, because they do not legally obligate in a direct way the general revenues of the municipality, can issue bonds without voter approval and without the debt counting as part of the municipality's overall debt. Of course, the source of funds used by the municipality to pay for renting the facility is in fact the general revenue fund.

Underwriting. Typically, the authority issuing a bond will secure the services of an underwriter, whose role is to arrange the actual sale of bonds to financial institutions. The top five municipal bond underwriting firms in 1996 were Goldman, Sachs & Co., Smith Barney Inc., Merrill Lynch & Co., PaineWebber Inc., and Lehman Brothers.[45] Individuals, banks, insurance companies, and bond funds invest in state and local bonds. Legal counsel retained by the issuing authority provides a legal opinion on the status of the issue, the legal authority to issue the bond, and the tax-exempt status of the bond.

Public Sale Versus Negotiated Sale. Historically, bonds have been offered for public sale, with purchasers such as larger financial institutions, who might be purchasing for their own portfolio or for resale, effectively determining the interest rate by their offers. A public sale is initiated by a widely published official notice of sale. The notice of sale typically includes information such as the denomination of bonds, bid conditions and requirements, and provisions for payment. More detailed information is provided in what is known as the *bond prospectus*. Sealed bids are submitted by interested institutional investors, brokerage firms, and even individuals, although individuals typically purchase through intermediaries. The issuing jurisdiction then is free to accept the lowest bid interest rate or reject the bid according to the terms and conditions of sale. Jurisdictions with good ratings prefer this method, as they are likely to attract numerous bidders and thus be able to choose lower interest rates.[46]

Becoming increasingly common, however, is the negotiated sale. Negotiated sales are conducted between investment banks and the issuing government. The underwriter acts as a broker between the issuing jurisdiction and the investment community.[47] If the issuer thinks the rates quoted by potential buyers are too high, the issuer is free to reject the bids, as in a public sale. A key advantage of a negotiated sale is that the bond issue can be spread over a period of time. If the interest rates in bids are high but the issuer cannot postpone the project, the issuer may sell only a portion of the total issue to start the project while the underwriter continues to seek additional bids.[48] One disadvantage of negotiated sales is that some investors, including some pension funds, cannot purchase state or municipal securities except through public sale. Overall, negotiated sales seem to cost about 30 basis points more than competitive bids.[49]

Bond Features. Bonds differ from each other in a variety of ways.[50] Some bonds, called *term bonds,* may be due and payable to the investors on a single date. *Serial bonds* are due on a specific schedule of payments over a number of years. In recent years, serial bonds have largely replaced term bonds, in part because of statutory prohibitions against term bonds. Investors holding term bonds obviously must be concerned with whether a jurisdiction is annually setting aside sufficient funds to be able to repay its debt.

Another difference is between *coupon* and *registered bonds*. Coupon bonds have coupons attached indicating the bond's maturity date and the amount of payment. Whoever presents the mature coupons receives payment. Registered bonds require that the owner register with the government issuing the bonds. The advantage of a coupon bond is that it is easily transferred from one owner to another, whereas a registered bond offers protection against loss or destruction of the bond itself. States and municipalities prefer coupon bonds because the issuing jurisdiction is not responsible for keeping records of the purchasers. However, a provision of the Tax Equity and Fiscal Responsibility Act of 1982 requires that state and municipal bonds be registered to retain their tax-exempt status, and that requirement was upheld in *South Carolina v. Baker*. As a consequence, the use of coupon bonds has all but disappeared, although state and local governments continue to lobby for federal legislation that would permit issuing nonregistered bonds that are tax exempt.

Another feature of bond sales is *discounting*. A bond is discounted when it is sold at some fraction of its face value. For example, a $10,000 bond may be sold for $9,800. It is thus discounted below par. When it matures and principal is payable, the investor will receive $10,000 in return for the $9,800 investment in addition to the interest payments the investor would have been receiving over the years. At times, a bond may actually be sold at a premium over its par value. This can happen when a bond whose fixed interest rate was set in a period of high interest rates is available for sale after interest rates have fallen. A potential new investor will be attracted to the higher interest rate bond, but the seller has less incentive to sell the bond because of the low return of other choices now available on the market. So the seller charges the new investor, say, $10,200 for a bond that will repay principal of only $10,000 at maturity. The bond investor must consider both the selling value—discounted, at par, or at a premium—as well as the interest rate in determining the return on investment. The secondary market, in which bonds already sold once are resold to other investors, rarely has bonds that are sold at their face value. Conditions now are almost always different from the time of issue causing the bonds to be valued greater or lesser than their face value.

Bonds are becoming increasingly complex in the structure of their terms. Traditionally debt issuers were concerned primarily with the interest or coupon rate of the bond and the various costs of debt issuance, discussed above. Increasingly, however, issuers are incorporating detailed features, usually with the help of a financial advisory service, to vary the conditions of sale, the conditions in which the issuer may pay off the bond early, and variations in cash flows at different points in the life of the bond. Called *structured finance*, designing features into a bond issue unique to the cash flow characteristics of the borrower offers ways for issuers to tailor a bond issue to their specific situations.[51]

Zero Coupon Bonds. The typical municipal bond pays interest at specified points until the maturity date, when the principal is paid. There is growing use of what are called zero coupon bonds. The coupon rate, in finance terminology, is the interest rate the bond will pay. A zero coupon bond is one which pays out no interest until maturity, when both principal and interest are paid at once. Attractive to the issuer because it means there are no annual cash flow requirements, zero coupon bonds naturally require some incentive to attract investors away from the more typical municipal bond, which pays in regular installments through the years until maturity. The usual means of attracting investors to zero coupon bonds is to sell the bonds for much less than their stated value—to discount the bond from face value. Zero coupon bonds typically call for the issuer to set aside funds with a trustee, on a regular basis, sufficient to pay off the debt at time of maturity.

Interest Rates. Interest rates, of course, are one of the most critical elements of bonds for both the issuer and potential buyers. As a hedge against changing interest rates or financial condition, the state or municipal authority may sometimes use what is called a *call* feature. This means the authority may call or repay the bond in part or in full before the maturity date. The issuer can thus take advantage of falling interest rates by paying off all or part of the bond issue. Exercising this feature usually involves the payment of some premium. Callable bonds typically carry a higher rate of interest since investors would otherwise be less attracted to an investment that may be repaid sooner and therefore at a lower profit. A similar feature, which favors the bond buyer, is the *put* option, which allows the buyer, at specified intervals, to require paying off the bond. For this feature, the buyer agrees to specified discount rates at the different put options.

Variable interest rate municipal bonds have become common, just as variable rate financing has become standard in the financial industry. Many state and municipal issuers have taken advantage of variable rates both at the time of original issue and also to refinance bond indebtedness.

The actual interest the jurisdiction will have to pay on a bond issue depends on many factors related to the financial condition of the jurisdiction and the general market for other investments at the time of the issue. The tax-exempt status of the interest earned by state and local bonds means that the interest rate paid will be lower than comparably safe investments that do not enjoy tax-exempt status. If the jurisdiction has a good record of previous debt management, it will be perceived as a lower risk than one that has had trouble meeting its financial obligations. Likewise, if the jurisdiction is located in a good regional economy with low unemployment rates and a high tax base, it will be able to sell its bonds at lower interest rates. The issuing jurisdiction also will provide potential investors with information about other long-term obligations, including other debt and also unfunded pension liabilities (see Chapter 13). A reputation for good financial management is cited as evidence of credit worthiness.

Bond Ratings. Investors rely heavily on standard ratings provided by independent services, such as Duff & Phelps Credit Rating Co., Fitch Investors Service L.P., Moody's Investor Service, and Standard & Poor's Corporation. Standard and Poor's uses nine ratings, from AAA for the highest rating (best risk) to D for the worst risk. Only bonds rated BBB– and above are considered investment grade quality.[52] Moody's scale ranges from AAA to C in a similar fashion.

The importance of bond ratings is illustrated by a change from an AA– rating to an A–. One study of cities showed that the difference could be as much as 40 basis points, just under half a percent of interest per annum. This could mean as much as $1 million additional cost to the issuer of term bonds, totaling $10 million and paid over 25 years.[53] A downgrade in rating may come about because of the issuer's own investment practices, as in the case of the Orange County, California, bankruptcy (discussed below). State and local governments that invest their own funds, such as pension funds and short-term deposit instruments can have their borrower status downgraded if they invest too heavily in high-risk derivatives.[54]

Credit Enhancement. One of the devices state and local governments use to control costs of debt and debt issuance is insurance. In 1990, less than 30 percent of all new bond issues carried bond insurance; in 1996, over half of all new issues were insured.[55] New York City's debt crisis in the 1970s and the Washington Public Power Supply System (WPPSS) defaults in 1983 were among the big contributors to the growth of municipal bond insurance. Bond insurance serves to earn the issuer a AAA rating. Usually through the payment of a one-time premium, the bond issuer purchases the guarantee that principal and interest payments will be made and will be made on time. The difference between the insurance cost and the interest costs of an A-rated bond versus a AAA-rated bond is in the issuer's favor. If the rating without insurance would be below A, the costs of insurance likely will exceed the interest savings as the risk to the insurer requires a high premium.

Another type of credit enhancement is a *bank-issued line of credit*. The line of credit assures the bond buyer that the issuer will not be delayed in meeting payments even if short-term fluctuations in cash flow cause a temporary problem. The line of credit can be accessed if necessary to meet the short-term cash flow problem.[56]

In some developing countries, central governments provide credit enhancements for local government borrowing through the use of an intercept mechanism. The central government agrees to intercept, if necessary, a stable source of revenues that otherwise would flow to the borrower, such as a portion of central revenue transfers to local government. This intercept is paid to the lender in the event of default or delayed payment by the local government.

Bond Trustee. A typical municipal bond issue will have a specified institution serve as the trustee to handle all transactions with the ultimate buyers. The trustee's function is to see that the contract between issuer and buyer is faithfully executed. The trustee ensures that all legal requirements are followed and acts as the holder of annual interest payments due and payable. If a feature of the bond requires the jurisdiction to make regular payments into a *capital accumulation fund* (or *sinking fund*) in order to be able to repay principal, the trustee sees that these payments are in fact made and secured.

Disclosure and Regulation

Municipal bond issuance is subject to the general regulatory functions of the Securities and Exchange Commission (SEC), as are all other public debt and equity issues in the U.S. financial markets. For decades, municipal debt instruments were specifically exempt from SEC regulation, but beginning in the 1970s, Congress began to increase the role of the SEC in regulating municipal bond issues. SEC regulations focus on the underwriter's role and set disclosure requirements that affect the type and quality of information underwriters must provide potential investors.[57] Significant new disclosure rules were adopted in 1990 that pertain to the consistency and timeliness of an underwriter's release of information provided by the bond issuer. The quality of the information itself and all releases by the bond-issuing jurisdiction are still considered to be the jurisdiction's responsibility. The underwriter does not assume any liability properly borne by the issuer.

Amendments to the Securities Exchange Act created the Municipal Securities Rulemaking Board (MSRB) in 1975 in the wake of New York City's financial crisis and the revelation that some dealers in state and municipal securities were involved in unethical and "dangerous" conduct.[58] MSRB's authority extends only to dealers and others involved in municipal bond transactions, not to the actual issuing governments themselves. It is MSRB that functions under the general authority of the SEC to ensure that the disclosure information is as accurate and timely as possible. The MSRB requires bond dealers to file repository copies of all official documentation on a municipal bond issue in order to make the information more widely available to all potential investors. Another step is to make bond pricing information more widely accessible, requiring dealers to report daily both inter-dealer transactions and retail transactions in municipal bonds.

A large step in public disclosure imposing requirements on the issuing jurisdictions themselves has been the implementation of Nationally Recognized Municipal Securities Information Repositories; there are five including such financial services organizations as Bloomberg Financial Markets, Moody's Investor Services, and Standard & Poors. Municipal debt issuers must at least annually, and more often if conditions change, report on their financial condition.[59] This reporting requirement extends for as long as the issuer has outstanding debt in the market, providing potentially valuable information to subsequent secondary market purchasers of municipal securities.[60] Also municipal debt issuers are required to maintain and report regularly on their overall financial condition, not just on the status of specific debt issues.

The additional disclosure requirements have caused considerable consternation among many of the participants in the municipal bond market.[61] One particular requirement that securities dealers feel is too vague is the requirement that brokers and dealers must judge whether or not a client is capable of understanding the risk involved in an investment before they issue a recommendation to a client. However, the Orange County, California, financial fiasco (see below and

Chapter 10) has discouraged critics from attempting to reduce disclosure requirements of both issuers and dealers in the municipal securities market.

DEBT CAPACITY AND MANAGEMENT

Since the federal government borrows for purposes other than capital investment, we continue in this section to focus on state and local governments, reserving the topic of federal debt for Chapter 15. Media discussions of the federal debt and the size of the federal deficit raise citizens' consciousness of government debt, but locally people are asked officially to approve debt (bond issues) for financing everything from schools to new fire stations. More importantly, citizens are not given the opportunity to vote on an even larger component of state and local debt—debt that is issued by special authorities or that does not involve the pledge of full faith and credit of the jurisdiction. The questions to be addressed in this section involve how much debt can be managed safely and which debt management practices will ensure sound future financial condition.

Size of Debt

The size of debt can be assessed in several ways. The total amount of debt is probably the least meaningful measure. The fact that state and local governments' total outstanding debt at the end of 1996 was $1,292 billion, although this figure may sound staggering, is not really instructive. Interest payments on general debt in 1995 amounted to $47 billion, or only 5.2 percent of total state and local expenditures, and interest payments have remained relatively constant over recent years at about 5 percent of total expenditures.[62] Individuals commonly devote more than 5 percent of their total expenditures on interest payments for home mortgages, car loans, and credit card debt.

Per Capita Debt. Per capita debt figures help put the total government debt in perspective. How much per capita do state and local governments owe? They owed in 1993 $3,942 per person. Is that too much, too little, or just about right? Is it growing, declining, or remaining more or less stable? The latter question is easier to answer than the former. Figure 12–2 charts state and local per capita debt from 1970 through 1992. Per capita debt has risen both at the state and local government levels, with local debt rising somewhat more rapidly than state debt. In addition, the amount of increase in the five-year period 1980 to 1985 was almost equal to the rate of increase for the preceding 10-year period (1970 to 1980), and the period 1985 to 1990 witnessed an even faster rate of growth. However, the recent trend is a slower rate of growth. Thus, state and local debt is rising faster than population, but is that cause for alarm?

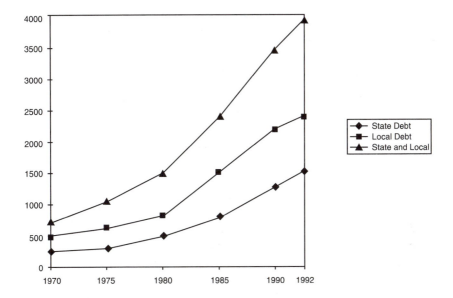

Figure 12–2 State and Local Debt per Capita, 1970–1992. *Source:* Data from *Statistical Abstract of the United States*, p. 274, 1985, U.S. Bureau of the Census; *Statistical Abstract of the United States*, pp. 287, 298, 1992, U.S. Bureau of the Census; and *Statistical Abstract of the United States*, p. 304, 1996, U.S. Bureau of the Census.

Ratio of Debt to Personal Income. Relating debt to personal income instead of population makes the picture begin to clear. Calculating total debt outstanding per $1,000 of personal income is one way of assessing whether debt is in danger of becoming an unreasonable economic burden. In 1992, state and local government debt per $1,000 in personal income was $184. These numbers are considerably less alarming. Over a 30-year period, combined state and local debt per $1,000 in personal income has remained very stable. Figure 12–3 charts this historical trend. State and local debt per $1,000 of personal income in the 1990s, although showing a trend toward increase after a 10-year decline from the 1970s through 1982, was no higher than the previous high of $205 back in 1972 and has even begun to decline in recent years.

Distribution of Debt

Ultimately, whether the size of state and local debt is reasonable is a subjective judgment. The main factors used in making such an appraisal are the financial bur-

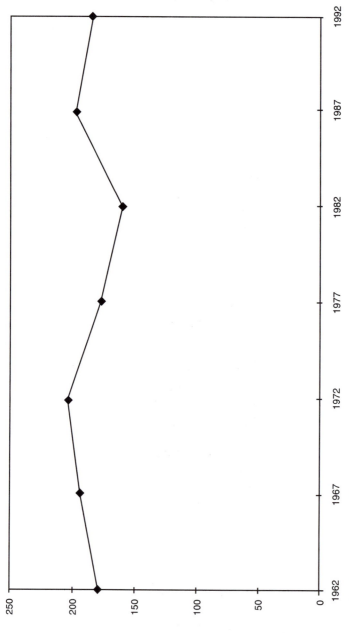

Figure 12–3 State and Local Debt per $1,000 Personal Income, 1962–1992. *Source:* Data from *Historical Statistics on Governmental Finances and Employment*, p. 113, 1984, U.S. Bureau of the Census; *Government Finances in 1985–86*, p. 3, 1988, U.S. Bureau of the Census; *Significant Features of Fiscal Federalism, Vol. 1: Revenues and Expenditures, 1992*, pp. 245 and 286, U.S. Advisory Commission on Intergovernmental Relations; *1992 Census of Governments, Vol. 4, Government Finances: No. 5, Compendium of Government Finances*, p. 152, 1996, U.S. Bureau of the Census.

den on individual taxpayers and the economy and the perceived value of the facilities and services purchased by the debt. Generally, debt varies somewhat with income and with the amount of state and local services. The state with the highest per capita debt in 1994, Alaska ($23,431), also was ranked fairly high—12th—in personal income per capita ($22,296).[63] Hence, Alaska presumably has the income level to support a higher debt (Alaska's high cost of living tends to inflate all of its statistics, of course). New York ranked second in per capita income and eighth in per capita debt. There is wide variation, however. Connecticut ranked first in per capita income and only 35th in per capita debt; California's debt and income was closely correlated, with a per capita income ranking of 14 and a debt ranking of 19.

Indebtedness is not distributed evenly among the various types of local government. Local authorities and special districts, including water and sewer authorities, school districts, and the like, account for the largest share of local debt issues—55 percent in 1995. Municipalities and townships account for another 30 percent of debt, followed by counties at 15 percent.[64]

Debt Default

It is important to remember that the figures on debt do not reflect the full scope of future financial obligations of governments. As will be seen in the following chapter, pension programs for public workers constitute a form of debt and often are inadequately funded. Debt defaults are correlated with economic cycles, but it also should be noted that there have been few defaults on state or local indebtedness since the Great Depression of the 1930s.[65] In that decade, about 4,800 state and local units defaulted on their obligations. While that number may seem large, the total number of governments then was 150,000. Most of the defaults involved small jurisdictions; less than 50 had populations more than 25,000.[66] Since that time, the number of defaults has been low.

In recent years, few public bond issuers have faced financial insolvency, although the exceptions have been noteworthy. In 1963, debt service payments on $100 million in revenue bonds for the Calumet Skyway in Chicago were interrupted.[67] In the mid-1970s, New York City came close to bankruptcy as a result of extensive borrowing to meet operating budget requirements and defaulting on some of its short-term debt. As a result, New York City was partially placed under the supervision of a financial control board (see Chapter 14). Only this intervention by the state government and the banking community prevented outright default on several bond issues. Also in the 1970s, Cleveland defaulted on just over $15 million in tax anticipation notes, largely because of poor financial management practices and inadequate accounting procedures.[68]

The largest failure has been the WPPSS. In 1983, after a more than decade-long program of construction of five nuclear power generating plants, WPPSS defaulted on over $2 billion in revenue bonds. The revenue bonds were issued in anticipation of the sale of electricity. WPPSS got caught in the situation faced by the power industry in many parts of the country in the 1970s—a combination of slower rates of growth in electricity demand, rapid escalation in the costs of nuclear power plant construction, and rising interest rates.[69] In 1993, WPPSS successfully issued $800 million in bonds to refund the debt.[70]

In reality, defaults by state and local governments recently have been far exceeded by failures of banks and savings and loan institutions, but periodic problems in the 1990s, headlined by the Orange County, California, financial collapse, keep the attention of both municipal bond market participants and the public. The financial collapse in both Bridgeport, Connecticut, and Cuyahoga County, Ohio, preceded Orange County, with Bridgeport attempting to declare bankruptcy, although the bankruptcy was not permitted by the courts. Cuyahoga County perhaps lost its place in history to Orange County, although they share some similarities. Neither got into trouble as a result of overextending debt. Both counties became mired in financial difficulties as a result of their investment activities with their own pension funds and other sources of cash, plus those of numerous other local governments for whom the counties acted as investment managers. Cuyahoga County lost $114 million on a $1.8 billion investment pool, but subsequently repaid most of the local government co-investors.[71]

Orange County, California, Bankruptcy. The bankruptcy of Orange County, California, set off shockwaves in the finance industry and in the press because it is so wealthy, no one imagined bankruptcy was even possible. The county was the investment manager for its own funds and almost 200 other local governmental units. At the high point, Orange County was investing over $7 billion. A high proportion of the investments were in *derivatives*, a hybrid form of financial instrument that depends on changes in the value of other financial instruments. In this case, Orange County invested in instruments that depended for their value on the interest rates on other instruments. In effect, Orange County was betting on a certain directional movement in interest rates—upward—and when interest rates fell, Orange County did not have cash in the pool sufficient to cover the funds invested. The strategy had been successful in previous years; the pool earned rates of return ranging from 7 percent to 9 percent from 1991 to 1994.[72] In late 1994, the county petitioned for bankruptcy under Chapter 9 of the U.S. Bankruptcy Code. Subsequently, the county defaulted on various taxable pension fund and taxable arbitrage notes.[73] Orange County then filed suits of its own against its former auditor KPMG Peat Marwick and the investment firm that managed most of the derivative and other investments, Merrill Lynch. Partly in continuation of trends toward increasing regulation of municipal debt and investment activities, and partly in response to Orange County's actions, the SEC has continued to increase its regulatory role, as discussed above.

Debt Capacity

Measuring Debt Capacity. Measuring debt capacity is an art rather than a science. In recent years, the public finance and budgeting profession has given considerably more attention to improving the level of the art. Three main factors influence debt capacity: expenditure pressures, resource availability, and the commitment of governmental officials to use resources to meet debt requirements.[74] Assessing resource availability involves analyzing all potential sources of revenue including own-source revenues; transfers from other levels of government; and types of self-financing including user charges, special assessments, impact fees, and a variety of other measures to collect fees or revenues sufficient to support the specific project or facility (see Chapter 4).

Expenditure analyses look at the present and potential future commitments of jurisdictions. Population growth, changing economic conditions, the state of the current capital facilities and infrastructure base, and the socioeconomic characteristics of the population are important influences on potential future expenditures. The willingness of lenders to purchase debt is reflected ultimately in the interest rate they will require to lend.

Revenue and expenditure analyses are used by state and local governments to support capital budgeting and debt management. Fiscal capacity analysis, focusing on the ability to generate revenues, and requirements analysis, focusing on expenditure needs, are used to determine present fiscal conditions and estimate future conditions. Against that backdrop, the financial requirements and budgetary impact of possible capital investments and debt financing alternatives can be assessed.

Debt Burden. The most common overall measure of debt burden is the ratio of debt to debt carrying capacity, which reflects the extent to which revenues are sufficient to cover debt service, in addition to operating expenses.[75] The World Bank often looks at the ratio of debt service to current revenues, the ratio of capital expenditures to total expenditures, and the excess of current revenues over ordinary operating expenditures as indicators of the ability of a city to incur additional debt. More refined measures focus not on actual revenues but on the revenue base itself. U.S. local governments commonly use the ratio of debt to the assessed value of taxable property, because that assessed value reflects a local government's basic ability to generate revenues. Beginning in 1962, the Advisory Commission on Intergovernmental Relations (ACIR) gradually developed a more sophisticated measure combining both tax capacity and tax effort, the latter being a measure of a state's willingness to tax.[76] These quick indicators are all useful, but ultimately they are interpretable only in the context of a jurisdiction's overall debt management strategy.

For enterprise-like operations, such as water authorities, conventional ratio measures of debt burden are in common use. The debt to equity ratio is a measure of the extent to which a utility is financing itself through debt relative to equity. The higher the ratio, the more risk there is in additional debt issues as lenders want to see borrowers also making significant commitment of their own resources (equity). Another common ratio—interest share of operating income—measures the amount of debt, as a percentage, that operating income has to cover.[77]

Debt Management. In general, sound debt management at the state and local levels involves restricting debt primarily to financing long-term investments. A general rule is that borrowing should not be used to meet current operating expenses. The much-publicized financial crisis experienced by New York City involved short-term borrowing to finance current expenses. Occasionally, short-term borrowing is used to deal with emergencies but often is refinanced as part of a long-term debt issue. Moreover, the payout period of the debt should correspond to the useful life of the facility or infrastructure financed.[78]

The rule to restrict debt to long-term capital financing does not apply to financial emergencies resulting from major flooding or unusually heavy snows during the winter, for example. But this rule, along with the rule to match the payout period for the debt with the expected life of the facility, should generally be followed. Adherence to these two rules ensures that the jurisdiction will more or less match the benefit flows from capital facilities with the opportunity costs (see Chapter 7 for more detailed discussion of cost and benefit streams and the concept of opportunity costs).

One of the major positive results of the financial difficulties of cities such as New York and the major cutbacks in federal aid in the 1980s has been an increase in the sophistication of the tools used in analyzing the financial condition of governments. Furthermore, state governments, in the last two decades, have become quite involved in regulating local government debt, not only by means of the more traditional statutory and constitutional provisions that govern the powers and authority of local governments but also by means of extensive state programs of technical assistance. Effective debt management requires the balancing of competing claims against the current annual budget and future annual budgets. As a consequence, state and local governments increasingly rely on methods to assess overall financial health and place potential bond issues in that context.

Debt Refinancing. State and local governments also have become more sophisticated in their transactions in the financial markets. One strategy in use is to swap the interest owed on outstanding bonds for more attractive interest rates. A traditional method for accomplishing that is to call in bonds that have higher interest rates when the market changes and rates have fallen. That is possible, of course, only with bonds having call features. An alternative that does not require any actual transaction with outstanding bonds is an interest rate swap. In this type of transaction, the borrowing authority agrees to pay a third-party financial investor a variable rate of interest over a fixed period of time in exchange for payment of a fixed rate of interest by the third party. This is a synthetic variable rate financing deal in that the bonds themselves remain as they were, with the terms and conditions unchanged.

The Port Authority of New York and New Jersey, for example, in 1991 entered into an agreement with a third party for a 10-year period during which the third party agreed to pay the authority at a fixed rate of 6.5 percent on a $10 million value. In return, the Port Authority agreed to pay the third party an indexed variable rate. The Port Authority felt, and initial experience bore them out, that the variable rate was likely to remain below the fixed 6.5-percent rate.[79] Subsequently, the Port Authority entered into a counter swap with the same third party, this time agreeing to pay the third party a fixed rate of 5.32 percent while receiving from the third party the indexed variable rate. What once had been $10 million in bonds outstanding at 6.5 percent was converted into the same value at 5.32 percent.

Wild speculation in interest rate swaps of course could put a state or local authority into a risky debt position. The Port Authority has a well-established debt management program with formally defined principles. The debt situation vis-à-vis the original bondholders remains unchanged in an interest rate swap. The state or local authority is simply trading in the financial market based on judgments about future interest rates. The original bond issue is not affected, in that investors will be paid according to the original terms. The borrowing authority, through a completely separate transaction, hedges against future interest rate changes and achieves, through a third party, a gain or experiences a loss based on the marginal interest rate differences. The risk analysis focuses on whether the overall portfolio of the borrowing authority has been exposed to higher or lower future interest payments. Recent trends in lower interest rates make interest rate swaps an attractive possibility for borrowers who issued long-term debt a few years earlier when interest rates were higher. This is different from the Orange County, California, strategy for its investments. In the interest rate swap hedges, the party involved negotiates a known risk and return range, and keeps its maximum risk exposure within bounds of good financial management practice. In the Orange County case, the county's investment manager was in effect borrowing to *bet* on interest rates rising. When they fell, the county could not pay off the borrowed money.

SUMMARY

Every day we use physical facilities and infrastructure provided by state and local governments. Few of us stop to analyze how those facilities are paid for or what impact their construction has on state and local taxes—unless the extension of new water and sewer lines or a major street repaving project results in a hefty assessment on our own property. However, it is increasingly common for state and local governments to highlight capital facilities planning and budgeting and to involve citizens more directly in the planning process. Most of the government services and assets the ordinary citizen benefits from, such as schools, roads, water, recreation facilities, libraries, and solid waste collection, require major investments. As a result, almost all state and larger municipalities have identifiable capital planning and budgeting processes. Many of these are closely integrated with the annual current budget planning and decision-making process, and the trend is toward greater integration.

Because of the long life of capital facilities and infrastructure, extensive use is made of long-term financing in the form of various types of bond issues. Some local governments still consider it financially prudent to borrow little or not at all, but state governments and virtually all large cities are unable to provide the services demanded by citizens without resorting to some debt financing for capital investments. Although it is generally accepted that future generations should not be saddled with unreasonable debt burdens about which they have no say, most citizens recognize that capital facilities will be enjoyed by future generations. Debt financing provides a means for those future generations to share the costs as well as the benefits.

The municipal debt market has undergone remarkable changes in the last decade. Sophisticated structured financing tools developed for private debt and equity transactions are being applied to municipal debt issues. In addition, municipalities are using increasingly sophisticated money management techniques to minimize their cost of debt and to maximize the returns on their own investments. Occasionally these techniques result in major financial disasters. As a result, the SEC, once hands off toward the municipal debt market, has adopted increasingly stringent disclosure requirements, and Congress has increased the SEC's regulatory role toward municipal debt.

Effective debt management requires that the amount of debt incurred not impose infeasible burdens on future taxpayers and that it not force future cutbacks in operation and maintenance expenditures necessary to maintain capital facilities. State governments, through constitutional provisions and statutory requirements, regulate their own borrowing as well as that of local governments. These regulations mainly focus on the commitment of the "full faith and credit" of the jurisdiction. Partly because of the restrictions imposed on general obligation bonds and partly because of the efficiency of tying repayment of debt to specific revenues generated by the investment, there has been tremendous growth in the use of a wide variety of debt instruments. Overall, however, state and local debt has grown little over the past 30 years in relation to personal income. State and local governments also have become more sophisticated in their financial analysis of capital investments and debt financing.

NOTES

1. U.S. Office of Management and Budget, *Budget of the United States Government: Fiscal Year 1998, Analytical Perspectives* (Washington, DC: U.S. Government Printing Office, 1997), 101.

2. U.S. Office of Management and Budget, *Budget of the United States Government: Fiscal Year 1998, Analytical Perspectives*, 140.

3. J.E. Petersen, Repairing America: Finding the Funding, *Governing* 8 (July, 1995): 69.

4. E. Rosell, The Chickens Can Come Home to Roost: The Anatomy of a Local Infrastructure Crisis, *Urban Affairs Quarterly* 30 (1994): 298–306.

5. B.S. Bunch, Current Practices and Issues in Capital Budgeting and Reporting, *Public Budgeting & Finance* 16 (Summer 1996): 8.

6. Bunch, Current Practices and Issues in Capital Budgeting and Reporting, 9; T.D. Lynch, C.E. Lynch, and R.A. Omdal, The State of Capital Budgeting in Louisiana's Local Governments, *Public Budgeting and Financial Management* 8 (1997): 555–577.

7. Details on functional categories for state and local capital outlays are from U.S. Bureau of the Census, *Government Finances in 1992–93* (Washington, DC: U.S. Government Printing Office, 1996); http://www.census.gov/govs/estimate/93stlus.wk1; accessed December 1997.

8. A. Halachmi and A. Sekwat, Strategic Capital Budgeting and Planning: Prospects at a County Level, *Public Budgeting and Financial Management* 8 (1997): 578–596.

9. *Capital Improvements Program for the Period 1996–2010 Including Five Year Capital Improvements Budget for the Period 1996–2001* (Carrboro, NC: Orange Water and Sewer Authority, 1996).

10. National Council on Public Works Improvement, *Fragile Foundations: A Report on America's Public Works* (Washington, DC: U.S. Government Printing Office, 1988).

11. Petersen, Repairing America: Finding the Funding, 66.

12. Congressional Budget Office, *Trends in Public Infrastructure Outlays and the President's Proposals for Infrastructure Spending in 1993* (Washington, DC: U.S. Government Printing Office, 1992), 15.

13. U.S. Office of Management and Budget, *Budget of the United States Government: Fiscal Year 1998, Analytical Perspectives*, 127.

14. S.R. Godwin and G.E. Peterson, *Guide to Assessing Capital Stock Condition* (Washington, DC: Urban Institute, 1984), 7–9.

15. R.W. Johnson and C.C. Barnett, *Urban Services Delivery in CEE and the NIS*, prepared for U.S. Agency for International Development Zagreb Conference on Local Government (Research Triangle Park, NC: Research Triangle Institute, 1996).

16. J. Brizius, *Deciding for Investment* (Washington, DC: National Academy of Public Administration, 1994), 8–9.

17. M.A. Glaser and J.W. Bardo, A Five-Stage Approach for Improved Use of Citizen Surveys in Public Investment Decisions, *State and Local Government Review* 26 (1994): 161–172.

18. S.A. MacManus, Democratizing the Capital Budget Planning and Project Selection Process at the Local Level: Assets and Liabilities, *Public Budgeting and Financial Management* 8 (1996): 406–427.

19. R. Berne and R. Schramm, *The Financial Analysis of Governments* (Englewood Cliffs, NJ: Prentice-Hall, 1986); S.M. Groves and M.G. Valente, *Evaluating Financial Condition: A Handbook for Local Government*, 3rd ed. (Washington, DC: International City/County Management Association, 1994).

20. B. Townsend, Development Impact Fees: A Fair Share Formula for Success, *Public Management* 78 (April 1996): 10–15.

21. Congressional Budget Office, *How Federal Spending for Infrastructure and Other Public Investments Affects the Economy* (Washington, DC: U.S. Government Printing Office, 1992), xv; C.L. Johnson, Alternative Debt Financing Mechanisms for Economic Development, *State and Local Government Review* 28 (1996): 78–89.

22. R. Miranda and N. Hillman, Reengineering Capital Budgeting, *Public Budgeting and Financial Management* 8 (1996): 360–383.

23. U.S. Office of Management and Budget, *Budget of the United States Government: Fiscal Year 1998, Analytical Perspectives*, 103.

24. *Report of the President's Commission on Budget Concepts* (Washington, DC: U.S. Government Printing Office, 1967), 34.

25. U.S. General Accounting Office, *Budget Issues: Incorporating an Investment Component in the Federal Budget* (Washington, DC: U.S. Government Printing Office, 1993); U.S. General Accounting Office, *Budget Issues: The Role of Depreciation in Budgeting for Certain Federal Investments* (Washington, DC: U.S. Government Printing Office, 1995).

26. U.S. General Accounting Office, *Budget Issues: Budgeting for Federal Capital* (Washington, DC: U.S. Government Printing Office, 1996).

27. National Council on Public Works Improvement, *Fragile Foundations: A Report on America's Public Works* (Washington, DC: U.S. Government Printing Office, 1988).

28. Several of these reports are summarized in U.S. Congress, Office of Technology Assessment, *Rebuilding the Foundations: State and Local Public Works Financing & Management* (Washington, DC: U.S. Government Printing Office, 1990).

29. U.S. General Accounting Office, *Budget Structure: Providing an Investment Focus in the Federal Budget* (Washington, DC: U.S. Government Printing Office, 1995).

30. D. Kittower, Municipal Bonds: The Deals of the Year, *Governing* 10 (March 1997): 56.

31. U.S. Bureau of the Census, *Statistical Abstract of the United States: 1996* (Washington, DC: U.S. Government Printing Office, 1996), 304.

32. M.R. Marlin, Did Tax Reform Kill Segmentation in the Municipal Bond Market? *Public Administration Review* 54 (1994): 387–390.

33. *South Carolina v. Baker, Treasury Secretary of the United States*, 485 U.S. 505 (1988).

34. For a discussion of the history of legal actions concerning state and local tax immunity, see M.T. Wrightson, The Road to South Carolina: Intergovernmental Tax Immunity and the Constitutional Status of Federalism, *Publius* 19 (Winter 1989): 39–55.

35. C. Kyle, Airport Financing: Let the Passengers Pay, *Governing* 7 (March 1994): 18–19; P. Lemov, A Groundbreaking Bond Takes Off in Little Rock, *Governing* 9 (July 1996): 51.

36. J.E. Anderson, Tax Increment Financing: Municipal Adoption and Growth, *National Tax Journal* 43 (1990): 155–163.

37. M. Kreps, Ups and Downs of Municipal Bonds' Volume and Yields in the Past Century, in *The Handbook of Municipal Bonds and Public Finance*, eds. R. Lamb, J. Leigland, and S. Rappaport (New York: New York Institute of Finance, 1993), 114.

38. L. Pohle, Marketing Mini-bonds: Lessons Learned from Denver's Successful First Issuance, *Government Finance Review* 7 (June 1991): 32–34.

39. C.L. Johnson and J. Mikesell, Certificates of Participation and Capital Markets: Lessons from Brevard County and Richmond Unified School District, *Public Budgeting & Finance* 14 (Fall 1994): 41–54.

40. L.H. Wadler, The Impact of Lending Velocity on Revolving Fund Performance, *Municipal Finance Journal* 16 (Spring 1995): 32–62.

41. Turning on the Tap, *Governing* 8 (April 1995): 48.

42. U.S. General Accounting Office, *State Infrastructure Banks: A Mechanism to Expand Federal Transportation Financing* (Washington, DC: U.S. Government Printing Office, 1996).

43. R. Forbes, Costs of Issuance on Tax-Exempt Debt: The Results of a 1988 Survey, *Municipal Finance Journal* 12 (Spring 1991): 29–40.

44. C.L. Johnson, An Empirical Investigation of the Pricing of Financial Advisor Services, *Municipal Finance Journal* 15 (Fall 1994): 36–52.

45. Kittower, Municipal Bonds: The Deals of the Year, 56.

46. P.A. Leonard, Negotiated versus Competitive Bond Sales: A Review of the Literature, *Municipal Finance Journal* 15 (Summer 1994): 12–36.

47. J.B. Kurish, *Pricing Bonds in a Negotiated Sale: How To Manage the Process* (Chicago: Government Finance Officers Association, 1994).

48. P.A. Leonard, An Empirical Analysis of Competitive Bid and Negotiated Offerings of Municipal Bonds, *Municipal Finance Journal* 17 (Spring 1996): 37–67.

49. W. Simonsen and M.D. Robbins, Does It Make Any Difference Anymore? Competitive versus Negotiated Municipal Bond Issuance, *Public Administration Review* 56 (1996): 57–63.

50. J.C. Joseph, *Debt Issuance and Management: A Guide for Smaller Governments* (Chicago: Government Finance Officers Association, 1994).

51. L.H. Wadler, *The Art of Structured Finance* (Chestnut Ridge, NY: The Linear Press, 1995).

52. *Municipal Finance Criteria* (New York: Standard and Poor's, 1996).

53. P.R. Aguila, Jr., and C.L. Holstein, The Cost of a Rating Downgrade, *Government Finance Review* 5 (August 1989): 38–39.

54. High Risk Can Earn Low Marks, *Governing* 7 (December 1994): 53.

55. Bond Insurance: A Sign of the Times, *Governing* 9 (November 1996): 60.

56. P. Tigue, *Purchasing Credit Enhancement: How to Decide if Bond Insurance Makes Sense* (Chicago: Government Finance Officers Association, 1994).

57. A. Levitt, The Municipal Bond and Government Securities Market, *Municipal Finance Journal* 16 (Summer 1995): 6–37.

58. R.W. Doty, The Role of the Municipal Securities Rulemaking Board and the Central Repository for Public Securities Dealer Regulation or Market Regulation?, *Municipal Finance Journal* 11 (1990): 7–51.

59. P. Lemov, Munis under the Microscope: The Disclosure Era Begins, *Governing* 8 (September 1995): 55.

60. P. Lemov, Ahead of the Fiscal Curve, *Governing* 9 (December 1996): 34.

61. P. Lemov, A New Investment Rule Requires "Suitable" Advice, *Governing* 9 (October 1996): 57.

62. All figures in this and the following paragraph are from U.S. Bureau of the Census, *Statistical Abstract of the United States: 1996*, 303–304, except the total debt outstanding for state and local governments figure, which is from E. Roy, Outstanding Municipal Debt Falls to Lowest Level Since 1991, Fed Says, *The Bond Buyer* 318 (December 13, 1996): 27.

63. All figures in this paragraph are from U.S. Bureau of the Census, *Statistical Abstract of the United States: 1996*, 307 and 453.

64. U.S. Bureau of the Census, *Statistical Abstract of the United States: 1996*, 304.

65. S. Dickson, Civil War, Railroads, and Road Bonds: Bond Repudiations in the Days of Yore, in *The Handbook of Municipal Bonds and Public Finance*, eds. Lamb, Leigland, and Rappaport, 166–173.

66. G.W. Mitchell, Statement before the Committee on Banking, Housing and Urban Affairs, *Federal Reserve Bulletin* 61 (1975): 729–730.

67. Dickson, Civil War, Railroads, and Road Bonds: Bond Repudiations in the Days of Yore,172; R.W. Collin, What the Law Says about Orange County: Creditors' Rights and Remedies on Municipal Default, *Municipal Finance Journal* 16 (Summer 1995): 52–89.

68. N.R. Cohen, Municipal Default Patterns: An Historical Study, *Public Budgeting & Finance* 9 (Winter 1989): 62.

69. J. Leigland and R. Lamb, *WPP$$: Who Is To Blame for the WPPSS Disaster* (Cambridge, MA: Ballinger, 1986).

70. H.D. Sitzer, The Washington Public Power Supply System: Then and Now, *Municipal Finance Journal* 14 (Winter 1994): 59–78.

71. P. Lemov, Two Down-and-Out Localities Are Back on the Fast Track, *Governing* 9 (December 1995): 49.

72. J.I. Chapman, The Challenge of Entrepreneurship, *Municipal Finance Journal* 17 (July 1996): 16–32.

73. C.L. Johnson and J.L. Mikesell, The Orange County Debacle: Where Responsible Cash and Debt Management Practices Collide, *Municipal Finance Journal* 17 (Summer 1996): 1–15.

74. R. Berne, Governmental Accounting and Financial Reporting and the Measurement of Financial Condition, in *The Handbook of Municipal Bonds and Public Finance,* eds. Lamb, Leigland, and Rappaport, 257–315.

75. R. Bahl and W. Duncombe, State and Local Debt Burdens in the 1980s: A Study in Contrast, *Public Administration Review* 53 (1993): 31–40.

76. R.W. Rafuse, Jr., *Representative Expenditures: Addressing the Neglected Dimension of Fiscal Capacity* (Washington, DC: U.S. Advisory Commission on Intergovernmental Relations, 1990).

77. R.W. Johnson, *Capital Financing for Municipal Infrastructure: Choices as Viewed by the Enterprise and the Investor* (Research Triangle Park, NC: Research Triangle Institute, 1996).

78. D.M. Lawrence, *Financing Capital Projects in North Carolina*, 2nd ed. (Chapel Hill, NC: Institute of Government, University of North Carolina, 1994).

79. J. Haupert, Using Interest Rate Swaps as Part of an Overall Financing and Investment Strategy, *Government Finance Review* 8 (April 1992): 13–15.

CHAPTER 13

Government Personnel and Pensions

In his classic work on government budgeting, A. E. Buck wrote, "Personnel is the most important single factor in government both from the operating and the fiscal point of view."[1] Yet, despite the importance of personnel administration to budgeting, rarely has there been any attempt to integrate the two. The literature on budgeting has been almost silent on government personnel policies and procedures, and the literature on personnel or human resources administration has been similarly silent on budgeting.

Aspects of government personnel are reviewed here in two main sections. The first section reviews the impacts of personnel decisions and expenditures on the budget and discusses the structure of personnel retirement systems. The second section suggests some of the reasons why budgeting and personnel administration have been separate activities and discusses budget staffs, including sizes, skill mixes, and training.

PERSONNEL IMPACTS AND PENSION PLANS

Personnel Considerations in Decision Making

Importance of Personnel Expenditures. The largest portion of any government's operating budget is typically devoted to personnel. In 1991 to 1992, salaries and wages on average accounted for 22 percent of direct government expenditures. That percentage does not include costs for employee insurance and pension benefits. Local governments spent the highest proportion (42 percent) and the federal government the lowest (12 percent), with the states being at the average (23 percent). The federal percentage is low because Social Security costs, which involve transfer payments rather than the delivery of services, are part of total expenditures.[2] The percentage of the budget spent on direct personnel services for governments in the United States is low compared with the figure for most other countries, where 60 or even 80 percent is common. In many of these countries, privatization of services and budget deficit reductions leading to layoffs are dramatically lowering these numbers.

Pay rates vary from jurisdiction to jurisdiction, but all governments try to keep salaries and wages competitive with those in the private sector. The federal government has moved to locality-based pay for white-collar workers so that pay depends upon what private sector salaries are in any given geographic area of the country.[3]

Public employment has been important for welfare purposes. Awarding government jobs to the economically needy and to the politically faithful has been a widespread practice. Patronage appointments have been common at all levels of government. State and local governments sometimes have residency requirements for their workers. Such requirements are based on the premises that employees who are residents are likely to be more dedicated to serving the government than nonresidents and that employee-residents will spend their earnings in the place where they reside, giving an economic boost to the local economy.[4]

Administrators have used personnel tactics to build empires. A large staff is often regarded as a sign of success for the administrator. Moreover, when staff increases, the administrator can make claims on other resources, namely, supplies, equipment, and the like. All administrators, of course, are not would-be kings. Attempts to increase staff result in part from sincere convictions that the additional personnel will enhance effectiveness.

Since personnel expenditures constitute a large percentage of total budgets, controlling budgets in the short and long term necessarily depends on controlling personnel costs. Presidents have from time to time frozen scheduled federal employee pay increases as a means of curtailing growth in expenditures and dampening inflationary pressures on the economy.[5] Actions such as these raise questions about whether public employees are unfairly denied pay increases that are due them and can lead to governments having difficulty attracting needed personnel because salary and wage levels are lower than those in the private sector. During budget execution, if revenues are lower than originally projected, hiring freezes and other personnel actions may be taken to reduce outlays.

In the longer term, governments sometimes make concerted efforts to reduce their work forces on a permanent basis. In 1993, for example, President Clinton issued a memorandum calling for the elimination of 252,000 civilian positions, or 12 percent or more of the work force, by October 1, 1999.[6] Congress in 1994 and again in 1996 legislated *buyout* programs, which authorized agencies to grant incentives for their workers to retire early, as a means of reducing the size of the bureaucracy and cutting personnel costs.[7] Periodic agency *reductions in force* have become more common in the federal government and in other governments, just as *downsizing* has become common in the private sector.

Personnel costs for state and local governments are uncontrollable regarding stipulations of the Fair Labor Standards Act (FLSA), which was originally adopted in 1938 and in more recent times extended to state and local governments.[8] The law provides for minimum wage standards and overtime pay for more than 40 hours being worked in a week. Employees are exempt from these standards if they are salaried *and* their duties are of a nonproduction nature; conversely, employees are entitled to FLSA protection if either of these factors does not apply. During the 1990s, many court battles have been fought by workers demanding backpay for overtime worked. The presumption had been that higher-paid workers were automatically excluded from FLSA protection, but through a variety of means, workers being paid even $100,000 have been able to gain coverage and win backpay awards. New York City, for example, was forced to pay 435 of its managers a total of $13.8 million.[9] One view is that the mandates in the FLSA impose unrealistic financial burdens on state and local governments (see discussion of unfunded mandates in Chapter 14).

Budget Documents. Given the magnitude of personnel expenditures, the use of employment for patronage purposes, and tendencies toward empire building on the part of agencies, it becomes obvious why budgeting decisions often have focused on personnel practices. Budgets of many years ago indicated the names of individuals and their earnings. The purpose was to guarantee that individuals were not receiving exorbitant salaries.

Today the practice of naming employees in the budget is far less common, although information on the wages and salaries of individual employees is available to the public for most government employees. Newspapers often report the salaries of the highest-paid state university employees, for example, and employees of nonprofit agencies sometimes receive the same attention. In contemporary budgets, salaries of heads of agencies are often reported in budgets, but itemized earnings of lower-ranked employees are not. Still, budgets usually at least report personnel expenditures by agency or bureaus within them and may provide considerable detail, such as by class of workers (trades, clerical, administrative, professional, and technical) and type of pay (wages, salaries, holiday pay, overtime pay, shift differential pay, and callback pay). Figure 13–1, drawn from the City of Los Angeles budget, illustrates one method for presenting personnel information. The number of positions in the police department, all other departments, and the total for the city are shown in graph and chart form for a multiyear period. Other governments report fire-fighter positions as well as police as distinguished from civilian personnel. Some governments, including the federal government, report *full-time equivalent* (FTE) personnel rather than simply the number of positions.

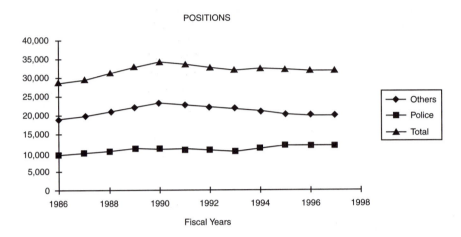

POSITIONS

Fiscal Year	Police	Others	Total
1986–87	9,640	19,167	28,807
1987–88	9,903	19,600	29,503
1988–89	10,479	20,870	31,349
1989–90	11,107	21,957	33,064
1990–91	11,171	23,046	34,217
1991–92	11,227	22,667	33,894
1992–93	10,754	22,152	32,906
1993–94	10,597	21,660	32,257
1994–95	11,364	21,326	32,690
1995–96	12,191	20,514	32,705
1996–97	12,183	20,182	32,365
6-30-1997*	12,183	20,104	32,287

*The 1996–97 figures are adopted position authorities. The final figures for June 30, 1997, assume attrition of 78 civilian positions during 1996–97.

Figure 13–1 Authorized City Staffing for City of Los Angeles, 1986–1996. Courtesy of City of Los Angeles, 1997, *Budget Summary, Fiscal Year 1996–97: Authorized City Staffing*, Los Angeles, California.

Personnel Complement Control. Sometimes personnel tables are included in budgets only for information purposes, that is, to provide the legislative body and the general public with information about the size of the personnel complement of agencies. In other cases, these displays exist for decision-making purposes. An agency may not be permitted to hire a new staff member, even though funds are available in its budget, without first receiving authorization for a new position.

Budget offices and personnel departments often exercise such control, and sometimes legislatures place specific limitations in appropriation bills. Exercising complement control is considered one method of limiting growth in the bureaucracy and the budget.

Costs Created by Personnel. Not only does paying employees lead to considerable costs for government, but the actions of employees can generate unwanted additional costs. Discriminatory employment practices by managers and coworkers can result in major financial burdens when a court awards compensatory damages to the injured workers. Some evidence suggests that occupations and government offices that have been historically dominated by men, including budgeting and finance offices, tend to be resistant to entry by women and tend to be more prone to instances of sexual discrimination.[10] Torts, especially acts of negligence by workers, can result in harm to coworkers and citizens, again leading to major financial awards (see Chapter 10).[11]

Labor–Management Relations. Labor unions have come to play an important role in personnel matters and budgeting.[12] Governments set salary and wage levels, as well as other benefits, particularly retirement benefits, in a variety of ways, including through legislative action and collective bargaining. Unions obviously are deeply involved in collective bargaining, but they also influence the process of determining compensation through legislation. By their lobbying efforts, unions have been able to persuade state legislators to pass laws setting minimum salary levels for teachers in local school districts, to impose standards for retirement systems, and to pass other related personnel legislation (e.g., laws mandating regular training for police officers).

Collective bargaining is well established in many governments. Close to 40 percent of all government workers are members of labor unions, and as of 1996, 43 percent were represented by unions in labor negotiations with their employers.[13] Membership in unions is slightly lower than the number of workers covered by bargaining units, since some workers covered by a bargaining agreement choose not to join a union. At the federal level, 1.9 million of the 2.8 civilian federal workers are represented by unions, with 750,000 in the postal service. About 60 percent of the federal workers in collective bargaining units are in the postal service, the Department of Veterans Affairs, the Internal Revenue Service, and the Social Security Administration.[14]

Collective bargaining greatly complicates the process of budgeting. Given the proportion of expenditures committed to personnel, a wage settlement can have a massive impact on the budget. Many labor contracts are valid for only one year, which means that year-round negotiations are likely to occur, causing great uncertainty over what personnel costs will be for the budget that is being prepared.

Bargaining Units. The number of bargaining units and unions further complicates the situation. Employees bargain as a unit that is said to have a *community of interests*; one unit might be clerical workers in a city government. Determination of the bargaining unit is made by an independent agency, such as a state labor relations board for both state and local governments within the state or, in the case of the federal government, the Federal Labor Relations Authority, except for postal workers who are under the National Labor Relations Board. Those responsible for budgeting, then, have no control over the number of bargaining units and the number of unions that will be involved in negotiations.

The greater the number of bargaining units, the more complex budget planning becomes. The federal government has well over 2,000 units, with some having thousands of employees and others only a handful.[15] A major difference between the federal government and other governments is that federal workers generally do not have the power to bargain over salaries, although there are important exceptions, such as the postal service. States have a total of about 1,000 bargaining units, and local governments have more than 35,000.[16]

Work stoppages or strikes have major budgetary implications as well as service implications. If workers go on strike, salary savings may occur, but backlogs in work may develop, later forcing payment of overtime. Federal workers are generally prohibited from striking, and the Federal Service Impasses Panel resolves impasses in negotiations between management and labor.[17] Where strikes do occur, the effects can be massive. Approximately 30,000 days of work were lost by an eight-day work stoppage in the San Diego schools in 1996.[18]

Bargaining's Impact on Personnel Costs. Although collective bargaining greatly influences the budgeting process, there is conflicting evidence on whether it leads to higher personnel costs and higher total spending. For one thing, the economic "health" of a jurisdiction will affect its ability to grant wage and salary increases to workers. During the recessions of the early 1980s and early 1990s, wage increases at the state and local levels were kept to a minimum largely because of tight budgets, regardless of worker unionization. However, political activity on the part of organized police officers, for instance, may protect jobs, result in hiring more police officers, lead to gains in nonwage benefits (hours of work, uniform allowance, and the like), but may not necessarily result in higher pay than in locales without unions.[19]

Further complicating matters are budget restrictions, such as tax and spending limitations, that prevent local governments from raising taxes. Unions often work actively to defeat such proposals on election ballots.[20]

Another factor in wage determination is the spillover of decisions within a community and from one community to others. If unionized police in a city win wage increases, clerical workers in the same city are likely to benefit even if they are not unionized. Similarly, if a union is successful in bargaining for increases in compensation in one city, other cities in response may grant increases to their workers in order to remain competitive in recruiting and retaining employees and in some cases possibly to avert unionization.

Labor Negotiations. To bargain for compensation increases, union leaders have had to learn about budgeting. Without a thorough understanding of a jurisdiction's budget, unions can be persuaded by management that funds simply do not exist to grant increases. The job of the union is to "find" budget surpluses that can be used to increase employee compensation. Some national unions help their state and local affiliates to analyze their governments' budgets.

Since the mid-1970s, important changes have occurred in the nature of bargaining between unions and management. In the early years of public sector collective bargaining, one of labor's main arguments was that salaries and wages in the public sector needed to be increased to match those in the private sector. While that argument is still used, negotiations have come to focus more on the productivity of workers. In some jurisdictions, wage increases have been dependent on measurable improvements in worker productivity. According to the concept of productivity bargaining, workers are entitled to benefit from the financial savings accruing from greater productivity.

Another change in bargaining has been management demands for concessions. As budgets have become tighter, some jurisdictions have demanded that workers take pay reductions. In other cases, agreements have been developed for hiring new workers at pay rates lower than current ones; this occurred in the postal service. Some negotiations have concentrated on job security—protecting workers from layoffs. While these types of negotiations are not nearly as common in government as in the private sector, the point is that collective negotiations in the public sector are no longer restricted to demands for greater pay and benefits.

The movement toward privatization of government services may have an unintended consequence in regard to labor relations. While many states have no policy on public sector labor relations, other than to ban strikes by public workers, most private sector workers may organize, bargain for wages, and strike. Shifts toward privatization, then, allow for more activity on the part of unions.[21]

Future of the Labor Movement. What the future holds for public sector unionism, collective bargaining, and its impact on budgeting and finance is uncertain. On the one hand, unions usually win representational elections of workers; in other words, if unions are successful in having an election held, they usually win.[22] Union membership has been declining sharply in the private sector, a fact that prompted the formation of a national commission to examine how to improve labor–management relations.[23] In the public sector, conflict between management and labor is common and growing in some areas such as the postal service.[24] The labor movement may face an extremely hostile environment in many locales, a factor that can result in bargaining stalemates, strikes, and general unrest that contribute to an atmosphere of uncertainty in terms of budget-ing.[25]

Comparable Worth. One other matter that causes considerable confusion in the personnel budgeting arena is comparable worth or *pay equity.* Simply stated, the concept of comparable worth maintains that workers should receive compensation according to their contribution to an organization. Where a problem arises is that many occupations in government that are held by women, although they require sophisticated skills, tend to be low paying (clerical secretaries, librarians, nurses, and teachers). Demands are made that compensation levels be greatly increased for such occupations to avoid situations in which lawn maintenance personnel or garbage truck drivers receive substantially more than secretaries, who are expected to master sophisticated office equipment and a variety of computer software programs. Labor unions often are torn on this issue. On the one hand, the unions want to be strong advocates for comparable worth, but, on the other hand, they do not want to lose the support of workers in other occupations.[26]

Employee Benefits and Pension Plans

Both personnel administrators and budgeters view personnel expenses in terms of total compensation, which consists of salaries and wages plus employee benefits. Given scarce resources, increasing benefits in any given year may preclude raising wage and salary rates.[27] Employee benefits include paid holidays, vacations, unemployment insurance, and Social Security retirement. Government contributions to Social Security and payments for laid-off workers have real price tags attached to them, but governments have come to recognize that other benefits such as paid holidays, vacations, and free parking are also expensive. Two benefits that are particularly expensive are health care and government-sponsored pension plans. Of concern to budgeters is that if the costs of these benefits are not controlled, the budget itself can get out of control. Decision makers may find themselves each year more concerned with how to cover the rising costs of employee benefits than how to deal with policy issues.

Health Care. No employer is immune from rapidly rising health care costs, including government employers, and as a result governments have sought alternative means of providing the health care that workers need at a cost that governments can afford. Governments are turning to managed care programs, which provide employees with a package of health services at predetermined costs. *Health maintenance organizations* (HMOs) have become popular because they provide services to employees at a set fee. Some governments allow employees to choose among HMOs.

In other cases, experiments are under way with *medical savings accounts* (MSAs). These accounts, often compared with individual retirement accounts, become the repository of tax-free contributions by both employers and employees and are used to pay employee health care expenses, with unused monies being rolled forward from one year to the next. The merits of the MSAs are being hotly debated regarding whether they should be made available to most workers. Proponents reason that the accounts are an effective means of reducing health care costs, and opponents contend that the accounts are most likely to be used by better-paid employees, leaving lower-paid employees with insufficient funding for their health care needs.[28]

More generally, employers are moving toward *cafeteria plans*, which allow employees to select the types of coverage they wish. Employees are given options and may choose to use some of their salaries and wages toward the purchase of additional benefits. Federal tax laws permit the establishment of tax-free *dependent care accounts* and *medical expense reimbursement accounts*. In the latter case, an employee decides prior to the beginning of the calendar year how much to contribute each pay period to such an account and then the money can be used to pay medical expenses not covered by the employer's health plan. The monies in these accounts must be used during the year in which they are collected.[29]

Structure of Retirement Systems. The most expensive part of an employee benefits package in a government consists of *public employee retirement systems* (PERSs). There are approximately 200 state-administered plans, some of which include local government employees as well as state employees, and about 2,500 locally administered plans.[30] In addition to these, there are thousands of other small plans involving annuity policies with private insurance carriers. The federal government has several plans, the main one being the Federal Employees Retirement System (FERS) for persons hired on or after January 1, 1984. Employees hired before that date may opt for FERS or remain in the Civil Service Retirement System (CSRS); most have chosen to continue with CSRS coverage.[31] Altogether, the federal government has about 50 retirement systems in which more than 12 million employees and retirees participate.[32]

Retirement systems—both public sector and private sector—must comply with federal laws. The Employee Retirement Income Security Act (ERISA) of 1974 governs private sector plans.[33] Sections 415 and 457 of the Internal Revenue Code exert major controls over public retirement systems. In 1996, Congress amended these provisions to allow greater flexibility on the part of state and local systems in complying with federal law.[34]

Retirement systems generally are based on an assumption that a person will use a variety of measures to cover living expenses during retirement besides that of pension checks. First, living expenses may decline as the individual becomes less active and has fewer demands on income, such as support for dependents. Second, savings are used to cover expenses. Third, many government workers are covered by Old-Age and Survivors Insurance, disability insurance, and health insurance (Medicare) of the Social Security Administration. Members of FERS are required to participate in Social Security, while federal employees who belong to CSRS do not participate. In FERS, workers may pay a percentage of their earnings into a tax-deferred plan, and the government matches part of the amount. These matching retirement accounts are similar to private 401K plans, referring to that section of the Internal Revenue Code that covers employer–employee matching tax-deferred plans.

Contributions into Social Security constitute one area of government budgets that are uncontrollable. State and local governments once had the option of joining and withdrawing from Social Security; governments withdrew when their calculations indicated greater returns could be made on their own investments than Social Security paid in benefits. In the 1980s, however, Congress passed legislation barring withdrawal from Social Security, and the Supreme Court upheld the law.[35] Additional legislation has required participation in Medicare, and when employees are not covered by an approved public retirement system, they must participate in Social Security.[36] The result is that state and local governments must budget each year for increased Social Security and Medicare costs regardless of their budget situations. Monies withheld are known as Federal Insurance Contributions Act (FICA) taxes.[37] About three-quarters of state and local workers participate in Social Security.[38]

Defined Benefits and Defined Contributions. Pension systems in the public sector historically have used *defined benefits*, in which benefits normally are determined according to some combination of years of services, wages or salaries (for example, average salary of the last three years of service), and age at time of retirement. The longer one has worked for a government and the higher one's salary, the higher pension benefits will be. More than 90 percent of state and local government retirement systems use the defined benefits plan.[39] Retirement benefits for state and local employees covered by Social Security average 58 percent of their final salaries, and for those not covered, 67 percent.[40] In addition to initial retirement benefits, *cost-of-living allowances* are usually assigned pensioners, in some cases on an automatic basis according to an economic barometer, such as the consumer price index, and in others on an ad hoc basis. In the latter instance, a government might decide one year to increase retirement benefits by the same percentage as salary increases being awarded current employees. Other benefits are provided for disability retirement (for people who retire early because of poor health), and for survivors' benefits (covering family members who continue to live after the death of retirees). The vast majority of benefits paid each year go to elderly retirees, with the remainder divided between disability retirees and survivors.

Defined benefits plans coupled with cost-of-living allowances provide income security to employees and retirees and place investment risks on employers. Since benefits are determined in advance of retirement, employers must take steps necessary to be sure that sufficient funds will be available when employees retire. Cost accounting standards require that private sector companies "fund" the future liabilities created by these defined benefit programs. If projected earnings from investments of a company's pension fund are less than projected payouts, then the company must take an accounting adjustment, generally a write down of profits, to cover the projected difference.

An alternative to defined benefits is the *defined contribution* plan. Under this plan, benefits are not defined in advance of retirement but rather, the employer commits to contributing regularly to an employee's retirement account (usually a percentage of compensation). The benefits received at the time of retirement are a function of the employer's and employee's contributions plus investment earnings on these contributions. While public employers use primarily defined benefits plans, most private employers (approximately 90 percent) use defined contribution plans.[41] A key advantage of a defined contribution plan for an employer is its predictability; all that need be done each year is to set aside a percentage of salaries and wages for depositing into retirement accounts.[42]

Funding. Pension plans are funded by a combination of contributions from government and employees and investment earnings on those contributions. In some cases, the retirement program is financed exclusively by government, but that practice is an exception to the rule. In 1996, earnings constituted 70 percent of receipts for state and local retirement systems. Government contributions accounted for another 19 percent, and employee contributions accounted for the remaining 11 percent.[43] The federal government permits state and local employees to make some contributions to their retirement plans on a tax-deferred basis; individuals later pay taxes on the income when they receive pension checks and are presumably in a lower tax bracket.

There are basically two methods of financing retirement programs—*pay-as-you-go* and *advance funding*. With the pay-as-you-go method, all that is required in any one budget year is to raise sufficient revenue to cover retirement benefit checks. This method is generally discouraged in that it allows for the accumulation of debt. Persons in the future will be owed benefits, and taxpayers at that time will be forced to meet those costs.

The preferred method is advance funding, in which monies are accumulated for workers while they are working and those monies generate income through investments while workers are on the payroll and during retirement as well. If using this method, a retirement system must invest prudently but effectively to avoid any *unfunded actuarial accrued liability* so that the system is "actuarially sound." Advance funding uses the concept of *present value*. That is, future receipts, particularly contributions and investment earnings, are compared with anticipated costs (benefits) in terms of current dollars. The concept is analogous to the discount rate used in analysis (see Chapter 7). Several methods are used in calculating actuarial assets and liabilities.[44]

Liabilities. Studies often have found many state and local systems to have substantial unfunded liabilities, but the situation has improved since the 1970s.[45] One survey of systems found that assets averaged 85 percent of liabilities or conversely, that 15 percent of liabilities were unfunded. The unfunded amount was a seemingly staggering $169 billion. However, this number may give a false impression of disaster lurking for these systems. The unfunded actuarial accrued liability does not fall due at some specific date in the future but instead is amortized on average over a 22-year period.[46]

Pension fund liabilities can cause serious problems. Meeting current operating needs and covering the costs of retiree benefits can easily put a budget out of balance and force a tax increase. Where jurisdictions are at their legal or political limits on tax rates, severe program cuts may be the only alternative. Pension fund liabilities can increase the cost of doing business, since interest rates may be higher for jurisdictions that have large outstanding pension debts.

Several options are available for improving the funding situation of retirement systems:

- An obvious option is to increase government and employee contributions.
- Another is to take advantage of economies of scale by combining systems; this may reduce administrative costs and make possible more lucrative investments.
- Retirement systems can pool their funds for investment purposes.
- A jurisdiction can make investments that are riskier but also have higher rates of return. The stock market crash of 1987 and the Orange County, California, bankruptcy of 1994 (Chapters 10 and 12), however, are sobering reminders of the loss that can result from nonguaranteed investments. Models are available that suggest how to balance high returns with acceptable levels of risk.[47]
- Some jurisdictions have sold bonds in order to obtain funds needed to cover retirement liabilities.[48]
- Pension systems can have their creditworthiness rated in terms of the systems' abilities to meet financial obligations. These ratings then can be used to back other entities for fees, consequently increasing the revenue for the pension systems.[49]

Although retirement fund administrators have focused primarily on increasing the rate of return on investments while not becoming overly speculative, a new objective has emerged—to use pension funds to advance social and economic goals. For instance, a pension plan that invests in local economic development projects not only earns retirement benefits for employees but furthers the economic vitality of the community. However, a pension fund may be forced to choose between investing in a local project at one rate of return or investing in opportunities outside of the community at higher rates of return.[50] Additionally, the local investment may entail greater risk than others, with the pensioners' future benefits possibly being put in jeopardy.

Accounting and Reporting. Three statements and a technical bulletin issued by the Governmental Accounting Standards Board are the governing documents for accounting and reporting of public pension systems:

1. Statement No. 25, Financial Reporting for Defined Benefit Pension Plans and Note Disclosures for Defined Contribution Plans
2. Statement No. 26, Financial Reporting for Postemployment Healthcare Plans Administered by Defined Benefit Pension Plans
3. Statement No. 27, Accounting for Pensions by State and Local Governmental Employers
4. Technical Bulletin 96-1, Pension Disclosure Requirements for Employers

The three statements were issued in 1994 but not implemented until 1996 for the first two statements and 1997 for the third in order to allow time for governments to adjust their accounting and reporting systems to the dictates of the statements. The technical bulletin provides guidance on implementing the statements. Overall, the statements require an annual reporting of assets, changes in assets from year to year, and actuarial information on the long-term prospects of pension funds. Statement No. 26 covers health care plans for retirees.

PERSONNEL OPERATIONS

Personnel Administration and Budgeting

Because decisions related to personnel have major effects on budgeting, some linkage between budgeting and personnel administration is needed. However, just as constant tensions exist between budget offices and line agencies, so do tensions persist between the budget and personnel offices.

Historical Differences. A fundamental problem is that budgeting and personnel administration stem from different origins. As has been seen in earlier chapters, budgeting arose to provide information to executive and legislative decision makers. Central budget offices are intended to aid the chief executive, an elected politician. Budgeting is frankly political. Personnel administration, on the other

hand, is a product of a reform movement designed to minimize political considerations and base personnel actions—appointments, promotions, and the like—on
what employees know and do on the job rather than on whom they know. Personnel administration is expected to be apolitical.

Not only do budgeting and personnel differ in their historical roots, but they
also differ with regard to organizational structures. Since passage of the Pendleton Act of 1883, which established a merit system of employment in the federal
government, the personnel function at all levels of government has tended to be
organizationally beyond the control of political executives.[51] The justification for
independent civil service commissions has been that they insulate personnel matters from the caprices of politics.[52]

A point of controversy is whether these independent commissions have out-
lived their usefulness and should be abandoned. Commissions are often seen as
having negative influences and as rarely innovative and supportive of improvements in managerial practices.

Reforms. At the federal level, reforms were instituted in 1978 with passage of
the Civil Service Reform Act.[53] The Civil Service Commission was dissolved,
and taking its place was the Office of Personnel Management and the Merit Systems Protection Board. The Office of Personnel Management, which reports
directly to the President, is expected to take personnel actions conducive to
implementing the policies of the political leadership, while the Merit Systems
Protection Board in effect is a watchdog guarding against political influences that
might affect hiring, firing, and other personnel actions.

Even when the central personnel agency reports to the chief executive, tensions persist between the agency and the budget office. The two may disagree
with each other on how to handle situations where their jurisdictions intersect.
Budget and personnel offices are linked with each other on such matters as
reclassification of jobs, complement control, collective bargaining, reductions in
force, in which employees are laid off, usually for financial reasons, and efforts
to "reinvent" government (see Chapter 5).[54]

Personnel in Budgeting

It takes people to operate budgeting systems—people at the central location of
a budget office, in line agencies, and in the legislative body. While only some
personnel are assigned full time to budget matters, all personnel are inevitably
involved with budgeting and budget decisions. In this section, we discuss the size
and skill mix of budget staffs.

Census data provide some overall perspective on the number of government
employees engaged in budgeting and finance. There were about 130,000 federal
full- and part-time employees in this field in 1995 or 4.5 percent of total federal

employment.[55] State employment in the field was equal to about 164,000 full-time equivalent employees or 4.2 percent of total employment.[56] The full-time equivalent figure for local government was 190,000 or only 1.9 percent.[57]

Federal Staff. At the federal level, both the executive and legislative branches have sizable staffs. The Office of Management and Budget has a staff of about 540, and each department has personnel whose main function is budgeting. Congress has the Congressional Budget Office (230 employees), staffs for standing committees, staffs for each representative and senator, the General Accounting Office (3,700 employees), the Library of Congress (4,500 employees, including the Congressional Research Service), and the Office of Technology Assessment. Staffs exist for the House and Senate Budget Committees, the House Ways and Means Committee, the Senate Finance Committee, and the House and Senate Appropriations Committees.

Altogether Congress has about 32,000 employees. Most of the people who work for Congress do not work on budgeting, such as employees of the U.S. Government Printing Office (3,800 employees) and the Architect of the Capitol, but many are assigned to work on budgeting and substantive matters with budgetary implications.[58]

State Staff. The sizes of state budget staffs vary greatly. New York State has about 300 professional staff members, while California has about 100, and Florida and Virginia have about 60. Other states with more than 40 professional budget office staff members include Connecticut, Illinois, New Jersey, and Pennsylvania. On the other hand, many states have fewer than 20.[59] Professional fiscal staffs are to be found in virtually all state legislatures, but, as would be expected, there is great variation.

Detailed information is unavailable on the professional staffs working in municipal budget offices and for city councils and other local legislative bodies. Local staffs generally are small, and local legislative bodies—city councils, school boards, and the like—often have to rely mainly on executive branch staff for budget information and analysis.

The question of how many budget staff members are needed on either the executive or legislative side of government depends on what the budget units are expected to do. Small staffs handling multimillion- or multibillion-dollar budgets obviously can be expected to do little more than superficially review materials prepared by agencies and perhaps devote in-depth effort to selected "hot" issues.

Skill Mix. Budget offices vary in the purposes that are pursued and the activities undertaken, both of which affect the mix of required skills. A budget office whose main purpose is to hold agencies accountable for spending in accordance with appropriations may prefer persons with business skills and accounting training. At the federal level and to a lesser extent at the state level, skills in public finance may be important for developing policies for economic growth. Still other skills may be sought by budget units engaged in policy and program analysis.

Budget office staffs at the state level have been increasing in their professionalism, especially in the last 10 to 20 years. Today, few offices hire people with less than a baccalaureate degree, except for clerical workers and technicians. Many state budget offices routinely hire persons with master's and doctoral degrees.

There has been a trend away from staffing state offices with persons having accounting and other business degrees. Whereas in 1970 the typical state budget office had two-thirds of its staff trained in these fields, only 12 states reported in 1995 having half or more of their personnel trained in accounting and business. Conversely, the social sciences have increased their representation in state budget offices. In 1995, 19 states reported that half or more of their staff were trained in public administration, economics, or other social sciences. Another 17 states had a majority of their staffs trained in neither business nor the social sciences.[60]

The typical state budget office staff now has a blend of educational backgrounds. Both business and the social sciences are represented along with other professional disciplines, including engineering, law, education, and labor relations. Indeed, categorization of staff has become difficult in that a staff member often has a baccalaureate degree in one field and one or two master's degrees in other fields.

Whether the composition of the staff has any bearing on the way a state budget system operates is unclear. Certainly, a staff cannot do something for which it is not trained. Only those trained in program analysis would be expected to be able to conduct such an analysis. On the other hand, it is possible that budget offices might recruit program analysts and not use their talents. The available evidence suggests that the use of effectiveness analysis in decision making is not significantly greater in social science–oriented budget units than in business-oriented units.[61]

Training. Aside from recruiting personnel with new talents, existing personnel can be upgraded through training programs. Budget offices routinely invest in training their staff either as a whole or selectively (e.g., by sending a few employees to special courses each year). The federal Chief Financial Officers Council has established a human resources committee, which is concerned with improving the recruitment, retention, and training of financial personnel.[62] Each year the Government Finance Officers Association offers several training courses, and professional associations hold conferences and various meetings that can help budgeting and finance people keep abreast of changes. The Association for Budgeting and Financial Management, for example, holds an annual conference that covers both budgeting and financial management subjects and which gives attention to all levels of government plus the nonprofit sector. In addition to skill training, financial management employees need training in ethics, conflict of interest laws, and the like.

The effectiveness of training depends in part on whether employees are given the opportunity to use newly developed knowledge and skills. Training an employee in a budget technique that is not used by the jurisdiction has a limited benefit. On the other hand, training can be an effective way for a budget office to acquire the type of talent needed for its mission.

Certification. The budgeting and finance field has operated on a market basis, with each employer determining independently whether job candidates have the requisite skills, knowledge, and ability needed for any particular job. An emerging question is the extent to which certification programs should be used to help ensure that qualified individuals are hired. The Association of Government Accountants has a system for issuing certificates in government financial management (CGFM), and in 1997, the Government Finance Officers Association launched an ambitious Certification Program in Public Finance. The latter consists of comprehensive examinations in five areas:

1. governmental accounting, auditing, and financial reporting
2. cash management and investments
3. debt management
4. operating and capital budgeting
5. pension and benefits, risk management, and procurement[63]

The examinations are only available to Government Finance Officers Association members, who have baccalaureate degrees from accredited institutions and have three years of government experience within the previous 10 years.

The Human Element. Finally, one should be mindful that professionals in budgeting and finance are people and deserve to be treated accordingly. This book covers numerous changes under way that must be implemented by a relatively small cadre of professional workers. Changes in how work is performed and increases in the amount of work to be performed can have a telling effect on employees. The Internal Revenue Service has encountered substantial problems in redeploying workers who have been displaced by redesigning of work, including the introduction of new technology.[64] Also budgeting and finance personnel need to know how to communicate and work effectively with line administrators; all too often, finance people are seen as roadblocks rather than facilitators in accomplishing the missions of agencies.[65]

SUMMARY

The impact of personnel costs on any government budget is immense. Because labor costs are a large segment of every operating budget, personnel may be the first to be cut during financially tight periods. Collective bargaining, while helping employees, has greatly complicated budgetary planning at the state and local levels; unresolved negotiations at budget time mean that personnel costs remain unknown.

Many retirement programs at the state and local levels are not actuarially sound and may present severe problems in coming years. In granting workers improvements in retirement benefits, government officials need to assess the current and projected impact on budgets. Advance funding is preferred over the pay-as-you-go method of financing retirement plans.

Despite the apparent linkages between the budget and personnel functions, the administration of these systems has often not been integrated. Tensions persist between the two, in part as a result of their differing histories. Budgeting is an openly political process whereas personnel administration is intended to be basically apolitical.

Executive and legislative staffs in recent years have expanded in size and changed in terms of their capabilities. Congress substantially increased its budget staffs with the creation of the Congressional Budget Office and the House and Senate Budget Committees. Persons with social science training increasingly staff state budget offices, whereas business administration had previously been the most common background. Many local governments need more budget staff but do not have adequate resources for additional hiring. Training can be a useful method of acquiring needed talent.

NOTES

1. A.E. Buck, *Public Budgeting* (New York: Harper and Brothers, 1919), 539.

2. U.S. Bureau of the Census, *Government Finances: 1991–92* (Washington, DC: U.S. Government Printing Office, 1996), 8.

3. U.S. General Accounting Office, *Federal Personnel: Federal/Private Sector Pay Comparisons* (Washington, DC: U.S. Government Printing Office, 1994).

4. E. Perlman, Placing City Limits on Public Employees, *Governing* 8 (May 1995): 39–40.

5. N. Kingsbury, for the U.S. General Accounting Office, *Federal Employment: Impact of President's Economic Plan on Federal Employees' Pay and Benefits* (Washington, DC: U.S. Government Printing Office, 1993).

6. W.J. Clinton, Memorandum: Streamlining the Bureaucracy, *Federal Register* 58 (1993): 48583.

7. Federal Workforce Restructuring Act, P.L. 103-226, 108 Stat. 111 (1994); Omnibus Consolidated Appropriations Act, P.L. 104-208, Sec. 663, 110 Stat. 3009 (1996).

8. Fair Labor Standards Act, ch. 676, 52 Stat. 1060 (1938).

9. J.C. Markoe, Fair Labor Standards Act: Public Sector Liability, *Government Finance Review* 11 (June 1995): 48–49; A.A. Hartinger, Fair Labor Standards Act: 1996 Salary Basis Test Update, *Government Finance Review* 13 (February 1997): 29–31.

10. B. Stanko and G.J. Miller, Sexual Harassment and Government Accountants: Anecdotal Evidence from the Profession, *Public Personnel Management* 25 (1996): 219–235; R.D. Lee, Jr., and P.S. Greenlaw, A Legal Perspective on Sexual Harassment, in *Public Personnel Management: Current Concerns—Future Challenges*, 2nd ed., eds. C. Ban and N.M. Riccucci (New York: Longman Publishing Group, 1997), 109–122.

11. R.D. Lee, Jr., Federal Employees, Torts, and the Westfall Act of 1988, *Public Administration Review* 56 (1996): 334–340.

12. M.A. Horowitz, *Collective Bargaining in the Public Sector* (New York: Lexington Books, 1994).

13. U.S. Bureau of Labor Statistics, Union Affiliation of Employed Wage and Salary Workers by Occupation and Industry, 1996: http://stats.bls.gov/news.release/union2.t03.htm; accessed December 1997.

14. T.P. Bowling, for the U.S. General Accounting Office, *Federal Labor Relations: Official Time Used for Union Activities* (Washington, DC: U.S. Government Printing Office, 1996).

15. M.F. Masters and R.S. Atkin, Bargaining, Financial, and Political Bases of Federal Sector Unions, *Review of Public Personnel Administration* 15 (1995): 5–23.

16. U.S. Bureau of the Census, *Public Employment: Labor–Management Relations* (Washington, DC: U.S. Government Printing Office, 1992).

17. G.W. Bohlander, The Federal Service Impasses Panel: A Ten-Year Review and Analysis, *Journal of Collective Negotiations in the Public Sector* 24 (1995): 193–205.

18. U.S. Bureau of Labor Statistics, Work Stoppages Involving 5,000 Workers or More Beginning in 1996: http://stats.bls.gov/news.release/wkstp.t02.htm; accessed December 1997.

19. K.M. O'Brien, The Impact of Union Political Activity on Public-Sector Pay, Employment, and Budgets, *Industrial Relations* 33 (1994): 322–345; K.M. O'Brien, The Effect of Political Activity by Police Unions on Nonwage Bargaining Outcomes, *Journal of Collective Negotiations in the Public Sector* 25 (1996): 99–116.

20. W. Orzechowski and M.L. Marlow, Political Participation, Public Sector Labor Unions and Public Spending, *Government Union Review* 16 (Spring 1995): 1–25.

21. D.A. Dilts, Privatization of the Public Sector: *De Facto* Standardization of Labor Law, *Journal of Collective Negotiations in the Public Sector* 24 (1995): 37–43.

22. K. Bronfenbrenner and T. Juravich, *Union Organizing in the Public Sector: An Analysis of State and Local Elections* (Ithaca, NY: ILR Press, 1995).

23. Commission on the Future of Worker–Management Relations, *Report and Recommendations* (Washington, DC: U.S. Government Printing Office, 1994).

24. M.E. Motley, for U.S. General Accounting Office, *U.S. Postal Service: Challenges in Improving Performance and Meeting Competition* (Washington, DC: U.S. Government Printing Office, 1996).

25. R.P. Engvall, Public-Sector Unionization in 1995 or It Appears the Lion King Has Eaten Robin Hood, *Journal of Collective Negotiations in the Public Sector* 24 (1995): 255–269.

26. S.J. Libeson, Reviving the Comparable Worth Debate in the United States, *Comparative Labor Law Journal* 16 (1995): 358–398.

27. J. Walters, The Trade-off Between Benefits and Pay, *Governing* 8 (December 1994): 55–56.

28. J. Harris and J. Markoe, Medical Savings Accounts: The Critical Factor in Health Care Debate, *Government Finance Review* 12 (October 1996): 44–45; Who Are Winners and Losers Under MSAs?, *Government Finance Review* 13 (February 1997): 2.

29. T.J. Cavanaugh, Participation in "Cafeteria" Plans, *Government Finance Review* 10 (October 1994): 48–49.

30. U.S. Bureau of the Census, Public Employment Retirement System Survey, 1996: http://www.census.gov/ftp/pub/econ/www/go0700.html; accessed December 1997.

31. For details on federal systems, see K.D. Whitehead, ed., *Federal Personnel Guide* (Chevy Chase, MD: Key Communications Group, published annually).

32. U.S. General Accounting Office, *Public Pensions: Summary of Federal Pension Plan Data* (Washington, DC: U.S. Government Printing Office, 1996).

33. Employee Retirement Income Security Act, P.L. 93-406, 88 Stat. 829 (1974).

34. Small Business Job Protection Act, P.L. 104-188, 110 Stat. 1755 (1996).

35. *Bowen v. Public Agencies Opposed to Social Security Entrapment*, 477 U.S. 41 (1986).

36. B. Dotson, IRS Pursues State and Local Government FICA Payments, *Government Finance Review* 13 (February 1997): 39–41.

37. Federal Insurance Contributions Act, ch. 2, 53 Stat. 175 (1939).

38. U.S. Bureau of Labor Statistics, *Employee Benefits in State and Local Governments, 1994* (Washington, DC: U.S. Government Printing Office, 1996), 80.

39. P. Zorn, *1995 Survey of State and Local Government Employee Retirement Systems* (Chicago: Public Pension Coordinating Council, 1996).

40. Zorn, *1995 Survey of State and Local Government Employee Retirement Systems*, 92.

41. U.S. General Accounting Office, *Private Pensions: Most Employers That Offer Pensions Use Defined Contribution Plans* (Washington, DC: U.S. Government Printing Office, 1996).

42. J.J. Jankowski, Jr., Defined Contribution Plans, *Pensions* 79 (February 1997): 14–17.

43. U.S. Bureau of the Census, Percent Distribution of Receipts, Benefits and Withdrawal Payments, quarter ending December 31, 1996: http://www.census.gov/ftp/pub/govs/qpr/964qprt3.txt; accessed December 1997.

44. M.J. Samet, T.P. Peach, and W.P. Zorn, *A Study of Public Employee Retirement Systems* (Schaumberg, IL: Society of Actuaries, 1996).

45. J.H. Dulebohn, A Longitudinal and Comparative Analysis of the Funded Status of State and Local Public Pension Plans, *Public Budgeting & Finance* 15 (Summer 1995): 52–72.

46. Zorn, *1995 Survey of State and Local Government Employee Retirement Systems*, 51; also see U.S. General Accounting Office, *Public Pensions: State and Local Government Contributions to Underfunded Plans* (Washington, DC: U.S. Government Printing Office, 1996).

47. K.J. Engebretson, A Multi-asset Class Approach to Pension Fund Investments, *Government Finance Review* 11 (February 1995): 11–14.

48. Pension Obligation Bonds: Practices and Perspectives, *Government Finance Review* 12 (December 1996): 42–44.

49. P. Young, Public Pension Fund Ratings, *Government Finance Review* 12 (December 1996): 45–47.

50. D.J. Patterson, Public Pension Funds and Economically Targeted Investments, *Public Budgeting and Financial Management* 6 (1994): 566–598.

51. A Bill To Regulate and Improve the Civil Service of the United States (Pendleton Act), ch. 27, 22 Stat. 403 (1883).

52. R.D. Lee, Jr., *Public Personnel Systems*, 3rd ed. (Gaithersburg, MD: Aspen Publishers, 1993).

53. Civil Service Reform Act, P.L. 95-454, 92 Stat. 1111 (1978).

54. D.F. Kettl et al., *Civil Service Reform: Building a Government That Works* (Washington, DC: Brookings Institution, 1996).

55. U.S. Bureau of the Census, Federal Government Civilian Employment by Function: October 1995: http://www.census.gov/govs/apes/95fedfun.txt; accessed December 1997.

56. U.S. Bureau of the Census, Public Employment Data: October 1995, Total, All States: http://www.census.gov/ftp/pub/govs/apes/95stus.txt; accessed December 1997.

57. U.S. Bureau of the Census, 1995 Public Employment Data: Local Governments: http://www.census.gov/govs/apes/95locus.txt; accessed December 1997.

58. U.S. Office of Personnel Management, *Federal Civilian Workforce Statistics: Employment and Trends as of May 1996* (Washington, DC: U.S. Government Printing Office, 1997), 19.

59. Unpublished data from 1995 Survey of State Budget Offices, conducted by School of Hotel, Restaurant, and Recreation Management, The Pennsylvania State University.

60. In the 1995 survey, two states reported a 50-50 split between business and the social sciences. The 1970 data are from Survey of State Budget Offices, conducted by Department of Public Administration, The Pennsylvania State University, in conjunction with the Budget Office of the Commonwealth of Pennsylvania and with the endorsement of the National Association of State Budget Officers; see R.D. Lee, Jr., A Quarter Century of State Budgeting Practices, *Public Administration Review* 57 (1997): 133–140.

61. R.D. Lee, Jr., Educational Characteristics of Budget Office Personnel and State Budgetary Processes, *Public Budgeting & Finance* 11 (Fall 1991): 69–79.

62. U.S. Office of Management and Budget and Chief Financial Officers Council, *Federal Financial Management Status Report and Five-Year Plan* (Washington, DC: U.S. Government Printing Office, 1996).

63. J.L. Esser, GFOA Certification: A Unique Opportunity, *Government Finance Review* 13 (April 1997): 3; N. Gleason, Start Studying: The First GFOA Certification Exam, *Government Finance Review* 13 (April 1997): 41–42.

64. U.S. General Accounting Office, *Tax Administration: Lessons Learned from IRS' Initial Experience in Redeploying Employees* (Washington, DC: U.S. Government Printing Office, 1997).

65. I.T. David, Implementing GAAP and Improving Financial Management, *Government Accountants Journal* 43 (Fall 1994): 29–34.

CHAPTER 14

Intergovernmental Relations

Each level of government has discrete financial decision-making processes that determine matters of revenue and expenditure. Decisions about revenues and expenditures at different levels of government, however, are interdependent. Budgetary decisions made at one level are partially dependent on budgetary decisions made at other levels. Nonbudgetary decisions made at one level also may have dramatic impacts on budgets at another level.

This chapter examines the financial interdependencies among the federal, state, and local governments.[1] The first section examines some of the basic economic and political problems that stem from having three major levels of government that provide various services and possess differing financial capabilities. The second section considers the patterns of interaction among the different levels, and the third section considers the main types of intergovernmental financial assistance programs. Devolution of responsibility from federal to state and local levels, especially welfare reform, are key topics. The chapter concludes with a discussion of current issues and alternatives for restructuring these patterns of financial interaction, including the controversial issue of unfunded mandates.

STRUCTURAL AND FISCAL FEATURES OF THE INTERGOVERNMENTAL SYSTEM

For convenience, we have commonly referred throughout this book to the three levels of governments, but at this point this simplification must be set aside. In this section, we consider the problems associated with having multiple levels and types of governments.

Areal and Functional Relations

Multiple Governments. In addition to the federal government and the 50 state governments, there are over 86,000 local governments and the District of Columbia.[2] The local "level" is not a single level in that most states have county governments (over 3,000 nationwide), and within their boundaries exist such general purpose governments as municipalities and sometimes townships. Superimposed over these are numerous independent school districts and special purpose districts such as irrigation and sewer districts. Special districts, of which there are over 33,000, are the most numerous.

These various local governments are not merely subunits of their state governments, nor are the states subunits of the national government. In a unitary system, policies are set by the national government, and their administration is delegated to lower levels of government, which are subunits of the central government. The United States and a few other large countries such as Canada, Germany, and India have federal systems. In a federal system, each constitutionally defined level of government has substantial autonomous decision-making authority defined in the constitution.

Many countries that heretofore have been characterized by high degrees of centralized governmental authority are implementing policy, legal, and constitutional reforms to increase the autonomous authority of regional, provincial, or local level governments, although that does not necessarily mean shifts from unitary to federal systems. India, for example, enacted in 1991 constitutional reforms to establish certain powers and responsibilities for local governments as a matter of national constitutional authority, effectively removing some aspects of state government control over local government. In the newly independent republics of the former Soviet Union, central authority over all governmental functions is gradually giving way to increased responsibility at the regional and city levels, but that authority is defined and delimited by the central government. In the United States, local governments are not constitutionally defined, but are instead subject to the discretion of their state governments.

Having myriad governments at different levels within a nation can be defended in several ways. By having multiple governments, an omnipotent, despotic type of government may be avoided. Another advantage is that the diversity of governments allows for differing responses according to the divergent needs of citizens in different locales. The Federalist framers and advocates for the U.S. Constitution defended a federal structure using three arguments: (1) it would promote a sense of community and affinity between citizens and the government; (2) it would promote efficiency by assigning functions that had mainly local importance to local governments and functions of national importance to the federal government; and (3) it would promote liberty by avoiding concentration of power in the hands of a few.[3]

The existence of numerous units of government increases the probability that individuals will be able to find communities to live in that suit them. For example, people may locate in communities that offer desirable mixes of taxes and services. Of course, we do not suggest that such economic calculations are the sole criteria on which people base their location decisions, but the existence of multiple governments enhances that important aspect of quality of life.

Another advantage is that having multiple governments allows the achievement of economies of scale; functions may be performed by the size of government that is most efficient in carrying out the functions. Just as it may be advantageous from the standpoint of efficient resource use for private, profit-oriented organizations to grow to a large scale, it also may be advantageous for one unit of government to conduct some government activities on a large scale.

On the other hand, to perform all government functions at the central level might result in inefficient conduct of some activities. Lessened flexibility of operations and other diseconomies suggest the need for some functions to be performed by units of government smaller than the federal government; geographically and economically smaller-scale activities are more efficient when carried out by smaller governments. Probably many services can be provided most efficiently at the local level.[4]

Of course, no government, no matter what the level, is free to do whatever it pleases. The Constitution provides for the federal government's powers (especially Article I, Section 8) and reserves all other powers to the states (Tenth Amendment). Local governments have fewer constitutional protections, because these governments have been created by their states. Within these legal parameters, a higher-level government may impose standards upon lower levels.

Coordination Problems. The existence of thousands of governments results in coordination problems both geographically and functionally. Municipalities in a metropolitan area need some coordinative mechanisms. Road networks, for example, need to be planned in accordance with commuting patterns within a metropolitan area, and such plans should not be restricted to the geographical boundaries of each municipality. Before the federal government became involved in highway programs, many highways did not connect sensibly across state lines. Recreation and parks programs may be provided on a metropolitan or area basis and thereby achieve economies of scale.

This rationale, based on economies of scale, has led some to argue for consolidation of the local governments in a metropolitan area, such as Miami–Dade County, Florida, and Nashville–Davidson County, Tennessee. However, some studies have shown that the savings expected from metropolitan consolidation have not been achieved. Rather, greater efficiencies seem to result from competition among the various local governments in a metropolitan area.[5] Where coordination is needed among the local governments of a metropolitan area, it seems achievable through cooperation and shared decision making rather than consolidation. However, there does seem to be evidence that consolidation has benefits in the case of very small local units of government.

Functional coordination among different levels is also necessary because the three main levels of government share responsibilities for some of the same functions. Criminal justice, for instance, is a shared function; some type of police, court, and prison system exists at each government level. The independent pursuit of similar objectives by different governments can result in wasted resources and ineffective services.

Multilevel overlapping and shared responsibility can make it difficult to design federal programs to achieve national objectives. A good federal assistance program for local governments in one state may be a poor fit in another state with a different allocation of responsibilities between state and local governments. Therefore, increasing emphasis has been given to developing mechanisms for functional integration.[6] While program specialists stress functional integration, however, policy generalists may stress areal integration. This conflict has been popularized by Deil S. Wright as picket fence federalism—each picket represents a function, such as mental health or education, and all three levels of government make up part of each picket.[7]

A Case Example: Coordinating Water Resource Management. Managing subsurface and surface water resources is a good example of the difficulties involved in achieving intergovernmental coordination. Supplying local drinking water would surely seem to be an example of a service that can be handled most effectively and efficiently at the local level. However, the actions of private citizens and industry within the watershed for a local community's water source can make it difficult for the local government to protect its water supply if those individuals or industries are outside the city limits. This situation can lead the county or the state to take on a role in watershed protection. In addition, the federal government has determined that overriding matters of public health give it the authority and responsibility to set minimum standards for drinking water purity, causing local governments to budget perhaps more than they might wish if left to their own residents' preferences. Furthermore, large bodies of water have multiple uses, and the federal government has invested heavily in flood control dams in the East and impoundments to create irrigation sources for farmers in several states in the West. As a result, the United States has literally thousands of public and private agencies and companies involved in coordinated, and sometimes uncoordinated, actions to manage water resources.[8] Environmental concerns overlay on this complex system numerous federal and state regulations that have budgetary consequences for lower levels of government as well as private business.

Fiscal Considerations

Vertical

Vertical Imbalance. The conflict between the organizing principles of geographic area and program function plays out within the context of need for services and the corresponding need for revenues, with differences in capabilities existing both within levels of government and among levels.[9] Vertical imbalance, or noncorrespondence, refers to the relative abilities of different levels of government to generate needed revenue. Although one level of government may have a comparative advantage in providing a particular service efficiently, it may not have the same advantage in obtaining revenue. Another level of government, on the other hand, may possess sufficient revenue capability but is not the most efficient unit to provide certain services. In the United States, it is typically the federal government that possesses the greatest revenue capacity but not the comparative advantage in providing many government services, while states and local governments have functional expenditure obligations that are greater than their ability to raise revenue.

This disparity is due largely to the different revenue sources used by governments. The federal government, relying on personal and corporate income taxes, has a more elastic tax structure in which revenues increase with any increase in economic activity. While state and local revenue sources are relatively more inelastic, the demand for services provided by these governments is quite elastic.

Superior fiscal capacity can be used by one level of government to entice or persuade another to provide a given service. For example, the federal government used its tremendous fiscal capacity to persuade the states to build an interstate network of highways. Had the federal government not been willing to pay 90 percent of the cost of the system, there would be far fewer highways today.[10]

Horizontal

Horizontal Fiscal Differences. Problems caused by differences in fiscal capacity also exist for governments at the same level. From state to state, there clearly are differences in income and wealth, which are the basic sources of government revenue. For example, U.S. per capita personal income in 1995 was $22,788, but Connecticut's was $30,303, or 133 percent of the national average, and Mississippi's was $16,531, or only 73 percent of the national average.[11] Differences in income and wealth lead to differences in revenue-generating abilities, tax burdens, and levels of public services, although there is no simple correlation between income on the one hand, and taxing and spending on the other.

There is disagreement over whether per capita income differences are a good measure, however, of the differing fiscal capacities of the states. Widely used since the 1930s as a measure to differentiate among the states' relative needs for federal assistance, per capita income does not fully capture ability to pay for services within a state. Other measures include retail sales and gross state product (the latter is a measure similar to the national gross domestic product, discussed in Chapter 15). Analysts often use full market property value to assess debt repayment capacity, but this measure reflects accumulated wealth and not necessarily the direct ability to generate revenues.[12]

Another consideration is how hard the state and its local governments are making the effort to tax the resources they have available.[13] Before it was eliminated in federal budget cutting, the U.S. Advisory Commission on Intergovernmental Relations (ACIR) calculated a more complex measure that estimated the revenues a state would raise if it were to use the average tax system employed throughout the country. This representative tax system measured tax capacity and, when divided by population, provided a gauge of a state's fiscal effort.[14]

The ACIR subsequently added the concept of representative expenditures including information about costs for public services to help measure different states' financial abilities. According to ACIR calculations (based on 1987 data), Connecticut could afford to finance outlays 52 percent higher than the national average, but its actual fiscal effort was 22 percent below the national average. Mississippi had the weakest fiscal capacity as measured by the representative tax system, but its actual fiscal effort was 16 percent higher than the national average.[15] Based on that criterion, Mississippi deserves some balancing assistance because it has a greater need and is making a greater effort to use its resources.

Any comparisons among states, or localities, based on income, wealth, tax effort, and so forth do not capture an essential feature determining levels of services and levels of taxation. Residents of each state do not make uniform demands for services. Even if ability to tax or charge for services were distributed evenly across the country, expenditures would differ since citizens desire different levels of services. From a strict demand point of view, a state would provide only those services that citizens are willing to pay for. But willingness to pay for services, measured by tax effort, still may not solve the problem. The need for many government services is greatest in those states where the fiscal capacity to meet those needs is lowest. Mississippi is a good example of a state that has high needs and, by the ACIR measures, makes a better-than-average effort to meet those needs, but still falls short. The problem is even more acute with respect to different local jurisdictions within the same state. Central city governments within large metropolitan areas face demands for services that increase at a faster rate than does the value of their revenue sources.

Fiscal Responsibilities. Another issue is the extent to which one government with greater revenue-generating capacity should be responsible for aiding other lower-level governments. The issue is whether and to what extent governments should redistribute resources among different segments of the population and geographic areas. Since the 1980s, there seemingly has been less support for redistributive activities, especially at the federal level, than in the decades beginning with the Johnson administration's War on Poverty. The two decades from 1960 through 1980 witnessed the largest effort ever by the federal government to redress disparities among the states and among regions within states. By 1979, questions were raised about the ability of the federal government to sustain such a redistributive effort, and the New Federalism of President Reagan implemented significant reductions in federal programs to transfer funds to impoverished individuals and low-income states and localities. Efforts to eliminate the federal budget deficit have prevented any significant renewal of overtly redistributive programs in the 1990s.

One governing principle is that a government should engage in such funding only when the problem addressed corresponds to its level of responsibility, that is, the federal government should deal with national problems and the states with state problems. In 1987 in issuing Executive Order 12612, President Reagan said: "It is important to recognize the distinction between problems of national scope (which may justify Federal action) and problems that are merely common to the States (which will not justify Federal action because individual States, acting individually or together, can effectively deal with them)."[16] This executive order can justify an extremely narrow definition of appropriate federal government assistance to states and localities.

It has not only been officials identified with the Reagan administration who have argued for shifting functional responsibilities toward state and local governments. Alice M. Rivlin, former director of the Office of Management and Budget (OMB) and former director of the Congressional Budget Office, has argued for a fundamental rethinking of federalism that would reduce the federal role significantly and for placing federal emphasis primarily on foreign policy and national defense, social insurance, and a few smaller programs, while eliminating most grant programs.[17] Significantly, however, Rivlin also argues that this requires a substantially altered tax system, with a high degree of tax sharing between the federal and lower levels of government.

Disparities in fiscal capacity among governments at the same level lead directly to another problem, that of external costs and benefits of government functions. People of low income moving from states with low services to states with high services create new burdens on the high-service states. This occurred, for example, in the migration of the 1930s from impoverished areas to the West Coast and in later migrations from the rural South to cities in the North and West. Proportionately more people who move from lower-income to higher-income states receive welfare payments and generate greater demands on other public services than do those moving from states with similarly high levels of income and services. The flow of illegal immigrants into some states exacerbates those states' difficulties in financing social services and education.

Some of the costs of the failure to provide comparable levels of service across state lines are borne by those outside the low-service states. But the situation has positive aspects as well. Providing services at the most economical level may also result in the benefits' spilling over into other areas. The most obvious example is education. Higher levels of education generally yield higher levels of income. Given the mobility of the population, the benefits produced by one local educational system may spread far beyond its geographic boundaries.

Economic Competition. Governments compete with each other in trying to attract businesses and industries.[18] Firms locate for a variety of reasons, such as access to markets, a good labor supply, and availability of other resources. Because businesses seek to minimize production costs, the advantage lies with jurisdictions that have a high service level and low taxes on industry. Whether these are the main reasons businesses actually move or not is irrelevant. As long as governments compete with taxes and services, the fiscal effects are the same.

Competition for businesses among political jurisdictions can have important consequences, one being distortions in revenue and expenditure patterns. When special concessions are granted to firms, needed revenues must be obtained elsewhere or the level of services must be reduced. Devoting resources to special facilities, such as industrial parks, which are frequently financed by long-term debt instruments, may affect a community's ability to finance other capital projects, such as a civic center or a new sewage treatment plant. The package of tax forgiveness and free services that Alabama gave Daimler Benz in return for locating its first U.S. manufacturing facility in the state was a gamble. So far the evidence has been discouraging. The cost to the state has been nearly $300 million, or $168,000 for every job created.[19]

Although intense competition among some states for industrial relocation does cause problems, there are important benefits from this competition. First, it serves as a market-like regulator, preventing states and local governments from overtaxation. Second, it increases the efficiency of the allocation of public sector resources. States and localities that offer uneconomical incentives to businesses ultimately cannot sustain those incentives. There is a tendency toward equilibrium in the balance of incentives and the taxes and other charges necessary to make services available to support industrial development. Some states have backed away from the use of high-cost incentives.

Overlapping Taxes. The taxes of jurisdictions overlap with each other and ultimately the same people and firms must pay the various governments. Tax overlapping also occurs when all levels of government tax the same specific source, such as when federal, state, and local governments all tax income. Overlapping or multiple taxation in some sense is unavoidable and not necessarily undesirable. It causes serious problems only when a government at one level in effect preempts another government's ability to raise sufficient revenue. This can occur if the state sales tax rate is so high that it discourages local jurisdictions from levying such a tax. Indeed, states may preclude their local governments from having sales taxes but may provide them alternative sources of revenue. The same kind of problem occurs as a result of heavy federal personal and corporate income taxes. States and local governments, while often criticized for failing to raise sufficient revenue to meet needs, may be largely preempted by the federal government from major reliance on income taxes. Rivlin's proposals for a major reallocation of governmental responsibilities among federal, state, and local governments would address tax overlapping directly by introducing a new shared tax—a value-added tax—and sharing corporate income and gasoline taxes. Differences in the latter two taxes among the states would be eliminated.[20] Shared taxes also would reduce tax competition among states.

PATTERNS OF INTERACTION AMONG LEVELS OF GOVERNMENT

The structural and fiscal features of the U.S. intergovernmental system ensure that there will be numerous interactions among the differing levels of governments. Multiple governments within the same nation interact in numerous ways that directly involve budgetary and other financial decisions as well as each government's fiscal condition. Intergovernmental revenue transfers, such as grants, are a common form of interaction, but they are by no means the only important form. Federal direct expenditures and taxes that occur within a state or local jurisdiction are also important, as is the financial assistance that one level of government gives to another. Finally, regulations, statutes, and other actions that do not directly involve taxing and spending but nevertheless affect taxing and spending shape budgetary decisions.

Direct Expenditures and Taxes

Discussions of intergovernmental finance too often concentrate exclusively on financial assistance and neglect the importance of direct expenditures. How much the federal government spends in a state, and in turn how much a state spends in specific local areas have large impacts. Direct federal expenditures have varying geographical impacts, and the same is true for state expenditures.

Nongrant Spending. Locating government-owned or -built facilities in a jurisdiction can substantially affect the jurisdiction's economy. Political considerations are crucial at the state level in regard to the location of highways, state hospitals, and parks. Local and state governments work actively to obtain federal projects in their jurisdictions as one means of guaranteeing future prosperity. At the federal level, military installations, the awarding of defense contracts to corporations, which of course are geographically based, and other civilian installations generate intensive lobbying.

In an attempt to reduce the political bargaining over which military facilities to close during defense downsizing, a nonpartisan commission makes recommendations that then must be approved by the President and Congress. Although some of the political bargaining is reduced, members of Congress still fight to save facilities in their home districts or states. For example, in 1997 the Senate voted 66 to 33 against closing two military installations recommended by the commission, despite strong arguments from the Department of Defense that the bases were neither needed nor economically sensible.[21] Recognizing the serious economic impact of closing military installations, in 1993 the Clinton administration strengthened existing programs by introducing the Revitalizing Base Closure Communities program, which provides funding and technical assistance to convert former defense facilities to civilian uses. Allegedly, one ingredient in President Clinton's strategy to win California's electoral votes in the 1996 election was assisting two California local areas to convert major defense facilities into local economic development facilities.

Beyond the physical items are various programs that disburse loans and grants to individuals and corporations. At the federal level, these include Social Security, Medicare, support to farmers, and small business loans. These direct and indirect payments to individuals account for more than half the federal spending distributed among the states.[22] States also distribute large welfare and other human services payments among local jurisdictions. Federal spending includes significant salaries and wages paid to federal employees and members of the military, most of whom live in one state or another—about 12 percent of federal spending in states. Federal contracts with private firms and individuals represent still another 12 percent of federal spending in the states. These contracts, federal salaries, and miscellaneous other small programs total more than twice the actual federal grants given to state and local governments.

Tax Collections. In addition to spending, tax collections have varying effects on locales, and the resulting balance between federal expenditures and revenues has significant effects upon jurisdictions. Generally, federal revenues raised in the Northeast and Midwest have tended to be greater than the federal expenditures in these regions. The opposite pattern has existed in the South and West, with the exception of Texas, California, Colorado, Nevada, and Oregon, where the federal tax burden also is greater than total federal expenditures.[23] Table 14–1 indicates the states with the highest and lowest per capita federal expenditures minus per capita federal taxes in 1991. New Mexico was at the top of the list; the federal government spent $3,295 per person more than all federal taxes collected per person. Connecticut was at the other end, "losing" a net $2,429. Where the

Table 14–1 States with Greatest and Least Per Capita Federal Expenditures Minus Federal Tax Burden, Fiscal Year 1995

	Greatest Net Per Capita			Least Net Per Capita Flow	
Rank	State	Net Flow	Rank	State	Net Flow
1	New Mexico	3,295	41	New York	−952
2	Virginia	2,620	42	Wisconsin	−958
3	Mississippi	2,003	43	Michigan	−1,180
4	West Virginia	1,895	44	Minnesota	−1,241
5	North Dakota	1,614	45	Nevada	−1,334
6	Montana	1,565	46	Delaware	−1,345
7	Maryland	1,562	47	New Hampshire	−1,389
8	Alabama	1,395	48	Illinois	−1,474
9	Kentucky	1,316	49	New Jersey	−2,129
10	Missouri	1,256	50	Connecticut	−2,429

Source: Data from P. Fleenor, *Facts and Figures on Government Finance*, pp. 64 and 84, © 1997, Tax Foundation.

balance is less than even, federal finance has a negative impact on a state's economy. This has been the case in the Great Lakes states, which are part of the so-called rust belt. Federal taxes exceeded expenditures in 1991 in each of these states: Illinois, Indiana, Michigan, Minnesota, New York, Ohio, and Wisconsin.

Table 14–1 compares federal spending with federal taxing per person without regard to estimates of need or ability to pay. If one of the federal responsibilities is to redistribute income from wealthier areas of the country to poorer areas, then it should not be surprising that some states send more taxes to Washington than the federal government spends in those states. Figure 14–1 illustrates the relationship between the net revenue flow of federal expenditures and federal taxes, for all 50 states, with state per capita income. If this net federal flow is generally redistributive, then we would expect the pattern to be generally downward sloping to the right, which indeed is what Figure 14–1 demonstrates. The lower the per capita income, the greater the net flow of federal funds to the state.

We inserted the overall, linear trend line in the figure; the correlation between net flow and per capita income is −.67, which is consistent with the hypothesis that net federal revenue and expenditure actions are redistributive. Of course, numerous other factors are involved. Figure 14–1 only illustrates the general tendency of total federal activities in the states to be redistributive. As we noted pre-

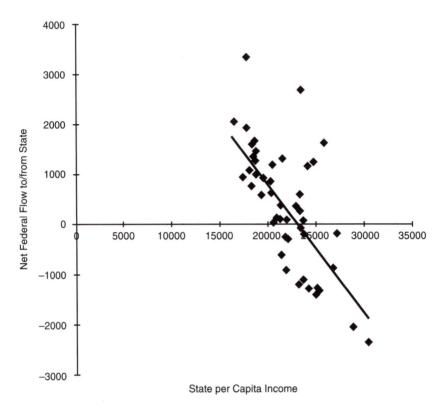

Figure 14–1 Net Federal Flow to/from State as a Function of State per Capita Income, 1995. *Source:* Data from P. Fleenor, *Facts and Figures on Government Finance*, pp. 64 and 84, © 1997, Tax Foundation; *Statistical Abstract of the United States: 1996*, p. 453, 1996, U.S. Bureau of Commerce.

viously, per capita income is not the only nor necessarily best indicator to try to estimate the redistributive character of federal spending. The figure is important though because it includes not just federal grants, but all federal spending in states. It would appear that total federal spending is more redistributive than federal grants alone.

Intergovernmental Assistance

State Aid. The literature on intergovernmental relations tends to overemphasize federal aid to state and local governments and underemphasize state aid to local government. In 1992, federal aid to states was $159.1 billion and to local governments \$20.1 billion.[24] State aid to local governments was \$195.8 billion, about 10 percent more than what the federal government provided to state and local governments combined. State support of local governments for most states is the largest element in the state budget. Of course, state aid probably would be much smaller were states not receiving substantial federal support. As noted in Chapter 2, states receive just over one-fifth of their revenue from the federal government. Local governments receive about 33 percent of their revenue from state governments and only 3 percent from the federal government; except for school districts, each type of local government obtains half or more of its revenue from its own sources.

Differences in federal and state support exist among the types of local governments (Figure 14–2). As of 1991 to 1992, 40 percent of all federal aid to local

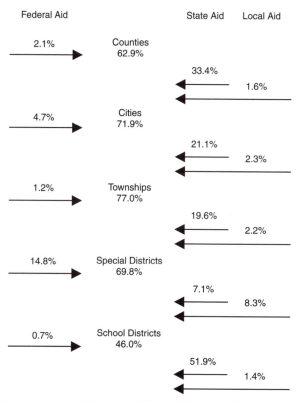

Figure 14–2 Intergovernmental Sources of General Revenues for Types of Local Governments, 1991–92. *Source:* Adapted from *Government Finances in 1991–92*, Table 6, U.S. Bureau of the Census, 1996.

governments went to cities, but these monies constituted less than 5 percent of city revenues. Special districts such as sewer and water districts are the most dependent on federal aid, which constitutes 15 percent of their budgets. Slightly more than half of state aid went to school districts, with these monies accounting for just over half of school district revenues (school districts are local governments that on average do not raise a majority of their revenues by themselves). Most of the other state aid was divided evenly between counties and cities.

These summary figures, of course, do not convey the great variety in patterns of state aid. Some states provide much greater assistance to local governments than other states; some states may provide a given service and thereby make direct expenditures, whereas other states may fund local governments to provide the service. New Hampshire, for example, provides only 13 percent of local government general revenues, much less than New Mexico, which provides 53 percent.[25] Several states provide more than $1,000 per capita to local governments—including Alaska, California, Minnesota, New Mexico, New York, and Wyoming. Others provide much smaller amounts—in addition to New Hampshire, the states providing the smallest amount of financial assistance to local governments are Hawaii, Rhode Island, South Dakota, and Tennessee.[26]

Aid to elementary and secondary education, as noted, constitutes the largest portion of state aid to local governments. Local school districts have not always depended as heavily on state and federal aid. Figure 14–3 shows that local sources in the early part of the century accounted for more than 80 percent of total funding, whereas it had declined to only 43 percent by 1980. Since then, local financing for education has been rising, to 48 percent by the mid-1990s. Just as state aid to local governments in general varies considerably from state to state, so too does state aid to education, with New Hampshire again providing the lowest percentage of funding.

Because of the importance of external, mainly state, funding, the manner in which funds are distributed to local school districts is often a matter of some controversy. States use a formula for distributing these funds. The *foundation plan*, as it is called, is geared to guaranteeing a minimum amount of educational expenditures either per pupil or per classroom. The word *foundation* connotes a definition of equality of educational opportunity, meaning that every student should have a minimum level of education—a foundation program. Formulas typically are geared to real estate property assessments, with districts having low assessments per pupil receiving more aid than districts having high assessments. Although relatively rare, some state formulas even have recapture provisions in which state aid to wealthier districts can be negative, the funds the state receives from wealthier districts being used to support the poorer districts. Separate formulas may be used for programs serving preschool, disadvantaged, and handicapped children as well as elementary-level children and secondary-level

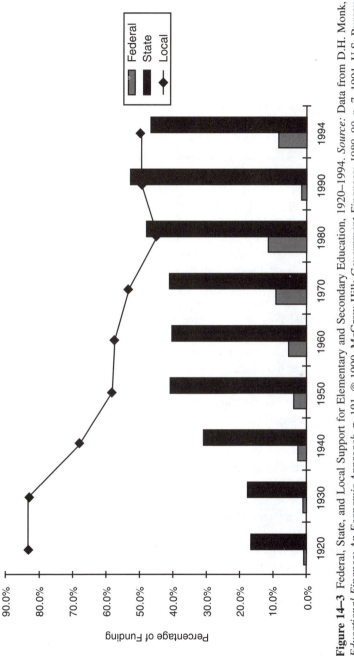

Figure 14–3 Federal, State, and Local Support for Elementary and Secondary Education, 1920–1994. *Source:* Data from D.H. Monk, *Educational Finance: An Economic Approach,* p. 101, © 1990, McGraw-Hill; *Government Finances: 1989–90,* p. 7, 1991, U.S. Bureau of the Census; and *Public Elementary–Secondary School System Finance Data,* 1994, U.S. Bureau of the Census.

children. A General Accounting Office study found that the foundation level itself does little to equalize opportunity; the foundation level in many states is below the average state contribution per student.[27]

These formulas were attacked in the courts starting in the 1970s as discriminatory; foundation plans were accused of failing to equalize educational opportunity among jurisdictions. While recognizing the great importance of education, in 1973 the Supreme Court decided in a Texas case, *San Antonio School District v. Rodriquez*, that the allocation of funds for education was a state responsibility and was not controlled by the Constitution.[28] The Court, in that case, was concerned that basing the formula on a macro measure such as the property tax base may not represent circumstances at the micro or individual level (e.g., extremely poor families might live in a wealthy district and not be receiving equal educational opportunity). Despite the Court's conclusion in Rodriquez, other cases have been won in state courts, so that many states have been required to alter their educational financing schemes to minimize disparities in per-pupil expenditures among districts. By 1991, courts in 12 states had overturned state formula financing systems, and courts had upheld existing systems in 14 other states.[29] Since 1991, 17 states have changed their equalization funding formulas or programs, although not necessarily in response to legal actions.[30]

Other state aid programs are comparatively small. Education is followed in size by welfare and highways.[31] Aid for these programs is usually geared to some type of formula (welfare programs are often per-client reimbursement programs). Virtually all states have some form of motor fuels tax-sharing formula that benefits local governments as well as the states.[32] General local government support, as opposed to specific functional aid, is higher than support for any functions other than education and welfare.

Overall, state assistance has been more predictable than federal aid because of the extensive use of formulas. Formulas facilitate budget planning at the local level because jurisdictions from year to year have some knowledge of what state funds will be. The only major controversies have centered on the factors used in the formulas. Aid to local governments in many states rise and fall depending upon the states' economic health. Local governments have shown resiliency in making up for state and federal decreases by drawing on their own resources and by placing greater reliance on user charges and other charges aimed at direct beneficiaries (see Chapter 4).

Federal Aid. Federal grants have been aimed at inducing state and local governments to increase the level of services in specified areas and are not intended to replace state or local spending with federal revenues. The inducement effect is based on the theory that the more separation there is between taxing and spending, the more taxpayers will not perceive the full costs of local services. This is known as the *fiscal illusion hypothesis*; empirical studies have shown that federal grants do induce more local expenditures than state grants to local governments.[33]

Matching provisions are usually required as a means of ensuring that grants will not merely result in a lessened tax effort by the recipients of the grants; without matching provisions, a $1 million federal grant could be offset by an equal reduction in local revenues supporting a program, thereby producing no increase in the level of services. A study conducted by the U.S. Treasury Department concluded that federal grants have only a minor effect on state and local expenditures, since matching requirements in federal grants have the effect of limiting spending by recipient governments as well as the federal government.[34] Other studies have shown that matching grants have the effect of inducing additional spending, whereas unconditional grants, such as general revenue sharing, tend to replace spending that the recipient government might otherwise make.[35] It is important to note, however, that substituting spending by a recipient government with a grant or transfer from another government may be the goal. States may want local governments to accept state aid and decrease reliance on the property tax.

During the 1960s, about 80 percent of all federal aid went for transportation and income security. As can be seen in Table 14–2, there have been substantial shifts since that time. Transportation, which accounted for more than 40 percent of the aid in the 1960s, declined at one point to less than 2 percent, but with new programs had increased again, to 11 percent by 1996. Health programs rose to 43 percent. Income security accounts for about 23 percent of the aid. It has fluctuated widely—up in the 1960s, down to the current levels, then a spike in the late 1980s to 1990 and back down again. Generally, the effects of rapidly rising health care costs and the number of individuals qualifying for income security programs account for most of the shifts that occurred between 1980 and 1996.

The amount of federal aid given to state and local governments varies among federal agencies. As can be seen in Table 14–3, the Department of Health and Human Services disburses the most aid by far, accounting for over half of all federal grants. A different perspective, however, is gained by looking at the portion of an agency's budget committed to grants. While the Department of Health and Human Services spends about 40 percent of its funds on grants, the Department of Education spends over half (55 percent) and the Department of Transportation and the Department of Housing and Urban Development spend 67 percent and 84 percent on grants, respectively.

Regional Differences. Just as total federal outlays are not uniform from state to state, so too are grants not uniform. In fiscal year 1995, the national average was $851 per capita in federal grants to state and local governments, up from $533 in 1990. The states receiving the highest per capita grants were Alaska ($1,846), Wyoming ($1,548), and New York ($1,321). The lowest group consisted of Colo-

Table 14–2 Percentage Function Distribution of Federal Grants-in-Aid, 1960–1996

	1960	1970	1980	1990	1996
Natural Resources and Environment	2%	2%	6%	3%	2%
Agriculture	3	3	1	1	0
Transportation	43	19	14	3	11
Community and Regional Development	2	7	7	4	3
Education, Employment, Training, and Social Services	7	27	24	19	15
Health	3	16	17	37	43
Income Security	38	24	20	30	23
General Government	2	2	9	2	1
Other	*	1	1	1	1
Total	100	100	100	100	100

Note: Includes grants-in-aid from federal funds accounts; does not include trust funds such as highway trust fund; totals may not equal 100 percent due to rounding.

*.5 percent or less.

Source: Data from *Special Analyses, Budget of the United States Government, 1989,* p. H-18, Office of Management and Budget; *Facts and Figures on Government Finance: 1992,* p. 103, © 1992, Tax Foundation; and *Historical Tables: Budget of the United States Government, Fiscal Year 1998,* Office of Management and Budget.

rado, Florida, Indiana, Kansas, Nevada, Utah, and Virginia with per capita amounts less than $700.[36]

These per capita grant figures must not be interpreted simply as revealing what areas are winners and losers in the federal aid game. As noted in the previous section, a state and its local governments might receive comparatively small amounts of grants but extensive economic support as a result of direct federal expenditures. Another consideration is what the corporations and individuals in a state pay in taxes. An apparent winner might turn out to be a loser when taxes paid are compared with federal dollars returned as direct expenditures or grants.

Assuming that the federal graduated income tax has the effect of drawing proportionately greater resources from wealthy states than from less wealthy states, federal aid could amplify or dampen this effect. For example, per capita federal aid to state and local governments might increase as per capita personal income declined, which would amplify the effect. This pattern, however, is not evident;

Table 14–3 Federal Agency Outlays and Grants to State and Local Governments, 1996 (in Billions of Dollars)

Agency	Total Outlays	Grant Outlays	Grants as Percentage of Total
Agriculture	54.3	17.1	31.5
Commerce	3.7	0.5	13.5
Education	29.7	16.2	54.5
Energy	16.2	0.2	1.2
Health and Human Services	319.8	129.1	40.4
Housing and Urban Development	25.5	21.4	83.9
Interior	6.7	1.7	25.4
Justice	12.0	1.4	11.7
Labor	32.5	7.0	21.5
Transportation	38.8	26.0	67.0
Treasury	364.6	0.4	0.1
Environmental Protection	6.0	2.8	46.7
Emergency Management	4.2	2.0	47.6
Other	649.5	2.0	0.3
Total	1560.3	227.8	14.6

Source: Data from *Budget of the United States Government, Fiscal Year 1998*, p. 326, Office of Management and Budget; and *Analytical Perspectives*, p. 193, 1997.

the correlation between state per capita federal grants and transfers and state per capita income, while positive, is only .27. This indicates that federal grants are somewhat higher as income increases. Other factors explaining the distribution of federal grants include the number of Medicaid recipients and the amount of federal land in the state, which brings money from minerals, timber, and grazing rights.[37] Again caution is necessary when interpreting only one measure of federal economic impact on states. The lack of a clear pattern is explained by the numerous federal grant programs that tend to offset each other in benefiting particular types of states.

Studies that have compared federal aid and state aid to urban areas have concluded that, while both are responsive to need, state aid is more responsive. Cities with greater fiscal problems receive greater per capita state assistance. An important factor in this is local initiative itself; some cities are much more aggressive and adept at securing federal and state aid, and this is not necessarily correlated with extent of need.[38] In recent years, state governments have tried to offset some of the decline in federal aid to local governments, particularly targeting their assistance to cities with the severest problems measured in terms of need, such as prevalence of poverty and low fiscal capacity.

Within metropolitan areas, fiscal imbalances also can cause problems in the pattern of services and ability to pay for those services. Capital flight out of central cities in the form of wealthier households and businesses moving to the suburbs exacerbates differences, especially in the older cities of the Northeast and Midwest, although cities in other parts of the country have been experiencing similar phenomena. One of the ways some metropolitan areas have combated this problem is to develop metropolitan area tax base sharing and other fiscal equalization strategies.[39] Although not a widespread practice, multiple municipal jurisdictions within the same metropolitan area have begun to see advantages in increased coordination as city regions look to their potential fate in a global economy.[40]

Federal aid to local communities can be provided directly to these communities or indirectly through the states. In the latter case, state officials are allowed some discretion in distributing federal funds, although federal regulations may require that a given amount pass through to localities and that some of this money be distributed according to set criteria, such as population. State enabling legislation often is required before a local government may receive funds directly from the federal government.

Devolution and Future Trends. The dollar volume of federal grants-in-aid continues to climb each year, but federal aid as a percentage of state and local outlays reached a peak in 1979 to 1980 and is not expected to grow again in the foreseeable future. The decline in federal assistance and the increasing responsibilities of state and local governments are changing the character of intergovernmental relations in the United States. As Figure 14–4 indicates, federal aid in 1980 was approximately 28 percent of state and local outlays; since then, that percentage has been slipping. On various comparative measures, federal aid is expected to continue to decline. In 1996, it was about 16 percent of the federal budget, somewhat higher than the preceding several years.[41] Federal aid has hovered between 2 and 3 percent of gross domestic product throughout the period covered by Figure 14–4.

The figure also indicates the substantial change in character in federal aid to state and local governments. In the 1960s, federal aid focused significantly on physical capital investments; almost 50 percent of total grant outlays were for capital investment. By 1993, capital investment outlays had declined to only 16 percent. During the same period, payments to individuals went from 35 percent (1960) of total grants to 63 percent (1993). Although President Clinton started his

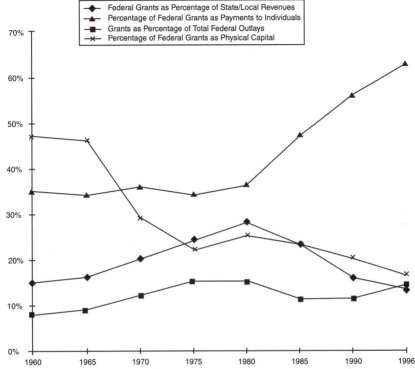

Figure 14–4 Selected Characteristics of Federal Grants to State and Local Governments, 1960–1996. *Source:* Adapted from *Budget of the United States Government, Fiscal 1997,* p. 194, Office of Management and Budget, 1997.

first term proposing an increase in federal support for capital investments, the proposal was largely abandoned due to deficit reduction measures. It is unlikely that significant federal support for physical capital or other investments will be renewed.

This shift to payments to individuals has meant a change from state and local government as an active agent in implementing federally funded programs to a role as a conduit for channeling federal funds to individuals.[42] During the 1960s, with extensive federal assistance to capital infrastructure programs, state governments mainly (but also local governments) were heavily involved in selection, design, and contracting for public works financed by federal dollars. Payments to individuals channeled by the states have meant hiring more staff to determine eligibility, to verify information, and to track benefits paid to recipients. Prior to welfare reform in the mid-1990s (discussed later in this chapter), the states were not very involved in program design.

Federal aid cutbacks have created difficulties for many governments and have been nearly devastating for others, especially when combined with reductions in revenue due to economic recessions and taxing limitations. The last recessionary period of 1990 to 1992 caused enormous hardship for state and local governments. The boom period since has enabled many state budgets to develop large budget reserve pools as revenue surpluses have accumulated with economic good times.

Prior to the 1960s, state and local governments had primary financing responsibility for domestic programs. Beginning with the 1960s and the antipoverty programs of the Johnson administration, the financial role of the federal government came to equal and, by the mid-1970s, even exceed the financial role of state and local governments. While state and local spending has not yet caught up with federal domestic spending with the substantial shifts in spending patterns of the last decade, growth in state and local government spending has been more rapid than growth in federal spending. Not only have federal grants for capital declined, but state and local spending for capital investment as a percentage of gross domestic product also has declined. Thus, states have had to scramble to keep services operating and in many situations have had little or no choice but to cut programs and sometimes eliminate them. The good news, however, is that state and local governments have responded by improving management and efficiency, increasing their own-source revenue generation, and moving toward employment of user charges and other mechanisms that limit expenditures more to what people are actually willing to pay, a change that is producing greater overall allocative efficiency in the economy. This signals a stronger role for state and local governments as determinants of domestic policy, and for many it is a welcome shift back toward a more decentralized political system in which federal management expertise is no longer seen as significantly greater than that of state and local governments.

Devolving greater responsibility and control to state and local governments became the companion theme to balancing the federal budget. As we will discuss in a following section, additional consolidation of federal grant programs and use of more block grants in lieu of more restricted programs is one of the hallmarks of the devolution campaign. But devolution has meant not only a relaxation in federal requirements, but it also has meant a fundamental shift in responsibility for policy, programs, and financing. Devolution involves outright reductions in federal aid to state and local governments, changing some programs from matching to non-matching grants, and of course greater flexibility.[43] Some critics point out, however, that devolution will have negligible impact on the total size of the public sector. One estimate is that if all functions except defense and foreign affairs, debt service, social security, and other federal payments to individuals were devolved to state and local governments, and if states proved to be able to carry out the devolved programs for 90 percent of the previous federal cost, the total cost of government would drop by less than half of one percent.[44] State and local governments face a large reorientation in policy formulation, program design, and program implementation in assuming responsibilities that have been determined by federal policy and program design since their origins.[45]

Welfare Reform as a Case Study in Devolution. The most prominent shift in devolving policy and program design has been reconfiguring the nation's welfare system. The Personal Responsibility and Work Opportunity Reconciliation Act (PRWORA) of 1996 shifted federal responsibility for setting welfare standards and replaced the long-standing approach of federal matching grants with a fixed block grant program.[46] This was preceded by considerable relaxation in federal requirements through granting states waivers, exempting them from many federal requirements. By 1995, 39 waivers had been granted to 34 states allowing a wide range of experimentation in the transition from welfare to work, in privatizing many aspects of program administration, in consolidating disparate low-income assistance programs, and a variety of other state innovations.[47] Under PRWORA, states now are responsible for determining eligibility, setting benefit levels, and program administration. A block grant to replace the Aid to Families with Dependent Children program—Temporary Assistance for Needy Families—required states to implement their programs by July 1997.

A key feature of the devolved welfare system is a limitation on eligibility for Temporary Assistance for Needy Families. Families have a lifetime limit of five years in which they may receive assistance, putting a premium on state program designs to get individuals employed and off welfare. Welfare system employees who once were responsible for eligibility determination and enforcement of standards have become job counselors, and the transition has proven difficult for many states.[48] States also are responsible for enforcing the five-year limitation on benefit eligibility, which raises serious questions about the adequacy of information systems to track welfare recipients who move from place to place, across state lines.[49] Although many states initially may experience funding increases, as the transition started during a time of relative budget comfort in many states, fiscal pressures will mount on state and local governments as the federal block grants remain fixed in time, especially when the next surge in unemployment occurs.[50]

Other Elements Affecting Intergovernmental Patterns

Direct expenditures and financial assistance provided by one level of government to another are not the only factors in the U.S. system of intergovernmental relations that affect budgeting. In addition to restrictions and requirements built into most financial assistance, the programs financed by the assistance also contain various requirements that influence how state and local governments plan and budget. Another element derives from the fact that state governments are the constitutional authorities for establishing local governments within their jurisdiction and thus have significant roles in determining what revenue sources local governments may use, what services local governments are responsible for providing, and under what circumstances local governments may enter into debt.

Features Associated with Financial Assistance. The preceding sections discussed the targeting aspects of grants provided by one level of government to another. Additional controls often are built into the assistance arrangement. One of the fastest growing budgetary components for all levels of government is the Medicaid program, which offers health assistance to the poor. Prior to 1991, some states adopted taxes on health providers as one of the means to raise the funds required by the state matching provision. In 1991, the Health Care Financing Administration (HCFA), through regulation, prohibited the use of health provider taxes and prohibited counting private donations to health providers as part of the state match.[51] From HCFA's point of view, this regulation relates to the program's intent to provide additional health care financial assistance to the poor and the concern that the federal assistance should provide additional funding and not be a replacement for other sources of funding. From the states' point of view, HCFA was imposing an unreasonable limit on their attempts to be innovative in securing funds. Nevertheless, the states were required to comply with HCFA's ruling, thereby creating major financial problems for them.

Features Not Directly Associated with Financial Assistance. In other ways, the federal government's authority under the Constitution has been used to preempt state authority, and state governments frequently preclude local action in various arenas. Since the late 1960s, coinciding with the development of many of the federal assistance programs, federal preemptions of state and local authority have increased at a rapid pace. From 1960 through 1995, more than 800 statutory actions were implemented preempting state policy or action in favor of federal policy or action.[52] Examples since 1990 include the Clean Air Act Amendments of 1990 (104 Stat. 2399), the National Highway Traffic Safety Administration Authorization Act of 1991 (105 Stat. 2081), and the Telephone Consumer Protection Act of 1991 (105 Stat. 2394). Many of these acts, such as the Clean Air Act Amendments, stipulate programmatic choices that states and local governments must make.

Critics of the growing federal preemption of state and local government authority cite the Supreme Court's 1985 decision in *Garcia v. San Antonio Metropolitan Transit Authority* (469 U.S. 528) as a bellwether. In that case the Court narrowly interpreted the extent to which the Constitution protects the powers and authority of the states. However, analysis of numerous other cases involving financial administration, personnel policies, and program management since *Garcia* suggests that there is no particular pattern of support either for a central government or state government position. To the contrary, there has emerged some "resurgence of federalism" in Court decisions in recent years, although no dominant trend has been established one way or the other.[53]

State Control of Local Governments. These issues are not limited to federal effects on state and local governments. Since state governments have full constitutional authority over local governments, significant limitations on local authority may stem from state actions. The trend would seem to be toward increased state controls over local financial management practices.[54] Statutory debt limitations, usually expressed as a maximum debt to the property tax base ratio, are common, and requirements that state legislatures approve through formal legislative enactment some local taxes, such as sales taxes, exist in many states.

A state also may assume direct control of a local government if it cannot exercise the capacity to govern itself. Instances of state takeover of municipal functions have been associated with some aspect or another of financial failure, but not usually bond debt failures. And it is not restricted to certain size cities. The State of Florida appointed a State Control Board in December 1996, to supervise the City of Miami's budget and finances after the city was unable to balance its budget in two successive years, which is against state law.[55] In 1997, the State of North Carolina took over the small town of Princeville, under a previously never used state statute dating back to 1931. The state's Local Government Commission took over city finances and revenue collections, while the town commissioners continued to govern otherwise. Town officials had been unable, or unwilling, to collect taxes due, and the city sewer system was overflowing into the streets due to neglected maintenance.[56]

Philadelphia, New York, and East St. Louis are among other cities with state-appointed oversight or financial control boards. New York's board, appointed in 1975, will continue at least until 2008.[57] Somewhat analogous has been the situation with the nation's capital, except it is the federal government that statutorily controls the District of Columbia. Like cities in many states, the District operates under the auspices of a home rule charter that grants considerable autonomy to the District, albeit like state home rule charters, subject to change by the legislature. In 1995, a financial control board was appointed to supervise the finances of the District of Columbia, similar to one created by the New York State legislature to supervise New York City's finances when it verged on bankruptcy in the 1970s.[58] As part of the 1997 Balanced Budget Agreement (see Chapters 9 and 15), Congress also developed a financial assistance package for the District of Columbia. The aid package focused on relieving the District of its unfunded pension liability, a tax credit package, Medicaid, and prison system financial relief.[59]

A state's assuming complete control over a city is a rare event, but serves as a reminder that local governments are statutorily governed by state governments with nothing comparable to the federal Constitution's Tenth Amendment reserving a broad array of powers to state governments.

TYPES OF FISCAL ASSISTANCE

Grant Characteristics

Of the numerous aspects of grants-in-aid, at least four are particularly important: (1) the purpose of the award, (2) the recipient, (3) the amount, and (4) the method of distribution. The purpose of awards will be discussed in some detail in the next subsection, but for the moment it should be noted that purposes range from narrowly defined functions to general support.

Recipients can be individuals or families who receive financial aid, as in the case of welfare payments or Medicaid payments to the poor and medically needy. When programs provide guarantees of aid to individuals and families, they are referred to as entitlements. Sometimes the term *entitlement* is used for programs providing funds to state and local governments, as in the instance of the community development block grant program, in which funds are promised in advance to local governments.

The third aspect is the amount of aid that is made available. Some programs are open ended in the sense that aid is provided to all persons who qualify. All persons meeting a needs test based on income, for instance, might qualify for aid; if the number of qualified applicants increases, then the amount of aid available must also increase. This type of grant, of course, complicates budgeting, because administrators do not know in advance what funds will be needed. An alternative is for the legislature to predetermine an amount that will be available regardless of the number of potential recipients. The Women, Infants and Children (WIC) supplemental food program is an example of a program in which the amount a family is eligible for is determined by a needs test but funding may or may not be made available for everyone who applies. Once the funding limit in a particular state is reached, other eligible candidates are placed on a waiting list. Since the early 1990s, WIC program funding has been sufficient to avoid eligible people being placed on waiting lists.

Fourth, there are different distribution methods. In one method, would-be recipients compete for awards by submitting proposals to indicate how funds will be used. This is common for demonstration grants available to private and non-profit institutions and several categories of grants available to state and local governments. Another method is to use a formula that allocates funds among eligible recipients. Formulas can be used to help target money where it is needed most. Gaining agreement on specific provisions in a formula among legislators can be difficult; for example, members of Congress evaluate proposed provisions of a formula in terms of how home districts or states will be affected. Sometimes the distribution is set by the legislative body, particularly in instances in which funds are provided for specified public works projects.

Categorical Aid

At the federal level, there are hundreds of grant programs, with *categoricals* being one of the most common types; states also have an extensive array of narrow grant programs. The number of federal categorical programs since 1975 has fluctuated. In 1975 there were 422 categorical grant programs. That number fell to 392 by 1984, but in the 1990s reached nearly 600.[60] The number, of course, does not signify the amount of assistance available, but it does indicate the diversity of programs.

Categorical programs have a narrow focus and target aid to deal with perceived problems. If rat infestations are seen as a major problem in poor neighborhoods, an aid program can be established to support efforts to eliminate or control rat populations. Categorical programs presumably allow the federal government to target aid to deal with problems that are perceived to be national in scope and allow the state governments to do the same in regard to state problems. Many categorical programs were created during the War on Poverty initiated by President Johnson in the late 1960s. Part of the motivation for creating categorical programs was that state legislatures, then dominated in many states by politicians from rural areas, were unresponsive to urban needs, especially the problems of large center cities. Many categorical grant programs were intended to channel funds directly to cities, bypassing the state legislatures.[61] Another reason for creating categorical programs was to target and restrict assistance in various ways in order to control the recipients' behavior.[62] For example, assistance for community development projects required extensive community participation to ensure that low-income groups had an influence over program design.

Categorical grants typically require would-be recipients to apply for aid by preparing proposals. These proposals indicate how problems will be addressed and what the expected benefits will be. During the application process, applicants are required to engage in considerable preplanning, which is expected to help increase the chances that the money will be spent effectively. Funding agencies, by means of an application review process, presumably can weed out unsound projects.[63]

Criticisms of categorical aid programs abound. Grants may skew local priorities. A jurisdiction might apply for funds for one type of project even though some other project, for which no grant funding was available, would provide greater benefits to the jurisdiction.[64] Another criticism is that much time and energy are consumed in drafting grant proposals. Still another is that some jurisdictions do not obtain their "fair share" of federal dollars simply because they lack adequate staff for proposal writing; small jurisdictions, in particular, may have little "grantsmanship" capability. Categorical grants make budget planning difficult because proposals may be held pending for months. Another problem is that grants are not coordinated. Furthermore, state legislatures resent being bypassed, and many grant recipients, governmental or private organizations, resent some of the restrictions that are attached to the use of funds.

One frequently made proposal is that the application process should be simplified. Simplification includes reducing the amount of paperwork involved and standardizing some forms and procedures to make the process comprehensible to applicants who may wish to seek funds from two or more agencies. OMB Circular A-102 and subsequent legislation reducing duplicative audit requirements have standardized some forms and procedures.

Revenue Sharing

General Revenue Sharing. A dramatic alternative to categorical grants is general revenue sharing (GRS), which at the federal level was created by the State and Local Fiscal Assistance Act of 1972. Under the original legislation, the federal government shared some of its revenue with states, counties, cities, and townships; in subsequent years, the states were dropped from the list of beneficiaries, in part because many had surpluses in their budgets and could hardly claim to be in need of general federal support.

Although general revenue sharing was allowed to expire in 1986, it is worthy of consideration in that it represents the opposite end of the spectrum from categorical grants. Three key characteristics of the now defunct program were:

1. pre-established amounts of aid
2. use of formulas for distributing the aid
3. considerable latitude to spend funds in terms of local priorities

When renewing the program, often for three years at a time, Congress set specific dollar amounts to be disbursed in given time periods. Such provisions allowed local governments to plan well in advance as to how GRS monies would be used; of course, the drawback from the point of view of the federal government was that this portion of the budget was relatively uncontrollable.

GRS allocations were made by a series of complex formulas. A ceiling was set to limit how much any jurisdiction would receive, as well as a floor to guarantee that most jurisdictions would receive some funds. A distinguishing feature of GRS was that jurisdictions received funds without having to make application for these monies.

GRS attempted to solve some of the problems associated with categorical grant programs. Jurisdictions had great freedom in deciding which functional areas would receive funds. Another benefit was that time and energy were not wasted in proposal writing. Jurisdictions that needed funds but lacked the staff capability to make application for categorical grants received GRS funds.

On the other hand, there were many criticisms of GRS. The formula was said to provide unneeded monies to some jurisdictions. The floor provision may have propped up basically inefficient jurisdictions that might otherwise have been forced by economics to consolidate their services with those of other governments. The ceiling, on the other hand, possibly denied needed funds to many deserving jurisdictions, particularly center cities. Communities allegedly were allowed to squander their GRS funds, whereas categorical grants required more planning.

GRS expired because a compelling case could not be made for its continuation. As the federal government faced annual budget deficits in excess of $200 billion, federal officials could convincingly argue that there simply was no revenue to share with local governments. Additionally, proponents faced the difficult task of identifying a national purpose being served by GRS. In the short run, eliminating the program caused serious budgetary problems for municipalities with shrinking tax bases. In addition, many local governments shifted to user charges, which in some cases were regressive (user charges are typically based on the cost of the service rather than the ability to pay).

While revenue sharing is no longer in operation at the national level, it is at the state level. States provide funds to local governments using formulas based on population and income. Fiscal pressures on state governments in the 1990s caused many to reduce amounts allocated to revenue sharing; for example, in 1992, New York cut local revenue sharing by $100 million, and numerous other states cut back on revenue-sharing funds.[65]

Block Grants. A form of compromise between GRS and categorical grants is special revenue sharing, or block grants. Under this system, a higher-level government shares part of its revenue with lower-level governments, but the use of funds is restricted to specified functions, such as law enforcement or social services. Sometimes a distinction is made between block grants and special revenue sharing, with the former requiring submission of an application and the latter not, but more often the terms are used interchangeably or the term *block grants* is used to cover both types of revenue sharing. State aid to education, using various formulas, is an example of a block grant, with the funds coming largely from state general revenue. State aid for local roads is another form of block grant, with monies coming from earmarked taxes on motor fuels.

Block grants at the federal level have been used as a method for consolidating categorical grant programs. These categoricals are grouped together so that jurisdictions have greater flexibility within specified program areas. The application process is greatly reduced, because a jurisdiction applies for only one grant instead of several. Early block grant legislation includes the Partnership for Health Act of 1966, the Law Enforcement Assistance Act of 1968, and the Comprehensive Employment and Training Act of 1973.

A landmark in block grant legislation is the Housing and Community Development Act of 1974.[66] The program provides entitlement funding to medium and large cities through the use of a formula and gives funds to states to award small cities on a discretionary basis. The law phased out programs for open space, public facility loans, water and sewer grants, urban renewal, model cities, and rehabilitation loans. Under the original legislation, entitlement cities were required to submit an application for funding; the process was considerably less detailed than had been required for the previous categorical programs. During the Reagan administration, the application process was dropped for the entitlement cities.

In 1981, the Reagan administration recommended numerous consolidations of categorical grants into block grants. Congress obliged by passing the Omnibus Budget Reconciliation Act of 1981, which among other things consolidated many existing categorical grant programs and created nine new block grants, four in health-related services, to be administered by the states.[67] Seven of the grants are controlled by the Department of Health and Human Services and the other two are controlled by the Department of Housing and Urban Development and the Department of Education. In subsequent years, other block grant programs have been added bringing the number to fifteen by the mid-1990s. The most recent round of consolidation and relaxing federal control created the Temporary Assistance to Needy Families, the initial major reform of welfare assistance in an attempt to devolve responsibilities from the federal government to states, as discussed above.

A distinctive feature of federal block grants is that monies are granted in lump sums to states, which determine how the money is to be used, and when it involves local government assistance, how funds are to be divided among governments within each state. This approach was championed as restoring power to the states. Available evidence indicates that states used this opportunity to improve the management of programs.[68] States standardized forms and the procedures used by local governments to apply for funds; the standardization sometimes cuts across block grants. OMB established standards for auditing these grants to ensure that local governments were operating according to provisions established in law and regulation.

Another distinctive characteristic of block grants beginning with the Reagan administration has been a substantial reduction in funds. These cuts were in part defended in the name of efficiency. Since the block grants provide more flexibility to state and local governments, fewer federal officials were needed to administer the programs and fewer state officials were needed to oversee local government operations. Another rationale has been that since the federal budget has had massive deficits, grant programs should not be immune from budget cuts.

State and local governments selectively have replaced some lost federal dollars, but overall the pattern has been for programs to be reduced in scope to reflect the cuts made in Washington. Some cuts in the Reagan years were postponed while categorical grants were being phased out and block grants phased in, but once the affected categoricals had been terminated, cuts took place in programs. States generally have increased their support of health and social services programs, in which they had been involved for many years, but have been less generous toward other programs, such as community services and low-income energy grant programs. Center-city governments tend to be harder hit by cuts than suburban and rural governments, since the former have a history of greater reliance on federal funding.

Figure 14–5 illustrates that state and local governments have generally maintained their overall revenue levels, although at slower rates of growth, despite relative declines in federal grants. State and local total revenues are shown in billions of dollars (left-hand axis), and the percentage of state and local general revenues constituted by federal aid is also shown (right-hand axis). State and local revenues as a whole have steadily increased, making up with their own sources for the drop in federal aid.

RESTRUCTURING PATTERNS OF INTERGOVERNMENTAL RELATIONS

Tax Laws

Tax Deductions. A substantive change that could be made is to adjust taxes in ways that would reduce the need for financial assistance. By increasing the taxing powers of lower-level governments, the need for grants-in-aid may be reduced. For example, taxpayers currently may deduct many state and local taxes from gross income before computing federal tax liabilities. Included are state and local income taxes, property taxes, and some other lesser taxes. Excluded are state sales, gasoline, and similar consumption and excise taxes. The Tax Reform Act of 1986 (TRA86) is responsible for removing the deductibility of some state

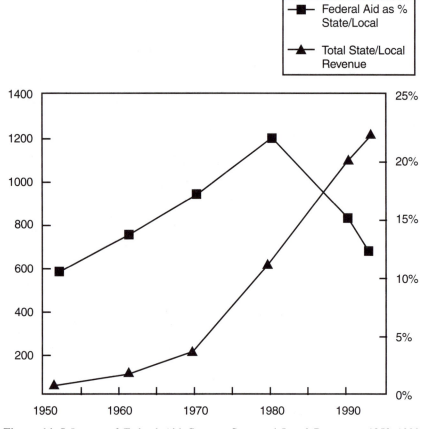

Figure 14–5 Impact of Federal Aid Cuts on State and Local Revenues, 1952–1993. *Source:* Data from *Facts and Figures on Government Finance: 1992*, pp. 230, 240, and 289, © 1992, Tax Foundation; *Facts and Figures on Government Finance: 1997*, p. 116, © 1997, Tax Foundation.

and local taxes, such as sales taxes. Federal tax law could be altered either to increase or decrease deductibility.

Economists have been particularly critical of deductions for property taxes in that this benefit is largely enjoyed by middle-income families. Lower-income families are less likely to own homes and therefore are unable to benefit from the deductibility, and higher-income families do not benefit appreciably from such deductions. The importance of the home building industry to the overall economy, however, has been used by lobbyists to argue in favor of property tax deductibility. TRA86 did limit mortgage interest deductions to only two homes, one of which must be a principal residence and the other a vacation or second home.

On the other side of the argument, tax deductions do provide some measure of latitude for state and local taxation. They reduce somewhat the differentials among states and among localities, and they mitigate some of the problems of tax overlapping. At least overlapping taxes may be held to a level that is not confiscatory. The strongest argument in favor of tax deductibility is that the practice is firmly entrenched and that any effort to eliminate deductibility for property taxes, for example, would be politically unacceptable without compensating tax relief.

Tax Credits. The institution of tax credits would be likely to cause a more substantial shift in revenue sources than would result from changes in tax deductibility. Tax credits would allow individual taxpayers to use taxes paid to one jurisdiction to reduce the tax liability owed to another jurisdiction. A tax credit reduces tax liability dollar for dollar, whereas a deduction of taxes paid to another jurisdiction from one's taxable income is worth only the marginal tax bracket percentage, the highest being 39 percent. One proposal sometimes made is to allow such credits for the federal income tax; the effect would be to redistribute revenue from the federal government to state and local governments. A tax credit on income taxes could encourage those states without income taxes to adopt them because the taxpayers would be less affected. However, if the tax credit is uniform regardless of income, it would benefit the wealthier states even more than the poorer ones.

Unemployment Insurance. The federal government has enticed or forced states to impose unemployment insurance taxes on employers by providing that most monies from such taxes may stay within each state; in the event that a state did not have an approved system, a tax presumably would be imposed by the federal government. Until TRA86, unemployment benefits were not treated as income under federal tax law, thereby providing an important benefit to individuals and creating a costly tax expenditure for the federal government. These benefits are now taxable. Inheritance taxes are practically forced on states by a federal tax provision deducting 80 percent of any state inheritance tax paid. Any state that did not adopt an inheritance tax would lose considerable appeal to retirees and other older citizens.

Taxes and Bonds. Another important benefit afforded state and local governments through federal tax law is the tax exemption on interest earned on bonds issued by these governments. Tax exemption has had the effect of allowing governments to pay lower interest rates to bondholders than if the bonds were taxable. An even more important impact of TRA86 on state and local revenues was the reduction in the types of municipal bonds that are eligible for tax-exempt status, particularly private purpose activity bonds (see Chapter 12). Some have argued that TRA86 has farther-reaching implications because provisions relating to required registration of tax-exempt municipal bond buyers and state reporting on arbitrage gains from tax-exempt bond proceeds undermine the autonomy of state and local governments within the federal system. The Internal Revenue Service has begun to audit some questionable tax-exempt bonds, suspecting that they may not meet the tax-exempt criteria.

Shared Taxes. Presently, the federal, state, and local governments in the United States have either exclusive or overlapping jurisdiction over various tax sources. Only the federal government may tax imports and exports. The federal government does not have a property tax or general sales tax. Federal, state, and local governments overlap in the use of personal and corporate income taxes. Some states benefit from linking their own personal income tax systems to the federal system. Individuals in North Carolina, for example, can file a state income tax form that bases taxes on the federal taxable income. This simplifies administration of the system and reduces state tax administration costs. When TRA86 expanded the federal tax base, it automatically expanded the base for most states, since their systems are tied in one form or another to the federal system. However, there is no shared link between the two—the federal Internal Revenue Service collects only federal income taxes, and state and local governments collect their own. State and local governments typically share a sales tax; it is collected by the state, but revenues are allocated to local governments that levy such taxes.

Some proposals for the adoption of a value-added tax have included the idea that it would be shared among levels of government. Sharing the tax means that it would be a common tax, so there would be no tax competition between states over the level of taxation. It would also mean shared administration, reducing the collection costs, and it would minimize the ability of one level of government to preempt other levels' use of a particular tax. State and local finance in the German federal system relies heavily on shared taxation. Any major realignment of responsibilities among levels of government also has to include changes in revenue systems as well.

Grant Requirements

Mandates. Other proposals to improve intergovernmental fiscal relations pertain to mandates. For instance, when a state legislature passes a law requiring school districts to adopt certain procedures in dealing with gifted children or children with learning disabilities, a mandate has been established that has budgetary implications. The federal government has tended to tie mandates to grants, making the stipulation that a government must meet specified conditions to qualify for funds. Notable crosscutting mandates—requirements that apply to most federal agencies and grant programs—require jurisdictions to pay locally prevailing wages, meet federal standards for architectural barriers for handicapped persons, and prevent discrimination based on race, sex, and the like.

Medicaid came under increasing fire in the early 1990s as a federal assistance program that ultimately imposes heavy costs on state governments. Federal mandates increasingly limit state control of Medicaid by specifying in great detail who is eligible and what costs are reimbursable. States have felt they are less able to make their own budgetary decisions.[69]

Unfunded Mandates. Another category for reform has been eliminating what many term unfunded mandates. These are federal or state mandates that are not necessarily tied to particular financial assistance programs. For example, federal laws and court rulings have set standards for state prison systems that in many cases require additional prisons to be built—without federal assistance. Clean air and water standards have forced local governments to build new solid waste treatment facilities, substantially change wastewater treatment systems, and adopt numerous other practices. The City of Columbus, Ohio, estimated that 13 environmental regulations may cost the city as much as $1.6 billion between 1991 and 2000.[70] Overall estimates are that local governments alone will be spending $48 to $50 billion a year by the year 2000, to maintain current environmental quality standards. Of course, one cannot argue that local governments would otherwise spend nothing and attribute the total spending to federal, unfunded mandates.[71]

State and local officials argue that these mandates should be accompanied by federal funding because they appear to be attempts to achieve goals previously set by the federal government through financial assistance programs and now, with federal aid cut owing to budgetary pressures, have become regulatory means to the same end. The furor over unfunded mandates perhaps was exemplified by what some argue was White House suppression of an ACIR report in 1996 that analyzed the 14 mandates state and local governments find most onerous. Among the report's recommendations were proposals to exempt state and local government employees from the Fair Labor Standards Act, the Family and Medical Leave Act, the Occupational Safety and Health Act, and other lesser annoyances.[72] Pressure on members of the ACIR eventually led to the report's being held without publication. In all likelihood, the ACIR's targeting for elimination several work force protection statutes was a key factor in the Clinton White House's opposition to the report.

The contrary view is that there are genuine national goals that relate to such public purposes as health and safety, environmental regulation, minimum living standards for every family, and so forth, and that these require federal action. Because there is a national purpose does not necessarily mean there should be a matching federal payment to assist in achieving that purpose. The same line of reasoning is employed by states in their use of mandates for local governments.[73]

The Clinton administration acted in 1993 through Executive Order 12875, Enhancing the Intergovernmental Partnership, to reduce unfunded mandates by requiring federal agencies either to provide funds necessary to comply with mandates or to show evidence of significant consultation with state and local governments before promulgating new regulations mandating state or local expenditures.[74] Then in 1995, Congress passed the Unfunded Mandates Reform Act, which requires any bill that would impose *new* unfunded costs greater than $50 million be subject to a point of order in either chamber.[75] This procedural hurdle makes it much simpler for either the House or Senate then to kill the bill; a majority of members would have to override the point of order.[76] Critics quickly pointed out that the law affects only new mandates, and hence does not provide any significant relief to state and local governments. Somewhat similar legislation was introduced in 1997 to require the Congressional Budget Office to analyze the effects on the private sector of new mandates that may have compliance costs in excess of $100 million.

The courts also have been somewhat involved in addressing federal mandates, although in cases not involving significant state and local financial issues. In 1995 in *U.S. vs. Lopez*, the Supreme Court struck down a federal statute that regulated possessing a gun in a school zone, and in 1997, the Supreme Court ruled that the provisions of the Brady Handgun Act requiring state and local law enforcement officers to conduct criminal background checks on persons applying to purchase guns were not enforceable.[77] Despite these cases, it is unlikely that the courts will be a significant source of relief for state and local governments for most categories of unfunded mandates.[78]

It is impossible to take any particular assistance program or any particular mandate and examine its effects in isolation. As shown throughout this chapter, some programs result in redistribution across states, other programs are intentionally targeted to the poorer states, and other programs are intended to affect classes of individuals wherever they might live. Intergovernmental questions are resolved, not by considering one program at a time, but by considering the entire system of programs. Many argue that state and local governments have been strengthened in recent years by having to rely more on their own resources, not weakened by the combination of decreased federal financial aid and increased mandated requirements.

Civil Rights. One particular controversy concerns the extent to which a jurisdiction's operations must comply with civil rights stipulations. In *Grove City College v. Bell* (465 U.S. 555), the Supreme Court ruled that only that portion of an organization affected by federal dollars had to comply with standards protecting against discrimination based on race, sex, age, and handicapping condition. In that instance, since the college's only federal support was for student-aid activities, only those had to comply. Congress in 1988 reversed that decision by passing the Civil Rights Restoration Act, which provides that all operations of a recipient government must meet federal standards; the law was passed over a veto by President Reagan.

Paperwork. Related to mandates are various reporting requirements that create paperwork and thereby create costs. States require local governments to submit numerous reports each year, and the federal government requires the same of state and local governments. The Paperwork Reduction Act, a 1995 revision of the 1980 statute, regulates agency requests for information from state and local governments, and from private corporations and individuals (see discussion in Chapter 10). Agencies are to reduce the information collection burden they impose on others by between 5 and 10 percent per year through 2001.

The Regulatory Flexibility Act of 1980 and Executive Order 12291 of 1981 require agencies to conduct regulatory impact analyses to determine the effects of proposed rules or regulations, including the effects on state and local governments. Executive Order 12498 of 1985 further requires agencies to develop annual regulatory plans that must be submitted to OMB; while it may not legally "veto" agency plans to issue regulations, by using this review process OMB can stall, if not block, plans that would increase the paperwork burden on state and local governments.

Another provision that attempts to deal with the problem of mandated requirements is contained in the State and Local Government Cost Estimate Act of 1981. The law requires the preparation of fiscal notes for proposed legislation that would cost state and local governments $200 million or more annually. Such fiscal notes, which explain the effects of the proposed legislation, are intended to aid legislators in their deliberations and to avoid unwittingly imposing severe financial burdens on these governments.

The Single Audit Act of 1984 is an additional paperwork reduction device (see Chapter 11).[79] Implemented through OMB Circular A-128, the act allows a state or local government receiving funds through numerous different federal programs to comply with those programs' audit provisions using a single financial compliance audit.[80] The 1990 Cash Management Improvement Act introduced prompt payment provisions that require the federal government to pay interest to the recipient when a transfer is late. A related provision requires states withdrawing federal funds early to pay interest to the federal government. Streamlining cash flow has been achieved through the provisions of this act.

Besides the reduction of mandates and paperwork, several other intergovernmental devices have been proposed and used. One concern is to ensure that jurisdictions have adequate information about grant programs. The General Services Administration, working with OMB, now publishes the *Catalog of Federal Domestic Assistance*; the catalog, which gives capsule descriptions of grant programs, can help a local government determine whether it might be able to secure federal funding for a contemplated project.

Grant Coordination. Another concern is to coordinate federal grants at regional and statewide levels. If a community is applying for a federal grant to assist elderly citizens, how would that grant complement other programs for the elderly in the region and how would the grant relate to state-level programs? In response to this type of question and as an outgrowth of the Intergovernmental Cooperation Act, the Bureau of the Budget (now OMB) in 1969 issued Circular A-95, which provided for the establishment of areawide and state clearinghouses responsible for reviewing and commenting on proposed projects. The review and comment process offered the potential for eliminating waste in the use of federal funds. Jurisdictions applying for these funds were expected to respond to any objections made by the clearinghouses and, where appropriate, modify the proposed projects.

On the negative side, the clearinghouse reviews produced delays in the grant process and frustrated mayors, their budget offices, and line agencies. For all of the time devoted to the reviews, projects in many cases were implemented much as originally intended, perhaps over the objection of various clearinghouses.

In 1982, President Reagan rescinded Circular A-95 by issuing Executive Order 12372, which was in turn amended the following year by Executive Order 12416. As part of an effort to provide "regulatory relief," the Reagan executive orders gave states responsibility for establishing appropriate review processes and allowed state and local elected officials considerable flexibility in determining what grant programs were to be submitted to the state single point of contact for comment and review. As a result, far fewer reviews are conducted than was the case under Circular A-95.

Federal counterparts to various state-level coordinating bodies have included federal regional councils, which were organized around the 10 federally standardized regions of the United States. The federal regional councils, consisting of representatives from federal domestic agencies, were intended to increase coordination among federal programs; these bodies, however, were eliminated by executive order in 1983 on the grounds that they were no longer needed.

Federal-state, interstate, and interlocal arrangements have been developed for the provision of services (as distinguished from forums for discussion), including metropolitan councils of governments that involve officials from various communities in a region. One of the most successful interstate organizations is the New York Port Authority, established in 1921 by New York and New Jersey.[81] The authority operates terminals, bridges, tunnels, and the World Trade Center.

At the local level, there are numerous types of cooperative arrangements. Some counties provide services such as water and sewage treatment on a contract basis for municipalities within their jurisdiction. The choice of such an arrangement may be at the discretion of municipalities, as in the case of the Lakewood Plan, whereby communities can contract with Los Angeles County for virtually all city services, or at the insistence of state governments, which may require city-county cooperation for services such as police and fire protection.

Management Capacity. With the increasing emphasis on block grants, greater attention has been focused on the abilities of state and local governments to manage themselves. Devolving to these governments decision-making authority over the use of federal funds has been accompanied by a concern that they improve their management capabilities. There have been suggestions that the federal government assume responsibility for management capacity building, but the federal government has shown only a limited inclination to accept any such obligation. In fact, management improvements and other innovations at the state and local levels in recent years have led many to look to them as a source of management ideas for the federal government. The influential book *Reinventing Government* was in part responsible for the creation of a commission chaired by Vice President Gore in 1993 that reviewed the means by which federal management productivity could be improved.[82] Washington does not necessarily have superior management capabilities that, if only transferred to the state and local levels, would produce quick results.

Realigning Responsibilities. A far more comprehensive strategy for relieving both states and localities of some of their financial burdens involves reconfiguring responsibilities for major functions among the three levels of government. President Reagan in 1982 advocated two types of major revisions that he called *swaps* and *turnbacks*.[83] The swap proposal was for the states to accept financial responsibility for Aid to Families with Dependent Children (welfare) and food stamps and for the federal government in return to relieve the states of the financial burden of funding Medicaid.

The turnback proposal was for the states to assume financial responsibility for 40 or more federal aid programs in social services, education, transportation, and community development. According to the proposal, over a period of several years these programs would be transferred to the states and federal funding eventually would be eliminated. A basic rationale of the proposal was that if these programs were important to the states, they would be willing to commit their own dollars for continuance; on the other hand, there was the presumption that lower-priority programs would be phased out by the states.

Neither the swap nor the turnback concept was well received by state and local governments. The administration's position called for a drastic cut in federal grants at a time when state and local governments were suffering through a major economic recession that had depleted their treasuries. Additionally, the term turnback was a misnomer in that programs were not being turned back or returned to state and local governments. The Reagan administration proposals were not enacted into law, but the idea of a major reorganization of government responsibilities remains an important proposal for improving how the overall government system meets the needs of citizens.[84]

SUMMARY

Fundamental issues arise in regard to the question of how to structure intergovernmental relations. Functional integration results in picket fence arrangements that may deter geographic integration. Fiscal capacities differ among and within levels of government, so that the government that perhaps should provide services often lacks the necessary funding capability. Failure to provide services results in externality problems.

Both direct spending and grants-in-aid are important for intergovernmental relations. Decisions by federal and state agencies on the location and expansion of capital facilities affect the economic viability of local jurisdictions. Despite more extensive attention often being devoted to federal aid programs, state aid to local government is larger. Some states provide much of their local governments' revenue while others provide little, a point that should be stressed to avoid unwarranted generalizations. Aid to education constitutes the largest portion of state aid, with monies typically allocated on a formula basis. Federal aid is concentrated in the areas of education, income security, health, and transportation.

Major changes are occurring in the intergovernmental fiscal landscape, with substantial responsibilities for welfare reform already having been devolved to state governments, and numerous other proposals up for consideration. Furthermore, substantial concern has prompted legislative and executive action to mitigate the impacts of unfunded federal mandates. However, the fiscal impact of these changes is likely to be small since they affect only newly proposed mandates.

Intergovernmental grants have at least four aspects: their purpose (narrow, broad, and general), the type of recipient, the amount, and the method of distribution. Categorical grants are criticized as deterring coordination, skewing local priorities, and needlessly wasting time in proposal preparation. On the positive side, the categoricals are said to force planning in the preparation of proposals and to allow for screening out inadequately conceived projects. GRS supported local priorities and provided funds to jurisdictions that did not have staff available to apply for categorical grants. GRS was criticized as not targeted at any national purpose and giving funds to many undeserving jurisdictions. The program was terminated at the federal level, but some states engage in revenue sharing with their local governments. Block grants, a cross between categoricals and GRS, have the advantages and disadvantages of both.

In addition to grant programs, numerous other devices are employed. These include provisions in federal tax law that benefit state and local governments and review and comment processes for grant proposals. Also, mechanisms have emerged for providing services on an intergovernmental basis, such as with the New York Port Authority and the Lakewood Plan in California. Proposals have been made for major reconfiguring of program responsibilities among the federal, state, and local governments. Since the 1980s, many state and local governments have shown a resurgence, resulting in what many see as a healthy redress of balance between the federal level and the state and local levels.

NOTES

1. P.E. Peterson, *The Price of Federalism* (Washington, DC: Brookings Institution, 1995).

2. U.S. Bureau of the Census, *Census of Governments: 1992*: http://www.census/gov/govs/gov-struc.txt; accessed August 1997.

3. D.B. Walker, *The Rebirth of Federalism: Slouching toward Washington* (Chatham, NJ: Chatham House, 1995).

4. C.M. Tiebout, A Pure Theory of Public Expenditures, *Journal of Political Economy* 44 (1956): 416–424; K.O. Park, The Impact of Special Districts on Local Expenditures in Metropolitan Areas: An Institutional Paradox, *State and Local Government Review* 27 (Fall 1995): 195–208.

5. C.B. Wagoner, Local Fiscal Competition: An Intergovernmental Perspective, *Public Finance Quarterly* 23 (1995): 95–114.

6. E.T. Jennings, Building Bridges in the Intergovernmental Arena: Coordinating Employment and Training Programs in the American States, *Public Administration Review* 54 (1994): 52–60.

7. D. Wright, *Understanding Intergovernmental Relations*, 3rd ed. (Pacific Grove, CA: Brooks/Cole, 1988), 83–86.

8. T. Arrandale, A Guide to Clean Water, *Governing* 8 (December 1995): 57–62.

9. The discussion is based in part on B.P. Herber, *Modern Public Finance*, 5th ed. (Homewood, IL: Richard D. Irwin, 1983).

10. D. Rapp, Route 66 Gets a Federal Fix, *Governing* 7 (March 1994): 100.

11. U.S. Bureau of the Census, *Statistical Abstract of the United States: 1996* (Washington, DC: U.S. Government Printing Office, 1996), 453.

12. R. Bahl and W. Duncombe, State and Local Debt Burdens in the 1980s: A Study in Contrast, *Public Administration Review* 53 (1993): 31–40.

13. D.N. Hyman, *Public Finance: A Contemporary Application of Theory to Policy*, 5th ed. (New York: Dryden, 1996), 587.

14. U.S. Advisory Commission on Intergovernmental Relations, *Significant Features of Fiscal Federalism, Vol. 2, Revenues and Expenditures: 1992* (Washington, DC: U.S. Government Printing Office, 1992).

15. U.S. Advisory Commission on Intergovernmental Relations, *Representative Expenditures: Addressing the Neglected Dimension of Fiscal Capacity* (Washington, DC: U.S. Government Printing Office, 1990).

16. Executive Order 12612, in *Federal Register* 52 (1987): 41686.

17. A.M. Rivlin, *Reviving the American Dream: The Economy, the States and the Federal Government* (Washington, DC: Brookings Institution, 1992); F.T. Herbert, Federalism Reconsidered and Revitalized, *Public Administration Review*, 57 (1997): 354–358.

18. *The Kiplinger Washington Letter*, March 7, 1997, 1.

19. A. Ehrenhalt, The Devil in Devolution, *Governing* 10 (May 1997): 7.

20. Rivlin, *Reviving the American Dream*, 126–152.

21. H.M. Sapolsky and E. Gholz, Indefensible Defense Costs, *Wall Street Journal Interactive Edition*, July 11, 1997, 1.

22. P. Fleenor, ed., *Facts and Figures on Government Finance* (Washington, DC: Tax Foundation, 1997), 64.

23. Fleenor, ed., *Facts and Figures on Government Finance*, 64 and 84.

24. U.S. Bureau of the Census, *Government Finances in 1991–92* (Washington, DC: U.S. Government Printing Office, 1996), 7.

25. Bureau of the Census, *Government Finances in 1991–92*, 22.

26. S.D. Gold and S. Ritchie, State Actions Affecting Cities and Counties, 1990–93: De Facto Federalism, *Public Budgeting & Finance* 14 (Summer 1994): 29.

27. U.S. General Accounting Office, *School Finance—State Efforts To Reduce Funding Gaps Between Poor and Wealthy Districts* (Washington, DC: U.S. Government Printing Office, 1997).

28. *San Antonio School District v. Rodriquez*, 411 U.S. 1 (1973).

29. K.K. Wong, State Reform in Education Finance: Territorial and Social Strategies, *Publius* 21 (Summer 1991): 125–143.

30. U.S. General Accounting Office, *School Finance—State Efforts To Reduce Funding Gaps Between Poor and Wealthy Districts*, 35.

31. Fleenor, ed., *Facts and Figures on Government Finance*, 173.

32. See current issue of *Highway Statistics*, prepared annually by the Federal Highway Administration.

33. P.J. Grossman, The Impact of Federal and State Grants on Local Government Spending: A Test of the Fiscal Illusion Hypothesis, *Public Finance Quarterly* 18 (1990): 313–327.

34. Office of State and Local Finance, U.S. Department of the Treasury, *Federal-State-Local Fiscal Relations* (Washington, DC: U.S. Government Printing Office, 1985), 154–157.

35. J.R. Bartle, The Fiscal Impact of Federal and State Aid to Large U.S. Cities: An Empirical Analysis of Budgetary Response, *Public Budgeting & Finance*, 15 (Winter 1995): 56–67; Hyman, *Public Finance*, 592.

36. Fleenor, ed., *Facts and Figures on Government Finance*, 64.

37. H. Hovey, Hal Hovey's State Scoreboard, *Governing* 9 (September 1996): 59.

38. M.J. Rich, Targeting Federal Grants: The Community Development Experience, 1950–1986, *Publius* 21 (Winter 1991): 29–49; D.J. Watson, Importance of Local Initiative in Targeting of Federal AID: The Case of UDAGs, *Public Budgeting and Financial Management* 6 (1994): 201–215.

39. S. Nunn and M.S. Rosentraub, Metropolitan Fiscal Equalization: Distilling Lessons from Four U.S. Programs, *State and Local Government Review* 2 (Spring 1996): 90–102.

40. K. Ohmae, *The End of the Nation State: The Rise of Regional Economies* (New York: Free Press, 1995).

41. U.S. Office of Management and Budget, *Historical Tables: Budget of the United States Government, Fiscal Year 1998*, CD-ROM version (Washington, DC: U.S. Government Printing Office, 1997), tables Hist01z1 and Hist12z2.

42. J.E. Petersen, Money for People, Not Places, *Governing* 9 (December 1996): 72.

43. S.D. Gold, Issues Raised by the New Federalism, Urban Institute: http://newfederalism.urban.org/html/ntj.htm; accessed December 1997; reprinted from *National Tax Journal*, June 1996.

44. J.D. Donahue, The Disunited States, *Atlantic Monthly* 279 (May 1997): 18–22.

45. J. Walters, Cry, the Beleaguered County, *Governing* 9 (August 1996): 31–37.

46. Personal Responsibility and Work Opportunity Reconciliation Act, P.L. 104-193, 110 Stat. 2105 (1996); C. E. Steuerle and G. Mermin, *Devolution as Seen from the Budget*, Urban Institute: http://newfederalism.urban.org/html/anf_a2.htm; accessed December 1997.

47. J. Walters, Walking in a Waiver Wonderland, *Governing* 8 (October 1995): 13; G.F. Seib, North Carolina's Welfare Reform Gets Corporate Help, *Wall Street Journal* 129 (February 20, 1997): 1; L.K. Foster, Working Toward Reform, *State Government News* 39 (November 1996): 10–12, 18.

48. R. Gurwitt, Cracking the Casework Culture, *Governing* 10 (March 1997): 27–30.

49. R. Gurwitt, Overload, *Governing* 8 (October 1995): 16–20, 22.

50. Fiscal Pressures under Welfare Reform, *Government Finance Review* 13 (February 1997): 3.

51. C.L. Eckl et al., *State Budget and Tax Actions: 1991* (Washington, DC: National Conference of State Legislatures, 1991), 13.

52. D.B. Walker, The Advent of an Ambiguous Federalism and the Emergence of New Federalism III, *Public Administration Review* 56 (1996): 271–280.

53. C. Wise and R. O'Leary, Intergovernmental Relations and Federalism in Environmental Management and Policy, *Public Administration Review* 57 (1997): 150–159.

54. U.S. Advisory Commission on Intergovernmental Relations, *State Laws Governing Local Government Structure and Administration* (Washington, DC: U.S. Government Printing Office, 1993).

55. Miami Gives State Control of Its Budgets and Pacts, *Wall Street Journal Interactive Edition*, December 24, 1996, 1.

56. C. Kirkpatrick, State Seizes Town Drowning in Debts, Failed Infrastructure, *Durham Herald-Sun*, February 5, 1997, 1, 8.

57. K. Berry, Dealing with Financial Crisis: Miami Emulates the Big Cities, *Wall Street Journal Interactive Edition*, December 27, 1996.

58. H.A. Upton, D.C.'s Financial Straits, *Government Finance Review* 12 (December 1996): 35–38.

59. M.H. Anderson and A. Keto, Negotiators Agree on Package of Aid for District of Columbia, *Wall Street Journal Interactive Edition,* July 31, 1997.

60. U.S. Advisory Commission on Intergovernmental Relations, *Characteristics of Federal Grant-in-Aid Programs: Grants Funded in 1991* (Washington, DC: U.S. Government Printing Office, 1992); U.S. Advisory Commission on Intergovernmental Relations, *Federal Grant Programs in Fiscal Year 1992: Their Numbers, Sizes and Fragmentation Indexes in Historical Perspective* (Washington, DC: U.S. Government Printing Office, 1993).

61. B.D. McDowell, Grant Reform Reconsidered, *Intergovernmental Perspective* 17 (Summer 1991): 8–11.

62. M. Givel, *The War on Poverty Revisited: The Community Services Block Grant Program in the Reagan Years* (Lanham, MD: University Press of America, 1991).

63. U.S. Office of Management and Budget, *Grants and Cooperative Agreements with State and Local Governments*, Circular A-102 (1997): http://www.whitehouse.gov/WH/EOP/OMB/html/circular/a102; accessed December 1997.

64. J.L. Mikesell, *Fiscal Administration: Analysis and Applications for the Public Sector*, 4th ed. (New York: Harcourt Brace Jovanovich, 1995), 453–455.

65. S.D. Gold and S. Ritchie, State Policies Affecting Cities and Counties in 1992, *Public Budgeting & Finance* 13 (Spring 1993): 10.

66. Housing and Community Development Act of 1974, P.L. 93-383, 88 Stat 739 (1994).

67. U.S. General Accounting Office, *Block Grants: Lessons Learned* (Washington, DC: U.S. Government Printing Office, 1995).

68. U.S. General Accounting Office, *Block Grants: Characteristics, Experience and Lessons Learned* (Washington, DC: U.S. Government Printing Office, 1995).

69. D. Liska, *Medicaid: Overview of a Complex Program* (Washington, DC: Urban Institute, 1997): http://newfederalism.urban.org/html/anf_a8.htm; accessed December 1997.

70. R.C. Hicks, Environmental Legislation and the Costs of Compliance, *Government Finance Review* 8 (April 1992): 7–10.

71. T. Arrandale, Environmental Mandate Maze, *Governing* 8 (February 1995): 47–52.

72. J. Walters, Fear of Federalism, *Governing* 9 (October 1996): 11.

73. O.L. Ervin, Understanding American Local Government: Recent Census Bureau and ACIR Contributions, *Public Administration Review* 55 (1995): 209–212.

74. W.J. Clinton, Enhancing the Intergovernmental Partnership, *Federal Register* 58 (1993): 58093–58094.

75. Unfunded Mandates Reform Act, P.L. 104-4, 109 Stat 48 (1995).

76. Law Restricts Unfunded Mandates, *1995 CQ Almanac* (Washington, DC: Congressional Quarterly, 1996), 3.15–3.20.

77. *U.S. v. Lopez*, 115 S.Ct. 1624 (1995); *Printz v. U.S.*, 117 S.Ct. 2365 (1997).

78. J. Kinkaid, Intergovernmental Deregulation? *Public Administration Review* 55 (1995): 495–497.

79. Single Audit Act, P.L. 98-502, 98 Stat. 2327 (1984).

80. U.S. Office of Management and Budget, *Audits of State and Local Governments*, Circular A-128 (1997): http://www.whitehouse.gov/WH/EOP/OMB/html/circular/a128; accessed December 1997.

81. U.S. General Accounting Office, *Federal Interstate Compact Commissions: Useful Mechanisms for Planning and Managing River Basin Operations* (Washington, DC: U.S. Government Printing Office, 1981).

82. D. Osborne and T. Gaebler, *Reinventing Government: How the Entrepreneurial Spirit Is Transforming the Public Sector from Schoolhouse to Statehouse, City Hall to the Pentagon* (Reading, MA: Addison-Wesley, 1992); D. Osborne and P. Plastrik, *Banishing Bureaucracy: The Five Strategies for Reinventing Government* (New York: Addison-Wesley, 1997).

83. T.J. Conlan and D.B. Walker, Reagan's New Federalism, *Intergovernmental Perspective* 8 (Winter 1983): 6–22.

84. A.M. Rivlin, A New Vision of American Federalism, *Public Administration Review* 52 (1992): 315–329.

CHAPTER **15**

Government, the Economy, and Economic Development

The sheer size of the government sector in the U.S. economy guarantees that government action will have a major impact on overall economic performance; the total government share of gross domestic product (GDP) now exceeds 18 percent. Recognizing the importance of the federal government's role in economic affairs, the first Clinton administration created the National Economic Council to coordinate the numerous cabinet and Executive Office of the President agencies advising the President.[1] The council's functions are to coordinate economic policy making and to ensure that any actions of the executive branch affecting the economy will be consistent with the President's economic policy. With the end of the Cold War, the government's economic policy apparatus has been raised to a point of parity with the national security policy system.

This chapter focuses on the impact of government budgets—primarily the federal government's budget—on the overall economy. The first section considers the U.S. economy and its interdependence with those of other nations. Other governments and private individuals in other countries react to actions taken by the federal government, and these external reactions sometimes can cause economic changes within the United States. To understand government and the economy, one first has to understand the conditioning factors of the world economy.

The second section summarizes the major objectives sought by government economic policy. Included is a discussion of deficit control and management of the federal debt. In contrast to state and local borrowing, which is basically used as a means to finance capital investment, federal deficit spending and subsequent borrowing function more as macroeconomic policy tools.

The third section is a brief discussion of how governments and businesses attempt to forecast the economic future. The fourth section follows with an examination of the principal tools used to influence the economy. For the federal government, these tools conventionally include fiscal and monetary policy, and for state and local governments, infrastructure investments and taxing or spending decisions that are intended to affect the local and state business climate. The chapter concludes with a discussion of the distributional effects of overall economic policy. That last section focuses on the role of government in securing equity through influencing the distribution of income in society.

THE UNITED STATES AND THE WORLD ECONOMY

OPEC Control of Oil Production

Most citizens once thought of the United States not only as the most significant contributor to, but also as the controller of the world economy. It took the shock of the Organization of Petroleum Exporting Countries' (OPEC's) curtailment of oil production in 1973 to 1974 to bring many to the realization that the world economy has significant controlling effects on the U.S. economy. Long gas lines and gasoline prices that more than doubled caused many people to recognize that economic conditions are not completely in the United States' own hands. Once several nations, including Japan and Germany, surpassed the United States in some economic measures (though not in total production), most in the United States realized that our economy, although still a major component of the world economy, is one of numerous important national economies. Since that first OPEC production cut and the subsequent strengthening of other economies relative to our own, citizens are more attuned to how much U.S. economic well-being depends on the economic behavior of billions of individuals around the world and on the economic policy decisions of dozens of other governments.

The United States as a Debtor Nation

A second significant event, although less immediately apparent to many citizens, occurred in 1985. For the first time, the United States became a net debtor nation. That meant technically that the value of foreign investments in the United States for the first time exceeded the value of U.S. investments abroad. By the mid-1990s, the market value of U.S. investments abroad exceeded $4.3 trillion versus the value of foreign investments in the United States just over $5.1 trillion.[2] This difference of over $800 billion represents about 6 percent of U.S. GDP. This means basically that the claims of foreign investors, both private and governmental, on assets in the United States exceed the claims of U.S. investors, private and governmental, on assets in other countries. Since 1985, the United States has remained a net debtor, with the cumulative value of foreign-owned assets in the United States exceeding the value of assets in other countries owned by U.S. investors.

Foreign assets in the United States are invested in descending order in three major categories—debt and equity securities of U.S. companies, U.S. government treasury securities, and property. This inflow of foreign capital has helped keep U.S. interest rates low because it fills part of the demand for borrowing created by federal budget deficits. In addition, foreign investment produces jobs in the United States. On the other hand, when the net inflow of foreign capital replaces domestic investment, it represents a short-run fix with a potentially serious long-run disadvantage. The potential long-run problem is that the U.S. savings rate may be too low to finance all the demand for investments, and therefore the economy is increasingly dependent on the confidence of foreign investors in the U.S. economy. Any major threat to their confidence could cause that source of external investment to diminish and could motivate foreign owners to dispose of their U.S. assets, disrupting the U.S. economy. That this has not happened is due of course to the strength of the U.S. economy, and the declining size of the annual federal budget deficit.

Value of the U.S. Dollar in the World Economy

The third phenomenon, noticed by many citizens, occurred in two phases in the 1980s. Many U.S. residents enjoyed low prices on imported goods or low-priced vacations in Europe as the value of the dollar relative to other currencies climbed to record highs. Then late in 1987 residents watched the flood of tourists reverse as European and Asian visitors came to the United States while prices for comparable trips for U.S. residents abroad climbed to new highs. Imported cars, stereos, and televisions that had been bargains a year before became unaffordable for many. This reversal occurred for two reasons. Per capita incomes grew faster in several other countries, and this increased purchasing power drove up prices for goods produced in those economies. Also, deliberate action by the U.S. government to lower the value of the dollar relative to other currencies, in order to increase the foreign purchase of U.S. goods and services, made foreign goods and services relatively more expensive to U.S. consumers. By the mid-1990s, the value of the dollar against other world currencies had become relatively stable, but we now understand that its value fluctuates with changes both within the influence range of the U.S. private economy and government action but also with changes in other economies. Since the mid-1980s, the U.S. dollar no longer dominates world currencies, but is one of several dominant currencies.

Competitiveness of the U.S. Economy

A fourth key economic phenomenon of the 1980s was the decreasing competitiveness of the U.S. economy relative to other emerging industrial powers.

Although "cheap foreign labor" had been considered a threat by many traditional U.S. industries, such as textiles, for more than two decades, the 1980s saw problems in industries in which innovation and technology had constituted the U.S. competitive edge. For the first time, the United States saw competitors in computer design, electronics, and other high-technology areas begin to produce not only cheaper but, in the minds of many consumers, better products.

A key issue that emerged in the 1990s, surfacing in President Clinton's first election campaign, was the extent to which the government should play an active and direct role in improving U.S. global competitiveness. Although President Clinton announced a program of investment in U.S. technology to build economic strength, appointed Vice President Gore to lead the effort, and strengthened the Office of Science and Technology Policy, other domestic policy concerns including health care and welfare reform, and the Republican takeover of Congress in the 1994 elections relegated this initially activist position to a low level of policy concern.[3]

A surge in the 1990s in U.S. productivity, led by significant private sector restructuring and manifested in part in downsizing the work force in many industries, helped move the issue of government stimulation of U.S. competitiveness further off the national agenda. Aided by private sector restructuring and declining budget deficits, by the middle of the 1990s the U.S. economy experienced both overall growth and strong competitiveness with other economies. The International Institute for Management Development annually publishes a set of world competitiveness rankings, and from 1993 through 1997, the U.S. economy ranked first among all nations.[4] Although the U.S. ranked high on virtually all the factors considered, the major factors contributing to the high ranking were the openness of the economy to world trade, investment in education, health of the financial sector, infrastructure, and technological innovation.

The preceding issues signal that the U.S. economy is so interdependent with those of other nations that no significant actions the United States takes are without repercussions around the world. Likewise, no significant economic events in other major industrial nations or groups of developing nations are without repercussions in the United States. Understanding the role of the government in the U.S. economy thus means casting a wider net and considering also the actions and reactions of major trading partners and major creditors.

OBJECTIVES OF ECONOMIC POLICY

The role of the federal government in the economy consists of several interrelated functions. First, the government provides the legal framework in which economic transactions take place, and second, it directly produces services, and some goods, and regulates private production. Also, it purchases significant quantities of goods and services and redistributes income among individuals and groups. Although not as accepted as these functions, some also argue that governments should promote their countries' economic competitiveness in the global marketplace.[5]

One goal of the government's regulation of economic transactions through setting the legal framework is sometimes described as maintenance of a "level playing field"—making sure that all economic actors play by the same rules and succeed or fail solely on the basis of their own strengths and weaknesses. Setting the legal framework is the subject of texts on regulation, business, and constitutional law. This section and the following one focus on the government's effects on the economy's overall performance.

Although Franklin D. Roosevelt's 1932 election platform promised to involve the federal government in the solution to economic problems brought on by the Depression, it was not until after World War II that the overall role of the government in stimulating the economy became formalized through legislative enactment. The Employment Act of 1946 set several macroeconomic policy objectives for the federal government. Primary among these were full employment, price stability, and steady economic growth. To these have been added in practice, if not formal legislation, equilibrium in the balance of transactions between the U.S. economy and other economies and debt management.[6] Most industrial nations share these objectives, whether they rely primarily on the private market, central planning, or a mix of central control and market activity to achieve them. Less industrial, developing, and emerging market countries also share these objectives, but the most prominent economic policy objective for these nations is the promotion of economic development. The success of Japan's economy through the 1980s and the apparent causal role of the Japanese government's activist production and trade promotion policies intensified the debate in the United States and other industrial countries on the proper role of the government in promoting development, but the mood in most industrial economies has favored a less activist role for government.[7]

The first three objectives are primarily domestic in nature. In many respects, they can be summarized in a single prescription: achieve a level of economic growth that produces full employment without unacceptable inflation. Economic growth is the engine that drives demand for employees. However, running that engine too fast or with too rich a fuel mixture may cause prices to rise unacceptably. The reformulation of these objectives into a single statement brings out the causal connection that exists between economic growth and employment. It also brings into the discussion two key value-laden terms: full employment and unacceptable inflation.

Full Employment

Definition of Full Employment. As a measure of economic performance, employment is the number of civilians over age 16 outside of institutions who are working in formal income-producing jobs. The most commonly used measure of employment is the complement of employment—unemployment. The unemployment rate is the proportion of the work force not employed at a given time. To be considered unemployed, one must be seeking employment. This definition was refined in 1994 to exclude individuals who reported they were discouraged by failure to find work but who had not looked for work in the last 12 months.

There is no legislated definition of full employment, although an unemployment rate of 3 to 4 percent was often cited as the criterion of full employment after the 1946 Employment Act. Until the 1980s, the thinking was that about 3 to 4 percent of the work force at any given time will be between jobs or otherwise temporarily unemployed, and thus we can never achieve employment below that threshold. Some members of the work force are considered at least temporarily unemployable because of changes in the nature of jobs and skill requirements. Some economists do not count these "structurally" unemployed as part of the base for calculating full employment. Homemakers returning to the work force, young people switching jobs voluntarily, and fluctuations in demand in the global economy also make it difficult to achieve a 3 to 4 percent target. Since unemployment has only approached even 5 percent once since before 1970 (just below 5 percent in 1997), we have come to accept an unemployment rate higher than 3 or 4 percent as consistent with the term full employment.

The adoption of a higher unemployment rate as the criterion of full employment is connected to the fact that the U.S. economy is much more susceptible to external events than it once was. As external economic shocks occur and consumer tastes change more rapidly, U.S. businesses simply cannot react as fast as once they could, leading at times to downturns and unemployment. When unemployment dropped below 5 percent in 1997, coupled with low inflation rates and an unexpectedly high rate of growth in GDP, the U.S. economy had reached its strongest point in decades. Since that point, debate has centered on whether this was a transitory, highly unusual conjunction, or whether it signals the advent of a new, long-term level, brought on by technology gains, the application of information technology to production, and other factors. The answer to that debate is unlikely to be known for years.

Political Acceptability of Unemployment. The political system has a varying capacity to accept unemployment. A nationwide unemployment rate of 9 or 10 percent, a rate reached in the early 1980s, is clearly unacceptable by current standards but is substantially lower than the peak of 24 percent unemployment during the Depression of the 1930s. As the rate declines toward 5 percent, acceptance increases. The extent to which society tolerates unemployment is partially dependent on who is unemployed. Though there may be a tendency to accept high unemployment among low-skilled, minority group, or younger workers, tolerance for unemployment quickly dissipates when it reaches middle-income, white-collar workers.

Politically, the unemployment rate is not the only important issue. Since the late 1980s, with the rate generally close to 5 percent, citizens have been more concerned with the types of new jobs that are being created. The concern is that many new jobs created have been either service jobs that pay only the minimum wage or are part-time jobs that pay no or few benefits. Another issue is the controversy over part-time work. Many people choose part-time work, but companies also have increased the number of workers they hire either as part-time workers or temporary workers. As companies downsized their work force during the 1990s, an increasing percentage of the national labor force was employed in part-time and temporary activity, although often amounting to full 40-hour or more weeks, but without the job security of regular employment and without the benefits of health insurance and pension plans. A major strike by United Parcel Service workers in 1997 focused primarily on part-time and temporary employment issues.

Controlling Inflation

Relationship Between Unemployment and Inflation. The more the unemployment rate declines, the more difficult it becomes to find workers, and as a result wage rates may be bid up, creating inflationary pressures. Certainly through the mid-1960s the traditional assumption that rising employment leads to price increases and declining employment to price decreases seemed to hold up. However, the mid-1970s recession saw both rising unemployment and rising prices. At the peak, 1974 prices rose 11 percent over those of the year before, and 1975 prices rose another 9 percent. During that time, unemployment peaked at over 8 percent. Figure 15–1 illustrates this heretofore unconventional relationship. During the 1980s, the more conventional pattern held with inflation and unemployment moving in opposite directions, until the sustained growth period of the 1990s. By the mid-1990s, the economy was achieving both the lowest inflation rates in 35 years and low unemployment rates, as the figure illustrates.

The 1990s experience has had economists reestimating what is called the *nonaccelerating inflation rate of unemployment* (NAIRU), which is the rate of unemployment below which excess demand for labor is thought to set off wage and price inflation. Previously considered to be in the 5 to 6 percent range, unemployment below this range presumably would set off wage-led inflation. In the mid-1990s, however, a lower rate of noninflationary unemployment, just below 5

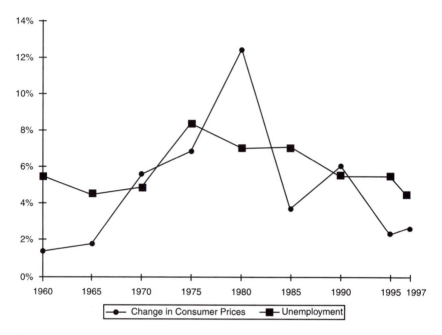

Figure 15–1 Inflation and Unemployment, 1960–1997. *Source:* Data from *Economic Report of the President: 1997*, pp. 370 and 421, 1997, Council of Economic Advisors; *Wall Street Journal*, p. 1, © September 1, 1997.

---

percent, did not result in wage-induced inflation.[8] This lower NAIRU, if sustainable, seems related to the fact that wage increases were more tied to productivity increases, which are noninflationary.[9] In addition, greater pressure on jobs from foreign competition holds wage rates down that are not the result of increased productivity. If wage demands grow too high too rapidly, companies may increase the search for foreign production sources.

Economic Growth

Economic Productivity. It must be noted that unemployment is not the only, and perhaps not the best, measure of the economy's health. Even if the rate of unemployment and the rate of inflation are both at acceptable levels, the overall productivity of the economy could be seriously declining. GDP is commonly used as an indication of economic productivity. For the United States, the average annual growth rate in productivity (GDP) from 1965 through 1991 was 3 percent. For Japan, the comparable figures varied between 4 percent and 6 percent.[10] Just as important, during that period the average annual rate of inflation in the United States varied between 4 percent and 6 percent, while for Japan inflation was less than 4 percent. Thus, during a 15-year period the productivity of the U.S. economy measured in terms of real output did not change. U.S. GDP actually dropped in 1991 (a recession year), but since 1992 the U.S. GDP growth rate has been above 5 percent a year, in current dollars, with inflation in the 3 percent range—meaning real production gains. No other industrial economy matched that during the early 1990s.

In 1996, the U.S. Commerce Department changed the way GDP is measured. Previously, real (inflation-adjusted) GDP was measured by comparing each year with the base year of 1987. Subsequent years' total production was adjusted for price changes using an index constructed on the base year, yielding real GDP growth rates. The problem with the methodology was that it implicitly assumed that all components of production changed prices the same amount and same direction, although particularly since the 1970s that has not been the case. The new methodology computes price changes annually using a rolling average, called a *chain-weighted* measurement.[11] Historical series reported by the Commerce Department and used by other agencies have been revised to reflect the new methodology.

Impact of Government on Productivity. Most economists think that the primary impact of the government on economic productivity and long-term growth is due to influences on knowledge development and investment in productive capacity.[12] Investment in knowledge and infrastructure was one of the initial themes of the Clinton administration, but it lost impetus due to more pressing concerns for health care and later welfare reform.

In addition to human capital investment, the government also invests directly in research and development (R&D) to produce technological breakthroughs and indirectly supports private investment in R&D. One mechanism for encouraging private R&D has been to allow a tax credit for increases in R&D expenditures over prior-year levels. The impact of the direct and indirect actions of government on improving the productivity of the economy can be measured only in the long run. For example, even if businesses substantially increase their expenditures for R&D as a result of government incentives, the payoff in productivity terms will show up only years into the future.

A Government Technology Policy. Whether the government should be more active in protecting and promoting critical high-technology industries emerged in the late 1980s through the beginning of the current decade as a key policy issue when the U.S. economy began to lose ground in all areas, not just markets dominated by inexpensive labor. The Bush administration was widely criticized for not protecting critical industries such as microelectronics, and President Clinton made stimulation of high-technology development an economic policy priority.[13]

However, the problem with providing more support to one segment of the economy than to another is that government rather than the marketplace "picks winners and losers," and there is little evidence that governments generally are good in that role.[14] The government has difficulty determining which particular elements in a volatile industry such as electronics are going to be the most important determinants of U.S. global competitiveness in high-technology markets five or ten years from now.[15] The more widely accepted view is that government actions, rather than overtly promoting particular industries, should be directed toward improving the human and capital base, should encourage and certainly not discourage savings and investment, and should promote the international exchange of ideas, goods, and services.[16]

Equilibrium in International Financial Flows

Important elements of government policy in this era of the global marketplace are actions designed to affect the balance of trade and other financial transactions between nations. Related to this balance is U.S. reliance on world capital markets to finance its domestic budget deficit. The U.S. financial position vis-à-vis the rest of the world is discussed in this section. A discussion of the overall deficit situation and debt management follows.

U.S. Transition from Creditor to Debtor. As noted earlier, in 1985 the United States became a net debtor nation. In the context of this chapter, net debtor means that there are more foreign demands on U.S. assets than there are U.S. claims on assets in other countries. Traditionally, a situation of net debtorship is caused when a country or its citizens purchase more abroad than is sold to other countries (a trade imbalance). That is a major contributing factor for the United States. The other major factor, as noted earlier, is the net balance of investments abroad and foreign investments in the United States.

Balance of Payments. Balance of payments refers to the value of goods and services and financial assets and liabilities flowing between the United States and other countries. Historically, the balance of payments objective was to avoid a situation in which imported goods and services plus financial transactions created the potential for drawing down on the U.S. gold reserve. Today, with the rate of exchange between the U.S. dollar and other currencies freely set by the market and unrelated to gold reserves, the balance of payments objective is primarily a matter of maintaining equitable trade relationships between the United States and other countries. Trade negotiations between the United States and Japan, for example, are contentious because of the much larger value of goods U.S. businesses and citizens purchase from Japan than vice versa.

The balance of payments consists of several components or measures. The net balance of goods purchased abroad versus goods sold abroad is the *simple trade balance*. In 1996, for example, the current account deficit increased to $148 billion (approximately $980 billion in exports and $1.13 trillion in imports, remittances, and other net transfers). For the entire year in 1996, the $148 billion deficit was the worst in 9 years.[17] To remedy an excess in net imports, either GDP must rise faster than domestic demand, domestic demand must fall, or some combination of the two must occur. Although the U.S. economy was experiencing ideal conditions in terms of unemployment, production, and inflation, the International Monetary Fund warned that U.S. purchase of consumer goods from abroad coupled with a low domestic savings rate was likely to create future problems. To the trade balance is added financial transactions, and, as noted earlier, the United States is a net borrower, which exacerbates the balance of payments problem.

Financing the U.S. Economy. The importance of movements in the trade balance lies in their implications for how the economy is being financed. Since the mid-nineteenth century until the mid-1980s, the U.S. economy was financed domestically.[18] National saving was sufficient to provide funds for national investment, with the surplus national saving being invested abroad. However, the net national savings rate, which averaged just over 7 percent of GDP in the 1970s, declined to below 4 percent of GDP throughout the 1980s, and generally has remained around the 4-percent level.[19] One result has been that U.S. claims on foreign assets now are well below foreign claims on U.S. assets. Part of the U.S. economy has been financed not by domestic savings but by foreign investments in the United States. These foreign investments represent a future claim on U.S. assets that are not matched by equal U.S. claims on foreign assets.

Concern about this situation is not chiefly motivated by nationalistic pride. Foreign investments in the U.S. economy represent foreign confidence in the economy. Foreign investors have found U.S. treasury notes an attractive investment because of the interest rates offered and because of their safety. Were the same foreign investment in U.S. industry's stocks and bonds, financing would be available for economic expansion. To the extent that the investment in U.S. government debt does not produce expansion of domestic U.S. production capacity, then the government's need for this investment competes with industry's need for financing. In macroeconomic terms, this external financing of the deficit creates a situation in which a greater quantity of U.S. goods and services has to be sold abroad in the long term to meet payments to foreign holders of U.S. debt. That quantity then is not available for U.S. consumption. Thus, the trade balance, as well as the overall balance of payments disequilibrium, is intertwined with the domestic federal government budget deficit. By the mid-1990s, the U.S. budget deficit had shrunk to such an extent that foreign borrowing to finance the deficit was becoming less of an issue. The 1997 balanced budget agreement should ensure that this continues, providing future congresses and presidents adhere to the agreement.

The Decline in National Savings. A critical change in the U.S. economy relative to other nations has been a decline in national savings. National savings represent the source of funds for new investment in equipment, plants, and other physical facilities that allow total production to grow. Figure 15–2 shows domestic savings for the United States relative to selected member countries of the Organization for Economic Cooperation and Development. The United States increased gross national savings from the roughly 13 percent level in the 1965 to 1969 period to 16 percent in 1994. This exceeded the United Kingdom, which experienced little increase during that same period, but still fell well below other countries. Economically strong countries in recent years, Japan and Germany, increased or maintained their high savings rate. Although not as high as some other countries, the growth in U.S. savings has financed increased investment and consequently an increase in the standard of living.

The data reported in Figure 15–2 are *gross savings* as a percentage of GDP. Gross savings are adjusted by subtracting the consumption of fixed capital to arrive at net national savings. Consumption of fixed capital essentially means equipment and facilities that become old and useless and are not replaced. Thus, gross savings could grow or remain constant while *net savings* actually falls because the rate of new investment is not sufficient to replace deteriorating production capacity. That is exactly what happened in the U.S. economy during the 1970s and 1980s. Whereas gross savings in 1991 was 16 percent, net national savings was less than 2 percent, only a fourth of the 8-percent rate of net national savings in the decade 1960–1969.[20] By 1994, net national savings had begun to increase again, to just over 4 percent.

Two changes that emerged in the mid-1990s, if continued, portend a continuing increase in national savings. Individual savings increased, particularly as the baby-boom generation in its peak earning years substantially increased investment in mutual funds, individual stocks and bonds, and other savings instruments. Second, the need for financing the government deficit dropped sharply.

Deficits and Debt Management

Chapter 12 described state and local debt primarily as long-term investment in physical infrastructure and other capital assets. It is therefore prudent for state and local governments to use short-term borrowing only for meeting the demands of short-term contingencies and to ensure that long-term borrowing is linked to the expected life of the investments financed. Federal debt policy, on the other hand, relates more to macroeconomic policy considerations than to capital investment requirements. Deficits in the federal budget accumulate as spending exceeds revenues whether the spending finances investments in long-term growth or meets operating expenses, pays interest on previous debt, or provides

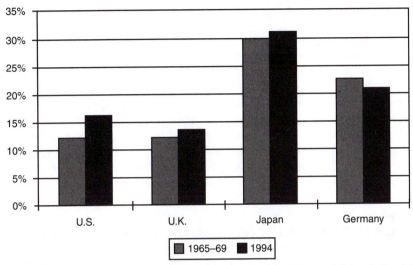

Figure 15–2 U.S. Gross National Savings Compared with Those of Other Industrial Countries, 1965–69 and 1994. *Source:* Data from *World Development Report, 1992*, p. 9, World Bank, 1992; *OECD Economic Surveys, United States, 1996*, annex 2, Organization for Economic Cooperation and Development, 1996.

transfer payments. While it is possible to make a numeric comparison between the investment levels in the federal budget and the size of the deficit, federal budget deficits have not been the result of conscious investment planning.

Developing Country Debt Management. For developing countries, prudent debt management is more comparable to that of U.S. state and local governments. Developing countries as a rule have excess or idle labor capacity. The long-run economic strategy is to invest in education to improve the productivity of labor and in physical infrastructure to facilitate the production and flow of goods and services produced by the private sector. Typically, a shortage of physical infrastructure, such as transport and communications facilities, retards the economic investment that would employ the excess labor capacity. Governments in developing countries borrow from donor agencies, such as the World Bank and from banks in industrial countries, to increase physical infrastructure and other capital investments. If they are economically sound, the investments will produce long-run economic growth sufficient to repay the indebtedness. More often than not, developing countries encounter debt troubles when borrowing finances current consumption rather than investment and when physical infrastructure assets that have been built are not maintained. The economy then does not maintain a sufficient level of growth, revenues do not increase as expected, and debt exceeds capacity to repay.

U.S. Federal Use of Debt. In the post-Depression era, the federal budget deficit has been used as an overt tool to influence total demand in the economy and thus overall economic performance. According to the prevailing economic theory of that era, deficits should be managed to provide stimulus to the economy without creating inflationary pressure. However, by the 1980s the size of the deficit had reached proportions that were out of step with economic policy objectives. Although there was general agreement on both sides of the political spectrum that deficit-reducing measures were necessary, it was not until 1997 that an overall agreement was reached between Congress and the President on specific tax and expenditure measures that promise a balanced budget by 2002. Independent of that agreement, however, the most sustained period of economic growth in decades produced deficits far smaller than even the most optimistic forecasts.[21]

Size of the U.S. Federal Debt. To understand the debate about government debt in recent years, it is first important to understand the relative size of the federal debt and then to consider its origins and implications. Figure 15–3 shows the debt as a percentage of GDP, a useful measure for comparing the growth of the debt with the growth of the overall economy. Total federal indebtedness in 1950 was equal to 94 percent of GDP, reflecting the financing of World War II. That figure steadily declined and between 1970 and 1980 reached postwar lows around 35 percent. Rapid increases after that brought federal debt up to 70 percent of GDP in 1995, the highest since 1955.[22] That trend, however, is not expected to continue as a result of economic improvement and the balanced budget agreement.

Effects of Economic Performance on the Size of the Federal Debt. Two circumstances explain the rapid rise in the federal government's debt after a long period of decline. First, the federal budget, in terms of both revenues and expenditures, is affected by the overall performance of the economy (see discussion below). Oil price shocks and high inflation led to unbalanced federal budgets throughout the 1980s. Overall growth in the economy was virtually zero for the decade in real terms. This lack of growth created pressure on the budget because of automatic increases in expenditures for some social welfare programs that expand as unemployment goes up. It also caused a decline in federal revenues. The reverse occurred in the mid-1990s as low unemployment and increased production combined to produce decreased demand for federal social welfare assistance and increased tax revenues.

Effects of Tax Cuts on the Size of the Federal Debt. The second circumstance affecting the 1980s was a set of policy decisions. On taking office, the Reagan administration initiated a sweeping set of economic reforms, including a major series of tax cuts beginning in 1981 and significant budget reductions in nonde-

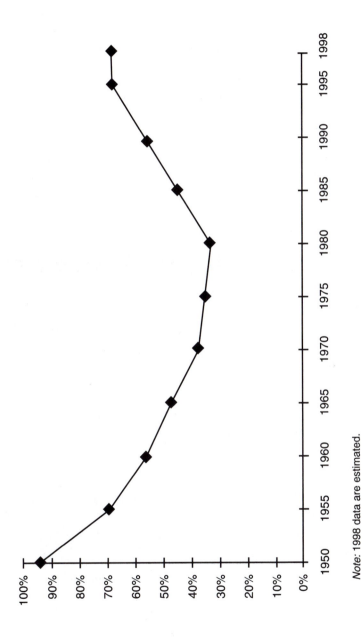

Note: 1998 data are estimated.

Figure 15–3 Federal Debt as a Percentage of Gross Domestic Product, 1950–1998. *Source:* Adapted from *Economic Report of the President: 1997*, p. 389, Council of Economic Advisors, 1997.

fense spending. However, as the program evolved, it proved politically impossible to reduce nondefense spending sufficiently to match increases in defense expenditures, and overall spending remained at prior levels or even went higher than before the tax cuts. The theory behind the tax cuts was that the funds not collected by the government would be better invested by the private sector, yielding in fact a future revenue dividend in the form of increased tax yields from the heightened economic activity. The fiscal dividend never materialized. Estimates of the revenue loss from the Economic Recovery Tax Act of 1981 for the first five years placed it at $635 billion unaccompanied by matching expenditure cuts.[23] Federal revenue levels grew more slowly than at any time since the 1960s, while defense spending, entitlement program outlays, and interest on the debt soared to new heights. The tax cuts adopted in 1997, unlike those of 1981, were accompanied by offsetting expenditure reductions.

ANTICIPATING ECONOMIC CONDITIONS

Both the private and public sectors need tools to measure economic change and anticipate economic trends. If businesses are to make sound investment decisions (including the decision to hire new workers or build new plant capacity), they have to anticipate future economic developments. If interest rates are expected to fall, it is not the time to borrow to buy new production equipment. If a tax incentive that reduces overall tax liability when funds are invested in new productive capacity is about to expire, it is a good time to make new investments. Some of these events can be predicted with relative certainty. An investment tax credit may have a specific expiration date, and it may be easy to see that Congress is not likely to renew it. On the other hand, it may not be as easy to predict how much change will occur in interest rates. Forecasting tools are a vital ingredient in business economic planning.

If the federal government is to achieve its economic policy objectives, it too needs sensitive and valid measures with which to predict the direction of the economy. It also needs models of change that predict what will happen if specific policy changes, such as a change in the maximum corporate income tax rate, are enacted. Although forecasting techniques are beyond the scope of this text, some familiarity with the measures that are watched closely by business and government and of the analytical models used by forecasters is important for understanding government economic policy.

Business and government forecasters watch closely a number of individual economic indicators.[24] Some indicators are related to the labor force, including unemployment, average weekly hours worked, and average hourly earnings. Other indicators reflect financial conditions such as interest rates and new starts in home building. Businesses, forecasters, and public policy makers watch such indicators closely to understand current economic conditions and to predict turning points when the economy will begin to move up or down from its current state.

Of particular importance for anticipating economic turning points are *cyclical indicators*, also known as *leading, coincident,* and *lagging indicators.*[25] Leading indicators presumably show in advance what the economy will do, revealing the turning points, whereas lagging indicators report what already has occurred. The Bureau of Economic Analysis of the U.S. Department of Commerce releases the cyclical indicators monthly.

Coincident Indicators

Gross Domestic Product. Coincident indicators, those that report what the economy is doing now, are the ones that most commonly reach the public's attention. GDP is one of the most important—it is a measure of the total goods and services produced by the nation. GDP is the aggregate of personal consumption expenditures, gross private domestic investment, net exports of goods and services, and government purchases of goods and services.

Formerly, a similar indicator, gross national product (GNP), was the common indicator of total production. In 1992, the federal government and most analysts switched to GDP for comparison purposes, since most other countries report production in terms of GDP. The main difference between the two is that GDP excludes the earnings of U.S. businesses and residents abroad. GDP thus reflects production within the U.S. economy as opposed to production by U.S. economic entities.

Most commonly reported as an indicator is the rise or fall in GDP. For example, U.S. GDP grew almost 5 percent in 1995. Care must be taken in interpreting that growth, however. Some of that increase was due to inflation. Adjusted for inflation, GDP growth in 1995 was actually 2 percent. For analysis purposes, therefore, both nominal and real (adjusted to remove effects of inflation) figures are used.

Net National Product and National Income. Two other coincident indicators, both derivatives of GDP, are net national product (NNP) and national income. GDP includes all capital investment, some of which does not produce new productive capacity but only replaces capacity that is being used up. NNP is the measure of investment after depreciation is removed. In 1995, the U.S. GDP was $7.2 trillion and the U.S. NNP was $6.4 trillion, meaning that approximately $.8 trillion of GDP represented no new production. NNP thus tells what consumption and investment is net of capital stock replacement. National income is derived from NNP by eliminating indirect business taxes included in the price of goods sold and business transfer payments. Table 15–1 summarizes the relationships among GDP, GNP, NNP, and national income from 1960 through 1995.

Prices. The four measures of national product and income indicate what is happening to the levels of production and income. Prices are another measure of what is happening. Wholesale prices may provide an earlier warning of potential problems than measures of national product because they indicate probable changes in prices about to be paid by consumers. The wholesale or producer price index covers about 2,800 commodities.

The consumer price index (CPI) is based on the cost of goods and services bought by urban wage and clerical workers. It is estimated from a sample of urban areas around the country. Change in the CPI is widely cited as an indicator of inflation. One of its most important uses is to adjust various government bene- fit programs, most prominently Social Security, for the affects of inflation; Social Security payments are automatically increased based on changes in the CPI. The methods used in constructing the CPI are controversial, largely because of the effect they have on the government budget and the deficit. A one-point decrease in the CPI in 1997 would have reduced government expenditures by $6 billion.[26] While there is general agreement that the CPI overstates inflation, there has been no agreement on a fix. Problems in the methodology revolve around inadequacy in the way the index handles changes in the quality of goods and services and changes in consumer buying patterns.

Unemployment. Two other measures provide good indications of the current state of the economy—unemployment and industrial production. Unemployment, a percentage measure of the people within the labor force who are not employed, is a common public policy target indicator. The measure is politically charged. A change in the unemployment rate of half a percent up or down is enough to send the President before the news media to announce significant economic progress or to have opposition leaders charge that the economy is failing. However, unem- ployment is subject to wide seasonal fluctuations, and the measurement of unem- ployment is subject to manipulation. Some job seekers may become discouraged and fall out of the count altogether. Women and members of ethnic minority groups may not be well represented in the count of job seekers because they may be convinced there are no jobs to seek or no jobs worth seeking. Therefore, unemployment always has to be interpreted with some care.

Industrial Production. The industrial production index, prepared by the Fed- eral Reserve System, is a measure of the manufacture of durable and nondurable goods. The durable portion of manufacturing is watched closely, particularly key industries such as steel. Steel sales reflect future intentions of manufacturing con- cerns. Rising sales may indicate the possibility of future investments in capital facilities. Falling sales may indicate lack of confidence in the economy and attempts by firms to keep inventories low. The value of this index has declined

Table 15–1 Relationships among Gross Domestic Product, Gross National Product, Net National Product, and National Income, 1960–1995 (in Billions of Dollars)

Item	1960	1965	1970	1975	1980	1985	1990	1995
Gross domestic product	526.6	719.1	1,035.6	1,630.6	2,784.2	4,180.7	5,743.8	7,253.8
Plus:								
Receipts of factor income from rest of the world	5.0	8.1	13.0	28.2	81.8	108.1	177.5	208.3
Less:								
Payments of factor income to rest of the world	1.8	2.7	6.6	14.9	46.5	87.7	156.4	215.3
Equals:								
Gross national product	529.8	724.5	1,042.0	1,643.9	2,819.5	4,201.0	5,764.9	7,246.7
Less:								
Consumption of fixed capital	60.7	74.9	111.9	200.1	368.0	519.5	693.1	825.9
Equals:								
Net national product	469.1	649.6	930.1	1,443.8	2,451.5	3,681.5	5,071.9	6,420.8
Less:								
Indirect business tax and nontax liability	45.5	62.7	94.3	140.0	212.0	329.6	444.6	595.5
Business transfer payments	1.4	2.2	3.2	5.2	11.2	20.9	26.5	30.8
Statistical discrepancy	-3.7	-1.4	1.0	11.2	27.4	4.4	16.1	-.9
Plus:								
Subsidies less current surplus of government enterprises	.3	1.7	4.9	8.1	15.2	21.9	25.3	18.2
Equals:								
National income	426.2	587.8	836.6	1,295.5	2,216.1	3,351.5	4,611.9	5,813.5

Note: Totals may not match due to rounding.
Source: Reprinted from *Economic Report of the President: 1997,* p. 326, Council of Economic Advisors, 1997.

somewhat as the size of the manufacturing segment of the economy relative to the services segment has declined.

Leading Indicators

Although the above are useful measures of the current or recent state of the economy, they often do not provide the lead time necessary to devise intervention strategies. The forecaster as a result turns to the leading indicators. A nonprofit research group, the National Bureau of Economic Research, identifies more than 30 leading indicators, only a few of which are discussed here.

Employment-Related Indicators. A key leading indicator is the *average work-week of production workers in manufacturing.* Its usefulness is based on the practice of most manufacturers to cut back on the length of the workweek rather than lay workers off if the demand for production starts to fall off. A somewhat later indicator is the *average weekly initial claims for unemployment insurance.* This indicator provides evidence of the extent to which layoffs are increasing or decreasing. Both measures indicate employers' estimates of the direction of change in the economy.

Housing Starts. Private, nonfarm housing starts provide a measure of the faith of builders and financial investors in the health of the economy. A decline in the number of starts can signal future economic decline. Housing is thought to be sensitive in that it reflects willingness to tie up investment dollars for several months to a year in an expensive commodity for which there may be no buyer at the time construction begins. However, housing starts are extremely sensitive to mortgage rates. During periods of extremely high rates, such as the early 1980s, many potential buyers were forced out of the market. In the 1990s, mortgage rates fell to their lowest points in recent years, and housing starts increased. A significant portion of financing activity, however, was in refinancing existing mortgages as opposed to newly constructed homes. In recent years, housing starts have become a somewhat less reliable leading indicator. Growth in the use of adjustable rate mortgages allows home buyers to hedge against cyclical swings in interest rates, which in turn keeps demand for housing higher in the initial stages of rising interest rates.[27] A closely related indicator is building permits issued.

Stock Markets. Stock markets are watched closely by the business community and government analysts, but their volatility makes them hard to use as a leading indicator. The New York Stock Exchange (NYSE) is the market most carefully watched, but the Tokyo and London markets also are watched. A substantial increase in investments in emerging markets and the volatility in these markets have given prominence to several other markets as well. The Hang Sen (Hong Kong) stock market index is reported daily, for example.

Several composite indexes of stock exchange transactions are used, the most notable being the Dow Jones Industrial and Standard and Poor's indexes. Changes are infrequent in the stocks listed in these indexes. For example, until a major change dropping four stocks and adding four others in 1997, the 30-stock Dow Jones Industrial index had remained largely intact since 1980.[28]

Stock transactions are useful as leading indicators in that they reflect the faith of investors in the stocks traded on the open market and thus in the companies whose stocks are traded. As a barometer of investor confidence, stock transactions may be helpful. In principle, the value of a stock is a reflection of the health of the firm. However, stocks may surge or decline wildly as a result of corporate takeover attempts and fights to prevent takeover. Furthermore, the crash of 1987 indicates that factors such as the mechanisms by which some firms automatically buy or sell stocks by computer (program trading) may sometimes have more to do with surges than with any underlying economic factors. To the extent that stock prices reflect these other factors rather than the economic health of the corporations, prices will be misleading as an economic indicator.

Composite Indexes. A variety of combined indexes are used to gauge economic changes and trends. The Bureau of Economic Analysis of the Commerce Department publishes a monthly series of indexes.[29] These composites combine several individual indexes (such as one composite combines 12 leading indicators). A related type of composite is a diffusion index. The numerical value of a *diffusion index* is equal to the percentage of components of the index that are moving in the same direction. For example, in the Dow Jones averages, if industrials, transportation, and utilities increase in price but general stocks decrease, the diffusion index value is 75 percent—three components out of four are increasing.

Forecasting

Despite the availability of a wide range of indicators and extensive historical series, forecasting remains a risky business. It is common to find two or more major federal organizations in substantial disagreement over expected economic trends. Rarely do the Office of Management and Budget (OMB) and the Congressional Budget Office (CBO) agree, for example, on the forecast of the federal deficit. One analyst noted that OMB and the CBO averaged errors of $58 billion and $35 billion, respectively, in estimates of the size of the deficit for the fiscal years 1979 to 1983.[30] Forecasts by the President's advisors, reflected in the annual budget, have tended to overestimate economic performance so that government receipts fall short of original estimates and expenditures tend to be higher due to programs such as unemployment benefits that kick in automatically. The CBO also has been overoptimistic but often more accurate than OMB.[31] Neither OMB nor CBO accurately forecast federal revenues in 1997, both underestimating—the CBO being further off than OMB in that case.

Economic forecasts are based on informed judgment or a combination of judgment and sophisticated econometric models (see the discussion on forecasting revenues in Chapter 4). Several university-based research groups and several private organizations employ econometric models that include numerous variables—from around 100 to as many as 1,200. Among the more famous private models are those of Wharton Econometric Forecasting Associates, Data Resources, Inc., and Chase Econometrics. Several organizations, including the Institute for Survey Research, University of Michigan, conduct surveys of ordinary consumers and expert analysts to obtain estimates of economic trends. Judgment regularly is used to adjust the sophisticated mathematical models.

Not surprisingly, during major economic changes both business and government are sometimes criticized for not having anticipated the degree of change or sometimes even the direction of change. The recession year of 1982 had been predicted in 1981 to be a year of modest economic growth. The recovery in 1983 was predicted to be a period of slow growth, whereas actual growth in GDP turned out to be more than twice that forecast. The recession that plagued the last two years of the Bush administration was reputed to be momentarily ending, but the Clinton campaign was able to make the case that recovery had not yet begun. Psychologically, many voters in 1992 seemed unprepared to believe that a recovery was beginning and opted for replacing the political party in control of the White House for the first time in 12 years. The economic boom of the mid-1990s has lasted longer than any analysts believed possible. Models seem to fail when major structural changes are occurring, such as OPEC's gain of control over oil production in the early 1970s. When the economy is stable, various models are fairly successful, and popular opinion then generally agrees with the expert forecasts.

Given the conflicting interpretations possible even with sound information, economic forecasters as well as political leaders interpret the data from their own perspectives. The technical problems involved are great, but inevitably forecasting succumbs not to technical problems but to political resolutions. The President and his staff may attempt to focus attention on one indicator that shows signs of progress, while members of Congress from the opposing party may focus on another. State and local political leaders are just as susceptible to coloring judgment with hope by trying to appear confident in the economic future while sometimes failing to address serious underlying economic and fiscal weaknesses.[32] We return to the issues involved in conflicting theories of economic behavior and the implications for government economic policy in the next section.

TOOLS AVAILABLE TO AFFECT THE ECONOMY

Automatic Stabilizers

Government actions intended to achieve economic policy objectives can be either discretionary or automatic. In the case of discretionary actions, policy makers discuss alternatives and reach a decision as to how to intervene in specific circumstances. Automatic or built-in stabilizers, on the other hand, do not require policy makers to take any special steps. Some government revenues and expenditures rise or fall automatically with changes in the economy. Revenues are especially sensitive to economic performance, with taxes falling due to falling incomes. Government expenditures, at least at the federal level, do not automatically fall with declining economic performance but in fact tend to increase. The combined tax declines and expenditure increases have an automatic stimulative effect tending to encourage economic growth.

The progressivity of the tax structure is an example of a built-in or automatic stabilizer. As the economy declines, corporate profits decline and workers' salaries decrease. Both corporate and personal taxes thus go down, with the result that proportionately more funds are left available to the private sector for investment, stimulating demand. Similarly, tax revenues rise as the economy expands, providing some brake on growth so it does not lead to inflationary pressures. One estimate is that a $1.00 decline in GDP produces an automatic $.25 fall in federal income and a $.08 increase in federal spending.[33]

Discretionary Policies

There are also nongovernmental stabilizers that are an inherent part of the economy and individual economic behavior. Recessions are resisted by individuals and corporations that use savings to maintain established levels of activities. Conversely, expansionary trends are resisted. As income rises, greater proportions of income are placed in savings rather than being used for consumption.

Discretionary interventions vary widely. They are based on economic theories of behavior, both micro- and macroeconomic, that anticipate the economy's responses to government actions involving taxing and spending and alterations in the flow of funds through the monetary system. The former actions are called fiscal policy; the latter, monetary policy. Fiscal policy and monetary policy are first reviewed separately, and then their integration into an overall strategy is discussed. A separate section is devoted to the public investment role of government, a role particularly important for developing countries and for U.S. state and local governments.

Fiscal Policy Instruments

The essential tools of fiscal policy are revenues, expenditures, and the implied surplus or deficit. Their use has evolved during the twentieth century, changing as different views of the role of government in the economy have held sway. The prevailing view early in the century was that little government intervention was necessary. If the economy seemed to be faltering, the government's role should be limited to an incremental increase in expenditures over revenues to "prime the pump." During the Depression of the 1930s, demand fell off so rapidly and to such a depth, however, that small actions by the government had virtually no effect. It was only the extraordinary production demands of World War II that stimulated sufficient growth to pull the economy out of the depths. The immediate postwar period rode on the demand for consumer goods that had been in short supply during the war, and there seemed to be little for the government to do for the economy one way or the other.

Keynesian Economics. Ideas about what the government should do in the event of a downturn have not stood still. John Maynard Keynes had argued in 1936 that the main cause of downturns was lack of demand.[34] The government's aim should be to stimulate demand by spending, thus ensuring that idle productive capacity is used. By 1946, the federal government assumed a formal role in the economy, and that role was guided by the prescriptions of Keynesian economics. Keynes focused on the problem of cuts in production in response to declining demand. Such cuts result in less purchasing power for consumers, which further reduces demand for goods and services. This still further decline in demand results in further reductions in production levels. The emphasis, according to Keynesians, should be on maintaining demand levels. The way to maintaining demand levels, in their view, is to spend at a level higher than revenues, in other words, to incur a deficit whenever economic fluctuations threaten to reduce demand to levels that will generate unemployment and general economic decline.

Supply-Side Economics. Keynesian economics was widely accepted until the 1970s, when a contrasting view of the basic problem in a fluctuating demand cycle was given wide circulation. Some economists began to argue that the basic problem lay, not on the demand side, but on the supply side.[35] So-called supply-side economics became the dominant viewpoint of the Reagan and Bush administrations. The supply-side view held that high tax burdens are the major contributor to reduced economic performance. The more taxes are collected, the less money is available for private investment and the less incentive there is to produce. If taxes are cut, production will be stimulated and additional workers will be hired. Although the tax rates are lower, the actual revenue yield will be higher because of increased corporate profits and increased take-home pay for workers.

Furthermore, the increased supply of goods and services available should have a dampening effect on inflation.

The more extreme version of the supply-side view provided the basis for the 1981 tax cuts (Economic Recovery Tax Act of 1981). However, the expected revenue windfall did not materialize. The prevailing explanation of why it did not is consistent with the theory that tax cuts generally stimulate growth; the accepted view is merely that tax revenues from that growth are usually less than necessary to offset the government revenue loss.[36]

The differences between the demand-oriented economists and the supply-oriented economists have moderated. The middle-of-the-road view is that specific and directed tax decreases or reductions in tax liabilities can be helpful, such as investment tax credits to encourage businesses to invest in capital facilities and an R&D tax credit to encourage private expenditures on research, but a major multiplier effect, in which tax reductions yield tax revenue increases, is unlikely. Capital gains tax changes seem to produce the greatest level of response. Contemporary views tend to emphasize somewhat more the supply side view than efforts to stimulate demand.

Contemporary Fiscal Policy. The contemporary view of fiscal policy is more pragmatic than theoretical. Budget deficits that overwhelm incremental fiscal adjustments have overshadowed theoretical debate among fiscal policy theorists. The current approach to fiscal policy calls for moderate fiscal efforts on the tax or expenditure side to counter trends rather than massive tax cuts or expenditure increases. Modest increases in government expenditures during periods of economic decline are expected to stimulate demand, which in turn will stimulate a higher level of production. Modest tax reductions, especially those designed to stimulate business investment, should have a similar stimulative effect on the supply of funds available to individuals. The Balanced Budget Agreement of 1997 contained significant tax cuts, but only with accompanying expenditure reductions to ensure that the tax cut excess of the early 1980s without expenditure reductions was not repeated.

Multiplier Effects. Extracting taxes from the economy or adding expenditures will not only have immediate effects but also multiplier effects, since any transaction will generate several other transactions. For each government expenditure paid to industry or an individual, part is taxed while the remainder is divided between consumption and investment. The private citizen or firm spends, and in doing so places dollars in the hands of others, some of which will be taxed and the rest spent or invested. Therefore, an increase of $100 in government expenditures will be multiplied in its effect on the economy.[37]

Expenditures have a stimulative effect when they exceed revenues. An initial government expenditure financed by the deficit puts money in the hands of producers and consumers, who in turn pay a portion in taxes, save a portion, and spend a portion. An excess of revenues over expenditures has a dampening effect. An extremely large federal deficit, however, confounds the fiscal policy effects. Large surpluses seem to have become an artifact of the past, regardless of the direction the economy may be moving. It remains to be seen whether the Balanced Budget Agreement and the economic upswing of the mid-1990s will yield regular annual surpluses, and if so, what the effects of those will be.

Response Lags in Fiscal Policy. One problem with implementing a modest fiscal policy is the gap between the time a revenue or expenditure response is necessary and the time it actually can occur. The lack of complete information about the economy produces a *perception lag*, the period of time that elapses between an event—such as the beginning of an inflationary period—and its recognition. The perception lag contributes to a *reaction lag*, the time between recognition and the decision to act. Pluralistic or decentralized political systems are often unable to avoid substantial reaction lags. For example, in January 1967 President Johnson proposed a surtax on income to dampen the inflationary effects of Vietnam War spending. The proposed legislation was not introduced in Congress until August and, though finally approved, was not signed into law until July 1968. To close this gap, several presidents have attempted to gain congressional approval for moderate discretionary authority to raise or lower taxes. However, Congress has jealously guarded its prerogative to initiate and approve tax actions.

After the reaction lag is the *implementation lag*, the time required before the action taken actually affects the economy. Tax measures clearly are felt within a short period of time. The introduction of a new tax does require time to establish the specific regulations and mechanisms for collection. Once the tax is established, however, comparatively little time is required to make the necessary adjustments to the tax rate.

In contrast, extended implementation lags are likely when expenditures are adjusted for fiscal policy purposes. In the short term, the apportionment process that allocates funds to agencies may have some marginal influence on spending patterns during the various quarters of the fiscal year (see Chapter 10). Potentially more powerful tools include budget impoundments, which, within certain limits, allow the President to defer or rescind expenditures (see Chapter 9). Many expenditures, however, are basically uncontrollable in the immediate future because of previous commitments (for example, entitlement programs that provide assistance to the elderly and the poor). Furthermore, a large component of the federal budget is now devoted to meeting interest payments on the debt or to refinance previous debt.

Capital construction has been suggested on occasion as one discretionary area where government expenditures could be used for fiscal policy purposes. The first Clinton term proposed grants to state and local governments for capital projects but failed to secure passage in Congress. Construction would be initiated during slack periods and curtailed during periods of high employment. To some extent, public construction has been used for this purpose, particularly by the federal government during the Depression. The central government in a developing country, which typically has a much larger role in public infrastructure construction, is often in a better position to use this type of discretionary expenditure control. The short-term use of "stockpiled" capital projects that can be implemented when needed for their stimulative effects should not be confused with the role of government investment in long-term economic growth, discussed later.

Monetary Policy

Control over the Money Supply. Both demand-side and supply-side economists focus on the role of taxing and spending in the economy. Although fiscal policy economists did not launch a major critique of demand-side theories until the late 1970s, other economists since the 1950s have argued that the government's main effect on the economy should not come through fiscal policy at all. Led by Milton Friedman, these economists argue that the main effects of government policy on the private sector come through control over the money supply. In a simple economy, a government controls the money supply through its monopoly power over the printing of money. As the economy expands, the demand for money increases, and ultimately government meets this demand by printing more money. In a sense, the government literally can print currency and use that currency to meet its spending requirements. The increase in the money supply (over and above printing replacements for worn currency) is called *seignorage*. Clearly, if the government resorts to printing money without regard to demand, the value of the currency printed declines in value. U.S. news media in the early 1980s showed film footage of individuals in Bolivia actually pushing carts full of currency to pay for a few dollars worth of goods as the annual inflation rate reached several thousand percent. Inflation affected currencies so much in Russia and Poland shortly after the demise of the Soviet Union that the governments issued new currency, eliminating three zeros to ease the use of currency in ordinary transactions.

In a more complex economy, paper money and coinage in circulation is not the major component of the money supply controlled by government. In the United States, only 25 percent of the principal money supply is paper money and coinage. The remaining 75 percent consists of demand deposits in banking institutions. Most financial transactions are conducted with checks and other paper documents that transfer bank account balances from one individual or institution to another. The banking deposit component of the money supply expands through credit or borrowing. When an individual borrows to purchase a new car, the bank increases the individual's bank balance, which allows a check to be written to the car dealer. In this case, the money supply grows by the amount of the loan. Similarly, banks can borrow from the Federal Reserve System, which also adds to the money supply. Deregulation of the banking industry and the growth of various stock and bond funds have further added to the number and types of negotiable instruments that constitute the money supply. Influencing the money supply thus grows increasingly complicated.

Role of the Federal Reserve System. In the United States, control over the money supply and interest rates, and hence monetary policy, is exercised by the Federal Reserve System, a quasi-public institution.[38] The system is headed by a board of governors consisting of seven members appointed by the President with the advice and consent of the Senate. The chairperson is designated by the President. The Federal Reserve Bank and its branches are augmented by all national banks and by state banks and trust companies that wish to join.

The Federal Reserve serves as a bank to the banking community. Financial transactions among banks and other financial institutions are cleared through the Federal Reserve. The system lends money to the member banks, which member banks then can relend to their customers. In setting these lending rates, the Federal Reserve influences the direction and magnitude of interest rates in the economy, in turn dampening or stimulating the credit system. The system also buys and sells government bonds ranging from short-term Treasury notes to long-term bonds (open market operations). The Federal Reserve also controls the reserve requirements for member banks—the amount of money a bank has to have available as a proportion of the total demand deposits of customers. Using these three tools—open market operations, lending, and control of reserve requirements—the Federal Reserve controls the money supply.

Importance of Open Market Operations. Open market operations and setting the discount rate are the most prominent operations because they occur daily. As the Federal Reserve purchases bonds, it increases the reserve holdings of the member institutions selling the bonds and hence increases the supply of money available to be lent. This increase in turn stimulates economic activity, because more investment funds are made available. As member banks buy bonds from the Federal Reserve, their cash reserves decrease, reducing the total supply of funds available to the economy.

Discount Rate. Frequently adjusted, the Federal Reserve's lending rate to member institutions, called the discount rate, has increased in prominence as a monetary tool. Banks borrow from the Federal Reserve to meet customers' demands for money. As the Federal Reserve increases the interest rate, the rate charged to final borrowers increases, which in turn decreases the demand for funds. Chairman of the Federal Reserve Alan Greenspan became almost a household name in the mid-1990s as the Federal Reserve exercised close watch on an economic boom that continued longer than any in recent history, accompanied by unprecedented growth in the stock market. Small adjustments up and down in the discount rate proved to be quite effective in smoothing out the business cycle, allowing the sustained growth to continue without creating inflationary pressures.[39]

Reserve Requirement. Changing the reserve requirements of member institutions is done infrequently. For every dollar in customer deposits, member banks are required to retain a specific percentage. By increasing this percentage, the Federal Reserve can immediately curtail the amount of money available. Historically changed only every few years, the reserve requirement in the 1980s became a more prominent feature of monetary policy, with adjustments often occurring on an annual basis. The 1990s reflect a return to infrequent changes in the reserve requirements.

Putting these monetary tools together, the government's monetary policy is described as loose or tight (or expansionary or contractionary). Loose monetary policy usually involves lowering the prime rate, purchasing securities from member banks, and sometimes involves lowering reserve requirements. These actions increase the money supply, which permits banks to lend more to customers. As a result, private investment goes up and unemployment falls. The side effects are lower interest rates and higher prices.

A tight monetary policy entails the reverse—the prime rate increases, the Federal Reserve sells securities, and reserve requirements may increase. These actions reduce the ability of banks to lend. Tight monetary policy is pursued generally to dampen inflationary pressures and to slow down a speeding economy. Loose monetary policy is pursued to stimulate growth and reduce unemployment.

Political Criticism of the Federal Reserve Board. Although the Federal Reserve Board is protected from direct coercion from the President because its members' terms are fixed without threat of removal, the board is periodically criticized for appearing to respond to political pressure. While there is little evidence of overt behavior in support of incumbent presidents, there is some indication that the Federal Reserve Board has done less than it could in some periods (for example in the 1960s and 1970s), to offset cyclic movements in the money supply and that this lack of action coincided with the interests of incumbent administrations.[40] Federal Reserve Chairman Greenspan got into some hot water, not from critics charging political machinations, but from remarks made about the stock market boom that temporarily sent the market tumbling. Following that reaction, Greenspan continued to keep close watch on the rapid growth in stock valuation, but tempered the nature of his remarks.

Combining Fiscal and Monetary Policy

Although economists differ on the emphasis given to fiscal versus monetary policy, the two sets of tools operate at the same time, whether deliberately or not.

Sometimes they are complementary, but sometimes the effects of fiscal policy actions are offset by monetary policy actions. Many analysts are wary of advocating frequent changes in fiscal or monetary policy in response to changing economic conditions. The inability to predict economic change sufficiently far in advance and the slow response of governments suggests to many economists that fiscal policy should be oriented toward long-term economic objectives and monetary policy should be used for effecting short-term adjustments. Although fiscal and monetary policy advocates disagree vigorously, most economists agree that the budget deficits of the 1980s and early 1990s were harmful.

Public Investment Role of Government

Government Investment in Infrastructure. Fiscal policy and monetary policy are basically tools of central governments. State and local governments typically have balanced budget requirements, making it impossible to incur debt strictly for fiscal policy reasons, and neither type of government has a major influence on the overall money supply. However, state and local governments have significant impacts on regional economies, and increasingly state and local governments adopt explicit economic development strategies. In this regard, state and local governments pursue strategies to create an effective economic climate to foster economic growth. And they inevitably change taxes and spending in response to general economic conditions, which, whether deliberate or not, has at least regional economic effects.[41]

One of the major strategic elements available is public sector investment in the physical infrastructure necessary for business expansion. As discussed in Chapter 12, serious concern emerged in the United States during the early 1980s regarding the loss in economic productivity due to the deterioration in the infrastructure base of roads, bridges, streets, water and sewer systems, and other public facilities. According to some, fewer technological innovations, decreases in labor productivity, and inadequate capital investment in infrastructure were the major contributors to an overall worsening of the U.S. economy.[42] In developing countries, inadequate operation and maintenance of existing facilities has in many cases led to deterioration of physical facilities long before their expected depreciation. This deterioration has in turn led to a decline in economic production.

State and Local Incentives for Private Sector Investment. Governments are a major source of total capital formation in many developing countries. Public sector investment in infrastructure as a percentage of all capital formation averages 25 percent for all developing countries and reaches 60 to 70 percent in some countries.[43] While state and local governments in the United States do not invest nearly as high a proportion in infrastructure, their role in creating a favorable economic climate also is important. Some state employee pension funds, for example, have been used as sources of venture capital and to capitalize industrial development funds to attract new business.[44] Federal policies, such as giving municipal bonds tax-exempt status, also influence state and local investment spending.[45]

Similarly, even in the face of reduced federal revenue transfers and difficult fiscal circumstances, state and local governments have increased both their relative share of infrastructure financing and the absolute amounts spent on public infrastructure. This stimulative effect, of course, required state and local tax increases.

State and local governments also actively compete with each other over the location of major industrial facilities.[46] However, to the extent that state and local governments offer special incentives, such as tax breaks and below-market-cost facilities for industrial expansion, little national economic growth is stimulated. Certainly it may be possible to induce a business to relocate or to locate a planned expansion by offering special incentives, but such a move represents for the national economy as a whole only a relocation of economic activity rather than net new economic growth. When public investment creates possibilities for new investment, however, not only the local economy but the total economy expands. A joint public-private venture, for example, participated in the redevelopment of the Baltimore harbor area, which created conditions in which net new economic investment was attracted. Similar ventures have occurred in Portland, Oregon, and Seattle, Washington. Riverfront revitalization projects in San Antonio, Texas, stimulated downtown economic growth and have been emulated since.[47]

Link Between Public Infrastructure and Economic Growth. The causal link between public infrastructure investment and real economic growth depends on two conditions. The lack of facilities or infrastructure has to be a barrier to investment, and the costs of the investment have to be in principle recoverable through economic gains. For example, if poor road conditions slow the movement of goods and services, then the costs of those goods and services increase. In addition, firms may hold back on new investments because of the expected difficulty in transportation. Investment in road improvements under these conditions then reduces transportation costs, which in turn either provides additional funds for investment or is passed on in savings to consumers, who in turn can increase either savings or investment. If the economic returns on the road improvements exceed their costs, it is a net economic gain to the economy. On the other hand, if there are insufficient centers of production and consumption linked by those roads, then the volume of transportation will not be sufficient to yield sufficient economic gain, and the investment will not have been warranted.

Unfortunately, determining when the investment will yield sufficient economic return is often difficult. Many local governments in the United States have invested in downtown revitalization, business incubator facilities, industrial parks, and other facilities without sufficient analysis of the local economy and have been disappointed with the returns.[48] Similarly, in developing countries inadequate consideration of whether there are genuine economic opportunities to be stimulated by an infrastructure investment at times has led to indiscriminate construction of roads where there were no real market and production centers to link. One study of U.S. highway investments suggested that instead of significant new capital investment in highways, greater economic impact could occur from decreasing congestion and other planning improvements—for little more spending than current levels.[49]

REDISTRIBUTIONAL EFFECTS OF ECONOMIC POLICY

Unintentional Redistributive Effects

To this point in the chapter, we have been concerned with the overall performance of the economy. Government involvement in the economy also has specific objectives focused on subsectors or individuals. Fiscal and monetary policy actions taken to control overall economic growth and price stability are not necessarily neutral in their effects on individuals and industries. If the government lowers corporate tax rates to stimulate business investment but increases other taxes in order to neutralize the effects on the budget balance, then those for whom taxes are raised are paying for the economic benefits whether they share in the benefits or not. Many developing country governments have attempted to address problems of the urban poor by imposing price controls on agricultural products. While the short-run effect may be to lower food prices in urban areas, the longer-run effect is to decrease agricultural production. In the short run, economic costs are imposed on one group, rural producers, for the benefit of another group, urban consumers. In the long run, overall economic performance declines. Developing country budgets, operating often in conditions of instability and uncertainty, frequently have difficulty achieving any specific policy objective, such as poverty alleviation, through the budgeting process.[50]

Economic policies aimed at stabilization also can have unintentional redistributive effects. Under inflationary conditions, persons on fixed or relatively fixed incomes lose purchasing power. This is especially true for retired persons living on pensions, but it is also true for workers who cannot command increases in wages. If the government takes no action to slow the rate of inflation, its inaction "redistributes" income from those on fixed incomes to those whose wages or other income rises with inflation. Higher interest rates favor income earnings from investments, usually held by upper-income families. Large federal deficits, which ultimately impose repayment costs on future generations, also may create intergenerational inequity (see Chapter 11).

Since the 1960s, the degree of inequality of income distribution in the United States has increased significantly. There was a sharp increase in inequality during the 1980s, attributed by many to a significant cut in federal corporate and personal income taxes, benefiting mainly the already wealthy, and cuts in programs of assistance to the poor.[51] Some economists critical of the "monetary policy only" view of the government's economic role argue that the government should mitigate the negative distributional effects of economic growth that leaves only the middle- and upper-income classes better off. According to these economists, policies such as aggressive employment subsidies to reduce the number of unemployed should be implemented as direct measures to lower the nonaccelerating inflation rate of unemployment.[52]

Income Stabilization Policies

The most deliberate income stabilization policy would be to institute a negative income tax.[53] This would involve determining an appropriate income guarantee, a benefit reduction rate, and a break-even income. The income guarantee is the amount of the transfer when the family income is zero, the benefit reduction rate is the rate at which the amount transferred is reduced as family income increases, and the break-even income is the point where family income reaches a level beyond which the family no longer qualifies for a transfer. The United States has no negative income tax, but its principles are incorporated to varying degrees in several income-related transfer programs.

Transfer Programs. Several transfer programs (Food Stamps; Supplemental Feeding Program for Women, Infants and Children; Medicaid) provide a minimum or floor level of benefits comparable to the income guarantee. Major reforms in the welfare system in 1997, however, have severely curtailed the benefits by imposing lifetime limits on the amount individuals may receive, and imposing strict work requirements (see Chapter 14).

Tax Policies. Expenditure programs are not the only form of income redistribution. As noted in Chapter 4, different taxes have different impacts on various groups. In addition, the overall structure of the entire tax system may operate to redistribute income among different groups. The Tax Reform Act of 1986 was in one basic aspect almost exclusively a redistributive act.[54] Throughout consideration of various possible changes, the basic principle followed was that the act had to be revenue neutral. In the face of huge budget deficits, neither political party was prepared to support a tax reform that reduced revenues, as the Economic Recovery Tax Act of 1981 had. As a consequence of the 1986 law, lower-income groups benefited from sharply reduced taxes, middle-income groups benefited from modest reductions, and upper-income individuals and corporations faced tax increases. In 1993, there were sharp increases in the top tax bracket, and in 1997 tax decreases focused on both ends of the income bracket.

While economic policy affects the distribution of income, it cannot be expected to address structural features of the labor market. For example, workers with minimal or obsolete skills will have difficulty finding employment even during periods of rapid growth. Economic policy also is of limited assistance in coping with readjustments in the economy, such as might occur if defense spending continues to be reduced throughout the 1990s. Other policies, of course, are designed to deal with more basic structural problems. Expenditures on education, both academic and vocational, are expected to increase the overall human resource base for the economy. Regulatory policies are expected to reduce private incentives to pollute the environment, which imposes an eventual economic cost when the environmental damage is repaired.

No redistributive policy is neutral in its economic impact, and indeed no economic act, no matter what the intended effects, is automatically neutral with regard to distribution of income. Designing redistributive policies should take into account the potential reduction in economic efficiency and try to mitigate any losses.[55] During a recessionary period, both the labor force and total plant capacity are underemployed, so that government action to stimulate the economy may do just that without causing significant unintended redistributive effects. But since recession is not the normal state of the economy, we have to assume for starters "that if the government expands its purchases of goods and services or provides additional benefits so that some group of private citizens can consume more goods and services, somewhere else in the economy purchases of goods and services for consumptionary investment, exports, or other government programs will have to be reduced."[56]

SUMMARY

Representing over 32 percent of total economic activity in the United States, federal, state, and local government budgets have a tremendous combined effect on the economy. The federal government acts deliberately to intervene in the economy to achieve aggregate economic objectives. The major economic policy objectives of most central governments include economic growth, full employment, stable prices, and balance in the flow of funds into and out of the economy. Increasingly, as national economies become more interdependent, governments, including the U.S. federal government, include specific competitiveness objectives as part of national economic policy. Because it has sometimes soared to unacceptable heights (politically and economically), management of the U.S.

federal budget deficit and the overall government debt also has been added as a major economic policy objective.

Fiscal policy and monetary policy are the main tools used to influence macro-economic performance. Fiscal policy encompasses the use of the government's taxing and spending powers to stimulate or dampen economic activity. An excess of expenditures over revenues (a deficit) stimulates demand and thus employment. A possible consequence, however, may be inflation. An excess of revenues over expenditures (a surplus) has a dampening effect on the economy. Monetary policy affects economic activity through control over the money supply. By changing interest rates and reserve requirements and by buying or selling bonds, the Federal Reserve can speed up or slow down the pace of economic activity. In the latter half of the 1980s, debates over the theory and detail of fiscal and mone-tary policy were overshadowed by the huge federal budget deficit. In the 1990s, the focus has shifted to deficit management and delicate adjustments in interest rates to sustain economic growth.

Although state and local governments do not exercise fiscal and monetary con-trol, their role in providing the basic infrastructure required for private sector business activity is important to regional economic performance. In this respect, state and local governments and developing country governments pursue similar ends. For developing country governments, their effective use of borrowed funds from donor agencies and commercial banks depends on putting the funds to use in increasing economic productive capacity.

Government policy interventions also have consequences for income redistri-bution. Changes in tax policy and increases or decreases in expenditures are almost never neutral as regards income distribution. In addition, there is general agreement that some level of redistribution of income is appropriate to address the problems of those with very low incomes. How extensive these programs should be, however, has been a controversial issue. A major welfare reform in 1997 set lifetime limits on the amount of public assistance individuals may receive and required welfare recipients to seek employment.

NOTES

1. Executive Office of the President, Executive Order 12835 of January 25, 1983, Establishment of the National Economic Council, *Federal Register* 58 (1993): 6189–6190.

2. Home Debts from Abroad, *The Economist* 344 (July 12, 1997): 24.

3. Executive Office of the President, *Technology for America's Economic Growth: A New Direction To Build Economic Strength* (Washington, DC: U.S. Government Printing Office, 1993).

4. International Institute for Management Development, *The World Competitiveness Yearbook: 1997* (Lausanne, Switzerland: International Institute for Management Development, 1997), 318.

5. Commission of the European Communities, *White Paper on Growth, Competitiveness and Employment* (Brussels-Luxembourg: ECSC-EC-EAEC, 1995): http://www.ispo.cec.be/infosoc/backg/whitpaper/top.html; accessed December 1997.

6. R.A. Musgrave and P.B. Musgrave, *Public Finance in Theory and Practice*, 5th ed. (New York: McGraw-Hill, 1989).

7. O.L. Graham, Jr., *Losing Time: The Industrial Policy Debate* (Cambridge, MA: Harvard University Press, 1992).

8. Back to the Glory Days? *The Economist* 345 (June 21, 1997): 27–28.

9. M. Mandel, How Long Can This Last? *Business Week* (May 19, 1997): 30–34.

10. World Bank, *World Development Report 1992* (New York: Oxford University Press, 1992), 241.

11. Executive Office of the President, *Economic Report of the President: 1995* (Washington, DC: U.S. Government Printing Office, 1995); Executive Office of the President, *Economic Report of the President: 1997* (Washington, DC: U.S. Government Printing Office, 1997), 48. The 1995 *Report* contains a detailed description of the methodology.

12. R. Reich, *The Work of Nations: Preparing Ourselves for 21st Century Capitalism* (New York: Alfred A. Knopf, 1991).

13. Executive Office of the President, *Highlights of the President's Economic Program* (Washington, DC: U.S. Government Printing Office, 1993), 4.

14. Don't Be Salesmen, *The Economist* 342 (February 1, 1997): 17–18.

15. G.M. Grossman and E. Helpman, *Innovation and Growth: Technological Competition in the Global Economy* (Cambridge, MA: MIT Press, 1992).

16. C. Farrell, The Triple Revolution, *Business Week* (December 12, 1994): 18–25.

17. U.S. Foreign Debt Rose 26.6% in '96, Commerce Agency Says, *Wall Street Journal Interactive Edition*, June 23, 1997.

18. R. Chernow, *The House of Morgan: An American Banking Dynasty and the Rise of Modern Finance* (New York: Simon and Schuster, 1990).

19. Congressional Budget Office, *Assessing the Decline in the National Saving Rate* (Washington, DC: U.S. Government Printing Office, 1993), 2; Organization for Economic Cooperation and Development, *OECD Economic Surveys, United States: 1996* (Paris: Organization for Economic Cooperation and Development, 1996), 22.

20. Congressional Budget Office, *Assessing the Decline in the National Savings Rate*, 2.

21. M. McNamee and D. Foust, How Growth Could End the Budget Wars, *Business Week* (May 19, 1997): 32–33.

22. Executive Office of the President, *Economic Report of the President: 1997,* 322.

23. L.T. LeLoup et al., Deficit Politics and Constitutional Government: The Impact of Gramm-Rudman-Hollings, *Public Budgeting & Finance* 7 (Spring 1987): 84.

24. N. Frumkin, *Guide to Economic Indicators* (Armonk, NY: M.E. Sharpe, 1990).

25. D. Levitan, How To Read the Economy: A Primer, *Government Finance Review* 9 (April 1993): 25–27.

26. J.L. Norwood, The Consumer Price Index, the Deficit, and Politics, *Government Finance Review*, 13 (February 1997): 32–33.

27. H.F. Myers, Housing Cycles Balance Economy: Buying Decline Cools It, Rise Leads Recovery, *The Wall Street Journal News Service*, October 16, 1988.

28. The Dow Jones Industrial Average Will Change Four Stocks, *Wall Street Journal Interactive Edition*, March 13, 1997.

29. U.S. Department of Commerce, Bureau of Economic Analysis, *Business Conditions Digest* (Washington, DC: U.S. Government Printing Office, published monthly); U.S. Department of Commerce, *Economic Indicators: Historical and Descriptive Background* (Washington, DC: U.S. Government Printing Office, 1980).

30. R. McNown, On the Uses of Econometric Models: A Guide for Policy Makers, *Policy Sciences* 19 (1986): 359–380.

31. The CBO's annual analysis *The Economic and Budget Outlook: Fiscal Years [ten year period]* always contains a chapter explaining the differences between CBO and OMB estimates. A mid-year publication, *The Economic and Budget Outlook: Update*, reflects changes in the months since publication of the *Outlook*. Congressional Budget Office, *The Economic and Budget Outlook: Update* (Washington, DC: U.S. Government Printing Office, annually).

32. R. Bahl and W. Duncombe, Economic Change and Fiscal Planning: The Origins of the Fiscal Crisis in New York State, *Public Administration Review* 52 (1992): 547–558.

33. C.L. Schultze, *Memos to the President: A Guide through Macroeconomics for the Busy Policy-maker* (Washington, DC: Brookings Institution, 1992), 204.

34. J.M. Keynes, *The General Theory of Employment, Interest and Money* (New York: Harcourt Brace, 1936).

35. A.B. Laffer and J.P. Seymour, eds., *The Economics of the Tax Revolt: A Reader* (New York: Harcourt Brace Jovanovich, 1979).

36. D.N. Hyman, *Public Finance: A Contemporary Application of Theory to Policy*, 5th ed. (Chicago: Dryden, 1996), 457.

37. D.J. Ott and A.F. Ott, *Federal Budget Policy*, 3rd ed. (Washington, DC: Brookings Institution, 1977), 80–85.

38. J.P. Freudreis and R. Tatalevich, *The Modern Presidency and Economic Policy* (Itasca, IL: Peacock Publishers, 1994), 117–119.

39. We Are All Fine-tuners Now. *The Economist* 345 (May 17, 1997): 81–82.

40. N. Beck, The Fed and the Political Business Cycle, *Contemporary Policy Issues* 9 (1991): 25–38.

41. P. Brace, *State Government and Economic Performance* (Baltimore: Johns Hopkins University Press, 1993).

42. *Saving More and Investing Better: A Strategy for Securing Prosperity* (Washington, DC: Competitiveness Policy Council, 1995).

43. World Bank, *World Development Report 1991* (New York: Oxford University Press, 1991), 139–145.

44. L. Litvak, *Pension Funds and Economic Renewal* (Washington, DC: Council of State Planning Agencies, 1981).

45. R.W. Eberts and W.F. Fox, The Effect of Federal Policies on Local Public Infrastructure Investment, *Public Finance Quarterly* 20 (1992): 557–571.

46. T. Segal, The Competitors, *World Business* 6 (January/February 1997): 32–37.

47. A. Jordan, River of Dreams, *Governing* 11 (August 1997): 26–30.

48. D. M. Markley and K. T. McNamara, Local Economic and State Fiscal Impacts of Business Incubators, *State and Local Government Review* 28 (1996): 17–27.

49. K.A. Small et al., *Road Work* (Washington, DC: Brookings Institution, 1989).

50. R.D. Lee, Jr., Linkages among Poverty, Development and Budget Systems, *Public Budgeting & Finance* 12 (Spring 1992): 48–60.

51. C.J. Niggle, Monetary Policy and Changes in Income Distribution, *Journal of Economic Issues* 23 (1989): 809–822.

52. Up the NAIRU without a Paddle, *The Economist* 344 (March 8, 1997): 92.

53. Hyman, *Public Finance*, 249–251.

54. J.H. Birnbaum and A.S. Murray, *Showdown at Gucci Gulch: Lawmakers, Lobbyists, and the Unlikely Triumph of Tax Reform* (New York: Vintage, 1988).

55. E.K. Browning, The Marginal Cost of Redistribution, *Public Finance Quarterly* 21 (1993): 3–32.

56. C.L. Schutze, Paying the Bills, in *Setting Domestic Priorities: What Can Government Do?*, eds. H.J. Aaron and C.L. Schutze (Washington, DC: Brookings Institution, 1992), 300.

Concluding Remarks

The field of public budgeting and finance in the coming years will be characterized by increased attention given to

- integration of planning, budgeting, accounting, and performance measurement systems
- financial management
- legislative-executive conflict over budgetary roles
- achievement of an acceptable balance between the provision of public services and their financing within an intergovernmental framework
- promotion of economic growth within an international context

A risk-free prediction is that budgetary decision systems will have increased capabilities to use program information. The steady development of systems oriented toward program information since the late 1950s shows no signs of abating. Whether the use of program information is desirable has been a moot question for years. The issue today is how to use program information, not whether to use it. The 1990s are showing renewed efforts in this area at all levels of government.

Advancements in computer technology—both hardware and software—help strengthen the trend toward use of program data. Networked microcomputers make possible relatively sophisticated information systems for small governments and may even give them an advantage over larger jurisdictions that still operate largely within a mainframe environment or some combination of mainframes, local area networks, and personal computers. Wider accessibility to computer technology also is spurring the rapid growth of tools that help decision makers use the technology. Expert systems and decision support systems will increase the capacities of decision makers to consider information, even under tight deadline pressures.

As planning, budgeting, accounting, and evaluation systems become increasingly sophisticated, the need for better integration increases. One of the essential emphases in program budgeting was, and is, to link budgetary, program, and accounting information into an integrated decision system. The trend toward integration, however, does not mean that political realities will be removed from budgetary decision making, as some critics have contended. All that is suggested here is that a greater array of information will be more readily available than in the past and that decision makers will need to choose among that information in determining what positions to take on difficult problems.

Financial management gained increased attention in the 1980s and has continued to be a central concern in the 1990s. Earlier, unrepressed inflation and serious taxpayer recalcitrance forced government leaders to realize resources were limited and budget trimming was essential. Economic problems at the local, state, and federal levels have continued to make for "tight" budget situations that call for frugal measures. Budget execution, therefore, will receive greater attention. Can savings be achieved through closer monitoring of program spending? Can improvements in accounting systems lead to savings? What alternative financial arrangements hold promise for reducing costs? To what extent should governments pursue contracting out of services, privatization, and leasing arrangements? Growth in government programs will be accepted grudgingly, if at all, by taxpayers, who remain skeptical of the ability of governments to do many things well.

Executives and legislative bodies will continue their struggles with one another over their relative roles in budgetary decision making. The increased ability to collect, store, and manipulate data through computer technology makes possible far more detailed legislative involvement than was possible only 10 years ago. Will that increased ability be translated into greater legislative authority and control, and in what ways? On the other hand, both executives and legislatures may be less than assertive in dealing with the most intractable problems. Gridlock existed largely from 1981 to 1993 when Republican Presidents Reagan and Bush controlled the White House and Democrats largely controlled Congress. The same gridlock developed in 1995 when the President was a Democrat, and Congress came under the control of Republicans. Although the two camps reached rapprochement in 1997, a lingering question was whether the fragile budget balancing agreement would be honored over time.

If Congress is to play an increased role in decision making, then one imperative is to realign powers and procedures within the two chambers. Legislative bodies have changed their operations, added staff, and more generally increased their ability to handle policy making. At the same time, Congress encompasses a complex maze of committees, processes, and political considerations that make difficult any coherent approach to policy making. In the second half of the 1990s, the congressional leadership has been unwilling to consider any thorough revamping of the organization and processes by which Congress operates.

During the remainder of the 1990s and into the next millennium, governments will continue to be confronted with competing programmatic needs that must be met within a context of limited resources and intergovernmental relationships. National security and defense, programs for the elderly (especially Social Security), and health care will continue to demand the attention of the federal government, while all levels of government will be called upon to deal with such intractable problems as AIDS, drug trafficking and drug abuse, and poverty and related conditions, such as homelessness. Whether addressed by the public sector or the private sector, the increased proportion of the population aged 65 and above is inevitable, and an increasing share of health expenditures as a proportion of gross domestic product can be expected. At the other end of the age spectrum, financing elementary and secondary education will require new approaches as traditional sources of finance decline or are limited by taxpayer resistance. Difficult choices must be made over how programs are to operate and how they are to be financed. Presidents, governors, and mayors may all lament the afflictions of AIDS and drug dependency, but where are funds to be obtained for dealing with these problems? Local governments may be willing to provide programs for the poor, but only if state and federal funds are available to support these efforts. The intergovernmental finance system will come under increasing scrutiny as the different levels of government vie for the same tax dollars.

Promoting economic growth for the nation as a whole will continue to be a priority. In addition, so-called rust belt states will continue their struggle to survive under conditions of fiscal distress. Other areas, such as those dependent on the price of petroleum, will continue through periods of boom and bust as petroleum supplies and prices fluctuate. The extent to which state and local governments can affect their economic futures will remain uncertain.

One of the most important causes of the uncertainty in promoting economic growth by all levels of government is the rapid emergence of an international economy. International economic factors have had a major effect on the United States throughout the 20th century, but starting in the 1980s the impact reached new levels of magnitude. What the U.S. economy makes and sells is intimately influenced by the economies of other nations. The industrial mix of the U.S. economy and its labor force is inevitably changing. These changes are occurring at a time when the U.S. labor force is aging due to the aging of the baby boomers. How budget systems will be able to respond to these challenges is unknown.

These themes do not capture all that is likely to transpire over the coming years. At the same time, they reflect many of the concerns of the future. One certainty is that budget systems will continue to undergo change as they are called upon to serve the needs of decision makers.

Bibliographic Note

This Bibliographic Note is intended to assist in finding materials for further reading on public budgeting systems. Because the preceding chapters are footnoted extensively, we make no attempt here to recapitulate everything cited earlier. Readers will find the Index a handy guide to footnote references. This Bibliographic Note is meant as an aid in identifying general references as well as sources that have produced and can be expected to continue to produce literature on public budgeting.

Until the mid-1990s, any search for budget materials most likely began in a library, but today the Internet and especially its World Wide Web allow searches from wherever a computer is connected. Throughout this book we have cited various Web addresses in chapter endnotes, and in Chapter 11 we noted specific Web sites that can be of great use. Sites typically have links to other sites, allowing the user to "click" on an address in hypertext and move from site to site, literally traversing the globe in search of information.

Because the Web is in its infancy and is undergoing extensive change on a daily basis, Web site addresses are in flux. In attempting to reach the sites identified throughout the book, the reader is likely to find that some addresses have changed. When this occurs, many sites provide links so a user is automatically transferred from an old address to the current one. If the reader is not so fortunate to be automatically transferred, then an attempt should be made to contact the homepage for the unit issuing the document cited. For example, if a document from the Census Bureau is cited and the specific location is no longer correct, go to the homepage of the Census Bureau and begin a search from that location.

Several services are available in helping to locate information on the Web. Netsearch provides important links to many of these services: http://

home.netscape.com/escapes/search/ntsrchrnd-2.html. Web guides that organize sites by subject matter include:

- CnetSearch: http://www.search.com
- EINet galaxy: http://www.einet.net
- Infoseek: http://www2.infoseek.com
- Lycos: http://lycos.cs.cmu.edu
- WWW Virtual Library: http://vlib.stanford.edu/overview.html
- Yahoo!: http://www.yahoo.com

Search engines, which search hundreds of thousands of sites for keywords that a researcher supplies, include:

- Alta Vista: http://altavista.digital.com
- HOTBOT: http://www.hotbot.com/index.html
- WebCrawler: http://webcrawler.com

Besides these search engines and guides, several other sources are useful starting points for searches relating to budgeting and finance. One useful site on the Web is Financenet, sponsored by the U.S. Chief Financial Officers Council: http://www.financenet.gov. Another is the site maintained by the Association for Budgeting and Financial Management: http://www.pubadm.fsu.edu/abfm/index.html. A useful document available in print and on the Web is *Investigators' Guide to Sources of Information*, prepared annually by the General Accounting Office—click on "Special Publications and Software" after reaching the Government Accounting Office site: http://www.gao.gov.

Numerous periodicals provide information about the theory and practice of administration in general and budgeting and finance in particular. As the World Wide Web develops, journals will be placed on-line, most probably on a subscription basis, although back issues might be posted and available at no charge. For the present, journals are mainly available in print form. Periodical indexes that are available in print, on CD-ROM, and on-line include *Public Affairs Information Service International* (New York: Public Affairs Information Service) and the *Social Science Index* (New York: H.W. Wilson).

There are several journals that produce articles on budgeting and finance. *Public Administration Review* (American Society for Public Administration) often publishes scholarly articles on budgeting. *Policy Studies Journal* and *Policy Studies Review* (Policy Studies Organization) include occasional articles related to budgeting in their regular issues and in related special symposia issues. *State and Local Government Review* (University of Georgia) frequently includes budget-related articles that are particularly helpful to practitioners as well as scholars. *Public Budgeting & Finance* (Association for Budgeting and Financial Management and American Association for Budget and Program Analysis) and *Public Budgeting and Financial Management* (Marcel Dekker) specialize in financial management and budgeting. *Government Finance Review* (Government Finance Officers Association) provides brief analytic pieces and news items on budgeting and finance.

Numerous journals cover the fields of public finance, policy analysis, and policy evaluation. Although occasional articles related specifically to budgeting systems appear in these journals, their usual focus is on specific budgetary subtopics. *Public Finance Quarterly* (Sage) and *Public Finance/Finances Publique* (H.J. Paris) both publish empirical and theoretical analyses of economic policy concerns, including government growth and size, tax policy, fiscal and monetary policy, and economic analysis. *Public Finance* is more international in orientation. There are a number of journals devoted to policy analysis and policy evaluation. In addition to *Policy Studies Review* and *Policy Studies Journal*, the journals *Evaluation Review* (Sage), *Evaluation and Program Planning* (Pergamon), and *Journal of Policy Analysis and Management* (Association for Public Policy Analysis and Management) all share that focus.

In addition to the periodicals focusing on budgeting, other professional journals include occasional articles of relevance. These include *Administration and Society, Administrative Science Quarterly, American Economic Review, American Political Science Review,* and *Management Science.* The Washington-based *National Journal* provides weekly news and analysis of the federal government, including budgetary events, and the *C.Q. Weekly Report* (Washington, DC: Congressional Quarterly) covers congressional actions in particular. Most of the journals listed have annual or occasional indexes to facilitate general search.

Government publications provide another major source of up-to-date analysis and data. An excellent reference work that explains various types of documents and their sources is Joe Morehead and Mary Fetzer's *Introduction to United States Government Information Sources*, 5th ed. (Englewood, CO: Libraries Unlimited, 1996). An annual index to many local, state, and federal documents is *Bibliographic Guide to Government Publications—U.S.* (Boston: Hall). Federal documents can be located through the *Monthly Catalog of United Sates Government Publications* (Washington, DC: U.S. Government Printing Office) and through the Government Printing Office's (GPO's) Web site: http://www.access.gpo.gov. Many GPO documents are posted and can be downloaded at no cost. For statistical information, refer to the *American Statistics Index*, which includes federal documents, and the *Statistical Reference Index*, which indexes state government publications, both indexes are published by the Congressional Information Service (Bethesda, MD).

Congressional documents can be identified and obtained through a variety of sources. A useful index is the *CIS Index to Publications of the United States Congress* (Bethesda, MD: University Publications of America). Many congressional documents are available through the U.S. Library of Congress' Web site: http://thomas.loc.gov. Congressional publications can be searched through *Congressional Masterfile* and statistics can be located through *Statistical Masterfile*, both of which are available from the Congressional Information Service on CD-ROMs. Information about legislation can be found through the Library of Congress Information System (LOCIS) at http://lcweb.loc.gov/homepage/online.html. Information about reports from the Congressional Research Service can be obtained in print and CD-ROM format from *Major Studies and Issue Briefs of the Congressional Research Service* (Bethesda, MD: University Publications of America). The General Accounting Office, which is an arm of the Congress, indexes its reports in *GAO Reports and Testimony*: http://www.gao.gov/reports.htm.

There are numerous on-line subscription databases related to government. Valuable subscription services include LEGI-SLATE (Washington, DC: Legi-Slate, Inc.) and LEXIS-NEXIS (Dayton, OH: Mead Data Control), which provide tracking of federal legislation and other important federal information. LEXIS-NEXIS and Westlaw (St. Paul, MN: West Publishing) are extensive databases for searching federal and state legislation, case law, legal periodicals, and the like. *Congressional Compass* (Bethesda, MD: Congressional Information Service) is a database containing congressional hearings, committee reports, bills, laws, members' interest group ratings, the U.S. Code, and the Code of Federal Regulations.

Students of budgeting and finance will generally find themselves returning regularly to several key government sources. The Office of Management and Budget, Council of Economic Advisers, Treasury Department, Congressional Budget Office, and General Accounting Office produce publications of major import to the field. Reports from these agencies are available in print and on the World Wide Web (see Chapter 11).

Several annual volumes from various agencies contain basic data on revenues and expenditures for local, state, and federal levels as well as intergovernmental transfers among levels. Considerable care must be exercised when working from more than one source since the figures do not always agree. The Census Bureau in the Department of Commerce publishes *Government Finances, Statistical Abstract*, and *Survey of Current Business*. In addition, the Census of Governments is conducted every five years and contains not only financial data but also a wealth of organizational information. The Census Bureau is located on the Web at http://www.census.gov.

Besides the Census Bureau, there are other providers of statistical information that are located on the Web. These include the University of Michigan's Statistical Resources on the Web: http://www.lib.umich.edu/libhome/Documents.center/ stats.html; FEDSTATS, maintained by the federal Interagency Council on Statistical Policy: http://www.fedstats.gov; and the Federal Statistics Briefing Room, maintained by the White House: http://www.whitehouse.gov/WH/html/briefroom. html).

Analyses of federal budgeting and finance are published by private organizations such as the American Enterprise Institute (Washington, DC), the Committee on Economic Development (New York), the Heritage Foundation (Washington, DC), the National Bureau of Economic Research (New York), the National Industrial Conference Board (New York), and the Tax Foundation (New York*). The Guide to the Federal Budget* is an annual publication that critiques the President's budget (publisher varies). The Brookings Institution (Washington, DC) publishes numerous books on budgeting and taxation. Many of these institutions have Web sites and an easy way of locating them is through the Policy Community: http://policy.com.

Books, of course, are an important source of information. Five of the classics in public budgeting, no longer subject to revision and updating, are William F. Willoughby's *The Problems of a National Budget* (New York: Appleton, 1918), A. E. Buck's *Public Budgeting* (New York: Harper and Brothers, 1919), Arthur Smithies' *The Budgetary Process in the United States* (New York: McGraw-Hill, 1955), Jesse Burkhead's *Government Budgeting* (New York: Wiley, 1956), and Aaron Wildavsky's *The Politics of the Budgetary Process* (Reading, MA: Addison-Wesley, 1984).

Histories of budgeting include Vincent J. Browne's *The Control of the Public Budget* (Washington, DC: Public Affairs Press, 1949), Bertram M. Gross's "The New Systems Budgeting" (*Public Administration Review* 29 [1969]: 113–137), C. W. Lewis' "History of Federal Budgeting and Financial Management from the Constitution to the Beginning of the Modern Era" (*Public Budgeting and Financial Management* 1 [1989]: 193–213), Irene S. Rubin's "Who Invented Budgeting in the United States?" (*Public Administration Review* 53 [1993]: 438–444), and Carolyn Webber and Aaron Wildavsky's *A History of Taxation and Expenditures in the Western World* (New York: Simon and Schuster, 1986).

Works on budgeting with a special focus, such as on the federal government, budget theory, budget politics, and the like, include Donald Axelrod's *Budgeting for Modern Government*, 2nd ed. (New York: St. Martin's, 1994); Robert L. Bland and Irene S. Rubins' *Budgeting: A Guide for Local Government* (Washington, DC: International City/County Management Association, 1997); Dall W. Forsythe's *Memos to the Governor: An Introduction to State Budgeting* (Washington, DC: Georgetown University Press, 1997); James L. Goslings's *Budgetary Politics in American Government*, 2nd ed. (New York: Garland, 1997); Thomas D. Lynch's *Public Budgeting in America*, 4th ed. (Englewood Cliffs, NJ: Prentice-Hall, 1994); John L. Mikesell's *Fiscal Administration,* 5th ed. (Orlando, FL: Harcourt Brace, 1998); Gerald J. Miller's *Government Financial Management Theory* (New York: Marcel Dekker, 1991); B. J. Reed and John W. Swain's *Public Finance Administration,* 2nd ed. (Thousand Oaks, CA: Sage, 1996); Irene Rubin's *The Politics of Public Budgeting: Getting and Spending, Borrowing and Balancing,* 3rd ed. (Chatham, NJ: Chatham House Publishers, 1996); Allen Schick's *The Federal Budget: Politics, Policy, and Process* (Washington, DC: Brooking Institution, 1995); and Aaron Wildavsky and Naomi Caiden's *The New Politics of the Budgetary Process,* 3rd ed. (New York: Longman, 1997).

Edited volumes provide reprints of journal articles and originally prepared pieces. Among these are *Budgeting Formulation and Execution,* edited by Jack Rabin, W. Bartley Hildreth, and Gerald J. Miller (Athens, GA: Carl Vinson Institute of Government, The University of Georgia, 1996); *Case Studies in Public Budgeting and Financial Management,* rev. printing, edited by Aman Khan and W. Bartley Hildreth (Dubuque, IA: Kendall/Hunt, 1996); *Government Budgeting: Theory, Process, and Politics,* 2nd ed., edited by Albert C. Hyde (Pacific Grove, CA: Brooks/Cole Publishing, 1992); *Handbook of Comparative Public Budgeting and Financial Management,* edited by Thomas D. Lynch and Lawrence L. Martin (New York: Marcel Dekker, 1993); *Local Government Finance: Concepts and Practices,* edited by John E. Petersen and Dennis R. Strachota (Chicago: Government Finance Officers Association, 1991); *Handbook of Public Budgeting,* edited by Jack Rabin (New York: Marcel Dekker, 1992); *Management Policies in Local Government Finance,* 4th ed., edited by J. Richard Aronson and Eli Schwartz (Washington, DC: International City/County Management Association, 1996); *Managing Local Government Finance: Cases in Decision Making,* edited by James M. Banovetz (Washington, DC: International City/County Management Association, 1996); *Public Budgeting and Finance,* 4th ed., edited by Robert T. Golembiewski and Jack Rabin (New York: Marcel Dekker, 1997).

A variety of simulations are available to assist students in appreciating the dynamics of decision making. Numerous simulations, directly or indirectly related to budgeting and finance, are listed on the Web site for the Association for Budgeting and Financial Management: http://www.pubadm.fsu.edu/abfm/index.html. The *Public Budgeting Laboratory* is a comprehensive set of materials prepared by Jack Rabin, W. Bartley Hildreth, and Gerald J. Miller. It consists of a book of *Readings,* noted above, by the editors, plus a *Workbook, Data Sourcebook,* and an *Instructor's Manual* (Athens, GA: Carl Vinson Institute of Government, The University of Georgia, 1996).

For literature on decision making, program budgeting, zero-base budgeting, accounting, economic policy, personnel management, program evaluation, and the like, the reader is encouraged to turn to the endnotes for each chapter.

Happy reading.

Index

A

Accountability, 7–14, 174
Accounting, 309–337
  account groups, 316
  basis of accounting, 322–329
  classification of receipts and expenditures, 318–322
    objects of expenditure, 319–321
    organizational unit, 319
    performance measurement, 322
    purpose and activity, 321
  comprehensive annual financial report (CAFR), 329
  defined, 309
  Federal Accounting Standards Advisory Board, 312
  formula, 317
  fund types, 314–316
  General Accounting Office, 311–312
  general purpose external financial reporting (GPEFR), 322
  Governmental Accounting Standards Board, 313
  measurement focus and basis of, 323–324
  Office of Management and Budget, 311–312
  organizations, 311–313
    Big 6 accounting firms, 312–313
  pension plan, 419
  performance measurement, 322
  principles, 313
  purposes, 310–311
  reporting, 329–337
  specified procedures, 317–318
  standards, 313
  structure and rules, 316–318
    double entry, 317
    journal, 318
    ledgers, 316
Accounting and Auditing Act, 311
Accounting entity, 314
Accounting firms, 312–313
Accounting formula, 317
Accrual accounting, 323–324
Activity measures, 104, 324
Activity-based accounting, 324
Activity-based management, 324
Administrative budget, 154
Advisory Commission on Intergovernmental Relations, 434, 463
Agency fund, 316
Allotment, 51, 266
Allowable cost, 327
Analysis. *See* Policy and program analysis
Analytical Perspectives, 152, 153
Annual budget, budget cycle, 56–57
Annual report, 329
Anti-Deficiency Act of 1950, 232
Apportionment, 266
  process, 51
Appropriation, 228–229
  See also Congress
Appropriation bill, 228–229
  budget, approval, 50

521

Appropriations Committee, 228, 254
Articles of Confederation, 8
Asset management, 363–378
    capital investment planning, 368–370, 371
Audit, 337–342
    guidelines, 340–341
    objectives, 338
    organizational responsibilities, 338–340
    standards, 341
    types, 340–341
Audit committee, 339–340
Authorization, 228
Automatic stabilizer, economic policy, 495
Average weekly initial claims for
    unemployment insurance, leading indicator,
    492
Average workweek of production workers in
    manufacturing, leading indicator, 492

B

Backdoor spending, 229–230
Balance of payments, United States, 482–483
Balance sheet, 330–332, 333
Balanced budget, 133–135
Balanced Budget Act, 245–247
Balanced Budget and Emergency Deficit
    Control Act. See Gramm-Rudman-Hollings
Balanced budget requirement, 252–253
Bankers' acceptance, 286
Bank-issued line of credit, 390
Base budget, 137, 216
Baseline, 238
Basis of accounting, 322–329
    need for different bases, 328–329
Benchmarking, 191
    budget preparation, 117–118
Benefits. See Cost-benefit analysis
Bicameralism, 214
Biennial budget, 257
    budget cycle, 56–57
Block grant, 457–459
    management capacity, 467
Blue book, 312
Bond bank, 384
Bond financing, 461–462
    bond prospectus, 387
    bond rating, 389–390

bond trustee, 390
    disclosure, 390–392
    discounting, 388
    features, 387–388
    importance, 379–381
    interest rate, 389
    issuance procedure, 385–390
    local government, 378–392
        participants, 385
        taxes, 380–381
    public sale vs. negotiated sale, 386–387
    ratings, 389–390
    regulation, 390–392
    Securities and Exchange Commission, 390–
        391
    state government, 378–392
        participants, 385
        taxes, 380–381
    structured finance, 388
    tax exemption, 380–381
    types, 381–385
    underwriting, 386
    voter approval, 386
Borrowing, 283
    budget preparation, 82
    See also Debt
Bowsher, C.A., 220
Budget
    appropriation bill, approval, 50
    defined, 14–16
    description, 15
    as explanations, 15–16
    as preferences, 16
    revenue bill, approval, 50
Budget and Accounting Act, 10
Budget and Accounting Procedures Act of
    1950, 10
Budget Appendix, 151–152, 154
Budget approval, 201–222. See also Congress
    authority, 211–212
    bicameralism, 214
    checks-and-balances system, 217–218
    committee responsibilities, 209–210
    compensation, 208–209
    conference committee, 206
    constituency differences, 212–213
    enrolled bill, 214
    executive fragmentation, 213–214
    federal aid to states, 214–216

fiscal note, 210–211
gridlock, 206
item veto, 216–217
legislative characteristics, 201–209
legislative committee, 206–207
legislative intent, 219
legislative oversight, 217–222
legislative process, 209–211
legislative roles, 211–222
legislative veto, 220–221
legislative-executive interactions, 211–217
Office of Management and Budget
  clearinghouse function, 214
parameters, 201–211
pork barrel, 212–213
staff, 208–209
standing committee, 206–207
strategies, 215–216
time, 207–208
Budget circular, 152
Budget cycle, 47–57
allotment, 51
annual budget, 56–57
apportionment process, 51
approval, 50–51
  executive veto power, 50–51
audit, 52–53
  location of audit function, 52–53
biennial budget, 56–57
budget year, 55–56
execution, 51–52
execution subsystems, 52
General Accounting Office, 52–53
impoundment, 51
intergovernmental factors, 55
overlapping cycles, 53–55
  federal level, 54
  links between phases, 54–55
phases, 47
preaudit, 51–52
preparation, 48–50
  chief executive responsibilities, 48
  fragmentation, 49–50
  location of budget office, 48–49
  political factors, 49
  steps, 49
preparation phase, length, 55
rationale, 47
scrambled, 53–57

submission, 48
Budget deal, Congress, 1
Budget deficit, 234, 237–239
budget preparation, 132
economic policy, 484–488
Budget document, 14–15, 151–162
alternative budget presentations, 155–156
approved budgets, 154
consolidated budget, 155
coverage, 154–156
expenditure, 156–157
federal documents, 151–152
format, 14–15
government personnel, 409, 410
information display, 156–163
number, 151–154
off-budget, exclusions, 155
on-budget, exclusions, 155
receipt, 163–164
specialized documents, 152–154
types, 151–154
unified budget, 155
Budget Enforcement Act, 239–242
Budget execution, 265–302
Budget of the United States Government, 151–152, 154
Budget preparation
benchmarking, 117–118
borrowing, 82
budget deficit, 132
budget request, 129–151
budget techniques, 116–121
  hybrid techniques, 116–117
chief executive, 130–133
  citizen preferences, 133
  intergovernmental relations, 132–133
  program priorities, 131
  relationships with legislative body, 132–133
  strategic concerns, 130–132
  tactical concerns, 132–133
current services budgeting, 107–108
decision process, 129–165
  final deliberations, 150–151
downsizing, 140–144
entrepreneurial budgeting, 117
expenditure side, 95–122
  early developments, 95–98
  nonbudgetary developments, 97–98

program information, 96–97
federal initiatives, 118–119
fixed-ceiling budgeting, 108
government employee retirement, 79
Government Performance and Results Act,
    118
local techniques, 120
multiyear request, 115–116
    cost projections, 116
    program projections, 116
    techniques, 120
    time horizons, 116
National Performance Review, 117–118
open-ended budgeting, 108
performance budgeting, 109
performance measurement, 102–107
    activities, 104
    choosing among program results, 106–
        107
    continuous quality improvement, 105
    goals, 106
    impacts, 103
    investments, 103
    management by objectives, 104
    need, 105
    objectives, 106
    outputs, 103–104
    productivity, 104–105
    program measures, 105–106
    quality of life, 102–103
    social indicator, 102–103
    suboptimization, 104
    total quality management, 105
    workload, 104
planning-programming-budgeting, 109–113
policy guidance, 115
preparation assumptions, 107–108
program budgeting, 109–113
program guidance, 115
reasons for adopting reforms, 121
re-engineering, 117–118
request process structure, 98–107
    preparation instructions, 98–102
    program information, 102–107
revenue, 59–89, 133–135
    balanced budget, 133–135
    source, 59–83
    tax earmarking, 134–135
    taxing limitations, 133

revenue estimating, 86–88, 133
    contingency reserve, 88
    deterministic models, 86
    econometric models, 87–88
    politics, 88
    rainy day fund, 88
    simple trend extrapolations, 86–87
revolving loan program, 81
rightsizing, 140–144
spending, 135–140
    agency expectations and deliberations,
        136–137
    commitments, 135
    entitlement, 135
    Office of Management and Budget and
        agency relations, 137–139
    Office of Management and Budget
        recommendations, 139–140
    Office of Management and Budget roles,
        136
    organizational competition, 135–136
spending cutback, 140–144
    budget reserves, 141–142
    budget systems, 144
    fiscal stress, 141
    items to cut, 143–144
    legislative roles, 142–143
    management, 141–144
    Office of Management and Budget roles,
        142
    rainy day funds, 141–142
state techniques, 119–120
strategic planning, 114–115
systems of budgeting, 107–121
target-base budgeting, 117
taxing and spending limitations, 83–86
techniques in other nations, 120
unemployment insurance, 79–80
zero-base budgeting, 113–114
    disadvantages, 113–114
    history, 113–114
Budget request
    budget preparation, 129–151
    decision making, 129–151
Budget stabilization fund, 284
Budget year, budget cycle, 55–56
Budget-in-brief, 151
Budgeting
    distinctions regarding public budgeting, 2–6

early history of, 95, 97
generational effects, 131–132
government personnel, 419–420
method, 1
process, 1
public and private sector differences, 6
public and private sector differences in
objectives, 2–4
profit motive, 3–4
resource availability, 2–4
public and private sector differences in
services provided, 5–6
externalities, 5
public goods, 5
stages, 12–13
Budgeting system
defined, 16–17
interconnectedness, 17
outputs, 16–17
Buck, A.E., 9
Build-operate-own
budget preparation, 80–81
private equity ownership, 379
Build-operate-transfer
budget preparation, 80–81
private equity ownership, 379
Bureau of the Budget, 10, 48–49
See also Office of Management and Budget
Burkhead, J., 97

C

Cafeteria plan, health care, 415
Call feature, 389
Capital accumulation fund, 390
Capital budgeting, 257, 363–378
evaluation, 374–378
federal capital budgeting, 375–378
separate, 366–368, 374–375
processes, 368
Capital expenditure
classification problems, 366
physical nature, 365–366
time duration, 365–366
Capital investment
current expenditure, 364–365
economic policy and, 364–365
Capital investment planning, 368–374

asset management, 368–370, 371
developing service objectives, 372
identifying environmental trends, 370–371
identifying financial resources, 372–373
identifying implications for future recurrent
costs, 373
identifying present service characteristics,
370
including first year in annual budget, 373–
374
multiyear plans, 368
preliminary listing of capital projects and
cost estimates, 372
selecting projects, 373
Capital project funds, 315
Cash accounting, 322–323
Cash and investment managers, cash
management, 291–292
Cash flow, 282–284
Cash flow statement, 335–337
Cash management, 282–292
cash and investment managers, 291–292
computer, 291
federal government, 290–291
checks, 290
currency and coins, 290
electronic fund transfer, 290
letter of credit, 291
intergovernmental relations, 291
Cash Management Improvement Act, 465
Casino, budget preparation, 82–83
Catalog of Federal Domestic Assistance, 465–
466
Categorical aid, 455–456
Causal relationship
policy analysis, 181–182
program analysis, 181–182
Certificate in government financial
management, 423
Certificate of deposit, 286
Certificate of participation, 384
Charitable contribution, budget preparation, 81
Checks-and-balances system, 217–218
responsible government, 7
Chief executive, budget preparation, 130–133
citizen preferences, 133
intergovernmental relations, 132–133
program priorities, 131
relationships with legislative body, 132–133

strategic concerns, 130–132
tactical concerns, 132–133
Chief Financial Officers Act, 311, 339
Chief information officer, 349
Circuit breaker tax, 69
Circular. *See* Office of Management and Budget
Civil rights, intergovernmental relations, 464–465
Civil Rights Restoration Act, 464–465
Civil Service Reform Act, 420
Civil Service Retirement System, 415
Cleveland, F.A., 9
Coincident indicator, 489–492
    consumer price index, 490
    gross domestic product, 489, 491
    industrial production, 490–492
    national income, 489–490, 491
    net national product, 489–490, 491
    price, 490
    unemployment, 490
Collective bargaining, 411–414
Collective goods, 26
Commercial paper, 286
Commission on Economy and Efficiency. *See* Taft Commission
Comparable worth, government personnel, 414
Competition, procurement, 295–296
Competition in Contracting Act, 295
Composite index, leading indicator, 493
Comprehensive annual financial report (CAFR), 329–330
Computer
    acquisition planning, 348–349
    cash management, 291
    information system, 348–350
    tax administration, 278–279
Computer imaging, 350
Computer Security Act, 355
Concession contracting, budget preparation, 80–81
Conference committee, 206
Congress
    budget approval, 227–258
        appropriation bill, 228–229
        authorization, 228
        backdoor spending, 229–230
        Balanced Budget Act, 245–247
        balanced budget requirement, 252–253
        biennial budgeting, 257

budget deficit, 234, 237–239
budget reforms 1974-1985, 230–236
budget resolution, 255
Bush years, 236–242
capital budgeting, 257
Clinton years, 242–247
continuing resolution, 255–256
controllability, 233, 236
deferral, 232
federal credit budget, 233
Ford-Carter era, 230–233
Gramm-Rudman-Hollings, 237–239
impoundment, 230–232
item veto, 249–252
joint resolution, 256
leadership, 255
1990 crisis and accord, 239–242
1993 accord, 242–243
1995–1996 debacle, 243–245
omnibus budget reconciliation bill, 256
policy making, 236
prior to 1974 reforms, 228–230
process issues of reform, 248–249
proposed Congressional reorganization, 253–255
proposed reforms, 247–257
proposed revisions in use of resolutions and budget summits, 255–256
Reagan years, 233–239
reconciliation, 231, 235
rescission, 232
Social Security, 246–247
substantive issues of reform, 247–248
Taxpayer Relief Act, 245–247
term limits, 255
budget deal, 1
Congressional Budget and Impoundment Control Act of 1974, 230–232
Congressional document, 518
Congressional Review Act, 275
Consolidated budget, 155
Consolidated cash statement, 154
Consolidated Financial Statements, 152
Constituency, responsible government, 7
Consumer price index, coincident indicator, 490
Contemporary fiscal policy, economic policy, 497
Contingency reserve, 88

Contingent valuation, 186–187
Continuing resolution, 255–256
Continuous quality improvement, 105
Contracting out, 269
Controllability of budget, 233, 236
Corporate income tax, 65–66
Cost accounting, 324–326, 327
   fixed asset, 325
Cost center, 325
Cost-benefit analysis, 179–180
Cost-effectiveness analysis, 179–180
Council of Economic Advisers, 133, 135, 136
Coupon bond, 387
Credit accounting, 327–328
Credit enhancement, 390
Credit liability, budget preparation, 144–150
   federal liability reforms, 148–149
   state and local government, 149–150
   types, 145–148
Crosswalking, 160
Current expenditure, capital investment, 364–365
Current services budgeting, budget preparation, 107–108
Cutback management, 141–143
Cyclical indicator, 489

D

Database manager, 350
Debt capacity, 392–399
   measuring, 397
      debt burden, 397–398
      debt default, 395–397
      distribution of debt, 393–395
      per capita debt, 392, 393
      ratio of debt to personal income, 393, 394
      size of debt, 392–393
Debt Collection Act of 1982, 280–281
Debt collection, taxpayer rights, 280–282
Debt default, debt capacity, 395–397
Debt financing, vs. pay-as-you-go, 379–380
Debt management
   debt default, 395–397
   developing country, 485–486
   distribution of debt, 393–395
   economic policy, 484–488
   per capita debt, 392, 393
   ratio of debt to personal income, 393, 394
   size of debt, 392–393
Debt refinancing, 398–399
Debt service funds, 315
Decision making, 18–20
   budget request, 129–151
   centralized, 6
   disjointed incrementalism, 19
   government personnel, 407–414
      importance of personnel expenditures, 407
   incrementalism, 19
   limited rationality, 19–20
   policy analysis, 192–194
   program analysis, 192–194
   rational decision making, 18–19
   simulations, 520
Decision support system, 343
Deferral, 232
Deficit. *See* Debt
Deming, W.E., 105
Department of Defense
   Five-Year Defense Program, 110–111
   planning-programming-budgeting, 110–112
Dependent care account, 415
Depreciation, 326
Derivative, 287
   Orange County, California, bankruptcy, 396
Design-and-build contract, 295
Developing country, debt management, 485–486
Diffusion index, 493
Direct loan, 145–146, 147
Disability insurance, 76
Disclosure, bond financing, 390–392
Discount rate
   in analysis, 187–189
   Federal Reserve System, 500–501
Discounting, bond financing, 388
Discretionary policy, economic policy, 495
Disjointed incrementalism, decision making, 19
Domestic Policy Council, 135
Downsizing, 268–270
   budget preparation, 140–144
Duff & Phelps Credit Rating Company, 389

E

Economic analysis, 179–180

Economic competitiveness, 475–476
Economic growth
    economic policy, 480–482
    public infrastructure, link between, 503–504
Economic indicators, 488–493
    types, 488–489
Economic policy
    anticipating economic conditions, 488–494
    automatic stabilizer, 495
    balance of payments, 482–483
    contemporary fiscal policy, 497
    debt management, 484–488
    deficit, 484–488
    discretionary policy, 495
    economic growth, 480–482
    fiscal policy, 497
    fiscal policy instrument, 496–499
    full employment, 478–479
        political acceptability of unemployment,
        478–479
    inflation, 479–480
    Keynesian economics, 496
    legal issues, 476–477
    monetary policy, 499–501
    multiplier effect, 497–498
    objectives, 476–488
    productivity, 480–481
    public investment role of government, 502–
        504
    redistributive effects, 504–506
    state and local incentives for private sector
        investment, 502–503
    supply-side economics, 496–497
    technology policy, 481–482
    tools to affect economy, 495–504
    U.S. as debtor nation, 474–475
    value of U.S. dollar, 475
Economic Recovery Tax Act of 1981, 233–234
Economic Report of the President, 152
Economics, policy and program analysis, 172,
    179–180
Educational finance, 440–444
Effectiveness
    policy analysis, 176
    program analysis, 176
Efficiency
    policy analysis, 176
    program analysis, 176
Electronic fund transfer, 290

Electronic mail, 351
Employee benefits, government personnel,
    414–419
Employee Retirement Income Security Act of
    1974, 415
Employment Act of 1946, 477
Employment-related indicators, leading
    indicator, 492
Encumbrance accounting, 323
English Consolidated Fund Act of 1787, 8
Enrolled bill, 214
Enterprise funds, 315
Entitlement, 135, 454
Entrepreneurial budgeting, budget preparation,
    117
Environmental pollution, 272
Equity, 184
Ethics and analysis, 192–193
Evaluation and analysis, 174–175
Executive accountability, 8
Executive budget system
    development, 8
    modern system, 9–10
Executive Orders
    12291, 175, 465
    12372, 466
    12416, 466
    12498, 465
    12837, 102, 137, 141–142, 271–272, 321
    12838, 272
    12839, 271–272
    12843, 296
    12845, 296
    12857, 272
    12861, 271
    12862, 117, 157, 220
    12866, 175
    12873, 296–297
    12875, 464
    12928, 298
    12931, 293, 297
    12969, 299
    12979, 295
    12989, 299
    12993, 339
    13011, 273
Executive veto power, 50–51
Expendable trust fund, 315
Expenditure

budget document, 156–157
  capital vs. current, 364–366
  classification, 318–322
  federal objects of expenditure classification, 319–320
  objects of, 319–321
  organizational unit, 319
Expenditure control, responsible government, 11
Externalities, 5, 183

F

Fair Labor Standards Act, government personnel, 409
Fannie Mae, 147, 148
Federal Accounting Standards Advisory Board (FASAB), 312, 326
Federal Acquisition Computer Network, 296
Federal Acquisition Reform Act, 297
Federal Acquisition Streamlining Act, 295, 297
Federal aid, intergovernmental relations, 444–445
  devolution, 448–451
  fiscal illusion hypothesis, 445
  future trends, 448–451
  regional differences, 445–448
Federal capital budgeting, 375–378
Federal civilian reform, planning-programming-budgeting, 112
Federal credit budget, 233
Federal Credit Reform Act of 1990, 148
Federal Deposit Insurance Corporation, 145
Federal Employees Retirement System, 415–416
Federal government, cash management, 290–291
  checks, 290
  currency and coins, 290
  electronic fund transfer, 290
  letter of credit, 291
Federal insurance program, 147, 148
Federal Managers' Financial Integrity Act of 1992, 271, 355
Federal mission PP&E, 326
Federal Procurement Policy, Office of, 293
Federal purchasing regulations, 296
Federal Reserve Board, criticism, 501

Federal Reserve System
  discount rate, 500–501
  monetary policy, 500
  open market operations, 500
Fees. *See* User charge
Fiduciary funds, 315
File transfer protocol, 351
Finance Committee, 228
Financial Accounting Standards Advisory Board (FASAB), 312
Financial condition
  responsible government, 11–13
  See also Debt capacity, Debt management
Financial Institutions Reform, Recovery, and Enforcement Act of 1989, 148
Financial management, responsible government, 11–13
Financial report, 329–330
Fiscal assistance, types, 454–459
Fiscal illusion hypothesis, 445
Fiscal note, 210–211
Fiscal policy
  combined with monetary policy, 501–502
  economic policy, 496–499
  implementation lag, 498
  perception lag, 498
  reaction lag, 498
  response lags, 498–499
Fitch Investors Service, 389
Five-Year Defense Program, Department of Defense, 110–111
Fixed asset, cost accounting, 325
Fixed-ceiling budgeting, budget preparation, 108
Float time, 282
Forecasting, 493–494
Foundation plan, 442
Fractional assessment, 68–69
Fraud
  organizational arrangements, 314
  waste and abuse, 271
Freddie Mac, 147, 148
Freedom of Information Act, 355
Full employment
  defined, 478
  economic policy, 478–479
    political acceptability of unemployment, 478–479
Full faith and credit bond, 378

Fund accounting, 314–316
Fund equity, 330

G

GAAFR *(Governmental Accounting, Auditing, and Financial Reporting),* 312–313
Gambling, budget preparation, 82–83
Garcia vs. San Antonio Metropolitan Transit Authority, 452–453
General Accounting Office
    accounting, 311–312
    auditing, 339
    budget cycle, 52–53
General obligation bond, 378, 381–382
General PP&E category, 326
General purpose external financial reporting (GPEFR), 322
General revenue sharing, 456–457
General Services Administration, 293–294
Generally accepted accounting principles, 313
Generally accepted auditing standards (GAAS), 338, 342
Generally accepted government auditing standards (GAGAS), 339, 342
Generational accounting, 328
Geographic impact of budgets, 437–440
Geographic information system, 346
Gini coefficients of inequality, 184
Goals, 106, 176–177
    multiple, 181
Gopher, 351
Government employee retirement, budget preparation, 79
Government expenditure, 35–36, 37
    by function, 40–42, 43
    geographic effects, 29–30
    industry effects, 29–30
    private sector, 28–29
    revenue sources, 38–40
    subpopulation effects, 30–31
    taxing and spending limitations, 83–86
Government Information Locator Service, 345
Government investment in infrastructure, 502
Government Performance and Results Act 118, 157
Government personnel
    budget document, 409, 410

budgeting, 419–420
    comparable worth, 414
    costs created by, 411
    decision making, 407–414
    employee benefits, 414–419
    Fair Labor Standards Act, 409
    labor-management relations, 411–414
        bargaining units, 412
        collective bargaining, 411–414
        costs, 412–413
        labor negotiations, 413
    operations, 419–423
    pension plan, 414–419
    personnel administration, 419–420
    personnel complement control, 410–411
    personnel in budgeting, 420–423
        certification, 423
        federal staff, 421
        skill mix, 421–422
        state staff, 421
        training, 422–423
    reduction in force, 408–409
    welfare, 408
Government publication, 517–518
Government shutdown, 244
Government size and growth, 31–38
Governmental accounting, 309–337
Governmental Accounting, Auditing, and Financial Reporting, 312–313
Governmental Accounting Standards Board, 121, 313, 323–324, 327–328, 329, 335, 338–339
    Statement 3, 328
    Statement 10, 327–328
    Statement 11, 323–324, 330
    Statement 18, 328
    Statement 26, 328
    Statement 27, 328
Governmental auditing, 337–342
Government-sponsored enterprise, 147, 148
Gramm-Rudman-Hollings, 237–239
    enactment, 237
    legal challenge, 237
    1987 budget accord, 238–239
    revision, 237
    sequestration, 238
    timetable, 237–238
Grant
    characteristics, 454–455

coordination, 466–467
requirements, 462–468
Gridlock, 206
Gross domestic product, coincident indicator, 489, 490, 491
Gross national product, 489, 490
Grove City College vs. Bell, 464
Guaranteed loan, 146–148

H

Health care, 415
cafeteria plan, 415
Health maintenance organization, 414
Heritage PP&E, 326
Homepage, 351
Hoover Commissions, 10, 96, 109
House Budget Committee, 230–231, 255
Housing and Community Development Act, 458
Housing start, leading indicator, 492

I

Immigration and Naturalization Service vs. Chadha, 221, 232
Impact fee, 75
Impact measures, 103
Impoundment, 51, 230–232
Income stabilization policy, redistributive effects, 505–506
Income tax. *See* Corporate income tax, Personal income tax
Incrementalism, decision making, 19
Indexing, 64–65
Industrial production, coincident indicator, 490–492
Inflation
economic policy, 479–480
unemployment, 479–480
nonaccelerating inflation rate of unemployment, 479–480
Information, 17–20
categorization, 343–345
government collection and dissemination of information, 272–274
types, 17–18
Information display, budget document, 156–163

Information resources management, 343
Information system, 343–356
computer, 348–350
issues and problems, 355–356
security, 355
Information Technology Management Reform Act, 119
Infrastructure. *See* Capital investment
Inspector general, 271
Insurance liability, budget preparation, 144–150
federal liability reforms, 148–149
state and local government, 149–150
types, 145–148
Insurance trust revenue, budget preparation, 76–80
Intelligent character recognition, 350
Interest rate, 187–189
bond financing, 389
Intergovernmental assistance, 440–451
Intergovernmental relations, 429–469
cash management, 291
civil rights, 464–465
direct expenditures and taxes, 437–440
economic competition, 436
federal aid, 444–445
devolution, 448–451
fiscal illusion hypothesis, 445
future trends, 448–451
regional differences, 445–448
financial assistance factors, 452–453
fiscal considerations, 433–437
fiscal responsibilities, 434–436
horizontal fiscal differences, 433–434
intergovernmental assistance, 440–451
management capacity, 467
nongrant spending, 437–438
overlapping taxes, 436–437
patterns of interaction among levels of government, 437–454
realigning responsibilities, 467
reporting, 465–466
restructuring patterns, 459–468
state aid, 440–444
state control of local government, 453–454
tax, 459–462
bond financing, 461–462
shared taxes, 462
tax credit, 461

tax deductions, 459–461
unemployment insurance, 461
tax administration, 279–280
tax collection, 438–440
vertical imbalance, 433
Intergovernmental system
fiscal features, 429–437
structural features, 429–437
Internal Revenue Service, 65, 276–277, 279, 281–282
Internal service funds, 315
International economy, 513–514
Internet, 350–355
Internet relay chat, 351
Investment
public investment role of government, 502–504
risks, 288–289
state and local incentives for private sector investment, 502–503
Investment instrument, 285–288
bankers' acceptance, 286
certificate of deposit, 286
commercial paper, 286
corporate securities, 286
derivative, 287
federal securities, 285
investment pool, 287
money market instrument, 286
repurchase agreement, 286
yield rate, 287, 288
Investment planning, 284–285
Investment pool, 287
Invitation for bid, 294
Item veto, 216–217, 249–252

J

Joint Financial Management Improvement Program, 312
Joint resolution, 256
Journal, 318, 516–517
Just-in-time ordering, 293

K

Key, V.O., 96

Keynesian economics, 496

L

Labor-management relations, government personnel, 411–414
bargaining units, 412
collective bargaining, 411–414
costs, 412–413
labor negotiations, 413
Leadership, political party, 205–206
Leading indicator, 492–493
average weekly initial claims for unemployment insurance, 492
average workweek of production workers in manufacturing, 492
composite index, 493
employment-related indicators, 492
housing start, 492
stock market, 492–493
Lease-purchase agreement, 293
Ledger, 316
Legal issues, economic policy, 476–477
Legislative apportionment, 203–204
Legislative clearinghouse, 271
Legislative committee, 206–207
Legislative intent, 219, 266
Legislative Reorganization Act, 229, 253–254
Legislative veto, 220–221
Legislature. *See also* Congress
budget approval, 201–222
authority, 211–212
bicameralism, 214
checks-and-balances system, 217–218
committee responsibilities, 209–210
compensation, 208–209
conference committee, 206
constituency differences, 212–213
enrolled bill, 214
executive fragmentation, 213–214
federal aid to states, 214–216
fiscal note, 210–211
gridlock, 206
item veto, 216–217
legislative characteristics, 201–209
legislative committee, 206–207
legislative intent, 219
legislative oversight, 217–222

legislative process, 209–211
legislative roles, 211–222
legislative veto, 220–221
legislative-executive interactions, 211–217
Office of Management and Budget clearinghouse function, 214
parameters, 201–211
pork barrel, 212–213
staff, 208–209
standing committee, 206–207
strategies, 215–216
time, 207–208
fragmentation in budgeting, 205
legislative apportionment, 203–204
single-member district, 203–204
term limit, 204
Letter of credit, 291
Liabilities, 144–150, 316, 317, 323–324, 330
pension, 418–419
Liability, tort, 300
License fee, budget preparation, 81
Limited rationality, decision making, 19–20
Line Item Veto Act, 217, 250–252
rescission, 250–252
Line of credit, 390
Loans, 145–148
Local government
bond financing, 378–392
participants, 385
taxes, 380–381
planning-programming-budgeting, 112–113
state control, 453–454
Lockbox, 283
Lorenz curve, 184
Lottery, budget preparation, 82–83
Luxury excise, budget preparation, 72–73

M

Management by objectives, 104
Management information system, 343–348
defined, 343
design, 347–348
structure, 345–348
Mandate, 462–463
unfunded, 463–464
MAX Decision Support System, 350

Measurement focus and basis of accounting, 323–324
Medicaid, budget preparation, 77
Medical expense reimbursement account, 415
Medical savings account, 415
Medicare, budget preparation, 76
reforms, 79
Meta-analysis, 182
Mill, property tax and, 69
Mission, 106
Monetary policy, 499–501
combined with fiscal policy, 501–502
Federal Reserve System, 500
money supply control, 499–500
open market operations, 500
Money market instrument, 286
Moody's Investor Service, 389, 391
Multiple governments, 430–432
coordination problems, 431–432
Multiplier effects, economic policy, 497–498
Multiyear request, budget preparation, 115–116
cost projections, 116
program projections, 116
techniques, 120
time horizons, 116
Municipal bonds. *See* Bond financing
Municipal minibond, 383
Municipal Securities Rulemaking Board, 391

N

National Bellas Hess, Inc. vs. Department of Revenue, State of Illinois, 72
National income, coincident indicator, 489–490, 491
National information infrastructure, 345
National Performance Review, 12
budget preparation, 117–118
National Security Council, 135–136
Need measures, 105
Net national product, coincident indicator, 489–490, 491
Net present value, 188–189
Netsearch, 515–516
New York City budget crisis, 12, 390
Nonexhaustive expenditures, 28
Nonexpendable trust fund, 315

Nongrant spending, intergovernmental
    relations, 437–438
Nonguaranteed bond, 378, 381–382

O

Objective, 106
Off-budget, budget document, exclusions, 155
Office of Management and Budget, 49
    accounting, 311–312
    cash management, 282–292
    circulars
        A-11, 98–102, 104, 152, 269, 350
        A-19, 271
        A-21, 341–342
        A-25, 74
        A-34, 266
        A-50, 342
        A-76, 269, 294
        A-87, 341–342
        A-94, 186–187, 189
        A-95, 466
        A-102, 456
        A-122, 341–342
        A-123, 119, 271, 310
        A-125, 283
        A-127, 270–271, 313
        A-128, 465
        A-129, 148, 280–281, 328
        A-130, 273, 349
        A-131, 325
        A-133, 342
        A-134, 313
        A-135, 272
    debt collection, 275–282
    downsizing, 268–270
    end-of-year spending, 268
    information, 272–274
    interactions on budgeting, 265–268
    management controls, 270–272
    midyear changes, 267
    Office of Information and Regulatory
        Affairs, 273–274
    planning, 266
    privatization, 268–270
    regulation control, 274–275
    relations, 265–275
    reorganization, 138, 268–270

    tax administration, 275–282
Office of Management and Budget 2000, 138
Office of Personnel Management, 272, 420
Offsetting collections, 156, 318
Old-Age and Survivors Insurance. *See* Social
    Security
Omnibus Budget Reconciliation Act, 242
Omnibus budget reconciliation bill, 256
Omnibus Consolidated Rescissions and
    Appropriations Act, 256
Omnibus Taxpayer Bill of Rights, 281
On-budget, budget document, exclusions, 155
On-line subscription database, 518
OPEC, oil production, 474
Open-ended budgeting, budget preparation, 108
Operating lease, 293
Operating statement, 332–335
Operations research, 178
Opportunity cost, 176
Optical character recognition, 350
Orange County, California, bankruptcy, 391-
    392, 396–397
    derivative, 396
Outcomes, 103, 118
Output measures, 103–104
Outsourcing, 269
Oversight of executive, 217–222

P

Paperwork Reduction Act, 119, 273–274
Pay-as-you-go
    capital financing, 379–380
    Congress, 241
    public pension plans, 417
PAYGO. *See* Pay-as-you-go
Pension plan
    accounting, 419
    cost-of-living allowances, 416
    defined benefits, 416–417
    defined contributions, 416–417
    funding, 417–418
    government personnel, 414–419
    liabilities, 418–419
    reporting, 419
Pension trust, 315
Performance audit, 341
Performance budgeting, budget preparation,
    109

Performance measurement
  accounting, 322
  budget preparation, 102–107
    activities, 104
    choosing among program results, 106–107
    continuous quality improvement, 105
    goals, 106
    impacts, 103
    investments, 103
    management by objectives, 104
    need, 105
    objectives, 106
    outputs, 103–104
    productivity, 104–105
    program measures, 105–106
    quality of life, 102–103
    social indicator, 102–103
    suboptimization, 104
    total quality management, 105
    workload, 104
Personal income tax, budget preparation, 63–65
  adjustments, 63–64
  deductions, 63–64
  enforcement, 65
  exemptions, 63–64
  indexing, 64–65
  rate structure, 64
  tax base, 63
Personal property tax, 71
Personnel, tax administration, 279
Personnel administration, government personnel, 419–420
Personnel complement control, 267
Planning
  defined, 110
  responsible government, 11
Planning-programming-budgeting system, 97
  budget preparation, 109–113
  Department of Defense, 110–112
  federal civilian reform, 112
  local government, 112–113
  state government, 112–113
Policy and program analysis, 171–195
  accountability, 174
  analytic unit, 190–192
  causal relationship, 181–182
  decision making, 192–194
  defined, 173

  economics, 172
  effectiveness, 176
  efficiency, 176
  equity, 177
  externalities, 183
  focus, 171–177
  implementation problem, 189–190
  institutionalizing use of, 194–195
  intellectual roots, 172–173
  internal validity, 185
  judgment criteria, 176–177
  methods and techniques, 177–190
  models, 178–181
  multiple goals, 181
  organizational locus, 190–195
  policy formulation, 173–174
  problems, 181–185
  productivity, 176–177
  program evaluation, 174
  program monitoring, 174
  quantification, 185–189
  redistributive effects, 183–184
  service delivery alternatives, 175
  social evaluation, 175
  social sciences, 172
  subjective information, 185
  uses, 173–175
Policy Development, Office of, 136
Policy formulation, 173–174
Policy guidance, budget preparation, 115
Policy sciences, program analysis, 172
Political party, leadership, 205–206
Politics
  analysis and, 192–194
  budget preparation and, 49, 129–151
  government expenditures and campaign expenses, 27–28
Popular annual financial report, 329
Pork barrel, 212–213
Postaudit, 338
Preaudit, 51–52, 267
President. *See* Chief executive
Price, coincident indicator, 490
Pricing, public service, 5–6
Privacy Act, 355
Private entity, public entity, comparison, 145–146
Private equity ownership
  build-operate-own, 379

build-operate-transfer, 379
Private purpose bond, 382–383
Private sector
    boundaries, 27–31
    government expenditure, 28–29
    size, 25–31
Privatization, 268–270, 293–294
Procurement, 292–299
    competition, 295–296
    contracting process, 294–296
    innovations, 298–299
    objectives, 293–294
    organizational configurations, 292–293
    problem areas, 298–299
    reform, 296–298
Productivity, 104–105
    analysis, 176–177
    economic policy, 480–481
    profit, 3–4
Program analysis. *See* Policy and program
    analysis
Program budgeting, 96–97
    budget preparation, 109–113
    defined, 110
Program evaluation, 174
Program guidance, budget preparation, 115
Program information
    in budget document, 157, 159–162
    legislature and, 220
    program measures, 102–107
Program monitoring, program analysis, 174
Program planning, responsible government,
    11–13
Program revisions, 160
Program structure, 159–160
Programming, defined, 110
Programs, projects, and activities (PPA), 238
Progressive tax, 60
Project-based accounting, 326
Prompt Payment Act, 283
Property, plant, and equipment (PPE), 326
Property tax, budget preparation, 66–71
    circuit breaker tax, 69
    consumption tax, 71–73
    databases for tax administration, 69–71
    fractional assessment, 68–69
    personal property tax, 71
    tax base, 67–68, 71–72
    tax increment financing, 67

tax rates, 69, 72
Proportional tax, 60
Proposition 13, 83
Proprietary funds, 315
Public budgeting, future trends, 511–514
Public choice, 172
Public employee retirement system, 415–419
    structure, 415–416
Public employment, 36–38
Public entity, private entity, comparison, 145–
    146
Public goods, 5
Public infrastructure, economic growth, link
    between, 503–504
Public sector, 25–44
    boundaries, 27–31
    expenditure, 35–36, 37
    growth, 31–38
    magnitude, 31–38
    reasons for growth, 26–27
        collective goods, 26
        demographic changes, 26
        economic hardships, 27
        externalities, 26
        government responses, 26–27
        high-risk situations, 27
        technological change, 27
    revenues, 31–35
    size, 25–31
    value questions, 26
Public service
    pricing, 5–6
    privatization, 80–81
Put option, 389

Q

Quantification
    policy analysis, 185–189
    program analysis, 185–189
Quill Corporation vs. North Dakota, 72

R

Rainy day fund, 88, 284
Rational decision making, 18–19
Receipt
    budget document, 163–164
    classification, 318–322

Reconciliation, 235
Redistributive effects
  economic policy, 504–506
  income stabilization policy, 505–506
  policy analysis, 183–184
  program analysis, 183–184
  unintentional, 504–505
Reduction in force, government personnel,
  408–409
Re-engineering, budget preparation, 117–118
Reform, procurement, 296–298
Reform movement, 9–10
Registered bond, 387
Regressive tax, 60
Regulation, bond financing, 390–392
Regulatory Flexibility Act, 275
Regulatory relief, 274–275
Reinventing government movement, 12
Reorganization, 268–270
Repo, 286
Reporting
  accounting, 329–337
  intergovernmental relations, 465–466
  pension plan, 419
  requirements, 465–466
Repurchase agreement, 286
Request for proposal, 294
Request for quotation, 294
Rescission, 232, 250
  Line Item Veto Act, 250–252
Research and development, 3–4
Reserve requirement, 501
Resolution Trust Corporation, 145
Responsible government, 7–14
  checks and balances, 7
  constituency, 7
  executive budget system development, 8–10
  expenditure control, 11
  financial condition, 11–13
  financial management, 11–13
  investment vs. consumption, 13–14
  management, 11
  planning, 11
  program planning, 11–13
  revenue responsibility, 10–11
  separation of powers, 7
Retail sales tax, 40, 71–73
Revenue, 31–35
  budget preparation, 133–135

  balanced budget, 133–135
  tax earmarking, 134–135
  taxing limitations, 133
Revenue anticipation note, 283
Revenue bill, budget, approval, 50
Revenue bond, 382
Revenue estimating, budget preparation, 86–
  88, 133
  contingency reserve, 88
  deterministic models, 86
  econometric models, 87–88
  politics, 88
  rainy day fund, 88
  simple trend extrapolations, 86–87
Revenue responsibility, responsible
  government, 10–11
Revenue sharing, 456–459
Reverse benefit principle of taxation, 73
Reverse repo, 289
Revolving fund, 384–385
Revolving loan program, budget preparation,
  81
Rightsizing
  budget preparation, 140–144
  See also Downsizing
Right-to-know laws, 272
Risk accounting, 327–328
Risk management, 299–301

S

Sales tax, 40, 71–73
San Antonio School District vs. Rodriquez, 444
Savings, United States, 484, 485
Scenario writing, 180–181
Search engine, 351, 516
Secondary effect, 183
Securities and Exchange Commission, bond
  financing, 390–391
Security, information system, 355
Senate Budget Committee, 230–231, 255
Separation of powers, responsible government,
  7
Sequestration, 237–242, 253
Serial bond, 387
Service efforts and accomplishments (SEA)
  reporting, 121, 322
Shadow pricing, 185–186

Shared taxes, 462
Simple trade balance, 482–483
Single Audit Act, 341–342, 465
Single-factor business tax, 66
Sinking fund, 390
Small Business Regulatory Enforcement
    Fairness Act, 275
Smokestack chasing, 66
Social evaluation, program analysis, 175
Social indicators, 102–113
Social sciences, program analysis, 172
Social Security, 246–247
    budget preparation, 76
    reform, 77–79
Software, 349–350
    spreadsheet, 349
South Carolina vs. Baker, 387
Special revenue funds, 315
Spending, budget preparation, 135–140
    agency expectations and deliberations, 136–
        137
    commitments, 135
    entitlement, 135
    Office of Management and Budget and
        agency relations, 137–139
    Office of Management and Budget
        recommendations, 139–140
    Office of Management and Budget roles, 136
    organizational competition, 135–136
Spending cutback, budget preparation, 140–144
    budget reserves, 141–142
    budget systems, 144
    fiscal stress, 141
    items to cut, 143–144
    legislative roles, 142–143
    management, 141–144
    Office of Management and Budget roles, 142
    rainy day funds, 141–142
Spillover effect, 183
Spreadsheet, software, 349
Stakeholder, 183
Standard & Poors Corporation, 389, 391
Standing committee, 206–207
State aid, intergovernmental relations, 440–444
State budgeting, reform, 9
State control of local government, 453–454
State corporate income tax, budget preparation
    single-factor business tax, 66
    smokestack chasing, 66

State government
    bond financing, 378–392
        participants, 385
        taxes, 380–381
    planning-programming-budgeting, 112–113
State revolving fund, 384–385
Statistical information, 518–519
Stewardship PP&E, 326
Stock market, leading indicator, 492–493
Strategic analysis, 180–181
Strategic planning, budget preparation, 114–
    115
Sumptuary excise, budget preparation, 73
Sunset legislation, 219–220
Supplemental Security Income, budget
    preparation, 76
Supply-side economics, economic policy, 496–
    497
Swap proposal, 467
System
    defined, 16
    interconnectedness, 17
Systems analysis, 173, 179
Systems theory, 97

T

Taft Commission, 9–10
Target-base budgeting, budget preparation, 117
Tax
    intergovernmental relations, 459–462
        bond financing, 461–462
        shared taxes, 462
        tax credit, 461
        tax deductions, 459–461
        unemployment insurance, 461
    overlapping jurisdictions, 436–437
    taxing and spending limitations, 83–86
Tax administration
    computer, 278–279
    intergovernmental relations, 279–280
    personnel, 279
Tax amnesty, 278
Tax and expenditure limitation, 83–86
    causes, 83–84
    impact, 85–86
    types, 84–85
Tax anticipation note, 283

Tax collection, intergovernmental relations, 438–440
Tax credit, 461
Tax earmarking, 134–135
Tax efficiency, budget preparation, 61
Tax enforcement, administration, 276–278
Tax equity, budget preparation, 60–61
  ability to pay principle, 60
  benefit received, 61
  progressive tax, 60
  proportional tax, 60
  regressive tax, 60
  spillover effects, 61
Tax expenditure, budget preparation, 62
  deductions from income, 62
  exemptions, 62
  federal budget, 62
  interest on municipal bonds, 62
Tax increment financing, 67
Tax Reform Act (TRA86), 62, 64, 383, 459–460, 461–462
Taxpayer Bill of Rights, 2, 281
Taxpayer Relief Act, 245–247
Taxpayer rights, debt collection, 280–282
Technical evaluation, program analysis, 175
Technology policy, economic policy, 481–482
Term bond, 387
Term limit, 204, 255
Total quality management, 105
Transfer payments, 60, 505
Treasury Bulletin, 152
Treasury Department, 10, 48, 133, 144, 152, 276, 282, 285, 286, 290, 311–312, 316, 328
True lease, 293
Trust and agency fund, 315
Turnback proposal, 467

U

Unemployment
  coincident indicator, 490
  inflation, 479–480
    nonaccelerating inflation rate of unemployment, 479–480
    political acceptability, 478–479
Unemployment insurance, 461
  budget preparation, 79–80
Unfunded mandate, 463–464

Unified budget, budget document, 155
United States
  balance of payments, 482–483
  as debtor nation, 474–475
  effects of economic performance, 486
  effects of tax cuts, 486–487
  federal debt size, 486, 487
  federal use of debt, 486
  financing U.S. economy, 483
  savings, 484, 485
  transition from creditor to debtor, 482
  U.S. economy competitiveness, 475–476
  value of U.S. dollar in world economy, 475
United States Congress. *See* Congress
United States Government Annual Report, 152
Unrestricted fund balance, 283
U.S. vs. Lopez, 464
Usenet news, 351
User charge, budget preparation, 73–75
  impact fee, 75
  rationale, 73–74
  tax subsidies, 75
  types, 74–75

V

Value engineering, 325
Value-added tax, budget preparation, 83
Veto
  appropriation bill and override, 217
  item, 216–217, 249–252

W

Washington Public Power Supply System default, 390, 396
Water resource management, 432–433
Ways and Means Committee, 228
Web site, 351
Welfare, government personnel, 408
Welfare reform, 451
Wide area information service, 351
Wildavsky, A., 19, 97
Women, Infants and Children (WIC) supplemental food program, 454
Word processing, 350
Workers' compensation, budget preparation, 80

Workload measures, 104
World economy, 474–476
    equilibrium in international financial flows,
        482–484
World Wide Web, 351
    sites related to budgeting and finance, 351–
        354, 516

Y

Yellow book, 339
Yield rate, 287, 288

Z

Zero coupon bond, 388
Zero-base budgeting
    budget preparation, 113–114
    disadvantages, 113–114
    history, 113–114
    sunset legislation, 219–220